# THE ACCOUNTING SAMPLER

# McGraw-Hill Accounting Series

# THE ACCOUNTING SAMPLER

## THIRD EDITION

THOMAS J. BURNS
The Ohio State University

HARVEY S. HENDRICKSON
Florida International University

McGRAW-HILL BOOK COMPANY

New York  St. Louis  San Francisco  Auckland  Düsseldorf  Johannesburg
Kuala Lumpur  London  Mexico  Montreal  New Delhi  Panama
Paris  São Paulo  Singapore  Sydney  Tokyo  Toronto

To
Carl L. Nelson
The George O. May
Professor of Financial Accounting
Columbia University

# THE ACCOUNTING SAMPLER

1 2 3 4 5 6 7 8 9 0 DODO 7 8 3 2 1 0 9 8 7 6

This book was set in Univers Medium by Intergraphic Technology, Inc. The editors were Donald E. Chatham, Jr., and Matthew Cahill; the designer was Anne Canevari Green; the production supervisor was Sam Ratkewitch.
R. R. Donnelley & Sons Company was printer and binder.


**Library of Congress Cataloging in Publication Data**

Burns, Thomas Junior, comp.
    The accounting sampler.

    (McGraw-Hill accounting series)
        1.    Accounting—Addresses, essays, lectures.
I.    Hendrickson, Harvey S.    II.    Title.
HF5629.B87    1976          657' .08          75-45498
ISBN 0-07-009202-8

# Contents

## 3. VALUATION IN ACCOUNTING

## 4. MANAGEMENT PLANNING AND CONTROL

## 5. THE RULE-MAKING AGENCIES AND SOME ISSUES

## 7. THE NEW ACCOUNTING

# List of Contributors

Mr. Harry B. Anderson is a reporter for the *Wall Street Journal.*

President of the American Accounting Association, Dr. Wilton T. Anderson, CPA, is chairperson of the accounting faculty at the Oklahoma State University.

Mr. Frederick Andrews is a reporter for the *Wall Street Journal.*

A Harvard faculty member, Professor Robert N. Anthony is a former controller of the U.S. Defense Department and a former president of the American Accounting Association.

Mr. Richard Armour is a humorist.

Editor of the *Soviet Accounting Bulletin*, Professor D. T. Bailey is at the University of Birmingham (U.K.).

Director of the Princeton University Press, Mr. Herbert S. Bailey, Jr., has also composed "The Bottom Line."

Dr. C. Richard Baker, CPA, is an assistant professor of business at Columbia University.

At Stanford University, Professor William H. Beaver, Ph.D., CPA, has received the AICPA Accounting Literature Award.

Mr. Kenneth H. Bergstrom was an industrial accountant with several companies.

Mr. Alan Breck is an English chartered accountant.

Professors Vincent C. Brenner and Paul E. Dascher are on the faculties at Louisiana State University and Drexel University, respectively.

At the City College of New York, Professor Abraham J. Briloff, Ph.D., CPA, is a widely known critic of certain accounting practices.

Mr. David Burnham is a writer for the *New York Times.*

Co-editor of this book, Professor Thomas J. Burns, Ph.D., CPA, is director of the Ph.D. program in accounting at the Ohio State University.

Formerly on the Columbia University faculty, Dr. John C. Burton, CPA, is chief accountant for the *SEC.*

Professor Steven M. Cahn is chairperson of the philosophy department at the University of Vermont.

Mr. Thomas J. Carroll, CPA, is a partner with Peat, Marwick, Mitchell & Co.

At the University of Sydney, Australia, Professor Raymond J. Chambers advocates current values in prize-winning literature.

Ms. Sau Lan Chan is an industrial accountant.

Mr. Robert H. Chenhall is an Australian accountant.

A graduate of the University of California at Berkeley in accounting, Mr. Michael Chetkovich, CPA, is a managing partner at Haskins & Sells.

Mr. Richard Cornuelle is a writer.

Both at Carnegie Mellon University, Dr. Richard M. Cyert is its president and Professor Yuji Ijiri, Ph.D., CPA, is an award-winning accounting researcher.

Former president of the American Accounting Association, Dr. Sidney Davidson, CPA, is the Arthur Young Professor of Accounting at the University of Chicago.

A pioneer in managerial economics, Emeritus Professor Joel Dean was at Columbia University.

William O. Douglas was a member of the U.S. Supreme Court for many years.

Drs. James Don Edwards, CPA, and Carl S. Warren, CPA, are both professors at the University of Georgia; Dr. Edwards has received the American Accounting Association's Outstanding Educator Award.

Mr. Robert K. Elliott, CPA, is a partner in the executive offices of Peat, Marwick, Mitchell and Co.

Mr. Charles T. Farley is a retired manager for the G.A.F. Corporation.

Ms. Helen Fearnley is news editor for *Accountancy*, the journal of the Institute of Chartered Accountants in England and Wales.

Professor Gerald A. Feltham, Ph.D., of the University of British Columbia (Canada), is currently visiting Stanford University.

The late Robert Frost was a worldfamous American poet.

Liz Roman Gallese is a reporter for the *Wall Street Journal.*

With an M.B.A. from the Harvard Business School, Mr. Donald E. Garretson is corporate vice president and treasurer at the 3M Company.

A former partner of Haskins & Sells, Mr. Oscar S. Gellein, CPA, is a member of the Financial Accounting Standards Board.

The best-known "professional shareholder" in the United States, Mr. Lewis D. Gilbert crusades for improved financial reporting.

Formerly an M.I.T. faculty member, Emeritus Professor Billy E. Goetz now teaches at Florida Atlantic University.

Assistant Professor Michael H. Granof is at the University of Texas at Austin.

Mr. Malvern J. Gross is a partner with the Price Waterhouse public accounting firm.

Mr. Walter E. Hanson is managing partner of Peat, Marwick, Mitchell & Co., the world's largest public accounting firm.

The late Professor Henry Rand Hatfield, of the University of California at Berkeley, was a prize-winning accounting author.

Mr. John M. Healy is assistant editor of *Dun's Review*.

Mr. John Heath, Jr., is director of business development for Marshall & Stevens, an international appraising firm.

Co-editor of this book, Dr. Harvey S. Hendrickson, CPA, is chairperson of the accounting and finance department at the Florida International University.

Dr. Leo Herbert is a retired U.S. General Accounting Office official.

A graduate of the Ohio State University, Mr. Ernest L. Hicks, CPA, is a partner with Arthur Young & Co. and author of AICPA Accounting Research Study No. 8.

A chartered accountant, Mr. Geoffrey Holmes is editor of *Accountancy*.

Oliver Wendell Holmes was a member of the U.S. Supreme Court for more than 50 years.

The well-known textbook author, Professor Charles T. Horngren, Ph.D., CPA, of Stanford University is president-elect of the American Accounting Association (which gave him its Outstanding Educator's Award in 1973).

Mr. Harold H. Jack has been the controller for the AFL-CIO unions since 1955.

Associate Dean at Stanford University, Dr. Robert Jaedicke, CPA, holds a chair in accounting at Stanford University.

Mr. Harvey Kapnick, CPA, is managing partner of Arthur Andersen & Co., Chicago.

Mr. N. R. Kleinfield is a reporter for the *Wall Street Journal.*

Dr. R. M. Lall, a chartered accountant in India, is senior lecturer at Singapore Polytechnic.

Dr. Charles W. Lamden, CPA, is a partner with Peat, Marwick, Mitchell & Co.; Dr. Dale L. Gerboth, CPA, is a staff member for the Financial Accounting Standards Board.

Dr. E. John Larsen, CPA, is an associate professor of accounting at the University of Southern California.

Dr. Charles Lawrence, CPA, is a professor of accounting at Purdue University.

Mr. Donald L. LoFranco, chartered accountant, is a manager with Gardner, McDonald & Co., Toronto; Mr. Herbert Hartley, chartered accountant, is a partner with Coopers & Lybrand in the same city.

Mr. Peter D. Louderback is with Peat, Marwick, Mitchell & Co.

The late John F. Loughlin was a manager in the Milwaukee office of Coopers & Lybrand; he held a degree in accounting from the University of Detroit.

A retired partner with Ernst & Ernst, Mr. Herbert T. McAnly, CPA, is known as "Mr. LIFO" for developing dollar-value LIFO.

Mr. David W. McHenry, who graduated in accounting from West Virginia University, now attends law school there.

Mr. Glenn McHugh is a former executive for the Equitable Life Assurance Society of the United States.

Mr. Robert L. McKinnell is a Canadian chartered accountant.

Mr. Thomas W. McRae, CPA, is research administrator for the AICPA.

Mr. Henry C. Marksburg is a writer for *The Arthur Young Journal*.

Well-known author and former teacher at the University of Illinois, Dr. Robert K. Mautz, CPA, is a partner with Ernst & Ernst in Cleveland.

Mr. George Melloan is on the staff of the *Wall Street Journal*.

Professor Philip E. Meyer, D.B.A., CPA, is chairperson of the department of accounting, Boston University.

A former faculty member at Michigan State University, Dr. Herbert Miller, CPA, is a partner with Arthur Andersen in Chicago.

A former director of research for the AICPA, Professor Maurice Moonitz, Ph.D., is on the University of California at Berkeley faculty.

Dr. Gerhard G. Mueller, CPA, is chairperson of the accounting faculty at the University of Washington (Seattle).

Formerly on the Northwestern University faculty, Professor John H. Myers, Ph.D., CPA, is at Indiana University.

Given the American Accounting Association's Outstanding Educator's Award in 1975, Dr. Carl L. Nelson is the first George O. May Professor of Financial Accounting at Columbia University.

Mr. David Norr, CPA and CFA (chartered financial analyst), is partner in charge of research at the First Manhattan Co.

Mr. Russell E. Palmer, CPA, is managing partner of Touche Ross.

An accounting historian, Professor R. H. Parker was appointed to a chair of accountancy at Dundee University (Scotland) in 1970.

Professor Emeritus of Accounting and Economics at the University of Michigan, Dr. William A. Paton, CPA, has been an author for over 50 years.

Formerly on the Louisiana State University faculty, Dr. James W. Pattillo, CPA, is the Peat, Marwick, Mitchell Professor of Accounting at the University of Notre Dame.

Mr. Bill Paul is a reporter for the *Wall Street Journal*.

Mr. Roger F. Pickering is a CPA in the state of Wisconsin.

Mr. Robert F. Randall is a freelance writer for business periodicals.

Mr. Frank Ryan is head of his own computer services firm; Drs. Arthur J. Francia and Robert H. Strawser are accounting professors at the University of Houston and Texas A & M University, respectively.

Mr. Telly Savalas is a totally bald actor in films and on television.

Professor George M. Scott, D.B.A., is on the accounting faculty at the University of Texas at Austin.

Professor C. D. Sears, of the Western Australian Institute of Technology, has extensive industrial accounting experience.

Dr. Lee J. Seidler, CPA, is a professor of accounting at New York University.

Mr. Theodore Shabad is a correspondent for the *New York Times.*

Mr. Keith Shwayder is vice president and general manager of the Samsonite corporation.

Mr. Lee Smith is a reporter for *Dun's Review.*

Dr. David Solomons, CA, is the Arthur Young Professor of Accounting at the Wharton School.

Mr. Edward Sorel is a writer.

Mr. Kenneth H. Spencer, CA, is a partner of Peat, Marwick, Mitchell & Co. in Melbourne, Australia.

A former president of the American Accounting Association and Stanford University faculty member, Dr. Robert T. Sprouse, CPA, is vice chairman of the Financial Accounting Standards Board.

Mr. Ron Stinson and Mr. Dick Faulk are former students of Professor William A. Paton at the University of Michigan; their present whereabouts are unknown.

A graduate of the Ohio State University, Mr. Thomas L. Stober is a doctoral student at the University of Chicago.

With two earned degrees, Mr. Richard W. Swalley is supervisor of Cost and Factory Accounting, Firestone Plastics Company, a subsidiary of Firestone Tire and Rubber Company.

On the faculty at Dundee University (Scotland), Mr. Iain W. Symon is a CA.

Ms. Ann Tomlinson is a reporter for *The Lantern*, the Ohio State University student newspaper.

Dr. Ivor E. Tower is a principal lecturer at the Bullamahanka College of Advanced Education, Australia.

Mr. William L. Ureel is chief accountant for Atomic Power Development Associates, Inc., in Detroit, Michigan.

Mr. George C. Watt, CPA, is a Price Waterhouse partner in charge of accounting standards research for his firm.

A graduate from the University of Oklahoma, Mr. Joseph T. Wells is a special agent with the F.B.I.

Mr. Donald Welsch is an economist with the Peat, Marwick, Mitchell & Co. public accounting firm.

Mr. Craig E. Wood, CPA, is finance vice president of the Maysteel Corporation.

A self-described "night-school accountant," Mr. Walter B. Wriston is chairperson of the First National City Corporation and its major subsidiary, First National City Bank.

An accounting historian, Dr. Stephen A. Zeff, CPA, is professor of accounting at Tulane University.

# List of Periodicals

*Abacus* is published semiannually since 1965 by the Sydney University Press (Press Building, University of Sydney, N.S.W., Australia). Its editor is Murray Wells.

*Accountancy* is a monthly first published in 1889 by the Institute of Chartered Accountants in England and Wales (56-66 Goswell Road, London, E.C.1, England). Its editor is Geoffrey Holmes.

*The Accountant*, the "accountant's newspaper," is a weekly first published in 1874 by Gee & Co. (Publishers), Limited, London. Its editor is Arthur E. Webb.

*The Accounting Historian* is published quarterly since 1974 by the Academy of Accounting History. Its editor is Gary Previtts.

*The Accountants' Journal* is a monthly first published in 1922 by the New Zealand Society of Accountants (Box 10046, Wellington, New Zealand). Its editor is J. C. Jamieson.

*The Accountant's Magazine* is a monthly first published in 1897 by the Institute of Chartered Accountants of Scotland (Accountant's Publishing Co. Ltd., 27 Queen Street, Edinburgh 2, Scotland). Its editor is E. H. V. McDougall.

*Accountants Weekly* is published weekly since 1973 by Morgan-Grampian (Professional Press) Limited (Calderwood Street, London). Its editor is Brian Hale.

The *Accounting Review* is a quarterly first published in 1926 by the American Accounting Association (653 South Orange Avenue, Sarasota, Fla. 33577). Its current editor is Don DeCoster.

*The Arthur Andersen Chronicle* is a quarterly first published in 1940 by the international accounting firm, Arthur Andersen & Co. Its editor is Charles E. Beall.

The *Arthur Young Journal* is a quarterly first published in 1953 by the international accounting firm, Arthur Young & Co. (277 Park Avenue, New York, N.Y., 10017). Its editor is Albert Newgarden.

*The Australian Accountant* is a monthly (except January) first published in 1936 by the Australian Society of Accountants and Australian Institute of Cost Accountants (Accountants Publishing Co., Ltd., 49 Exhibition Street, Melbourne, Australia). Its editor is Dagnija Misins.

*Barron's* is published weekly since 1921 by Dow Jones & Co. (22 Cortland St., New York, 10007). Its editor is Robert M. Blaiberg.

The *Beta Alpha Psi Newsletter* is published three times a year by the National Council of Beta Alpha Psi. Its editor is Doris Cook.

*Business Week* is a weekly first published in 1929 by McGraw-Hill, Inc. (1221 Avenue of the Americas, New York, N.Y. 10020). Its editor is Lewis H. Young.

*California Management Review* is a quarterly first published in 1958 by the Graduate Schools of Business Administration of the University of California, Berkeley, Los Angeles, and Irvine (Berkeley, Calif. 94720). Its editor is Robert N. Katz.

*Canadian Chartered Accountant* is a monthly first published in 1911 by The Canadian Institute of Chartered Accountants (69 Bloor Street E., Toronto, Canada). Its editor is L. J. Reesor.

*Certified Accountants Journal* is a monthly first published in 1905 by the Association of Certified and Corporate Accountants (22 Bedford Square, London, W.C. 1, England). Its editor is Robert Bell.

*The Certified General Accountant* is published five times a year by the Certified General Accountants' Association of Canada (25 Adelaide St. E., Toronto, Canada). Its editor is Gordon W. Fuller.

*The Chartered Accountant in Australia* is a monthly first published in 1930 by the Institute of Chartered Accountants in Australia (Box 3921, B.P.O., Sydney, Australia 200). Its editor is William T. Brown.

*Columbus Evening Dispatch* is published daily in Columbus, Ohio, since 1870 by Columbus Dispatch Printing Co. (34 S. Third St., Columbus, Ohio 43215). Its editor is Carl DeBloom.

*Coopers & Lybrand Journal* is published quarterly since 1920 by the International accounting firm, Coopers & Lybrand (1252 Avenue of Americas, New York, N.Y. 10020). Its editor is Morton Meyerson.

*Cost and Management* is a bimonthly first published in 1926 by the Society of Industrial and Cost Accountants of Canada (154 Main Street East, Hamilton, Ontario, Canada). Its editor is Jacqueline H. Hewer.

*The CPA Journal* is published monthly since 1960 by the New York State Society of Certified Public Accountants (600 3d Avenue, New York, N.Y. 10016). Its editor is Dan G. Kramer.

*Dun's Review* is published monthly since 1893 by Dun & Bradstreet Publishers (666 Fifth Avenue, New York, N.Y. 10019). Its editor is Raymond Brady.

*Esquire* is published monthly since 1933 by Esquire, Inc. (488 Madison Ave., New York, N.Y. 10022). Its editor is Don Erickson.

*Financial Analysts Journal* is published six times a year since 1945 by the Financial Analysts Federation (219 East 42d Street, New York, N.Y. 10036). Its editor is Jack L. Treynor.

*Financial Executive* is published monthly since 1934 by The Financial Executives Institute (633 3d Avenue, New York, N.Y. 10017). Its editor is Carl Cerminaro.

*Forbes* is published semimonthly since 1917 by Forbes, Inc. (60 5th Avenue, New York, N.Y. 10011). Its editor is James Michaels.

*Fortune* is published fourteen times a year by Time, Inc. (Time and Life Building, New York, N.Y. 10020). Its editor is Hedley Donovan.

*Harvard Business Review* is published every two months since 1922 by the Harvard Business School (Soldiers Field, Boston, Mass. 02163). Its editor is Ralph F. Lewis.

*H&S Reports* is published quarterly since 1964 by the international accounting firm, Haskins & Sells (2 Broadway, New York, N. Y. 10004). Its editor is Harry Levy.

*The Journal of Accountancy* is published monthly since 1905 by the AICPA (666 5th Avenue, New York, N. Y. 10019). Its editor is Lee Berton.

*Journal of Accounting Research* is published semiannually (plus a supplement on the proceedings of the University of Chicago's annual accounting conference) since 1963 by the London School of Economics and Graduate School of Business, University of Chicago (Chicago, Ill. 60637). Its editor is Nicholas Dopuch.

*Journal of Contemporary Business* is published quarterly since 1972 by the Graduate School of Business Administration, University of Washington (Seattle, Wash. 98195). Its editor is Nancy L. Jacob.

*Management Accounting* (formerly the *NAA Bulletin*) is published monthly since 1919 by the National Association of Accountants (919 3d Avenue, New York, N.Y. 10022). Its editor is Ervin S. Koval.

*Management Science* (merged with *Management Technology* in 1965) is published monthly since 1952 by The Institute of Management Sciences (146 Westminister Street, Providence, R.I. 02903). Its editor is Martin K. Starr.

*Managerial Planning* (formerly *Budgeting*) is published bimonthly since 1952 by the Planning Executives Institute (P.O. Box 70, Oxford, Ohio 45056). Its editor is Henry C. Doofe.

*New York* is published weekly (except for a combined issue the last two weeks in December) since 1968 by the NYM Corporation (755 2d Avenue, New York, N.Y. 10017). Its editor is Clay S. Felker.

The *New York Times* is a morning newspaper published daily in New York since 1851 by the New York Times Co. (229 W. 43d St., New York, N.Y. 10036). Its managing editor is A. M. Rosenthal.

*Newsweek* is published weekly since 1938 by Newsweek, Inc. (The Newsweek Building, Livingston, N.J. 07039). Its editor is Osborn Elliott.

*The Ohio CPA* is published quarterly since 1942 by the Ohio Society of CPA's (P.O. Box 617, Worthington, Ohio 43085). Its editor is Henry C. Pusker.

*The Practical Accountant* is published bimonthly since 1968 by the Institute for Continuing Professional Development, Inc. (119 W. 57th St., New York, N.Y. 10019). Its editors are Robert A. Behren and Alex Cohen.

*Price Waterhouse Review* is published quarterly since 1955 by the international public accounting firm, Price Waterhouse. Its editor is Arden Eidell.

The *San Francisco Chronicle* is published daily in San Francisco since 1865 by the San Francisco Newspaper Publishing Co. (905 Mission St., San Francisco, Calif. 94119). Its editor is Randolph Hearst.

The *Wall Street Journal* is published each morning Monday through Friday since 1889 by Dow Jones & Co., Inc. (30 Broad Street, New York, N.Y. 10004). Its editor is Edward Cony.

The *Wisconsin CPA* is published monthly since 1933 by the Wisconsin Institute of Certified Public Accountants (Room 400, 600 E. Mason St., Milwaukee, Wis. 53202). Its editor is Robert N. Berkopes.

*World* is a quarterly published since 1967 by the international public accounting firm, Peat, Marwick, Mitchell & Co. (345 Park Avenue, New York, N.Y. 10022). Its editor is Gerald J. Barry.

# Preface

As the first published readings book developed chiefly for introductory courses, the third edition of *The Accounting Sampler* reflects the strengths of the first two editions while improving upon them in several major ways.

Drawing on the experience of those using the *Sampler*, the selections included are on the average shorter, more people-oriented, and more straightforward than those included in earlier editions. Since most of the articles are shorter, the editors have been able to increase this number by about two-thirds (to 153 items) without adding appreciably to the length of the book. It is also substantially a different collection since only slightly over 10 percent of the articles included were in the previous edition. The contents of this book were drawn from 75 sources and from the leading accounting and business periodicals of several countries. In addition to the study questions prepared on the articles (as per our previous editions), we have included in this edition for the first time both a selected bibliography for most articles and an index for all the selections. Where it seemed appropriate, we have prepared brief comments on individual articles. We have also included a chart which shows how each selection may be studied to complement the appropriate chapter of thirteen leading elementary accounting textbooks. We have included at the start of the book a list of the authors (and their backgrounds) and a list of periodicals in which their articles appeared (together with the periodical's address and the name of its editor). For the use of instructors, a Solutions Manual has been prepared which contains answers to the study questions and digests of every selection.

The articles in this collection could be read very profitably with or without previous or subsequent class discussion. The editors have provided a blend of both old (up to 50 years) and new materials. There are several types of articles which have not been included in the earlier editions. There are pieces on international accounting, nonprofit organizations, social accounting, accounting organizations, the rule-making agencies, accounting history, and even the Accounting Hall of Fame. There are articles by a Peace Corps accountant, a movie accountant, a young CPA, an accountant in the FBI, two retiring accountants, an accountant for artists, sports accountants, management accountants, a controller, and many more. There are selections on accounting for cattle ranching, a drive-in diner, Jack Nicklaus, United Fund Agencies, football teams, nuclear fuel, and others. Many distinguished scholars have authored selections; there are also articles by many leading practitioners from government, industry, and the profession. For example, there are selections by representatives of the three accounting policy makers: the FASB, the SEC, and the CASB. There are also pieces by four managing partners of Big Eight firms. Material is included on many current controversies or recent developments in accounting: forecasts, leases, pensions, inflation accounting, franchising, human assets, multinationals, segment reporting, tax allocation, goodwill, GAAP, the Trueblood report, auditor's liability, extraordinary items, and others. Yet there are many selections on more conventional subject matter, such as financial statement items and the statements themselves, including both fund statements and budgets.

Special recognition should be made of the many users of the earlier editions who with their suggestions have helped us in preparing this edition. This book continues to be dedicated to the first George O. May Professor of Accounting at Columbia University, and a contributor of several articles in this edition. We are proud that the American Accounting Association has given him its Outstanding Educator Award in 1975. As a teacher, advisor, and friend, he has had a remarkable influence on our lives. Whatever our contributions may be to this book, the most worthwhile aspects can be traced to the influence of Professor Carl L. Nelson.

Thomas J. Burns
Harvey S. Hendrickson

# Correlation Table: How Sampler Selections Relate to Chapters of Various Elementary Accounting Texts

| TEXT (AUTHORS) | 1 | 2 | 3 | 4 | 5 | 6 | 7 |
|---|---|---|---|---|---|---|---|
| Anthony-Welsch (2 vols.) | 1/1 | 2-5, 12, 15 | 6-11 | 1-16 | 14 | 1/15/16 | 16 |
| Burns & Hendrickson | 1 | 3-6 | 2 | | 7-11 | 1, 12 | 12 |
| Gordon & Shillinglaw | 1 | 2-3, 5-18, 15-17 | 10-14 | 1, 4, 18-25 | 10-16 | 9, 17, 18 | 1, 8, 10 |
| Gray & Johnson | 1 | 7, 8, 9 | 3 | 2-15 | 6 | 16 | 16 |
| May, Mueller, & Williams | 1, 2 | 4-6, 15 | 7-14 | 1-2, 3 | 17 | 3, 2 | 4, 17 |
| Meigs, Mosich, & Johnson | 1 | 2-6, 8-9, 13, 15-19, 21 | 10-12 | 7, 22, 27 | 28 | 20 | 6 |
| Meigs, Mosich, & Meigs | 1 | 2-5, 7-10, 15 | 11-12 | | 13-14, 17 | 1, 16 | 6 |
| Niswonger & Fess | 1 | 2-12, 15-18, 26 | 8-10 | 19-22, 24, 25 | 14, 23 | 27-28 | 13 |
| Perry | 1 | 2-5, 7, 9, 14-17, 20 | 5, 9-13 | 23-25, 26 | 18-19 | 19-22 | 8 |
| Pyle & White | 1 | 2-5, 8-9, 13, 15-19, 21 | 10-12 | 7, 22-27 | 28 | 20 | 6 |
| Thacker | 1, 2 | 3, 5-9, 13-14 | 4, 10-12 | 10-14 | 15 | 3, 10-14 | 4, 16 |
| Thomas | 1 | 2-9 | 10-13 | | 13 | 13 | |
| Tracy | 1 | 2-4 | 5-11 | | 14 | 1, 13 | 13 |

Numbers at top of the columns refer to the parts of *The Accounting Sampler*. Numbers to the right of the authors' names refer to chapters in each of the texts.

# Part 1
# The Accounting Environment

# 1

## WHAT DOES IT STAND FOR?*

Institute of Chartered Accountants of Scotland

| | |
|---|---|
| AAA: | American Accounting Association |
| ACA: | Association of Certified Accountants |
| ACA: | Associate of ICAEW |
| ACA: | Associate of ICAI |
| ACCA: | Associate of ACA |
| ACMA: | Associate of ICMA |
| AICPA: | American Institute of Certified Public Accountants |
| AISG: | Accountants' International Study Group |
| AJPC: | Accountants' Joint Parliamentary Committee |
| APB: | Accounting Principles Board (now FASB) |
| ARS: | Accounting Research Study |
| ASA: | Australian Society of Accountants |
| ASR: | Accounting Series Release (of SEC-US) |
| ASSC: | Accounting Standards Steering Committee |
| AUTA: | Association of University Teachers of Accounting |
| | |
| BAFA: | British Accounting and Finance Association |
| BCS: | British Computer Society |
| BE: | Bureau Elargi (EEC accountancy bodies) |
| | |
| CA: | Chartered Accountant |
| CAPA: | Conference of Asian and Pacific Accountants |
| CASB: | Cost Accounting Standards Board (US) |
| CASSL: | Chartered Accountants Students' Society of London |
| CCAB: | Consultative Committee of Accountancy Bodies |
| CICA: | Canadian Institute of Chartered Accountants |
| CIPFA: | Chartered Institute of Public Finance and Accountancy |
| CPA: | Certified Public Accountant |
| | |
| DM: | Discussion Memorandum, FASB |
| | |
| ED: | Exposure Draft, FASB |
| EEC: | European Economic Community |
| | |
| FASB: | Financial Accounting Standards Board (US) |
| | |
| GAAP: | Generally Accepted Accounting Principles |
| Gd'E: | Groupe d'Etudes (EEC accountancy bodies) |
| GNP: | Gross National Product |
| | |
| IAAC: | Inter-America Accounting Conference |
| IASC: | International Accounting Standards Committee |

*From *The Accountant's Magazine*, November 1974, pp. 440–442. Reprinted by permission of the publisher.

ICAA:        Institute of Chartered Accountants in Australia
ICAEW:       Institute of Chartered Accountants in England and Wales
ICAI:        Institute of Chartered Accountants in Ireland
ICAS:        Institute of Chartered Accountants of Scotland
ICCAP:       International Co-ordination Committee for Accountancy Profession
ICMA:        Institute of Cost and Management Accountants
ICRA:        International Centre for Research in Accounting (Lancaster)
IdW:         Institut der Wirtschaftsprüfer in Deutschland
IFIP:        International Federation for Information Processing
IMTA:        Institute of Municipal Treasurers and Accountants (now CIPFA)
INSEAD:      Institut Européen d'Administration des Affaires
IRRAF:       International Register of Research in Accounting and Finance

LGAA:        Local Government Auditors (Scotland) Association

MBO:         Management by Objectives

NAA:         National Association of Accountants (US)
NCC Ltd:     National Computing Centre Limited
NIvRA:       Nederlands Instituut van Registeraccountants

OR:          Operations (al) Research

RA:          Registeraccountant (Member of NIvRA)

SACA:        South African Chartered Accountant
SCAH:        Scottish Committee on Accounting History
SEC:         Securities and Exchange Commission (US)


## QUESTIONS

1. What is the only country in the world that has CPAs?
2. What is the equivalent of a CPA in other countries?
3. Why are such initials as MBO and OR included in the listing?
4. What initials might be added to the list?

# 2
# DEVELOPING ACCOUNTING PRINCIPLES*
Stephen A. Zeff

Attempts by the American accounting profession to establish accounting "principles" or "standards" have been characterized by an increasing degree of collaboration with both enforcement agencies and affected parties. Several factors explain this tendency.

In marked contrast to the professional accountancy bodies in Canada, England, Scotland and Australia, the American Institute of Certified Public Accountants (AICPA) is a voluntary association of CPAs. Although the accountancy bodies in most countries of the British Commonwealth themselves award accounting qualifications to successful candidates, American CPAs are licensed under state law. Upon becoming a CPA and satisfying a minimum experience requirement, one may apply for membership in the AICPA. While the institute's current membership of 90,000 members (out of a total of about 140,000 CPAs) includes virtually all the partners in the major CPA firms, the institute has not always enjoyed such a broad base of support. Indeed, between 1921 and 1936, the institute coexisted with a rival organization known as the American Society of Certified Public Accountants. For these reasons, the American Institute has sought the cooperation of enforcement agencies in the establishment of accounting principles.

A second important reason, at least since 1934, for the institute's reliance on support agencies has been the existence of the Securities and Exchange Commission (SEC). The SEC, which is advised by an accounting staff headed by a Chief Accountant, has broad powers to determine the accounting and auditing practices employed in the preparation and verification of financial statements issued by the largest and most important U.S. corporations. The AICPA hardly could ignore the opinions of the SEC and its accounting staff in the formulation of its own policies on accounting and auditing. In fact, due to the urging of the SEC, the Institute in 1939 launched a program resulting in the issuance of a series of pronouncements on accounting principles.

The institute's collaboration with support agencies and affected parties intensified during the 1960s, when powerful segments in the public and private sectors "discovered" accounting. One by one, these segments became aware that accounting was beset by controversies and that accounting practices could be treated as variables instead of as system parameters. As forces began to coalesce in opposition to proposed accounting reforms, the leaders of the profession began to sense that the achievement of important progress in accounting required political and diplomatic skills as well as technical and professional expertise. Public hearings and extensive liaison activities typified the profession's approach to controversial questions in the closing years of the decade.

*From the *Journal of Contemporary Business*, Spring 1973, pp. 41—50. Reprinted by permission of the publisher.

## EARLY INITIATIVES

Sporadic attempts to fashion accounting principles were registered between 1917 and the late 1930s, both by the AICPA and the American Accounting Association. In 1917, a pamphlet which not only was concerned with auditing procedures but which also touched upon accounting and disclosure questions was published by the Federal Reserve Board on the recommendation of the Federal Trade Commission and a special committee of the AICPA. Revisions of the pamphlet were published in 1929 and 1936.

In the following year, 1918, another special committee of the institute recommended against acceptance of a controversial accounting practice which was being urged in the journals, and its report was adopted at the institute's annual convention. For the first time, institute members were requested to abide by an accounting recommendation of one of its committees.

During the ensuing decade, nothing of major significance occurred concerning accounting principles, although an AICPA committee exchanged suggestions for improved financial reporting with a committee of Robert Morris Associates, an organization of bank loan officers.

In 1930, the New York Stock Exchange accepted an invitation to join with the American Institute in elevating the financial reporting standards of listed corporations. George O. May, senior partner in Price Waterhouse & Co., was responsible for bringing the two parties together. May was aware of the need of the AICPA to collaborate with support agencies, and he regarded the exchange as an important prospective partner. May was named chairman of the special committee of the institute to cooperate with the exchange. He continued to be at the cutting edge of most of the institute's significant initiatives in accounting principles until the early 1940s, and he remained a potent force into the 1950s.

Quintessential to May's accounting philosophy, which permeates the report which the institute's special committee on cooperation with the exchange issued in 1933-1934, was that listed companies should clearly formulate and publicly disclose their accounting policies. Several specific accounting principles were recommended by the special committee and were adopted by the AICPA membership at the 1934 annual meeting.

As the institute and the exchange were consummating their collaborative effort, Congress passed two major securities acts which regulated, among other things, the nature and scope of financial disclosures by corporations which issue large amounts of securities in interstate markets or whose securities are listed on national exchanges. The second of these acts, the Securities Exchange Act of 1934, established the Securities and Exchange Commission. A year later, the commission created the Office of Chief Accountant. Carman G. Blough, the first incumbent, immediately began taking steps to encourage the standardization of accounting practice. Blough urged the profession to establish norms of good practice. Little of consequence was heard in response—in part, perhaps, because the institute was engaged in protracted discussions over a possible merger with its chief rival, the American Society of CPAs. But it seems plausible to believe that leading members of the institute seriously doubted that it should "dictate" accounting practices to its members. May's philosophy was one of flexibility coupled with the disclosure of the accounting principles which corporations believed were most appropriate in their particular circumstances. To recommend standard accounting practices, apart from general guidelines, would have been anathematic.

Leading university accounting educators were critical of the institute's weak response to the SEC's challenge. Largely in order to fill this void, the American Association of University Instructors in Accounting reorganized itself in 1935-1936 as the American Accounting Association and launched a research program aimed at articulating and clarifying the concepts underlying accounting practice. In 1936, the association's executive committee issued a report containing a concise statement of basic accounting principles. The association's leaders hoped that this document would stimulate the kind of discussion which was envisaged by the SEC, with the eventual outcome of promoting greater rationality in financial reporting. But the institute ignored the association's statement and in 1938 published a report that had been commissioned 3 years earlier by a large accounting firm. With characteristic caution, the institute withheld its endorsement of the authors' recommendations.

The American Accounting Association commenced a series of monographs and, in 1940, published *An Introduction to Corporate Accounting Standards* by W. A. Paton and A. C. Littleton, which was intended to be an elaboration of the association's 1936 Statement. The association's 1936 Statement was revised and reissued in 1941, 1948 and 1957.

## COMMITTEE ON ACCOUNTING PROCEDURE

In 1937-1938, the SEC reached a critical juncture in the development of its policy on accounting principles. In prior years, acting mainly through the Chief Accountant, the SEC had sought to encourage the accounting profession to codify and reduce the number of its diverse accounting practices. When it became clear that this strategy was unavailing, forces began to build within the commission for unilateral action. The Chief Accountant took advantage of a temporary impasse among the commissioners to issue an Accounting Series Release which said that financial statements filed with the commission would be presumed to be misleading or inaccurate if they were prepared in accordance with accounting principles for which there was no "substantial authoritative support." The message to the profession was abundantly clear. Unless it took steps to provide the SEC with "substantial authoritative support," the commission would make its own declarations of "generally accepted accounting principles."

Thus prodded by the commission, the institute authorized its Committee on Accounting Procedure to develop and issue pronouncements on accounting principles, without the necessity of obtaining prior approval from either the executive committee or the council. Representatives from all the large CPA firms were appointed to the committee, which promptly assumed front-rank importance in the institute's affairs. A research staff was set up to assist the committee. At first, it was headed by a part-time director; in 1944, the services of a full-time director were secured.

Between 1939 and 1959, the institute's committee issued 51 Accounting Research Bulletins, including 8 which dealt exclusively with terminology. The committee worked in close liaison with the SEC's accounting staff. Seldom did the committee proceed with a proposed bulletin when it was known that the SEC opposed the recommended treatment. Yet, for the better part of the committee's 22-year history, it was locked in disagreement with the SEC's accounting staff over the propriety of special charges and credits in the retained earnings account. A bulletin issued by the committee in 1947 provoked the SEC Chief Accountant to publish a letter expressing his disagreement. In 1950-1951, a proposed bulletin on upward quasireorganizations which had received CAP's unanimous approval was pigeonholed once the SEC communicated its unequivocal disagreement with the contents. However, in the large majority of instances, the committee and the SEC's accounting staff were in general accord.

During the period 1939-1959, other organizations expressed an interest in the committee's work. On several occasions, notably involving the accounting for stock dividends, the New York Stock Exchange requested the committee to issue a pronouncement. The exchange advised the presidents of listed companies that it endorsed the committee's position on stock dividends.

In the 1940s, the institute's research staff began to expose drafts of proposed pronouncements to interested parties. Among these recipients, one of the most vocal was the Controller's Institute of America, especially when three bulletins were promulgated by the committee in 1947 without first issuing exposure drafts. One of the bulletins expressed the committee's disapproval of the accounting recognition of replacement-cost depreciation.

By and large, however, during the 1940s and 1950s, the determination of "generally accepted accounting principles" was left to the accounting profession, specifically the American Institute's Committee on Accounting Procedure. Only infrequently were accounting questions discussed in the financial press. The accounting profession, for its part, sought the assistance of outside parties chiefly through the exposure process. Of course, it regularly consulted with the SEC, and, with few exceptions, the SEC looked to the accounting profession for "substantial authoritative support." As one SEC chairman, himself a CPA, later said of the commission's attitude toward accounting principles, "It was my experience [as SEC Chairman] that the commission generally considered promulgations by the institute's Committee on Accounting Procedure as correctly representing applicable accounting principles."[1]

## ACCOUNTING PRINCIPLES BOARD (APB)

During the middle and late 1950s, criticism within the profession of the direction and pace of the Committee on Accounting Procedure (CAP) began to grow. It was believed

---

[1]Affidavit by Donald C. Cook, 6 May 1959 in "The AICPA Injunction Case; RE ARB 44 (Revised)," *Cases in Public Accounting Practice*, Vol. 1 (Chicago: Arthur Andersen & Co., 1960), p. 74. Cook was SEC Chairman from 1952 to 1953.

by some that the committee was reaching unacceptable compromises on important questions, while avoiding other issues altogether. The absence of in-depth research preceding formulation of the committee's recommendations contributed, in the opinion of some observers, to shallow and poorly reasoned bulletins. In response to the mounting dissatisfaction with the work of the CAP, the institute (in 1957) appointed a blue-ribbon panel to recommend changes in its overall approach to developing accounting principles. Among the panel members was a representative of the Controllers Institute, which had lately been intensifying its communications with the CAP. In 1958, following several months of meetings and study, the panel recommended that the CAP be replaced by an Accounting Principles Board (APB to be supported by a full-time accounting research staff). At the outset, the research input was to consist of studies on basic postulates and broad accounting principles which, it was hoped, would lay the groundwork for the board's future pronouncements on specific topics. Subsequent research studies were to be commissioned on each subject on which the board sought to make a pronouncement. Therefore, implicit in the panel's recommendation was the belief that research, particularly into the basic concepts underlying accounting practice, would facilitate a resolution of the complex issues that were likely to come before the board. The institute's executive committee and council accepted the panel's recommendation, and the new plan was put into effect in 1959.

Unlike the old CAP, the APB was, by edict of the institute's executive committee, composed of the managing partners of individual firms. Through the participation of the firms' top partners, it was believed that the board would carry even greater weight with members of the profession. However, it soon became clear that this expectation was matched by a less than satisfactory performance by some of the managing partners. In a number of instances, they were too busy in their firms to prepare adequately for board meetings and they were often strong-willed individuals who disliked compromise. Therefore, beginning in 1964 they were gradually replaced by the senior technical partners in their firms. In addition to partners in CPA firms, the board membership also included academics and, for the first time on institute committees concerned with accounting principles, CPAs employed in industry.

A research director was appointed in 1960, and within 2 years the board had in hand a pair of monographs proposing postulates and broad principles for use in their deliberations. But the researchers' conclusions were judged to be so incompatible with accepted practice that the APB peremptorily discarded the two studies. Instead of initially establishing the precepts which would underlie its future pronouncements on specific questions, as was envisaged by the Institute's special panel in 1958, the board proceeded to deal directly with the specific questions.

The impact of subsequent research studies on the board's decisions was only somewhat more positive than was that of the postulates and principles studies. Of the 31 Opinions and 4 Statements issued by the Board through 1973, only 11 were preceded by research studies on the same subject. Of these eleven, only two could be said to have been proximately influenced in any material respect by the prior research. This disappointing record is a product of the lack of a research tradition among accounting professionals. Members of the profession are basically experiential in orientation—i.e., they look to the wisdom of accumulated experience rather than to the findings of research and investigation.

Aside from the failure of research to have an important effect on the outcome of board deliberations, the most noteworthy development during the board's 14-year tenure has been the growing interest, involvement and intervention of other affected parties in the determination of accounting principles. On three occasions between 1962 and 1971, the federal government frustrated attempts by the board to determine appropriate accounting practice for the investment credit. At various times, powerful industry groups conspired to stop the board from issuing pronouncements on marketable securities, leases and intangible drilling costs. Industry was also a potent factor in the government's decisions on the investment credit. Although the board was the object of countervailing pressures from government and industry when it was debating a pronouncement on pooling-of-interest vs. purchase accounting, the most serious obstacle to a resolution of the problem was the board's own inability to muster a two-thirds vote for any combination of pooling and goodwill opinions. Finally, during all but 4 years of the board's life, financial journalists wrote extensively and critically about accounting abuses and the failures and frustrations of the board. Criticisms of accounting practices by Abraham J. Briloff in *Barron's* and other journals further sensitized the market to the potential variability and capriciousness of companies' accounting practices.

Industry's growing interest in accounting principles stemmed from the financial community's more careful scrutiny of corporate earnings reports. During the 1960s, corporations were coming under increasing pressure for profit performance, and some companies changed accounting methods apparently to improve their market profiles. These stratagems, once they were laid bare in analysts' newsletters and reports, intensified the concern of the financial community over the pliability of "generally accepted accounting principles." This heightened concern with the quality of financial reporting, coupled with the growing importance of the bottom line, drew the attention of the financial and business communities to the efforts of the APB to improve the standards of accounting practice. Those who believed that particular pronouncements by the board would adversely affect their standing in the eyes of the financial community, went to considerable lengths to persuade—and if that failed, to prevent—the board from carrying out its intent.

In its middle years, the board decided to take a more sensitive reading of the views of aggrieved and otherwise affected parties. The exposure process alone did not reveal the depth of feeling held by those with contrary opinions. Private meetings with industry groups soon were expanded into closed-door symposia which were intended to educate both the critics and the board members. The symposia, in turn, evolved into full-dress public hearings followed by the publication of the written submissions and oral testimony. Opponents of proposed pronouncements who sensed an unwillingness by the board to reconsider its views, appealed to the SEC, the Congress or both. In the words of two prominent analysts, accounting had become too political.

Pressures which otherwise would have been directed at the SEC were thus deflected to the APB, a body without statutory authority to enforce its own will. While the SEC continued to make known its intent to support board pronouncements, the APB's tentative positions on several of the more controversial issues either elicited a tepid response from the Commission's accounting staff or otherwise represented departures from long-standing commission policies. Unlike most of its actions in the 1940s and 1950s, the profession was not merely seeking to implement reforms which already had the support of the SEC. The board was trying to break new ground. Also unlike the experience of earlier decades, some of the board's positions were stoutly opposed by powerful industry and government forces.

This is not to suggest that the board's tenure was one of constant frustrations and little accomplishment. Its Opinions on pensions, extraordinary items, income tax allocation, bank accounting, intercorporate investments, funds statements and accounting policies introduced into financial statements, in the opinion of many, very salutary changes. Some, to be sure, would dispute this claim. The Opinions on earnings per share, pooling of interests and goodwill, while perhaps more generally criticized than most of the others, were believed by many observers to do much to correct a number of accounting and reporting abuses. But the board has been stymied on currency translations, diversified reporting (save for its innocuous Statement), marketable securities, oil and gas accounting, leases and the investment credit. As already noted, not all of these defeats were self-administered. As the board has matured, the game of establishing accounting principles has itself changed.


## CONCLUSION

The question has become whether practicing CPAs, buttressed by the presumed support of the SEC, can deal effectively with the determined opposition of industry. In-depth research and the exposure of tentative drafts for informed comment will continue to be important. The ongoing development of a broad base of support for the profession's pronouncements among practicing accountants, accounting educators and members of the financial community is still essential. But the lesson of the 1960s and the early 1970s is that the major battles may be fought in the political arena, not in the sedate milieu of the professional world.

EDITORS' NOTE: Additional material on developing accounting principles, particularly of a current nature, is located in Part 5. The APB was replaced by the Financial Accounting Standards Board in mid-1973.


## QUESTIONS

1. What reasons does Zeff offer for the increasing degree of collaboration between the American accounting profession with enforcement agencies and affected parties in attempting to establish United States accounting standards?

2. What have George O. May, Carman B. Blough, W. A. Paton, and Abraham J. Briloff contributed to the development of accounting standards?

3. Contrast and compare the CAP with the APB.

4. What has been the role of the SEC in developing accounting standards?

## SELECTED BIBLIOGRAPHY

Moonitz, Maurice, *Obtaining Agreement on Standards in the Accounting Profession*, Studies in Accounting Research No. 8, Sarasota, Fla.: American Accounting Association, 1974.

Storey, Reed K., *The Search for Accounting Principles*, New York: American Institute of Certified Public Accountants, 1964.

# 3

# GROWTH OF ACCOUNTABILITY KNOWLEDGE, 1775-1975*

Leo Herbert

EDITORS' NOTE: See the illustration on the following page for the growth of accountability knowledge.

## QUESTIONS

1. Use Kohler's dictionary or some other reference to define bookkeeping, income statement, balance sheet, auditing, and cost accounting.

2. Why has the growth of accountability knowledge increased so rapidly during the past 25 years?

## SELECTED BIBLIOGRAPHY

Kohler, Eric L., *A Dictionary for Accountants*, 5th ed., Englewood Cliffs, N.J.: Prentice-Hall, 1975. (Or see one of the earlier editions.)

Zeff, Stephen A., "Chronology of Significant Developments in the Establishment of Accounting Principles in the United States, 1926-1972," *Journal of Accounting Research*, Spring 1972, pp. 217-227.

*From "Schools of Accounting—Pros and Cons," Occasional Paper, American Assembly of Collegiate Schools of Business, August 1975, p. 6. Reprinted with permission of the author.

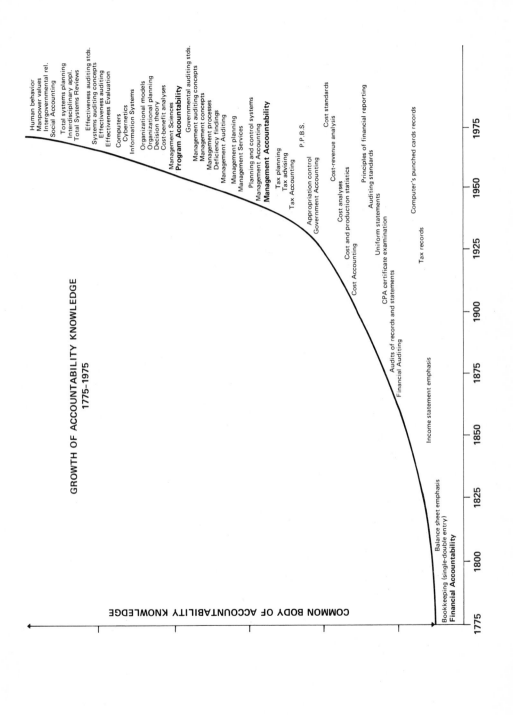

GROWTH OF ACCOUNTABILITY KNOWLEDGE
1775–1975

COMMON BODY OF ACCOUNTABILITY KNOWLEDGE

Financial Accountability
Bookkeeping (single-double entry)
Balance sheet emphasis
Income statement emphasis
Financial Auditing
Audits of records and statements
CPA certificate examination
Uniform statements
Principles of financial reporting
Tax records
Computer's punched cards records
Auditing standards
Cost Accounting
Cost and production statistics
Cost analyses
Cost-revenue analysis
Cost standards
Government Accounting
Appropriation control
Tax Accounting
Tax advising
Tax planning
P.P.B.S.
Management Accounting
Management Accountability
Management Services
Management planning
Planning and control systems
Management Auditing
Deficiency findings
Management processes
Management Accounting
Management auditing concepts
Management concepts
Governmental auditing stds.
Program Accountability
Management Sciences
Cost-benefit analyses
Decision theory
Organizational planning
Organizational models
Information Systems
Cybernetics
Computers
Effectiveness Evaluation
Effectiveness auditing
Systems auditing concepts
Effectiveness auditing stds.
Total Systems Reviews
Interdisciplinary appl.
Total systems planning
Social Accounting
Intergovernmental rel.
Manpower values
Human behavior

1775   1800   1825   1850   1875   1900   1925   1950   1975

# 4
## MONEY*
Richard Armour


Workers earn it,
Spendthrifts burn it,
Bankers lend it,
Women spend it,
Forgers fake it,
Taxes take it,
Dying leave it,
Heirs receive it,
Thrifty save it,
Misers crave it,
Robbers seize it,
Rich increase it.
Gamblers lose it . . .
I could use it.


# 5
## THOUGHTS ON WRITING†
E. John Larsen


In *Horizons for a Profession: The Common Body of Knowledge for Certified Public Accountants* (AICPA, 1967), Roy and MacNeill wrote:

> To the CPA the ability to express himself well is more than the hallmark of an educated man, it is a professional necessity. . . . We feel justified, therefore, . . . in being unequivocal about this requirement of the common body of knowledge for beginning CPAs: *candidates who cannot write the English language at least as well as a minimum-threshold should be denied admission to the profession, if need be on this account alone.*

---

*From "A Satirist Looks at the World," 2nd Annual Wm. McInally Memorial Lecture, Graduate School of Business, University of Michigan, 1967. Reprinted by permission of the publisher.

†From *The Journal of Accountancy*, September 1973, p. 102. Reprinted by permission of the publisher.

Similarly, the American Accounting Association's *A Guide to Accounting Instruction: Concepts & Practices* (South-Western Publishing Co., 1968) contains the following passage:

> Probably no other personal quality is more important than having the ability to communicate well—both in writing and orally. . . . Although accounting instructors are not supposed to be English teachers per se, it would be shirking a responsibility to the student if an extra effort was not made in this area.

I am guided by the above statements in my approach to the teaching of accounting. Accordingly, I am providing some thoughts on writing to guide my students in this critical area of their performance.

1. In all written communication, remember Socrates' query to Phaedrus: "At any rate, you will allow that every discourse ought to be a living creature, having a body of its own and a head and feet; there should be a middle, beginning, and end, adapted to one another and to the whole?"

In applying this to expository writing, make certain your exposition flows smoothly from beginning to end. The easiest way to achieve this goal is to write very much as you would speak, except, of course, for slang, excessive idioms, and the like.

2. Write principally in the *third person*. There is no need for using first or second person in most expository writing. For example, "We should avoid situations which will threaten our independence" is less desirable than "CPAs should avoid situations which will threaten their independence"; and "You confirm receivables by direct written communication with the debtors" is inferior to "The CPA confirms receivables by direct written communication with the debtors."

3. Write principally in the *active voice*. Passive voice passages are tedious to read and often result in "dangling modifiers." For example, "Most CPAs believe" is much smoother than "It is believed by most CPAs."

4. Avoid irrelevancies. Write only what is required, and no more. Irrelevant "regurgitation" appended to an examination answer often is inaccurate or contradicts the main response.

5. Avoid such grammatical shortcomings as incorrect *number*, changes in *tense, dangling modifiers, fragmentary sentences*, and long unwieldy, awkward sentence structure. With respect to the latter, it is advisable to write like a Hemingway rather than a Henry James. In Hemingway's famous short story "The Killers," for example, the first three sentences—twenty-three words in the aggregate—provide setting, three of the principal characters, and the beginning of the plot:

> The door of Henry's lunch-room opened and two men came in. They sat down at the counter.
> "What's yours?" George asked them.

In contrast, after three sentences (173 words) at the beginning of Henry James's equally famous *nouvelle*, "The Beast in the Jungle," the reader has yet to know the identity of the principal characters other than their sex and knows little of the setting or plot.

6. Learn the correct spelling and/or usage of the following words. Misspellings and/or incorrect usages of these words have frequently been found in written communication of CPA firms staff accountants, and in examinations and papers of university students majoring in accounting:

| | | |
|---|---|---|
| absorption | deferred | preferred |
| accelerated | disbursement | principal |
| accountant | effect | principle |
| accrual, accrue | evidential | procedure |
| affect | existence | profession |
| arm's length | independence, | questionnaire |
| auditor | independent | reconciliation |
| capital | judgment | relevant |
| comparative | lessee, lessor | separate |
| competent | mortgage | substantiate |
| confidential | obsolescence | supersede |
| consistent | occurrence | their |
| counsel | paid | there |
| current | practitioner | whether |

7. Recall, or learn, the correct use of the *apostrophe* in the possessive case.

8. Avoid using pronouns with vague—or missing—antecedents.

For guidance in improving your writing, consult the following:

William Strunk, Jr. and E. B. White, *The Elements of Style* (New York: The Macmillan Company, 1959).

Mary C. Bromage, "A Matter of Wording," *The Journal of Accountancy*, January 1963, pp. 59-62.

## QUESTION

1. What are common misspellings and/or incorrect usages of the following words: accrual, deferred, judgment, principle, procedure, and reconciliation.

# 6

# THE LANGUAGES OF ACCOUNTING*

R. H. Parker

Accounting, we like to think, is the language of business. But what are the languages of accounting? If we accept the authority of the second edition of the *UEC Lexicon*,[1] there are at least eight: French, German, English, Dutch, Danish, Italian, Spanish and Portuguese. The Lexicon not only defines terms in each of these languages but also allows for differences of usage within them. The English definitions are based on British usage, but the alternative American terms are given as well. (The first edition had an American-English bias.) The French definitions have been supplemented by corresponding terms found in the French-speaking areas of Belgium and Switzerland; the German definitions by corresponding terms in Austria and German-speaking Switzerland; the Dutch definitions by terms used in Flemish-speaking Belgium; the Spanish definitions by terms used in Spanish-speaking Latin America; and the Portuguese definitions by terms used in Brazil. Danish has been chosen as the representative Scandinavian language, but the corresponding Norwegian and Swedish terms are also given.

The first edition of the Lexicon was published in two volumes in 1961 and 1964. The second edition has been ten years in preparation. It is the product of the UEC Lexicography Committee. . . .

The UEC Lexicon is not a dictionary in the usual sense. It does not normally give for each specific term the corresponding word in other languages. To do so would be extremely difficult and often misleading. Instead, the meaning of each term is explained by definitions which are translated into each language.

The list of definitions is arranged in the alphabetical order of the French terms. The French language, however, seems to have given very few words to the international language of accounting, defining the latter as those accounting words or phrases which are identical or almost identical in all languages. Those in the Lexicon include: cash, capital, cartel, cash flow, cheque, configuration, discounted cash flow, factoring, and the banking terms "nostro" and "vostro". "Cartel" in its business sense is of German origin, and "cheque" came into English *via* French, but in the main these terms, as used in accounting, are either Italian or English in origin, reflecting firstly the early dominance of the Italian city states in bookkeeping and banking, and secondly the Anglo-American dominance of accounting in the last hundred years or so.

## QUESTION

1. What explanations can you offer for the fact that most accounting terms are either Italian or English in origin?

*Excerpt from *The Accountant's Magazine*, December 1974, p. 504. Reprinted with permission of the publisher.

[1]Union Européenne des Experts Comptables Economiques et Financiers: *Lexique UEC* (Düsseldorf: Institut der Wirtschafsprüfer in Deutschland e. V., 2nd edition, 1974), 1,100 pages.

# 7

## INTRODUCING MATHEMATICS TO ACCOUNTANTS*
C. D. Sears

Perhaps the main areas in mathematics and statistics useful to the modern accountant are:

1. Discounted cash flow techniques.
2. Basic probability theory and statistics.
3. Model building.
4. Probability theory and decision models.
5. Inventory models—economic order quantity, without shortages and with constant buffer stocks. Also possibly, those using the regret matrix.
6. Linear programming—graphical solutions of the two-variable type.
7. Linear programming—simplex models using maximizing and minimizing techniques.
8. Games theory—$2 \times 2$ and $2 \times n$ games as applied to decision theory.
9. Markov chain analysis—applied to the solution of marketing problems.
10. Basic simple queuing.

All of these techniques are reasonably easy to use and can be mastered by a person motivated to get up to date with recent developments. The mathematics of cash flow techniques can be mastered by a person with a reasonably good knowledge of arithmetic and basic algebra. Moreover, the other topics, enumerated above, although involving some knowledge of algebra and logarithms, can be mastered by a person with an elementary knowledge in these subjects. . . .

The reader may feel that this article suggests a massive dose of mathematics. Perhaps it does, but it can be taken in reasonably sized doses and is good medicine for accountants. . . .

### QUESTIONS

1. Which if any of these mathematical and statistical topics have you already studied?
2. Which topics do you plan to study? How?
3. What applications of these topics do you know about that can be found in accounting and business?

*From *The Australian Accountant*, June 1972, pp. 203—204. Reprinted by permission of the publisher.

# 8

## THE ECONOMIST AND THE ACCOUNTANT*
Donald Welsch

The increasing rate of change in business activity created by modern industrial and communication technology has brought the economist and accountant closer together in their concerns. The path connecting the past, the present, and the future has shortened. The roles of the attestor and the analyst are more closely linked. The economist relies on the accountant to provide a more accurate representation of the present; the accountant relies on the economist to integrate this representation into the external environment.

The economist and the accountant, in spite of surface differences, deal with similar problems with consistent complementary approaches. The main orientation of the accounting profession has been toward historical information recorded in financial terms. The economist focuses on the relationships inherent in historical information as a basis for explanation of the process by which his client reacts to the environment. These relationships can be used to test the sensitivity of the client's operations to changes in external events, to describe the probable impact of external events, and to project the probable consequences of a client's decision created by external conditions.

The economist relies on financial and economic data to provide an understanding of the underlying trends and fluctuations in the client's operations.

The tools of the economist (and his recent mathematical counterpart—the econometrician) are not new. The still popular theory of economic value derived in a free marketplace is rooted in the concepts of Adam Smith in his *Wealth of Nations* some 200 years ago. Wesley Clair Mitchell established the role of quantitative economic analysis in 1913. His work, entitled *Business Cycles and Their Causes*, provided the framework for the current practice of economic statistics. John Maynard Keynes, in 1936, defined the roles of producer, consumer, and government in his *General Theory of Employment, Interest and Money*. His analysis provides the basic framework for most modern economic analysis. . . .

*Excerpt from "Econometrics and Auditing," *World*, Summer 1975, p. 45. Reprinted by permission of the publisher.

# 9

## WHAT MAKES AN ACCOUNTANT?*
Alan Breck

### MUST ACCOUNTANTS BE ABLE TO COUNT?

The novitiate in any field of activity will generally have doubts about his mental or temperamental suitability for the career which he has chosen, or which more probably has been chosen for him; and will raise questions with himself or with his mentors. But this question "Must accountants be able to count?" will strike most, at first reading, as a stupid question. It may be so, but it is not so silly as some which you will be asked by clients later in your careers; and the ability to answer which will be found important.

In these random comments on some attributes of value to an accountant, I hope to show that, even if it is found that my opening question must be answered by at least a qualified affirmative, it by no means follows that the proposition "I am a good counter" will support the inference "I shall be a good accountant".

That inference was thought to be valid in my young days, but it is a long time since and the qualities looked for in an accountant have changed greatly in that time.

One of the more obvious changes in the environment in which the accountant operates is the proliferation and increasing sophistication of the mechanical and electronic devices available to take the drudgery out of counting. When I entered the profession it was really necessary for the apprentice—though possibly not for the accountant—to be able to count. Cash books, wages books, day books, all kinds of columns of figures had to be added, with, at any rate in the case of those being trained in a small office, no assistance but their ten fingers. Now it is beginning to be realised that for the accountant it is more important to know what sums should be done than to be able to do them, and fortunately the technical apparatus and the technicians to do the sums are available.

That it is not yet fully realised that the accountant's role is not that of "arithmetician extraordinary", however, is shown by a note which appeared in "Notes and Comments" in *The Accountant's Magazine* in May 1972, at page 214, where an advertisement for a portable electronic calculating machine was quoted as describing its owner as having his "own super Chartered Accountant at [his] finger tips and IT never gets tired". As the member who drew attention to this advertisement commented, "maybe prospective candidates should be warned that they are only worth £55 and at that price are available 24 hours a day".

*From *The Accountant's Magazine*, December 1972, pp. 619—621. Reprinted by permission of the publisher.

## SOME ANALOGIES WITH OTHER PROFESSIONS

If the accountant is no mere calculating machine neither is he merely a recorder of facts, a compiler and custodian of financial data banks. His real role has a more creative side, and to illustrate this analogies can be drawn with other professions.

The most informative analogy is possibly with engineering. The designation "engineer" has perhaps even more meanings than the designation "accountant", and, as in our profession, the general term is loosely applied to many who are not professional engineers at all but are mechanics, tradesmen, craftsmen or what you will. Broadly the distinction could be drawn by the stating that the "engineer" has such professional skill as to enable him to determine what bits of material, in what shapes and in what combinations will make a useful product—and the product may range in size and complexity from a child's toy to a whole industrial plant or a complete hydro-electric scheme—but under his guidance mechanics or tradesmen, with the help of suitable equipment, also designed by engineers, can then shape and assemble the bits and pieces into the end product. Similarly, the "accountant" knows what financial data can be recorded and how it can be analysed, assembled and presented to serve useful purposes for managers, investors or other users. The actual recording, analysis and so on, which is the part which involves the "doing of sums", can be left to clerks or technicians, again with appropriate mechanical or other aids. Unfortunately, in accountancy, there is no term which corresponds to the engineering mechanic; which may help to perpetuate the confusion as to what an "accountant" really is and does.

In the construction industry, probably because of its age, the same confusion does not exist between the architect and the builder, though the role of the former has evolved historically from that of the master-builder. It could be said that in the field of business finance the accountant's function is in some ways analogous to that of the architect and is evolving from simpler functions in something of the same way.

In parts of his work the architect calls on the assistance of quantity surveyors, or measurers as they were often called in my youth. This separate profession, the members of which, however highly skilled, would never confuse themselves or be confused by others with architects, may be matched in the financial field by the emergence of a separate profession of data processors or computer technologists. This is already happening; but again, however highly skilled these people may be, they are not accountants and should never be regarded as potentially replacing accountants, whose skills are quite different.

## THE ABILITY TO ASK QUESTIONS AND QUESTION THE ANSWERS

One function of the accountant, then, is to decide what sums should be done. That is to say, he must know what questions must be asked and answered if the information on which decisions about action will be based is to be available in a reliable and readable form. More importantly, he must be able to recognise whether the answers provided are such as to provide a satisfactory basis for decision-making. This involves the design of systems for recording and communicating data, and, in the exercise of the accountant's attest or auditing function, the critical assessment of the structure and operation of such systems.

If the proper routines for obtaining and processing the data required to answer his questions have been prescribed, the accountant should be able to assume that the answers are at least arithmetically correct. Arithmetical correctness by itself, however, is not enough. Knowing what can go wrong, and recognising when it has, is not merely a matter of detecting arithmetical errors. Indeed, in so far as the detection of fraud is part of an auditor's function it is likely that only in the simpler or minor cases will it be revealed in this way. One of the first requisites for the perpetration of a successful fraud is the clever concealment of it by expert manipulation of the arithmetic so as to make the records appear flawless in that respect. It can at times be positively dangerous to assume that, because the figures are correct, no further enquiry into the situation which they purport to portray is necessary. This does not mean that the accountant must view with suspicion every answer to every question, but the ability to recognise when further enquiry is needed and to question the answer given is one of the essential qualities he must have.

To take a simple, if extreme, example in which the need for some enquiry will be obvious to the veriest novice—if it is reported that the books of a business are in perfect balance and all entries arithmetically correct, and that the debtors amount to £80,000 while the sales for the year have been £100,000, some explanation is plainly required. To present the position as stated may be arithmetically true; it is not necessarily, and indeed is unlikely to be, fair. The word "unlikely" in the previous sentence is used advisedly to draw attention to another quality which the accountant must possess. He must exercise deliberate judgment and not jump to conclusions, unless it be the conclusion to make further enquiries. Even that conclusion is usually better reached deliberately, in case there is a simple explanation which reflection would suggest and to overlook which could expose either ignorance or incompetence, two qualities which, if not unknown in accountants, must never be injudiciously or indecently exposed.

## JUDGMENT IS THE THING

Odd though some may think it, an accountant is seldom required to certify anything. As auditor he is not required to certify accounts but to express an opinion about them. In other capacities he is more commonly called on to make a report, which will embody opinion, than to issue a certificate. The ability to form a sound and balanced judgment is, therefore, an essential quality for an accountant.

No judgment needs to be exercised in determining that $2 + 2 = 4$. It always does. But profit or loss arises from an assessment that the whole (the end result) is greater or less than the sum of the original parts, so the existence and the declared amount of the profit or loss are matters of judgment. This is a truth, acceptance of which is essential for the proper understanding of the accountant's function and authority, and the non-acceptance of which is responsible for many of the criticisms made of the profession by those who wrongly assume that the formulation of accounts for a live business enterprise is no more than an exercise in arithmetic, which being subject to immutable rules is, by itself, dead.

A calculating machine, if in good mechanical order, will always produce the arithmetically correct answer—it cannot exercise judgment. Even the most sophisticated electronic equipment only appears to exercise a power of selection, or judgment, because the programme on which it operates has been framed to reflect the judgment of the programmer or of those instructing him, a judgment which the machine cannot change—hence GIRO, garbage in, rubbish out. Only when machines are defective do they, in a sense, exercise judgment by departing from the prescribed programme, with dire results. The converse should not, of course, be applied to the live accountant, to produce the conclusion that only those who cannot or do not add or calculate correctly can exercise judgment.

## THE ABILITY TO EXPLAIN

I have indicated that a large part of an accountant's work consists in forming and formulating judgments and opinions. It is, of course, easier to form an opinion than to find out the real facts. It is also easy to assume, as I have suggested earlier, that arithmetical correctness or consistency in setting out the data is proof that the facts which the data purports to represent have been indubitably established. The accountant must never make this assumption and be satisfied with mere arithmetical correctness. His opinion, to be worthwhile, must be based on a thorough expiscation and informed assessment of all the ascertainable facts. It may also require, and must in any event be capable of, explanation.

While computers can calculate and analyse but cannot explain, accountants, even if they cannot calculate, must be able to explain. There are two facets of explanation—knowing the explanation, and communicating it. To form a sound judgment or opinion it is necessary to be able to think in an orderly, logical manner. To communicate the opinion formed so that it is precisely the intended meaning which is conveyed, that ability must be allied to an ability to formulate and set down one's thoughts in an equally orderly and lucid fashion. This formulation may, as the case demands, be mainly in figures or mainly in words, and often the words are more important than the figures. The opinion, nevertheless, will have been founded on facts capable of numerical representation, and the accountant who is alternatively the purveyor, or the interpreter and critic, of financial information which is capable of such representation must be presumed to be at home with figures. It must always be remembered that the reader (customer) may not similarly be equally at home, but may be more literate than numerate. Hence the need for care in the verbal descriptions or explanations, and the desirability that the accountant be equally at home with words as with figures.

## A RETURN TO THE ORIGINAL QUESTION

These ramblings may, I hope, have given prospective accountants an inkling of some of the qualities, possession of which they are likely to find helpful and which, indeed, will be demanded of them. But they have not directly answered the original question, and though it is at times helpful to be able to avoid answering difficult questions to do so will usually detract from that complete integrity which it is rightly demanded an accountant should possess as a primary attribute.

I must, therefore, attempt an answer to the "stupid" question with which I began. An accountant is something far beyond an arithmetician. He must be able to account rather than simply count; but it is helpful if he can also do the latter. The chances are that if he is a good accountant he will have this ability but it is not an essential prerequisite. A good accountant is likely, then, to be a good counter—a good counter will not necessarily, and certainly not on the strength of that qualification alone, be a good accountant.

## QUESTIONS

1. Why is a good accountant likely to be a good counter but a good counter will not necessarily be a good accountant?

2. Why must the accountant be as at ease with words as with figures?

3. What is the difference between a computer technologist and an accountant?

# 10

## THE MANY WORLDS OF RICK JOHNSON*
H&S Reports

The vibes weren't good for Rick Johnson in May 1967 when he sat for the CPA Examination in Lincoln, Nebraska. At four sittings out of five he happened to draw seat No. 13. Yet the following month he received his bachelor's degree from the University of Nebraska safely enough, and in a few weeks he learned that he had passed all parts of the exam.

What made the feat remarkable was that for the previous fourteen years Rick had been spending much of his time with his mind on the stars, while his classmates were concentrating on their textbooks. Ever since he built his first telescope at age eight or nine with the help of his dad, Rick has successfully combined his formal schooling and the start of a professional career in public accounting with a very busy off-duty schedule as an accomplished amateur astronomer-photographer-lecturer-electronic tinkerer. . .and lots more.

*From "The H & S Scene," *H & S Reports*, Autumn 1972, pp. 28–30. Reprinted by permission of the publisher.

Now in his third year in the Omaha office of H&S, Rick relishes his dual life. "I enjoy accounting very much—I wouldn't be in it if I didn't," he says to people who ask how he balances two interests that seem so far apart. "I have always wanted to have my hobbies totally divorced from my work. I can concentrate on accounting during the day, and I can switch to my telescopes, or take pictures, or give an astronomy talk to a club in the evening. No problem." Nor, apparently, is there any problem about his switching back to an audit job the next morning and tuning out last night's stars.

Rick came to accounting naturally. His father, Philip G. Johnson, heads his own CPA firm in Lincoln. In fact, the elder Johnson started out in 1937 with Irwin-Imig Co., the Omaha firm that merged with H&S in 1956. So Rick grew up in an atmosphere of auditing and tax practice, and even got in some experience as an assistant in his father's office while he was an undergraduate student. And because in those days he was also busy putting on illustrated talks before astronomy clubs and student audiences. . . .

Diploma and CPA certificate in hand at age twenty-two, Rick decided to take a law degree at Nebraska. "I wanted more education—a broader education. I thought I'd get more of a taste of the real world with law added to accounting," he says, looking back on it. And the elder Johnson had set the pace by studying law in addition to accounting. So Rick did not come to our Omaha office until 1970, three years after sitting for the CPA exam.

After the accounting workday is over, Rick may be found at his bachelor pad on the west edge of town tinkering—as he puts it—with one of five telescopes (two others are at his family home in Lincoln), or adapting a camera to fit to the 'scope if the evening sky looks clear. As in all photography of the stars, which move during exposure of the film, Rick's equipment is controlled by a tracking mechanism ("I bought some of it, and made the rest.") to compensate for the motion of the earth. How well he has succeeded is abundantly clear when he puts on one of his color slide shows, which startle audiences who did not realize how many colors there are in the faint pin-points of light we see as distant star clusters. One of Rick's most colorful slides is of a grouping he calls "the Christmas Tree." Another shows the Andromeda Galaxy, about two million light-years away, which required a camera exposure of 34 minutes.

Rick's remarkable collection of astronomical color slides and black-and-white prints have made him a popular speaker in Nebraska. His show-and-tell has been on the road for years, with new material added as he gets better and more interesting results with his cameras. He has developed a light, conversational manner of presentation which permits those who know nothing about astronomy to understand and appreciate the talk. Yet when members of the audience throw the tough questions at him, Rick can answer with confidence. When he doesn't know, he says so.

"I'll speak to any group that asks me," he says. "I find that some of the junior high school age kids are at a level that has left the older ones far behind."

Another of Rick's interests is rocketry. "I got hooked on rockets when I was seventeen. A friend of mine who was working in a hardware store had a customer who came in to buy a lot of asbestos. He said he wanted it for a rocket launching pad. We were invited to the launch—and I was hooked." Now Rick assembles most of his rockets from scratch (he makes a few from kits) and uses them to send up cameras and mice, which float softly back to earth on a colorful plastic parachute. He takes pride in not having lost a rocket-borne camera or a mouse yet. Rick's 10-second color movie, taken back toward the ground from the nose of his 30-inch rocket as it blasts upward in a whirl of smoke, is a mini-spectacular. And it is a laffer when Rick projects it backward.

So what else has this young accountant in Omaha done with his time?

Helped organize the Lincoln-Prairie Astronomy Club when he was fifteen.

Played the French horn in school and college bands and the University of Nebraska horn choir.

Got his general license as a ham radio operator, call letters WAØCKY.

Learned to fly his father's Cessna 182 Skylane, but has not taken the training course required for a pilot's license.

Wrote articles in popular astronomy magazines, and started work on a basic astro-photography book in collaboration with others.

Put together his own color TV set in a couple of days last winter, when a blizzard closed all the roads around Lincoln and Omaha.

Built a Theramin, an electronic sound-producing machine that gives forth all kinds of mysterious sounds as the operator moves his hands in its wave path.

Fished on vacation trips to Minnesota, photographed bald eagles and ospreys in the wild, climbed mountains in Colorado, read his way through mountains of murder mysteries, and raised tropical fish.

Lately, however, Rick has been experimenting with laser beams, which he firmly believes will be the basis for most communications in the future. His generator, which sends out the narrow, red laser beam, and the demodulator, or receiving instrument, both are Johnson-made, mounted in plywood boxes. When they are placed at opposite ends of Rick's main room, Rick can demonstrate how the laser (super high radio frequency) beam can be used in place of a wire to play radio music, at a distance. He waves his hand in the beam's path, and the music is cut off. He moves it away, and the radio blasts out. "With time to fool around lining this up, I could hit a doorknob at ten miles," Rick says of his laser equipment. . . .

## SELECTED BIBLIOGRAPHY

Beeson, Lynda J., "An Accounting Internship in Industry," *Management Accounting*, March 1975, pp. 59-61.

Bradshaw, W. A., and H. E. McCandless, "John Weeks, CA," *Canadian Chartered Accountant*, January 1973, pp. 34-35.

*H&S Reports*, "Well, You Don't Look Like an Accountant," Summer 1975, pp. 20-22. On female accountants.

Nolan, James, "Honors Students in Accounting Gather at Ohio State University," *The Journal of Accountancy*, December 1972, pp. 22-23.

# 11

# THE DUAL PRACTICE OF LAW AND ACCOUNTING*
David W. McHenry

The dual practice of law and accounting is the concurrent practice of both professions by a person who is dually qualified. This means he is qualified and licensed under a state law to be both a lawyer and a Certified Public Accountant.[1] The dual practitioner must be differentiated from a person who is a lawyer and who also does elementary bookkeeping or accounting functions, or a Certified Public Accountant who has had some legal training and also offers clients some elementary legal advice.

Before 1951, the dual practice of law and accounting was considered by most lawyers and accountants to be very unethical. However, in 1951 by the efforts of The National Conference of Lawyers and Certified Public Accountants, a statement was adopted by both the American Bar Association and the American Institute of Certified Public Accountants. This statement contained the "Principles Relating to Practice in the Field of Federal Income Taxation," which were designed for members of both professions.[2] Included in the statement were guidelines regarding the roles of both lawyers and Certified Public Accountants concerning federal tax matters. This action was the first major step toward liberalizing the old prohibitions of being a dual practitioner in accounting and law.

At the time of this 1951 conference, the accounting profession had been plagued by litigation involving accountants charged with unauthorized practice of law. Representatives of the two professions met as adversaries in the courts, in congress and in the press. The two professions argued with each other in a manner that reflected badly upon both of them.[3] The job of the conference was to promote cooperation between the professions of law and accounting and to mediate disputes about what is properly the practice of accounting and what is properly the practice of law concerning tax matters. The guidelines which the conference eventually recommended only helped identify the roles of lawyers and accountants regarding federal tax matters. The conference did not attempt to define the practice of law or federal taxation. It urged the two professions to work together in the public interest and recommended that services and assistance in federal tax matters be rendered by both lawyers and Certified Public Accountants but counseled them to avoid conflicts.[4]

*From *Beta Alpha PSI Newsletter*, Spring 1975, pp. 5 and 9. Reprinted by permission of the publisher.

[1] Louis S. Goldberg, "Lawyers and CPA's: A Study of Methods of Practice," *The Journal of Accountancy*, April 1971, pp. 53–54.

[2] "Lawyers and Certified Public Accountants: A Study of Interprofessional Relations," *The Journal of Accountancy*, August 1970, pp. 62–66.

[3] "Lawyers and CPA's: The Era of Co-operation," *The Journal of Accountancy*, June 1967, pp. 29–30.

[4] "Lawyers and Certified Public Accountants: A Study of Interprofessional Relations," op. cit.

Later conferences of lawyers and Certified Public Accountants found that it was not in the public interest for a person to engage in the practice of both public accounting and law.[5] Their reasoning was that the public could not be expected to understand or evaluate competence and that the public was likely to be misled and confused by dual titles. However, they specified many areas and activities where lawyers and Certified Public Accountants should work more closely together. A few of these areas are: estate planning, establishing or terminating a business, mergers, reorganizations and SEC registration.

In the early 1960's, the American Bar Association issued Opinion Number 272 which stated that the dual practice of law and accounting was unethical when practiced from the same office but it refused to prohibit a person from practicing both from different offices.[6]

The prohibitions on dual practice became increasingly more lenient through the 1950's and 1960's. Recently the American Bar Association adopted its new Code of Professional Responsibility. This code permits a lawyer to practice in more than one profession. Basically the only prohibition is that the letterhead or sign of the dual practitioner, which is seen by the public, must not specify that he is a member of both the professions.[7]

The principal argument against the dual practitioner is that it is difficult to keep abreast of the changes in one profession and practically impossible to maintain a high level of competence in both. This argument is strengthened by the contention that the formal entry education of both professions is just a starting point for the acquisition of the knowledge and experience necessary to maintain the level of competence needed. On the other hand, the supporters of dual practice contend that the dual practitioner does not strive to be competent in all areas of both professions. Therefore, by specializing in an area common to both professions he is better able to serve his clients. Also the public is helped because the small businessman needs to hire only one individual rather than two, thus reducing his expenses.[8]

There are additional arguments against dual practice, but they are not as strong as the first one. The opponents of dual practice contend that one profession acts as a feeder for the other profession and that the independence relating to the auditing function is impaired. Meanwhile the supporters reply that most activities of a professional "feed" his practice so why should a dual practitioner be singled out. They also state that Certified Public Accountants who are not lawyers also engage in activities which limit their independence in the auditing function, such as tax matters and business negotiations. One last argument for dual practice is that training in both areas helps reduce conflicts and misunderstandings between the two professions.[9]

[5] Ibid.

[6] Burt A. Leete and Stephen E. Loeb, "The Dual Practitioner: CPA, Lawyer or Both?" *The Journal of Accountancy*, August 1973, pp. 57–63.

[7] Ibid.

[8] Ibid.

[9] Ibid.

Today many students with accounting degrees are going on to law school. One main reason for this is the flexibility and freedom of the lawyer, who may take a tax case into court without "overstepping the bounds of ethical propriety," after having exhausted administrative remedies.[10] The dual practice of accounting and law is a growing practice with all indications that it will continue to grow for some time in the future, thus providing a rewarding career for many competent professionals qualified in both the professions of accounting and law.

## QUESTIONS

1. What are the arguments for and against the dual practitioner?
2. Which profession has more responsibilities for society in general rather than just to its clients? Why?
3. Which profession has the more favorable television image? Why? Are these images accurate ones?
4. What are the current economic opportunities for beginning lawyers? Beginning CPAs and accountants? What are the future economic opportunities for both professions?

# 12
# A DAY IN THE LIFE OF AN AUDIT PARTNER*
C. Richard Baker

The organization and operation of large public accounting firms are of interest to many groups including students, researchers, practitioners, partners, and employees of public accounting firms, and the general public. Traditionally, and for valid reasons, these firms have been reluctant to provide an inside look at their operations, especially at the manager and partner level. During the course of some recent research on the organizational structure of accounting firms, I had an unusual opportunity to observe the operations of certain firms at the executive level. This article, with some literary license, is based upon notes taken during several months of observation. It is a synthesis of typical working days in the lives of audit partners.

[10]William H. Westphal, "The Future of the CPA in Tax Practice," *The Journal of Accountancy*, June 1969, pp. 40–44.

*From *The CPA Journal*, September 1975, Vol. XLV, no. 9, pp. 40–43. Reprinted by permission of the publisher.

## THE AUDIT PARTNER

Partners in large public accounting firms are the elite of their profession. They have prestigious positions, a certain amount of power, and substantial income. A partner does not reach this position overnight. Normally, about ten years with a firm are necessary before one is considered for partnership. A partner has great responsibility simply because he is able to sign the firm name. Through this signing, a partner binds his fellow partners professionally, legally, and morally. Thus, individuals are carefully evaluated before admission to membership in the firm.

Partners are the executives of the firm. There are many kinds of partners—administrative, technical, promotional, practice, or audit partners, and others. In each firm there is a certain hierarchy and deference and ritual, but theoretically, and to the view of outsiders, partners are equal. An *audit* partner has charge of a domain of clients which he serves, within the rules of the firm, according to his own style.

For all kinds of partners, including audit partners, there are ranges of style. Some are entrepreneurs, regularly seeking new business for the firm. Some are technicians, happiest when solving difficult problems of systems, accounting or tax theory. Some are trouble-shooters, who are skilled in resolving serious client relationship problems. There are those who are active in professional organizations and participate in establishing professional standards. There are the administrators, who work their way up to leadership positions, perhaps becoming a managing partner or member of his staff. And there are those who simply take pride in their work, enjoy the prestige and the remuneration, but have no desire to lead the firm.

A partner is a consultant, problem solver, public relations person, administrator, mediator, and negotiator. He is rarely an ordinary technician, doing routine tasks. His day is usually full and varied; flexibility and adaptability mark his style.

## THE AUDIT PARTNER'S DAY

Partner Robert Morris' office is located on the top floor of a relatively new office building. The firm occupies half the floor and has been in this location for about six years. This is a satellite office of a larger metropolitan headquarters. The office has a general practice in audit, tax, and management services, with a degree of specialization in real estate, savings and loan companies, entertainment, and banking. There are four partners in the office (three audit and one tax). One is designated the managing partner. There are 12 managers (six audit, four tax, and two management services). There are 19 seniors and 12 staff assistants. Staff assistants are also borrowed from the metropolitan office from time to time as needed. Morris' office is spacious and attractively decorated. There is a view of the city from a picture window.

*8:30 a.m.* I arrive before partner Morris. His secretary Miss Anne Thrope is already there. She seats me in his room telling me he'll be in shortly. She offers me a container of coffee, which I take gratefully.

*8:45 a.m.* Morris arrives, says "Hello," unloads his briefcase of last evening's homework, buzzes his secretary and asks for his usual coffee. I note with interest that *his* coffee comes in china service. (I will note throughout the office that one of the truest hierarchical tests is the quality of coffee containers.) His mail is already opened, in two piles, one of letters and the other of reading material of various types. He spends about ten minutes reading and scanning. Most of the reading material is laid aside for later perusal. Several letters are marked for certain managers with the notation "Please handle." Four letters need an immediate answer and Miss Thrope is called to take dictation (and to bring more coffee).

*9:45 a.m.* Morris asks Arthur Benson, an audit manager, to come to his office.

MORRIS: Art, I know this is going to be a bit difficult, but the managing partner wants some current billing information on these jobs. Can you pull it together?

BENSON: It'll take a while, but I can do it.

MORRIS: Good. I don't know why he can't get it from bookkeeping but there's no point in arguing with him.

Also, can you handle something rather confidential for me? I've had some contact with a major stockholder in a company which is not a client. Some of the company's minority stockholders are clients, and they have asked me to check into the possibility of trading their minority interests for certain of the corporate assets. The majority stockholder is not interested in this, but he would like to take the company private. He wants to know what would be involved and if we can help him. If I give you the file will you investigate the possibilities and get back to me?

BENSON: I'll look it over and check with you later.

*10:00 a.m.* Morris continues sorting his mail and performing various administrative details. John Reilly, the partner in charge of the office, calls and asks Morris if he can step in for a moment.

REILLY: Bob, a client of the Dallas office is considering the acquisition of a small printing company in our area and wants a purchase investigation. You know the industry. Can you take it on?

MORRIS: I can handle it, John, if I can line up some staff. We're tight, you know.

REILLY: I realize that but we have to do a good job for Dallas on this just like it was one of our own office clients. If you've any trouble with personnel let me know.

MORRIS: OK, we'll do the best we can. Let me have the Dallas letter of instructions and I'll acknowledge it.

*10:30 a.m.* Morris receives a telephone call from Mike Brown, a manager in the firm's Chicago office.

MORRIS: Mike, how are you? How's everything in Chicago?

BROWN: OK, Bob, except for a little problem with one of your clients.

MORRIS: Tell me more.

BROWN: You audit a company called Ace Specialty. It's 20 percent owned by Johnson Manufacturing out in Oak Park.

MORRIS: That's right and no problems I know of.

BROWN: Well, the Johnson Company is entering into merger negotiations and will need audited statements at an interim date. As you know, Johnson is not a client, but the partner of the Chicago firm that audits them called me as a matter of convenience. They want to know what they can get from you in the way of a 'comfort letter' on the four month period since the last annual audit.

MORRIS: Mike, we can't give them a thing unless we do some additional work. We've had very little contact since the end of the year.

BROWN: What would be involved?

MORRIS: We'd have to carry out our usual review of the subsequent period—you know, read the minutes, review the monthly financial statements, get representation letters, and the like. It would take a week or ten days to do, so give us as much notice as you can.

BROWN: Right, I'll talk with the partner out here and give you a call tomorrow probably.

*10:45 a.m.* Morris looks over the notes on his calendar and calls Oliver Falk, an audit manager, to remind him that on the following day they are to go to a seminar on the entertainment industry sponsored by the local CPA society.

He also reviews a typed memo he had drafted concerning the promotion of a new work for schools and colleges, and comments to me about a recent trip: "A couple of small colleges are my clients. One of their people invited me to attend a meeting of the Regional Association of College and University Business Officers. It was an interesting meeting. I played some tennis with several of the business officers, and managed to lose a few games, and we may develop some additional work through these contacts."

Morris then scans a memo on a tax point prepared by the office's tax department. It was detailed and quite lengthy. He doesn't enjoy reading such memos. He prefers to obtain the information by discussing the problem directly with a tax manager. He agrees that the formal memo is necessary as documentation and support but feels it is not a substitute for face-to-face discussion. However, since the tax manager who wrote it is out of town, he has no alternative.

*11:45 a.m.* Morris and I go to lunch at the Executive Club, a nearby businessmen's lunch club. James Adams, a vice-president of a small bank, joins us to discuss possible cooperation in developing new clients for the firm and new customers for the bank. We have cocktails and lunch. After a few good stories and the usual discussion of golf scores, the conversation turns to how useful audits are to bankers.

ADAMS: Bob, we rely pretty heavily on audited financial statements in a good many situations. In others we don't, but probably should. In new situations, the audit is very important in evaluating our risks.

MORRIS: I think you could help us identify young companies with good growth potential who would develop into good clients for us and good customers for the bank.

ADAMS: We'd like that because we're both trying to help businesses grow and prosper. Certainly no conflict of interest there.

*1:30 p.m.* During lunch "hour" a call had come in from Bill Johnson, Controller of ABC Textile Company. Morris calls him back.

JOHNSON: Bob, what is this SEC proposal on quarterly reports all about? What are they trying to do now?

MORRIS: Bill, you know the SEC has wanted to get the auditors involved in interim reports for some time. This is only an exposure draft and it's very ambiguous, I think. First they say that the quarterly results must be included in the footnotes which, in effect, make them part of the audited statements, and yet they say it will not require audits of the interim results, as such. Our firm has written a strong letter opposing it and several other major firms have too.

JOHNSON: Well our chairman is upset about it. He says we pay you guys too much as it is.

MORRIS: Now Bill, you know our fees are always reasonable but the chairman has a point. Why don't you draft a letter for him to send the SEC. I'll be glad to work with you on it.

JOHNSON: Fine. Let me draft something and I'll give you a call later in the week.

*2:00 p.m.* Morris interviews a recruit who is graduating in a few months from the Wharton School. This recruit has already been screened in a campus interview and has been invited to spend a day in the firm's offices to learn more about the organization. Morris describes the audit function, tells him something about the work he would be assigned in his first year and answers a wide range of questions about the firm and its policies. Morris and the other partners and managers whom the recruit meets during the day are selling the firm as a career opportunity, and at the same time, they are sizing up the recruit. Immediately after the interview, Morris prepares a short summary of his impressions and has Miss Thrope hand-deliver it to the personnel manager who will conduct the final employment discussion that day.

*2:45 p.m.* Richard Newton, an audit manager, stops in the office.

NEWTON: Mr. Morris, I had a call from a personal friend who is a financial analyst. He want me to introduce him to the financial executives of some of our clients. I told him I'd have to check it out with you.

MORRIS: I'm not too happy about it. I don't think it's appropriate for outsiders to trade on the name of the firm. Maybe in a particular case it might be OK if your client relationship is close enough. If the client wants to make the contact, then of course you should introduce your friend.

NEWTON: Thanks. Your answer will help to cool him off on the idea.

*3:00 p.m.* Frank Cohen, one of Morris' clients, telephones primarily to chat for a few minutes. Cohen is interested in a possible merger candidate for his company, and while he is going over a few details two more buttons light up on Morris' telephone. Morris' secretary puts a note in front of him that the editor of *The CPA* is on one line and Mrs. Morris on the other. Morris gets his wife first and tries to make the conversation short but ends up asking her to hold. He then switches to the editor on his speaker phone.

MORRIS: Doug, I know I promised you a draft of an article on Financial Reporting for Schools and Colleges but I've been completely snowed under. By the way, you're on my speaker phone.

DOUG: I understand, Bob. I just wanted to remind you our deadline is the tenth.

MORRIS: I'll get it to you before then.

DOUG: Thanks, Bob.

Pressing the next button, Morris brings his wife up-to-date on his plans.

MORRIS: Dear, I know I should have called you earlier. You know I'm going to that dinner at the Economics Club tonight.

MRS. MORRIS: I know but I wanted to find out what train you'll be on.

MORRIS: If I don't call, make it the 10:05.

MRS. MORRIS: Fine. See you then.

Morris called two managers he wanted me to meet and asked Miss Thrope to bring some coffee.

MORRIS: Rich, this is Joe Edwards and Gene Martin. They handle mostly real estate and banking audits but they can do any job that comes along. I'm going to ask Miss Thrope to hold my calls. It's getting a little hectic around here. Have some coffee.

EDWARDS: Rich, what do you think about public accounting by now? Want to join up?

BAKER: Well, I can see why you fellows need nice long vacations. I don't suppose you ever really have a quiet uneventful day.

MORRIS: Not very often. Maybe on a holiday when most clients are closed and we're open.

*3:30 p.m.* After our coffee break, Mr. Morris has his secretary call Larry Jones, the manager on the Zone Shipping Company audit, to come to his office to discuss the presentation of a footnote dealing with a legal action against the client.

MORRIS: Larry, do you have that footnote drafted?

JONES: Mr. Morris, I have the footnote but now we have a new problem.

MORRIS: What's that?

JONES: Well, the company's attorneys now say they can't give us the opinion we want that this suit is without merit.

MORRIS: You should call company counsel, Sullivan, and get him involved. If we can't get a "no merit" legal representation we have to consider a possible certificate qualification. Let me know what Sullivan says. If necessary set up a threeway meeting.

*3:45 p.m.* Samuel Foley, Treasurer of a client, calls. He is concerned about the necessity of disclosing the compensation of the directors of an Australian subsidiary. Morris advises Foley that he does not know the answer offhand but will contact the Sydney office of the firm to find out. He drafts a Telex for his secretary to telephone in to the Telex operator in the metropolitan headquarters office.

*4:00 p.m.* Morris begins reviewing the working paper files on a current audit. He moves quickly through the sheaf of legal size papers, stopping here and there to scan the work done in specific areas. He pays particular attention to the summary of work done and the conclusions reached on each section of the accounts. He makes notes for later discussion with the manager on the job.

MORRIS: Rich, I suppose you think that most of my time is spent on the telephone, but actually I put in a lot of concentrated hours reviewing working papers.

BAKER: Do you find it boring?

MORRIS: No. Not if the papers are well organized and complete. What I don't like is a half-finished set of working papers that raise more questions than they answer. Then I tend to get annoyed. Generally speaking, our fellows do a thorough job and I rarely have to send them back to the field to fill in the gaps.

BAKER: How do you view audit working papers in the overall scheme of things?

MORRIS: They're the foundation for nearly everything we do. No matter how good the auditing, or the judgment decisions, if the evidence is not clearly set forth in the working papers, we could be in trouble. That's the reason we spend so much time in reviewing the papers, to see that the evidence supports our opinion, but this file has got to wait until morning. I have to change.

*5:00 p.m.* Morris had left the office in order to attend a black tie dinner at which the Secretary of the Treasury was to give a speech on the state of the economy. I could not attend, as I wanted to go to the metropolitan office to attend a training session.

*6:00 p.m.* About 20 second-year staff accountants are assembled in the large modern training facility of the metropolitan office. A partner and two managers are acting as instructors. The topic is recent releases of the SEC. The session utilizes TV cassettes and workbooks prepared by the New York office for use throughout the firm.

*7:30 p.m.* As the last event of the day, I attend a quarterly meeting of the firm's partners and managers. The managing partner of the region is to present operating statistics for the period. He gives figures on hours billed, lost time, numbers of professionals, numbers of clients, etc., all in comparison with last year and with budget. There are brief reports from partners who have investigated possibilities for new business in specific areas. There is a discussion of certain lawsuits pending against the firm. After the business meeting, the bar is opened and dinner follows.

## OBSERVATION

The experiences of this hypothetical audit partner during a working day typify the range of problems and situations he faces. They also highlight an unusual combination of internal administration, client relations, technical problems, and promotional activities. In all these functions, the need for skill in communication and in personal relations is paramount. It is equally clear that there is pressure arising from constant demands for service, largely unpredictable, from other partners, other offices, clients, and the public. It is not an easy day, but it is certainly challenging.

## QUESTIONS

1. Explain why a public accounting firm employs many different types of accountants.

2. Do you feel that the quality of your accounting homework problems is related to the quality of accounting working papers? Why?

## SELECTED BIBLIOGRAPHY

Montagna, Paul D., "The Career Pattern of a Large-Firm Accountant," in *Certified Public Accounting*, chap. 3, Houston: Scholars Books Company, 1974, pp. 41-58.

# 13

## SIR HENRY BENSON MOVES ON FROM COOPERS*
Geoffrey Holmes

Sir Henry Benson GBE FCA retired on 31 March after more than 40 years as a partner in Coopers & Lybrand. Sir Henry was born and educated in South Africa. He claims that he didn't choose the profession of chartered accountancy—

SIR HENRY: It was chosen for me.

When he was 14 years old, his mother brought him over to the United Kingdom because she wanted to see her family.

SIR HENRY: We had three hours to spare at the end of a very short visit, and she said 'Let's go down and look at the office'. We went down, and she met the partners at that time, with whom she had been brought up as a girl because she was the daughter of the third of the Cooper brothers. Nobody had anything to say—it was a rather

---

*From *Accountancy*, May 1975, pp. 46—48. Reprinted by permission of the publisher.

sticky meeting because everyone was rather shy, and at the end of it, in desperation, the senior partner, Stuart Cooper, said: 'Well, if you would like this lad to be articled when he has finished school, you can send him home to England here'. And my mother said: 'That's it—that's what will happen', and that's how I became a chartered accountant.

So Sir Henry began life holding the right cards. But he played them well. In January 1932, he qualified as an associate of the Institute, with honours (fourth place). The year 1940 saw him commissioned in Grenadier Guards—he later attained the rank of colonel. From September 1943 to July 1944, he was seconded by the Army to the Ministry of Supply, to advise the Department on the reorganisation of the accounts of the Royal Ordnance Factories, and in December 1943 he was appointed Director of Ordnance Factories to carry out the reorganisation. In March 1945, he was released from the Army for government work, and appointed Controller of Building Materials, Ministry of Works. In October 1945, he was given a special three-month appointment to advise the Minister of Health on housing production. He returned to Coopers in 1946, and in the Honours List of that year was made a Commander of the Order of the British Empire.

From then on, his career is a history of appointments to advisory committees, government working parties, development corporations and related bodies. The range of his activities has been immense. He was a member of the advisory committee on legal aid, a member of the tribunal under the Prevention of Fraud (Investments) Act 1939, he undertook an inquiry into the methods adopted by London Electricity Board for the disposal of scrap cable, investigated and reported on the position of the railways in Northern Ireland, and the list goes on and on. He was a joint inspector into the affairs of Rolls Razor Limited, president of the Institute in 1966/67, vice president of the Union Européenne des Experts Comptables Economiques et Financiers, and only in 1974 he was appointed a member of the Governor's City Liaison Committee.

Sir Henry's retirement may enable him to devote more time to his three hobbies, shooting, sailing and golf; but he is not letting go of the reins altogether: he continues to hold a number of directorships, remains chairman of the International Accounting Standards Committee, and is expected to be appointed treasurer of the Open University in May this year.

Would Sir Henry still choose accountancy as a profession?

SIR HENRY: From what I know now, without any question. I think it's the golden age of the accountancy profession.

What are his most vivid recollections as an accountant? Has he any exotic memories?

SIR HENRY: No, you know you can't have any particular memory in a life so full and varied in commercial practice. Apart from anything else, the things that are probably most exciting are the things that you can never disclose because of professional secrecy. The one or two really exciting things that have happened in one's life affect other people, and one's professional relations with clients, so it's not really possible to say anything about them.

Which is a pity, because outsiders tend to see accountancy as a boring profession.

SIR HENRY: I think it's the most exciting profession in the world.

I asked Sir Henry what qualities Coopers sought in choosing qualified staff.

SIR HENRY: First and foremost, above everything else, character. You will no doubt ask: 'What is character?' It's almost impossible to define it in a few words without being extremely pompous, but a very large number of people have roughly the same quality of intelligence, and roughly the same amount of training. What we are looking for is the man who can show some sign of leadership, who can show decision when decision is required, who will have a sense of judgement in a situation—all these things make up a man's character.

When a man comes to you, either to be articled, or as a potential member of the qualified staff, is it possible to test for 'character' in an hour or so of interview?

SIR HENRY: No, not at all. You can get a rough idea—you know from his answers to the questions that you put to him whether they are the sort of answers you would expect from a man with the qualities that you need. But you can only in fact judge his character by a long period of assessment; and above all by putting him under a certain strain and stress from time to time to see how he reacts.

What about a potential partner? What qualities does he need?

SIR HENRY: Exactly the same qualities—character above everything else. Of course he must have a high technical competence—he would be of no use to clients if he hadn't high technical competence.

It always seems to me that Coopers' partners tend to work hard and play hard. Is this the firm's philosophy?

SIR HENRY: It is my philosophy.

But in other partners I have seen the same sort of philosophy.

SIR HENRY: I think it has always been the philosophy of the firm.

I asked Sir Henry whether Coopers was the same place it was 30 years ago.

SIR HENRY: When I joined the firm, which was in 1926, the total strength everywhere, all over the world, was about 150 people. The only offices we had were London, Liverpool, Brussels and New York. The total strength now, world-wide, is 17-18,000, and we carry on business in 77 different countries.

Was it a better place 50 years ago?

SIR HENRY: It is certainly a different place. It is a better place now in the sense that the range of work is vastly greater than it was, the opportunities both for partners and staff are immeasurably broader, and the type and quality of work is so much more interesting—nobody need ever be dull.

Sir Henry, I said, you played an important part in building the firm from 150 staff to 17,000—a growth of more than 100-fold. Have you any regrets about that growth?

SIR HENRY: None whatever. I think if you don't grow, you die.

Moving away from Coopers a little, I asked Sir Henry what qualities he regarded as essential in an auditor?

SIR HENRY: The quality of inquiry. An auditor who goes round and does the audit by rote and by rule along established lines will never be a good auditor. He must have a sense of inquiry, a sense not so much of suspicion, but of 'Why?'. He must be sufficiently perceptive to see that there is something slightly unusual, something slightly out of the ordinary, something that puts him on inquiry to go a little further, and to penetrate deeper in his work.

Is Sir Henry satisfied that present training methods in both large firms and small firms alike inculcate these qualities?

SIR HENRY: I don't think you will ever inculcate them if they are not there in the man's makeup in the beginning. I think it's got to be in the man's character from the start. You can, of course, help to train him, and guide him, but the sense of inquiry must always be there.

What about audit quality? Was Sir Henry in favour of post-audit review, I asked?

SIR HENRY: Undoubtedly, it is essential today.

Have you always done it?

SIR HENRY: We have done it certainly for the last 20 years plus.

You regard it as necessary even in a firm as large as Coopers?

SIR HENRY: Imperative.

What do you do when you find something you don't like?

SIR HENRY: Get hold of the partner, or the member of staff responsible, point out that the quality of what he had done was not good enough, point out the deficiencies, and indicate that we don't want it to happen again.

What about peer review? Over the last two or three years, the idea has developed in the United States of one firm of accountants looking at the methods and procedures of another, and reporting upon them, either as a result of an SEC directive, or by the voluntary agreement of the firms concerned. What does Sir Henry think about peer review?

SIR HENRY: I am against peer reviews.

You feel it should be unnecessary?

SIR HENRY: It should be unnecessary. I can't see that it's going to help very much if a firm is conscious of the need for watching its own standards the whole time. This should be a continuous process.

Do you feel the same if one is talking about a small firm? Do you feel that one or two partners should be capable of ensuring their own standards?

SIR HENRY: I can see no reason why not. I don't think it makes any difference the number of partners; it is what is in the mind of the partner himself.

How do you view statistical sampling?

SIR HENRY: Not with enormous enthusiasm. It has obviously got advantages in particular circumstances, we don't use it to a very large extent in this firm except in particular cases when the range and type of the work make it necessary.

What about the size of some audit samples? Was there not a danger that some unhappy auditor was one day going to be faced in a court of law with a statistical sampling expert who said that a sample-size of 25 or 30 was a ridiculously small sample?

SIR HENRY: I think that anybody can question the size of any sample, whether it be big or small, if things go wrong, because critics invariably have hindsight, saying that it should have been done differently. But of course the sampling is really only the second stage. The first stage is to be sure that the internal control and the internal procedures are right. The sampling thereafter is largely a matter of ensuring that those controls and procedures are operating.

I asked Sir Henry whether he thought auditors were at greater risk in present economic circumstances? Was there, when their clients were in economic difficulties, a greater risk of the auditor being sued?

SIR HENRY: Yes.

I asked Sir Henry whether he is in favor of auditors having limited liability.

SIR HENRY: I used not to be, for a number of reasons. Partly because if you limit liability, you are, or you might be, put under some obligation to the government, and I think it best for a profession to be detached from government. Secondly, I had the feeling that a profession should not be insulated from the effects of negligent work. But I am beginning to change that view, partly because of the size of the possible claims, the fact that a single slip could have the effect of breaking a firm of great standing which had been carrying on business for many years.

In this, is Sir Henry affected by the prevailing climate in the United States, where there are far more professional negligence claims against all the professions than there are here?

SIR HENRY: The law is different, and the climate of approach between business and its professional advisers is different from what it is here. I prefer the climate of opinion here, where it is recognised that a professional man, 99 times out of 100, does the very best that he can, and if he does slip, as every human slips from time to time, it is not usually held against him in the sense of seeking damages from him.

In the past, rights and responsibilities have tended to go hand in hand, have they not?

SIR HENRY: Yes. This is another reason why I am wary about limited liability.

Turning to Sir Henry's interest in International Standards: Forbes magazine the other day attacked International Standards on a number of counts, suggesting that they were a device of the Anglo-Saxon nations, that they wouldn't really be enforceable.

SIR HENRY: It was a damaging article.

How much truth is there in it?

SIR HENRY: When International Standards began, everybody thought they were an extraordinarily good idea. Nobody could dissent from the principle. A great many people didn't think that they would be very successful, or that they would be every effective. The International Accounting Standards Committee has now got to the point where it is suffering, not from failure, but from its success. It is in fact issuing Standards at regular intervals, and it is issuing Standards which are precise, which have bite in them. But now people are beginning to wonder whether they do want International Standards—whether they wouldn't prefer to go on in the old way. What the International Accounting Standards Committee now faces is the necessity of convincing people that their original enthusiasms have got to be sustained. What is most encouraging is the fact that a number of relatively small nations are crying out for International Standards, because firstly they want them and have not the research facilities to make them themselves, and secondly they want the power and authority which the International Accounting Standards Committee agreement gives them to impose those Standards in their countries.

Forbes suggests that the International Accounting Standards Committee is no more than an Anglo-Saxon venture designed to impose Anglo-Saxons views on the world. This is of course total nonsense.

Would you not define them as Anglo-Saxon?

SIR HENRY: I don't really know what Anglo-Saxon is. I wish I did know; the article seems to imply that Anglo-Saxon is practically confined to the UK. The article then goes on to suggest that the Standards are not likely to be applied by the very countries who have subscribed to the agreement and constitution. That is the damaging parts about it.

Is there any truth in this?

SIR HENRY: I think that it will take a period of education and propaganda to be sure that the Standards are applied and the disciplinary procedures are imposed by the various professional bodies. But this, I think, is a necessary concomitant of an international movement of this kind. It is going to take time to get it fully established in the way it was intended to be.

Are we not in danger of having too many Standard-setting bodies?

SIR HENRY: Yes, we are. But I hope that as the IASC grows in stature and prestige, its work will receive routine international acceptance, and that all that it will be necessary to do locally will be to impose stiffer, or more restrictive, Standards than the International Standards.

Do you ever see International Standards overtaking, say, the Standards in this country and the Standards in the United States?

SIR HENRY: I think they will in the sense that I have just mentioned.

But can International Standards ever be so far up to the developments of the profession they would manage to beat best practice in the United States and best practice here?

SIR HENRY: No, I don't think so, because International Standards by their very nature must always be a furlong or two behind the field.

I asked Sir Henry what he regarded as the contribution of International Accounting Standard 1 to this country? Was it not a pity that it neither used the British wording nor the American wording, but we now had a third wording on the same basic concept?

SIR HENRY: Yes. But you see, an International Standard has to accommodate the views of nine separate great nations. It is a good Standard, and I hope that in the course of time perhaps it may be accepted as *the* Standard—not necessarily because it is better worded, or better drafted, but merely because if we can remove Standards which say the same thing, we can cut down the total number.

Did he not ever envy the small practitioner down in Minehead who walked comfortably down the hill to his office at 8:55 am each morning?

SIR HENRY: Sometimes I envy what is called the small practitioner very much indeed. Usually he lives closer to his work, he lives close to the countryside, and the pressures which inevitably fall on one in practice in London are not there. There are other compensations.

## QUESTIONS

1. What qualities does Sir Henry feel are most important for becoming an accountant? Compare with those given by Alan Breck (Selection 9).

2. Critique Sir Henry's views on auditor liability, peer review, and statistical sampling.

## SELECTED BIBLIOGRAPHY

Alumkal, Margaret, and John Paranilam, "Profile of Accounting Executives in the United States," *The Accountant*, Feb. 6, 1975.

Maynard, Brian, "On His Way to the Top," *Accountants Weekly*, June 13, 1974, p. 8.

# 14
## ACTUARIES*
World

Actuaries are one breed of professional who are mathematically equipped to handle a wide assortment of problems. An actuary might be found in a 3 a.m. strategy session with a client, advising on a pension plan to be offered at the bargaining table the next morning. Another might be called upon to examine the adequacy of the reserves of a multi-billion dollar insurance company. Yet a third could be helping a client to analyze the employee benefits program and pension fund liabilities of a company which the client wants to acquire.

Lots of people are confused by the word "actuary." As one actuary observed, common cocktail party reactions to his profession range from ". . .A what? Never heard of such a thing!" and ". . .They work for insurance companies, don't they?" to a knowingly facetious ". . .When am I going to die?"

Faced with such misinformation, an actuary could try to give his profession some definition by explaining that an actuary is a statistician who deals with the contingencies of life, a kind of mathematical soothsayer—or morbid bookie. Actuaries' two traditional preserves have been the computation of life insurance company premiums, and reserves, based on complex mortality tables, hence the proverbial connection made between actuaries and extinction; and the design and pricing of employee benefits packages. Both areas require the ability to assess the financial consequences of events which may—or may not—occur many years in the future. This requires long-range forecasting on such factors as mortality, salary levels, rates of investment return, and patterns of employee mobility and retirement.

Today, actuaries are ready to take on many practical business or social questions that involve mathematical projections into the future. The U.S. Congress depends on actuarial advice for the financing of the Social Security program. State governments, seeking increased professionalism in law enforcement, turn to the actuary to develop a statewide retirement system for police officers. And the actuary's ability to manipulate quantified data has led top management to ask him for advice on long-range corporate financial planning. Where there is an uncertainty and it can be reduced to numbers, an actuary can be called in to do a little figuring.

There is good reason why the term "actuary" tends to draw a blank in most people's minds. Most people have never come across one in the flesh. At the end of 1972, there were only 4,301 U.S. and Canadian actuaries holding membership in the Society of Actuaries, the principal professional organization in North America. It takes the average actuarial hopeful seven or eight years to pass all 10 parts of the Society's examinations, making him a "Fellow" of the Society and bestowing the right to post-fix his name with "F.S.A." After passing the first five exams, the aspirant is an "Associate" member. A candidate specializes after the eighth exam when he must

*From **World**, Summer 1973, pp. 2, 4, 5, 6. Reprinted by permission of the publisher.

decide between the I route (advanced material relating to insurance companies) or E route (advanced employee benefit topics). The meager number of accredited actuaries is in growing demand, a demand which far outstrips the supply. The bulk of them are still employed by some 200 insurance companies and 90 consulting actuarial firms. The rest are sprinkled throughout various federal and state government agencies, universities, and an occasional labor union or large corporation. . . .

Unlike physicians, lawyers, and accountants, actuaries are not licensed under state laws. And without this legal sanction, actuaries have not been altogether successful in carving out a preserve for themselves. There is nothing stopping any accountant who gets the urge from engaging in some back-of-the-envelope figuring on an actuarial problem—nothing, that is, except a limited acquaintance with such intimidating esoterica as Boolean algebra and differential and integral calculus. To tackle this problem, the American Academy of Actuaries was organized in 1965 by the other professional bodies, with the primary purpose of presenting a united front in seeking recognition and accreditation at the Federal and State levels.

As a consequence, many other professionals are beginning to see actuaries as mathematical theoreticians who have stepped down from their Ivory Tower and are ready and willing to apply their erudite know-how to real-life problems.

### QUESTIONS

1. How does the actuarial profession overlap with the accounting profession?

2. Several public accounting firms employ actuaries. For example, Peat, Marwick, Mitchell & Co. employ forty. What duties would an actuary have with a public accounting firm?

3. Several United States universities offer master's degrees in actuarial science. Investigate one of these programs at your library as to prerequisites and subject matter.

# 15

## WOULD YOU RECOMMEND ACCOUNTANCY AS A CAREER?*
The Accountant's Magazine

You would, according to a survey of some 500 accountants, carried out in November 1974, by *Accountants Weekly*. The sample was drawn from the English Institute, the

*From "Notes and Comments," *The Accountant's Magazine*, January 1975, p. 8. Reprinted by permission of the publisher.

Scottish Institute, the Association and the Institute of Cost and Management Accountants, with a few members from the Irish Institute.

To the question "If asked, would you advise a young person for or against choosing accountancy today?", the most enthusiastic "Yes" came from CAs and FCMAs, both of whom scored 100%. All of the four bodies analysed in the results of the survey (the Irish sample was too small to include in the analysis) were enthusiastic about the prospects in accountancy: the other scores ranged from 82% (ACAs) to 91% (FCAs).

Probably linked with the above question was the response to this one: "Do you consider that your professional body is doing enough to encourage young people to qualify as accountants?" Here the Scottish Institute scored the highest (89%), the other categories of accountants (Fellows and Associates of the other three bodies analysed) ranging from 54% (ACAs) to 78% (FCCAs and FCMAs).

When the overall results were aggregated and then divided crosswise into accountants in industry and commerce and accountants in practice, the results showed the first category rather more enthusiastic than the second. For the first question 85% of accountants in industry said "Yes" (78% in practice). The second question produced a 71% (64%) result.

## QUESTION

1. What social and economic arguments could be presented for choosing accounting as a career objective?

## 16
## THE ACCOUNTANT'S ROLE IN THE FBI*
Joseph T. Wells

As the chief investigative arm of the United States Department of Justice the jurisdiction of the Federal Bureau of Investigation includes a wide range of responsibilities in the criminal, civil, and internal security fields. Special Agents are charged with the duty of investigating violations of the laws of the United States, collecting evidence in cases in which the United States is or may be a party in interest, and performing other duties imposed on them by law. Special Agent Accountants have the primary responsibility of curtailing "white collar" crime involving fraud and embezzlement, as well as other schemes such as bribery, obstruction of justice and conflict of interest. Additionally, they develop evidence in civil investigations showing

*From *Management Accounting*, April 1975, pp. 24—26. Reprinted by permission of the publisher.

just compensation to the citizen as well as the United States Government in the prosecution and defense of civil suits of which the United States Government is a party of interest. These investigations have saved millions of dollars for the American taxpayer.

## THE SPECIAL AGENT ACCOUNTANT

The Special Agent Accountant is an internal designation used within the FBI. Of approximately 8,600 FBI Special Agents, about 700 are Special Agent Accountants. To be considered for the position of Special Agent Accountant, an applicant must have reached his 23rd and not have reached his 36th birthday. He must meet rigid physical standards and be free of defects which would interfere with the use of firearms or with participation in dangerous assignments. The candidate must also be a graduate of a four-year state accredited college, have a bachelor's degree with a major in accounting and have at least one year of practical accounting and/or auditing experience. Although the certified public accountant certificate is desirable, it is not a mandatory requirement.

Applicants for this position come from virtually all segments of private industry as well as public accounting. The entrance salary of $14,117 is increased upon completion of the New Agents training to $17,653 to reflect additional fixed compensation for irregularly scheduled overtime. While engaged in investigative work, the Agent can advance to a grade which has a salary range from $25,352 to $31,895, including overtime. Many Agents promoted to supervisory positions receive higher salaries, up to the present maximum of $36,000 per annum.

All Agents, including the Agent Accountant, must be able to cope with investigative problems as they occur. Agent accountants must be qualified to handle any type of investigation. In fast-breaking situations such as a bank robbery, kidnapping, or an extortion, the Agent Accountant will join in the hunt for the perpetrators of the crime.

## AGENT TRAINING

Since he or she is expected to handle all types of investigations, the Agent Accountant is afforded the same training as other agents in the New Agent's Training School, which is located at the newly constructed FBI Academy near Quantico, Virginia. During this rigorous 14 week course, the Agent Accountant is given an intensive grounding in FBI rules and regulations, investigative techniques, the laws of evidence, and federal criminal court procedure. He must become proficient in the use of fingerprint identification and other tools of the investigator. Before graduation, he has to qualify in firearms and defensive tactics. The standards during this training are high. The trainee is given frequent examinations, and failure may result in his being dropped from the class.

Training in the FBI is a continuous process for all Agents. Each Agent is required to qualify with a variety of firearms and the use of defensive tactics eight times annually. In addition, Agent Accountants are periodically given specialized in-service training to keep abreast of the latest accounting and auditing theories, techniques, and procedures. The training includes an overview of auditing techniques and the utilization of computers and other automated record-keeping devices as they relate to government, banking, and private industry.

After graduation, the Agent is assigned to one of the FBI's 59 field offices. Although personal preferences are given consideration, assignment locations are naturally based on the FBI's needs. The new Agent Accountant's first experience is usually in general investigative matters. Later he is assigned to assist one of the more experienced accountants, who will plan and supervise his work. After receiving this on-the-job training, the new Agent will be assigned accounting cases on his own.

Many factors govern the type of investigative assignments an agent will receive. As in public accounting, one of the influencing factors is the size of the field office to which he is assigned. The smaller the field office, generally, the less the Agent will specialize. Other factors include the nature and type of ongoing investigations and the special talents or interests of the individual Agent.

## TYPES OF ACCOUNTING VIOLATIONS

Investigations with accounting implications can be criminal or civil in nature. They are usually limited to audits and special examinations which are designed to determine whether certain specific allegations of federal law violations are true. Some of the more common criminal activities that are investigated include various violations of Title 18, United States Code, pertaining to bank fraud and embezzlement, the National Bankruptcy Act, and certain federal antitrust laws, as well as various types of fraud against the United States Government. Civil investigations are made upon request from the Justice Department. These investigations include cases such as an individual's financial ability to pay a government obligation, as well as matters involving the Renegotiation Act and the Court of Claims Act.

Investigations concerning bank fraud and embezzlement generally include criminal violations by officers and employees of a banking-type institution insured under various federal laws, and in certain instances, by persons who borrow from these institutions. Investigations involving the National Bankruptcy Act often originate when it is learned that a bankrupt individual or firm has converted or concealed assets in contemplation of bankruptcy. Most perpetrators of these crimes foresee the possibility of an investigation and consequently go to great lengths to prepare voluminous fictitious records and supporting documents. From an accounting standpoint, these investigations can be very challenging.

Allegations of fraud against the government often arise when parties under contract to certain governmental agencies submit false claims for payment. In recent years, schemes devised by unscrupulous contractors and realtors to defraud the Federal Housing Administration and unsuspecting homeowners have caused special prosecutive efforts to be directed in this area.

Investigations involving the criminal aspects of certain antitrust laws are also conducted by the FBI at the specific request of the Department of Justice. When compared to some other areas, the number of antitrust convictions appears to be small. However, ongoing complex investigations spanning a year or more are not uncommon, and the resultant fines, savings and recoveries attributed to these investigations are among the highest of any violation.

Civil investigations involving the Renegotiation Act and Court of Claims Act are somewhat similar in that they both generally arise from monetary disputes between the government and one or more civilian contractors. The FBI is requested to make an independent inquiry which often involves a detailed analysis of both parties' records and accounting procedures. Opinions of Special Agent Accountants are generally rendered in civil investigations such as Court of Claims and Renegotiation Act matters. However, there are rare instances when an Agent will be called upon to express his opinion in criminal cases.

## TRENDS IN WHITE COLLAR CRIMES

Exhibit 1 indicates that dramatic increases in certain white collar crimes have occurred over the past few years. Although the list is by no means totally inclusive, it is illustrative. Fines, savings and recoveries, the total funds attributable to FBI investigations, have increased dramatically in all areas, while increases in the number of convictions have been effected in only two of the four areas shown. This indicates that efforts aimed at reducing the number of violations have been successful to a degree, but that the average dollar amount per conviction is rising at an alarming rate. Unfortunately, the development of more sophisticated systems coupled with greater utilization of EDP has produced a bolder, more knowledgeable criminal.

**Exhibit 1   Comparison of Certain "White Collar" Crimes for the Fiscal Years 1969 and 1973**

| | TOTAL CONVICTIONS | | | TOTAL FINES, SAVINGS, RECOVERIES | | | AVERAGE PER CONVICTION | | |
|---|---|---|---|---|---|---|---|---|---|
| | 1969 | 1973 | PERCENT INCREASE (DE-CREASE) | 1969 | 1973 | PERCENT INCREASE (DE-CREASE) | 1969 | 1973 | PERCENT INCREASE (DE-CREASE) |
| Bank frauds and em-bezzlements | 730 | 1,064 | 46 | $10,209,419 | $19,984,683 | 96 | $ 13,896 | $ 18,783 | 35 |
| Antitrust matters | 139 | 43 | (69) | 28,548,200 | 42,493,825 | 49 | 205,382 | 988,228 | 374 |
| Frauds against the government | 117 | 175 | 50 | 2,396,178 | 3,434,746 | 43 | 20,480 | 56,307 | 175 |
| National Bank-ruptcy Act | 34 | 28 | (18) | 341,164 | 836,927 | 145 | 10,034 | 29,890 | 198 |

Source: FBI Annual Reports, 1969 and 1973.

## INVESTIGATIVE ACCOUNTING VERSUS AUDITING

There are many similarities between conducting an audit and conducting an accounting investigation. However, some fundamental differences do exist due to the scope of the respective examinations. Most audits are designed to render an independent opinion on a company's financial statements, and are not aimed at detecting defalcations or irregularities. The criminal accounting investigation, on the other hand, is normally based upon specific allegations of fraud or concealment.

Other differences are readily apparent in the area of working paper preparation. The Agent Accountant invariably expects his working papers to become the basis for testimony or supporting evidence in court, and he attempts to prepare his documentation in such a manner as to facilitate explanation of the concepts involved to non-accountants. Also, the Agent is often the object of legal rebuttals designed to lessen the impact of the evidence as admitted, or to reduce or destroy his credibility as a witness. Therefore, he must be sure that his working papers and his testimony are as accurate as possible and are able to withstand the closest scrutiny, even in seemingly unimportant detail.

Rarely can the Agent utilize previous working papers, inasmuch as most investigations are not of a recurring nature. Also, attempts to standardize techniques of working paper preparation have met with limited success because of the diversity of the information available in each particular situation.

FBI accounting investigations many times require investigative techniques unrelated to accounting. In the instances where the criminal is not an accountant, it is sometimes necessary for the Agent to set aside his formal training in order to follow the thought processes of the criminal.

## CONCLUSION

Accounting investigations in the FBI are often a curious mixture of accounting knowledge, fundamental psychology and common sense; and each investigation, because of the human element, is truly unique. The accountant's role in the FBI is indeed an important and challenging one.

## QUESTIONS

1. What are the duties of special agent accountants?
2. What are the qualifications for becoming a special agent accountant?
3. What are the differences between auditing and accounting investigations?

# 17

## ACCOUNTING BY SAM*
Robert F. Randall

He had just finished working on the "Three Days of the Condor," starring Robert Redford and Faye Dunaway, and he thought it would be a hit at the box office.

Predicting what a motion picture will make at the box office, however, is not his forte. It's predicting how much it will cost to make the film. His name is Sam Goldrich and he is a production accountant for motion pictures and television shows.

A lean, articulate man, Sam Goldrich has worked in the movie industry since 1952. "I started out to be a producer, writer or genius." He ended up being one of a small group of highly skilled accountants who specialize in the film making industry. His own "credits" run from "Porgy and Bess," TV's ill-fated "The Trials of O'Brien," and the more successful "Patty Duke Show," to the recent sleeper, "Death Wish," and the blockbuster, "Serpico."

When he's not on location or in the office working for Producer Dino DeLaurentiis, Mr. Goldrich manages to get down to The New School in New York City for a couple of hours to teach motion picture accounting. His lectures replete with quips ("A production accountant's main function is to tell the producer he's in trouble"), Hollywood lore and film making anecdotes entertain as well as inform young aspiring producers, directors and production accountants themselves.

"If you don't have a sense of humor, forget it," Mr. Goldrich advises accountants who want to become production accountants. It is a "pressure job," he really admits, but he likes working in film because "It pays well and it's more fun" than other endeavors.

The production accountant is the guardian of the producer's money. The producer is the individual who initiates the film making process. He selects the property, a book or a play, for example, and hires a screenwriter to turn it into a usable script. He hires the director and with the director casts the picture. When the production is far enough along to the shooting stage, he also hires a production manager and production accountant.

The production manager breaks down the script into shooting days and then with the assistance of the production accountant budgets the script. "They will say we can shoot this thing in 54 days for two-and-a-half-million dollars," Sam Goldrich illustrates.

This is the stage where the expertise and the experience of the production accountant are needed. The producer depends on his forecast of the cost of shooting the picture. The heyday of the big Hollywood studios and runaway production budgets is over. Cost accounting, by necessity, rules supreme in all movie companies and is likely to continue to do so.

*From *Management Accounting*, June 1975, pp. 51–53. Reprinted by permission of the publisher.

"It's very crucial to get a schedule that you can live with," Mr. Goldrich says. "But there are so many 'ifs,' you know. You can't predict human nature. Some directors can take a picture and be a whiz."

Director Sidney Lumet, with whom he worked on "Serpico," is one of the directors he holds in high regard. "I respect him as a man, as an artist, as a good director, but the crews sometimes get unhappy because there's no overtime! He goes in and shoots like a whirlwind."

Two other directors with whom he has worked also have his respect and admiration: Michael Winner, a man with an excellent sense of humor, with whom he usually trades barbs; and Sydney Pollack who in his view is a painstaking craftsman and a *mensch* ("a real human being")—an accolade that Mr. Goldrich rarely gives anyone in the industry.

Some directors, successful in the past, will unaccountably flounder and, as a result, go over budget on the picture. So the production accountant's knowledge of a director's pacing can be crucial in putting together the budget for the picture. His relationship with the production manager is also important to the budgeting process. Mr. Goldrich has learned that production managers and producers almost always tend to underestimate the cost of shooting a picture.

## "ABOVE THE LINE"

The budget itself is broken up between "above the line" and "below the line" categories. "Above the line" consists of the talent: the writers, the major actors, actresses, extras, bit players and the director, among others. "Below the line" is everything else, including production staff, rental of cameras, set construction, film cutting and laboratory costs.

The cost of shooting a picture runs on the average $12,000 to $15,000 a day, and the post-production costs including editing, dubbing sound and musical score are enormous, too. These costs, however, can be controlled. What is difficult to control is the cost of shooting a picture. If an actor or actress gets sick, the picture may be delayed or if the set is unavailable for some reason or other, the production crew may be unable to shoot the scenes scheduled.

In one movie on which Mr. Goldrich worked, the production crew was all ready to shoot in a large deserted warehouse. At the last minute a lawyer representing the owners said the warehouse could not be used. This decision threatened to delay the shooting and cause the picture to run over budget. Fortunately, an enterprising production manager improvised and worked around the obstacle so the crew could shoot as scheduled. That's why, he says, a good production manager is so important to the success of a picture.

"I have learned, being a bit of a philosopher as well as an accountant, that once the picture starts, the picture takes over," Mr. Goldrich says. He calls the period just before the shooting starts "the honeymoon" because there is little pressure, compared to when the crew is on the set shooting the film.

One of the most important responsibilities of the production accountant once shooting of the picture has begun is to give the producer a weekly estimate to complete. A good production accountant has to be constantly on the set in order to make this estimate.

"The reason I go on the set is that when you make up your costs to complete you want to know exactly what's going on the set. You talk to certain people on the set because what you're trying to give the producer is as close and honest an estimate as possible as to what the picture is going to cost and what kind of bread he's got to get up, and the mark of a good man is to give it to him accurately and quickly as possible."

The average moviegoer would be thrilled to watch the filming of motion picture but the actual shooting is not very exciting, says Mr. Goldrich. "People are always dying to get on a set but when they get there, it's very dull! You'll be shooting the same scene over and over again four or five times. They shoot it in bits because you can't have too long a scene; the light will burn out."

## BILLS DRIBBLE IN

What does the production accountant do on the set? "You get to know the people you can trust," he says. "You talk to the script supervisor, the girl who keeps track of everything that is shot. You talk to the set construction people to find out how much more is needed. Construction can run a lot of money. Are we finished? Do we have to build more? Do we need more paint, more lumber? You try and look through your purchase order file to see what bills have not come in yet. Bills have a way of dribbling in."

He continues, "I take notes when I go on the set. I talk to people. If any sudden change comes up, for example, based on what I tell them, sometimes they rewrite the script."

In a tongue-in-cheek illustration of the cost pressures on a moving picture, Mr. Goldrich told his class that "Three Days of the Condor" started out as "Six Days of the Condor." "In the accounting department, we called it 'The 4½ days:' we split the difference."

The financing of a motion picture, Mr. Goldrich explains to his class, flows from "The Bible," the producer-distributor contract which runs more than 100 pages and defines the duties, rights, prerogatives and percentages of the principals. Even before they are shot, most pictures are already sold to a distributor who extends a line of credit to the producer who draws upon it as he needs it. If the motion picture goes over budget, the producer loses "points" or percentages of the profit. A skilled production accountant, therefore, can be the producer's most important asset.

The production accountant must know the small print of every contract, including standard clauses of the different unions and the tricky clauses that can cost the producer more money than he had banked on. "It's money if you make a mistake computing actors," Mr. Goldrich explains. "I've seen new accountants overpay actors something fierce. On the other hand, if you know your contract well enough you can save your company money."

In an industry dedicated to the artistic muse, it is noteworthy that the accountant's continuing revision of the estimate to complete during the actual shooting of a picture is an art all by itself. (Only about 10 top notch production accountants work in the New York area.) "Your estimates have to be done while you go along," he stresses, "otherwise, what's the good of economy after the picture's all shot and saying, 'oh, boy, did we take a beating!' "

"If you took a CPA, for example, who thinks that accounting is accounting and threw him into it, I think he would be completely out of his depth," Mr. Goldrich says, emphasizing the highly specialized function the production accountant fulfills.


## BUDGET VARIABLE: TALENT

The production accountant does not deal only with people, and the budget figures can vary in direct proportion to the egos of the "talent." Mr. Goldrich's definition of a producer makes the point: A producer is a man walking through Grand Central station and off in the distance he hears a phone ringing and he *knows* it is for him!

Producers are not the only people who have egos. A star can throw a picture off the budget track by interfering with the director. Whether or not he is allowed to depends on the director's own personality. After 23 years of working in the industry, Mr. Goldrich knows many of the people on the artistic side and on the commercial end and his knowledge often is tapped by producers or production managers.

His acquaintance with vendors is useful in saving the producer money. "You learn how to manipulate your money," Mr. Goldrich explains. Sometimes on the set he is called upon to give an estimate on what a change contemplated by the director or production manager will cost, so his familiarity with all phases of movie production is invaluable.

Obviously, Mr. Goldrich loves his work and enjoys the people who work in the industry. When a production crew is put together and meets for the first time on "distant location," it is like "old home week" as people who worked together before on other productions meet again. "One of the things I enjoy about it is you see some great artists at work. I don't mean only the directors. A good lighting man who knows how to light up a set is a joy to behold!"

Sam Goldrich spent ten years in Hollywood and then moved to the New York City area in 1962. During that time he has worked on many productions for studios, independent producers and as a consultant. The producer, he now works for—Dino DeLaurentiis—headquartered in New York City, has made more than $20 million worth of motion pictures in the last few years, including "Serpico," "Crazy Joe," "The Valachi Papers," "Three Tough Guys," "Stonekiller" and "Mandingo." "Death Wish," starring Charles Bronson, is also one of his movies.

But in the film industry no matter how many successes you have had in the past, it's the latest film that counts. That's why Production Accountant Sam Goldrich is looking forward to sometime this summer when "Three Days of the Condor" is released in first-run theaters throughout the United States and the credit "Accounting by Sam" flickers on the screen.

Industry people will know who "Sam" is.

**QUESTIONS**

1. What are the duties of a production accountant for motion pictures and television shows?

2. Compare and contrast the accounting period for a motion picture with that for a business organization.

# 18

## YOU NEED A SENSE OF HUMOR*
Peace Corps Accountant

The 26-year-old author had two goals: to help people and to work as an accountant. He managed to combine both of these ambitions during a two-year stint with the Peace Corps in Malaysia.

Elaborating on his Peace Corps experience, the author, Daniel G. Dorian, said he was assigned as an accounting advisor to the Auditor General of Malaysia to help introduce Program and Performance Budgeting (PPB) into that government. After about a year, he was transferred to the Secretary General of the Ministry of Agriculture and Lands, where he wound up his tour.

The experience was exhilarating. Mr. Dorian says, but many of his basic assumptions were challenged. For example, when he tried to obtain some computer time from the Treasury Department, he asked the manager how much the system was used. "Well, we use it about 20 hours," was the reply.

"I said, 'that's not too bad, 20 hours a day; that will leave us at least four hours a day.' "

"Wait a minute," said the man in charge of the computer operation, "We use it 20 hours a week." This revelation was a surprise to Mr. Dorian who says, "I am used to computer operations that run five days a week, 18 hours a day at least, if not more, and some 24 hours a day—six or seven days a week."

The point he makes is that it did not help the Malaysians very much to make computer programs more efficient because they were not using anywhere near the amount of computer time available. "So doing what is right for the U.S. in U.S. terms, saving computer time, is not accomplishing much here."

"My basic argument" he continued, "is that we should get away from the concept of improving things in our terms and get with the concept of doing something of value in local terms. We are dealing with a basically different kind of society and should make different kinds of assumptions than those applicable to the U.S. or any developed economy."

*From *Management Accountant*, May 1974, p. 64. Reprinted by permission of the publisher.

Salability is one talent the management accountant needs in a developing country, he says. "It is very hard to convince somebody who has always thought of accounting as an accurate, to-the-penny science to drop a few digits on the end of his million dollar numbers. It was a challenge even to convince some people to round off on a budget—not even an actual accounting statement—a budget. Getting people to drop these end digits, even up to the hundredth level, let alone going to thousandths, was a radical, radical thing to do. When you think about it, taking those end digits away from someone used to dealing with them is like removing a security blanket, which even supposedly advanced economies still hang onto."

Does he think his Peace Corps tour was worthwhile for him and the host country? "I would have to say enthusiastically, yes, in the first case and probably yes in the second." Whether or not the systems he helped to establish were of value is secondary, he believes, to the more important result that he and the people he worked with were exposed to different views on techniques in management accounting. The first adaptation to the new is always the hardest, he says, so the next time should be easier. Of course, Mr. Dorian learned from his experience, too.

"Would I urge other accountants to join the Peace Corps? Sure, if you are crazy enough to try, you will enjoy it." He says it was not a great hardship. Thanks to the generosity of the U.S. Government, he lived in a large cement house and was even able to provide free room and board to a student attending a university.

If nothing else a Peace Corpsmen should have a sense of humor. "That is probably the most important piece of baggage you can carry. The sense of humor is vital because if you take yourself or the assignment too seriously, you lose patience and are going to feel frustrated and become cynical. I would say developing a sense of humor and patience has probably been the most significant result of my being in the Peace Corps."

While he was working in a government office in Malaysia, a farmer came in and asked for a job. When Mr. Dorian said he had nothing to do with giving out jobs, the man asked for a recommendation. That earnest job seeker symbolized for him the reason for his entire Peace Corps experience. "What I really want to do is find that guy a job and what impressed me about Malaysia was that that man really wanted to work."

If he has anything to do about it, Mr. Dorian will return to Malaysia and help create jobs. "I am hoping that within two or three years when I have built up a base of experience in accounting that I will be able to go back to Malaysia and make a significant contribution in terms of assisting industry in making a profit, and by making a profit, creating jobs, and by creating jobs, improving economic opportunities for Malaysians.

## QUESTION

1. Define PPB and budget.

## SELECTED BIBLIOGRAPHY

Dorian, Daniel G., "Management Accounting in a Developing Country," *Management Accounting*, May 1974, pp. 15-18.

# 19

## GROUP PORTRAIT WITH ACCOUNTANT*
Esquire

EDITOR'S NOTE: The photograph described below is not reproduced.

This is a sort of historic picture of about as much artistic talent as has ever been packed into one photographer's set at one time. We'll get to its greater meaning in a minute; first, the identities. On this page, top to bottom, Wolf Kahn, Marisol, Jackie Winsor, Nancy Graves, Jo Baer; on the other page, left to right, back row, Emily Mason, Cy Twombly, John Chamberlain, John Clem Clarke; next row forward, Michael Balog, Robert Rauschenberg, Robert Petersen, Robert Indiana, Malcolm Morley, Claes Oldenburg, Richard Serra; the three men sort of in the middle are Larry Rivers, Joseph Kosuth and James Rosenquist; Andy Warhol down in front you know; but the one to really watch, the normal-looking one to the left of Andy, is Rubin L. Gorewitz. Rubin is not a famous artist, he's a certified public accountant whose practice is artists—about six hundred in all. Rubin looks after the books so the artists can look after the art. But Rubin is a man of vision, too, and at present his vision observes that some of the laws affecting artists are iniquitous. For one thing, an artist's tax deduction for a charitable contribution of his own work is limited to the cost of the materials, whereas a private citizen who donates a painting by somebody else that he only *paid* for can deduct the whole thing. For another, when an artist dies his estate is taxed at fair market value, even though the necessity to sell art to pay the tax may kick the bottom out of the market. "It's as though the law were made to penalize the artist, coming and going," says Rubin; "under one set of regulations he's penalized when he's alive, and under the other he's penalized after he's dead." Rubin is working with Congressman John Brademas and Senator Jacob Javits on a proposed bill to remove the inequity; meanwhile he's seeking royalty legislation to give artists a share of the profits when their works change hands between collectors, and he's got a couple of Congressmen interested in this one too. And after that? "I am also trying to have a law written classifiying artists as ministers of the gospel, so they can get the benefit of Section 107 of the Internal Revenue Code, which gives them a parsonage allowance. They could deduct a hundred percent of rent and utilities. The worst artist I know is more spiritual than the best priest or rabbi I know; their artworks are their flock. Artists are the only pure beautiful type of people in the world today; let them be artists all the time, let them think art, and let accountants . . . be the liaison between the artists and that other world that artists must deal with but shouldn't." Let us pray that our net worth increases as fast as Rubin's clients'.

## QUESTION

1. How does the necessity to sell art reduce its fair market value? Illustrate.

*From *Esquire*, November 1974, p. 124. Reprinted by permission of the publisher.

# 20

## SPORTS ACCOUNTANTS*
Robert F. Randall

The script is a familiar one every Sunday afternoon in the Fall. Joe Namath or Bob Griese drops back to pass and millions of sports fans lean forward, hoping for that one exciting play which makes up for all the hours of routine play actions viewed in front of the TV set or in a stadium watching professional football.

If it's not football, it may be the flashing game of hockey with Rod Gilbert of the New York Rangers or Bobby Orr of the Boston Bruins slapping a puck into the net.

Whatever their preference, sports fans never had it so good. Neither have major sports teams. The millions of dollars poured into the coffers to the teams is proof of that. As any fan will tell you, it's almost impossible to get tickets to major league football games. Attendance at games reached an all-time high in 1970 when 13,488,708 fans flocked to stadiums all over the United States to watch 22 men scramble for a pigskin.

Just emerging from its Canadian deep freeze, hockey has not yet become a national sport with a following the size of football, but it's well on its way. With the creation of another league and the resulting dramatic surge in salaries, as the new World Hockey Association began competing with the established National Hockey League for players, the ice arena may eventually rival the gridiron for the attention of sports fans.

Thanks to television, sports enthusiasts see practically all the action on the field or the rink. But what happens in the front offices of the major league teams, particularly in the accounting end? Given the millions the sports industry reaps every year, what happens to it? How is it accounted for?

One football magazine estimated that total gross revenue for major league teams will reach $200 million in 1972. Split evenly among the 26 teams, that would come to about $7.6 million per club. Of course every team does not sell out its stadium every year, and most teams are privately owned, so the real bottom line figures are hard to come by.

There are some exceptions. The New England Patriots are publicly owned, and the Green Bay Packers team is set up as a nonprofit corporation with stockholders limited to 200 shares. The Packers do not pay dividends; profits not used for capital improvements go into the club's surplus funds or are earmarked for charitable causes. The late Vince Lombardi said that when he took over the team in 1959, total income was $600,000. Thanks largely to his driving genius for coaching victorious teams, by 1967 it had grown to $5,500,000.

But Clint Murchison, owner of the Dallas Cowboys, recently complained to *Forbes* that most people don't understand that "most professional teams don't generate much profit." A member of the "Big Eight" surveyed NFL teams several years ago and the

*From *Management Accounting*, December 1972, pp. 56–58. Reprinted by permission of the publisher.

results tended to confirm this opinion. Average after-tax earnings per club were estimated at about only $235,000.

Hockey teams on the average are even less profitable. There are a number of reasons. Hockey arenas do not have the seating capacity of stadiums; hockey has not yet caught on nationally to the extent where it can tap a larger portion of the TV-radio entertainment dollar; and many new franchises have growing pains.

Most franchises are not started to make money even though NFL franchises are estimated to be worth more than $8 million today. Usually a franchise is picked up by an individual or group of individuals who love the game and also want a tax write-off. Team accountants generally do more than just the accounting for the team. Many also do the accounting for the stadium, arena or corporation that owns the franchise.

Madison Square Garden Corp., for example, owns the New York Rangers—a top-notch hockey team—and the Knickerbockers, a major basketball team. In addition to the activities at the Garden itself, it conducts real estate operations and owns racetracks.

At least one accountant, Frank Wall, is president of a major league team. Mr. Wall, for many years a partner in the firm of Garrett & Wall, CPAs, helped with the financial arrangements for the purchase of an NFL franchise in Atlanta. When the Falcons were created in 1965, he became the treasurer. Then he was promoted to general manager and in 1970 was named president.

## INCOME IS PREDICTABLE

There are basic similarities in accounting for major league teams whether the game is played on ice or astroturf. Major sources of income are ticket sales and radio-TV rights. Major expenses are player salaries and rental of the stadium or arena.

Accounting for the team is pretty simple, according to Miss Magda Kende, assistant treasurer of the Detroit Lions. She has been with the team 17 years. It has "a very predictable income" from the sale of tickets, television and radio rights. "Tickets go on sale at 9 Monday morning, by 10 o'clock they're all gone."

The team operates on a fiscal year of January 1 to December 31. If it makes the play-offs, the income will be carried over in the books for the next fiscal year. Players are given annual contracts, and trades are on a player-for-player basis. The stadium where the team plays home games is rented from the Detroit Tigers. Miss Kende works up financial statements every month and usually actual results are within 5% of the budget.

Accounting for the New York Jets falls into the same pattern. Bonus payments for players are amortized over a period of four to eight years. The team realizes most of its income from sale of tickets and radio-TV rights. Shea Stadium is rented from New York City for home games. Other expenses include travel, maintenance and the cost of equipment. (The team spends about $8,000 or $9,000 a year for footballs alone.)

## FINANCIAL IMPORTANCE OF WINNING

Agreeing with the notion that accounting for professional sports teams is not too difficult is William W. Combs, vice president and treasurer of Missouri Arena Corp., which owns the franchise for the St. Louis Blues hockey team. "Once you have the pattern, there's really not much to it," he said. "You'll find it's not the only job for many accountants. Most are involved in accounting for the overall operations. Most of us are tied into the building operation."

As an illustration of the predictability of the income, he explained that the Blues have 18,000 seats available and usually 17,000 are sold on a seasonal basis. The fact that the Blues have never finished worse than third place in five years helps to ensure that every game is a sell-out. He estimates that 5% of the team's income is derived from TV and radio rights.

One unusual aspect of accounting for hockey is that, unlike professional football teams, visiting hockey teams do not share in the gate receipts with the home team. Player contracts are on an annual basis but there is a trend toward multi-year contracts, Mr. Combs says. In depreciating player contracts, he reckons on the basis of a player's useful life of five years. (As in any business, there are exceptions. Jean Beliveau, an all-time all star, played 20 years for the Montreal Canadians before he retired last year.)

The importance of having winners to ensure that the bottom line figure is black rather than red is stressed by Kent Bowen, vice president and treasurer of the Pittsburgh Penguins hockey club. An expansion team created in 1967, the team is still struggling to generate sufficient interest to sell out the home games. The opener this year drew 11,000 fans. That and other indications lead Mr. Bowen to think "We have made it." He believes that sports buffs in the Pittsburgh area now realize the city has a hockey team.

It has been a long struggle. The team has had three owners in five years. The fact that the team has won few games has not helped attendance figures. "It took us a long time to even get national TV coverage," Mr. Bowen pointed out.

Things are looking up for the team. It made the Stanley Cup play-offs last year and has a good chance to do so again. Mr. Bowen forecasts reaching the breakeven point "this year possibly and next year definitely."

"We work on a tight budget," he said. Player and staff salaries are the major expenses, followed by road travel. "There are only two or three items after October 1 that could be variable." These items include gate receipts and the weather. In depreciating player contracts, the general manager, assistant manager and scout get together and try to estimate the length of a player's useful life to the club. "Basically, it's a five- to six-year life," he said.

Like the stars on the field and on the rink, the financial men in the front offices for big league teams maintain an unofficial camaraderie. They compare notes on how to handle common aspects of the business. Admittedly, theirs is not too difficult a task, as compared to—say—the accounting for the diverse operations of a conglomerate. But it isn't boring—not when you can get season tickets to all the home games.

## QUESTION

1. Identify the financial statement items that would appear on the income statement for the New York Jets. On the balance sheet.

## SELECTED BIBLIOGRAPHY

Krise, Shirley A., "Tax Aspects of Sport Enterprises," *World*, Spring 1975, pp. 21-26.

# 21
# A GOAL ACHIEVED
## A Reason for Pride*
H&S Reports

In 1896 Frank Broaker of New York State became the first certified public accountant in the United States. Since that time hundreds of thousands of men and women have studied and worked for years to earn the privilege of taking a rigorous four-part, three-day, $19\frac{1}{2}$ hour examination. Their goal and the reward of those who pass: the right to place the initials "CPA" after their name.

Certification is official recognition that an accountant has achieved the levels of competence and proficiency demanded of those who want to call themselves certified public accountants. Like the licensed physician and practicing attorney, the CPA is a professional who must not only take and pass required college courses but also satisfy a "jury of his peers" that he is competent to practice his profession.

For the applicant who has satisfied the educational requirements (in addition to several years of actual work experience in some states) the CPA test is the final hurdle. Behind the more obvious mechanics of the test—which covers accounting practice, accounting theory, business law and auditing—is the complex structure consisting of national organization, state professional groups, practicing CPAs and educational institutions whose efforts are required to produce semi-annual examinations that reflect the changing requirements of U.S.—indeed international—business, law and finance. And overshadowing it all is a rich tradition and heritage stretching back more than 75 years.

All U.S. CPA exams today are developed and administered by the American Institute of Certified Public Accountants (AICPA), first incorporated in 1887 as the American Association of Public Accountants. At the end of its first year the AAPA, designed to foster more respect in this country for the profession of accounting and modeled after the Institute of Chartered Accountants in England and Wales, had a membership of 25 fellows and seven associates. Today the AICPA has some 90,000 members.

In 1893 the New York Board of Regents granted a charter for incorporation to the New York School of Accounts, the first school of accounting in the United States. Seven pupils enrolled in the first class.

*From *H & S Reports*, Autumn 1973, pp. 22—24. Reprinted by permission of the publisher.

Three years later, in 1896, New York became the first state in the Union to establish legal requirements for anyone wanting to call himself a CPA: He had to be a citizen of the U.S., a resident of New York or doing business in that state, of good moral character, and he had to possess a university certificate attesting to the fact that he had the qualifications to practice as a public accountant.

If the "good moral character" requirement of the 1896 legislation has a quaint ring to it, we might point out that today some 40 states require CPA candidates to take and pass supplementary ethics exams before they can be certified. A CPA found guilty of unethical practices can lose his certification, as can one convicted of criminal charges. Charles Waldo Haskins, who with Elijah Watt Sells founded Haskins & Sells in 1895, took an active interest in passage of the 1896 Act to Regulate the Profession of Public Accountancy in New York. Mr. Haskins qualified as a CPA under the Act and was named first president of the Board of State Examiners of Public Accountants, which was established by the Act. Mr. Haskins also played a key role in the founding in 1900 of the School of Commerce, Accounts and Finance of New York University and was its first dean.

In 1917 the AAPA changed its name to American Institute of Accountants and on June 14 and 15 of that year held its first CPA examinations. One hundred twenty-one candidates sat for that test, and 93 passed. (More than 30,000 candidates sat for the November 1972 exams.)

Most state accounting laws were passed between the turn of the century and the early 1930s. It was not until 1952 that the last of the states—Pennsylvania—adopted the AICPA uniform exam for CPAs, and it was only in 1962 that New Jersey became the final state to utilize the advisory grading service of the AICPA.

As presently structured the CPA exam is unique: It is a national examination whose results are generally accepted in 54 jurisdictions, including the 50 states, District of Columbia, Puerto Rico, Guam and the Virgin Islands. Earlier, individual states had administered their own CPA tests, a system far more expensive than the present arrangement. Even more serious were the certification problems that sometimes arose because of differences in state tests and requirements for CPAs moving from one state to another. One of the major advantages of the present system lies in its making the passing of one standardized test mandatory for anyone anywhere in the country who wants to be a CPA.

Exactly how does the CPA exam system work? If the AICPA forms the broad organizational base for the program, the 16-member Board of Examiners is the operational group charged with development, administration and grading of each test. Members of the Board, about half with primary interests in the practicing profession and the other half from the academic world, are selected by the president of the AICPA and serve a three-year term. Roughly half the Board's membership is made up of current or former members of state boards of accountancy. All are CPAs and usually chosen because of a particular field of expertise, such as taxes, law statistics or computers. Because of the important relationship that must be maintained between the profession and the college and university system, most of the practicing accountants on the Board have some association with the academic world.

The Board of Examiners meets twice a year and works at least three examinations in advance, a procedure demanded by the complex logistics involved in giving the same exam to more than 30,000 people simultaneously in 93 cities across the United States and in Puerto Rico. (Some 50,000 copies of each exam are printed and the security that must be maintained would give nightmares to the head of security at Fort Knox.)

After the tests are taken, all papers—identified only by serial number to guarantee anonymity of the candidate and impartiality of the grader—are forwarded to AICPA headquarters in New York City for grading, which is done by practicing CPAs, CPA educators or by attorneys. Each grades only one question. While the true-false and multiple choice sections may be machine graded, the essay questions offer not only more latitude to the candidate taking the test but more of a challenge to the grader responsible for that question.

There is no single "proper" answer for many of the questions. The "best" answer is one in which the candidate grasps the question in sufficient depth to recognize the peripheral implications involved and then presents a broad, solid analysis which "replies" on several levels to the question posed.

Obviously this makes the grader's task more difficult, since a grading point system is used to differentiate between a "basic" treatment of a question and one that probes deeply into more subtle, complex areas. However, the nature of accounting and the AICPA's interest in having the test scores reflect the knowledge and ability of the candidate require this more demanding and time-consuming grading procedure.

The CPA exams are given every May and November, and 75 is passing grade for each section. Only about 10 percent of the candidates pass all four sections the first time they sit for the exam. Other statistics are not readily verifiable since the AICPA has no information on whether the candidate has written all parts not previously passed, only those for which presently qualified, or only those chosen for the current examination. The Elijah Watt Sells Award, the profession's highest honor for CPA candidates, goes to those with the top grades who pass all four sections when they take the exam. The awards include a gold medal, silver medal and a variable number of honorable mentions.

Grading can be reviewed and almost always is for grades that are just below the passing level. Although the AICPA does the grading, the state boards are usually charged by law with final grading decisions. However, few changes are ever made by the state boards because of the problem this would create for a certificate holder in obtaining reciprocity in another state. Thus, if an accountant relocates to another state and applies for certification in his new home state, the latter might request the original certificate-granting state to verify that the candidate has received a passing grade on the AICPA-prepared and graded examination.

Although certain state procedures and requirements can complicate matters for a very small number of CPAs, in most instances certification by the states is granted automatically where application is made to state boards and the applicant has fulfilled legal and professional requirements. The ideal situation, according to some in the profession, would be automatic certification in all states—in effect a "national certification"—for all those passing the exam. While this may be highly desirable, there seems little chance of such a development in the near future. Most state boards still insist that all final decisions on certification remain at the state level.

The validity of any test depends on the quality and relevance of the questions presented. Where do the questions for the CPA exam originate and how are they developed?

Each test is first outlined by the Board of Examiners. After the general "outline" is put in final form, the Board goes into the specifics of questions. Potential questions are submitted by major accounting firms, by the American Accounting Association, by accounting professors and students, by state accounting societies and state boards, and by members of the Board itself. Most of the questions submitted have to be reworked by the AICPA staff.

Every test must be different, of course. As a first step in preparing an outline, the Board analyzes exams given in the past. New topics are selected for inclusion, "holes" in past tests filled in, stress put on important new areas. Questions are always included to reveal whether the candidate is keeping abreast of new accounting policies and procedures.

Other questions are designed to determine the candidate's awareness of the changes taking place in our society that affect his profession.

The Board monitors all developments in legal, business and financial areas that bear on questions of accounting and auditing, commercial law, taxes and related areas. When anything takes place that highlights the possible need for a change in procedures or underlines the necessity for more caution in certain situations, test questions are included which reflect these developments.

Emphasis on various subjects can shift over the years. Areas such as management advisory services and statistics are being given more attention today than in the past because of their growing importance to the profession of accounting.

While it may appear mechanical on the surface, the process of developing, administering and grading the exams is by no means routine. There is a constant interplay of tensions between the AICPA, state associations and the academic world. The colleges and universities generally tend to take a more advanced view of what a CPA should be required to know, while state boards often lean toward the conservative side.

As one example, most of the better schools today are teaching more advanced mathematics to accounting majors than many state boards believe necessary. On the other hand, many schools used to teach so-called accounting courses that were really little more than procedurally-oriented bookkeeping. Thanks to the efforts of the AICPA and some state boards, an increasing number of schools are giving more advanced conceptually-oriented accounting courses.

Several states (New York is one) require two years of practical work experience before anyone can qualify as a CPA. Candidates are not permitted to take certain sections of the exam in some states until they meet this requirement. The AICPA has suggested that a five-year college course be substituted for the present four-year term, with subsequent elimination of the work requirement. The question is under discussion and may be adopted in the future, although there is considerable resistance to it in some quarters.

The AICPA also believes more emphasis should be placed on written and spoken English. At present this has only an indirect influence on test grades since major concern is for technical competence. The CPA must not only have the required knowledge and background, the AICPA insists, but he should be able to communicate this knowledge in the most effective and efficient manner. And this requires a good command of written and oral English.

While almost everyone agrees that more stress should be placed on communications skills, no really practical method has yet been found to incorporate an evaluation of communications skills in the CPA exam system.

If there are complaints that the AICPA moves too slowly on one hand, there also are those who insist that it tries to change policy and procedures too rapidly. The truth, as one might expect, lies somewhere in the middle. In 1963, the AICPA and the Carnegie Corporation of New York jointly financed a study commission charged with fixing and determining the common body of knowledge required of all practicing CPAs. The group was headed by Elmer G. Beamer, at that time H&S partner in charge of the Cleveland office. (Mr. Beamer retired in June 1972.) The subsequent report, published in 1967 under the title "Horizons for a Profession," not only triggered major revisions in education and experience policies adopted by the AICPA, but continues today as a goal and ideal toward which the profession is working.

If history lends perspective to the present, can it also be helpful in projecting what the future may bring? Today's CPA exam is far more complex than in the past, reflecting the growing complexity of our society, of business and the regulations governing it and of the very function of the CPA. This process can be expected to continue, perhaps even to accelerate, and the CPA candidate sitting down to take the 1980 exam may find himself faced with questions undreamed of today.

The day may also come when the accounting student will work toward his CPA, and the CPA will study for a "specialist" certificate, much as a medical student works first for his M.D. and then may continue on toward a recognized specialty. The nature of business in the years ahead may demand the skills not only of the CPA as we know him today, but also of CPAs who have received considerable advanced training in specialities such as taxes, law, management advisory services or data processing. Such specialists already represent a vital segment of the profession. All that would be required would be establishment of minimum training and educational requirements and formal recognition of these specialties by the profession.

This ever-increasing complexity of life may also require that tomorrow's CPA continue his education after he is certified. Twelve states now insist that a minimum number of seminar hours or college credits be taken by practicing CPAs if they want to remain certified. It is quite probable that continuing education requirements may eventually become the rule rather than the exception.

The CPA examination is not simply a group of questions designed to test an indivdual's familiarity with a common body of knowledge. It also is intended to ensure that every CPA possesses certain basic working skills and techniques. Even more important, perhaps, is its challenging of CPA candidates to measure their awareness of how outside developments are affecting their chosen profession, to fix their ability to grasp key concepts and apply them to specific problems and, in the final analysis, to decide whether a given individual has the mental capacity and maturity to qualify as a certified public accountant. The CPA exam tests far more than a candidate's memory of what he was taught in school. Anyone who has qualified has good reason to wear his title with pride.

QUESTIONS

1. How does one qualify to be a CPA?
2. What subjects are covered in the CPA examination?
3. What is a "specialist" certificate?

SELECTED BIBLIOGRAPHY

Stewart, James C., "The Emergent Professionals," *The Accountant's Magazine*, March 1975, pp. 113-116.


# 22
# CPA REQUIREMENTS OF THE STATES*
Wilton T. Anderson


The CPA certificate is awarded to an applicant who meets the statutory and accountancy board requirements of the political jurisdiction to which he applies. These requirements vary considerably, and the principal ones are tabulated and explained on the following pages.

All fifty states, the District of Columbia, Guam, Puerto Rico, and the Virgin Islands, use both the examination and grading service offered by the American Institute of Certified Public Accountants. While most of the jurisdictions have statutes which specify that candidates will be examined in at least theory of accounts, accounting practice, auditing, and business law, the content of the examination is changing within these four broad question groupings. The examination is discussed in the July, 1971, issue of *The Journal of Accountancy* in an article entitled "The Changing Content of the CPA Examination" by H. S. Hendrickson.


## SOME CHANGES

### Education and Experience

In preparing the tabulations of state requirements, several changes in recent years were noticed. One of the changes has been for a number of states to increase the education requirement to the baccalaureate degree. This change provides greater protection to the public by upgrading the professional preparation. It is likely that more and more jurisdictions will enact this educational requirement. Quite often the increase in education is accompanied by a reduction in the required time of work experience under the supervision of a CPA. It is unlikely that the AICPA recommendation of a

*From *Collegiate News and Views*, Spring 1972, pp. 11, 12, 14, 15. Reprinted by permission of the publisher and the author.

five-year educational program and no work experience will become law in very many states for several years.

### Conditioned Credit

Another significant change has been for state boards of accountancy to accept conditioned credit (passed parts of the examination) from other states. It is quite common for a CPA candidate to take the examination in one state, pass enough parts to receive conditioned credit, then accept employment in another state. In those states having reciprocity of passed parts, the candidate must pass only the previously failed parts in order to receive the CPA certificate.

### Minimum Grade in Failed Subjects for Conditioned Credit

Another change has been for more states to require a candidate to earn a minimum grade in failed subjects in order to receive conditioned credit in passed parts of the examination. This requirement is ordinarily a board regulation instead of by means of a statute. It is a good regulation in that it forces candidates to prepare for all parts of the examination. All jurisdictions require candidates to write all parts for which conditioned credit has not been awarded.

### Examination Fees

Examination fees have increased in numerous states. The examination and grading service cost to state boards has been increased. Since most state boards must be self-supporting, it was necessary to pass the higher charge on to candidates.

### Licensing of All Public Accountants

Most states are licensing all public accountants. Ten years ago only a limited number of states had "permissive" accounting laws which would allow anyone to practice as a public accountant. In a "permissive" state the initials "CPA" can be used only by those people who meet education, experience, examination, and other requirements authorizing the use of those initials. The principal reason for licensing all public accountants has been due to the wording pertaining to auditing grants, agencies, and corporations with which the federal government is involved. The words "licensed or certified public accountant" often appear in regard to who is considered to be an approved auditor. Many noncertified public accountants, therefore, requested their legislatures to enact an accountancy law which would license them so they would be eligible for these audits.

### Continuing Education

A few other significant factors pertaining to the statutes or state board regulations affecting CPAs are beginning to emerge. The governing council of the AICPA has taken a position urging the enactment of accountancy statutes which will require continuing education on the part of CPAs. It is in the public interest that the competence of CPAs be maintained by study after they are licensed. Considerable latitude is allowed in the types of programs in which they can study such as collegiate courses, professional development courses and the like so that hardships are minimized.

### Corporate Form of Business in Practice of Public Accounting

Some states have enacted statutes permitting the corporate form of business in the practice of public accounting. Very recently this type of legislation became law in Massachusetts, Nebraska, and South Dakota. Tax regulations pertaining to pension funds had a great deal to do with the change in attitude of the profession about restricting public practice to individuals and to partnerships. Limited liability is rarely permitted in this type of statute.

### Meaning of CPA Certificate

The meaning of the CPA certificate is being altered. This alteration takes place rather slowly as new accountancy laws are enacted. In all except a few jurisdictions, the certificate has been construed to be a license to practice as a certified public accountant. In practically all states CPAs are considered competent to make opinion audits. The present policy of the AICPA is that the CPA certificate is evidence of basic competence of professional quality in the discipline of accounting. Most interpretations of this new meaning consider experience to be of little significance for licensing. This new meaning of the certificate has been adopted in only a few states; however, as the speciman statutory bill advocated by the AICPA, called the "form" bill, is adopted by the legislative bodies of the states, the meaning of the certificate likely will be altered.

### QUESTIONS

1. What are the requirements for becoming a CPA in your home state?

2. Are the requirements in your state more or less exacting than in most other states? Give possible rationale.

3. What are continuing education requirements for CPAs in your home state?

# CPA Requirements

Residence, Education, Experience, and Examination Conditioning

| STATE | STATE RESIDENCE REQUIRED (a) | PLACE OF BUSINESS FULFILLS RESIDENCE REQUIREMENT | REQUIRE POST HIGH SCHOOL EDUCATION | YEARS OF ACCOUNTING EXPERIENCE (e) | PUBLIC ACCOUNTING EXPERIENCE REQUIRED | OTHER ACCOUNTING EXPERIENCE SUBSTITUTIVE | EDUCATION SUBSTITUTIVE (WHOLE OR PART) FOR EXPERIENCE | EXP. OR EDUCATION MANDATORY BEFORE COMPLETION OF CPA EXAM | EXAM FEE (i) | SUBJECT PASSES REQUIRED FOR CONDITIONED CREDIT | LIFE OF CONDITIONED CREDIT | RECIPROCITY OF CONDITIONED CREDIT |
|---|---|---|---|---|---|---|---|---|---|---|---|---|
| Alabama | NS | Yes | Bach. | 3 | Yes | | (g) | Yes | $65 | 2 or P | 5NE | Yes |
| Alaska | NS | | 2 yr. | 4 | 4 | Yes | (g) | Yes | $25 | 2 or P | 5Y(k) | Yes |
| Arizona | NS | | Bach. | (d) | Yes | Yes | (g) | Yes | NS | 2 or P | 3Y | Yes |
| Arkansas | NS | (b) | Bach. | 1-2 | No | | (g) | Yes | $40 | 2 | 5NE | |
| California | Yes | Yes | (c) | 3-4 | 3-4 | Yes | Yes | (h) | $45 | 2 or P | 3Y | Yes |
| Colorado | Yes | Yes | (c) | 1-3 | 1-3 | Yes | (g) | (h) | $50 | 2 | 3NE | Yes |
| Connecticut | Yes | Yes | Bach. | 2 | 2 | Yes | No | (h) | $50 | 2 or P | 3Y | Yes |
| Delaware | 1 yr. | Yes | (c) | 2 | Yes | | No | NS | $50 | 2 or P +50% | 5NE | |
| District of Columbia | 1 yr. | Yes | 60 hrs. | 2-4 | Yes | 1½:1 | (d) | | $50 | 2 or P | 5NE | |
| Florida | 6 mo. | | Bach. | 1 | Yes | (f) | (g) | Yes | $75 | 2 | 5NE | |
| Georgia | NS | Yes | Bach. | 2 | 1 | 2:1 | (g) | No | $35 | 2 | 5NE | |
| Hawaii | 1 yr. | No | Bach. | (d) | (d) | (f) | Yes | Yes | $35 | 2 | 6NE | |
| Idaho | NS | Yes | Bach. | (d) | Yes | 5 | Yes | (h) | $35 | 2 or P +50% | 5NE | Yes |
| Illinois | NS | Yes | 120 hrs. | 3 | Yes | Yes | (g) | Yes | $65 | 2 or P +50% | (k) | Yes |
| Indiana | 6 mo. | | (c) | 3 | 3 | 3-6 | (g) | (h) | $50 | 2 | 6NE | Yes |
| Iowa | 6 mo. | | (c) | 1 | 1 | (f) | | No | $25 | 2 or P +50% | 4NE | |
| Kansas | NS | Yes | (c) | | 2 | | (g) | (h) | $50 | 2 + 50% | 6NE | Yes |
| Kentucky | NS | Yes | (c) | 1-6 | 1-6 | IRS | Yes | Yes | $50 | 1 + 50% | 4NE | Yes |
| Louisiana | 1 yr. | | (c) | 1-3 | 1-3 | Yes | Yes | (h) | $35 | 2 + 45% | (k) | Yes |

| State | | | | | | | | | | | | |
|---|---|---|---|---|---|---|---|---|---|---|---|---|
| Maryland | 1 yr. | | (c) | 2 | 2 | | (g) | Yes | $50 | 2 or P +50% | 5NE | Yes |
| Massachusetts | NS | Yes | Bach. | 3 | 3 | (f) | (g) | No | $50 | 2 or P +50% | 6NE | Yes |
| Michigan | NS | Yes | (c) | 2-4 | 2-4 | Yes | (g) | | $25 | 1 | 6NE | |
| Minnesota | NS | Yes | | 3 | 3 | Yes | (g) | Yes | $50 | 2 + 50% | 5NE | |
| Mississippi | 1 yr. | Yes | (c) | 1-2 | 1-2 | 1-3 | Yes | Yes | $60 | 2 or P +45% | 10NE | Yes |
| Missouri | NS | Yes | Bach. | 1-3 | 1 | 5 yr. | (g) | Yes | $50 | (j) | 2NE | Yes |
| Montana | 1 yr. | Yes | (c) | 1 | 1 | Yes | | Yes | $25 | 2 or P | 2Y | Yes |
| Nebraska | NS | Yes | | 4 | 4 | (f) | (g) | | $30 | 2 or P | 9NE | |
| Nevada | NS | Yes | Bach. | 2 | 2 | No | No | Yes | $50 | 2 or P +60% | Unlim. | |
| New Hampshire | NS | (b) | | 4 | 4 | Yes | | No | $75 | 2 | | |
| New Jersey | 1 yr. | Yes | Bach. | 3 | 3 | (f) | | | $35 | | 3Y | Yes |
| New Mexico | NS | Yes | Bach. | 1-3 | Yes | | (g) | Yes | $50 | 2 | NS | Yes |
| New York | NS | Yes | Bach. | 2-15 | | | (g) | Yes | $40 | (j) | 5NE | Yes |
| North Carolina | 1 yr. | Yes | 24 hrs. | 2 | 2 | (f) | (g) | (h) | $35 | 2 or P | 5NE | Yes |
| North Dakota | 1 yr. | | Bach. | (d) | | | (g) | | $100 | 2 or P | 5NE | |
| Ohio | NS | Yes | (c) | 2-4 | 2-4 | Yes | Yes | Yes | $40 | 1 | 8Y | |
| Oklahoma | 1 yr. | | No | (d) | 3 | Yes | Yes | Yes | $35 | 2 or P | (k) | |
| Oregon | NS | Yes | (c) | 0-2 | 0-2 | Yes | Yes | Yes | $30 | 2 or P | 6NE | Yes |
| Pennsylvania | NS | Yes | Bach. | 2 | 2 | Yes | (g) | Yes | | | | |
| Puerto Rico | NS | Yes | (c) | 0-6 | Yes | Yes | Yes | Yes | $25 | 2 | Unlim. | |
| Rhode Island | NS | Yes | (c) | 2-4 | 2-4 | No | Yes | Yes | $25 | 2 or P | NS | Yes |
| South Carolina | NS | | Bach. | (d) | 2-3 | | No | No | $50 | 2 or P +40% | 3NE | Yes |
| South Dakota | NS | Yes | Bach. | 1 | 1 | No | No | Yes | $50 | 2 or P | NS | Yes |
| Tennessee | 1 yr. | Yes | (c) | 2 | | | Yes | Yes | $35 | 2 or P | 6NE | Yes |
| Texas | NS | Yes | (c) | 1-6 | | | Yes | Yes | $50 | 2 | Unlim. | |
| Utah | NS | Yes | Bach. | 2 | 2 | No | (g) | (h) | $40 | 1 | 6NE | |
| Vermont | NS | Yes | 0 | 2 | 2 | | (g) | No | $50 | 2 | NS | Yes |
| Virginia | NS | Yes | 120 hrs. | 2 | 2 | (f) | | Yes | $40 | 1 | 2NE | Yes |
| Virgin Islands | NS | Yes | (c) | 2-6 | 2-6 | Yes | | (h) | $25 | 2 | NS | |
| Washington | NS | Yes | (c) | 1-2 | 1-2 | 2-4 | | (h) | $40 | 2 or P | 3Y | |
| West Virginia | NS | Yes | Bach. | (d) | | | Yes | | $40 | 1 | 3Y | |
| Wisconsin | NS | Yes | Bach. | (d) | 3 | Yes | (g) | Yes | $30 | 2 + 50% | (k) | |
| Wyoming | NS | No | (g) | 3 | 3 | (f) | (g) | (g) | $75 | 2 or P | (k) | Yes |

*a. Age and Citizenship.*  All jurisdictions require that an applicant be 21 years of age except Alaska (19), Kentucky (18), Maine (20), Montana (no requirement), and Wisconsin (23). Most states further specify that an applicant be a citizen of the U.S. or officially declare intent to become a citizen. No citizenship is specified in the statutes of Indiana, Kansas, and Washington. The following states require U.S. citizenship: Delaware, Georgia, Louisiana, Massachusetts, Mississippi, New Hampshire, New Jersey, and Oklahoma. Fifteen states specify the length of residency required before an applicant can take the examination.

*b. Place of Business Fulfills Residence Requirement.*  Arkansas, Maine, and New Hampshire require that, in addition to having a place of residence in the state, an applicant must have a place of business or be employed in a place of business in the state. Other states marked "Yes" allow a person who is not a resident of the state but who has a place of business in the state to become a CPA in that state. Hawaii specifically states that a place of business will not satisfy the residency requirement. All states require at least two character references, most require three, and some require five.

*c. Post High School Education.*  In Column 3 "Bach." means bachelor's degree in accounting or the equivalent thereof as determined by the respective state boards. *California:* College graduate plus 3 years' experience or junior college plus 4 years' experience or public accountant plus 4 years' experience. *Colorado:* Bachelor's degree with one year of experience or high school diploma with 3 years' experience. *Delaware:* Bachelor's degree with 2 years' experience or junior college with 4 years' experience. *Indiana:* No post high school education required until 7/1/72. Between 7/1/72 and 7/1/75, a degree will be required. After 7/1/75 a bachelor in accounting will be required. *Iowa:* Bachelor in accounting or 3 years' experience. *Kansas:* Bachelor in accounting or bachelor with 2 years' public accounting experience. *Kentucky:* Bachelor in accounting plus 2 years' experience or master in accounting plus one year's experience or bachelor plus three years' experience or high school plus 6 years' experience. *Louisiana:* Before 9/1/75 a completed course in higher accountancy plus 3 years' experience. After 9/1/75 a bachelor in accounting plus 1 year of experience. *Maine:* Until 7/1/74, 2 years' college plus 4 years' experience. After 7/1/74 a bachelor with 2 years' experience or a master with 1 year experience. *Maryland:* Until 6/30/74, 2 years or 72 semester hours plus 2 years' experience. After 7/1/74 a bachelor in accounting, no experience. *Michigan:* Prior to 1/1/75, bachelor plus 4 years' experience. After 1/1/75 bachelor in accounting plus 2 years' experience. *Mississippi:* Bachelor in accounting plus 1 year experience or bachelor plus 2 years' employment with CPA or 3 years' government experience or teaching experience. *Montana:* Prior to 1/1/75, two years of college required. After 1/1/75 bachelor's degree required. *Ohio:* Two years' business college plus 4 years' experience or bachelor in accounting plus 2 years' experience or master plus 1 year experience. *Oregon:* Bachelor in accounting substitutes for all experience. Otherwise 2 years' experience required. *Puerto Rico:* Six years' experience required. With degree 4 years' required. With bachelor in accounting, no experience required. *Rhode Island:* Prior to 6/10/73, 2 years of college with 4 years' experience. Between 6/10/73 and 6/10/76, 2 years of college in accounting with 4 years' experience. After 6/10/76 bachelor in accounting plus 2 years' experience. Master's degree substitutes for all but one year. *Tennessee:* Prior to 3/10/73, 2 years in accounting. After 3/10/73 bachelor in accounting. Master substitutes for one year of experience. *Texas:* Junior college in accounting plus 6 years' experience or bachelor in accounting plus 2 years' experience or master in accounting plus one year experience. *Virgin Islands:* High school plus 6 years' experience, degree plus 3 years' experience, or degree in accounting plus 2 years' experience. *Washington:* Business school or degree plus 2 years' experience plus accounting plus one year experience.

*d. Experience.*  *Arizona:* 2 years in a CPA office or 4 years in a PA office. *District of Columbia:* Credit given for one year of experience for each 30 hours of business education with a maximum of 2 years credit. *Hawaii:* 3 years, 2 public; or 4 years, 1 public; or 5 years, 0 public. *Idaho:* 3 years employed by CPA, 4 years employed by self or PA. *New Mexico:* Registered PA must have 3 years' experience. A bachelor's degree in accounting will substitute for 2 years. *New York:* 15 years' experience required for persons without degree. *North Dakota:* 4 years' experience in public accounting substitutes for bachelor's degree. *Oklahoma:* 3 years of experience (one of which must have been in Oklahoma). Bachelor in accounting substitutes for all experience. *South Carolina:* 2 years employed by CPA or 3 years employed by PA. *Wisconsin:* 3 years as senior accountant required. Degree in accounting substitutes for 1½ years of experience.

**e.** Some states do not explicitly allow accounting other than public accounting to fulfill experience requirements. Column 6 is blank for those states. Other states allow substitution of experience as an IRS agent, a state audit agent, etc., for public accounting experience. For these states Columns 5 and 6 should be read together. A "Yes" in Column 5 with a "Yes" or numbers in Column 6 indicates that public accounting experience is required but substitutions are specifically mentioned in the statutes and regulations. A number in Column 6 indicates the number of years of nonpublic accounting which are required. A ratio indicates the number of years of nonpublic accounting which will substitute for one year of public accounting.

**f.** Some states allow accounting other than public to satisfy the experience requirement. *Florida:* If under the supervision of a CPA. *Hawaii:* 3 years in post audit for federal or state government. *Iowa:* One year of government accounting or three years as an assistant professor. *Massachusetts:* Two years with IRS or state auditor substitutes for experience. *North Carolina:* Two years with IRS or state auditor substitutes for experience. *Virginia:* 4 years of IRS or state or federal auditing. *Wyoming:* College teachers with master's or IRS grade 11 must have 3 years experience.

**g.** *Education Substitutes for Experience.* In the following states the master's degree in accounting substitutes for one year of experience: Alabama, Arkansas, Georgia, Indiana, Massachusetts, Michigan, Missouri, New York, North Carolina, Pennsylvania, and Utah. In Arizona a master's degree substitutes for half of the experience. In Colorado and Kansas a master's degree substitutes for all the experience. In Vermont, Minnesota, and Oklahoma, a bachelor's degree substitutes for all the experience. In Alaska, Illinois, Nebraska, and New Mexico, a bachelor's degree substitutes for two years' experience. In Florida an additional year of accounting courses beyond the bachelor's degree substitutes for all the experience required.

**h.** In some states a candidate may take the CPA examination before he has completed his experience or educational requirement. An applicant must be within 120 days of graduation in California and Washington; within 90 days in Idaho, Kansas, and North Carolina; within 60 days in Colorado and Indiana; and within 45 days in Louisiana. In Utah the applicant may be in his last semester; and in the Virgin Islands and Connecticut he may not take the practice portion of the exam before he completes the experience requirement.

**i.** All states use the examination grading service of the AICPA. The following states require an applicant to pass an exam in ethics in addition to the uniform exam of the AICPA: Alabama, Florida, Nebraska, New Mexico, Oklahoma, Utah, Wyoming, and Virginia. Iowa requires an exam in taxation and general commercial knowledge; Michigan requires an exam in finance and economics. The fee noted in the table is the fee for the first application and examination. Reexaminations are usually offered at a reduced fee.

**j.** Conditioning requirements are listed in the table. The symbol "2" or "P" means that an applicant must pass two parts of the exam other than practice or practice alone to receive conditional credit. The symbol "+50%" means that in all subjects not passed an applicant must have a score of at least 50% for the passed parts to receive conditional credit. In Missouri the experience requirement is two years for those applicants who pass practice and auditing on the first try. If only one of these is passed on the first try, the experience requirement is 3 years. In New York auditing must be taken after the experience requirement has been fulfilled. To condition one must pass theory and law or practice. All states require a candidate to take all sections of the examination for which he qualifies the first time. Candidates who are members in good standing of the bar in their state need not take the law portion of the exam. If a candidate has conditioned on some parts of the exam, he must take all other parts each time he sits for the exam in the future.

**k.** *Life of Conditional Credit.* "3Y" means three years. "3NE" means three next examinations. In the following states the number of the next successive exams which must be taken to retain conditional credit is noted: Alaska, 1 per year; Illinois, 3 of 6; Louisiana, 1 of 4; Oklahoma, 1 out of 3 for 10 next exams; Wisconsin, 3 of 6; Wyoming, 4 of 6. In the District of Columbia an applicant must sit for all of the next five exams. All states extend the life of the condition for time spent in the Armed Services of the United States.

**l.** All the states marked "Yes" under Column 12 make some provision for recognizing conditional credit earned in another state if that courtesy is reciprocated by the state from which the applicant transfers his credits.

# 23

## ACCOUNTING'S BIG EIGHT FIRMS
### A Capsule View*

EDITORS' NOTE: In 1975, Peat, Marwick, Mitchell & Co. reported estimated revenue of $500 million. The firm has 21,000 employees and more than 1,400 partners; average partner compensation is about $90,000. Arthur Andersen & Co., in its 1975 annual report, reported revenue of $386.3 million. The firm has 884 partners; the average partner compensation is $95,152. The growth of accounting firms for 1967-1973 is shown below:

| | NUMBER OF PROFESSIONALS EMPLOYED | | | |
|---|---|---|---|---|
| FIRM NAME | 1967 TOTAL | 1967 RANK | 1973 TOTAL | PERCENT-AGE GROWTH |
| Peat, Marwick, Mitchell & Co. | 1,636 | 1 | 2,751 | 68% |
| Arthur Andersen & Co. | 1,513 | 2 | 2,422 | 60% |
| Ernst & Ernst | 1,339 | 3 | 2,354 | 76% |
| Coopers & Lybrand | 1,145 | 5 | 2,031 | 77% |
| Haskins & Sells | 1,129 | 6 | 1,989 | 76% |
| Price Waterhouse & Co. | 1,279 | 4 | 1,903 | 49% |
| Arthur Young & Co. | 913 | 7 | 1,729 | 89% |
| Touche Ross & Co. | 690 | 8 | 1,469 | 113% |
| Alexander Grant & Co. | 233 | 10 | 700 | 200% |
| Laventhol & Horwath | 157 | 12 | 623 | 297% |
| Main LaFrentz & Co. | 324 | 9 | 551 | 41% |
| Elmer Fox & Co.* | 88 | 16 | 382 | 334% |
| Seidman & Seidman | 100 | 15 | 358 | 258% |
| S.D. Leidesdorf & Co. | 205 | 11 | 358 | 75% |
| J.K. Lasser & Co. | 87 | 17 | 299 | 244% |
| Harris Kerr Forster & Co. | 110 | 14 | 232 | 111% |
| McGladrey Hansen Dunn & Co. | 83 | 18 | 209 | 152% |
| Hurdman & Cranstoun | 71† | — | 186 | 162% |
| Wolf & Co. | 58 | 21 | 162 | 179% |
| A.M. Pullen & Co. | 110 | 13 | 154 | 40% |

Source: Adapted from "Market Place" by Robert Metz in *The New York Times*, May 1, 1973. Columns 1 and 3 show the number of accounting professionals working for each of the biggest firms.

*In 1975, the firm merged with another one. It is now known as Elmer Fox, Westheimer & Co.

†Hurdman & Cranstoun 43, L.H. Penney & Co. 28.

*From *Business Week*, Apr. 22, 1972, p. 54. Reprinted by permission of the publisher.

**MAJOR CLIENTS**

ITT, Texaco,
General Telephone, Kraftco
Tenneco, Occidental Petroleum,
General Dynamics, Marcor,
United Airlines, Commonwealth
Edison.

Audits 380 companies on New York
and American stock exchanges.

Ling-Temco-Vought,
McDonnell Douglas, R. J. Reynolds,
Gulf & Western, Coca-Cola,
TRW, BankAmerica,
Western Bancorporation,
Ashland Oil, Republic Steel.

Audits 265 companies on New York
and American stock exchanges.

General Motors,
Procter & Gamble,
International Harvester,
North American Rockwell,
Continental Can, Monsanto,
A&P, Southern Pacific,
TWA, Pacific Gas & Electric.

Audits 245 companies on New York
and American stock exchanges.

AT&T, Ford,
Atlantic Richfield, Firestone,
Sun Oil, American Can,
Sperry Rand, Alcoa,
Kroger, Pan American.

Audits 260 companies on New York
and American stock exchanges.

General Electric,
Singer, Burlington Industries,
Xerox, Cities Service,
Beatrice Foods,
First National City,
Chase Manhattan,
Safeway, Penney.

Audits 330 companies on New York
and American stock exchanges.

Standard Oil [N.J.],
IBM, Gulf Oil,
U.S. Steel, Westinghouse,
Standard Oil of Calif.,
Standard Oil [Ind.],
DuPont, Shell,
Consolidated Edison.

Audits 350 companies on New York
and American stock exchanges.

Chrysler,
Boeing, Greyhound,
Litton, Sears, Mead,
Federated Department Stores,
Jewel Cos., Prudential,
American Motors.

Audits 150 companies on New York
and American stock exchanges.

Mobil Oil,
Western Electric, RCA,
Swift, Continental Oil,
Lockheed, Phillips Petroleum,
Textron, American-Standard,
American Airlines.

Audits 160 companies on New York
and American stock exchanges.

| FIRM | HOME OFFICE |
|------|-------------|
| Arthur Andersen & Co. | Chicago |
| Ernst & Ernst | Cleveland |
| Haskins & Sells | New York |
| Coopers & Lybrand | |
| Peat, Marwick, Mitchell & Co. | New York |
| Price Waterhouse & Co. | New York |
| Touche Ross & Co. | New York |
| Arthur Young & Co. | New York |

*Note:* Unlike the thousands of publicly held corporations they audit, CPA firms are organized as partnerships. Data on revenues, operating costs, and other significant financial figures are not a matter of public record and traditionally have been closely guarded secrets. The above table represents 1972 estimates of Big Eight operations, together with other important dimensions of the nation's best-known accounting firms in 1972. The firms are listed in alphabetical order.

| | |
|---|---|
| 41 U.S. offices | 650 U.S. partners and principals |
| 108 U.S. offices | 390 U.S. partners and principals |
| 75 U.S. offices | 400 U.S. partners and principals |
| 70 U.S. offices | 450 U.S. partners and principals |
| 106 U.S. offices | 660 U.S. partners and principals |
| 54 U.S. offices | 250 U.S. partners and principals |
| 60 U.S. offices | 450 U.S. partners and principals |
| 60 U.S. offices | 370 U.S. partners and principals |

**ESTIMATED U.S. NET BILLINGS**

$190 million
65% audit
17.5% tax
17.5% consulting

$180 million
60% audit
20% tax
20% consulting

$155 million
70% audit
20% tax
10% consulting

$135 million
78% audit
17% tax
5% consulting

$225 million
65% audit
20% tax
15% consulting

$180 million
70% audit
18% tax
12% consulting

$110 million
58% audit
25% tax
17% consulting

$100 million
66% audit
17% tax
17% consulting

## QUESTIONS

1. Rank from 1 to 8 the Big Eight firms on each of the following criteria: estimated United States net billings, number of offices, number of partners and principals, number of companies on stock exchanges that are audited, percentage of United States net billings from audits, percentage of United States net billings from tax work, and percentage of United States net billings from consulting.

2. What were the total number of professionals employed by the Big Eight firms in 1973? By the top twenty firms?

## SELECTED BIBLIOGRAPHY

"How Do You Measure Accountancy Firms?" *Accountancy*, April 1975, p. 16.

# 24

# PROFILE OF A PUBLIC ACCOUNTING FIRM
Anonymous

See page 75 for the profile of a public accounting firm.

| POSITION | HE WEARS | HE DRIVES | HE EATS | HE BELIEVES | HE HOPES | HE KNOWS | HE WANTS | HE'LL SETTLE FOR |
|---|---|---|---|---|---|---|---|---|
| Partner | $250 dark suit | A Buick Electra | At the Racquet & Tennis Club | The client's wrong | He's right | Everything | A large new client | A small new client |
| Manager | $160 dark suit | A Buick Le Sabre | At the Athletic Club | He's the backbone of the firm | He's in-dispensable | He isn't | A 4-week vacation | A Sunday off |
| Senior | $350 custom-tailored suit | A Jaguar | With managers | He can audit | The manager agrees | He doesn't | All easy jobs | One easy job |
| Experienced assistant | Loud shirts | A Ford | Anywhere | He can make senior | The senior won't write any review notes | He will | Partner recognition | Senior recog-nition |
| New assistant | Sport coats | In a bus | From a brown bag | He should have majored in finance | The payroll test will tie in | It won't | To move up fast | Keeping his job |
| Tax man | $75 suit & white socks | A Vega wagon | At Walgreens | In the Code | It won't change | It will | To bill 100% of his time | Billing 25% of his time |
| Systems man | Bell bottoms | Auditors crazy | Promptly at 11:30 | His job is important | He can prove it | He can't | To be an auditor | Some charge-able time |
| Office manager | Old dark suits | Himself | Rolaids | Staff scheduling should be someone else's job | We've hired enough new assistants | We haven't | Cooperation | A raise |
| Office support person | Anything | To work with a friend | In the cafeteria | He runs the office | He doesn't get caught loafing | He won't | To go home early | Going home at 5:00 |

# 25

## TEN MOST READ BUSINESS PERIODICALS BY CPAs*

Vincent C. Brenner and Paul E. Dascher

| PERIODICAL | NUMBER OF RESPON-DENTS READING | MEAN SCORE | FREQUENCY (PERCENTAGE OF YEARLY ISSUES READ) | | | MEAN SCORE | THOROUGHNESS (PERCENTAGE OF EACH ISSUE READ) | | |
|---|---|---|---|---|---|---|---|---|---|
| | | | 0-33% | 34-67% | 68-100% | | 0-33% | 34-67% | 68-100% |
| 1. *Wall Street Journal* | 137 | 58.93 | 36 | 30 | 71 | 49.12 | 43 | 56 | 38 |
| 2. *Business Week* | 75 | 62.01 | 16 | 17 | 42 | 53.94 | 19 | 29 | 27 |
| 3. *Fortune* | 69 | 52.75 | 24 | 16 | 29 | 44.01 | 25 | 32 | 12 |
| 4. *Forbes* | 52 | 54.87 | 15 | 15 | 22 | 46.46 | 18 | 22 | 12 |
| 5. *Barron's* | 19 | 50.32 | 7 | 5 | 7 | 48.58 | 6 | 8 | 5 |
| 6. *Harvard Business Review* | 16 | 56.66 | 4 | 5 | 7 | 37.72 | 7 | 8 | 1 |
| 7. *Financial Executive* | 12 | 70.00 | 1 | 3 | 8 | 41.96 | 4 | 7 | 1 |
| 8. *Kiplinger Letter* | 11 | 77.91 | 0 | 2 | 9 | 77.91 | 0 | 2 | 9 |
| 9. *Nation's Business* | 10 | 46.90 | 5 | 1 | 4 | 43.60 | 4 | 4 | 2 |
| 10. *Dun's Review* | 6 | 55.92 | 2 | 1 | 3 | 44.67 | 3 | 1 | 2 |

EDITORS' NOTE: The above excerpt was based upon a mail questionnaire survey conducted by the authors of 500 CPAs randomly drawn. In the same survey, the CPAs were asked about their most read nonaccounting or nonbusiness periodicals. The results, in order of frequency were: (1) *Time*; (2) *Newsweek*; (3) *U.S. News & World Report*; (4) *Reader's Digest*; (5) *National Geographic*; (6) *Playboy*; (7) *Sports Illustrated*; (8) *Saturday Review*; (9) *Gold Digest*; and (10) *Consumer Reports*.

*From *The CPA Journal*, December 1973, pp. 1054, 1102. Excerpt reprinted by permission of the publisher.

# 26

# THE NATIONAL ASSOCIATION
# OF BLACK ACCOUNTANTS*
Thomas W. McRae

The National Association of Black Accountants (NABA) is a relatively new professional accounting organization composed primarily of black accounting professionals. NABA was organized to serve the special needs of a growing new breed of professionals, accountants from minority groups. The membership of the organization comprises CPAs in practice as individuals or in partnership with others, members of accounting faculties at colleges and universities, CPAs and other professional accountants on the staff of CPA firms, professional accountants at all levels in industry, government, and other organizations. In addition, students majoring in accounting at colleges and universities are accepted as student members of the organization. The integration of professionals and students in a single professional organization represents a significant departure from other professional organizations in accounting.

The objectives of NABA do not compete with those of other professional organizations in accounting. Instead, its objectives complement those of other organizations. Most of the professional members of NABA are also active in one or more of the older professional organizations. NABA members are active in the American Institute of CPAs, State Societies of CPAs, the National Association of Accountants, The American Accounting Association, the Federal Government Accounting Association, and the Financial Executive Institute.

## EARLY HISTORY

NABA was conceived at an informal meeting of nine black staff accountants in New York City in December 1959. The participants in that meeting consisted of three CPAs—Ronald Benjamin, Frank Ross, and Michael Winston—and six staff accountants—Earl Bigget, Donald Bristow, Kenneth Drummond, Bertram Gibson, Richard McNamme, and George Wallace. These young men, primarily staff accountants from the major CPA firms, discussed the problems that they faced in their firms and decided that many of their problems differed significantly from the problems faced by their white peers. They concluded that an organization uniquely structured to deal with the problems that they perceived was needed. They left that meeting with a conception of a national organization that could address effectively the many problems common to the rapidly increasing number of blacks and other minorities in the accounting profession and that could effectively recruit and ease the transition of others into the profession.

*From *Wisconsin CPA*, March 1975, p. 23. Reprinted by permission of the publisher.

The organization was chartered in New York in August 1970. A group of young men, who, for the most part, were fresh from the colleges and universities of the nation and endowed with impeccable professional credentials, formed the core of the organization. They were fully prepared to make their mark in the accounting profession and in the business community and were impatient with what they perceived to be halfhearted efforts and pious platitudes about equal opportunities for minorities.

At first, NABA was basically a local New York City organization with about fifty members. Frank Ross, a CPA who was then a manager with Peat Marwick Mitchell & Co. and who later joined with other young black CPAs to establish a firm in New York City, served as the first president (1970-71). William Aiken, a CPA who was then on the staff of Arthur Young & Company and has since established a firm with two other young black CPAs, served as president of the organization for the two years 1971-72 and 1972-73. He was succeeded as president for the year 1973-74 by Theodore Wilson, a CPA who had been a manager at Arthur Young & Company and had joined Mr. Aiken in the new firm. Fred Moultrie, a partner in the Los Angeles office of Alexander Grant & Co., was elected president of the organization for the year 1974-75.

## RAPID GROWTH OF MEMBERSHIP

Under the leadership of those young men, the organization has grown from a single chapter in New York City with about fifty members to several professional and student chapters throughout the country with over 1500 members. It is growing rapidly.

## PROGRAMMING IN COOPERATION WITH CPA ORGANIZATIONS

The organization has developed several innovative programs. The professional chapters of NABA conduct extensive projects designed primarily to enhance the professional development of members, improve the working climate and opportunities for advancement in firms, aid minority businessmen, and provide educational assistance to minority students. In several of its undertakings, NABA has cooperated with other professional organizations, such as the National Business League, the American Institute of CPAs, State Societies of CPAs, and the National Urban League.

In 1971 NABA sponsored and published a research study, *The Black Experience in Large Public Accounting Firms—Fall 1971.* Its newsletter, *Spectrum*, has been widely distributed and well received. NABA has held three Annual Awards Dinners in New York City to recognize publicly the achievements of outstanding individuals in the accounting profession and to express its appreciation to nonmembers who contribute significantly to the achievement of the goals of the organization.

A professional organization, like a human being, comes to life after an appropriate period of gestation; must be carefully nurtured in its infancy; suffers growing pains in its childhood and adolescence; matures, ages, and will die if not properly supported and periodically rejuvenated by the infusion of new life. In a society like ours and in a profession with a history like that of the accounting profession of almost total exclusion of minorities, an organization like NABA comes to life to fill a special role and will wither away only when the role no longer has meaning or purpose. That day will come when America's racial and ethnic minorities have been fully integrated into the accounting profession and the business community and the American ideal of a fully integrated society has been achieved.

# 27
## OTHER U.S. ACCOUNTING ORGANIZATIONS*
Harvey S. Hendrickson

EDITORS' NOTE: Additional information on many of the organizations listed by Mr. McRae in the second paragraph of his article is given elsewhere in this volume, e.g., see James Pattillo's article, Number 134, pp. 494 to 506. The tableau also presents some interesting highlights on these and other accounting organizations in the United States. This is not a complete listing of United States accounting professional organizations; there are many others including The Academy of Accounting Historians (which publishes *The Accounting Historian*) and the Accounting Researchers International Association.

See page 80 for the table listing some U.S. accounting organizations.

### QUESTIONS

1. What is a certified internal auditor?
2. What is a certified management accountant?
3. Give the circulation figures of the United States accounting periodicals most widely distributed.
4. Examine four different accounting journals at the library, and write a one-paragraph description of each one.
5. Identify the major accounting journals in any foreign country with which you are familiar.

*Prepared for this publication.

| NAME | SPECIAL ACCOUNTING NEED OR INTEREST SERVED | PROFESSIONAL EXAMINATION AND CERTIFICATE PROGRAM | STUDENT MEMBERSHIPS (S) AND/OR STUDENT SUBSCRIPTIONS TO PERIODICAL(S) (P) | APPROX. 1975 MEMBERSHIP [REGULAR (R) AND STUDENT (S)] | PERIODICAL |
|---|---|---|---|---|---|
| American Accounting Association | Teaching of accounting | None | S | R: 12,000 S: 2,000 | The Accounting Review (quarterly) |
| American Institute of Certified Public Accountants | Public accounting and auditing | Certified Public Accountant | P | 110,000 | The Journal of Accountancy (monthly) The Tax Adviser (monthly) |
| American Society of Women Accountants (Affiliate of ASWCPA) | Women accountants | None | S | R: 4,600 S: 100 | The Woman CPA (quarterly) |
| American Woman's Society of Certified Public Accounts (Affiliate of ASWCPA) | Woman CPAs | None | Students may join ASWA; Associate memberships now available for persons who have passed the CPA exam. | R: 1,800 Associate: 200 | The Woman CPA (quarterly) |
| Association of Government Accountants* | Accountants employed by U.S. government | None | S | R: 8,500 S: 300 | The Federal Accountant (quarterly) |
| Financial Executives Institute | Accounting and financial managers within firms | None | P | 8,600 | Financial Executive (monthly) |
| Institute of Internal Auditors | Auditors and controllers within firms | Certified Internal Auditor | S | R: 8,500 S: 900 | The Internal Auditor (bi-monthly) |
| National Association of Accountants | Accounting within firms | Certified Management Accountant | S | R: 70,500 S: 2,300 | Management Accounting (monthly) |
| National Association of Accountants for the Public Interest | Provide accounting counsel without fees to other non-profit public interest organizations | None | None | 100 | The API Newsletter (bi-monthly) |

# 28
# ACCOUNTING HALL OF FAME*
The Accounting Historian

The Accounting Hall of Fame was established in 1950 at the Ohio State University . . . for the purpose of honoring accountants who have made or are making significant contributions to the advancement of accounting since the beginning of the twentieth century. In 1975 the 35th accountant, Leonard Spacek, was elected to the Hall.

While selection to the Hall of Fame is intended to honor the people so chosen, it is also intended to be a recognition of distinguished service contributing to the progress of accounting in any of its various fields. Evidence of such service includes contributions to accounting research and literature, significant service to professional accounting organizations, wide recognition as an authority in some field of accounting, and public service. The 35 elected members of the Accounting Hall of Fame are:

| | |
|---|---|
| Arthur Edward Andersen | George Oliver May |
| Thomas Coleman Andrews | Hermann Clinton Miller |
| George Davis Bailey | Robert Hiester Montgomery |
| Andrew Barr | Lloyd Morey |
| Carman George Blough | William Andrew Paton |
| Samuel John Broad | James Loring Peirce |
| Percival Flack Brundage | Donald Putnam Perry |
| John Lansing Carey | Thomas Henry Sanders |
| Arthur Lowes Dickinson | Hiram Thompson Scovill |
| Marquis George Eaton | Elijah Watt Sells |
| Harry Anson Finney | Leonard Paul Spacek |
| Arthur Bevins Foye | Charles Ezra Sprague |
| Paul Franklin Grady | Maurice Hubert Stans |
| Henry Rand Hatfield | Victor Hermann Stempf |
| Roy Bernard Kester | Joseph Edmund Sterrett |
| Eric Louis Kohler | Robert Martin Trueblood |
| Anaias Charles Littleton | William Welling Werntz |
| Perry E. Mason | |

## QUESTION

1. Write a paragraph about the accomplishments of any three members of the Hall of Fame.

*Excerpt from *The Accounting Historian*, Summer 1975, p. 4. Reprinted by permission of the publisher.

# Part 2
# The Accounting
# Model

# 29
## AN ENQUIRY INTO THE NATURE OF ASSETS*
R. M. Lall

Strangely enough, without adequately vouching the conceptual veracity of assets, writers have taken great pains in dealing with their classification and valuation at considerable length. They seem to have taken for granted what the term 'assets' stands for. Practically all writers, whether old or new, have developed the nature of assets implicitly rather than explicitly, and in doing so, some of them have conceived the subject matter in their own way. It would perhaps be not incorrect to say that today there is no general acceptance of a definition of assets or of the basic common characteristics of assets. The main object of this paper is to bring out the homogeneous pattern of salient ingredients of assets that we account for.

## DISTINCTION BETWEEN ASSET AND NONASSET

In practice it is generally implied that "assets are simply all those items which are listed on the left side (in certain countries, on the right side) of the balance sheet." This view, however, fails to explain how one can distinguish an asset from a nonasset. Obviously this view is open to a serious criticism that although the relevant side of the balance sheet bears the caption "assets," yet on that very side certain items are displayed, as for example, debit balance of profit and loss account, preliminary expenses, deferred revenue expenditure, discount on issue of shares and debentures, and so on, the items which can, by no stretch of imagination, be called "assets." Thus this view is too vague and unscientific for common acceptance.

## VARIOUS DEFINITIONS

### Acquisition Basis

Some authors prescribe the specific method of acquisition of an item as a pre-condition to its being christened an asset. Sanders, Hatfield and Moore opine that items can be treated as assets only when "the business has acquired them at a cost."[1] Perhaps no special efforts are needed to rebut this contention, for there is no denying the fact that accountants do record assets which have come in just as a gift or by discovery, and in the acquisition of which no cost was incurred. To a similar charge is exposed the definition of an asset as given by W. A. Paton who identifies an asset with "any consideration, material or otherwise, owned by a specific business enterprise and

*From *The New York Certified Public Accountant* (now *The CPA*), November 1968, pp. 793–797. Reprinted by permission of the publisher.

[1]Thomas Henry Sanders, Henry Rand Hatfield, and Underhill Moore, *A Statement of Accounting Principles*, A.A.A., 1959, p. 58.

of value to that enterprise."[2] Furthermore, Paton's definition does not provide any tests by which an asset can be differentiated from a nonasset; nor does it not state what specific operations must be performed to constitute a consideration so as to bring about the existence of an asset.

## Transaction Basis

There are well-known writers who hold that assets cannot be acquired except as a result of a transaction. To quote Mautz, Zimmerman, DeMaris, Fess, Moyer, and Perry: "They (assets) are the result of enterprise transactions."[3] In the same way Sprouse and Moonitz maintain that rights to assets must "have been acquired by the enterprise as a result of some current or past transaction."[4] Such qualifications to the definition of assets are of little significance.

A transaction need not necessarily precede the acquisition of an asset. Unless used in some special sense, a transaction implies a transfer of goods or services from one person to another. One can cite a number of instances where no transfer of goods or services takes place from one enterprise to another, nevertheless assets are acquired, as for example on certain changes in personnel, finances, materials etc. occurring within an enterprise itself. In the same manner, amendments to laws, enactment of new laws, completion of a phase of a programme for expansion, or occurrence of natural causes, hardly have the colour of transactions, yet all the same they may add new assets or diminish the existing assets of an enterprise. In evolving a definition of assets, the factor of how they were acquired is not relevant.

## Unamortized Cost

Some writers have defined assets in terms of 'unamortized costs.' According to Paton and Littleton, "Assets are those factors acquired for production which have not reached the point in the business process where they may be treated as 'cost of sales' or 'expenses'. Under this usage, assets or costs incurred would clearly mean charges awaiting future revenue, whereas expenses or costs applied would mean charges against present revenue."[5]

In a sense this definition has a decisive merit in as much as it precisely states how in the accounting process assets come into being and what they are held for. All the same it too does not provide any indicator by which assets can be distinguished from nonassets. Further, the definition is not comprehensive enough. There is little doubt that bank balances, bills receivables and such other financial claims are well-recognized

[2]W. A. Paton, *Accounting*, 1924, p. 28; *Essentials of Accounting*, 1938, p. 23.

[3]Group Study at the University of Illinois, *A Statement of Basic Accounting Postulates and Principles*, Center for International Education and Research in Accounting, 1964, p. 16.

[4]Robert T. Sprouse and Maurice Moonitz, *A Tentative Set of Broad Accounting Principles for Business Enterprises*, Accounting Research Study No. 3. AICPA, 1962.

[5]W. A. Paton and A. C. Littleton, *An Introduction to Corporate Accounting Standards*, 1940, pp. 25 and 26.

examples of assets. They would, however, be excluded from assets under this definition, for the simple reason that they are neither 'charges awaiting future revenue' nor are they 'charges against present revenue'. Moreover, this definition excludes all items from assets, which are not represented by 'costs' or which are not subject to amortization.

### AICPA Position

The American Institute of Certified Public Accountants offers a comparatively better definition of assets in these words: "Something represented by a debit balance that is or would be properly carried forward upon a closing of books of account according to the rules or principles of accounting (provided such debit balance is not in effect a negative balance applicable to a liability), on the basis that it represents either a property right or value acquired, or an expenditure made which has created a property right or is properly applicable to the future."[6]

It highlights the importance of trial balance and specifies the point of time when assets are shown in the process of income determination. Further it so defines assets as to exclude a loss. It does not, however, bring out very clearly the homogeneity of substance of assets, nor does it state expressly for whom the assets represent rights. According to this definition, an expenditure, which creates a property right *ipso facto* qualifies as an asset, but the fact is that howsoever valuable the property right so created, it should not be regarded as an asset unless it is of current or future benefit to the enterprise. This definition therefore needs a further restatement.[7]

## MISCONCEPTIONS ABOUT ASSETS

At times a few misconceptions about the concept of assets seem to be prevalent. The first misunderstanding is that all assets are legal rights. As a matter of fact, legal title is no determinant of the existence of an asset. A mortgaged property or a leasehold is as good as an asset as land with absolute right of ownership. Likewise with ample justification special advertising campaign, research expenditure or deferred charges in certain cases are treated as unquestionable examples of assets notwithstanding the fact that none of them is evidenced by a legal title.

A second misconception is that assets are necessarily physical or material in the sense that they can be seen, touched or felt. Physical characteristic like the one in question is not relevant to asset determination. This phenomenon is not common to all assets. Tangible assets like building, plant and fixtures are as good assets as intangible assets like goodwill.

A third misunderstanding is that assets are but money values. Often assets are referred as plant is $50,000, building is $35,000 or cash, $25,000, and so on. Assets

---

[6]The Committee on Terminology, AICPA, *Review and Resume*, Accounting Terminology Bulletin No. 1, 1953, p. 13.

[7]The Committee on Terminology originally gave the definition in 1941 and then restated it in 1953.

are what they are made of, that is, the usefulness they promise to bring in to the enterprise which holds them. Monetary unit is a convenient though not necessarily a sound yardstick in terms of which assets are expressed. Logically it is wrong to identify a measure with the object measured.

## COMMON PROPERTIES OF ASSETS BASIC TO DEFINITION

In coining a definition of assets, the underlying approach should be to pinpoint the common properties of assets. It appears that an item to be called an asset must possess the following characteristics:

### Future Benefits—Service Potential

First, the item must ensure some specific future benefits or service potentials to an enterprise. In fact it is its usefulness to the enterprise that makes the subject-matter of an asset. To the extent an item ceases to be useful, it ceases to be recognized as an asset. This statement has two implications.

First implication is that an item does not have usefulness in general. The issue of its being useful can be answered only by reference to the question: useful to whom?, because nothing can be useful to all persons at the same time generally. The answer to this question is "useful to the enterprise or the person who possesses the item."

The second implication is that usefulness means some positive benefit or service potential. For example, a machine with a negative value in the sense that it has been rendered obsolete and its cost of removal would exceed its residual value, cannot be considered as an asset. Again, expired capital outlay is not an asset. No doubt, in certain cases formidable difficulties may be experienced in determining the quantum of usefulness or service potential of an item, but this factor would affect the valuation without changing the nature of the asset.

On a deeper reflection it would be apparent that what accountants actually account for is usefulness or service potential, and not the forms in which these attributes are embodied. These forms are designated as land, building, plant, machinery, fixtures, receivables, advances, bank balances and so on. When a certain form ceases to be of economic benefit to the enterprise, it is excluded from assets.

It is aptly remarked by Paton and Littleton: "Behind accounting's array of figures, . . . lie the tangible and intangible embodiments of services."[8] The concept of assets favoured herein is in keeping with the basic approach of accounting theory. Incidentally it may be stated that the service potential nature of assets has not been emphasized as much as it deserves. Happily enough during recent years there has been

[8] Paton and Littleton, op. cit., p. 13.

a growing realization that assets are essentially in the nature of "aggregates of service potentials,"[9] "future economic benefits,"[10] or "rights to prospective benefits."[11]

## Legal Rights

Secondly, assets must necessarily have the protection of law in the sense that the enterprise to which they belong should have a legal claim to their enjoyment. An asset is not worth its name unless it is in the nature of a legal right. Rights to assets are not confined to property rights;[12] they may as well arise under the law of obligation. They may represent rights in personam (those rights which avail against certain person or persons), or rights in rem (those rights which avail against persons generally). They may arise from ownership or from possession, or *nemo dat mod non habet*. They may be right to real property or personal property, corporeal or incorporeal. They may just be 'profits a prendre'.

It is immaterial whether these legal claims to enjoyment or ownership are evidenced by contracts, written agreements or legal title. If the legal claims are liable to be withdrawn at any time without any compensation by other parties, they should not be called assets. What is important is that the enterprise must have a reasonable chance of the enjoyment of the legal claims, whether at present or in the future.

## Other Aspects

Incidentally it may be stated that a concept of assets must possess two qualifications. First, the economic potentials or legal claims constituting assets must arise from some economic event. Economic events is a broader term than 'transactions,' and includes all significant economic changes concerning an enterprise which must be recognized in the accounting process in order to make accounting reports not misleading to their users.

Second, economic potentials or legal claims are considered only in reference to an enterprise. Items not meeting any of these qualifications are not the concern of the accountant. Perhaps an explicit statement of these qualifications is not warranted for the simple reason that Accounting records data arising from economic events relating to an enterprise.

Thus assets may be defined as embodiments of present or future economic benefits or service potentials measurable in terms of monetary units, accruing to an enterprise as a result of economic events, the enjoyment of which by the enterprise is secured by the law.

[9]AAA Committee on Concepts and Standards, Accounting and Reporting Standards for Corporate Statements and Preceding Statements and Supplements, 1957, p. 3.

[10]Sprouse and Moonitz, op. cit.

[11]Moonitz and Jordon, *Accounting, An Analysis of Its Problems*, rev. ed., 1963, vol. I, p. 163.

[12]More often than not, assets are stated to represent at best property right excluding other legal claims.

## QUESTIONS

1. Select any asset reported on a conventional balance sheet and explain how it possesses the common properties of assets according to Lall.

2. Why is the source of an asset not relevant in defining the asset?

3. What misconceptions exist because of confusion between asset definition and asset measurement?

## SELECTED BIBLIOGRAPHY

Henderson, H. S., "The Nature of Liabilities," *The Australian Accountant*, July 1974, pp. 328-330, 333-334.

# 30

# CHARACTERISTICS OF A LIABILITY*
Maurice Moonitz

The following four characteristics will serve as a starter to establish an accounting definition of liabilities:

1. A liability involves a future outlay of money, or an equivalent acceptable to the recipient.

2. A liability is the result of a transaction of the past, not of the future. "Transaction" is used here in its primary sense of an event involving at least two accounting entities—an "external transaction."

"Transactions" encompass the following types of financial events: (a) the receipt of money from someone outside the enterprise; (b) the payment of money to someone outside the enterprise; (c) the acquisition of goods or services—materials, supplies, power, services of human beings of all types and grades, equipment, land, mineral deposits, leaseholds, etc.; (d) sales of goods or services of all types; (e) lending and borrowing of money on a short- or long-term basis; (f) the imposition and collection of taxes.

Accruals of all sorts are omitted from this list, so are the amortization of costs, as well as all "internal transactions" such as the transfer of work in process to finished goods. These accruals, amortizations, and transfers, however, are all consequences of the transactions listed above, and hence fit into the picture neatly as arising from past events. What does not fit in so neatly are events that have not yet occurred, e.g., next month's payroll, next year's purchase of fixed assets, next quarter's borrowings against

*Excerpt from "The Changing Concept of Liabilities," *The Journal of Accountancy*, May 1960, pp. 41—46. Reprinted by permission of the publisher and the author.

a bond issue, etc. Therefore, none of these future events will qualify as a liability under this second characteristic.

3. The amount of the liability must be the subject of calculation or of close estimation . . . .

4. Double-entry is taken for granted. If, for example, we do wish to consider the presence and influence of *future* purchases of depreciation assets, for any reason, we should consider the obligation to pay for the blamed things.

## REVENUE AND EXPENSE*

Carl L. Nelson

Assets are customarily shown in the accounts and on the balance sheet at cost. In most cases the assets are acquired as a result of a purchase for cash or the promise to pay cash in a short period of time; in this case cost is the amount of money which has been paid or will be paid. In other cases, assets are acquired as a result of exchanging other assets, issuing long-term obligations to pay money (bonds or long-term notes), or issuing proprietary claims. Cost here means the fair market value of the assets surrendered or the liability or proprietary equity that is created. As a generalization, the cost of any asset is the fair market value of the cash or other consideration transferred in exchange for the asset.

Assets are sometimes (but rarely) acquired as a result of a gift. These assets are costless, but to place them on the records at this zero cost would not yield the most useful results. Accountants therefore record them at their market value. This is not a departure from the general pattern, for placing assets on the records at cost also places them on at market value at the date of acquisition; cost is the value arrived at as a result of negotiations between the buyer and the seller. The effect of this transaction is to increase proprietorship, for no other asset has been surrendered and no liability has been created. This proprietorship should be clearly segregated from other proprietorship; it has been created neither as a result of an investment by the owners nor as a result of a sale of an asset or service at a price in excess of cost.

Other assets are received as a result of a revenue transaction and hence are not shown at cost. A claim on a customer is received as a result of a sale on account. This asset (accounts receivable) is recorded at the same amount as the amount of revenue created as a result of this transaction. For this reason, the asset side of a balance sheet cannot be understood without a realization as to what revenue is and under what conditions accountants record revenue. Revenue also is the starting point for the

---

*Unpublished paper. Reprinted by permission of the author.

computation of profit; how much revenue is recorded will have an important effect on the profit for a period.

The typical net income or net profit is an estimate. Revenues and expenses are both estimates until all assets are turned into cash. Normally this is done only when a business is about to discontinue activity (and sometimes not even then), so that only then can accurate results be determined. No one is interested in the profitability of the business at that time so that waiting until that time is useless. The users of accounting data want an annual (or more frequent) determination of income, even though it is an estimate.

Revenue creation is not the function of one individual or department in a business. The buyer, the personnel man, the advertising man, salesman, credit man—all play a part. For the typical merchandising or manufacturing business, the sale may be the point at which the accountant recognizes revenue, but this does not mean that the salesman produces the revenue. Rather, it is due to the existence of two conditions: (1) most of the activity necessary to produce the revenue has already been performed, and (2) a reasonably accurate measure of revenue is possible. Each of these requires elaboration.

In most merchandising or manufacturing enterprises, the sale is an important operation. Important as buying or producing may be, most firms expand considerable sums on the sale process. Thus it is a rare situation under which revenue recognition should precede the sale. When this sale has occurred (and by this the accountant means the delivery of the goods), the only remaining function is to collect the money; this is ordinarily not a time-consuming or costly process. With the sale (delivery), most of the activity to produce the revenue has been performed.

By revenue the accountant means the inflow of assets as a result of the business operations. With the sale, an account receivable is received, but the value of this receivable can only be estimated until the cash is received or the receivable sold. It is possible that a particular receivable may be worthless but in most cases the loss due to bad debts may be estimated fairly accurately and hence the revenue may be recognized. The revenue should be the amount which the firm expects to collect from the customers, that is the billed price less the estimated discounts which will be taken and the estimated amounts which will be uncollectible. The accounts receivable should then be valued at the amount of revenue less the estimated cost of collection. In practice, the sales discounts which will be taken and the collection cost which will be incurred are frequently ignored; because these amounts ordinarily are small, the error is not a serious one.

In other cases, the facts may be different. In some, the sale is an unimportant step and revenue can be estimated before the sale takes place. In others, the collection process is a difficult one and the revenue cannot be reliably estimated until the cash is received.

If the price of a product is set at a fixed amount (ordinarily by government action) and if the market (the government is usually the buyer under these conditions) will absorb any quantity at this price, the sales department has no function. When the production process is complete only delivery of the goods and collection of proceeds is lacking to complete the series of transactions. These ordinarily require little effort and their cost can ordinarily be accurately estimated. Under these circumstances, revenue can be as accurately estimated when the goods are produced as when they are sold. It should then be shown at that time. The amount will be the estimated amount that will be received from the buyer (price less discounts and uncollectible amounts). The effect is that the inventory should be priced at selling price less the cost of delivery, the cost of collection and estimated uncollectible amounts and discounts. Gold production is an illustration of this type of activity.

At times, the price may not be a fixed amount, but the market will absorb the output of a particular producer without price variation. This situation may be described as one in which the producer faces a demand curve that is perfectly elastic (elasticity approaching infinity). The producer could sell his output when the production process is completed. To hold it (as he sometimes does) is not a costless process; this course of action is desirable only if an increase in price is forecast. The firm is then engaging in two separate activities—production of a commodity and speculation in its price. The results of each should and can be measured. The revenue from production is the selling price that could be secured less estimated delivery costs, discounts, and uncollectibles. The inventory would then be priced at this amount less collection costs. All of these adjustments to price are likely to be small. An illustration of such a producer is the typical farmer.

Some producers operate under contracts which set the price before the production process is started. Such is frequently the case for a construction company. It obtains a contract to build a structure at a price of $1,000,000. The contract ordinarily provides the monthly payments of 90% of the contract price of the work performed during the previous month. This is only an estimate, of course, but for certain types of contracts, a reliable estimate is possible. If the estimate is reliable, revenue may well be shown as work progresses; the work has been accomplished (there is no sale problem and ordinarily no collection problem), and an accurate measure of revenue can be made. Accounts receivable will reflect the estimated contract price of work performed for which cash has not yet been received.

In all the above cases, revenue recognition preceded delivery and passage of title. In others, revenue recognition should be deferred until after delivery and collection.

If uncollectible accounts are large and difficult to forecast or if the collection process is a costly one, revenue recognition at the time of sale is inappropriate. The process is not complete until cash is collected and no reliable estimate of revenue can be made until then. The account receivable should be valued at the costs incurred up to the point of delivery of goods or services. The country doctor is often in this situation.

A special case of uncertainty exists in certain types of installment sales. If collection is uncertain or costly (both conditions may exist), the seller of goods on the installment basis should recognize revenue only as the cash is collected. At the time of sale (if no down-payment is received), no revenue should be shown; the account receivable should be valued at the costs incurred. The amount billed would be shown in the Accounts Receivable account; the difference between this amount and the costs incurred should be shown in a Deferred Profit account with the balance sheet presentation as follows:

Accounts receivable       XX
Less: Deferred profit     XX
                                    ─────
                                    XX

As amounts are collected, revenue will be shown.

At times the collection of cash will precede the delivery of the product or the service. Subscriptions to magazines, the transportation of persons, the rental of real estate—in all of these cases, the receipt of cash is frequently the first step in the business process. There is then no problem of determining the amount of revenue, but the revenue has not been earned—that is, very little of the activity necessary to produce the revenue has been performed. A railroad corporation's primary function is to provide transportation, not to sell tickets. Hence the receipt of cash produces no revenue; it results in a liability to provide the service. When the service is performed (or the product delivered), revenue results and the liability is eliminated.

Departures from these general principles are common in practicable application. Early recognition of revenue for income tax purposes results in early payment of taxes. If the law permits, deferral of revenue for tax purposes may therefore be desirable; the result is an interest-free loan from the government. In some cases, the income tax law requires that the accounting records be kept on the same basis as is used on the tax return; in others, this practice may be followed in order to minimize the record keeping. As the receipt of cash is usually the last step in the business process, recognition of revenue at this time is most desired by the business man. Hence many service enterprises and installment dealers use this as the basis of their accounting even though uncollectible accounts are small. Other dealers in merchandise and manufacturers are barred from the use of this method for tax purposes but may use it despite its prohibition. From this same stimulus comes the shunning of the production basis; revenue is deferred until the time of sale even though more useful results might otherwise be available.

Previous discussion has been directed to the seller of a product or service. From among the other types of activity, attention will be directed to the long-term investor in bonds and the investor in stocks.

An insurance company may purchase a $1,000, 10 year, 4% bond for $960.44. This price will result in the buyer receiving a return of $4\frac{1}{2}$% on his investment. This bond entitles the owner to receive:

| | |
|---|---|
| At maturity (in 10 years) | $1,000.00 |
| Periodically, $40.00 (4% of $1,000) | |
| per year for 10 years | 400.00 |
| | $1,400.00 |

The cost of the bond being $960.44, the insurance company will earn a total of $439.56 ($1400.00 less $960.44) over the ten year period.

Although accountants are agreed that the total revenue is $439.56, there is no general agreement as to the revenue per year. Some accountants would use $43.96

(one-tenth of the total) for each year. Others would use $4\frac{1}{2}$% of the investment as the revenue; the revenue the first year would then be $43.22.

During the first year revenue of $43.96 (or $43.22) would be shown but only $40.00 in cash would be received. The difference $3.96 (or $3.22) can be shown as revenue because (1) the revenue is received as a payment for the use of money and a year's use of money has been provided and (2) the amount is specifically provided for by contract. The only justifiable exception to this procedure would be if receipt of the $1,000.00 is doubtful. The revenue not currently received in cash will be received when the bond matures; hence the asset, first carried at its cost of $960.44 increases by $3.96 (or $3.22) the first year and by similar amounts in later years.

Some firms may show revenue of only $40.00, for only $40.00 is taxable during the life of the bond. This is another illustration of the effect of income taxes on accounting procedure.

Some firms own common stock which has an active market and own such a small number of shares that their action does not affect the market. On December 31, 1975 such a firm purchases one share at a cost of $40.00. During 1976 the issuing corporation earned $4.25 per share (total net income divided by the number of shares outstanding), and paid dividends of $3.00 to its stockholders. At the end of the year (December 31, 1976), the price of the stock was $38.75 per share.

The revenue is earned by the investor as a result of owning the stock and taking a risk for a period of time. This investor has performed this function for one year. The $38.75 (December 31, 1976 price) and the $3.00 (the dividend) are accurately measured amounts. Hence we can say that the revenue from ownership of a share of stock is $1.75, calculated as follows:

| | |
|---|---|
| Market value, Dec. 31, 1976 | $38.75 |
| Dividend received | 3.00 |
| | $41.75 |
| Market value, Dec. 31, 1975 | 40.00 |
| Revenue | $ 1.75 |

Although cash has increased by $3.00, the investment has decreased by $1.25.

Despite the measurability of this revenue, accountants ordinarily will show $3.00 revenue for this investment. This can be defended as a method of eliminating the need for judgment; at times the question of whether the investor could have realized this price is a difficult one. The number of shares owned by this firm and the activity of the market must be considered.

The determination of income requires the determination of expense as well as of revenue. In general, the accountant assigns costs to periods of time on the basis of association with revenue. If $10,000.00 revenue is recognized in 1976, the income statement should include all costs associated with that revenue, whether these costs have been incurred in past years, are incurred in the present year, or will be incurred in future years.

The cost of merchandise, for instance, is not necessarily charged as an expense in the year in which the merchandise is purchased or in the year in which payment is made. The total cost of merchandise purchased during 1976 is not treated as an expense for 1976; only that portion related to revenue is so considered; the result is an asset carried forward to 1977.

The same process is carried on with such assets as buildings and equipment. The portion of the total cost that is related to the current year is charged to current revenue (and called "depreciation"); the remainder is carried forward to be charged against the revenue of subsequent years.

Sometimes the cash is paid in the following year. Employees' services may be used to produce revenue for 1976 but may not be compensated until 1977. The expense is recorded in 1976; a liability will also be shown.

The application of this principle is one of the difficult (and still unsolved) problems of accounting. Advertising costs incurred in 1976 (to sponsor a television program, for example) will probably benefit 1976 and later years. Yet we are not sure that any revenue will be produced by the program. Even if we are, we do not know what portion of the benefit will be received in 1976 and how much in later years nor do we know how many years will benefit from the expenditure. The accountant usually is "conservative" and charges all of the 1976 advertising cost to the 1976 revenue. The same problem arises with research and experimental costs.

In the case of inventories and fixed assets, we may agree that some of the costs are expenses and some are assets. Despite this, making this division is not an easy task; the process is largely an arbitrary one.

In some cases the problem is largely one of estimating future events. A roof applied in 1976 may be guaranteed for five years; necessary repairs during this period will be made by the roofing company. As an expense for 1976 there should be shown costs which will be incurred during 1977 to 1981 inclusive. These must be estimated and the estimation process may be a poor one. Frequently, therefore, the accountant will not show these costs as expenses until they are incurred. Revenue of 1981 may be charged with expenses that should have been shown on the income statement for 1976.

At times accounting procedure is difficult to rationalize. Sales made late in 1976, may result in collection costs being incurred in 1977, discounts being incurred in 1977, or accounts receivable being collected in 1977. It is common (almost universal among larger firms) to charge bad debts to 1976 (as an adjustment to revenue) by setting up an Allowance for Bad Debts. It is not common to follow similar procedure for collection costs and sales discounts. These are ordinarily shown as an expense (Collection Expense) and as a revenue adjustment (Sales Discounts) for 1977.

For general purposes, the following are the basic ideas which require understanding: (1) measurement of both revenue and expense requires estimates; (2) these estimates are not easy to make and will differ from accountant to accountant and from business organization to business organization, and (3) because of difficulty of estimation or the small amount involved, the revenue or expense may deliberately be placed in the wrong period.

## QUESTIONS

1. What is the "cost" of an asset?

2. At what amount should gifts of assets be recorded? How should the "ownership" be reflected in the proprietorship section of the position statement?

3. Under what circumstances does the firm's net income or loss become more than an estimate?

4. How can you justify recognition of revenue at the time of sale even if there is a possibility of not collecting the receivable?

5. Under what circumstances might revenue be recognized prior to the sale? Subsequent to the sale?

6. Why may income tax considerations lead to deviation from the general principles of revenue recognition? What might be done by accountants and others if this results in departure from general accounting principles?

7. How can we justify recognizing the discount on the purchase of bonds as revenue during the life of the bond? What in essence is the discount on a bond?

8. What is the "conservative" approach employed by most accountants in treating advertising and research and development expenditures which "may" enhance future revenues?

## SELECTED BIBLIOGRAPHY

Robinson, Allen, "What Is Profit?" *The Australian Accountant*, April 1974, pp. 140-144.

# 32
# THAT'S HIS PROFIT
Anonymous

A Greek restaurant-owner in Canada had his own system for bookkeeping. He kept his accounts payable in a cigar box on the left-hand side of his cash register, his daily cash returns on the cash register, and his receipts for paid bills in another cigar box on the right.

When his youngest son graduated as a chartered accountant, he was appalled by his father's primitive methods. "I don't know how you can run a business that way," he said, "How do you know what your profits are?"

"Well, son," the father replied, "when I got off the boat from Greece, I had nothing but the pants I was wearing. Today, your brother is a doctor. You are an accountant. Your sister is a speech therapist. Your mother and I have a nice car, and city house, a country home. We have a good business, and everything is paid for. . . ."

"So, you add all that together, subtract the pants, and there's your profit!"

# 33

## THE CRITICAL EVENT AND RECOGNITION OF NET PROFIT*

John H. Myers

Let us assume for accounting purposes that profit is the same as the profit of the economist, a reward for having taken the risks of enterprise. This being the case, profit is earned by the operating cycle, the round trip from one balance sheet position back to that position, whether the starting point be cash or inventory or any other factor. Even in a simple merchandising business several steps occur: buying, selling, collecting. The question arises as to when during that cycle any profit should be recognized. Should the profit be recognized when a specific point on the cycle is reached, or should it be spread over that cycle in some manner? If it should be recognized at a point, what is that point? If it should be spread, what criterion should be used? In order to set some limits on this article, I have assumed that profit should be recognized at a single moment of time. This article will be devoted, therefore, to a consideration of the moment of time at which to recognize the profit. Perhaps after considering carefully the implications of the assumption we shall be in a better position to consider the question we have by-passed.

If profit is to be recognized at a moment of time, we must select that moment. The economist gives a clue in the function of entrepreneurship as the function of directing a business, bearing the pain of the risks, and reaping the rewards of astute decisions. This suggests that profit is earned at the moment of making the most critical decision or of performing the most difficult task in the cycle of a complete transaction. Just what event this is may not be easy to distinguish in many cases. Although in most types of business we recognize profit at the moment inventory is converted into accounts receivable, such timing is far from universal.[1] . . .

Merchandising is one of the most common businesses. The merchant generally performs three steps: (1) wise buying, (2) effective selling, and (3) efficient collecting. If "wise," "effective," and "efficient" permit, there is a profit. We recognize the profit at the time the second step, selling, is performed. Two reasons commonly are given for recognizing profit at this time: (1) an asset has been transferred for a valid claim (transfer); (2) the merchant's opinion as to value is not needed (objectivity). To claim that any profit was realized at the time of purchase would be contrary to our past heritage, but to defer profit until cash has been collected is not uncommon. Major reasons for deferring profit realization until receipt of cash are the risk of collecting in full and the possibility of incurring additional expense. Bad debt and collection expenses are common, but most businesses feel that they can set up adequate reserves

*From *The Accounting Review*, October 1959, pp. 528–532. Excerpt reprinted by permission of the publisher.

[1]One clue to the most difficult or crucial task in the operating cycle may be the function of the business from which the president was selected. Was he in sales, manufacturing, collection or something else? A background in sales would tend to confirm most present accounting practice.

for the estimated expense. Thus, it sounds as if the real principle behind current practice were certainty, but that cannot be so for we do prepare income statements in spite of such major uncertainties as unaudited income tax returns and renegotiable contracts.

The principle of the critical event seems to fit the situation of the merchant very well. Where collection is a critical problem (and I doubt if there are many cases where it is), profit may be taken up at collection time. For most businesses, most of us would agree that selling is the critical event and that profit should be recognized at that time. In rare cases buying might be critical, as where an extremely good price is paid for some rapid-turnover, staple item.

A manufacturer's business is much like that of a merchant except that an extra step is added, converting the purchased raw materials into salable units. This gives an extra point at which profit might be recognized, i.e., time of efficient manufacture. In general we do not use this time because of uncertainty as to eventual sale price. However, in the case of gold refining where the market is assured, profit is recognized at the time of manufacture. The same reasoning as in the case of the merchant seems to apply; again it is the certainty principle. The critical event principle also is pertinent. Selling is very important in most cases; in gold mining it is a mere clerical detail, for the market and the price are assured by the government.

However, in contracting and manufacturing goods to order, especially if the manufacturing time will extend over several fiscal periods, the situation is quite different. In many cases there is no assurance the goods can be made at the contracted price. Therefore, profit is recognized when it becomes certain, when the goods have been made. The critical event theory, if applied to this situation, might be construed to come to the same answer as the certainty theory. In many cases it probably will. However, there may well be cases when profit should be recognized at sale date before the goods are manufactured. If a manufacturer regularly makes standard items for stock, it does not seem right to defer profit recognition beyond sale date merely because the item is temporarily out of stock. Somewhere between these two extremes there will be a twilight zone in which determination of the critical event will be difficult, but knowing that such an event is the determining factor would clarify thinking considerably.

Some people argue that profit can be recognized only when a transaction has been completed, when both purchase and sale have taken place. They argue that both of these elements are necessary and that the sequence of the two is immaterial. This almost assumes that the normal position is to have nothing but cash and that any other position is one of risk. A merchant would consider himself on dangerous ground, assuming he plans to stay in business, if he did not have a stock of merchandise. Anyone who has maintained a heavy cash position in the last decade or so has been assuming a position in which risk (of price level change) has been high. Consider an individual who has accumulated more funds than needed for current living and for an emergency cushion. The normal position for him is to have an investment in stocks or bonds. When he is out of the market, he is assuming substantial risk until he reinvests. There is a real question if he is to measure profit from purchase to sale of a security or to measure from the time he gets out of the market until he again assumes his normal position with respect to the market. Point of view seems all important. What is the critical function in making a profit? This question may be a most useful over-all guide.

Profit is recognized by magazine publishers in the period when the magazines are distributed. In most cases sale occurs and cash is received at the time the subscription is booked. Manufacturing costs are incurred shortly before distribution date. Advertising revenue as well as sale price are considered earned at the time of publication. There is serious question if this routine is correct even using the theory of certainty typically followed by manufacturers. Long in advance of publication date, the sales of magazines (by subscription) and of advertising are known. Printing costs are usually incurred under long-term contracts, so no element of uncertainty appears here. The only other element is the editorial one. Since most or all of the editorial staff will be paid fixed salaries, no uncertainty exists here. If the certainty theory is to be used, profit should be recognized at the time the subscription is sold. Among the currently used theories, only the completed contract theory explains the present practice.

Under the critical function theory we must determine whether sales of magazines, sales of advertising, or production of the magazines is the critical function. Without good advertising contracts, the firm cannot prosper. Since advertising rates are based on circulation, sales of magazines seems all important. However, unless the editorial work pleases the subscriber, he soon will fail to renew his subscription. The readers' response will be felt much more quickly in newsstand sales. Choice as to which of these functions is the critical one may well not be unanimous. If it is agreed that editorial work is critical and that editorial work culminates in publication, then the current practice is appropriate.

Lending agencies. . . generally recognize profit over the period a loan is outstanding. When the note is discounted at the inception of the loan, the banker has, in a sense, collected the fee in advance. The fact that this fee is called interest might lead the unwary to assume that it should be spread over the period, because the payment is based on time. However, closer inspection shows that the theory behind the lending agency's recognition of gross income over the period of the loan is that many expenses (particularly interest paid on money loaned out and collection and bookkeeping expenses) are spread fairly evenly over the loan period. If expenses of setting up the loan are also spread over the collection period or are minor, the matching of revenue and expenses is well done. The resulting net income is spread over the loan period. In a sense the situation is somewhat comparable to the contractor and magazine publisher in that the customer has been "sold" at the beginning and only rendering of service is left to be performed. Profit is taken up as each piece of the service contract is completed. However, a fundamental difference exists, the manufacturer and banker have different responsibilities after "sale." The manufacturer or publisher must incur many costs to complete the service to the buyers. The banker's role is much more passive; he has only to wait for payments in the normal order of business.

The current practice of recognizing income during the period the loan is outstanding does not seem to agree with the critical function idea. The only things happening while the loan is outstanding are (1) the money borrowed to lend is incurring interest charges and (2) the economic situation is changing, especially as regards the borrower and his ability to pay. If the loan requires periodic payments there is an additional bookkeeping function. Perhaps in individual cases the critical function is the decision to loan or not to loan. If that is so, profit probably is earned at that time even though collection and exact determination of the amount might be delayed quite some time. This delay is, I am sure, one of the reasons profit is measured over the life of a loan. The service-rendered concept might be another reason for accruing profit over the life of a loan, but my experience is that the borrower receives the greatest service at the time he gets the money. Many merchants selling on the installment plan recognize all profit at time of sale of the merchandise and set up adequate reserves for loss. Their situation is only slightly different from that of a lending agency. The goods are sold and the loan is made in a single transaction. In the merchant's case, more rests upon this event than does in the case of merely making a loan. Nevertheless, a satisfactory or unsatisfactory lending policy, it seems to me, is the one thing that makes loans profitable or unprofitable.

A company owning and renting real estate presents an interesting case. Typically, rents are taken into income in the period to which the rent applies. Expenses are recognized as incurred. A major function of such a firm is providing various building services through payment of taxes, insurance, and the costs of maintenance, heat, and elevator operation. Rental of small dwelling units on a month-to-month basis is very different from rental of large areas for manufacturing or office use. Not only may more service be required for commercial purposes, but also the term of the lease will probably be considerably longer so that the tenant may feel justified in making many improvements to suit his operations. Even though the lease term may be short, there will be a strong presumption to renew because of the large expenses of moving. Under these circumstances, is profit really earned merely by serving the present tenants? When a major tenant occupying a whole floor or two is secured or lost, it would seem a renting firm would have real cause for a feeling of profitability or loss thereof. I would suspect the agent securing a long-term tenant would be well paid in recognition of his great service to the real estate company. The critical function theory would seem to demand that all profit for the term of the lease be recognized at this time. Practical difficulties of determining the ultimate profit from such a contract are large. The basic cause of the problem is the custom of determining profit at least annually. Although this custom is the root of the whole problem discussed in this paper, the problem is larger here because of the length of term of the contract. The practical difficulties of applying the theory in this case must not be the cause of rejecting the theory. If the critical function theory should be correct theoretically, then we must strive to find a way to apply it to the practical situation.

The theory of the critical event as the moment at which to recognize profit or loss on a transaction seems very useful. In the types of business which we have considered, it rather closely matches current practice and gives insight into the true nature of the business. It is a theory based on a fundamental economic process rather than upon such frequently used rationalizations as convenience, conservatism, certainty, tax timing, and legal passage of title.

## QUESTIONS

1. What are the events which may be critical for the recognition of net profit, and why may they be regarded as critical?

2. On July 9, 1971, the Federal Trade Commission dismissed complaints by thousands of former *Saturday Evening Post* subscribers who claimed they should have received cash refunds instead of substitute subscriptions when the magazine ceased publication in 1969. The FTC reported that the termination of the *Post* was due entirely to its financial position, that every effort was made to furnish a magazine of comparable value to subscribers, and that the money received from most subscriptions covered only a small fraction of the total cost of publishing and distributing the *Post*.

If this last factor is generally descriptive of the prevailing situation for most magazines and newspapers (or if money from advertisers covers a large percentage of the cost of publishing and distributing), of what significance is it in determining the critical event for magazine and newspaper subscriptions?

3. Defend (or attack) Professor John H. Myers' suggestion that the critical event for lending agencies in individual cases is the decision to loan or not to loan.

# 34

## THE GREAT FATHER*
Ron Stinson and Dick Faulk

Our Father, Paton,
Which art at Michigan,
Hallowed by thy word.
Thy day will come
When things are done
In business as they are at Michigan.

Give us this day
Thy sacred word
And forgive us our confusion,
As we forgive you for confusing us;
And lead us not into purchase discount income,
But deliver us from Finney,
For thine are the debits,
And the credits,
And the retained earnings,
Forever and ever.                      Amen.

*From *The Monroe Street Journal*, Nov. 20, 1950, p. 6. Reprinted by permission of the publisher.

EDITOR' NOTE: Probably the most prominent of all United States accounting educators in this century, William A. Paton has been an influential teacher and writer for over 50 years. For most of his career, he was a professor at the University of Michigan. The late Professor Finney was a leading textbook author to generations of accounting students.

## QUESTION

1. Why should a purchase discount not be classified as income (revenue)?

# 35

# TAKING STOCK*

Harry B. Anderson

Things were finally starting to look a little rosier at Paterson Parchment Paper Co., a big office-supply and paper concern.

At the end of the first nine months of 1972, Paterson Parchment showed a small operating profit, compared with a year-earlier loss. An official predicted that the company would also have an operating profit for all 1972, after several years of big losses. True, the company was facing a large write-down from the sale of its copying-machine division, but the division had been a loser, and in the long run Paterson Parchment stood to gain by disposing of it.

However, things didn't turn out as well as expected. Last month Paterson Parchment announced that the company had another big loss in 1972 despite the encouraging gains of the first nine months. The reason? A chagrined management explained that accountants at a key division, in effect, had been counting the same inventory more than once. The blunder made it necessary to write down earnings in the three years since 1970 by a whopping $1.3 million.

Paterson Parchment's woes may be extreme, but inventory problems are hardly uncommon. Despite the advent of computerized accounting and sophisticated management techniques, keeping tabs on inventories is still full of pitfalls—as increasing numbers of companies seem to have discovered lately. One dramatic example: Whittaker Corp., a big Los Angeles conglomerate, was recently forced to buy back two subsidiaries it had sold to another company when a $6.3 million inventory shortage in the subsidiaries' accounts was uncovered.

## FROM OVERBUYING TO THEFT

Inventory problems that have been reported recently range from simple overbuying of goods to outright theft. For example, Wichita Industries Inc., based in New York, said

*From the *Wall Street Journal*, Apr. 25, 1973, p. 40. Reprinted by permission of the publisher.

that write-downs of slow-moving inventory in its mechanical-controls division accounted for as much as $20,000 of the company's 1972 net loss of $91,767. Drug Fair Inc., a Washington-based drug retailer, said a recent downturn in earnings can be attributed partly to what is euphemistically known as inventory "shrinkage"—warehouse pilferage and shoplifting—as well as overbuying of goods that later had to be sold at discounts.

Paterson Parchment's problems were apparently the result of inexperience. A company spokesman says that in 1970 and 1971, it made "major changes" in accounting personnel at its Kee Lox Manufacturing Co. division, leaving the unit "without top-level poeple" to look after the books.

One of the worst mistakes occurred when the division, which makes inked ribbons and carbon paper, reworked a substantial amount of finished goods to improve the inking. The accountants failed to remove the original value of the reworked inventory from the books. Instead, they made duplicate entries. The error was eventually discovered through a physical inventory, but in the meantime the company had been seriously underestimating the division's cost of goods sold. This is a key figure that many companies arrive at by subtracting the value of year-end inventories from the year-earlier figure. Consequently, profits were being overstated.

Nobody knows how many companies have inventory problems. There has been a spate of news stories on the subject in recent months, and some management experts say that as the economy heats up—and inventories increase—the problems may intensify. According to the Commerce Department, inventories have been rising rapidly in recent months, climbing $1.8 billion in February to $197 billion. It was the seventh consecutive monthly rise of more than $1 billion.

## SURPRISES AHEAD

"You're going to see much more activity in the inventory area," predicts Emanual Weintraub, a member of the Institute of Management Consultants in New York. "Inventory management is better when things are bad and worse when business is good. I'd be willing to bet that nearly every time you find a major surprise in earnings, you'll find a major surprise in inventories."

Such surprises aren't new, of course. Retailers long have made systematic provision for inventory losses as a result of shoplifting or light-fingered employes. Every now and then, a major scandal points up the seemingly endless possibilities for inventory frauds. Such a case was the salad-oil swindle of the early 1960s, in which vast sums of money were lent against nonexistent stores of vegetable oil. The back-office problems that put a number of brokerage houses out of business in the late 1960s were in reality inventory problems—keeping track of the millions of pieces of paper that are the raw materials of the securities industry.

Great strides have been made in inventory control in recent years, management experts say. "Inventory control is a highly refined science dealing with measurable variables," says David Boodman, vice president of Arthur D. Little Inc., the Boston management-consulting firm. Successful control techniques "have become commonplace in a lot of industries," he says, "and they're in all the textbooks." But, he is quick to add, "the surprise is that there are still lots of companies" that aren't using them.

Inventory control takes more than fancy management techniques. According to Jack Brier, chairman of Kleinert's Inc., an apparel and shoe concern, inventory-control systems are only as good as the people who use them.

Mr. Brier should know. For the year ended last Oct. 7, Kleinert's reported a net loss of $67,000, in contrast to a year-earlier operating profit of $689,000, or 80 cents a share. In a letter to shareholders last December, Mr. Brier said that one reason for the deficit was a breakdown in a new inventory-control system at the company's newly acquired Danoca division. "We had a standard cost-accounting system, but it wasn't applied," Mr. Brier asserts. "The people didn't have the capability to understand it or follow through." Some have since been fired.

## TRACING THE PROBLEM

Sometimes inventory problems can be hard to pin down. RPS Products Inc., a Baltimore-based auto-parts distributor, had been expecting earnings for the year ended last June 30 to top 95 cents a share. But the company discovered a huge inventory shortage and wound up reporting a new loss of $449,000, in contrast to a year-earlier profit of $1.1 million, or 89 cents a share. Now it is believed that about 25% of the inventory that the company should have had on hand wasn't there. How it was lost—or whether indeed it was ever present—isn't known. The company hadn't taken a general physical inventory for over a year.

Physical inventories, which are conducted about once a year by most firms, generally catch any discrepancies between recorded inventories and actual stocks. But interim financial reports, usually based on estimates of inventories, can often be misleading. RPS Products, for example, reported earnings of nearly $1 million in the first nine months of 1972, before it discovered its shortages.

Knowing the exact amount of inventories is important because it is used to calculate the cost of goods sold; this, in turn, is subtracted from sales receipts to arrive at a gross-profit figure. The cost of goods sold is calculated by subtracting the amount of inventories on hand from the amount of inventories at the beginning of the reporting period, plus inventories acquired during the period. Between physical inventories, these figures are often rough calculations at best.

Physical inventories don't necessarily prevent errors. In the case of Whittaker, the Los Angeles conglomerate that had to buy back two subsidiaries when shortages were found, professional investigators found that the discrepancies had developed over four years. The shortages were "concealed by the alteration of accounting records, including physical-inventory quantities," according to Whittaker.

Just who was tampering with Whittaker's books wasn't disclosed. The company's outside accounting firm, Arthur Andersen & Co., recently took the unusual step of paying Whittaker $875,000, but the firm denied any legal liability in the matter.

## QUESTIONS

1. Why is determining the exact amount of inventories so important to an accountant?

2. What is the difference between a physical inventory and an inventory estimate?

3. What kinds of inventory problems have been reported?

# 36

## LIFO HURTS TOOL MAKER'S PROFIT PICTURE*
Columbus Evening Dispatch

LIFO

A switch to last in-first out inventory valuing cost Warner & Swasey Co. $4.5 million or $1.29 per share last year, the company has reported.

Warner & Swasey President Joseph Bailey said the switch was made to avoid accounting distortion due to "the unprecedented increase in costs, primarily material prices."

The company, a tool manufacturer reported that net sales for the final quarter of 1974 were $61.5 million, up 10.6 percent from $55.5 million a year earlier. Sales for the whole year were $242.9 million, an increase of 14.2 percent over $212.6 million over 1973.

## QUESTIONS

1. If a switch to LIFO (last in, first out) inventory valuation reduced profits, were the general prices of inventory items increasing or decreasing? Why? If it increased profits?

2. Record in two T accounts the entry to show the result of switching inventory valuation methods?

## SELECTED BIBLIOGRAPHY

Bray, Thomas J., "New Sets of Books: More Companies Alter Accounting Methods to Neutralize Inflation," *The Wall Street Journal*, Oct. 7, 1974, pp. 1 and 10.

*From the *Columbus Evening Dispatch*, Feb. 22, 1975, p. B-5. Reprinted by permission of the publisher.

# 37
# HOW LIFO BEGAN*
Herbert T. McAnly

During the latter part of the 19th century and the early part of the present century, some companies, particularly those engaged in the processing of basic raw materials, designated a fixed portion of their inventory as base stock and valued it at a constant low arbitrary price. They did this to minimize the distortion of profits from mere fluctuations in price levels of this necessary inventory investment.

At the inception of the Federal income tax law in 1913, only actual inventory cost was accepted. Later, in the early '20's, the lower of cost or market was recognized as acceptable in the pricing of inventories. The use of the base-stock method was proscribed by regulation. The U.S. Supreme Court in *Lucas v. Kansas City Structural Steel Company* [281 U.S. 264 (1930)] upheld these regulations and held against any form of the base-stock inventory method which froze an arbitrary quantity at an arbitrary price.

In 1938, the last-in, first-out (LIFO) method, an adaptation of the base-stock method, was recognized by Congress as acceptable for ore processors of basic metals and for tanners of hides. The LIFO method in substance corrected the objections to the former base-stock method by defining both the quantity and the price of this base stock. It permitted the portion of the quantity of the ending inventory equalling the beginning inventory to be valued at the beginning inventory price and only any increase in the quantity of the ending inventory over the beginning quantity to be valued at current costs.

The limited 1938 legislation was deemed discriminatory, and in 1939 Congress extended the right to adopt LIFO to all taxpayers. However, since LIFO originated in industries where the levels of inventories could be readily measured in quantities of common product units, the early regulations issued by the Treasury Department were written to deal only with quantities of items, implying specific identification of goods of uniform physical likeness or composition. Thus, the extension of LIFO to all industries, as interpreted by the original regulations dealing only in comparable physical units, was impracticable, due to style or design changes, temporary fluctuations of quantities of individual items at any specific inventory date, substitutions of materials, changes in production methods, etc. The Treasury Department did not propose to broaden the regulations to make LIFO practicable and continued this negative attitude for the ensuing ten years.

In order to accomplish the real objective of LIFO, *i.e.*, to charge against current operations the increased cost of carrying required continuous inventory investments, the dollar-value LIFO method was conceived in 1941.[1] This calls for dealing with

---

*From *Management Accounting*, May 1975, pp. 24–26. Reprinted by permission of the publisher.

[1]Developed by H. T. McAnly and published with his addresses delivered at the Central States Conference, Chicago, Ill., in May, 1941, under the auspices of CPA State Societies, Loyola University and the American Institute of Accountants.

inventory as a composite in terms of dollars and computing an index of price change contained in the ending inventory compared to the beginning-of-year costs. The index of price change applied to the end-of-year inventory cost makes possible the determination of inventory equivalents at beginning-of-year price levels. If there was an increase in the aggregate quantity of inventory measured in terms of beginning-of-year cost dollars, the increase would be valued at current-year cost by adding to such increment the price increase factor.

The dollar-value LIFO method was adopted by a number of industrial companies and large department stores in 1941. The then Bureau of Internal Revenue contended that LIFO could only be applied where there was a matching of specific items, and a Tax Court case resulted, involving Hutzler Brothers Co., a Baltimore department store.[2] Trial before the Tax Court occurred on November 13, 1945. On January 14, 1947, the Court, in a 14-2 decision, held in favor of the taxpayer. The court held that specific identification of goods was not required, that the inventory could be expressed in terms of departmental total dollars, and that the application of indexes of price changes resulted in compliance with Section 22(d) of the (1939) Internal Revenue Code.

On March 4, 1948, Treasury Decision 5605[3] was issued, permitting retailers to use the dollar-value LIFO method, and retroactively so if they had elected to use that method and had been denied its use by the Bureau of Internal Revenue. On November 2, 1949, Treasury Decision 5756[4] was issued. This administrative release permitted the use of the dollar-value LIFO method by any taxpayer—not just retailers. Thus, ten years after Congress extended the right to use LIFO to all taxpayers, the Treasury Department reluctantly approved measures to make its application conveniently practicable. In this ten-year period, prices had more than doubled and many companies had been misguided and deterred from LIFO elections that might otherwise have been made. As the author has observed elsewhere, the interpretation of legislative provisions follows, but rarely precedes, business practice.

During the past twenty years there have been many discussions with the Treasury Department and the Internal Revenue Service regarding the mechanics to be employed in using the dollar-value LIFO method, primarily related to pooling or grouping and to index calculations. Actually, a single group or pool for the entire inventory investment, coupled with a reasonably sound index of price change, is the appropriate way to reflect income under dollar-value LIFO. As a compromise with Treasury thinking, which favored multiple pools and tended to generate more taxable income, the natural business unit concept emerged. Thus, a single pool is permitted for each "economic activity" within a business. A broad interpretation of an "economic activity" generally should permit the use of a single pool. Regulations relating to the

---

[2] *Hutzler Brothers Co.*, 8 TC 14 (1947). Mr. McAnly served as the expert professional accounting witness in this trial. The legal firm of Ivins, Phillips & Barker of Washington, D.C., represented the taxpayer.

[3] 1948–1 CB 16.

[4] 1949–2 CB 21.

dollar-value LIFO method were finally issued on January 20, 1961—more than 20 years after LIFO was extended to all taxpayers by Congress. . . .

It is interesting to note that while the use of lower-of-LIFO cost or market is not permitted taxwise, a reserve to market when lower than LIFO cost is permitted for financial income determination. This would seem to be in conflict with the provision which calls for taxable and financial income to be on the same basis under LIFO.

It is also interesting to note that LIFO, which has had a 30-year struggle to get established for taxable income determination, is followed by the U.S. Department of Commerce in its computation of national income. This was first seen in the 1951 edition of its National Income Supplement which states: "The LIFO method of inventory accounting yields results most akin to national income practices." Subsequent editions have followed the practice.

## REFINEMENTS URGED

The LIFO technique has come a long way but additional refinements should be considered. Regulations pertaining to the development of indexes of price changes should be broadened so that all reasonably accurate and practical procedures are available. Department stores on LIFO are permitted to use National Indexes of Departmental Price Changes developed for the industry by the Bureau of Labor Statistics in the computation of their dollar-value LIFO inventories. Perhaps it is in order to suggest that indexes developed by other recognized Government agencies may prove to be acceptable in dollar-value LIFO calculations. . . .

In an inflationary period, such as currently exists, the use of LIFO by taxpayers with inventories results in a more uniform and realistic reporting of profits for tax, dividend, wage and price purposes. On the other hand, it produces less immediate national taxable income since it removes from current income the increased cost of carrying basic inventories until it is realized as profit through future price declines or reductions in quantity.

## QUESTIONS

1. How is LIFO computed?
2. What is the real constraint on using LIFO for tax returns? Why?
3. What are the effects of LIFO?
4. Contrast these effects with those of other inventory valuation methods.
5. What is the objective of dollar-value LIFO, and how is it computed?

# 38

## DEBIT, CREDIT, AND INPUT-OUTPUT TABLES*
Billy E. Goetz

In "Professorial Obsolescence" I was somewhat critical of the explanation of "debit and "credit" given in the most widely adopted introductory texts.[1] I contended that "A debit is a left-hand entry" is neither useful nor true. Here I will try to do better.

Conceive of a square table with the complete chart of accounts of an enterprise as row headings and as column headings, with a zero balance in each cell.[2] This table is placed in a computer's memory and becomes the general ledger of the enterprise.

As financial transactions occur, documents are prepared and filed in the usual way. Each transaction is analyzed into one or more pairs of equal debits and credits. Each such pair is entered in a magnetic tape as four numbers: a file number, the number of the account debited, the number of the account credited, and the dollar amount. This tape is a two-column general journal, restricted to a single debit and an equal single associated credit for each event entered.

The tape is fed into the computer, which is programmed to ignore the file number, to choose the table row headed by the debited account's number and the column headed by the credited account's number, and to add the dollar amount to the total in the cell thus designated. In this way, the journal entries on the tape are posted to the table ledger in the computer's memory.

Figure 1 is a skeletonized table showing the rows and columns for Cash, Common Stock, Retained Earnings, and Sales only. All the other accounts are understood to be listed in both row and column headings.

Thus, the first journal entry, assumed to be

Dr. Cash . . . . . . . . . . . . . . . . . . . . . . . . . . . . . . . . . . . . . . . . . . . . . $A
    Cr. Capital Stock . . . . . . . . . . . . . . . . . . . . . . . . . . . . . . . . . . . . . . $A

is posted by adding $A to the zero balance in the cash-row, common-stock-column cell as shown in Figure 1. Cash sales are similarly posted by adding to the total in the cell labeled B. A purchase of common stock to be retired would be entered by adding to the total of the cell labeled C. And so on, each journal entry is posted by adding its dollar amount to the total in the appropriate cell. Each entry is a debit to a row account *and* a credit to a column account.

National income accounting was created on the enterprise accounting model. It was vigorously developed by economists and statisticians, who converted the double-entry accounts and trial balances into input-output tables of the national economy. Now

*From "The Teacher's Clinic," *The Accounting Review*, July 1967, pp. 589–591. Reprinted by permission of the publisher and the author.

[1]*The Accounting Review*, January 1967.

[2]Richard Mattessich, *Accounting and Analytic Methods* (R. D. Irwin, 1964), refers to similar formulations by other authors, pp. 88 and 91. My matrix formulation was inspired by the U.S. Input-Output Table for 1947, as discussed in articles by Leontief and by Richard Ruggles, and Nancy D. Ruggles, *National Income Accounts and Income Analysis* (McGraw-Hill, 1949).

**Figure 1    The Table Ledger**

| OUTPUTS | CASH | ... | COM-MON STOCK | RETAINED EARNINGS | SALES | ... | DEBIT TOTALS |
|---------|------|-----|----------------|--------------------|-------|-----|--------------|
| Inputs |  |  |  |  |  |  |  |
| Cash |  |  | A |  | B |  |  |
| ... |  |  |  |  |  |  |  |
| Common stock | C |  |  |  |  |  |  |
| Retained earnings |  |  |  |  |  |  |  |
| Sales |  |  |  |  | E |  |  |
| Sales |  |  |  |  |  |  |  |
| ... |  |  |  |  |  |  |  |
| Credit Totals |  |  |  |  | D |  |  |

national income accounting can repay its debt to enterprise accounting. Figure 1 is an input-output table of an enterprise.[3]

We are now prepared to give useful and true meanings to "debit" and "credit." Debits are inputs and credits are outputs, either in private enterprise or in national income accounting.

Between the file of original evidences, the magnetic-tape general journal, and the input-output table ledger, we have sketched a simplified model of an accounting system. There remains the task of periodic adjusting and closing. Periodically, or whenever desired, the computer is instructed to compute row and column totals, and to print out a list of account titles with their debit (row) totals in one column (the left, if you insist!) and their credit (column) totals in an adjoining column. If you prefer, the computer can be instructed to deduct the credit total of each account from its debit total and print out only the balance: positive balances (debits or inputs) in one column and negative balances (credits or outputs) in the other. This yields a second (equivalent) useful and true meaning for "debit" and "credit." Debits are positive numbers, credits are negative numbers, and adding and subtracting are done algebraically. This gets rid of the confusion caused by the conventional definition of a debit as an increase in an asset or an expense or an increase in a liability, a proprietorship, or an income. Now, debits are simply increases, always and everywhere, and credits are decreases always and everywhere.[4] To see this, we need only remember that −12 is less than, or smaller than −8. Adding a −4 (a credit) to a −8 balance, *reduces* this balance to −12. This may confuse oldsters,

---

[3]This table, is, of course, a matrix. But since this article included no matrix juggling since this is written for non-mathematicians, I prefer to call it a "table."

[4]Accountants have faced and rejected both the input-output and the positive-negative definitions of debit and credit, but have never given adequate or persuasive reasons for so doing.

but youngsters, who know their freshman high school math, find it clear and simple.

To continue with the adjusting, closing, and reversing entries, we conceive of a stack of tables, one similar to Figure 1 for each period, separated by alternating layers (tables) whose function is to separate balance sheet items from income statement items and to close the latter to retained earnings. A document or voucher is prepared in quite the traditional manner for each adjusting entry. It is entered in the magnetic-tape journal as are all other journal entries: reference file number, debit account number, credit account number, and amount. These are posted, as before, to the cell occupying the intersection of the debited row and credited column. If desired, the computer can be programmed to produce an adjusted trial balance.

Income accounts are closed by posting amounts equal to their credit balances in the Retained Earnings column opposite the appropriate row headings. E.g., the Sales account is closed by adding the column total D in Figure 1 to the cell labeled E. Similarly, expense accounts are closed by posting amounts equal to their debit balances in the Retained Earnings row under appropriate column headings. Finally the computer offsets row and column totals for each account and carries the balances forward to the next table as row totals if positive or as column totals if negative.[5]

Nor are we confined to a three dimensional input-output by periods analysis; nor to a single set of adjusting and closing layers. We can construct sets and subsets of tables for product lines, or for organizational units, or for territories, or however management wants the operations broken down into a variety of hierarchies. Alternative adjusting interleaves can introduce price-level adjustments, or convert data to current costs, or split fixed items from variable. We can support summary accounts with detailed breakdowns. We can extend the time dimension and swallow budgets for as many future periods as we desire into our pile of tables, adding as many layers as we care to project.

This is a summary of the accounting cycle.

## QUESTIONS

1. What is Goetz's definition of debit and credit? Contrast with those given in your textbook.

2. How does Goetz use national income accounting to provide insight for understanding enterprise accounting?

3. Prepare a table to illustrate another accounting application of input-output analysis.

---

[5]For another method of adjusting and closing see Charnes, Cooper, and Ijiri, "Breakeven Budgeting and Programming to Goals," *Journal of Accounting Research*, vol. 1, pp. 16—41, 1963.

# 39

## BUCKEYE INTERNATIONAL POSTS RECORD RESULTS FOR FIRST 12 WEEKS*

Wall Street Journal

Buckeye International Inc. reported record first quarter sales and earnings due to sharply higher results from its foundry operations.

Net for the 12 weeks, ended March 22, rose to $1 million, or 72 cents a share, from a restated $17,900, or one cent a share, a year earlier. Sales rose to $25.5 million from $19.6 million.

The year-earlier profit was restated to reflect a year-end switch to the last-in, first-out method of accounting for certain inventories. The change reduced earnings by assuming that the most recently purchased items, usually the most expensive, were used in operations.

Buckeye International originally reported 1974 first quarter earnings of $256,500, or 20 cents a share.

Rowland C. W. Brown, president, said the foundry operations had a strong first quarter, based on high demand from all major customers. Railroad-car ordering is down from the torrid pace of 1973 and 1974 but still reflects strong long-term demand, he said. Demand hasn't fallen from other customers, such as producers of earth-moving equipment, mining products, off-highway haulers and military armor, he said. The backlog of about $120 million stretches into 1977, he added. Productivity and costcutting improved in all divisions, Mr. Brown said.

While the downturn in automotive, appliance and home-furnishings industries reduced sales in the company's automotive and plastics operations, they remained profitable, Mr. Brown said.

Baby-products operations had sales and earnings gains because of strong demand for a new child auto-restraint system, he said.

### QUESTIONS

1. What was the reduction in first quarter net income for Buckeye International due to the switch in inventory valuation methods?

2. What is the merit of reporting both FIFO and LIFO inventory valuations on the same statement?

*From the *Wall Street Journal*, Apr. 3, 1975, p. 11. Reprinted by permission of the publisher.

# 40

## AN ACCOUNTANT'S ADVENTURES IN WONDERLAND*
Henry Rand Hatfield

Wonderland was a place of strange conditions. What was unquestioningly accepted as being a baby turned out to be a pig; an old lady knitting was found to be a sheep; a substantial cat faded into thin air leaving only a smile, and even that vanished. It was a place where heated disputes arose over a word, and when some dissented from recognized authority, the woman's last word was "off with their heads." But Alice found her excursion into this realm an adventure not without interest, indeed on the whole pleasant.

I invite you to venture with me into unfamiliar fields and to consider some unusual aspects of accounting. Some of them may seem as strange as a vanishing cat (or a surplus which vanishes without leaving a smile), as superficially absurd as the song of the Walrus and the Carpenter.

But what I have to say, despite the form in which it is presented, may really contain a core of accounting theory, may perhaps present problems which, if one could confidently solve them, would extend to unexpected reaches.

The first adventure is entitled:

Hickory Dickory Dock,
The mouse ate up the stock.

I once owned a $1,000 bond. It was due in two years, bore 10 per cent interest payable annually, evidenced by two coupons of $100 each. Just before the end of the first year a mouse ate the second coupon. Accordingly I collected the first coupon, but not the second, which was part of the internal revenue of the mouse. At the end of the second year, I collected the principal of the bond, but the treasurer would not cash the mouse. The hidden reserve was not available.

Did I have $100 income in the first year, none in the second? Yes, says the Internal Revenue Bureau. To be sure, I received $100 cash, but the bond originally worth par declined to the discounted value of $1,000 due in one year, that is, to $909. Was there more than $9 income, that is, more than $100—$91? And did I not begin the second year with an asset worth $909 and end it with $1,000? Undoubtedly my income during the two years was $100, but was it divided in the ratio of 100 to 0, or of 9 to 91?

"'Have you guessed the riddle yet?' the Hatter said. 'No, I give it up,' Alice replied, 'What's the answer?' 'I haven't the slightest idea,' said the Hatter."

The second adventure may, for want of a better title, bear the motto:

Income, income, who's got the
    income?

*From the *Journal of Accountancy*, December 1940, pp. 527–532. Reprinted by permission of the publisher.

A testator leaves an estate of $1,000,000 yielding an annual income of 10 per cent. The income for two years is to go to A; at the end of two years the corpus goes to B. The questions to be considered are: Who gets income during the specified two years, and how much, and why?

I shall use the word "income" in an ordinary accounting sense. We accountants agree that interest accruing on a note and also the increasing value of a discounted non-interest-bearing note constitute income. Economists are sometimes less rational than accountants and use the term "income" in ways which seem peculiar to the verge of weirdness. Thus one of the most distinguished economists has argued that even though a savings bank dividend has been entered in my bank book, no income has as yet come to me. "'It's really dreadful,' Alice muttered to herself, 'the way all the creatures argue. It's enough to drive me crazy.' "

Such economists are perhaps suffering from what Bacon might have called the "Idol of the dictionary," or Freud the "Etymological complex." Those who assert that income is something which in a material way must have "come in" probably still consider that all Barbarians are dwellers on the Mediterranean Coast; and that our national bird, sacrificed on our high altars each Thanksgiving Day, really came to us from Turkey.

Perhaps even accountants are also sometimes victims of this etymological complex. Some there are who think that a depreciation reserve, because of the derivation of the word, is something kept back, like an army corps; when, instead of being something one keeps, it is something which he hasn't kept, just because he used it up by wear and tear. One might as well think that a sinking fund has something to do with financial shipwreck, instead of being something which may serve to keep the concern afloat.

But to come back to the question, Who is it, in the case cited, who during the two years, receives income? And, as Humpty-Dumpty said, "When I use the word 'income' it means just what I choose it to mean—neither more nor less."

The answer is obvious. The tenant receives $200,000 during the two years, the remainderman nothing during that period. This answer is perfectly obvious. As obvious as that the sun goes around the earth, as obvious as the fact that interest *is*, and is *not*, a cost of production—both of the latter statements being said by accountants to be obvious.

It is interesting to analyze the situation a little further. On January 1, 1939, A, the tenant, is possessed of an easily recognizable, legally enforceable right, of definitely ascertainable value. This consists of two parts: (1) a right to receive $100,000 at the end of the year; and (2) a right to receive a like sum at the end of the second year.

Surely no accountant can question the legitimacy of counting such rights as assets. They are similar to ordinary receivables and are to be valued in a similar manner. Assuming for convenience that 10 per cent is the proper rate of discount, the right to $100,000 due in one year is worth $90,909.09, the value of the second right is $82,644.63, or, for convenience, using very round figures, A is possessed of two things, one worth $91,000, the other $83,000, or a total value of $174,000.

How does he stand one year later? He indeed receives $100,000 in cash, but his accounts receivable have declined from $174,000 to $91,000, a decrease of $83,000. One asset, cash, has increased $100,000; another asset, receivable, has decreased

$83,000. By a most simple proposition in bookkeeping, his proprietorship has increased $17,000. And all of you who count receivables as assets and include the amortization of discount as a part of income, must perforce admit that A's income during the first year is not $100,000 but $17,000. A similar analysis will show that A's income during the second year is $100,000–$91,000, or $9,000.

How is it with the supposedly incomeless remainderman? On January 1, 1939, he owns a definite right to $1,000,000 due two years hence. The value of that right is $826,000. Two years later he has property worth $1,000,000, an increase of $174,000.

The estate as a whole has unquestionably yielded $200,000 during the two years. The purpose of the testator is that all of his income should go to the tenant, none to the remainderman, and this is generally supposed to take place. It is an interesting paradox to see that the division, instead of being in the ratio of 200,000:0, is in fact in the ratio of 26:174. If the income-tax officials do not approve of this, they should alter the provision that a gift is not taxable income, but that income from the gift is so taxable.

The third adventure is called:

"What's in a name?" or "Things
are not what they seem."

I hold a two-year bond with 10 per cent annual interest worth par. It is assumed by all accountants that the payment of each coupon is altogether a payment of interest. Can this be questioned?

The bond is made up of three parts, the main part promising to pay $1,000 and the two coupons, each for $100.

The three parts of the bond might have been bought by three different persons. If so, the prices paid would have been:

| | |
|---|---:|
| For the face of the bond ($826.45) | $  826 |
| For the coupon due in one year ($90.91) | 91 |
| For the coupon due in two years ($82.64) | 83 |
| .    Total | $1,000 |

At the end of the first year the holder of the first coupon would receive $100, that is, he would be repaid his investment of $91 and receive 10 per cent interest, or $9. Of the $100 actually received by the holder of the first coupon, only one-eleventh is interest. The holder of the other coupon receives nothing until the end of the second year, when he is paid $100. But he had paid $83 for the coupon, and the additional $17 is compound interest on $83 for two years at 10 per cent. Not $100 but only $17 is income.

Similarly the holder of the main part of the bond receives no cash until two years have elapsed when he is paid $1,000 for what cost him $826—an increase due to compound interest of $174.

The cashing of the two coupons, assuming they were held by different persons, meant only $26 interest, not $200. The bulk of the interest was paid to the third person, the holder of the main part of the bond. Does it make any real difference whether the three promissory notes constituting the bond, i.e., the face of the bond and the two coupons, are bought and held by three separate persons or all by one? If I discount two notes, one at the First National Bank, and the other at the Second National Bank, is not the nature of the notes the same as if both were discounted at one bank? "I am afraid I cannot put it any more clearly," Alice replied very politely, "for I can't understand it myself to begin with."

Adventure four:

Ten little . . . boys all went out to
    dine,
One stuffed his . . . self and then
    there were nine.

The tragic poem goes on, in grim sequence, showing reduction to eight, to seven, until the climax:

One little . . . boy living all
    alone,
He got married . . . then there was
    none.

Through this there is the clear inference that just one tenth disappears in each of ten successive fiscal periods. Is this not clearly symbolic of straight-line depreciation? Almost everything is symbolic in Wonderland. I have no objection to straight-line depreciation, but I am greatly amused at one of the main arguments in its support. It is said that it is superior to curved-line depreciation because the latter introduces the unreal element of interest, that it gives not cost but cost plus, while straight-line depreciation charges off each year the *cost price actually paid* without any frills or additions.

This fallacy can be made clear by taking a case involving time, but not contractual interest. A butcher buys cattle for slaughtering. The proper age for slaughtering is three years. He is willing to buy a three-year-old steer, ready for slaughter, for $100. A farmer offers him three steers, one three years old, one two years old, and one a yearling. The butcher will not pay $100 each for the three steers for one is not available for a whole year, the other not for two years. He might, however, take the three for $270. He immediately slaughters the oldest steer.

Advocates of straight-line depreciation should say that production should be charged $90, asserting that this was the actual cost of the unit consumed. By the simple and obvious method of short division, this must be so. Even children in the elementary schools know that much. "Now, children," says the teacher, "If three apples cost twenty-seven cents, how much does one cost?" In glad chorus all reply, "If three apples cost twenty-seven cents, one apple costs one third of twenty-seven cents, or nine cents." "However," said Alice, "the multiplication tables don't signify." When applied to the steers, the error is apparent. It comes from a source prolific of many errors, not all so easily detected. It is the error of assuming that things called for convenience by a common name are identical. If the problem had been stated to the children as follows: "A man pays twenty-seven cents for three pieces of fruit, an orange, a peach, and an apple; how much did the apple cost?" the answer would not be so glibly forthcoming. The three head of cattle, while each called a steer, are no more truly identical than the three fruits, for one is a three-year-old, one a two-year-old, and one a yearling.

Cannot this idea be profitably carried over to the field of depreciating machinery? One pays $270 for a machine which will last three years. He is really buying three successive years' service to be rendered by that machine. But these three services are not yet identical. Some are not full grown. Only one is immediately available, the next comes along after a year, the third is a wobbling little creature, small in size (as seen through the perspective of time) and of relatively little value. Like Alice, it has eaten from the left-hand side of the mushroom and become small. A price paid for the sum of such a series of services does not imply that each one cost an equal percentage of the total price. If keeping the steer a year is worth only $10, the three cost, respectively, $100, $90 and $80. But if upkeep is figured at $50 per annum, the prices would be $140, $90 and $40. The mere statement that three steers of varying ages cost $270 gives no indication of the cost of each. It does give one incontrovertible statement, namely, each did not cost one third of the total. Similarly with the machine. The only thing we know is that the price paid for the service of successive years is not the same. To know just how the total amount paid is to be divided, an additional factor is needed. This is the rate of interest. Without that the problem is insoluble. Of course, if we know the rate is zero, the problem can be solved, just as it can if the rate is taken at 5 per cent or 10 per cent. If the rate is taken as zero, or the time is so short that the amount of interest is presumably zero, it does not affect the calculation. But this cannot be, where time runs into years. No sane businessman, bound to pay $100 on January 1, 1940, and similar payments in 1941 and 1942, will commute the three payments for $300. (It is fair to ignore peculiar circumstances, such as the desire to secure the release of a mortgage, or as I have myself done, in prepaying all four quarterly instalments of a small income tax, because the convenience of making a single payment and the insurance against penalties due to professorial forgetfulness more than offset the loss of six months' interest.)

Straight-line depreciation, which charges a uniform sum each year, is popularly supposed to deal with exact cost price of each unit consumed. "'Contrariwise,' continued Tweedledee, 'if it was so it might be, if it were so, it would be, but as it isn't, it ain't. That is logic.'"

Adventure five:

A bird in the hand is worth 1.79
    birds in the bush, *or*
Blessings lessen as they take their
    flight.

Every accounting text and, so far as I know, every accountant in practice, makes much of the depreciable value of a machine, that part of its cost which is consumed, or disappears during its service life. It is this amount which by one or another scheme is to be allocated as an operating expense over the successive periods in which it is of service.

If a machine costs $10,000, and will have no residual value when no longer serviceable, the entire $10,000 is to be properly allocated.

*But*, and this is where the catch lies, if it is reckoned that it will have a residual value of $1,000, the accepted formula for straight-line depreciation says that the amount to be charged as expense during the useful life of the machine is $10,000–$1,000, or only $9,000. This is demonstrably false.

The matter may be made clear without using many figures. If a given sum represents the value of the services, or if you prefer the cost paid for the services which the machine will yield, it certainly will properly command a higher price, if in addition to the functional services it promises to yield for ten successive years, it will ten years later also furnish some calculable residual value. Surely, again, the extra price above that attributable to its anticipated services will depend on the amount of this residual value. It will depend on the amount but will not equal it.

The price paid for the machine—and I am assuming rational calculation—is made up of two items, present value of a series of services, and the *present* value of the residual sum. Surely no one is going to pay $1,000 today for $1,000 due in ten years. Interest somehow enters into the calculation. Even the Government pays all of one per cent on some of its loans. If, for instance, 6 per cent is taken as the interest rate, then the present value of $1,000 due in ten years is $558.40. Hear, then, the conclusion of the whole matter. The formula for straight-line depreciation is *not* to subtract the residual value from the cost and divide by the number of years. The formula is cost less the *present* not the *future* value of the residual sum. What one pays for the chance of receiving cash ten years hence has nothing to do with the cost of the services rendered by the machine.

In the illustration already used, the total depreciation is not $9,000 (i.e., $10,000 − $1,000) but $9,441.60 (i.e., $10,000 − $558.40). The annual charge is not $900, but $944.16.[1]

" 'Oh, don't bother me,' said the Duchess, 'I never could abide figures.' "

Adventure six:

Opposed equal forces moving in opposite directions do not offset each
   other.

The Interstate Commerce Commission provides that premium and discount on bonds shall be credited and debited to the same account. A corporation issuing $1,000,000 five-per-cent bonds at 105, and an equal amount of identical bonds at 95, by both debiting and crediting $50,000 to the same offset account, would reduce that account to zero, and neither discount nor premium would appear in its trial balance. The $50,000 paid each half year would then presumably represent the actual interest expense, there being no premium and no discount to amortize. This is simplicity itself.

---

[1]This discussion relates only to the ascertainment of the total amount of depreciation, not to its apportionment. The two are distinct. Premium on bonds is based on interest calculation. Its apportionment according to a most eminent accountant, may legitimately be by the straight-line method.

But while the unamortized discount and premium are equal in amount at the beginning, they cease to be so when the first coupons are paid, for the amount by which the $50,000 discount is decreased is not the same as the amount of premium written off, if the correct interest expense for the period is to be shown.

To illustrate: Assume that $2,000,000 five-per-cent bonds are issued at par, the actual interest expense each half year is $50,000 which is the amount paid on coupons. But if $1,000,000 of the bonds are issued at 95, and $1,000,000 at 105, the actual interest expense each half year is not $50,000, but a different amount varying from period to period. Surely this seems an utter absurdity. In either case the borrower receives the same amount, $2,000,000; in either case the same amount, $50,000, is paid out by cashing coupons; in either case the same principal, $2,000,000, is paid at the same time, when the bonds are redeemed, and yet, with this threefold identity, the interest charge is not the same for each period.[2]

I feel sure that most of you are in the same state of mind as Alice, for "The Hatter's remarks seemed to her to have no sort of meaning, and yet it was certainly English."

If you question my thesis, I cannot, like the Queen of Hearts, say, "Off with your heads," but if you retain your heads with the brains in proper working order, you will, in contradicting me, have also to hold that the basis on which all bond tables are prepared is incorrect.

I close with a final quotation from our fount of wisdom: "But Alice couldn't help thinking to herself, 'What dreadful nonsense we *are* talking.' 'Tut, tut, child,' said the Duchess. 'Everything's got a moral if only you can find it.' "

## QUESTIONS

1. What criticisms does Hatfield make about accounting?
2. Are all his criticisms still valid 35 years later? Explain.
3. Which of the criticisms do you feel are most significant, and why?

# 41
## TEXACO WILL DISCLOSE EFFECT ON
## ITS EARNINGS OF ACCOUNTING POLICY*
Wall Street Journal

Texaco Inc. will disclose in its 1974 annual report the effect on its earnings of certain accounting practices it follows for oil-exploration costs.

[2]See my article, "An Accounting Paradox," in *Accounting Review* for December 1928, where arithmetical illustration and algebraic formula are given.

*From the *Wall Street Journal*, Feb. 14, 1975, p. 17. Reprinted by permission of the publisher.

A maverick among the major oil companies in this regard, Texaco uses full-cost accounting and capitalizes exploratory costs. The company also follows a policy of deferring to earnings of future years the tax effect of deducting so-called intangible drilling costs for income-tax purposes.

Most other major oil companies follow a different accounting procedure by charging exploratory costs to expense. Also, many oil companies take into current income the increase in earnings from deducting intangible drilling costs on their income-tax returns rather than deferring such tax impact as Texaco does.

There has been considerable debate in the oil industry over whether companies should capitalize or expense their exploratory costs. Texaco has drawn some criticism for its policy. The question has been raised that the company might have overstated its earnings through use of its full-cost accounting procedure.

But Texaco said the net effect on the company's earnings of its accounting procedures, as compared with alternative policies, has been minor. "The comparison," Texaco said, "shows that the effect has been a net reduction in reported earnings totaling $14.9 million over the entire period of 24 years during which the accounting policies involved have been followed."

Texaco said the tabulation in the annual report "will disclose the earnings effect of the present full-cost accounting policy of capitalizing exploratory costs and the policy of deferring to earnings of future years the tax effect of deducting intangible drilling costs for income-tax purposes, as compared with assumed alternative policies of charging exploratory costs to expense and taking into net income currently the increase in earnings from deducting drilling costs for income-tax purposes."

Under the "assumed" policies to be used by Texaco for the tabulation, exploratory costs including all dry holes would be charged to expense as incurred, both in the U.S. and abroad. Nonproductive leases would be amortized on the basis of estimated average holding periods. The income-tax effect of deducting drilling costs for tax purposes as incurred would be taken into income currently, with certain exceptions outside the U.S. where deferred tax accounting for drilling costs is mandatory.

Texaco has followed full-cost accounting since 1963 and has had a policy of deferring the tax effect on intangible drilling costs since 1951.

## QUESTIONS

1. What is the difference between full-cost accounting and the alternative method for exploratory costs?

2. Show how Texaco might disclose the effect on its earnings of its accounting policy for exploratory costs.

3. Explain what the tax effects are for deducting intangible drilling costs for income-tax return purposes even though these are not deducted as expenses on the income statement.

# 42

## ALTERNATIVE INCOME MEASUREMENTS*
Carl L. Nelson

Primary attention is being given today to narrowing differences in accounting treatment of various revenues and expenses . . . .

Such an aim is commendable, but it would appear that some accountants would carry this to the extreme of endorsing uniformity regardless of the agreed methods of uniformity. In other words, uniformity is to be achieved whether the resulting data have any significance or meaning at all. The goal should, rather, be to determine what kind of accounting data would assist the consumer to make better economic decisions and then to produce these data.

One approach the accountant might take is to develop a concept of income which is economically significant and yet operational. It is possible that an income oriented toward capacity would meet these specifications.

A second approach would be to measure something that the accountant calls "income" (or profits) and that consumers of accounting data can rely upon because they know that there is uniform practice among all accountants and because they have faith in the competence of accountants. It may have no economic significance, but the decision-maker will never know this; he will never know that he has been led astray because he will blame the unpredictable events of the modern dynamic world rather than his accounting data for his mistakes. Accounting data then become a more expensive Miltown—a non-oral tranquilizer.

A third possibility is to abandon the idea of presenting a measurement of income and to substitute various kinds of information in an annual report. Included in this report might be: (1) measure of activity during the year—volume of sales classified by product and by area and volume of production classified by product and by area and measured by sales price, material cost, and labor cost; (2) year-end cost functions by product; (3) production capacity for various products (but capacity itself is a tricky concept); (4) cost of current capacity; (5) reproduction cost of current capacity; (6) engineering estimates of probable remaining life of capacity; (7) cash-flow statement; (8) amount of research expenditures (can "research" be defined?); (9) amount of advertising expenditures; and (10) a description of manpower development programs.

Perhaps the most useful information would be publication of the plans of management concerning the quantity and price of goods sold, quantity and cost (not including amortization of outlays of previous years) of goods manufactured, outlays on selling costs, research, and so forth, at the beginning of the year, followed by a report of actual events with an explanation of significant variances. The danger of this, of course, is that the plans would undoubtedly be affected by the reluctance of management to display them before the public. This reluctance is understandable.

*Excerpt from "An Accountant's View of Profit Measurement," *Profits in the Modern Economy*, Harold W. Stevenson and J. Russell Nelson (eds.), University of Minnesota Press, 1967, pp. 73–81. Reprinted by permission of the publisher and the author.

Anything new is always terrifying to a human being, and fear of competitors is sometimes an imagined, sometimes a real threat. The pure profit of the economist exists because of imperfections of the market. Information removes imperfections, and hence removes what management wishes to maximize.

To summarize, accounting information on profits represents the results of an imperfect measuring system manned by imperfect human beings. Valuable as the information may be, it is subject to misuse, and among the individuals most likely to misuse it are imperfectly informed scholars and practitioners in economics and finance.

## QUESTIONS

1. Describe an income oriented toward capacity.

2. Rank the four alternative income approaches suggested by Nelson according to ease of measurability. Ease of disclosure. Give reasons to support rankings.

3. In the nearly ten years since this article was published, have any of the four alternative approaches been partially adapted? Explain.

4. Indicate what progress has been made in the last decade in narrowing differences in accounting treatment of various revenues and expenses.

## SELECTED BIBLIOGRAPHY

Clay, Michael J., "Measurement of Performance: The Accounting Function," *Accountancy*, June 1973, pp. 10-13.

Treynor, Jack L., "The Trouble with Earnings," *Financial Analysts Journal*, September-October 1972, pp. 41-43.

# 43

# FTC TELLS 4 BIG RETAIL CHAINS TO RETURN CHARGE CUSTOMERS' UNCLAIMED BALANCES*
Wall Street Journal

The Federal Trade Commission ordered four major department store chains to return unclaimed balances to charge-account customers.

The companies agreed to the tentative orders in settlement of FTC charges that they failed to notify charge-account customers of their right to ask for cash refunds of credits—generated either through overpayments or the return of merchandise—and

*From the *Wall Street Journal*, Apr. 4, 1975, p. 2. Reprinted by permission of the publisher.

then kept the unclaimed balances if customers failed to either use them or request them.

The agency provisionally accepted consent agreements covering all the retail divisions of:

Associated Dry Goods Corp., New York, which owns Lord & Taylor Inc.

Carter Hawley Hale Stores Inc., Los Angeles, which owns Bergdorf Goodman Inc., Broadway Department Stores, Emporium Capwell, Weinstock's and Neiman-Marcus.

Gimbel Brothers Inc., New York, which owns Gimbels. Gimbel Brothers is a unit of Brown & Williamson Tobacco Co.

Lerner Stores Corp., a unit of McCrory Corp., itself a subsidiary of Rapid-American Corp., New York.

A fifth retailer, Genesco Inc. of Nashville, Tenn., and its Bonwit Teller division, didn't reach a settlement with the FTC, and the agency issued a formal complaint against the concern. The charges will be tried before an FTC administrative law judge.

In preliminary complaints last September, the FTC charged that all the retailers except Broadway Department Stores removed credits from accounts if the customer failed to ask for a refund or use the credit after a certain period. According to an FTC staff estimate, the stores kept a total of at least $2.8 million in customer funds over the last five years.

The consent agreements, which are for settlement purposes only and don't constitute an admission of illegal activity, require the companies to:

Refund all unclaimed credit balances of $1 or more created since June 30, 1972. An FTC official estimated that those refunds will be substantially more than $1 million.

Notify each customer with a credit balance of his right to a cash refund and provide each customer with at least three statements of his credit in the six months after the credit is created.

Stop writing off unclaimed credits and automatically refund unclaimed credit balances after a period of inactivity in a customer's account. If the company doesn't plan to refund balances of less than $1, it must tell the customers.

The agency asked for public comment on the tentative settlements by June 2. After reviewing the comments, the agency may formally accept or cancel the consent agreements.

Maurice Gregg, vice president and treasurer of Gimbel Brothers, said the company is pleased that it has been able to work out with the FTC the return of unclaimed balances to charge-account customers.

Attorneys for Associated Dry Goods and Lerner Stores acknowledged that the companies had agreed to the settlement and said they hadn't any further comment. Only one division of Associated Dry Goods, Lord & Taylor, was involved in the original complaint last September.

A spokesman for Carter Hawley Hale Stores said it has already implemented procedures to comply with the FTC order.

## QUESTIONS

1. Show in T-account format the entry to write off unclaimed credit balances in customer charge accounts.

2. Show in T-account format the entry to record the transaction required by the FTC in this situation.

3. If, at the end of the accounting period, some customer charge accounts have credit balances and refund checks will not be issued until the next accounting period, show in T-account format the adjusting entry required.

# 44
# CLOSING THE BOOKS*
Ernst & Ernst

Habit is a wonderful saver of mental effort. But too close adherence to habit in business limits efficiency by shutting off initiative.

This is particularly true in the adherence of general business to the habit of following a fixed date for closing the so-called "fiscal" year.

The best date for closing the books and preparing financial statements for the "fiscal" year is when business is in its most liquid condition—when bank loans and other liabilities are lowest, accounts receivable reduced, and, especially, when the inventory is at a minimum.

The most logical date for closing *your* "fiscal" year is that time when *your* business is logically over for the twelve months—when stocks are lowest—when prices are normal—when selling is not being forced—when you are not buying heavily—when profits can be most accurately determined—when your accounting department is not working nights, or your bank is not burdened with December 31st reports. In other words, close *your* books when *your* business is most naturally through with the rush of *your* year, when proper time and attention can be given, and your public accountants can serve you best.

EDITOR'S NOTE: Yes, this piece was originally published more than 50 years ago.

## QUESTION

1. Why is the calendar year not an optimal fiscal year for many enterprises?

*From *Management and Administration*, May 1924, p. 503. Reprinted by permission of the publisher.

# 45

# ACCOUNTING FOR A DRIVE-IN DINER*
Sau Lan Chan

The drive-in diner business is highly competitive and requires a marketing strategy that stresses low price. Also, the perishable products and inventory of the business pose special problems. In this particular instance, all food is prepared on the premises and no food is kept overnight, so there is no work-in-process or finished-goods inventory. Another unique consideration is that the only source of income is from cash sales so that no accounts receivable are kept. However, because of the nature of the business, it is not only important that accurate accounting records be kept, but that a computerized financial reporting system be utilized for cost control purposes.

All accounting information and reporting can be divided into three categories:

1. Operating data
2. Tactical data
3. Strategic data

Operating data are derived from the lowest information level, the transactions which result from the organization's activities. They provide the basic record of "what happened." The initiation and placement of purchase orders, the paying of vendors and employees, the individual sales; all of these transactions represent operating data. The appropriate compilation of the data then results in various reports such as labor distribution, payroll, expense and cost ledgers and other operating transaction records.

Tactical data are needed in order to control an organization's operations. To do this, a summary of the operating data must be made. Data are summarized into the general ledger account structure and trial balances are computed. These provide accounting detail for analysis and an overview of financial operations. Tactical data highlight problem areas in specific financial reports.

Strategic data are obtained when the financial analysis is prepared. These data incorporate such statistics as the working capital position, non-food inventory balances, the ratio of current assets to liabilities, net investment, profit and its associated detail. Strategic data require minimal management review and analysis for assessing the situation and making appropriate decisions.

## FUNCTIONAL PROCEDURES

In designing a good computerized financial reporting system, we must examine the data and information flow as they relate to specific procedures. Whenever there is a substantial volume of similar operations which reflect essential business activities, a special procedure evolves as a subsystem within the total system. Examples of such procedures are cash receipts and disbursements, cash sales, accounts payable, payroll, and many others.

*From *Management Accounting*, May 1975, pp. 39—42. Reprinted by permission of the publisher.

## Cash Receipts and Disbursements

One of the major subsystems is cash receipts and disbursements. From the various documents and work sheets, the accounting office can classify the data into different sources for cash receipts and different types of disbursements. The computer will then account for the increase or decrease in the cash balance. The details of all receipts and disbursements are first entered in the "cash receipt/disbursement ledger." The summarized data are then journalized and entered in the general ledger.

## Cash Sales

Selling is the lifeblood of any business, and in the drive-in, it is also the sole source of cash receipts. Two basic characteristics of this business's selling function are that: (1) All sales are cash sales, so there is no accounts receivable subsystem, and (2) there is no sales returns and allowance procedure. Therefore, cash received from customers requires a specific control procedure. A cash register records the cash sale transaction and the sales receipt becomes the initial data source. The manager sends the money together with two deposit slips to the bank. One validated deposit slip will later go to the accounting department to serve as a check figure against the deposit amount stated in the work sheet. The manager also prepares for the accounting office a daily work sheet (called the cash register tape and deposit reconciliation) which reports the amount of cash received from each cash register and which has been depositied in the bank. The work sheet is processed, and the amount passes through the "cash receipt/disbursement ledger" into the "general ledger."

## Accounts Payable

The main function of the accounts payable subsystem is to record liability payment transactions for materials and services purchased and for other miscellaneous incurred expenses. The manager of the drive-in has full authority for purchasing. He is the one who prepares the purchase order and sends it to the vendor. A copy of the purchase order is sent to accounts payable by the manager to preserve information for later computer processing. When the purchased material is received, the receiving department makes out a receiving memo and forwards it to accounts payable department. The information is input to the system and merged with the purchase order record.

Upon receipt of an invoice from the vendor, accounts payable enters the data directly from the invoice to the computer. The data are edited, audited, and merged with the purchase order and receiving memo files. The purchase order number on the invoice is matched against the actual purchase order number to determine if such an order exists. If it matches, the computer will carry on the mechanical comparison. If it does not match, the computer will reject the data and call for an investigation. Material quantities, dollar values, due dates, terms and unit prices are also compared. If there are differences after the mechanical comparison, an exception report will be output. The report will be directed to accounts payable for investigation and correction.

If there are no differences from the mechanical comparison, a vendor invoice transaction is created which is used to update the master file and also to create registers and vendor payment checks. The vendor master file is entered into the processing activity in order to provide information (i.e., vendor name and address) for the issuance of checks. The monthly distribution journal is prepared and it in turn provides data for the cost accumulation system and the "general ledger."

When the data processing department receives the "to pay" list from accounts payable, it will start the payment processing procedure. The check, voucher, and the disbursement register will be produced mechanically. Accounts payable will audit the checks to the list they submitted for payment and also to the disbursement register. Variances will be resubmitted to data processing in the form of adjustments to the files. After the checks have been approved, they will be sent back to be processed through a check signer device for signature imprint, and to an address device which will stuff the check and print the vendor name and address on the envelope.

## Payroll

Payroll processing can be one of the more complicated procedures. However, mechanical processing can eliminate errors and save time as well. The accounting department collects employee time-clock cards twice a month for payroll processing. The department reconciles the time-clock cards to the working schedule prepared by the manager of the drive-in to make certain that the employee has worked the number of hours recorded on the working schedule. The data are input to the computer together with the employee master file which contains information like employees' names, addresses, wage rates, deductions, and tax tables. After the computer operation, the master file is updated and the pay checks are generated mechanically. The computer produces a descriptive check for each employee with all the necessary information like employee's name, total earnings, federal income tax, state tax, F.I.C.A., etc., printed on it. The total of the payroll is accumulated in the direct cost file for later use and the tax data are stored in the tax file for making tax statements and for reporting to the Internal Revenue Service.

## Inventory

In the accounting system for the drive-in, the only inventory kept is for non-food materials. There is no account for finished goods, or work-in-process since the perishable food product cannot be kept overnight.

The amount of material received can be obtained by adding all the receiving memos together; however, the lack of documentation for the issuance of material makes it impossible to directly compute the level of ending inventory. Since materials are released from the storeroom without any paper document or record, the ending inventory has to be determined by physical count. Every Monday, materials are ordered so as to return the stock to a fixed pre-determined level. Thus, every Monday, the manager takes a physical inventory and submits his count to data processing. The amount of material that needs to be ordered is computed by subtracting the ending inventory from the pre-determined level. This amount is output in report form to the manager who will then prepare the purchase orders. Ending inventory is also utilized to update the inventory master file. Ending inventory of this period will become beginning inventory of the next period. The update process includes noting the amount of materials used in the material cost file.

The material cost file, when updated, provides data for the cost control system. All inventory designated items are catalogued by commodity or material group and are identifed within the group by a serial number. Transaction data are forwarded to data processing for file updating.

## GENERAL LEDGER

The basic need for a general ledger system is to properly establish the account structure that will satisfy the needs of the organization and provide flexibility to meet changing requirements. The account structure, however, should be kept simple, logical, readily understandable and relative to recordkeeping and reporting purposes. In this instance, all entries into the general ledger are made via journal vouchers in order to meet the needs of the detailed expense and cost subsidiary ledger requirements. Journal voucher numbers are established to designate the type of transactions (purchases, payables, cash, etc.).

The general ledger includes the descriptions and numbers of the accounts, the calendar month of the data, the journal voucher number, the beginning balance by control and subaccounts, the transaction (journal voucher) activity (either debit or credit amount), and the ending balance. The journal voucher number reference is provided to establish an audit trail back to the journal detail for verification of the data. The ending general ledger balances and post-closing adjustments are summarized to the working trial balance schedule and the data are balanced. This information is then used in the preparation of the two prime financial schedules—the profit and loss statement and the balance sheet.

## CONCLUSION

The primary objective of this financial accounting system is to provide a capability for summarizing the detailed data into meaningful financial statements in order that an assessment can be made of performance, costs, and profit for the operating statement and also to determine and evaluate the status of the balance sheet accounts. The types of financial reports prepared for the drive-in can be divided into four categories:

1. Formal financial statements—The computer is used to produce required financial statements.

2. Budgeting—The computer has proved valuable in this area. It stores historical statistics and cost-volume relationships and computes the budget figures, as well as interperiod comparisons, as soon as volume figures are available.

3. Periodic statistical analyses—Many routine analyses which provide the information base for management decision-making are now available as by-products of the

accounting process. Examples are analyses of sales by product, branch and inventory status.

4. Special studies—The financial manager is responsible for the numerous special studies which measure the impact on profits of price changes, new products, etc.

## QUESTIONS

1. Prepare a set of T accounts for a drive-in diner, and record therein the routine transactions for a drive-in diner that might occur during a week. Describe each transaction recorded in a listing of transactions.

2. Prepare a diagram illustrating cash receipts and cash disbursements for a drive-in diner.

3. Prepare a diagram illustrating the accounting for the purchase of materials, supplies, and services for a drive-in diner.

4. Prepare models of an income statement and a balance sheet for a drive-in diner.

## SELECTED BIBLIOGRAPHY

Henderson, Robert H., "Day Care: A Business Operated for Profit," *Management Accounting*, April 1975, pp. 39-42.

# 46

## LINKS TO BUSINESS: JACK NICKLAUS*
Coopers & Lybrand Journal

Famous for his remarkable concentration and thoughtful approach to his golf game, Jack Nicklaus has also been accused of, and sometimes penalized for, being too slow. Nicklaus would reply, "It didn't seem slow to me. Just long enough to think it out and hit the ball." In 11 years of pro playing, he has thought it out long enough to win 17 major championships—the record so far—and amass, as one of the game's biggest money-makers, over $2 million. He has applied that same concentration and acumen to the investment of those earnings in the various enterprises that make up Golden Bear Inc., his solely owned corporation, and one of Coopers & Lybrand sports clients. (The company's name is derived from an old nickname for Nicklaus—"golden" for his blond hair and "bear" because he was quite heavy about 10 years ago.)

The 35-year-old Nicklaus is not a mere "endorser" of products but a successful entrepreneur in his own right: He owns an auto agency; he is Eastern Airlines' flying

*Excerpted and updated from *Coopers & Lybrand Journal*, Fall 1973, pp. 64—65. Reprinted by permission of the publisher.

golf pro, and also helps it set up golf tournaments. He is a golf-course designer of wide renown, with 12 courses already constructed or in process, in such diverse locations as Hilton Head, South Carolina, Cincinnati (two), Palm Beach, Columbus, and Japan (four). In addition, Jack Nicklaus represents companies that produce and market golf clubs, apparel, and other golf-related items—all carrying his trademark.

Running a company of these dimensions clearly requires skilled managerial ability. To help him operate Golden Bear, Nicklaus relies on a partnership of seven men—himself plus six others—whose alliance is based on a simple handshake. While each man has his own specialty, he is directly accountable to Nicklaus in all projects involving the corporation. Of the seven, Tom Peterson is the only man on salary. Putnam "Put" Pierman, with heavy construction experience in the Midwest, is titular head of the executive committee. Dave Sherman is a Columbus attorney who concentrates on land purchases and contracts, Ken Bowden deals with the communications end from New York, and Bill Sansing handles marketing and advertising from Austin, Texas. Jerry Halperin of the Detroit Coopers & Lybrand office is Nicklaus's tax and financial adviser and coordinator of the work of the other C&L offices outside Detroit concerned with Golden Bear activities.

Halperin and Nicklaus and his associates meet throughout the year, often at major golf tournaments. (As for Jerry Halperin's golf game, he claims it's superlative— though, out of consideration for his client's feelings, he always makes a point of losing to him.) The engagement also entails periodic trips to Japan and Europe to supervise Nicklaus's substantial overseas interests. In addition to the usual accounting and tax services, the Firm has designed a computer program to test the economic feasibility of a proposed golf course and has structured the details of certain foreign operations.

Five Coopers & Lybrand offices other than Detroit service various aspects of Golden Bear activities: Palm Beach (where the main corporate office is located), recurring audit and tax returns; Columbus, public stock offering and registration statement related to a land development project; New York, the International Consulting Services group; Chicago, management consulting; and Cincinnati, golf construction and maintenance companies.

## QUESTIONS

1. What accounting services would be needed by a golfer playing for the first time in the professional golf tournament circuit?

2. What kinds of accounting services are needed by a business organization? A nonbusiness organization? A member of a profession? A nonprofessional person?

# 47

# CATTLE ACCOUNTING*
John F. Loughlin


Realistic general and cost accounting methods and procedures are as important to successful operations in the cattle industry as they are in manufacturing or other industries. The application of accrual basis accounting and cost accounting principles to a large cattle operation, however, raises questions and problems which differ from those encountered in other industries. Some questions involved in accounting for the breeding, raising, and marketing of cattle are:

1. What are the components of the cost of a calf?
2. How should the cost of breeding animals be allocated?
3. How should operating expenses be allocated?
4. How may costs be allocated between purebred and commercial operations? . . .

The basic production of cattle operations is represented by the calves produced and the value added to commerical or immature breeding animals. Depending on operating considerations, calves may be sold in their year of birth, they may be retained for breeding purposes, or they may be raised for future sale as commercial beef. Although operations may involve primarily raised animals, it is not uncommon that they will also include purchase of commercial animals for short-term retention and sale, which would, of course, occur when pasture availability and market prices indicate that such operations may be profitable.

Mature breeding animals represent the production facilities of a cattle operation. It is an accepted practice in the cattle industry that animals which have completed their second year are considered to be breeding animals. Breeding animals will normally consist of some top grade purchased animals and improved animals developed in the breeding operations. Upgrading of breeding herds may include the annual identification of less desirable animals and the sale of substantial numbers of such animals as breeding stock. Operations also include the annual identification of nonproductive or substandard animals which are culled from the herds for commercial sale. Considering the average productive life of breeding cattle, it is generally agreed that a life of from seven to eight years from the two-year old breeding classification is realistic as the average useful life of breeding cattle.


## VALUATION OF CATTLE AT COST

Depending on intended future disposition, calf production may represent finished inventory, inventory in process or productive facilities in process. Generally accepted accounting principles indicate that in these circumstances, calves should be recorded at cost in the year of birth. Costs of maintaining commercial animals after the year of

*From *Management Accounting*, Dec. 1974, pp. 31–37. Reprinted by permission of the publisher.

birth also represent inventory costs, and should be added to initial animal costs. Similarly, costs of maintaining immature breeding animals represent additional costs of productive facilities, and should be added to initial animal costs until the animals reach breeding age.

The cost of calves generally may be considered to consist of the applicable costs of the breeding animals which produced the calves. Calf cost, therefore, should include operating expenses and depreciation of breeding animals. Although calves may be born at various times during the year, it is most expedient for cost computations to be made on the basis that all calves are born at year-end. This approach is realistic since most operating expenses apply to breeding animals as opposed to being directly applicable to calves. On this basis, operating expenses are allocated to breeding animals, immature breeding animals and commerical inventory animals, and the amounts for breeding animals are allocated to calf cost. Operating expenses so allocated should include only normal expenses, and any abnormal expenses should be expensed currently and excluded from allocations to animal costs. Depreciation charges represent the allocation of the basic cost of breeding animals to the calves produced, over the estimated useful lives of the breeding animals. With costs computed in this manner, the net cost of breeding animals produced internally would consist of their calf cost, plus maintenance costs in their first and second year, less accumulated depreciation thereafter. Purchased breeding animals would be valued at their purchased cost, plus similar maintenance costs, if any, less accumulated depreciation.

Since generally accepted accounting principles require the recording of inventory at the lower of cost or market, an adjustment to this general basis of valuation is required when the computed cost of inventory animals exceeds their net realizable value. In a profitable commercial operation, such a situation would be unusual. If this were to occur, however, it would be appropriate to write-down inventory animals costs to net realizable value.

## PHYSICAL INVENTORY OF CATTLE

Accurate determination of the cost of cattle operations requires physical verification of cattle quantities on at least an annual basis. In order that accounting computations may represent an effective control over operations, the physical inventory of cattle should be controlled and supervised by the accounting function. The unique nature of this inventory will present an interesting challenge to the accountant, and certainly a radical change from normal accounting activities.

Considerations involved in the physical inventory will be dependent on the nature of the particular operation. The counting of purebred animals is normally the easiest because they are maintained in restricted areas and are subject to accurate record-keeping as required for breed registration purposes. Other breeding animals and commerical beef cattle may be maintained in larger pastures or in large areas of open range, presenting greater inventory problems. Since interim counts of births and deaths of these animals are normally reported for operating purposes on an estimated basis, an accurate physical inventory is very important in determining the results of operations.

When cattle are maintained in smaller pastures, it may be possible to obtain accurate counts by driving a jeep through the pasture and having counts made by several individuals as the cattle pass by. In other instances, it may be necessary to have the cattle herded into a corner of the pasture and count them as they are cut out in a line along the fence. For large numbers of cattle maintained in larger pastures or on open range, it is normally necessary for riders to round up the cattle, move them to pens, and count them as they are run through a chute. It is most expedient if such inventories are made in connection with a "roundup" when cattle are gathered for operating purposes. As in other physical inventories, it is necessary for the accountant to control movement of the cattle during the inventory, and to establish an accurate cut-off for comparison of quantities with accounting records.

## BASIS OF ACCOUNTING

The breeding, raising and marketing of cattle is essentially an agricultural activity, and therefore may often be accounted for on the cash basis which is predominantly used for federal income tax purposes in the agricultural field. Indeed, certain areas of the Internal Revenue Code seem to presume that only the cash basis is used in accounting for cattle operations. The cash basis, however, may result in material omissions or inaccuracies, and therefore is not a proper basis for developing meaningful financial information. In order that the financial information will be realistic and accurate, the full accrual basis should be used in financial accounting for cattle operations.

The accounting procedures discussed in this article were developed to account for operations involving production of purebred and crossbred breeding cattle and commercial beef cattle, as well as feeder operations for commercial beef cattle. The procedures consider allocation and accumulation of costs, including depreciation of breeding animals, in herd cost centers, and allocations to determine average costs of calves produced and costs added to immature breeding cattle and commercial beef cattle. In financial statements, breeding cattle are reflected as fixed assets at cost less accumulated depreciation, and costs of commercial beef cattle are reflected as inventory.

Cattle operating expenses may generally be classified as labor, supplies and property cost. The nature and amount of expenses vary considerably, depending on the nature of the operations. Purebred operations, for instance, would involve higher cost of labor, improved pastures and feed, which would be much smaller or not applicable for commercial cattle operations.

## CATTLE ACCOUNTING PROCEDURES

The following discussion describes cattle accounting procedures which apply accrual basis cost accounting principles to a purebred and commercial cattle operation. Operations involved in these computations include two primary purebred herds identified as Herds A and B, and a significant crossbred breeding herd identified as Herd D. Other purebred bulls which are used in crossbreeding are recorded in Herd C, and the remainder of crossbred breeding animals are recorded in Herd E. Commercial beef cattle are recorded in Herd F. As indicated by the description of the herds, these operations involve the production and sale of purebred and crossbred breeding animals as well as commercial beef cattle.

In the design of these cost accounting procedures, it was apparent that significant differences in values existed between the classifications of purebred and crossbred breeding animals and commercial beef animals. The herd designations and procedures for allocation of costs, therefore, were designed to reasonably allocate costs to these classifications.

Cost computations are prepared at year-end as a basis for adjusting amounts recorded during the year. The cost computations are supported by detailed asset record cards containing the cost of raised and purchased animals by herd and year of birth. The asset record cards are used to identify the costs of sales, mortalities and transfers. In preparation for the cost computations, quantities of transactions are determined by month and year of birth for each herd from monthly operating reports and accounting records. These quantities are adjusted based on an annual physical inventory for use in the cost computations.

## Herd Schedule

The herd schedule is used to summarize animal activity and costs computed in the remainder of the computations. Cost of sales, mortalities and transfers are recorded in the total amounts reflected on the herd schedules. Allocation of operating expenses and depreciation, including calf ratio allocations, are described in the following comments.

## Allocation Factor—Animal Months

Operating expenses are allocated to the herds based on the number of animals and the time that they were held during the year. This allocation factor is known as an animal month, one animal on hand for one month. Because of the volume of sales, mortalities, etc., during the year, these transactions are detailed by month in order to more accurately allocate the expenses. They are scheduled by year of birth because animal months for sales and mortalities and total animal months for first and second year animals are required for allocation of the expenses. Calves are treated as if born at the end of the year for purposes of expense allocations, and therefore no animal months are computed for calves. Transfers recorded on these schedules may consist of crossbred calves born in the purebred herd and transferred to the other breeding or beef cattle herds. Mature breeding animals culled from the breeding herds are also recorded as transfers to the beef herd. In the animal month computation, animals transferred are treated as if held all year in the herd to which transferred on the basis that they functioned as a member of the herd to which transferred.

In the month of purchase, sale, etc., animal months are computed as held one-half month. The number of animals are multiplied by the months held to compute the animal months. The animal months are subtotaled by type of transaction and by year of birth, and the total animal months are determined for the herd as shown.

### Classification of Operating Expenses

Expenses are segregated into three classifications: Feed costs, Special expenses and Ordinary expenses. Certain other expenses are classified as selling expenses for statement purposes and are not allocated to the cattle costs. Feed costs are recorded by means of standing work orders by herd classification. Since the actual herd distribution of feed costs is available, this expense is stated separately. Of the remaining expenses some apply more to certain herds than to other herds, and other expenses apply equally to all animals. It is considered that the Herds A, B, and D are given more attention and care than are the other herds. Therefore, expenses relating to this preferential treatment are classified as special expenses. The remaining expenses which are considered to apply to all animals equally are classified as ordinary expenses.

### Allocation of Expenses to Herds

For allocation of special expenses, it has been determined that in total these expenses apply to the animals in an average ratio of three parts to the special herds to one part to the other herds. On this basis the animal months for the special herds are weighted three to one and the special expenses are distributed to the herds in the ratio of the weighted animal months. The ordinary expenses are distributed in the ratio of the original animal months. As mentioned previously, feed costs are distributed to the herds based on actual usage.

The allocation of the special expenses as described above has been adopted as an average method of allocating these expenses. Since each of the special expenses would apply to the various herds in differing degrees, it is not considered practical to allocate these expenses in a more exact manner. It is considered that this method results in a fair and reasonable overall distribution, reflecting the additional costs of maintaining these special herds.

After the total operating expenses applicable to the herds have been determined, these totals are divided by total animal months of the herds to compute the cost per animal month for each herd. Cost per animal month is the computed average cost of maintaining one animal for one month in the particular herd. This factor is used to allocate the operating expenses to the animals within the herds.

With the data available at this point, the operating expenses for all animals by year of birth and by type of transaction can be computed by multiplying the cost per animal month by the number of animal months.

As mentioned above, operating expenses of mature breeding animals are components of the cost of the calves produced, and operating expenses of immature animals are additions to the cost of these animals. The one exception to the statement is considered to be the operating expenses for sales and mortalities. In specific instances, the animals may or may not have taken part in calf production, but in general it is considered less likely that they have. Therefore, an assumption is made that sales and mortalities were not involved in calf production, and related operating expenses are charged to the cost of sales or mortalities.

## Depreciation

The second component of calf cost is depreciation of the cost of mature breeding animals. Depreciation is computed by the straight-line method. This allocation of the cost of breeding animals to the cost of calves is begun when the animals have completed their second year, the age at which they are considered to be breeding animals, and is continued based on an average estimated useful life of eight years. Estimated salvage value of $90 per head is deducted from the animal cost before computation of depreciation. In accordance with the half-year convention, one-half year's depreciation is recorded for all additions and retirements during the year.

| | | |
|---|---|---|
| Asset balance  beginning of year | $28,313.35 | |
| Less reserve balance, beginning of year | (8,423.76) | |
| Net asset amount | $19,889.59 | |
| Less salvage value, 65 animals X $90 | (5,850.00) | |
| Value subject to depreciation | $14,039.59 | |
| Divide by remaining life | ÷ 5 | |
| Total annual depreciation | $ 2,807.92 | |
| Divide by number of animals | ÷ 65 | |
| Annual depreciation per animal | $      43.20 | |
| Animals held all year | 40 | |
| Depreciation per animal | X $43.20 | $1,728.00 |
| Sales | 15 | |
| Depreciation for ½ year per animal | X $21.60 | 324.00 |
| Mortalities | 10 | |
| Depreciation for ½ year per animal | X $21.60 | 216.00 |
| Total depreciation for animals | | $2,268.00 |

Depreciation for sales and mortalities is included in the cost of these retirements on the same basis as the operating expenses applicable to these animals. The balance of the depreciation is allocated to calf cost. Of the total depreciation of $25,300 for the herd, $5,300 is recorded as cost of sales and mortalities and the balance of $20,000 is allocated to calf cost.

## Calf Ratio Allocation

Depreciation and applicable operating expenses of the mature breeding animals to this point are allocated to calf cost within each herd. This would result in proper calf cost if all breeding animals were employed only within their particular herds. Under the crossbreeding program, however, the purebred animals are crossbred between the purebred herds, and are crossbred extensively with the other breeding herds. In this situation, a portion of the costs applicable to purebred animals should be allocated to calf cost in the herd in which the calves are born.

This situation is considered in the cost computation by reallocating the calf costs based on the ratio of the total calves to the total mature breeding animals, termed the calf ratio. The calf ratio is computed as follows:

Total calves, all herds

Total mature animals at year-end, all breeding herds

$$= \frac{5,200}{4,000} = 1.3$$

This calf ratio indicates that on average it required 1.3 mature breeding animals to produce one calf. The effect of the crossbreeding is reflected in the cost computations by limiting purebred calf costs by application of the calf ratio, in this case by limiting calf cost to 130 percent of the costs of a mature animal in the particular herd. The calf ratio allocation results in excess costs being allocated from Herds A, B, C, and D to Herd E. Although this procedure does not result in actual allocation of the costs of breeding animals in the crossbreeding program, the overall results of the calf ratio allocation are considered reasonable.

## Completion of Computations

After the calf ratio allocations, the allocation of costs to the herds is completed. The costs of sales, mortalities and transfers are then determined in the following manner. For calves, the average cost of calves produced is computed, and is used to record these transactions. For immature breeding animals, transactions are recorded at the average cost at the beginning of the year. Transactions for other animals are recorded at costs determined from the asset record cards for the applicable animals, generally representing average costs for animals produced internally. As described previously, operating expenses and depreciation which have been allocated to sales and mortalities are added to the cost of these sales and mortalities. No operating expenses are involved in recording transfers between herds because, for allocation of operating expenses, transfers are treated as if the animals were held all year in the herd to which transferred. The herd schedules are then completed by recording purchases at actual cost and any returned sales at cost recorded in the year of sale.

In addition to the previously described accounting computations, operating personnel prepare an annual computation of the estimated market value of the cattle by herd and age classification. The only accounting use of this market valuation is to assure that costs of beef cattle recorded in inventory are not stated in excess of net realizable value. Although realizable value considerations are not applied to breeding animals which are recorded as fixed assets, market value comparisons for these animals are very useful to management in evaluating the overall results of operations and formulating policy regarding the retention or sale of breeding animals.

## CONCLUSION

As in other industries, realistic and accurate financial information is important for successful operations in the cattle industry. In order to produce such information, basic principles of accrual basis cost accounting must be applied to the circumstances of the particular cattle operation. The procedures illustrated in this article are considered to produce the desired financial information in a reasonable and practical manner. The application of these principles presents an interesting challenge to the accountant for a cattle operation.

## QUESTIONS

1. What is the difference between the cash basis and the accrual basis of accounting? Illustrate from *"Cattle Accounting."*

2. Prepare a listing of routine transactions that would be recorded in accounting for cattle.

3. Prepare a listing of the titles of accounts that would be utilized routinely in accounting for cattle.

4. Prepare models of financial statements for producers of cattle.

## SELECTED BIBLIOGRAPHY

Bassett, R. E. G., "The Mechanics of Garage Accounting," *Accountancy*, April 1973, pp. 18-22.

Wendell, Paul J., "Accounting Problems of Magazine Publishers," *The New York Certified Public Accountant* (now *The CPA Journal*), December 1971, pp. 922-928.

# 48

# REPORTING FOR UNITED FUND AGENCIES*
Charles T. Farley

Although the United Fund dollar represents a small percentage of the total expenditure for local health, welfare, and recreation services, the agencies receiving United Fund support administer a large percentage of the nontax money expended for these services. United Fund budgeting, therefore, is focused on the community as a whole on maintaining a service program and a system of reporting which serves the entire community. It takes into consideration the needs of the community, the attitudes of the contributing public, and the financial resources of the agencies requesting the funds. Programs of other agencies, both governmental and voluntary, not associated with the United Fund are included to determine what services are available to meet community needs.

For some agencies, the United Fund is the only source of financial support. With other agencies, the United Fund dollar represents a small percentage of total expenditures for health, welfare, and social services. In general, the United Fund has a budget balancing function in the financing of member agencies. This emphasizes the importance of budgeting and planning of health and welfare services for the entire community so that a relatively limited expenditure can produce the best results.

## THE ANNUAL CAMPAIGN FOR FUNDS

The United Fund is primarily engaged in raising funds for member agencies and judiciously allocating these funds to meet the community's health and welfare needs. It is customary in most instances for the campaign to be conducted in one year and for the funds to be expended in monthly or quarterly allocations to the agencies throughout the following year. The budgeting and accounting for these activities can best be illustrated by describing the operation of a typical United Fund Agency and its relationship with its member agencies.

Prior to the start of the fund raising campaign, usually during May or June, the agencies are asked to submit estimates of their needs for their next fiscal year to the General Budget Chairman of the United Fund. These estimates are in summary form and are accompanied by a written explanation of the increases or decreases over the current year if they are substantial in amount. At this first step, the purpose is to obtain a total needs figure for campaign purposes. Proposed expansion of programs entailing additional staff may be referred to the Community Council, the planning agency associated with the United Fund, for study and recommendation. During July and August the general budget committee of the United Fund submits estimates of total needs to the Executive Committee of the Fund and the campaign goal is established.

*From *Management Accounting*, December 1973, pp. 28—29, 30. Reprinted by permission of the publisher.

During September and October, the agencies submit detailed budgets and program material to the United Fund, whose staff reviews this material, confers with the agencies as needed, and prepares budget folios on each agency for the United Fund budget panels. For the purpose of uniformity in supplying budget information, the agencies are required to submit their budget requests on the forms furnished them by the United Fund. The use of a uniform budget form is necessary to comply with the standard classification of accounts adopted by the United Community Funds and Councils of America. Agencies are asked to develop their own classification of accounts to conform with this classification in order to facilitate budget analysis.

The forms provide for the following information:

1. Actual figures for the last complete fiscal year
2. Figures for the current fiscal year based on figures to date
3. Budgeted figures for the current year
4. Proposed figures for the new budget year

The budget forms prepared by the agency's staff are reviewed by its board of directors and formally approved before submission to the United Fund. When the budget forms are received by the United Fund, its staff assembles them by budget panel groups whose responsibility is to review these requests with the agencies and recommend to the Budget Chairman of the United Fund an allocation that will enable the agency to provide its services for the new budget year.

## THE BUDGET AND ALLOCATIONS COMMITTEE

The responsibilities of the Budget and Allocations Committee are second to none in the United Fund. It must consider community needs and establish priorities based on these needs after taking into consideration the overall funds available as a result of the campaign. To accomplish this the committee is broken down into budget panels, the number of which is determined by the number of agencies associated with the particular United Fund. The following organization chart illustrates the structure of the Committee:

Executive Committee
Budget Chairman
Budget and Allocations Committee

*Panel 1*
Area Social Agencies

Children's Home
Children's Aid Society
American Red Cross
The Salvation Army
Community Services
Family Counseling

*Panel 2*

Local Health Agencies

Visiting Nurse Assn.
Mental Health Assn.
Retarded Children
Homemaker Service
United Cerebral Palsy

*Panel 3*

Character Building Agencies

Y.M.C.A.
Y.W.C.A.
Youth Center
Boys' Club
Boy Scouts
Girl Scouts

## RESPONSIBILITIES DEFINED

The responsibilities of the Budget and Allocations Committee are defined by the United Funds and Councils of America as follows:

1. To define and identify the problems toward which agency services are directed and then to look at those services to measure their cost and effectiveness

2. To use United Fund money to balance the community's budget for a total program of services which includes all tax-supported and voluntary agencies

3. To gear the spending of the United Fund dollar to a long-range plan which takes into account changing needs and changing ideas as to how needs should be met

4. To deal equitably with the financial needs of the particular group of agencies the United Fund is currently supporting

5. To see that the funds contributed to United Fund campaigns are used in the best interests of the community and that the agencies operate in the most economical and efficient way possible

6. To work actively with the Community Health and Welfare Council and to cooperate and plan with tax-supported local, state and federal agencies

## BUDGET PANELS

It is customary for each budget panel to consist of a panel chairman, vice-chairman, and six or more panel members, depending upon the number of agencies the panel is responsible for. These panels represent a cross section of the community including contributors, management, labor and professional groups. They have the responsibility for reviewing agency budgets, meeting with the agency boards and staff, and recommending to the general budget chairman a suitable allocation that will enable the agency to provide its particular services. The panel's recommendation is reviewed by the General Budget Chairman and the Executive Committee of the United Fund, who determine the final disposition of funds to the agencies based on campaign results.

Once the allocations are agreed upon, payment is made to the agencies monthly or quarterly depending on the arrangement between the particular agency and the United Fund. Periodically, the agencies are required to submit quarterly reports of actual support revenue and expenses for the current quarter and projected figures for the following quarter. The payments to the agencies are charged against their allocation for the year, and they may not exceed their approved budget without special review and approval by the Executive Committee of the United Fund.

If an agency does not need the full allocation at the end of the year, it must return the unused portion to the United Fund after allowing for an agreed upon working balance. Such balance normally reverts to the United Fund either through a remittance or by treating the surplus as a payment against the succeeding year's allocation. The United Fund cannot assume responsibility for unauthorized deficits in agency service operations.

It should be pointed out that the formal agreement drawn up between the United Fund and the agency usually requires that the agency provide annually a statement of its income and expenditures and a statement of financial condition prepared by an independent certified public accounting firm.

## CONCLUSION

Voluntary health and welfare agencies receive their support from a variety of sources: donations from the public, service fees from tax supported government agencies, governmental grants, endowments, and gifts restricted for specific purposes. In the past, with each agency recording and reporting in a different manner, contributors and purchasers of services found their financial reports incomplete and misleading. They did not show, for example, from what sources the agency obtains its income, how much is spent to provide its services, and how much is spent on supporting services such as administrative costs and campaign costs, if any. Furthermore, this information was not presented in a uniform and understandable manner.

Then, too, many agencies report on a cash basis instead of an accrual basis. Pledges and fees for services that the agency has coming at the year end, when not disclosed because the agency is reporting on a cash basis, can be very misleading to the reader.

To correct these shortcomings in accounting and reporting, "Standards of Accounting and Financial Reporting for Voluntary Health and Welfare Organizations" were adopted by the United Community Funds and Councils of America. The budget forms described are in conformity with the Standards.

## QUESTIONS

1. Why do nonprofit organizations regard the budget as their chief accounting statement instead of the balance sheet or a statement of receipts and disbursements?

2. Illustrate why a nonprofit organization should account on an accrual basis rather than a cash basis.

3. How does accounting for a nonprofit organization differ from accounting for a profit-making organization?

## SELECTED BIBLIOGRAPHY

Buerke, Edwin A., "The Small-Business Accountant," *Management Accounting*, November 1972, pp. 51-52.

Finnell, Jack C., "Accounting for Country Clubs: A Different View," *Management Accounting*, July 1972, pp. 16, 17, 20.

# 49

# NUCLEAR FUEL ACCOUNTING*

William L. Ureel

Accountants employed by the electric utilities will soon be called upon to perform their accounting services for the new nuclear fueled power plants. The development of fast breeder reactors that will be needed to meet our expanding power needs will present many new problems to the accountant. Since breeder reactors produce more fuel than they consume when operated, the accounting implications can only be imagined, especially with regard to the nuclear fuel that is used in their operation. . . .

Atomic power plants are really nothing new; they have been on the American scene for more than a decade. The first commercial nuclear power plant became operational in 1959, and by June 30, 1972, approximately three percent of all power generated in the United States came from the 25 operable nuclear plants. Today, there are approximately 50 plants being constructed, and 60 more are planned. This will allow the United States electric power industry to satisfy the ever-increasing demand with minimal impact or disruption of the environment.

During the past ten years, the demand for power has roughly doubled in our highly industrialized society. We can, therefore, appreciate some of the problems faced by the power industry in satisfying this demand during a period of rapidly rising construction costs, and of great public concern about air and thermal pollution. The trend to this new source of electrical energy is also heightened by the shortage and rising cost of low sulphur coal, oil, and natural gas which is especially acute in certain areas of our country. On the other hand, the demand for nuclear power plants is tempered by delays in construction schedules and excessively lengthy licensing procedures.

## THERE IS NO EXPERIENCE OR PRECEDENT
## FOR REFERENCE

Until recently, all nuclear fuel was supplied by the United States Atomic Energy Commission (AEC) on a lease basis. The accounting, therefore, was much simpler,

*From *Management Accounting*, July 1973, pp. 14–16, 24. Reprinted by permission of the publisher.

requiring only a lease expense treatment.[1] Now the utilities are required to purchase the fuel or to lease it from private firms. Since the nuclear fuel cycle varies from three to six years, this will greatly affect the complexity of nuclear fuel accounting. In addition, the accounting for nuclear fuel will require the solving of many unique problems. There is virtually no body of practical experience or precedent for reference. The accountants for the AEC and the private fuel fabricators do, of course, have some experience, but it is not in the commercial area of a utility.

## THE FUEL CYCLE

Before the accounting function can be explained, a description of the fuel cycle in present-day nuclear plants which use water as a heat transfer agent is necessary. The nuclear fuel cycle begins with the mining of the uranium ore. The uranium ore is then refined and is sent through a chemical conversion process which both purifies the uranium and prepares it for insertion into the gaseous diffusion plant. In the diffusion plant, the uranium is enriched. This simply increases the relative abundance of $U_{235}$ in the uranium fuel. The enriched uranium is then chemically converted into its final form, pressed into small pellets, and inserted into long tubes of zirconium or stainless steel. A fuel assembly consists of a number of these jacketed uranium-filled rods held together in a fixed lattice arrangement. The finished assemblies are shipped to a plant site where they are placed in the reactor for use. There, the outer jackets prevent the release of fission products into the coolant and the lattice arrangement permits the water to circulate between the uranium-filled rods so that the heat may be removed and converted to steam. The steam is then used to generate electricity in turbines in the same way that it is done in a coal-fired boiler generating plant. The fuel as it is used gradually loses its enrichment as the fissionable uranium is consumed. What remains of the spent fuel has a large residual value due to the amount of uranium remaining and to the plutonium that has been created during the reaction process. On the average it is expected that one-quarter to one-third of the fuel assemblies will be replaced each year during the annual plant shutdown period. The used fuel is highly radioactive and must be cooled for four to six months after removal from the reactor. Then it is shipped to a chemical processing plant where the assemblies are dissolved and the uranium and plutonium are recovered.

## THE FEDERAL POWER COMMISSION CHART OF ACCOUNTS

On January 1, 1970, the Federal Power Commission, after a two-year special study of nuclear fuel accounting, established a system of accounts which the utilities are to use to account for the ownership of special nuclear materials. Its stated purpose is to account for each phase of the fuel cycle including the salvage value of the spent fuel assemblies which may be sold, placed in storage, or reused by the utility in the

[1]After January 1, 1971, the United States Atomic Energy Commission withdrew from the business of leasing uranium for fuel. The uranium it has on existing lease, however, continued until June 30, 1973.

fabrication of new fuel assemblies. All power utilities with annual revenues greater than one million dollars must follow these regulations.

The account numbers and titles are described below. Account numbers 120.1 through 120.5 are utility plant accounts, number 157 is a current asset account, and number 518 is an operation and maintenance expense account. The sum of all the 120 subaccounts represents the net book value of all the nuclear fuel a utility has in its operations except for nuclear materials held for sale. The rules established for the use of each of these accounts or subaccounts follow:

**Account No. 120.1:** Nuclear Fuel in Process of Refinement, Conversion, Enrichment, and Fabrication

This account is used to accumulate the costs or investment related to the acquisition of nuclear fuel assemblies including all processing of the uranium, fabrication, and shipping costs to the plant site. The salvage value of any nuclear materials being processed for reuse in fuel assemblies is also recorded in this account. Exhibit 1 illustrates the estimated costs for the initial fuel loading of a typical 1,000 megawatt light water reactor. After all the original charges are recorded and the fuel assemblies are at the plant site, the total cost is transferred to another 120 subaccount, depending upon whether the fuel is placed into storage or directly into the reactor.

**Account No. 120.2:** Nuclear Fuel Materials and Assemblies—Stock Account

This is an account established to handle various storage situations. It is to be debited and Account No. 120.1 is to be credited for the original acquisition cost of the fuel assemblies while they are waiting to be placed into the reactor or to be held as spares. Nuclear materials valued at cost (which are being held by the firm for future use) are shown in this account. Also recorded in this account is the original cost of partially irradiated fuel assemblies being held in stock for reinsertion into a reactor, testing, etc.

**Account No. 120.3:** Nuclear Fuel Assemblies in Reactor

The initial cost of all the fuel assemblies which are within the reactor are debited to this account while either Account No. 120.1 or 120.2 is credited. (A core of a large boiling water reactor contains about 800 fuel assemblies with a value of approximately $40,000,000. A pressurized water reactor contains about 200 assemblies with nearly the same total value.)

**Account No. 120.4:** Spent Nuclear Fuel

The original costs of the fuel assemblies removed from the reactor and in the process of cooling are transferred from Account No. 120.3, "Nuclear fuel assemblies in reactor," to this account. It takes about four to six months for the assemblies to cool enough—as far as heat and radioactivity are concerned—to permit shipping and reprocessing. This account is credited and Account No. 120.5, "Accumulated provision for amortization of nuclear fuel assemblies," is debited with the original cost of these assemblies after they have cooled.

**Exhibit 1    Typical Investment in Initial Fuel Loading for a 1,000 Megawatt Nuclear Plant**

| DESCRIPTION OF ITEM | AMOUNT IN MILLIONS |
|---|---|
| Uranium ore including refinement | $13.0 |
| Conversion | 1.8 |
| Enrichment | 12.0 |
| Fabrication | 11.0 |
| Shipping and miscellaneous engineering | .8 |
| Interest during construction | 2.0 |
| Total investment | $40.6 |

**Account No. 120.5:** Accumulated Provision for Amortization of Nuclear Fuel Assemblies

This account is to be credited and Account No. 518, "Nuclear fuel expense," (an operating expense account) is to be debited for the amortization of the net cost of the fuel assemblies used to produce electrical energy. Net cost is equal to the original cost, less or plus the expected value of the uranium and plutonium produced, plus the reprocessing and shipping costs. This account should also be credited with the net salvage value of uranium, plutonium, and other by-products when such items are sold, transferred or otherwise disposed. It will be easiest to charge reprocessing costs and credit the value of these salvage items directly to this account in all cases. Exhibit 2 illustrates the major factors related to salvage value of nuclear fuel. In addition, this account is to be debited with the original cost of these assemblies after they have cooled and Account No. 120.4, "Spent nuclear fuel," is to be credited.

**Exhibit 2    Typical Salvage Value and Reprocessing Costs for a 1,000 Megawatt Nuclear Plant**

| DESCRIPTION OF ITEM | AMOUNT IN MILLIONS |
|---|---|
| Salvage value of uranium | $4.5 |
| Salvage value of plutonium | 7.0 |
| Less reprocessing costs | −5.0 |
| Net salvage value | $6.5 |

Note: Normally only one batch is processed at a time; the dollar values above are for a full fuel loading and are presented only for illustration.

**Account No. 157:** Nuclear Materials Held for Sale

This account includes the net salvage value of uranium and other materials held by the company for sale or other disposition that will not be reused by the company in its operations. Differences between the values carried in this account and the amount received at time of sale are to be debited or credited as appropriate to Account No. 518 at the time of the sale.

**Account No. 518:** Nuclear Fuel Expense

Charges to this expense account are made on the basis of the net cost of the fuel (original cost less net salvage value) distributed according to the thermal energy produced in such periods. Adjustments due to significant changes in the estimated net salvage values of materials held in Account No. 157, "Nuclear materials held for sale," and the amount realized upon the final disposition of the materials are debited or credited to this account. Significant market price declines of materials held in Account No. 157, "Nuclear materials held for sale," may be recognized at the time the market decline occurs. If the change in market value occurs when the nuclear fuel is in the reactor, the decline is to be amortized over the remaining life of the fuel. (No details are given as to how market increases are to be recorded. Most likely they should be recorded through adjustments to the amortization rate over the remaining life of the fuel.)

## THE EFFECTS OF NUCLEAR ACCOUNTING

The following are some of the significant impacts which this accounting system for nuclear fuel will have upon the utility industry in the United States. It does, of course, affect the balance sheet of the firm, but it also affects the firm's financial posture in other ways. For instance, fixed assets possessed by a utility are a good secure base for a loan or bond issue. Financing through leasing is also a possibility for some of the utilities, and many investors are showing an interest in this area. Since the accounting treatment of nuclear fuel is not entirely clear, one of the most significant effects may be to treat the nuclear fuel as a fixed asset. This permits the firm to include a substantial investment in its rate base.

Some of the practical problems which the accountant will have to cope with, as we envision them, are listed below. First, obtaining sound values or dollar amounts for the estimated salvageable uranium and the plutonium by-product will be extremely difficult. One reason is that the economic laws of supply and demand have not had an opportunity to exert themselves on these elements as yet. In addition, the extent to which plutonium will be used as a nuclear fuel and its relative value is not entirely clear. The prospect of utilizing plutonium as a nuclear fuel is bright, but this source of fuel is just now undergoing development and testing. The disposition of radioactive waste materials could also have quite an effect on operations. Aggressive environmentalist activity in this area could add considerably to the cost. At the present time, various methods are being studied. The burial of solidified wastes in natural salt deposits is one method receiving serious consideration.

Since they are to be treated as fixed assets, the depreciation of the nuclear fuel assemblies would not be handled on a time basis as is customary with most fixed assets (i.e., straight line, sum of the years digits, etc.) but would be related to the thermal energy produced. In calculating the quantity of thermal energy produced in a given period, the nuclear fuel specialist will be confronted with many variables such as the electrical energy produced, plant efficiency, plant design, fuel specifications, and the location of the assemblies within the reactor. The management of nuclear fuel is a new career specialty for physicists which requires the use of complex computer programs to obtain maximum utilization of the fuel. . . .

The accountant will, of course, require technical assistance to obtain the information he needs to make his monthly amortization charge to fuel expense. The accountant handling the accounting for nuclear fuel should understand the basics of the use of this fuel so that he may apply the general rule of reasonableness and correlate his records with actual events.

## SELECTION OF UNIT TO RECORD COSTS

An area in which the accountant plays a major role is the selection of the unit to be used to record costs and to be used as a basis for amortization calculations, accounting entries, and records. Should this unit of record be a core, one complete plant loading of fuel, a batch, or an individual assembly? The core loading may be too large a unit of record because all of the fuel will not be replaced at one time. Usually, only one-fourth to one-third of a core is replaced at a time. On the other hand, a batch, or an assembly, does not present this problem and would work satisfactorily as a basis for accounting. A "batch" of fuel is a group of assemblies which are inserted into the core at the same time and are removed from the core at the same time. This method would keep the details down to the bare minimum for average plant operations, and the average unit cost and amortization could be calculated in the event it was necessary to remove a fuel assembly for testing.

However, accounting records kept on a per-assembly basis may actually be the best course of action. For one thing, they would be more accurate whenever exceptions to the normal one-third or one-fourth batch were made. The physicist, for his purposes, will also require that his computer programs be operated on a per-assembly basis, and all the accounting information could be contained in these same programs. Thus, the accounting cost would not be increased except in the allocation of some common bills such as freight and insurance charges. The input of cost factors into the computer programs would then be the responsibility of the accountant. These would include, for example, cost accumulation, the rates used to determine the interest on construction, and changes in the net salvage value due to variations in the market price.

## TREATMENT OF FUEL AS A FIXED ASSET

The interest costs, or carrying charges, related to the investment in nuclear fuel during the different phrases of fabrication, initial testing of the core during its use, cooling and storage have not yet been completely defined. The interest on the investment of

$40,000,000 for a nuclear fuel core during mining, conversion, enrichment, and assembly fabrication would be comparable with the treatment of other fixed assets in the realm of plant accounts. For the first core, the split between "interest during construction" and normal carrying charges would most likely be made on the commercial power date. This is the date usually noted by utilities. However, should the carrying charge also be computed and capitalized for the period when a batch of fuel is spent in low-power-testing, cooling, and reprocessing phases of the nuclear fuel cycle? It is probably more reasonable that carrying charges during these operating phases of the fuel cycle are not capitalized, since the utility now has an opportunity to earn a reasonable return on its fuel investment. During periods of low-power testing, cooling, and fuel reprocessing, the utility will have some funds, probably in excess of $5,000,000 in active assets. However, unless interest expense is recorded by the utility in some manner such as a reprocessing cost, the utility will not be compensated for this investment.

The audit aspects are interesting to explore since, due to the radiation hazard of nuclear fuel assemblies, a visual examination or a physical inventory is not practical. Therefore, the records required by the Atomic Energy Commission related to the purchase, movement or sale of nuclear material must be used by the auditor to verify the physical presence or location of the fuel. However, the amortization, especially the related net salvage values, will be difficult to verify until experience is gained throughout the utility industry.

## CONCLUSION

It is important that the accountant, to reflect the financial aspects of a transaction properly, have a working knowledge of the nuclear fueled operation. To obtain it, he will require time—approximately five to ten years—to allow for practical experience on all phases of the nuclear fuel cycle. In the meantime, discussions and rulings will be needed before we find a uniform method of handling this form of accounting in all its phases.

## QUESTIONS

1. Set up T accounts for Accounts 120.1 through 120.5, 157, and 518; write in each account descriptions of the transactions that increase or decrease it.

2. What are the effects that the accounting for nuclear fuel will have upon a customer of the United States utility industry?

3. Discuss the unit problem in accounting for nuclear fuel.

# 50
## A LOOK AT ACCOUNTING DOWN UNDER*
Kenneth H. Spencer

At first glance financial statements issued by accountants in Australia appear quite different from those issued in the United States. Not only are the assets and liabilities shown on the wrong sides of the balance sheet (from the U.S. viewpoint) but some items are called by the wrong name. Stock to an Australian (or Englishman) is inventories to an American and debts to an Australian are receivables. A deeper examination of the differences, however, reveals that they arise in a limited number of areas and are largely of form rather than of substance.

In the United States the requirements of both form and substance were developed as a package by the professional accounting bodies within the legislative body (the Securities and Exchange Commission) also pronouncing on both aspects. In Australia, the lead in pronouncing on "form" has been very much the domain of the legislature while pronouncements on "substance" has been the prerogative of the profession. This pattern reflects the opinion of Lord Justice Lindley who, in the English case of Lee vs. Neuchatel Asphalte Co. (1889) said: "There is nothing at all in the Acts about how dividends are to be paid, nor how profits are to be reckoned; all that is left, and very judiciously and properly left, to the commercial world."

Legislation covering the form of financial statements is embodied in a series of Companies Acts which are similar to the United Kingdom Companies Act. Each of the six States and two Territories of Australia have Companies Acts. These Acts, which are broadly uniform, contain requirements on accounting and auditing matters including:

Public filing of financial statements of public companies and subsidiaries of local and foreign public companies;

The form and content of financial statements of all companies, whether or not their accounts must be filed;

The appointment of auditors.

While referring to the Companies Acts it is important to know that in Australia (and certain other countries) the parent company, whether local or not, is not liable for the debts of its subsidiaries. As a result the Companies Acts require a company to appoint an auditor to audit and report (along with directors and principal accounting officers—the Australian equivalent of the financial controller) on the truth and fairness of the consolidated financial statements and the separate financial statements of the parent and each subsidiary; the subsidiary company statements are not circulated to shareholders of the parent but are publicly filed. This requirement to audit and file the financial statements of each subsidiary contrasts with U.S. practice and is often not readily understood by overseas companies incorporating subsidiaries in Australia. The Companies Acts in fact go further and provide that in the case of private or family

*From *World*, Spring 1975, pp. 33–35. Reprinted by permission of the publisher.

investment types of companies they must either have their financial statements audited or file publicly a set of unaudited financial statements. The audits referred to in all cases are full scope examinations.

While company law has historically been the responsibility of each state, the federal government broke precedent by introducing into the federal parliament in December, 1974, the Corporations and Securities Industry Bill which, if enacted, will provide *inter alia* for foreign corporations and local public companies to become subject to its provisions. The accounting requirements follow those of the states but also require disclosure of turnover by classes of business—this is not required by the state acts. This bill is seen by many as a forerunner to a bill establishing a Securities and Exchange Commission which may also break precedent and defy Lord Lindley by legislating on accounting principles. Although Australian accountants have been critical of the seemingly meaningless mass of information required by recent amendments to Companies Acts to be disclosed in financial statements, earlier Companies Acts in their time were progressive legislation. The Victorian Companies Act of 1938 is believed to be the first corporate legislation in the world to require the issue of consolidated financial statements. It was not until 1948 that the United Kingdom Companies Act contained a similar requirement.

Before turning to pronouncements on accounting practices it is worth noting that there are two main accounting bodies in Australia: The Institute of Chartered Accountants in Australia whose members in the main consist of public accountants and their staff, and The Australian Society of Accountants whose members are drawn more from industry and the public service.

Partners in the larger local and international firms are almost invariably chartered accountants. A merger of these two bodies was attempted in 1969 but proved unsuccessful. However, since that time the two bodies have worked closely together and pronouncements on accounting practice (called Statements of Accounting Standards) are now issued by a joint committee of the two bodies. It is not unreasonable to expect a continuation of efforts to amalgamate the two groups. . . .

The Institute requires its members, whether acting as director, principal accounting officer or auditor, to conform with Statements of Accounting Standards. Directors and principal accounting officers have separate reports in front of the financial statements. Where the financial statements contain a significant departure it should be disclosed and explained. The nature of the departure may give rise to the need for a member to issue a qualified report.

Statements of Accounting Standards issued to date include: Presentation of Balance Sheets, Profit and Loss Statements, Accounting for Company Income Tax, Materiality in Financial Statements, Disclosure of Accounting Methods Used in Preparing Financial Statements, Depreciation of Non Current Assets.

Exposure drafts are current on: Accounting for extractive industries, Accounting for changes in the purchasing power of money (preliminary exposure draft based on the United Kingdom statement), Equity Accounting, Inventories, Events occurring after balance date, Translation of amounts in foreign currencies.

In addition the accounting bodies will be issuing a statement later this year dealing with replacement value accounting. It is expected that this would take the form of a preliminary exposure draft.

The Statements of Accounting Standards issued by the Australian bodies are broadly comparable to statements issued in the United States and United Kingdom. There are exceptions, of course. In Australia, as in the U.K., it is accepted (and common) practice to allow upward revaluations of non current assets. The surplus arising from the revaluation does not form part of the net profit for the period but is taken directly to a reserve account (surplus account) and included in the shareholders' funds (shareholders' equity) section of the balance sheet.

A bonus issue of shares (stock dividend) is often made from this reserve but it is not regarded as an available source of profits from which to pay a cash dividend and only in a rare situation would such a dividend be paid.

A provision of the Companies Act which influences accounting and which is at variance with U.S. practice is a provision that a company cannot acquire its own shares, or for that matter finance the acquisition of its shares by another legal entity. The provision does not preclude an Australian company from redeeming its redeemable preference shares but does mean that it cannot hold treasury stock in the way its American counterpart can.

Although Australian accounting standards and legal requirements have been influenced greatly by the United Kingdom, auditing practices have been influenced significantly by United States practices and experience; although, again, this may not be obvious from the form of the audit report.

As referred to earlier, the audit appointment of companies is a statutory one under the provisions of the Companies Acts and the form of the auditors report is prescribed by those Acts. The report in addition to expressing an opinion on the financial statements must also state whether or not they comply with the provisions of the Companies Acts. It does not contain separate scope and opinion paragraphs nor references to generally accepted auditing standards or generally accepted accounting principles applied consistently. However, it is accepted in Australia that these must be satisfied as conditions precedent to the issue of an unqualified audit report.

Auditing standards in Australia have not been formalized to the extent that they have in the United States. However, a number of statements have been issued which bear a similarity to statements issued in the United States. . . .

Finally, it should be noted that the Companies Acts provide for the appointment of an auditor by the shareholders on a permanent basis. Except in the case of private family companies the appointment can only be terminated with the approval of a statutory body or at the time that a company becomes a subsidiary of another company or he dies.

In summary, accounting and auditing practices in Australia have been derived in their legal aspects substantially from the United Kingdom. Once the differences of form and terminology are mastered the differences in approach with the United States are minimal. In many ways the procedures and practices are a half-way house between those of the U.K. and U.S.

## QUESTIONS

1. What are the differences between financial statements issued by accountants in Australia and those issued by accountants in the United States?

2. What are consolidated financial statements?

3. What are the principal differences between auditing in Australia and auditing in the United States?

## SELECTED BIBLIOGRAPHY

Asselman, Rorer J., "Accounting in Belgium and Luxembourg," *Accountancy*, April 1973, pp. 10-16.

Barbier, Guy, "Accounting in France," *Accountancy*, October 1972, pp. 10-17.

Goettsche, Hans G., "Accounting in Germany," *Accountancy*, August 1972, pp. 24-31.

Tenz, Walter, "Accounting in Italy," *Accountancy*, November 1972, pp. 20-30.

# 51
# BOOKKEEPING MADE EASY
## Maurice Stans*
Edward Sorel

At last, a book on accounting for those who can't even make their checkbooks balance. The author, a member of the Accounting Hall of Fame, shows that it isn't really necessary to keep books to be a bookkeeper. One method readers will like is to write down carefully all income on any scrap of paper that's handy—even the inside of a matchbook will do—and keep them all together in a safe place that you're likely to forget. The neophyte accountant will appreciate Mr. Stans's simple, concise language as he explains the basic difference between multiplication and subtraction, why cheap pencils without erasers may prove more costly than expensive pencils with erasers, and how to make your amnesia work to your advantage.

EDITORS' NOTE: The above excerpt is a parody of a book that might be written by Maurice Stans. Mr. Stans was the only accountant and former government official to be indicted in the Watergate investigation. Mr. Stans achieved prominence in accounting before becoming a Cabinet officer in the Eisenhower and Nixon administrations. This satire is based upon Mr. Sorel's interpretation of the testimony Mr. Stans gave at the congressional Watergate hearings.

## QUESTIONS

1. Speculate about the possible effects of the Watergate investigation on the public accountability of organizations.

*From "Perish and Publish," **New York**, Oct. 29, 1973, p. 45. Reprinted by permission of the publisher.

2. Although practically every individual involved in the Watergate investigation was a lawyer, what do you feel are possible implications for the accounting profession?

# 52
# THE NATIONAL CHART OF ACCOUNTS OF THE U.S.S.R.*
D. T. Bailey

The period immediately following the October Revolution of 1917 was unpropitious for the development of accounting in Russia. Because of the dislocation caused by the civil war, the wars of foreign intervention and the regime of War Communism (1918-1921), during which there was an attempt to abolish the use of money, the practice of accounting declined. An opportunity to resuscitate accounting was provided by the change from War Communism to the New Economic Policy. N.E.P. was marked by the restoration of a monetary economy, the stabilization of the unit of currency, and the competitive coexistence of state-owned and private enterprises. The Supreme Council for the National Economy (V.S.N.Kh.) attempted to bring some semblance of order into the keeping of accounts by state enterprises. Progress was slow. In 1921 V.S.N.Kh. had requested its 220 subordinated trusts to compile balance sheets as at 1 November, but only 106 companies complied.[1]

The leaders of the revolutionary regime in Soviet Russia placed considerable importance upon accounting as an indispensable mechanism for overseeing, or monitoring, the operation of the economy. In the words of Lenin, ". . . widespread, general universal accounting and control, the accounting and control of the amount of labour performed and of the distribution of products—is the essence of the socialist transformation . . .".[2] During the 1920s successive congresses of the Russian Communist Party underlined the urgent need for an adequate and dependable system of accounting. For this reason a comprehensive standardized accounting was developed gradually and applied throughout industry and commerce. The initial step was the creation of a national chart of accounts.

The first *plan schetov* or chart of accounts, was drafted at a Conference of the Book-keepers of State Industry and published in the official journal *Accounting* in 1925.[3] The development of the chart of accounts was motivated by the desire to

*From *The Australian Accountant*, June 1975, p. 286—289. Reprinted by permission of the publisher.

[1] S. A. Shchenkov, *Sistema Schetov i Bukhgalterskii Balans Prepriyatiya*, Moscow 1973, p. 6.

[2] V. J. Lenin, "How to Organize Emulation," in *Questions of the Socialist Organization of the Economy*—articles and speeches, Progress Publishers, Moscow, undated, p. 88.

[3] S. A. Shchenkov, op. cit., p. 7.

increase control over the nationalized enterprises by the state authorities. Its adoption was obligatory for all state enterprises. Primarily, the accounts chart was a device for strengthening administrative control over, and for ensuring a proper accounting for resources allotted to, the enterprises. It was not intended, except incidentally, to be either a device for aiding enterprise management, which was expected to be guided by the requirements of the state plan, or a tool of national economic management, which was effected through the state planning mechanism. Hopefully, the chart of accounts would contribute to the task of reducing production costs, it being considered to be "the central problem of industry to which all other tasks must be subordinated" according to the directives of the XV Party Congress held in 1927.[4] The chart of accounts was characterized by:

1. a classification of accounting data under headings useful to the supervising authorities;
2. a structuring of accounts enabling the supervising authorities to exercise, largely through the state banking network, an on-going control over the financial activities of enterprises.

Summarized balance sheets for all-union state manufacturing industry were compiled by V.S.N.Kh. for each of the years 1923-1928, and for the years 1938 and 1939 by the Commissariat of Finance, further work being prevented by the outbreak of war. At the present time the Central Statistical Administration summarizes the major financial indicators concerning profit earnings, turnover tax, profit appropriations, profitability, fixed and circulating capital and bank credit.[5]

At the beginning of 1932 V.S.N.Kh. had been divided into three commissariats for the heavy, light and forestry industries and in later years additional commissariats for particular industries were established. The commissariats assumed responsibility for the development and application of the chart of accounts within their respective industries. Gradually, as the commissariats on behalf of their own industries incorporated modifications into the national chart of accounts, there evolved a series of mutually incompatible charts for different industries.

With the aim of eradicating the discrepancies between the charts of accounts for different industries the Commissariat for Finance, in 1940, prepared a unified chart of accounts for industrial enterprises.[6] This accounts chart was intended for adoption by union, republican and local industrial enterprises, irrespective of the accounting system employed. Because of the Nazi invasion of 1941 the adoption of the new chart of accounts was delayed, its implementation not becoming obligatory until 1946. At that date a simplified version of the accounts chart for application in local enterprises was published.[7] Three years later, in 1949, a shortened version of the chart of accounts was

[4]Op. cit., p. 10.
[5]Op. cit., p. 42.
[6]Op. cit., p. 26.
[7]Op. cit., p. 30.

recommended for use with the journal voucher system of accounting[8] which was being introduced into some major enterprises. The journal voucher system embraced the use of matrix accounting, and the supporting standardized cost collection and cost distribution schedules provided an alternative means for the classification and accumulation of expenditures under appropriate headings. With the use of this accounting system some of the monthly returns, required to be submitted to the supervising authorities, could be prepared directly from the supporting schedules, thereby by-passing the main ledger enshrining the chart of accounts.

To obviate the necessity for more than one chart of accounts in industry the Ministry of Finance, in conjunction with the Central Statistical Administration, issued in 1954 a revised accounts chart for use by union and republican enterprises.[9]

In spite of the continual developments extending over a period of 30 years, in the late 1950s separate charts of accounts were being employed in manufacturing industry, construction, supply and marketing organizations, motor transport and so on. In 1960 the Ministry of Finance and the Central Statistical Administration promulgated a new version of the chart of accounts for adoption by all enterprises, whether under union, republican or local control, in all branches of the state sector of the economy, including manufacturing industry, construction and agriculture (i.e., state farms).[10] Technically the collective farms belong to the co-operative sector of the economy and, consequently, the introduction of the new unified chart of accounts was not obligatory although it is being increasingly adopted.[11] With minor modifications the 1960 chart of accounts is still in operation.

Before turning to a consideration of the 1960 chart of accounts it may be useful to outline briefly the nature of Soviet accounting.

The supersession of the Tzarist term *schetovodstvo* (account keeping) by the Soviet term *uchet* (recording) reflected the disappearance of the demarcation between business accounting and business statistics. The genus uchet consists of the species:

1. *bukhgalterskii uchet*, or double-entry book-keeping, which records the stocks and flows through the enterprise in monetary terms;

2. *operativnyi uchet*, or operational accounting, which comprises both production statistics and minutiae of cost accounting maintained in either monetary or non-monetary terms;

3. *statisticheskii uchet*, or descriptive statistics, which is concerned with the abstraction of a battery of plan fulfilment indicators from the records of bukhgalterskii uchet and operativnyi uchet.

Bukhgalterskii uchet, unlike operativnyi uchet, is an integrated part of the all-union standardized accounting system. The former is subordinated to the requirements of

[8]Loc. cit.

[9]Op. cit., pp. 31–32.

[10]Op. cit., pp. 38–39.

[11]M. Z. Vaitsman, *Uchet, Analiz i Reviziya pri Zhurnal'no–Ordernoi Forme Schetovodstva*, Kishinev 1964, p. 13.

the state authorities, the latter to the needs of the enterprise. Bukhgalterskii uchet is a comprehensive system of accounting administered by the chief book-keeper of the enterprise. Operativnyi uchet comprises an assorted collection of records maintained, according to inclination, by various supervisors and managerial specialists. As a first approximation, bukhgalterskii uchet may be equated with financial accounting and operativnyi uchet with cost accounting.

Such a distinction helps to identify their respective contents, but not the manner of maintaining the records. There are not separate systems of financial accounts and cost accounts employing different schemes of expenditure classification. Instead, in an integrated system of industrial accounting, expenditures are classified functionally. Bukhgalterskii uchet comprises first, second and third order accounts, which are called synthetical accounts, subaccounts and analytical accounts, respectively corresponding to major control accounts, subsidiary control accounts and ledger accounts. For example, the synthetical accounts include the control accounts for raw materials, production (i.e., work-in-progress) and finished goods. The individual items of stock are accommodated in the analytical accounts. Generally speaking, the analytical accounts contain a detailed breakdown of the assets and liabilities summarized in the synthetical accounts. Accounting for the costs of operations, processes and the manufacturing cost of individual products falls within the ambit of operativnyi uchet. The general effect has been to "tie-in cost accounting in a way that does not disturb . . . the closing of the books".[12]

The officially sanctioned chart of accounts is restricted to the major and subsidiary control accounts.

Two digits within the range 01-99 are allotted to each of eighty-odd major control accounts grouped into eleven divisions:

| I | Basic Means of Production |
| II | Production Stocks |
| III | Production Expenditure |
| IV | Completed Output, Commodities and Realization |
| V | Monetary Resources |
| VI | Current Accounts |
| VII | Appropriations |
| VIII | Shortages and Losses |
| IX | Funds and Provisions |
| X | Bank Credit and Finance |
| XI | Financial Results |

The classification follows the cycle of business activity. Basic means of production, or fixed assets, are obtained, production stocks laid in, expenditures incurred, products manufactured and sold and, ultimately, financial results obtained. In grouping the accounts no distinction is drawn between:

1. Balance sheet accounts and income statement accounts; or between
2. Operating and non-operating income and expenditure; or between
3. Long-term assets and liabilities and current assets and liabilities.

[12]K. Käfer, "European National Uniform Charts of Accounts," *The International Journal of Accounting*, Fall 1965, p. 80.

Subsidiary control accounts are distinguished from major control accounts by the addition of a third digit. . . .

Division I includes only those fixed assets which have been created by the expenditure of human effort on the construction of buildings and equipment. Such natural resources as land and mineral deposits not being valued are not featured in the accounts. In correspondence with the cycle of manufacture, raw materials fall into Division II, work-in-progress into Division III, and finished goods into Division IV. A distinction is drawn between finished goods that are either an industrial or commercial responsibility. No. 40 Completed Output a/c is provided for finished goods, mainly consumer goods, in the distribution network.

Monetary resources are represented by a range of accounts for funds earmarked for specific purposes held at the State Bank. There being no capital market in the U.S.S.R., no monetary resources are represented by official or commercial paper (e.g., Government stocks or shares).

Current accounts are equivalent to accounts receivable and payable although, because of the strict State Bank control exercised over the credit taken or granted by enterprise, the volume of credit is measurable generally in terms of days rather than weeks or months. . . .

Division VII contains accounts for the appropriation of profits and for other appropriation, such as withdrawals of working capital. . . .

An enterprise is not permitted to build up financial reserves in excess of those calculated to be needed for realizing the goals of the current plan. Any excess resources, whether of profit earnings or of capital, are siphoned into either the appropriate industrial ministry's financial pool or into the State Budget.

Division IX contains the accounts for specific funds represented by moneys held at the State Bank. . . .

The operating profit is calculated in No. 46 Realization a/c in which the cost of sales and sales income are brought together. Credit is not taken for sales revenue until the settlement of the customers' accounts has been assured by the State Bank. The operating profit is transferred to No. 99 Profits and Losses a/c, as also are the non-operating profits and losses (e.g., penalties arising from the breach of contractual obligations and losses from natural calamities). Division IV includes the former, and Division XI the latter account. Interim accounting statements showing the cumulative effects of the current year's activities are prepared monthly. The accounts are closed annually at the end of December.

The chart of accounts contains no accounts for either intangible assets (e.g., goodwill, patent rights) or proprietary claims (e.g., share capital, debentures) and reflects the state ownership of enterprises operating in a non-market economy. The state ownership of enterprises and the consequent primacy of state interests in the drafting of the chart of accounts is underlined by the inclusion of an additional eleven accounts, numbered 001-011, intended principally for the recording of assets not the legal property, although in the physical possession of the enterprise (e.g., assets held on lease, for sale on commission, for repair or for safe custody). These accounts do not form part of the double-entry accounting system.

Both financial and cost accounting categories are integrated into the chart of accounts through appropriately designated control accounts. The integration dates from the 1920s when the initial accounts charts were drafted and probably was attributable to:

1. The absence of a vested professional interest due to the retarded development of an accounting profession; (The traditional differentiation between financial accounting and cost accounting in many advanced countries during the period after, say, 1920 was attributable in large measure to the divisions, if not dissensions, within the accounting profession.)

2. The elimination of a rentier class with its concern for a purely financial interpretation of business activities; (The Petrograd Stock Exchange was closed down shortly after the 1917 October Revolution.)

3. The Soviet regime's need, following the dismantling of the market economy, to fall back on cost data as a guide both to relative efficiencies and for price formulation.

The third order, or analytical accounts are not specified in the chart of accounts. Consequently, the national chart of accounts coding is confined to two digits. The accounts for individual assets and liabilities, such as suppliers, customers, employees are opened in compliance with the needs of the enterprise, additional digits being assigned in, for example, the fourth and fifth positions for their numbering. The operational accounts for the costs of processes, operations and products also are excluded from the chart of accounts. The control accounts for production expenditure contained in Division III are not broken down into subsidiary control accounts. For the extended classification of production expenditures employed in operational accounting identifying digits may be allotted up to a further five positions.

The chart of accounts is supplemented by a uniform plan of accounting which "stipulates procedures relevant to a complete process of accounting, i.e., the initial recording of transactions to be accounted for, the classification and summarization of these transactions, and finally the reporting of accounting data to users of financial information".[13] Some of these aspects of Soviet accounting have been considered elsewhere.[14] The Soviet standardized accounting system also embraces "the uniform treatment of all accounting methods, procedures and concepts",[15] the organization of the accounting office, time-tables for the completion of the accounting work and the utilization of accounting aids (e.g., abacus, mechanical and electrical calculation and accounting machines, and so on).

Standardized accounting was first developed in the two major state controlled economies—Nazi Germany and Soviet Russia. Compared with the development of standardized accounting in Germany[16] during the years 1936-1944 the rate of progress

[13]G. G. Mueller, *International Accounting*, Macmillan, New York 1967, p. 92.

[14]D. T. Bailey, "Enterprise Accounting in the U.S.S.R.," *Accounting and Business Research*, Winter 1973, pp. 43—59.

[15]Op. cit., p. 53.

[16]See H. W. Singer, *Standardized Accountancy in Germany*, N.I.E.S.R. Occasional Paper V, C.U.P., London, 1943.

achieved in Russia may seem to have been comparatively slow. Germany had an advantage, not enjoyed by Russia, "as a result of having had a generation of business economists, large numbers of university-trained accountants, auditors, book-keepers and the like were available to operate a complicated system".[17] Germany, unlike Russia, was the most highly developed of the European industrial powers. With the decline of the *laissez-faire* economy and the rise of the administered economy in which the state becomes increasingly deeply involved in micro-economic management (e.g., through the setting of prices and wages agreements) accounting ceases to be merely the private concern of the individual firm. As accounting becomes a matter of public concern more countries may be expected to develop standardized accounting systems, the first step being the preparation of a national chart of accounts.

An exposition of the major features of the national chart of accounts of the U.S.S.R. has been attempted in this article. It has been shown that an enduring concern of the Soviet state, since the consolidation of its political power in the early 1920s, has been with the development of a system of standardized accounting of which the national chart of accounts forms an integral part. The first accounts chart was drawn up by V.S.N.Kh. in 1925 and intended for adoption by state enterprises. In subsequent years the chart underwent extensive modifications and revisions. In 1960 a final version of the national chart of accounts, which is applied in all branches of the national economy, was published.

## QUESTIONS

1. Why are the financial and cost accounting systems integrated in the U.S.S.R.?

2. Why does the U.S.S.R. double-entry accounting system not include accounts for intangibles, ownership equity, and assets not legally owned?

3. Contrast U.S.S.R. accounting with national income accounting. Note: Information on the latter can be found in any elementary macroeconomics text.

## SELECTED BIBLIOGRAPHY

Bailey, D. T., "The Business of Accounting: East and West," *The Journal of Management Studies*, February 1975, p. 28.

Hole, Roderick C., and Michael A. Alkier, "German Financial Statements," *Management Accounting*, July 1974, pp. 28-34.

[17]Op. cit., p. 13.

# 53

# THE ACCOUNTANTS' EXTRAORDINARY DILEMMA*
Thomas J. Carroll


From 1947 to 1965 the most definitive pronouncement on "extraordinary items" was Accounting Research Bulletin No. 32, issued in December 1947. Its language was essentially retained in Chapter 8 of Accounting Research Bulletin No. 43, issued in 1953. ARB No. 32 stated that there is a general presumption that all items of profit and loss recognized in the current period should be used in determining the figure reported as net income. The only possible exception to this presumption would be items which "are materially significant in relation to the company's net income and are clearly not identifiable with or do not result from the usual or typical business operations of the period." Unfortunately, the Bulletin did not attempt to define "usual or typical business operations of the period." Instead, examples of "extraordinary items" were listed and it was stated that misconceptions could arise if such items were included in the determination of net income. The Bulletin expressed its preference that "extraordinary items" be charged or credited directly to surplus with complete disclosure as to their nature and amount.

In 1966 the Accounting Principles Board, in response to the increased emphasis on, and interest in, the financial reporting format of business entities and the nature of the amount reported as net income in the financial statements, restudied the problem of extraordinary items, publishing its conclusions in Accounting Principles Board Opinion No. 9, *Reporting The Results of Operations*. The Board maintained that all items of profit and loss recognized during the period should be reflected in net income of the period with the sole exception of those rare material items related to the operations of a specific prior period or periods. In addition, it held that extraordinary items included in net income of the period should be segregated and reported separately in the income statement. Recognizing that the identification of extraordinary items requires the exercise of judgment, Opinion No. 9 defined them as "events and transactions of material effect which would not be expected to recur frequently and which would not be considered as recurring factors in any evaluation of the ordinary operating processes of the business." Opinion No. 9 went on to give examples of events or transactions which could be considered extraordinary items if they met the criteria in the definition, such as "the sale or abandonment of a plant or a significant segment of the business."

During the years following the issuance of APB Opinion No. 9, it became increasingly difficult to determine if particular events or transactions met its subjective criteria for extraordinary items. Yet, for a variety of reasons, the number of companies reporting extraordinary items increased significantly. *Accounting Trends and Techniques* reported that in 1969, 156 out of 600 companies surveyed presented extraordinary items in their income statements. In 1972, 204 out of 600 companies

---

*From *World*, Summer 1974, pp. 15–18. Reprinted by permission of the publisher.

surveyed presented extraordinary items, a 31% increase. It had become clear that the criteria for extraordinary items in Opinion No. 9 were so subjective as to invite a wide divergence of interpretation and had, in fact, become virtually unimplementable. The accounting profession and the business community, recognizing the difficulties encountered in the application of those criteria, looked to the Accounting Principles Board for more definitive criteria. The Board responded with the issuance of APB Opinion No. 30 in June 1973.

The stated purposes of APB Opinion No. 30 are "(1) to provide more definitive criteria for extraordinary items by clarifying and, to some extent, modifying the existing definition and criteria, (2) to specify disclosure requirements for extraordinary items, (3) to specify the accounting and reporting for disposal of a segment of a business, (4) to specify disclosure requirements for other unusual or infrequently occurring events and transactions that are not extraordinary items." This language diverges from that in Opinion No. 9, for despite the modest notice of changes in the definition of extraordinary items, it has removed from the extraordinary item category the "disposal of a segment of a business." In fact, the Board created an entirely new section of the income statement for reporting the effects of a disposal of a segment of a business. This development was much influenced by the consequences of an attempt to do away altogether with a category "extraordinary" which called for subjective determination and by circumstances which made drastic changes in financial reporting untimely.

There was a great deal of sentiment among members of the Board to abolish the accounting category of "extraordinary" because it was based upon a subjective determination. This group, which had strong support from investment analysts, preferred to set out separately in the income statement any material event or transaction or group of events and transactions which appeared to be unusual or nonrecurring without calling them extraordinary or anything else. In their view there would be but a single income amount on the income statement, that being "net income," and it would be up to the user of the financial statements to decide how to deal with each separately set forth item in his analysis of the results of operations. Whether the items would be captioned "extraordinary" or not, the proponents of this theory still face the problem of defining criteria for the items which would be separately set forth. Broad, inclusive criteria mean that a large, complex company might have several pages of one-line items in the income statement followed by pages and pages of footnotes describing each item. If the criteria were narrowly defined, the number of separate lines in the income statement would be restricted to the several major items of revenues and the several major items of expense. In either case guidelines based upon a subjective determination would be required—the very type of criteria this group cited when opposing the concept of extraordinary items. In addition, with the impending inauguration of the Financial Accounting Standards Board and with the Trueblood Committee yet to report, the APB was reluctant to opt for such a drastic change in financial reporting. As a result, the Board chose to define extraordinary items so as to permit little more than the acts of God and governments (and even then not in all cases) to be classified as extraordinary, to create a new section of the income statement for reporting the effects of a disposal of a segment of a business, and to require separate disclosure in income from continuing operations for events and transactions which are neither extraordinary nor disposals of a segment of a business but nevertheless are material and either unusual in nature or infrequently occurring. . . .

In order for an event or transaction to be classified as an extraordinary item, it must be both unusual in nature and infrequent in occurrence when judged with due consideration for the environment in which the entity operates. According to the Opinion, the environment in which an entity operates "includes such factors as the characteristics of the industry or industries in which it operates, the geographical location of its operations, and the nature and extent of governmental regulation." Thus, when we consider the factors in a railroad's environment, such as extensive track systems and large property holdings, we could conclude that a loss due to flood damage would not be unusual in nature for a railroad. On considering the factors in a bank's environment, such as the extent of regulation by the Federal Reserve Board, we could conclude that a loss on divestiture of a subsidiary in accordance with a Federal Reserve ruling might not be unusual in nature.

Because of the Opinion's narrow criteria for extraordinary events, users of financial statements will now have to identify and understand events of abnormal financial effects which are not extraordinary by an overall analysis of the financial statements and by careful review of the relevant notes. . . .

In dealing with events which are either unusual or nonrecurring but not both, the APB acted to curb special treatment accorded certain transactions by many companies in their income statements. The special treatment usually consisted of presentation on a net-of-tax basis as well as prominent disclosure of the earnings-per-share effect. They were not captioned extraordinary items, but in all other respects they certainly were presented in the same manner as extraordinary items. In fact these items might be termed "first cousins" to extraordinary items. In Opinion No. 30 the APB has in effect said that you should tell us about these events but do not present them in the income statement in any way which implies that they are extraordinary. This should help the readers of financial statements immensely because it will reduce the number of earnings-per-share figures that the reader must evaluate as a result of "special charges and credits" and because it will be very clear that such events are not extraordinary.

This provision has been criticized on the grounds that management can often control the timing of these transactions and that if their financial effects are included in operating income, a distortion of the operating income can occur merely by controlling the timing of the transaction. The critics seem to attach some sort of mystical significance to that term "operating income," and one wonders just how they would define the types of transactions which should be included in determining operating income. . . .

As discussed in the Interpretation of APB Opinion No. 30, the process of determining the appropriate place in the income statement for reporting items which appear to be unusual, infrequently occurring, or extraordinary should follow a decision chart such as the following.

APB Opinion No. 30 will, no doubt, cause a marked reduction in the incidence of reported extraordinary items. The Opinion also represents a significant step toward a truly "all-inclusive" income statement with but a single reported income—net income. On the other hand as discussed previously, confusion may result because of the manner in which a segment of a business is defined. In addition, because of the tight criteria given to extraordinary items, distortions in net income caused by events of abnormal financial effect which are not extraordinary will now have to be determined through analysis of the income statement and related notes.

EDITORS' NOTE: The APB is discussed in Stephen A. Zeff's article, Selection 2, Part 1, on page 8. Articles on the FASB and other rule-making agencies are found in Part 5. Since this article was written, the FASB has softened its position somewhat by permitting the temporary classification of gains or losses from early retirement of debt as extraordinary.

### QUESTIONS

1. How should extraordinary items be reported in the income statement?
2. What can be reported as an extraordinary item?
3. Referring to "alternative income measurements," which approach has been followed in regard to extraordinary items? Explain.
4. Has the current-operating concept of income determination been followed with regard to extraordinary items or the all-inclusive concept? Explain.

## 54

## HUMAN ASSETS ACCOUNTING IN THE PROFESSIONAL SPORTS INDUSTRY*
Philip E. Meyer

In recent years, the accounting literature has contained an increasing number of articles concerned with "human resource accounting." Such efforts typically focus on some innovative aspect of human assets and/or develop "models" with which such resources might be measured. Although such endeavors may provide value of an intellectual nature, persons engaged in the practice of accounting seek insights which can be related to their own ongoing interest in their chosen profession.

To obtain such a perspective, a research inquiry was undertaken to discern the "disclosure" aspects of human resources in an industry where such assets are universally regarded as being the most crucial. Even the most casual observer is aware that professional athletics has become endowed with the halo of being "big business." With the creation of new franchises and entirely new leagues, and the use of computers to assist in the selection of prospective professional players, the valuation of athletic teams is an important matter. To the extent that the worth of such an organization is inextricably based on its player personnel, one encounters a very real "human asset" situation. Because it is such individuals' performances that constitute

*From The CPA Journal, May 1973, pp. 417–419. Reprinted by permission of the publisher.

the primary source of teams' revenue-producing efforts, such persons, in turn, represent human assets to their employers even though they are not "owned" in the usual sense.

Accordingly, it is the objective of this report to present the findings of an empirical study into the nature of accounting practices utilized by such business enterprises. The subsequent sections of this paper discuss the accounting issues, the study and the findings as well as the author's conclusions.

## THE FINANCIAL REPORTING ISSUES

The focal point of the research effort was the financial statements of professional sports organizations. The overriding emphasis of the study was the responsiveness of such statements to the following tenets of accounting:

Profit is computed by matching revenues with related expenses.

If the revenue-producing character of a current expenditure is expected to occur in some future fiscal period, recognition of that expense is deferred accordingly (via capitalization as an asset).

The cost of an "intangible" asset should be amortized by systematic charges to income over the period estimated to be benefited (not exceeding forty years).

Specifically considered were the capitalization of various expenditures relating to player personnel. These included bonus contracts which arise when a payment is made to a player in some amount above his regular first-year salary, in order to secure exclusive rights to his services. Note that a player is generally precluded from negotiating with other teams until such time as his team sells or trades its exclusive rights to negotiate with him. It can thus be observed that such bonus payments provide benefits (to the team) extending beyond the period of the actual expenditure and would thereby qualify for capitalization as an asset.

Also examined was the multi-year contract whereby a player makes a commitment to play for the team beyond one (less-than-calendar-year) season. Such an agreement is in exchange for some pre-negotiated level of salary for each of the contracted years. The accounting question is whether such a contract warrants disclosure on the balance sheet as an asset and a liability.

Deferred payment player contracts emerged in recent years in response to prominent players' resultant high income tax bracket. The procedure essentially involves payment of a particular season's salary to be spread over a predetermined number of subsequent years. This phenomenon also suggests balance sheet implications.

A more subtle issue is that of costs associated with a player playing for a "farm club." The situation reflects the case where a prospective player employed by the team does not yet have the ability to be a regular performer for the team. He therefore plays for an affiliated team in the (lower level) minor leagues while his (major league) team absorbs the cost of his salary. The accounting question is whether such salary (and related) costs should be capitalized on the basis that the (revenue production) benefits do not occur until the player graduates to the major leagues. If the situation is perceived to be analogous to maintaining a "research and development" laboratory, a more overriding question would arise. Specifically, would all of the costs related to (subsidizing) a minor league operation warrant capitalization and, in turn, amortization against future revenues

Other questions considered include (internal) developmental, training, medical and therapy costs being capitalized, accounting for salaries paid to injured, temporarily inactive players, and capitalization of salaries and commissions paid to "scouts." The function performed by the latter group is to assist teams in locating, evaluating and recruiting prospective, uncommitted players. A final area of inquiry concerns accounting for the franchise costs associated with membership in the respective professional league.

## THE STUDY AND ITS FINDINGS

A fourteen (14) question questionnaire was mailed to ninety-two (92) professional sports organizations. All of these firms possessed franchises in the so-called major leagues of the four primary spectator team sports in the United States—baseball (24), football (26) basketball (23), and ice hockey (14). [Of the ninety-two teams, four (4) were located in Canada.] The responses to the individual questions on the questionnaire were to be offered in terms of yes, no and not applicable with stated provision for detailed answers where appropriate. The questionnaire was deliberately brief in length so as not to generate possible non-cooperation due to excessive consumption of time on the part of respondents. Responses were recorded on the basis of the four types of major sports groups.

Of the organizations contacted, 43.5% acknowledged receipt of the request for information; more than 80% of these replies responded to the questionnaire. This nearly 36% response reflected an approximate 50% return for baseball and football teams and about a 20% return for hockey and basketball teams. (This disparity might be associated with the occurrence of the survey during the latter two sports' active seasons and with the fact that the greater number of newer franchises in hockey and basketball may tend to be less organized.)

A summary of the responses appears in Table 1.

The question of capitalizing bonus contracts drew a 50% "yes", 50% "no" response. 7 of 12 baseball teams and 1 of 3 hockey teams responded affirmatively while the basketball and football replies were even. The question of balance sheet disclosure of multi-year player contracts generated a "not applicable" response from 28% of the respondents. Of those organizations reporting experience with such contracts, only 22% indicated the presence of such disclosure. The matter of balance sheet disclosure of deferred payment contracts drew an opposite response. Of the 87% of the teams involved in such a situation, 70% reporting making such disclosure.

With regard to the costs of players performing for its minor league clubs, 87% of the basketball and football teams reported that the question was not applicable to their operations. And of the 56% of all respondents participating in such an arrangement, none reported capitalization of these costs. Of a similar nature, only 1 of 32 respondents reported any capitalization of "training, developmental, medical or therapy" costs. In addition, none of the teams indicated capitalization of salaries paid to injured, inactive players, salaries paid to regular scouts, or commissions paid to free-lance scouts. As an aside, it was reported that 67% of the teams capitalize franchise costs paid to their respective leagues.

## CONCLUSIONS

The data suggest that professional sports enterprises make no attempt, in their formal financial statements, to measure the cost or value of their human assets. It is acknowledged that many of the capitalizable items suggested by the survey would at best be only crude indicators of the relevant information. It is further noted that aside from the conceptual validity of such measurements, there is the very real practical problem of subsequently matching such capitalized costs with generated revenues.

## Table 1

|  | YES | NO | NOT APPLI-CABLE | NUMBER OF RESPONSES |
|---|---|---|---|---|
| 1. Publicly held corporation | 5 | 28 | 0 | 33 |
| 2. Controlled by parent corporation | 6 | 26 | 0 | 32 |
| 3. Published financial statements | 4 | 29 | 0 | 33 |
| 4. Consolidated statements only | 1 | 5 | 24 | 30 |
| 5. Bonus contracts capitalized | 16 | 16 | 0 | 32 |
| 6. Balance sheet disclosure of multi-year player contracts | 5 | 18 | 9 | 32 |
| 7. Balance sheet disclosure of deferred payment player contracts | 19 | 8 | 4 | 31 |
| 8. Capitalization of costs relating to minor league play of prospective star players | 0 | 18 | 14 | 32 |
| 9. Capitalization of training, developmental, medical or therapy costs | 1 | 31 | 0 | 32 |
| 10. Capitalization of salary paid to injured, inactive players | 0 | 32 | 0 | 32 |
| 11. Capitalization of salary paid to scouts | 0 | 31 | 0 | 31 |
| 12. Capitalization of commissions paid to free lance scouts | 0 | 31 | 1 | 32 |
| 13. Capitalization of franchise costs paid to "league" | 20 | 8 | 2 | 30 |
| 14. Any intangible assets disclosed on balance sheet | 20 | 12 | 0 | 32 |

Despite these observations, it seems that the nature of a professional sports team particularly lends itself to the phenomenon of accounting for human assets. Even at the present time, the output of athletes is presumed to be measurable in terms of well-known sports statistics reflecting home runs, touchdowns, goals, assists, etc. Furthermore, there exists the frequent occurrence of trading (the rights to negotiate a contract with particular) players among the various professional teams. The nature of such trades implicitly suggests valuation of athletes' future services. It would appear therefore that the accounting procedures relating to human resources might parallel those which apply to inanimate assets such as plant, property and equipment.

In summary, the empirical inquiry (reported herein) indicates that for financial reporting purposes no sophisticated techniques are now used to measure the cost and value of human resources of sports teams. That the nature of these enterprises lends itself to such measurement seems apparent; that accountants should address themselves to this issue appears desirable.

What is being set forth as a mandate for accountants, therefore, is the proposition that complete accounting systems be established. During its infancy stage, the matter of human asset accounting warrants imaginative and creative thinking so that it might eventually be developed to the extent that it can be incorporated into the classical financial reporting model.

EDITORS' NOTE: Although human asset accounting is a comparatively recent development, the accounting problems, particularly of measurement, associated with it are similar to those associated with older forms of intangible assets such as goodwill, copyrights, and trademarks.

## QUESTIONS

1. What are the measurement problems involved in setting up the costs related to developing a professional athlete as an asset on the balance sheet of the employing sports organization?

2. Which of the various criteria of an asset would a human asset have most difficulty in meeting? Why?

3. What "sophisticated techniques" are available that could be "used to measure the cost and value of human resources of sport teams?" Illustrate.

# 55

## WHY NOT IMPROVE YOUR PRESENTATION OF THE "STATEMENT OF CHANGES?"*

Charles Lawrence

The Statement of Changes in Financial Position should be thought of as something that is still being developed. Formerly called Source and Application of Funds, the statement passed a milestone when APB Opinion No. 19 on "Reporting Changes in Financial Position" called for its inclusion regularly in the published financial statements of corporations. It is time now to seek further improvement in the presentation of the Change Statement.

The quest for progress in financial reporting has already been advanced by a succession of improvements in published statements. The balance sheet evolved from a report of rudimentary aggregates into the present classified, well-described report of dissimilar elements. Likewise, the income statement developed from a single line in an equity account into a well-developed statement setting forth dissimilar items in a framework of logical classification. Probably neither statement is in its final form: each will evolve as additional needs are uncovered and met by inclusion of still more information.

One objective of APB Opinion No. 19 is "to summarize the financing and investing activities of the entity. . . ." At first reading of the opinion, one might presume that financing and investing activities were but a single concept. There is no definition or list of divergent characteristics of financing and investing activities in the opinion. However, in commenting on transactions that do not affect cash or working capital, the opinion notes that "issuing equity securities to acquire a building is *both* [italics supplied] a financing and investing transaction. . . ."

Having suggested that these activities are different, the opinion indicates that Change Statements "should disclose *separately* [italics again supplied] the financing and investing aspects of all significant transactions that affect financial position during the period." But such disclosure is difficult without a working definition of the two basic activities. If the first objective of Opinion No. 19 is to be reached, investing and financing activities need to be defined for separate display and summarization by activity. This paper suggests (1) a method of differentiating between financing and investing activities, and (2) a form of Change Statement which will enable the presentation to "summarize the financing and investing activities" of an entity.

### CURRENT PRACTICE

The usual sequence for reporting comparative changes in financial position is: (1) to summarize all sources of working capital under a heading such as "sources of funds," (2) to summarize all the dispositions of working capital under a heading such as "application of funds," and (3) to present the net change in working capital either as a

*From *The CPA Journal*, May 1974, pp. 41—44. Reprinted by permission of the publisher.

final "increase" or "decrease" caption, on the one hand, or as an equalizing item under the "sources" or the "applications" heading, on the other hand. This statement is generally followed by another statement analyzing the changes in current assets and current liabilities that make up the net change in working capital.

If investing and financing activities are conceded to be different, and the Change Statement is truly designed to "disclose all important aspects of [the entity's] financing and investing activities," then surely the data pertaining to these separate activities should appear prominently in the statement. A glance at Exhibit I indicates that such is not presently the case. What the Change Statement presents, as to both source and disposition of working capital, is combined totals for financing and investing.

Is there a simple way to present financing and investing activities separately? Would such a separate presentation be useful to the reader? Fundamental to such analysis is a differentiation between financing activities and investing activities. What are their characteristics?

## CHARACTERISTICS

Perhaps APB Opinion No. 19 failed to differentiate between these terms because the difference was too obvious; or perhaps the task was too complex. In either case, for

**Exhibit I    Consolidated Statement of Changes in Financial Position for the Years Ended August 3, 1976 and July 28, 1975**

|  | 1976 | 1975 |
|---|---|---|
| Source of funds |  |  |
| Income (loss) before extraordinary items | $ 7,148 | $(63,846) |
| Charges (credits) not requiring use of working capital: |  |  |
| Depreciation and amortization | 16,067 | 16,260 |
| Deferred income taxes | (400) | (1,691) |
| Funds provided (required) by operations |  |  |
| exclusive of extraordinary items | 22,815 | (49,277) |
| Extraordinary items | 5,663 | — |
| Sale of preferred stock | — | 35,000 |
| Proceeds from issuance of long-term debt | — | 30,000 |
| Proceeds from sale of property, plant, and equipment | 10,111 | 11,507 |
| Total funds provided | 38,589 | 27,230 |
| Use of funds |  |  |
| Plant and equipment expenditures | 5,508 | 4,549 |
| Reduction of long-term debt | 9,634 | 4,310 |
| Other | 54 | 1,800 |
| Total funds used | $15,196 | $ 10,659 |
| Working capital increase | $23,393 | $ 16,571 |

the purpose of developing a format for separate display of investing and financing totals, the following guidelines are useful: Investing activities involve changes in long-term assets and include such activities as buying or selling long-term assets and investments. Financing activities involve increases or decreases in long-term equities. Examples of financing activities are issuing or repurchasing capital stock or bonds.

A special case of an equity change is the reported income of an entity. When viewed as a matter of "ploughing back earnings," net income (adjusted for non-working-capital items) becomes a source of working capital that qualifies as financing. Although some accountants might want net income to be shown as a third category, it is consistent with the objectives of APB Opinion No. 19 to categorize it as a financing activity.

## PROPOSAL

Since the financing and investing are not identical concepts, summaries of financing and investing activities call for two groupings: (1) changes in working capital due to financing activities, and (2) changes in working capital due to investing activities. Moreover a complete presentation requires that the two groups be further segregated ino the following four elements:

Increases in working capital from
a. decreases in investing (i.e., selling long term assets)
b. increases in financing (i.e., issuing capital stock, bonds)
Decreases in working capital from
c. increases in investing (i.e., purchasing long-term assets)
d. decreases in financing (i.e., paying dividends, redeeming bonds)

What guidance as to format is furnished by APB Opinion No. 19? The opinion is the essence of individual reporting freedom. Its only format clue, aside from identifying some of the items that should be included in the statement, is the admonition that "related items should be in proximity when the result contributes to the clarity of the Statement." Following this spirit of reporting-format freedom, Exhibit I has been cast into an alternative format (Exhibit II) which has the merit of showing separately net investing changes and net financing changes in working capital.

This form of Change Statement clearly fulfills the objective of APB Opinion No. 19 by showing separately the effects of financing and investing activities. Such a separation highlights the interesting situation (in this case) that over 40% of the increases in working capital for each of the two years came from investing activities, i.e., from disposing of assets of the firm.

|  | 1976 | | 1975 | |
|---|---|---|---|---|
| Working capital provided from financing changes | $13,181 | 56% | $ 9,613 | 58% |
| Working capital provided from investing changes | 10,212 | 44 | 6,958 | 42 |
| Working capital increase | $23,393 | 100% | $16,571 | 100% |

**Exhibit II   Alternative Form of Comparative Statement of Changes in Financial Position (on a Working Capital Basis) for the Years Ended August 31, 1976 and July 28, 1975**

|  | 1976 | 1975 |
|---|---|---|
| Financing changes which increased working capital: | | |
| Income before extraordinary items | $ 7,148 | — |
| Charges (credits) not requiring the use of working capital: | | |
| Depreciation and amortization | 16,067 | — |
| Deferred income taxes | (400) | — |
| Funds provided by operations | $22,815 | |
| Issuance of preferred stock | | $35,000 |
| Issuance of long-term debt | | 30,000 |
| Total increases in working capital from financing changes | $22,815 | $65,000 |
| Financing changes which decreased working capital: | | |
| Loss before extraordinary items | | 63,846 |
| (Charges) credits not requiring the use of working capital: | | |
| Depreciation and amortization | | (16,260) |
| Deferred income taxes | | 1,691 |
| Funds required by operations | | $49,277 |
| Reduction of long-term debt | $ 9,634 | 4,310 |
| Other | — | 1,800 |
| Total decreases in working capital from financing changes | $ 9,634 | $55,387 |
| Net increase in working capital from financing changes | $13,181 | $ 9,613 |
| Investing changes which decreased working capital: | | |
| Plant and equipment expenditures | $ 5,508 | $ 4,549 |
| Write-off of computer programs and equipment | 3,139[a] | — |
| Other | 54 | — |
| Total decreases in working capital from changes | $ 8,701 | $ 4,549 |
| Investing changes which increased working capital: | | |
| Proceeds from sales of land, plant, and property | 10,111 | 11,507 |
| Proceeds from extraordinary sale of land | 3,032[a] | — |
| Use of tax benefits of prior years | 5,770[a] | — |
| Total increases in working capital from investing changes | $18,913 | $11,507 |
| Net increase in working capital from investing changes | $10,212 | $ 6,958 |
| Net increase in working capital | $23,393 | $16,571 |

[a]Combined in a single extraordinary item in the statement as originally published.

Manifestly, this summary presents a useful view of management's activities. Within the financing activities, this format emphasizes (in the case) the interesting situation that, in 1975 when no funds were derived from operations, other financing activities were used to raise funds for the business. Certainly the theoretical extremes would be interesting to a reader interpreting the statements: if all funds came from reduced investment, the reader would draw very different conclusions than if all funds were raised from financing activities.

Another interesting aspect of this type of classification is illustrated in the presentation of extraordinary items totaling $5,663. This single item actually comprises three investing components: (1) a $3,139 write-off of computer programs and equipment, (2) a $3,032 credit on sale of land, and (3) a using up of $5,770 in tax benefits from prior years. With the new and expanded classification of financing and investing activities, these items come up as results of investing activities instead of being shown as an add-on to ordinary operations.

Although the primary reason for adopting the proposed format is to disseminate more information about the financing and investing activities of a reporting entity, another reason for adopting such a format is the resultant increase in reporting consistency that normally would be gained. The adoption of the proposed format would definitely locate that "source-application chameleon" in the present Change Statement—the negative results of operations. Typically the company illustrated in this article represented its 1975 loss of working capital from operations differently in the two successive years 1975 and 1976. (See Exhibit III.) As a result, the total funds provided for the year 1975 was stated as $76,507 in the 1975 report and as $27,230 in the 1976 report. Accountants can perhaps understand that the reason for this difference of nearly $50,000 in representing the identical item differently in two successive years was that it was matched and compared with an operating profit for the year 1976 in the 1976 report, and with an operating loss for the year 1974 in the 1975 report. However, in perspective, it does seem inconsistent and unnecessary to represent the same element differently in two successive years. With the adoption of a format such as this paper proposes, the loss of working capital from operations would always be shown in the financing section in the manner presented in Exhibit IV. Certainly the reader will appreciate this consistency in presentation.

Has any significant information been lost? No. Both total sources and total dispositions of working capital have been downgraded; however, either can be easily reconstructed from the face of the statement by combining two totals.

Have there been gains in information? Though the presentation is less simplistic when analyzed into financing and investing elements, much more information about management's activities in these two areas is made explicit.

Finally, there are always problems which accompany any proposed change in financial statements. The imposition of fixed rules or forms appears to be particularly unwelcome to many accountants. But aside from the philosophical issue of "reporting freedom" (a fundamental but unresolved issue), there seems to be no additional problem involved in this change. A reader can reconstruct total sources and

**Exhibit III   Comparative Statements of Changes in Financial Position for the Year Ending July 28, 1975**

| | THE YEAR 1975 AS PRESENTED: | |
| --- | --- | --- |
| | IN THE 1976 ANNUAL REPORT | IN THE 1975 ANNUAL REPORT |
| Source of funds | | |
| Income (loss) before extraordinary items | $(63,846) | — |
| Charges (credits) not requiring use of working capital: | | |
| Depreciation and amortization | 16,260 | — |
| Deferred income taxes | (1,691) | — |
| Funds required by operations | (49,277) | |
| Sale of preferred stock | 35,000 | $35,000 |
| Proceeds from issuance of long-term debt | 30,000 | 30,000 |
| Proceeds from sale of property, plant, and equipment | 11,507 | 11,507 |
| Total funds provided | 27,230 | 76,507 |
| Use of funds | | |
| Net loss for the year | | $63,846 |
| Items not requiring current outlay of funds: | | |
| Depreciation and amortization | | (16,260) |
| Reversal of deferred income taxes | | 1,691 |
| Funds required by operations | | 49,277 |
| Plant and equipment expenditures | $  4,549 | 4,549 |
| Reduction of long-term liabilities | 4,310 | 4,310 |
| Other | 1,800 | 1,800 |
| | 10,659 | 59,936 |
| Net working capital increase | $ 16,571 | $16,571 |

distribution of funds information easily from the information on the face of the statement, if he so desires.

### SUMMARY

The history of financial reporting is replete with changes to statement presentation, both in form and content. Changes are usually espoused because they present statement data in a new or more informative light: thus, classification is a frequent

## Exhibit IV   Statement of Changes in Financial Position
(Working Capital Basis)

| | |
|---|---:|
| Financing changes which increased working capital: | |
|    Issuance of preferred stock | $35,000 |
|    Issuance of long-term debt | 30,000 |
|       Total increases in working capital from financing changes | $65,000 |
| Financing changes which decreased working capital: | |
|    Loss before extraordinary items | $63,846 |
|    (Charges) credits not requiring the use of working capital: | |
|       Depreciation and amortization | 16,260 |
|       Deferred income taxes | (1,691) |
|          Funds required by operations | 49,277 |
|    Reduction of long-term debt | 4,310 |
|    Other | 1,800 |
|       Total decreases in working capital from financing changes | $55,387 |
|       Net increase in working capital from financing changes | $ 9,613 |
| Investing changes which decreased working capital: | |
|    Plant and equipment expenditures | $ 4,549 |
| Investing changes which increased working capital: | |
|    Proceeds from sales of land, plant, and property | 11,507 |
|       Net increase in working capital from investing changes | $ 6,958 |
| Net increase in working capital | $16,571 |

subject of change. This article proposes the classification of the Changes Statement into financing and investing components.

It is reasonable to expect that the Changes Statement will be modified over time. Classification may well be the best way in which it can be modified now.

## QUESTIONS

1. What is working capital?

2. Which deductions on the income statement do not decrease working capital? Why?

3. Set up equations representing the statement formats for those shown in Exhibits I and IV.

4. What is the change in format that Professor Lawrence is recommending, and what are its merits?

## SELECTED BIBLIOGRAPHY

Spiller, Earl A., and Robert L. Virgil, "Effectiveness of APB Opinion No. 19 in Improving Funds Reporting," *Journal of Accounting Research*, Spring 1974, pp. 112-142.

# 56

## INCREASING THE UTILITY OF FINANCIAL STATEMENTS*

Charles T. Horngren

EDITORS' NOTE: The following excerpt is from a 1959 article.

To discover more views on the funds statement, this writer circulated a fairly detailed and technical questionnaire to a random selection of 350 security analysts. One hundred twenty replies (34 per cent) were received.

Analysts cited the following information as being revealed by a funds statement:

1. Major sources from which funds were obtained (i.e., profits, borrowings, stockholder investment)
2. Financial management "habits" of the company (i.e., managerial attitudes toward spending and financing)
3. Proportion of funds applied to plant, dividends, debt retirement, etc.
4. Determination of the disposition of profits
5. Impact of spending upon working capital position
6. Indication of the trend of general financial strength or weakness of the company
7. Indication of impact of sources and uses of funds upon future dividend-paying probabilities

The following specific comments by analysts in their answering of the questionnaire may clarify the uses cited above:

1. There is probably no more useful analytical tool in statement analysis than the flow of funds, and we incorporate it in all our financial reports, whether for loan or investment purposes. In very concise terms, it manages to blend balance sheet and profit and loss together into meaningful terms and gives a quick bird's-eye view of what happened to a business in the period under review. There is no doubt in my mind that its use will increase, and it will emerge, if it has not already, as an absolutely essential financial schedule, included in all audit and annual reports.

2. Its importance ranks with balance sheet and income statement. It reveals [all uses cited above], plus the fact that if its usage became commonplace or universal in annual reports it would be a common tool of intra- and inter-industry analysis.

3. Use to judge whether the company (1) is likely to increase or cut [the] dividend, (2) is likely to have to do financing, and (3) is expanding vigorously.

4. In evaluating common stocks we frequently consider "funds flow" as exceeding in importance reported profits—particularly where large capital expenditure programs are under way.

5. Use the funds flow statistics as a means of judging whether company can finance further additions without additional financing and/or increase dividends or retire debt.

*Excerpt from "Increasing the Utility of Financial Statements," *The Journal of Accountancy*, July 1959, pp. 36—46.

6. Not only to determine the manager's past ideas but to project possible policies into the future, the funds statement is vital to me.

7. The funds statement is essential to equate earnings statements by adjusting for partially discretionary noncash charges (policy differences, etc.) and to attempt to predict financing (outside sources).

# 57
# THE ACCOUNTING ENTITY*
Philip E. Meyer

## INTRODUCTION

The entity concept in accounting relates to the identity of the matter or activity for which an accounting is to occur and the relationship assumed to exist between the entity and external parties. Reference to the accounting literature indicates that the controversy and confusion which surround the concept have serious effects on the consequential discussion of financial reporting. Some writers have engaged in direct debate about the nature of the entity; others not directly concerned with the controversy have employed implicit but divergent views of the entity. The entity is variously regarded as a proprietary unit, an economic unit, a managerial unit, a social unit, and a collection of rights and restrictions on their exercise.

It is the objective of this paper to examine the entity concept controversy. An attempt is made to classify the many apparently different views which have been advanced, in the hope that, by identifying their similarities and differences, it may become easier to establish some general understanding or consensus.

Eight possible conceptions of the accounting entity are identifiable in the literature. They seem to fall into three categories which will be referred to as the proprietary, pure entity and functional approaches. A tabular summary of the features of the eight concepts is given as an appendix of this paper.

## THE PROPRIETARY APPROACH

The three views which comprise the proprietary group are the 'traditional proprietary', the 'residual equity' and the 'equity' concepts of the accounting entity. They are classified as 'proprietary' because each focuses upon the effect of the relationship between the entity and some well-defined group of 'owners'.

*From *Abacus*, December 1973, pp. 116–126. Reprinted by permission of the publisher.

### The Traditional Proprietary View

The traditional proprietary view assumes that the owner acts in the best interests of the business and the firm acts in the best interests of the owner(s). The firm is merely an instrument used by owners to increase their wealth.

Business assets are seen as being owned by the stockholders and business liabilities are therefore liabilities of the owners. The firm's managers are representatives of the stockholders and are presumed to act in their best interests. The objective of accounting is to present to stockholders a report which describes the growth in their wealth over a period of time and the amount of their wealth as of a particular point in time. The balance sheet equation appears as 'assets less liabilities equals owners' equity'.

Net income is the measure of the growth of the entity's net worth before distribution of assets to owners. Income to the firm accrues at once to the owners; the company, as such, has no income. Since both interest charges and income taxes represent payments to parties other than owners, they are expenses. The payment of cash dividends to stockholders is merely a withdrawal by owners of their own assets; it is a transfer from one location to another, and not income to them nor expense to the business entity. A stock dividend, in turn, is not income to the owner nor expense to the business, nor even dilution of the interest of owners in the assets in the entity's possession. . . .

### The Residual Equity View

The residual equity view . . . focuses attention on that portion of owners' equity which is 'residual' in nature. Invariably, this denotes the interest of investors in common stock; if there are two or more classes of common stock, the interest of only the most junior class is considered to be 'residual'. Supporters of this view consider the traditional proprietary theory to be inadequate since it treats as identical the interests of various stockholder groups which are basically antagonistic to each other. Such antagonism is said to result from the desire of the lowest ranking investors always to want to minimize the returns to the highest ranking investors while the latter seek to maximize these returns.

On this view, the balance sheet equation takes the form 'assets less senior equities equals owners' equity'. Cash dividends paid to senior stockholders are tantamount to the payment of interest to creditors, while dividends paid to residual stockholders are mere distributions of what they already own. Even stock dividends distributed to senior stockholders would be considered as expenses. Such dividends represent a dilution of the residual equity since such equity in assets is transferred from the residual stockholders to the senior stockholders. Stock dividends distributed to residual equityholders, however, are regarded in the same manner as under the traditional proprietary view.

### The Equity View

Under this view both creditors and investors are regarded as having equities in the corporate assets; the balance sheet equation becomes 'assets equals equities', and the term 'liability' represents creditors' equities in the business assets. Each equity group represents a distinctive type of control, is subject to a distinctive type of risk, and has a distinctive type of claim; within each group there may be both long-term and short-term investors. . . .

Cash dividends and even interest charges are distributions to equityholders and therefore are not expenses from the point of view of equityholders. . . . Income taxes are considered as distributions of income and not an expense, as the government has an equity in the business entity even though it is not explicitly identified on the balance sheet. . . .

## Summary

The fundamental difference among these three conceptions of the entity is their respective definitions of the primary equityholding parties. The consequence is that the most restrictive definition ('residual equity') yields most opportunities of classifying distributions of revenue as expenses, while the least restrictive definition ('equity') generates the least number of opportunities of classifying such distributions as elements of profit. Yet, all three of these approaches are concerned with the equity interests of some well-defined 'owner' group; hence their treatment here as members of the 'proprietary' category.

## THE PURE ENTITY APPROACH

The two views to be considered here are the 'self-equity' view and the 'social' view of the accounting entity. They are classified as 'pure entity' views because both reject the necessity of considering the relationship of the entity to some well-defined group of equityholders. As the following discussion indicates, the two views lead in altogether different directions.

### The Self-Equity View

What is suggested . . . is that the company be regarded as an institution in its own right. It is not assumed to act in the best interest of stockholders but rather in its own self-interest. It is in its best interest to pay dividends, so that if and when it must again seek capital funds in the primary securities market, its stock will be attractive to prospective suppliers of capital.

It is the entity that holds the equity in the firm's assets. Income to the entity is a measure of the growth in assets retained by the business after recognition of payments due to all external parties. Since all such parties have provided some benefit to the entity, payments therefore are costs to the entity. Those parties whose 'contributions' are represented by economic resources with future service potential are identified on the equities side of the balance sheet. The balance sheet equation, therefore, appears as 'assets equals sources of assets'.

These sources are creditors and stockholders; the former will be repaid, while the assets provided by the latter become the net worth of the entity for which there exists no obligation (to repay). The net worth thus is a measure of the entity's equity in itself, its self-equity as it were, such that any diminution of the self-equity such as income taxes, interest charges and cash dividends constitutes an expense. Stock dividends are not expenses nor are they distributions of income; they constitute a recapitalization designed to provide a more attractive investment atmosphere for future financing.

### The Social View

This view focuses attention on the role of the business enterprise in satisfying the many demands of society including those of employees, creditors, lessors, stock-holders, customers, suppliers, and the community at large. Because enterprise objectives cannot and do not coincide with those of its many participants, management decisions are mediatory in nature. As opposed to the self-equity point of view, which divorces the interests of the organization from those of its participants, the social approach views the business as an institution manifesting the interests and aspirations of all its participants. . . .

The business entity is an integrative mechanism through which the respective goals of each group might be attained. The firm, as such, owns no assets and enjoys no income; it is merely a convenient means for achieving sectional goals by joint action, as each of the various participants contributes in order to derive benefits. The balance sheet equation is of the form 'assets equals investors' input contributions'. From the point of view of all participants, all payments (disbursements of assets) to any participant are distributions of revenue. Therefore, income taxes, interest charges and cash dividends are distributions. Inasmuch as stock dividends do not represent the transfer of assets, they would not qualify as distributions.

### Summary

Although the self-equity and social views profess no concern with accounting for the interests of specific external equityholders, they differ from each other in their respective attitudes toward external parties in the aggregate. Accordingly, they parallel the earlier differences in the sense that what is classed as 'profits' and 'distributions of profit' is a function of the degree of restrictiveness inherent in the definition of equityholders.

## THE FUNCTIONAL APPROACH

Three conceptions comprise the functional group: the names 'enterprise', 'fund' and 'commander' identify them. They are classified as 'functional' because attention is focused on the function of financial reports. Ownership or other interests in the entity or its assets are neither played up nor disregarded. The consequences of its dealings with and the state of its relationships with all other parties are disclosed in financial statements. The function of these statements is to disclose information about the entity, regardless of the identity and the different financial interests of equityholders.

## The Enterprise View

The enterprise view is . . . that, on the corporate balance sheet, creditor *and* stockholder interests comprise a section termed 'equities'. The business enterprise enjoys net income and a portion of that income is enjoyed also by certain external groups—stockholders, holders of interest-bearing debt, tax-collecting agencies of government and beneficiaries of profit-sharing plans. Thus use is made of two concepts of net income. 'Enterprise net income' is a measure of the surplus that accrues to stockholders in terms of their legally defined equity in the business assets.

It is apparent that the enterprise view is similar to both the residual equity view, which concentrates on the interests of junior common stockholders, and the equity view which focuses on the various types of investors. It also has a resemblance to the social view to the extent that it regards the accounts as portraying the operations of the enterprise in terms of its relationship to the total society. It might therefore be considered as a synthesis of various other conceptions of the accounting entity.

## The Fund View

The 'fund' theory was developed . . . as a response to the ongoing debate over the nature of the stockholder/enterprise relationship.[1] Vatter contended that financial statements should be regarded merely as statistical summaries with no inherent or implicit attachment to any or all interests of any or all possible interested parties.[2]

For every identified fund, there exists a hierarchy of restrictions upon the asset collection such that the balance sheet equation becomes 'assets equal restrictions upon assets'. The one final and pervasive restriction, which indicates that the 'collected' assets are devoted to the purposes and operations of the fund in which they appear, is called the 'residual equity'. To the extent that there are specific restrictions—for debt, for preservation of initial stockholder investment or for particular management purposes—the residual equity is less than it would otherwise have been.[3]

Avoiding the problems of defining, computing and reporting a particular net income or profit, the fund theory is concerned only with reporting the results of changes in asset collections and restrictions thereon. Disclosure of the various account balances enables users of accounting information to combine or relate the figures in any way they choose for their own purposes. Thus, interest charges, tax payments and dividends are not inherently of one nature or another; instead each acquires its character 'through the eyes of the beholder'. . . .

In summary, the fund theory view is concerned only with the grouping of economic resources and with the restrictions to which they are subject. *Vis-à-vis* the various theories cited earlier, two observations may be made. The 'residual equity' view seems

---

[1] William J. Vatter, *The Fund Theory of Accounting and Its Implications for Financial Reports*, Chicago, 1947.

[2] William J. Vatter, 'Corporate Stock Equities—Part I', in Morton Backer (ed.), *Modern Accounting Theory*, Englewood Cliffs, 1966, p. 256.

[3] Vatter, 'Corporate Stock Equities—Part 1', p. 256.

to be a personalization of the fund theory, in the sense that the neutral 'residual equity' of the chronologically earlier fund theory is used by proponents of the residual equity view to denote the ownership interests of the most junior shareholders. Second, the fund theory can be seen as having an affinity with the self-equity view to the extent that the proponents of both find it unnecessary to postulate a specific class of equityholders as the primary class of interest.

### The Commander View

The 'commander' theory focuses upon persons having 'command over resources'.[4] Such commanders need not also own the resources. Stockholders are commanders over their respective shares of stock while managers are commanders over the corporate assets. Financial statements are reports by commanders at one level to commanders at another level, reflecting, in effect, the concept of 'chain of command'.

Managers' command over corporate assets is accounted for in terms of success in adding to resources and satisfying existing claims. And although each side of the balance sheet is oriented toward the position of different commanders, the balance sheet is prepared also for the information of still other commanders of resources, including labour unions, customers and competitors.

The income statement portrays the effect of a particular fiscal period's events. Profit is a measure of the growth in the quantity of economic resources which management commands. Because interest charges and tax payments are costs incurred by managers, they are expenses. Dividend payments constitute transfers of assets from the command of managers to the command of stockholders. Inasmuch as stock dividends do not represent transfers of resources, they are neither expenses nor distributions.

The commander theory distinguishes resources which managers command from those which external parties command. It is similar to the equity view inasmuch as it does not differentiate among the various types of investors for whom accounting data are prepared. It is also akin to the fund theory to the extent that it views the opposite sides of the balance sheet as being almost mutually exclusive sets of financial data. . . .

### Summary

The three functional views are not explicated in 'ownership' terms. Instead, each takes a more general stance by virtue of which ownership is only one of the relationships of interest. Yet the three conceptions do, in fact, relate to the issues that surfaced with respect to the earlier viewpoints. Rather than advocate a dominant interest group to which the accounting is directed, the functional views tend to neutralize differences represented by other views, and to accommodate seemingly disparate points of view.

[4]Louis Goldberg, *An Inquiry into the Nature of Accounting*, Menasha, Wisconsin, 1965.

## THE EIGHT CONCEPTIONS

Eight seemingly distinct views of the accounting entity have been identified and examined. Each view was considered in the context of its underlying assumptions as to the objectives of accounting, the balance sheet equation, the domain of assets and the nature of profit. Interest charges, income taxes and dividend declarations were taken as illustrations of the unique nature of each of the conceptions of the accounting entity.

As a first step in the reduction of complexity and confusion, it is necessary to distinguish substantive differences in viewpoint from differences which are purely verbal. How deep-seated, then, are the differences among the cited conceptions of the entity? Are there in fact eight mutually exclusive, equally valid points of view? Are they irreconcilable? Is their number irreducible?

When engaged in discussions of particular concepts or conventions—realization, matching, conservatism, the going concern, the entity—it is the common practice to examine in depth the origins, nuances and intricacies of each singly, as if it stood on its own. It is the exception to find analyses which treat the several ideas of any author, or the several ideas of any school of opinion, as components of an integral set of concepts. Under piecemeal analysis, however, it is easy to overlook incompatibilities or internal inconsistencies between the avowed ideas or concepts of any author. One important reason for this is that more writers write on particular concepts than on systems of concepts. They may have in mind particular ideas about other things—for example, particular ideas about 'the going concern' when writing specifically about 'the accounting entity'—but these particular ideas are not expounded at the same time.

To deal with a particular concept in isolation is to disregard the crosschecks, or the advantages of the crosschecks, which the idea of 'system' implies. Consider a problem in the context of the present article. The assets of a corporation are, in fact, owned by the corporation and under the control of its management. They are not owned and controlled by the stockholders or the combination of stockholders and senior equityholders. Any author who at some point alludes to managerial decision-making is debarred from suggesting that the assets of a company are the assets of its stockholders. He is debarred logically, since managers and stockholders cannot both control the same assets at the same time. It is not possible to hold (in support of the idea that the assets of a company are the assets of its stockholders) that it is economically realistic to look behind the 'corporate facade'; for the company is no less real than the stockholder. Therefore the author would be debarred also on empirical grounds from holding the view in question. The example may seem trivial; but there are some authors who write as though stockholders may take actions in respect of company assets.

For present purposes, the point is that at least some of the eight conceptions which have been identified may come to be eliminated if the views of the authors on other concepts (other parts of the system of ideas which constitute a theory of accounting) were found to be inconsistent with their views on the accounting entity.

The present paper has not attempted to deduce what proponents of each of the eight conceptions of the entity have advocated or would advocate regarding other important accounting conventions. It therefore is subject to the limitations suggested in the preceding paragraphs. Nevertheless, it seemed valuable as a preliminary to more systematic analysis, to explore the similarities and differences in the conceptions which have been espoused in the literature.

## APPENDIX
### Eight Conceptions of the Accounting Entity

| CONCEPTION | ORIENTATION | BALANCE SHEET EQUATION | PROFIT |
|---|---|---|---|
| 1. Traditional proprietary | Stockholders | Assets less liabilities equal owners' equity | Revenues less costs other than dividends |
| 2. Residual equity | Common stockholders | Assets less senior investors' equities equal owners' equity | Revenues less costs other than dividends to residual stockholders |
| 3. Equity | Equityholders | Assets equal equities | Revenues less costs other than dividends, income taxes, and interest |
| 4. Self-equity | The entity | Assets equal sources of assets | Revenues less all costs (including dividends) |
| 5. Social | Society | Assets equal investors' input contributions | Revenues |
| 6. Enterprise | The enterprise | Assets equal equities | Dual concept a. Similar to 'equity' (above) b. Similar to 'traditional proprietary' (above) |
| 7. Fund | The fund | Assets equal restrictions upon assets | A mathematical residual: asset inflows not specifically restricted less asset outflows not specifically restricted |
| 8. Commander | Commanders: managers and investors | Resources over which managers have command equal resources over which investors have command | Revenues less costs other than dividends |

## QUESTIONS

1. Classify the eight concepts of the accounting entity into three categories.
2. What is the income statement classification of the following items under the eight concepts?
   a. Dividends      c. Interest
   b. Income taxes

# Part 3
# Valuation in
# Accounting

# 58
## WHAT IS VALUE?*
John Heath, Jr.

What is value? Can you answer this question? Before you try, what about other common-place words used in and by the business community? Such words as appraisal, valuation, opinion, worth, cost, merger, acquisition, pooling, purchase, reproduction, replacement, depreciation deterioration, tangible, intangible, fair market value, actual cash value?

These words are similar, but for some who use them they might as well be in different languages because they mean different things to different people. Unfortunately, they are often misunderstood and misused.

It is not surprising that businessmen are somewhat confused when even Webster's Dictionary is not very clear or precise on valuation terms. It defines "worth" as "monetary value, and equivalent of specific amount," and then defines "value" as "monetary worth, marketable price—see worth."

### DEFINITIONS

To prevent further confusion, let's then attempt to define various terms used in appraising values and discuss each in light of current business practices. The 10 most common terms are the following: reproduction cost, replacement value, depreciated reproduction cost, actual cash value, original cost, book value, tax basis, liquidation, fair market value, and subjective value—value to an appreciative owner.

*Reproduction cost* is the amount it would cost to reproduce a particular property, based upon an analysis of current market prices of materials, labor, contractor's overhead, profit, and fees. It presumes replacing the property in question in new condition of exactly like kind and as a complete unit at one time.

*Replacement value* is the cost to replace the property in question with a modern unit in new condition and of equivalent capacity. Replacement cost takes into consideration modern materials and design concepts. In most instances, the replacement cost may be quite different, either higher or lower, than the cost of reproduction described above.

*Depreciated reproduction cost* is reproduction cost, as defined previously, less an allowance for accrued depreciation as evidenced by observed physical deterioration and condition, age, utility, remaining serviceable life, with consideration given to functional and economic obsolescence. Also normally considered is the assumption that the facilities will be continued in use at the present location and for the purposes designed.

*Actual cash value* is a term used in insurance policies, but, to our knowledge, not defined by insurance companies. In many states, this term has taken on a meaning the same as depreciated reproduction costs as defined above. Other states permit the "board evidence rule," wherein market factors can be considered.

*From *Financial Executive*, June 1971, pp. 13—15. Reprinted by permission of the publisher.

*Original cost* is the initial capitalized cost of the item in the hands of the present owner, for accounting and tax purposes. It generally includes the purchase price of an item, but it may or may not include such items as sale tax, freight, cartage, and installation labor.

*Book value,* sometimes called net book value or unrecovered cost, is the capitalized cost for the item in question, less depreciation taken for accounting purposes, which is based on the adopted corporate method for computing depreciation over the useful life of the asset.

*Tax basis* is the capitalized cost less depreciation taken for federal income tax purposes wherein depreciation is computed in a prescribed manner over the allowed or allowable life for tax purposes. It may or may not be the same as the book basis.

It is important to realize that the accountant's concept of depreciation—determined by a fixed method over a given life period—is entirely different from the appraiser's connotation of the same word. The latter considers loss in value based on facts and circumstances embracing wear and tear, age, utility, and functional and economic obsolescence.

*Liquidation* is the amount in dollars the property in question is likely to bring under forced sale conditions within a specific amount of time. Very often liquidation is associated with an auction.

*Subjective value* is sometimes defined as the "value to an appreciative owner." It is the amount the object is worth to its owner, generally for emotional reasons, regardless of its worth or value to another. An example of something that has subjective value might be an old picture of one's ancestors, a serviceman's flag from World War I and II, a ticket stub to a national convention, or some other memorabilia.

*Fair market value* is the price at which property would change hands between a willing buyer and a willing seller, each having reasonable knowledge of all pertinent facts and neither being under compulsion to buy or sell.

Fair market value is without a doubt the best-defined valuation term. As a result of many court cases, attorneys, appraisers, and others involved in valuation work generally agree on the aforementioned definition.

In actual practice, however, there is more to determining fair market value of certain assets than considering the willing buyer, willing seller concept. One must properly consider such matters as the terms, conditions, and limiting factors, such as to whom, for what, and when the property is sold. When these factors receive proper consideration, they may change the answer radically from the willing buyer, willing seller concept.

It is one thing to express an opinion as to the fair market value of a property at a given time, but it is entirely another problem to express an opinion of the fair market value of a business entity. In the latter situation, the proper determination of fair market value embraces the deliberate consideration of past earning performances, future earnings potential, economic climate of the industry, and in any particular business, a study of the health, ability, vitality, and the age of the personalities involved.

Since appraising is not an exact science, most valuation processes contain an element of opinion. The expression of an opinion of the fair market value of a business or a group of assets is subject to considerable subjective thought and deliberation, and consequently the determination of fair market value can generate wide divergence of opinion among appraisers. Furthermore, the answer to a fair market value study can be somewhat theoretical or even fictitious. Seldom do the circumstances surrounding determination of fair market value include a complete willing buyer and a complete willing seller, each having reasonable knowledge of all pertinent facts and equal negotiating ability.

Let's consider just one example to illustrate the point. Recently an aerospace company wished to acquire the government equipment located at its plant. The government was willing to sell the equipment—at fair market value. Here we had a willing buyer and a willing seller. But—what was fair market value? The original cost to the government of some 1600 pieces of equipment of all kinds installed in the contractor's plant between 1950 and 1969 amounted to $22 million. Assuming maximum utility by the aerospace company and earnings to justify a proper return on the investment and other relevant factors, the appraiser felt that the equipment assembled in place for continued use had a value to the company of $15 million. However, if the company had told the government to remove the equipment, and the government had to sell the equipment in an orderly manner on the open market, it would bring only about $4.5 million.

Both sale of the equipment to the aerospace company and sale of the equipment on the open market contained the factors of a willing buyer and a willing seller; the terms and conditions radically changed with the selling price, hence the value.

One further comment: fair market value should not be confused with purchase price. Sometimes it is synonymous, but fair market value is the theoretical answer, and purchase price is the amount at which a transaction actually takes place and depends on the ability of the negotiators involved and the relative value of the assets in question to one or the other of the parties involved in the transaction.

## COMPARISON OF VALUES

Now that we have defined terms prevalent in valuation work, we must strongly emphasize that there is no set relationship between any of the foregoing terms used in valuation work. Here are a few examples.

First, let's take the case of an old castle being used as a machine shop. The insurable value, based on the reproduction cost less depreciation, with today's labor, would be an astronomical figure. However, if the castle was to be sold, its fair market value would probably be considerably less. Who could afford to maintain and operate a castle today and to what business purpose could it be put because of its obsolete design?

As a second example, let's consider the buildings erected by a fast-food carry-out business which operates nationally on a franchise basis. Each building in the chain is virtually the same, whether built five years ago or yesterday. As such, the reproduction cost is nearly the same at any time for any building. However, the fair market value of a particular building may be higher or lower than the reproduction cost, depending on whether the franchise is attached to it. In other words, a building with a franchise is a special-purpose structure and is worth considerably more than the same building without the franchise.

It is hoped that these examples illustrate and emphasize the fact that there is no set relationship between these terms used in valuation work. There is no formula to convert one term to another.

## DIFFERENT VALUES

Let's take one last example which will show how a given item or an entire industrial complex can be worth various amounts under different circumstances. As an example, a machine was purchased new in 1960 and given a 16-year useful life. Today it has the following "values":

*Reproduction cost,* because of inflation factors, would be $45,150.

*Replacement value,* because of modern technology, would be $58,815.

*Depreciated reproduction cost,* considering normal maintenance, etc., $33,962.

*Actual cash value,* excluding the foundation since it would be excluded for insurance purposes, might be $33,300.

*Original cost,* including freight, cartage, and installation, was $33,825.

*Book value,* for accounting purposes, using straight-line depreciation, would be $12,684.

*Tax basis,* using an accelerated method of depreciation, would be $5,223.

*Liquidation value,* if disassembled and placed on the loading dock for sale to a used machinery dealer, might be $24,000.

*Fair market value,* considering continued use in place as part of a going concern involved in a merger or acquisition, $28,000.

*Subjective value,* or value to its appreciative owner, might vary from zero—if the company has had trouble with the machine—up to $50,000 or even $100,000 if by chance the owner placed sentimental value on it.

How much is something worth? Many answers may be proper. It depends upon the usage and conditions.

## QUESTIONS

1. Some accountants use only the term "cost" in discussing their work and never refer to "value." For example, in 1936 the American Accounting Association stated: "Accounting is thus not essentially a process of valuation, but the allocation of historical costs . . . to the current and succeeding fiscal periods." ("A Tentative Statement of Accounting Principles Underlying Corporate Financial Statements," *The Accounting Review,* June 1936, p. 188.) Why do you suppose this is so?

2. The basic dichotomy in accounting valuation is often based upon whether entry or input prices (when the asset enters the firm) or exit or output prices (when the asset leaves the firm) are used. Classify the values given by Heath on this basis.

3. Determine the ten values discussed by Heath for any major asset you own (car, stereo, camera, etc.).

# 59
## QUICK, WHAT ARE YOU WORTH?*
Robert M. Randall

Some people figure their net worth in a furtive moment, dreading the awful reckoning as if they feared that either a wrathful God or an overeager insurance salesman were peering over their shoulder. In fact, the impulse to sum up your financial situation is a healthy one. A systematic calculation of net worth is a good first step toward getting control of your financial life.

Your bank has elaborate forms that it produces, say, when you apply for a mortgage. But if the calculation is to be approximate and for your information only, you can do it easily, yet comprehensively by using the form on page 195. In most cases, you will find that you are worth more than you thought. If so, you can plan new ways to make your assets work for you. Should your worth be less than you expected, you will need to rethink your personal financial strategy.

Professional money managers believe that the net-worth figure can be a help in setting some specific money goals: perhaps you should decide to start a savings program, set up an investment plan, or opt for buying a house instead of continuing to rent. Once you know your present worth, you should establish net-worth goals for the future and keep a careful record of yearly progress. Many professionals consider a 10% annual increase in net worth appropriate for average families.

Before you start to value and add up your assets and liabilities, you should consider what you want to find out. Literally, net worth consists of exactly what you could get in cash for your assets, less your liabilities, at a given point in time. Normally, that point in time is the present. But you might instead be interested in finding out what your estate will be worth to your survivors, and this calculation could change some values. You might also be curious to learn what you will be worth when you retire, or if your Aunt Jennie leaves you her millions. You could label one calculation "What I'll be worth ten years from now if fortune smiles on me." Another might be headed "What I'd be worth next Thursday if we decided to move to Australia." To find out what you are, might or will be worth, simply make the computation several times, substituting figures appropriate to the circumstances.

If you happen to have $3,500 to spend, you can get a computer to do the calculations for you. For the past two and a half years, a team at the New York brokerage firm of Donaldson, Lufkin & Jenrette, Inc. has been working out a computer program that can show a client what would happen to his finances under a wide range of conditions and can calculate the results of current decisions projected ten years ahead. The service is most often purchased by corporations for top executives. Despite net worths of $100,000 to $10 million, these men are often badly organized in their personal finances.

Specialists in the management of personal wealth have learned that there are some mistakes even seasoned businessmen make when they appraise their assets and lia-

*From *Money*, October 1972, pp. 78—79. Reprinted by permission of the publisher.

bilities. "One client of ours likes to say that his stock is worth $2 million," says a partner in a major New York accounting firm. "True, he's not exaggerating about the value of the stock, but if he sold it, he might have to pay as much as $800,000 in taxes. To figure his net worth, both sums would have to be considered."

Some other common mistakes in calculating net worth:

Failing to include retirement or pension plans and other benefits. Your firm's personnel department may be able to give you an estimate of the present value of your pension and perhaps help you figure out the potential worth of stock options, if and when you are eligible to exercise them. In any case, they should be able to tell you how much your profit-sharing or thrift plan amounts to and roughly what your pension will be at the time you retire.

Appraising property at replacement rather than market value. Bankers and accountants take a stony view of the value of cherished possessions—houses, stocks or collections of snuff boxes. They have to ask, "How much would be realized from the immediate sale of this property?" Their approach is almost certain to disillusion the man who prefers to value his snuff boxes at what they would be worth to just the right fellow snuff-box connoisseur. Even the value of a house depends somewhat on how much time is available for selling it. . . .

Figuring your own net worth makes sense. . . . If you continue to manage your financial affairs on your own, you will have a good bench mark for measuring where you are and where you are going. If you solicit advice from others, you will be able to appraise their suggestions better—and for the very reason that you are able to discuss your situation with precision, the advice itself may be of better quality.

## QUESTIONS

1. What is the name of the financial statement Mr. Randall discusses? How is it used?

2. With what other versions of the given equation (assets minus liabilities equal net worth) are you familiar? Explain.

3. Prepare a statement similar to the one for question (6) for yourself as of the date you graduated from high school and compare it with the one prepared for question (6).

4. Prepare a statement similar to question (6) for the day when you will have been a college graduate for 10 years. You will have to predict the assets and the liabilities you expect to have on that date. Contrast this statement with the one prepared for question (6), and note the changes.

5. Prepare a statement for your father (or guardian) as of this date according to the equation given.

6. Prepare a statement for yourself as of this date according to the equation given.

## SELECTED BIBLIOGRAPHY

"The Executive's Personal Budget," *Business Week*, Feb. 2, 1974, pp. 67-74.

| ASSETS | LIABILITIES |
|---|---|

**Real estate**

Homes _____
_____

Other _____
_____

**Cash**

Savings accounts _____
Checking accounts _____
Savings bonds _____

**Marketable securities**

Stocks _____
Bonds _____
Other _____

**Personal property**

Home furnishings _____
Clothing, furs _____
Jewelry _____
Automobiles _____
Art, antique
collections _____
Other (animals,
equipment, musical
instruments, etc.) _____
_____

**Long-term assets**

Insurance _____
_____
Annuities _____
Pensions _____
Benefits
(options, profit
sharing, etc.) _____
Patents, royalties _____
Value of business
interests _____

Total

---

**Mortgages**

Homes _____
_____

Other _____
_____

**Current bills**

Medical, dental _____
Charge accounts _____
_____
Rent, utilities _____
_____
Alimony,
child support _____
Other _____
_____
_____
_____

**Prepaid taxes on
investments**

Federal _____
State _____
Local _____

**Debts to individuals**

_____
_____
_____
_____

**Installment debts**

Auto loans _____
Home-
improvement
loans _____
Personal loans _____
Education loans _____
Other _____

Total

If you
want to deter-
mine what you
*will* be worth,
project the value
of your home and
other real estate
based on the trend
of prices for
property in the area.
If you want to
know what you are
worth *now*, list
the price you might
have to take
for your house in
a quick sale.

Don't forget
mortgages on your
summer home
or on other real
estate you hold as
an investment.

Remember to
list taxes that
would be owed on
stocks if you were
to sell them to
raise cash. Be
sure to include
assessments (for
sewer lines, road
improvements,
etc.). Remember
that people not on
salary owe
federal taxes
quarterly.

If you are
trying to determine
what you will be
worth to your heirs,
list the face value of
your insurance.
Otherwise, follow
standard accounting
procedures and
list the cash value.

**Assets minus liabilities equals net worth**

The two columns of this form are for adding up what you own and what you owe.
Made annually, this calculation will show whether you are gaining or slipping financially. Items on the form are positioned to show how some categories of assets and
liabilities correspond. The form should be studied across—for instance, do you have
enough cash to pay current bills and still cover emergencies? It should also be read
up and down—are your assets unduly concentrated in just one category?

# 60

# THE ACCOUNTANT AS A VALUER*
William A. Paton

Even more serious than failure to recognize the decline in the purchasing power of the monetary yardstick in handling recorded financial data is the stonewall resistance to recognition of major changes in the values of specific assets. Accountants cheerfully certify to financial statements in which land is shown at a fraction of unquestioned current value and such additions to resources as accretion of growing timber are neglected. And there is even some resistance to reporting the current market value of securities owned if above recorded cost. I've written at length on this subject and will be brief here. The general point is this: as evidence of current financial position and as a basis for judgment as to utilization the only truly significant measurement of any resource is its current value, carefully determined. What an asset cost once upon a time, even with cost correctly expressed, is of no significance in planning.

The position is often taken in this connection that the accountant is not a valuation man, an appraiser, and hence must steer clear of any gesture in the direction of finding and reporting what assets are worth. This position has been greatly overemphasized. Actually financial measurement is meat and drink to the accountant. The accountant's business is recording, classifying, measuring, reporting, interpreting *economic data.* He is really the valuation man par excellence. He has long been involved in the process of determining expirations of value, decreases in economic significance. He has no hesitancy in assisting—or taking charge of—the determination of an allowance for uncollectible receivables, in recording a decline in the market value of securities owned, in estimating and recognizing the loss in inventory values from price declines and other causes, in determining the impact of absolescence and other factors on plant value, in suppressing or amortizing organization and development costs and intangibles generally. It's only when it comes to increases in value that he turns his back. This is not high-level professional conduct and never has been.

The present-day posture of persistent allegiance to the "historical-cost" basis is of course especially unfortunate in view of what has been happening to prices in general and in particular. It stands in the way of permitting accounting to serve its underlying purpose of providing management and owners with essential, pertinent information. It also tends to clip the capable accountant's wings. Actually there is no one better qualified than the experienced accountant to take the lead in the process of the valuation of a business enterprise as a whole in connection with mergers, estate settlements, security issues, etc. Long since he should have recognized his opportunity to move in as the key man in this area, with resulting advance in professional stature.

*Excerpt from "Accounting Today—A Bird's-Eye View," *Michigan Business Review*, January 1974, pp. 22—24. Reprinted by permission of the publisher.

# 61
# VALUE CHANGES*
Oscar S. Gellein

The extent to which information about current values and changes in them should become a part of the financial statements is a key issue in formulating a framework for the attainment of financial statement objectives. An ideal portrayal of enterprise earning power, if foresight only were as all-seeing as hindsight, would be future periodic cash flows for the indefinite future. In this ideal state, income for a period would be measured by the change in the present value of the future cash streams between the beginning and end of the period, adjusted, of course, for capital changes. This ideal is unattainable but furnishes a guide. Current values of asset benefits are usually better indicators of likely cash flows than are cost measures. Accordingly, the predictive value of financial statements generally would be enhanced if current values were shown.

There is a wide range of views concerning the direction and extent of use of current values in financial statements. Some would move rapidly toward their extensive use in the belief that the information they furnish is necessary to measure the economic position and economic income of an enterprise, that is, its change in well-being. Others would see a period of evolution, starting perhaps with disclosure outside the financial statements proper, but looking forward to including current values and changes in them as an integral, but separately disclosed, part of the statements. Others question whether current values should be shown except as a matter of disclosure where current values differ significantly from original costs. These various views were held also by members of our group. Our views were unanimous, however, that no one value system taken as a whole and by itself furnishes maximally useful financial statements. Further, there was agreement that to whatever extent current values and related changes are a part of the reporting system, no one system furnishes universally relevant measures for particular assets and liabilities. Instead, a choice should be made among replacement value, exit values and discounted cash flow measures, asset by asset, on the basis of the relevance of the measure for estimating enterprise cash-generating ability. There is a consensus in our group that based on user needs as they are now constituted, income measured in terms of highly probable cash effect should be shown separately from any income reported as a result of asset value changes.

EDITORS' NOTE: When Mr. Gellein refers to his group, he means the AICPA Committee on the Study of the Objectives of Financial Statements (usually referred to as the Trueblood Committee). This committee published a report in October 1973; material from this report is included in Selection 111.

## QUESTIONS

1. Why does Mr. Gellein feel current values of assets are better than the cost values of the same assets?

*Excerpt from "Objectives of Financial Statements," Selected Papers 1973, New York: Haskins & Sells, 1974, pp. 32–33. Reprinted by permission of the publisher.

2. Which of the various views concerning the direction and extent of use of current values do you conclude is the most feasible, and why? Illustrate.

3. Why does Mr. Gellein argue that the relevance of a value measure is based on its estimation of cash-generating ability?

# 62
## AN APPRAISAL*
Glenn McHugh

You have asked me to read and review (if possible) your new edition of the manual. I have read it, mindful ever of your favorite admonition to the earnest, budding evaluator that there is no judgment in a lead pencil. I have read it also with another admonition in mind—that of Mr. Justice Holmes, who once said of the common law, that it was not "a brooding omnipresence in the sky, but the articulate voice of some sovereign...that can be identified."

Perhaps you hope, as I do, that these appraisers of ours will remember that admonition of the Justice's—first because they should be able to identify the property which means they have seen it, and second because they should not treat it like "a brooding omnipresence in the sky" but rather should not be confused or enveloped by it because of the perplexities of its nature or the uncertainties of its value.

Do you have in your mind's eye the ideal of what an appraiser should be and how he should function? And would this approach it? A man of maturity and judgment, keen-eyed and skeptical, who has just completed his appraisal performance with the inevitable formulas, who has wrestled with capitalization rates and affected a defensible compromise, who has assuaged his conscience on reproduction costs and depreciation and now must face the final phase—the determination of a value which he must now and forever (or at least for a year or so) subscribe to. In that tremulous moment of darkness and groping he will revisit the scene of his struggle, resurvey this erstwhile brooding omnipresence, settle down on the nearby curb and, before comfort or complacence overwhelms him, write out an amount which he as a cautious and prudent grandfather would pay for the property for the long term use and benefit of his grandchildren.

If you can induce your fellow appraisers to do that with this manual, you will have fulfilled a great destiny for you will have enrolled a galaxy of educated guessers, strong, stalwart men who have patience to search for and who have experience to select the pertinent facts, who have time to ruminate about them, and who finally have the humility and the courage to assign values to them which the rest of us must

*Letter by Glenn McHugh addressed to Frank Hall, January 1946, The Equitable Life Assurance Society of the U.S. Reprinted by permission of the corporation.

rely upon, must act upon, can pretend to understand, will carp about occasionally and will hope we can be thankful and content that we have them in our files.

## QUESTIONS

1. Given the above description of an appraisal, which of the following characteristics best describes an appraisal, and why? Relevance, reliability, freedom from bias, comparability, consistency, or understandability.

2. It is not uncommon for two appraisers both appearing as expert witnesses in a court case to report two very different market values for the same asset. Why?


# 63
# VALUATION OF ASSETS
Robert T. Sprouse and Maurice Moonitz

EDITORS' NOTE: This excerpt is from *A Tentative Set of Broad Accounting Principles for Business Enterprises*, Accounting Research Study No. 3, AICPA, 1962. Eleven of these research studies have been published by the AICPA during the past decade. Among them, critics generally consider this one to be among the most scholarly. Its conclusions were conventional for U.S. practice except for those accountants advocating replacement cost as the basis for valuing inventories and long-lived assets. Unlike the Netherlands practice, replacement cost is not now accepted for U.S. accounting practice.

The proper pricing (valuation) of assets and the allocation of profit to accounting periods are dependent in large part upon estimates of the existence of future benefits, regardless of the bases used to price the assets. The need for estimates is unavoidable and cannot be eliminated by the adoption of any formula as to pricing.

1. All assets in the form of money or claims to money should be shown at their discounted present value or the equivalent. The interest rate to be employed in the discounting process is the market (effective) rate at the date the asset was acquired.

The discounting process is not necessary in the case of short-term receivables where the force of interest is small. The carrying-value of receivables should be reduced by allowances for uncollectible elements; estimated collection costs should be recorded in the accounts.

If the claims to money are uncertain as to time or amount of receipt, they should be recorded at their current market value. If the current market value is so uncertain as to be unreliable, these assets should be shown at cost.

2. Inventories which are readily salable at known prices with readily predictable costs of disposal should be recorded at net realizable value, and the related revenue taken up at the same time. Other inventory items should be recorded at their current (replacement) cost, and the related gain or loss separately reported. Accounting for

inventories on either basis will result in recording revenues, gains, or losses before they are validated by sale but they are nevertheless components of the net profit (loss) of the period in which they occur.

Acquisition costs may be used whenever they approximate current (replacement) costs, as would probably be the case when the unit prices of inventory components are reasonably stable and turnover is rapid. In all cases the basis of measurement actually employed should be "subject to verification by another competent investigator."

3. All items of plant and equipment in service, or held in stand-by status, should be recorded at cost of acquisition or construction, with appropriate modification for the effect of the changing dollar either in the primary statements or in supplementary statements. In the external reports, plant and equipment should be restated in terms of current replacement costs whenever some significant event occurs, such as a reorganization of the business entity or its merger with another entity or when it becomes a subsidiary of a parent company. Even in the absence of a significant event, the accounts could be restated at periodic intervals, perhaps every five years. The development of satisfactory indexes of construction costs and of machinery and equipment prices would assist materially in making the calculation of replacement costs feasible, practical, and objective.

## QUESTION

1. It has been argued that valuation in accounting is either direct or indirect. Assets are valued directly when the benefits expected to be realized from the assets are measured; assets are valued indirectly when the sacrifices made are measured (on the assumption that the benefits will be at least equal to the sacrifices). Which of Sprouse's and Moonitz's recommendations on valuation are direct and which are indirect?

## SELECTED BIBLIOGRAPHY

Carlson, Arthur E., "A Case for Current-Cost Reporting," *Management Accounting,* February 1973, pp. 33-35, 44.

# 64

# THE FOUNDATIONS OF FINANCIAL ACCOUNTING
R. J. Chambers

EDITORS' NOTE: This is the appendix to a paper presented by R.J. Chambers at a University of California (Berkeley) Symposium on the Foundations of Financial Reporting, January 13th and 14th, 1967. The body of the paper advocates current values or C.C.A. Professor Chambers' book, *Accounting, Evaluation and Economic Behavior,* received the AICPA's literature award in 1966.

A choice must be made between alternative systems of accounting if vacillation and recurrent exposure to recrimination are to be avoided, and indeed if accounting is to perform a specialized function well. An attempt is made here to present an evaluation of the main types of system used or suggested.

The main differences between the systems relate to methods of asset valuation and the five systems compared differ primarily in this respect; the names used reflect the general principles of asset valuation employed; variants are disregarded in all cases. The systems are:

*Original cost accounting* (O.C.A.): the general basis of asset valuation is the initial purchase price of each asset in possession at balance date.

*Price level accounting* (P.L.A.): the general basis is the original cost modified by application of a general index of changes in prices. Because of its link with original cost, this system has many of the characteristics of O.C.A.

*Discounted value accounting* (D.V.A.): the general basis is the discounted expected net product of each asset. In essence all such values are based on sets of hypotheses about the future, including the primary hypothesis that the firm's operations will remain substantially the same.

*Replacement cost accounting* (R.C.A.): the general basis is the replacement cost of assets. This entails that replacement is intended and feasible, and is thus akin to D.V.A. in the assumption that the firm's operations will remain substantially the same.

*Continuously contemporary accounting* (C.C.A.): the general basis is the measure given by prices of assets held as they are evidenced, at balance dates, in the resale markets of those assets. The system is the system alluded to in the paper, and developed at length in the writer's *Accounting, Evaluation and Economic Behavior.*

In the following table the criteria are of two classes: A, technical accounting questions, and B, questions on the practical utility of the products of the systems. The questions in each group and in the set as a whole are not mutually exclusive, so that the mere number of "yes" and "no" entries is not to be taken as giving the weight of evidence conclusively. These numbers do, however, indicate the relative positions of the systems in such an evaluation scheme. There may be other criteria, and the reader may not agree with the scores given in every case. But, if a choice is to be made, some such scheme must be employed, and must include at least these questions.

## SELECTED BIBLIOGRAPHY

Backer, Morton, "A Model for Current Value Reporting," *The CPA Journal,* February 1974, pp. 27-33.

## Comparison of Five Accounting Systems

|  | O.C.A. | P.L.A. | D.V.A. | R.C.A. | C.C.A. |
|---|---|---|---|---|---|
| A1  Is it, in principle, a double entry system? | Yes | Yes | Yes | Yes | Yes |
| A2  Are its transaction inputs, in principle, facts? | Yes | Yes | Yes | Yes | Yes |
| A3  Are its transformations (depreciation, inventory valuations, etc.), in principle, facts? | No | No | No | Yes | Yes |
| A4  Are its transformed magnitudes measures? | No | No | No | Yes | Yes |
| A5  Are its transformed magnitudes contemporary? | No | No | Yes | Yes | Yes |
| A6  Do its transformations give prompt effect to relative price changes? | No | No | No | Yes | Yes |
| A7  Does it give a comprehensive history of the relationships and transactions of the firm? (Is it isomorphic?) | No | No | No | No | Yes |
| A8  Is aggregation of measures of items logically possible? | No | Yes | Yes | Yes | Yes |
| A9  Is it a representation of facts, or, alternatively, does its theory provide for other ways of getting contemporary facts? | No | No | No | No | Yes |
| B1  Are the results neutral as to specific future actions? | Yes | Yes | No | No | Yes |
| B2  Are individual measures relevant at stated dates to choice or adaptation? | No | No | No | No | Yes |
| B3  Is income a measure of general command of goods and services? | No | No | No | No | Yes |
| B4  Do magnitudes provide a basis for comparison of present operations with future potential variants? | No | No | No | No | Yes |
| B5  Is a valid current ratio given? | No | No | No | No | Yes |
| B6  Is a valid debt to equity ratio given? | No | No | No | No | Yes |
| B7  Is a valid rate of return given? (Is rate of return comparable with rates of return on pure money contracts and other opportunities?) | No | No | No | No | Yes |
| B8  Are interfirm comparisons of ratios valid? | No | No | No | Yes | Yes |
| B9  Do balance sheets and income accounts fairly present positions at stated dates and changes between those dates? | No | No | No | No | Yes |

# 65

## S.F. APPEALS BOARD GIVES XEROX TAX BREAK*

San Francisco Chronicle

San Francisco's Assessment Appeals Board voted yesterday to give a tax break of nearly $250,000 to the Xerox Corp.

At the same time, the three-man panel also voted to lower property taxes on the 25-story Equitable Life Insurance Co. building and on ten businesses at Fisherman's Wharf.

The board decided in a 2 to 1 vote to lower the full cash value of hundreds of leased Xerox machines in San Francisco from $38.8 million to $31.1 million.

### SAVINGS

It was not the $11 million reduction sought by attorneys for Xerox, but it will save the huge company about $240,000 in actual San Francisco taxes on its property for the current fiscal year.

San Francisco was the first stop for the Xerox representatives in their statewide effort to convince assessment appeals boards that California assessors have been unfairly pegging the value of their copying machines for tax purposes.

Their arguments convinced local board members Jackson Hu and Thomas Brady to lower the value of Xerox machines in San Francisco from $38,866,416 to $31,116,684. The third member, Robert Grassilli, dissented.

### VALUE

In another 2 to 1 vote, the board decided to lower the full cash value of the Equitable Life Building at 120 Montgomery Street from $17,296,700 to $15,300,000.

The life insurance company, which had asked a reduction in value to $14.1 million, will save approximately $63,000 in property taxes from the lower value.

Grassilli again dissented, but was overruled by Hu and alternate member Michael Perri, Jr.

There were no dissenting votes in the Fisherman's Wharf cases, in which Hu, Brady and Grassilli agreed to lower assessments on ten businesses for the second year in a row.

Altogether, the full cash value of the ten properties were lowered from $6,015,000 to $5,181,500—a reduction of $833,500 and an actual tax saving of about $25,200.

### QUESTIONS

1. Referring to Selection 63, what basis of valuation do you conclude that the San Francisco Assessment Appeals Board uses in reviewing property tax assessments?

*From the *San Francisco Chronicle*, Mar. 15, 1973, p. 22. Reprinted by permission of the publisher.

2. What basis of valuation do you think the Xerox Corporation used in valuing the machines on its balance sheet? Given that the Xerox Company has leased these machines out on contract, could you argue convincingly that the corporation might have used another basis of valuation? Explain.

3. What basis of valuation do you think the Equitable Life Insurance Company uses on its balance sheet (or position statement) for its building? Why?

4. What basis of valuation do you think the 10 businesses on Fisherman's Wharf use on their position statements? Why? Compare with the basis used by the Appeals Board.

# 66
# IF AT FIRST YOU DON'T SUCCEED, QUIT*
Steven M. Cahn

We must realize that becoming an educated person is a difficult, demanding enterprise. Just as anyone who spoke of intense physical training as a continuous source of pleasure and delight would be thought a fool, for we all know how much pain and frustration such training involves, so anyone who speaks of intense mental exertion as a continuous source of joy and ecstasy ought to be thought equally foolish, for such effort also involves pain and frustration. It is painful to have one's ignorance exposed and frustrating to be baffled by intellectual subtleties. Of course, there can be joy in learning as there can be joy in sport. But in both cases the joy is a result of overcoming genuine challenges and cannot be experienced without toil.

It is not easy to read intelligently and think precisely. It is not easy to speak fluently and write clearly. It is not easy to study a subject carefully and know it thoroughly. But these abilities are the foundation of a sound education.

If a student is to learn intellectual responsibility, he must be taught to recognize that not every piece of work is a good piece of work. In fact, some work is just no good at all. A student may be friendly, cooperative, and sensitive to the needs of mankind, but he may nevertheless turn in a muddled economics paper or an incompetent laboratory report.

And that he means well is no reason why he should not be criticized for an inadequate performance. Such criticism, when well-founded and constructive, is in no way demanding, for the willingness to accept it and learn from it is one mark of a mature individual. Yet criticism of any sort is rare nowadays. As student opinion is given greater and greater weight in the evaluation of faculty, professors are busy trying to ingratiate themselves with the students.

Indeed, college education is gradually coming to resemble the Caucus-race in

*From the *New York Times*, Dec. 29, 1974, p. E13. Reprinted by permission of the publisher.

"Alice's Adventures in Wonderland" in which everyone begins running whenever he likes and stops running whenever he likes. There are no rules. Still everyone wins, and everyone must receive a prize.

A democracy, however, cannot afford to transform its educational system into a Caucus-race, for the success of a democracy depends in great part upon the understanding and capability of its citizens. And in the complex world in which we live, to acquire sufficient understanding and capability requires a rigorous education. If we fail to provide that education, we shall have only ourselves to blame as misguided policies in our universities contribute to the decay of our democracy.

# 67
## DEPRECIATION*
Charles W. Lamden and Dale L. Gerboth

"Depreciation is a joint cost par excellence. It is joint with respect to the several time periods during which a plant asset is used. It is joint with respect to the products that are turned out utilizing any piece of equipment. It is joint with respect to the individual units of production that are turned out during any given time period. Economic theory suggests to us that joint costs cannot be allocated satisfactorily. Yet in a variety of circumstances we are faced with the problem of allocating these joint costs—costs which are joint to an extent unmatched by almost any other kind of cost."[1]

The observation by Sidney Davidson clearly states the depreciation accounting dilemma: accountants must allocate costs which cannot be allocated satisfactorily. This is the dilemma that is faced by the AICPA-sponsored research study on accounting for depreciable assets. By ruling out the substitution of current value or some other basis of valuation in place of historical cost,[2] the study focuses squarely on joint cost allocation.

In pointing out that joint cost allocation procedures are inherently unsatisfactory, it is generally explained by economists and accountants alike that "they are—arbitrary, in the sense that each allocation represents a selection, determined in accordance with human judgment, out of several possible criteria, some of which may be regarded as

*From **World**, Winter 1973, pp. 43—47. Reprinted by permission of the publisher.

[1]Sidney Davidson, **The Meaning of Depreciation**, Selected Papers No. 2, Graduate School of Business, University of Chicago (1962), p. 2.

[2]For a description of the study and its constraints, refer to Charles W. Lamden, "Depreciation—A Reliability Gap," **World**, Autumn 1971, p. 33.

having equal validity with the one selected."[3] Moreover, there appears to be no conclusive basis for accepting one alternative method over another.[4]

More important than the generally acknowledged view that joint cost allocation is theoretically indeterminable is the contention that rational criteria for choosing an allocation scheme nevertheless exist or can be developed. Accordingly, the issue that is of primary concern is whether the cost of depreciable assets can be allocated by a method that is not universally defensible but is rational when judged by some criterion. Grant and Norton express this concept as follows: ". . . there is no one right method for distributing the difference between the first cost of a fixed asset and its salvage value among the years of its life. The best that can be done is to develop criteria for judging the merits of alternative methods. . . ."[5]

## THE SEARCH FOR CRITERIA

The critical questions are—what are the criteria? and how can they be developed? Some of the bases for such criteria found in the accounting literature are set forth below.

### Criteria Based on Accounting Conventions

Accountants have long dreamed of constructing a theoretical system in which accounting procedures could be logically deduced from some agreed-upon set of postulates and principles. That concept was the basis of the research program visualized for the Accounting Principles Board.[6] To date, however, no comprehensive system is available for developing criteria on which the allocation of historical costs of depreciable assets can be based.

Despite the fact that a comprehensive deductive system does not exist, however, some of the fundamental accounting conventions provide at least a partial basis for formulating criteria. An analysis of the accounting concept of "matching costs with revenue," for example, can provide an overall criterion for evaluating cost allocation. At least it identifies the reason the allocation is required.

The American Accounting Association Committee on The Matching Concept explained "matching" as follows:

"In business operations, costs, defined as resources given up or economic sacrifices made, are incurred with the anticipation that they will produce revenue in excess of the outlay. Within this frame of reference, one can then say that costs constitute one measure of business effort, and revenues represent accomplishments coming from

---

[3] Louis Goldberg, *Concepts of Depreciation* (Melbourne: The Law Book Co. of Australia Ltd., 1960), p. 21.

[4] Arthur L. Thomas, *The Allocation Problem in Financial Accounting Theory* (Evanston, Illinois: American Accounting Association, 1969).

[5] Eugene L. Grant and Paul J. Norton, *Depreciation* (New York: The Ronald Press Company, 1955), p. 184.

[6] "Report to Council of Special Committee on Research Program," *The Journal of Accountancy*, December 1958.

those efforts. Appropriate reporting of costs and revenues should therefore relate costs with revenues in such a way as to disclose most vividly the relationship between efforts and accomplishments."[7]

To the extent that there is a direct relationship between costs and revenues no problem arises in applying the concept of "matching." But in the case of depreciable assets, often there is no direct means of associating cause and effect in any given period. In such circumstances, as stated in APB Statement No. 4, accountants resort to "systematic and rational" allocation,[8] which is an indirect means of associating cause and effect. Accordingly, even though matching is the reason allocation is required, it cannot be used as the criterion for selecting one cost allocation method over another.

## Criteria Based on User Needs

Some authorities view accounting as existing primarily to provide the information that best satisfies the legitimate needs of users of financial statements.[9]

The principal advantage of developing criteria from user needs is that it acknowledges useful information as the desired end product of accounting activity and seeks to develop accounting procedures based on that objective. If the criteria for judging the merits of the allocation method can be based on user needs, then the effectiveness of the allocation can be tested by empirical means.

Unfortunately, however, major obstacles must be overcome before allocation procedures can be based on user needs. There are many types of users, each of whom has a legitimate claim to accounting information but whose information needs may not coincide. In addition, it has been observed that users are often unable to recognize and express their needs for accounting information.[10] Efforts to overcome this deficiency by utilizing user decision models have been thwarted by a lack of acceptable models.[11]

Nevertheless, because of the seemingly great potential of basing allocation methods on user needs the authors utilized a survey designed to identify those needs.[12] The results of the survey, however, did little more than confirm the observation that users are unable to express their information needs. Thus, despite the promise of a user oriented basis, it produced no criteria for evaluating cost allocation methods.

[7]"The Matching Concept," *The Accounting Review*, April 1965, p. 369.

[8]"Basic Concepts and Accounting Principles Underlying Financial Statements of Business Enterprises," APB Statement No. 4 (New York: AICPA, 1971), par. 159.

[9]See APB Statement No. 4, paragraph 134.

[10]See, for example, George H. Sorter, "An 'Events' Approach to Basic Accounting Theory," *The Accounting Review*, January 1969, p. 13, and William K. Vatter, "Obstacles to the Specifications of Accounting Principles" in Robert K. Jacdicke, Yuji Ijiri, and Oswald Nielsen, eds., *Research in Accounting Measurement* (Evanston, Illinois: American Accounting Association, 1966), p. 78.

[11]See, for example, "Report of the Committee on Accounting Theory and Verification," *The Accounting Review*, supplement to Vol. XLVI, 1971, p. 68.

[12]For a description of the survey and its findings, refer to Charles W. Lamden and Dale L. Gerboth, "Depreciation—The Incantation and the Reality," *World*, Autumn 1972, pp. 6–13.

## Criteria Based on Practice

The most common procedure for developing criteria to evaluate accounting procedures is to base them on those procedures that have already achieved some degree of acceptance in practice. The weakness of this approach has often been pointed out. It generally does not provide an adequate basis for judging the worth, as opposed to the popularity, of the criteria.[13]

Nonetheless basing criteria on practice has some advantages. To the extent that practices have developed and survived because they are based on logical and pragmatic solutions to the allocation problem, usable criteria have been developed. This does not reduce or eliminate the utilization of alternative methods, however, since such criteria support a variety of accounting procedures which may be in conflict with each other.

## ANALYSES OF ARGUMENTS IN SUPPORT OF ALLOCATION METHODS

The allocation methods currently in use are supported in the accounting literature by one or more arguments, most of which are based on some criteria, expressed or implied.

Some of the arguments for the various allocation methods are set forth below.

### The Straight-Line Method

The straight-line method is the most commonly used method of allocation.[14] It is supported by two principal arguments:

1. Some of the factors contributing to the eventual exhaustion of an asset's usefulness are related to the passage of time.[15]

2. The method is as reasonable and equitable as any other method without relying on questionable assumptions and complicated calculations.[16]

The underlying criterion of the first argument is that the cost of a depreciable asset should be allocated on the basis of the incidence of events over time contributing to the eventual exhaustion of an asset's usefulness. If, for example, an asset will become useless because of circumstances that can be related to the passage of time, then each year of the asset's life should be charged with an equal share of the asset's cost.

The underlying criterion which can be implied from the second argument is: the method used should be the simplest to apply.

---

[13]See, for example, Robert R. Sterling, "On Theory Construction and Verification," *The Accounting Review*, July 1970, p. 449.

[14]Charles W. Lamden and Dale L. Gerboth, op. cit., pp. 6–13.

[15]See, for example, William A. Paton and William A. Paton, Jr., *Asset Accounting* (New York: The Macmillan Co., 1952), pp. 269–270.

[16]See, for example, Perry Mason, *Principles of Public Utility Depreciation* (Chicago:AAA, 1937), p. 69.

## The Units of Production and Units of Service Methods

The units of production and units of service methods are variations of the straight-line method as far as "allocation" is concerned. They differ only in that production and service methods substitute units produced or units of asset use (e.g. operating hours, miles) for time as the basis for allocating cost. Accordingly the units of production and service methods are based on the same criteria as the straight-line method except that the factors contributing to the exhaustion of an asset's usefulness are a function of use rather than time.

## The Decreasing-Charge Methods

There are several formulas for computing decreasing-charge depreciation (e.g. declining balance and sum-of-the-years digits), but all have the same general effect and generally the same supporting arguments.

Decreasing-charge depreciation is supported by four general arguments:

1. Depreciation should be recognized in proportion to the contribution of a depreciable asset to the operation of the firm. That contribution, whether measured by operating efficiency, or revenue produced, typically follows a descending curve.[17]

2. Even if an asset's contribution to operations is equal in each period of its life; a rational purchaser values more highly those services immediately received than those to be received in the more distant future.[18]

3. Depreciation should be recognized in proportion to the value of assets in the used asset market. Those values characteristically follow a descending curve.[19]

4. Other asset-related costs, particularly repairs, typically increase as an asset ages and should be offset by depreciation so as to equalize each period's total of depreciation and other asset-related costs.[20]

The criterion underlying the first argument is based on the "matching principle." In other words, the argument presumes a positive correlation between depreciation computed by the decreasing-charge method and the revenues against which the costs would be offset.

The second argument views the purchase price of a depreciable asset as the sum of the discounted costs of all services provided by the asset. The underlying criterion, therefore, is: each period's depreciation should be equal to that period's portion of the discounted present value of the cost of the services provided by the asset.

The criterion underlying the third argument is that the periodic decline in an asset's value in the used asset market is an acceptable measure of its contribution to that period's revenue.

[17]Robert L. Dixon, "Decreasing Change Depreciation—A Search for Logic," *The Accounting Review*, October 1960, pp. 591–592.

[18]Ibid., p. 592.

[19]George Terborgh, *Realistic Depreciation Policy* (Washington, D.C.: Machinery and Allied Products Institute, 1954).

[20]Eldon S. Hendriksen, *Accounting Theory*, Revised Edition (Homewood, Illinois: Richard D. Irwin, Inc., 1970), p. 414.

The criterion underlying the fourth argument is based on the concept that maintenance and repairs increase in the later years of an asset's life and that an equalized periodic cost should be matched against revenue.

### The Increasing-Charge Methods

Increasing-charge depreciation is supported only in special situations. The argument for such methods is based on the contention that the percentage of net income based on the asset's depreciated cost should be the same each year under conditions of relatively equal annual revenue and operating costs (other than depreciation). The criterion underlying this argument is that the allocation method should have an equalizing effect on the rate of return based on the asset's depreciated cost.

## SUMMARY OF CRITERIA UNDERLYING THE VARIOUS METHODS

The following criteria have been identified:

Depreciation should be related to revenue on the basis of a direct cause and effect relationship, or when no direct relationship can be identified, on a basis that indirectly associates cause and effect (the overall criterion of "matching").

Depreciation should be recognized on the basis of the incidence of events (either over time or on the basis of use) contributing to asset exhaustion.

Depreciation should be computed by the simplest method.

Each period's depreciation should be equal to that period's portion of the discounted present value of the cost of the services provided by the asset.

The periodic decline in an asset's value in the used asset market is an acceptable measure of its contribution to that period's revenue.

Depreciation should be computed so as to equalize each period's total of depreciation and other asset-related costs.

Depreciation should be computed so as to tend to equalize the rate of return based on the assets' depreciated cost.

While a listing of the various criteria does not answer the basic question of which method should be used to allocate costs in a "systematic and rational" manner to the periods for which benefits are provided, it does constitute the first step in establishing guidelines to narrow the alternative choices.

For example, if a company has engineering studies and historical records which give clear evidence that the utility of an asset is greater in the early years of its life or decreases in the later years, this would lend support to an accelerated method of depreciation by meeting the criterion of relating depreciation to the services rendered by the asset. If the studies show a clear pattern of increased maintenance and repairs and if an accelerated method will equalize each period's total depreciation and other asset-related costs, then the criterion for that method would have been met.

## THE APPARENT NEEDS FOR ARBITRARY RULES

The analysis of accounting literature and practices has not produced any evidence to deny the conclusion reached by engineering authorities that there is "no one right method" of allocating an asset's cost over its useful life.[21] Accordingly even after criteria are identified, the rules related to the selection of methods must be relatively arbitrary if economically sound and consistent procedures are to be established in the area of depreciation accounting.

While straight-line depreciation does not always correlate directly with the services rendered by the asset or the revenue derived therefrom, it does give recognition to the incidence of events over time contributing to asset exhaustion. And, very important, it is the simplest method to apply.

Accordingly, the following set of arbitrary rules may be a starting point as a basis for narrowing the alternatives in the selection of a depreciation method.

If methods other than straight line or units of production or service methods are to be used they must meet specifically identified and justifiable criteria, and must be supported by specifically identified empirical tests.

In all other cases only the straight-line method should be allowed.

Once adopted the same method must be used consistently and arbitrary shifts between methods should be prohibited.

## CONCLUSION

The purpose of this article was to present an analysis of the problems and procedures involved in the search for criteria for an allocation method in depreciation accounting. While the authors have identified certain criteria which can be used as the basis for selection of a method, no evidence was found that such criteria could be based on postulates or principles or were superior in concept or application, in all cases, as a basis for selecting an allocation method. Perhaps more definitive or better criteria can be established. The authors will continue their analysis and research and will welcome any suggestions.

## QUESTIONS

1. What is meant by saying that "depreciation is a joint cost par excellence?"

2. What is meant by "matching?" What difficulties arise in applying this concept in the case of depreciable assets?

3. What was the result of a survey conducted by the authors which was designed to identify user needs for cost allocation methods?

4. Evaluate the criteria that underly the straight-line method.

5. What is the difference in function between the straight-line depreciation method and the production and service methods of depreciation? Explain.

6. What criteria underly the decreasing-charge methods of depreciation? The increasing-charge methods of depreciation?

7. What is the case the authors make for straight-line depreciation, and why do you agree or disagree with it?

[21]Eugene L. Grant and Paul J. Norton, op. cit., pp. 39, 184, and 365.

## SELECTED BIBLIOGRAPHY

Balmford, John D., "Depreciation of Buildings—The Accountant's View," *The Chartered Accountant in Australia*, July 1972, pp. 4-7.

# 68

## WHEN GOODWILL IS BAD NEWS*
Forbes

One of the big problems of the accounting profession is that it must lay down general principles to deal with specific cases. The general principles, however, like ready-made suits, do not fit every specific case. That, in essence, explains the excitement now going on over the accounting requirement that intangible assets, especially goodwill, must be amortized.

Such intangible assets are a queer breed. Accountants define them as what you buy in a company if you pay more than the fair market value of the company's tangible assets—plant, machinery, inventory, land, receivables and the like. When high-stepping conglomerators of the 1960s paid outrageously inflated prices for companies, the excess was called "goodwill." Using goodwill, hustlers created huge, often fictional asset growth with no corresponding penalty, since in those days the accountants did not require that goodwill be written off. It could sit on the asset sheet forever, looking impressive, but often worth nothing or less than nothing.

That abuse was finally outlawed in October 1970 when the accounting profession adopted Accounting Principles Board Opinion 17. It said *no* asset has an eternal life; therefore all intangibles, including goodwill, must be amortized. The amortization period set was 40 years.

A decent general principle, but it apparently does not fit all the specific cases. There has been an increasing outcry against it from a variety of companies—truckers, for instance, whose most essential possession is the Interstate Commerce Commission license (an intangible asset) that permits them to haul freight across state lines. And newspaper publishers, who insist that the most important things they buy, when they acquire a new paper, are the intangibles of an established name and circulation base.

Most seriously affected are the broadcasters. Here's why:

Take the case of New York-based Lin Broadcasting Corp. (1974 revenues: $26.5 million). In November 1974 Lin acquired KXAS-TV in the lush Fort Worth-Dallas market. Lin paid $35 million. Of that, only $11 million was assigned to KXAS's tangible assets. The other $24 million was paid for the station's Federal Communications Commission license and its lucrative NBC network affiliation, both intangibles.

*From "The Numbers Game," *Forbes*, Nov. 1, 1975, p. 72. Reprinted by permission of the publisher.

This is common practice in broadcasting. When another broadcast company, Metromedia, bought a Chicago FM station for $2.8 million, a trivial $20,000 was assigned to tangible assets. The rest went for the FCC license and other intangibles.

Under Opinion 17, those intangibles must be charged to profits within the next 40 years. So the KXAS-TV deal will cost Lin some $600,000, or 26 cents per share, annually. Considering that Lin's 1974 per-share net was only 95 cents, that charge hurts plenty.

On top of it all, the Internal Revenue Service generally will not allow amortization of the intangibles as a deductible item for tax purposes. So, the penalty to earnings is equivalent to $1.2 million pretax, rather than just $600,000. "Put another way," says Arthur Andersen & Co. partner Charles Johnson, "a 40-year amortization period with no tax benefit is really only a 20-year write-off. That's what really hurts these companies."

The broadcasters agree that Opinion 17 is a good thing for stopping the abuses of conglomerators. But they argue that the broadcast industry is in a different class. Its intangibles are almost certain to increase in value, since the licensing system limits its market entry. Michael O'Sullivan, Lin's controller, puts it this way: "These intangibles have continuing value, and I don't see why we should have to amortize them."

He has a point. Back in 1962 Lin bought three radio stations for $2.5 million, of which $1.8 million was for intangibles. Last May Lin sold the same three stations for $8.7 million to Multimedia Broadcasting Corp. Of that $8.7 million, Multimedia figures it paid $5 million for intangibles. So Lin's intangibles *increased* some 200% in value.

The industry also argues that Opinion 17 affects it far worse than other industries, since typically 60% of a broadcast company's assets will be intangibles. "One-fortieth of very little is very little," says Ron Irion of the National Association of Broadcasters. "But one-fortieth of a hell of a lot can be a hell of a lot."

Another inequity, claim some, is that the young and growing broadcast companies are penalized more than the industry giants like CBS or NBC, which purchased most of their stations before the rule went into effect. Thus, their amortization burden is much less than it is for the younger companies.

# 69
## PRICE-LEVEL ADJUSTMENTS
## U.S. Viewpoints*
James Don Edwards and Carl S. Warren

Accounting is fundamentally a measuring and reporting process. Information presented in financial statements serves as a basis for informed economic decisions about

*From *The Accountant's Magazine*, May 1975, pp. 174—177. Reprinted by permission of the publisher.

business organisations. Although there has been no widely accepted identification of the exact uses of financial information, the American Institute of Certified Public Accountants' Study Group on the Objectives of Financial Statements cited three assumptions with respect to users' needs:[1]

(1) Users of financial statements seek to predict, compare, and evaluate the cash consequences of their economic decisions.

(2) Information about cash consequences of decisions made by the enterprise is useful for predicting, comparing, and evaluating cash flow to users.

(3) Financial statements are more useful if they include, but distinguish, information that is primarily factual, and therefore can be measured objectively, from information that is primarily interpretive.

Given these assumptions, the basic purpose of financial accounting is to provide information for predicting the future cash flows of business organisations.

## HISTORICAL COST AND THE CHANGING DOLLAR

The generally accepted valuation basis within the U.S. is historical cost—the exchange price at the date of acquisition. Assuming an arm's length transaction, cost at acquisition properly reflects current economic conditions and is unequivocally the best valuation base as of that date. The monetary unit (the dollar) used to describe cost at acquisition is a surrogate for the sacrifice to the firm in its ability to command other goods and services. Implicit in the use of a monetary unit as a measuring device is the assumption of stability of that unit.

The assumption that the dollar is a stable measuring unit cannot be defended on the basis of empirical evidence. The primary question is not whether the dollar is a stable valuation measure; it is not. The primary question is whether or not financial information prepared utilising the stable dollar-measuring-unit assumption is more helpful in predicting future cash flows than price-level adjusted statements.[2]

## A DISCUSSION MEMORANDUM

In February 1974, the newly organised Financial Accounting Standards Board (FASB) issued a discussion memorandum on issues related to reporting the effects of general price-level changes in financial statements.[3] The FASB's justification for taking up this

---

[1]AICPA Study Group on the Objectives of Financial Statements, *Objectives of Financial Statements* (New York: AICPA, October, 1973), pp. 13–14.

[2]Price-level adjusted statements should not be confused with current value statements. Price-level statements only reflect changing values in the unit of measure (the dollar) and not changes in values of specific assets. Price-level adjustments will only coincidentally result in a measure of current value.

[3]Financial Accounting Standards Board, *Financial Accounting Standards Board Discussion Memorandum: Reporting the Effects of General Price-Level Changes in Financial Statements* (Stamford, Conn.: FASB, 1974), p. 1.

issue was based upon recent trends in general price-levels combined with the need for disclosing the inflationary effects of the dollar upon different business entities.[4]

The basic question addressed in the discussion memorandum was: "Should reporting of the effects of general price-level changes be required as supplemental information to the conventional historical-dollar financial statements?"[5] The memorandum presented for consideration four major arguments, favourable and unfavourable, to general price-level adjustments. These arguments are briefly summarised below.[6]

### (1) Expression of Dollar Amounts in a Common Unit of Measure

**Pro**    Since the purchasing power of the dollar has changed over time, historical-dollar cost of assets acquired in previous years, say 10 years ago, cannot be directly compared with historical-dollar costs of assets acquired today.

**Con**    Measurement in terms of the number of dollars actually given up is a common unit of measure. Restatement of historical-dollar financial statements for variations in the purchasing power of the dollar is actually a change to another basis of accounting measurement.

### (2) Meaningful Interperiod Comparisons

**Pro**    Measurement in terms of dollars of constant purchasing power facilitates interperiod comparisons.

**Con**    Because of technological changes in goods and services that a firm acquires and because of changes in the operations of a firm over time, interperiod comparisons may not be meaningful even with adjustments for changes in the purchasing power of the dollar.

### (3) Income Measurement

**Pro**    The instability of the dollar presents a question as to the meaningfulness of net earnings reported using traditional historical-dollar earnings statements when perceived as a measure of the ability of an enterprise to keep its command over goods and services in general.

[4]Since 1969, the inflationary rate in the United States has increased appreciably. During the 1950–1958 period, the Gross National Product Implicit Price Deflator increase averaged 2.3% per year; for the years 1959–1968 the increase averaged 2.0% per year; and, for 1969–1973 (September 30, 1973) the yearly increase averaged 5.1% (ibid., pp. 3–4).

[5]Financial Accounting Standards Board, op. cit., p. 1.

[6]Ibid., pp. 6–8.

**Con**    Price-level adjusted net income is not an adequate measure of the ability of a firm either to maintain or to increase its command over goods and services. Only in adjusting for changes in the current values of a firm's assets and liabilities will net earnings be a measure of real earnings.

### (4) Disclosure of the Effect of Inflation on Individual Enterprises

**Pro**    It is not possible for users of historical-dollar financial statements to calculate the effects of inflation or to recast the financial statements in terms of dollars of common purchasing powers.

**Con**    Price-level adjusted statements confuse the users of this information rather than enlighten them. Many users falsely believe price-level adjusted statements to be approximations of the current values of the assets and liabilities of the firm. Price-level adjustments do not, except coincidentally, approximate current values.

The discussion memorandum sought comments from all interested parties—business entities, accounting firms, non-profit entities, the academic community, and public officials—on the main issue of whether or not the effects of price-level changes should be required as supplemental information to conventional historical-dollar financial statements. Comments were also solicited on the following issues:[7]

Is financial information which has been restated for changes in the general price level useful?

Do benefits of making price-level adjusted accounting information available outweigh the costs involved?

To which entities should a requirement for presentation of price-level adjusted financial information apply?

Restatement techniques (which price level index/restatement in dollars of current purchasing power/distinction between monetary and non-monetary items/income tax allocation/presentation).

Transitional problems.

### RESPONSE TO THE DISCUSSION MEMORANDUM

The comments presented in response to the discussion memorandum were varied. Most of the comments presented in open testimony to the FASB agreed that historical-cost financial statements needed improvement, but there was considerable lack of agreement about what corrective steps should be taken. The majority of *industry* respondents were *opposed to mandatory reporting* of price-level adjusted information; while the *academic community* strongly *favoured mandatory reporting*. Considerable disagreement existed among *accounting firms*. Although a *majority* of the firms supported *mandatory disclosure,* a *substantial minority* would leave such disclosure on a *voluntary basis.*

[7]Ibid., pp. 9—15.

It may be of interest to note (with emphasis supplied in most cases) specific positions taken by some of the respondents to the discussion memorandum:[8]

### Industry Response

### Commonwealth Edison

We believe that financial information restated for changes in general price levels *would be useful,* provided that the price-level *restatements* and the presentation of the results can be *simplified* enough to be understandable and *meaningful* to *readers* of the financial statements. *If required,* they should be presented as supplemental information. If financial statements adjusted for price level changes become generally accepted by the financial community, we believe that benefits would outweigh the additional costs involved to prepare the information.[9]

### Exxon Corporation

Exxon Corporation *would support* an FASB recommendation for supplemental statements statistically restated for general price level changes to show estimates of the impact of inflation on earning and financial position. We feel that such information would serve as a basis for determining rates of return that are deflated to remove the effects of inflation. This, we believe, represents the primary usefulness of price level adjusted statements. . . . we feel it is essential that both *preparers* and *users* of financial and statistical information *be aware* of the *nature* and *limitations* of such supplemental data.

It should be *emphasized* that *price level adjusted statements do not purport* to *represent current* fair values.[10]

### Standard Oil Company of California

The existing inflationary trends in both the United States and foreign countries have caused a need for a means to gauge financial positions and performance in a different light from historical costs. We realize that this need has been created and while we agree that price-level accounting is one reasonable means of meeting that need, we *strongly urge* that any recommendations for *adoption* of supplementary price-level accounting be made *only after* a clear *understanding* of it is *developed* by the *users* of this data and their *likely interpretations* of it. There will be a natural tendency to view price-level adjusted amounts as current or replacement values regardless of the techniques used in calculation.[11]

[8]Haskins and Sells: *The Week in Review* (May 24, 1974), p. 5.

[9]Robert J. Schultz, Vice-President of Commonwealth Edison (Chicago, Illinois): Letter of response to the FASB Discussion Memorandum on Price Level Changes in Financial Statements.

[10]Views of Exxon Corporation on Issues Related to Reporting the Effects of Several Price-Level Changes in Financial Statements, p. 1.

[11]Sellers Stough, Comptroller, Standard Oil Company of California (San Francisco): Letter to the FASB on the Discussion Memorandum on Reporting the Effects of Price-Level Changes.

## The Gillette Company

The Gillette Company would like to go on record as being opposed to (1) reporting price-level changes in financial statements, and (2) the procedure followed by the FASB in this instance.

... we cannot help but feel that any such restatement will deeply confuse, rather than inform, users of financial statements who will not understand the difference between price-level restatement and current value accounting. In our opinion, any alleged benefits of this theoretical accounting approach would be offset, many times over, by the excessive costs required. ... [12]

## W.R. Grace & Co.

We share the Board's concern that inflation may be significant and that price level statements may be required. We believe, however, that conceptual and practical compliance problems are presently insurmountable, both because the average user of financial statements does not understand price level movements and their effect upon common purchasing power and accounting has never purported to measure purchasing power and may not have developed to date the appropriate measurement techniques. [13]

## The Academic Community

## The American Accounting Association

All members of our subcommittee agree that reporting the effects of price changes as price-level changes in financial statements should be required. [14]

## Accounting Firms

## Touche Ross

Based on our understanding of the 'Report on Objectives of Financial Statements' (AICPA Study Group Report, op cit.), we have concluded that the needs of financial statement users are not served by such information. We believe users are interested in prospective cash flows, and future inflation instead of prior inflation. Moreover, any supplementary price level data that might be presented is subject to possible misinterpretation by users (excepting CPAs) as indicative of

[12]Edward G. Melaugh, Senior Vice-President-Finance, The Gillette Company (Boston): Letter to the FASB in regard to its Discussion Memorandum on Reporting the Effects of Price-Level Changes in Financial Statements.

[13]Albert E. Bollengier, Vice President and Controller, W. R. Grace & Co. (New York): Letter to the FASB on its Discussion Memorandum on Reporting the Effects of Price-Level Changes in Financial Statements.

[14]Charley Zlatkovich, Chairman, Price-Level Reporting Subcommittee, The American Accounting Association: Statement Prepared for Financial Accounting Standards Board, p. 1.

current values, even if a warning about the nature of such data is prominently displayed.[15]

... we recommend that *reporting* of the *effects* of *general price level changes* as information supplemental to conventional historical dollar financial statements should be *strongly discouraged,* and in no event should it be required.[16]

## Ernst & Ernst

*Conceptually, we support* the ideas (1) that the effect of inflation on financial statements *should be measured* and *disclosed* and (2) that application of a general price level index to adjust conventional accounting data to a common and current dollar basis may be the most useful way to do so. For *practical reasons,* however, we are *wary* of *imposing* such a *requirement* on *industry generally,* or even on all listed companies. We remain uncertain of the benefits to be obtained by such a provision and highly skeptical of its usefulness to privately held companies.

... There has *never been* any great *demand* for *price-level adjusted* financial statement either *on the part* of *preparers* or *users.* No evidence has been presented that such demand exists today.[17]

## Haskins & Sells

... we think inflation is increasingly significant to business enterprises and the techniques for reporting its impact in financial statements are available. We believe such information would be useful. ... We suggest that the best, indeed the only way to resolve the issue of usefulness of the information is to develop it and use it.

... *Accounting objectives* should and will continue to *emphasize* the *need* to provide accounting *information* that is *useful* for *making economic decisions* and the *purpose* of *reporting* the *effects* of *general price level changes* is *to serve this need better.*[18]

## Peat, Marwick, Mitchell & Co.

Our recommendations are premised on the continuation of the basic concepts and accounting principles underlying financial statements of business enterprises, and we are aware that the adoption of a different accounting model would necessitate a reconsideration of the subject. We believe the presentation of general price-

[15]Topical Index Docket, Touche Ross & Co. (April 26, 1974), p. 1.

[16]Touche Ross & Co.: Letter to Financial Accounting Standards Board (April 5, 1974) in regard to its Discussion Memorandum on Reporting the Effects of Price-Level Changes in Financial Statements.

[17]Statement by Ernst & Ernst to the Financial Accounting Standards Board (April 5, 1974) concerning its Discussion Memorandum on Reporting the Effects of General Price-Level Changes in Financial Statements, pp. 1–3.

[18]Haskins & Sells: *The Week In Review* (May 24, 1974), pp. 5–6.

level adjusted financial information is useful; it would serve some of the needs of investors, creditors, government officials, and other users of financial statements who are concerned with the economic affairs of business enterprises and other entities. *Reporting of* the *effects* of general price-level changes *should be required* as *supplemental information* to the conventional historical-dollar financial statements.

*Users* of financial statements should be *provided data* with which to *gain perspective* on the effects of inflation upon business enterprises and other entities. *Supplemental* general price-level adjusted financial *information* is meaningful data which *should enable users* of financial statements to *obtain* the *needed perspective.*[19]

## Arthur Young & Company

The basic question outlined in The Discussion Memorandum is: 'Should reporting of the effects of general price-level changes be required as supplemental information to the conventional historical-dollar financial statements?' Our answer is a qualified 'yes'. The *enhancement* of *financial statement usefulness* by *adding price-level adjusted data increases* as the general price level increases. We have concluded that the degree of inflation in the United States of America—both annual and cumulative—is now so great that the effects of financial statement information should be disclosed.

. . . our major concern is that there may not have been sufficient experimentation or sufficient publication of the results to disclose any unanticipated defects or to appraise compilation costs or delays.[20]

## Arthur Andersen & Co.

. . . *supplementary financial statements should be presented* to support the effects of general price-level changes. Our conclusion rests upon our belief that the existing *rate* of *inflation* in the United States *has reduced* the *usefulness* of *historical-dollar financial statements* and has increased the likelihood that misleading conclusions can be drawn from analyses of such statements; *our conclusion* that the effects of general price-level changes should be reported in supplementary financial statements *contemplates* the *continued use* of historical-dollar accounting.[21]

---

[19]Peat, Marwick, Mitchell & Co.: Letter to The Financial Accounting Standards Board (April 5, 1974) concerning its Discussion Memorandum on Reporting the Effects of General Price-Level Changes in Financial Statements, pp. 1—2.

[20]Arthur Young & Company: Reporting the Effects of General Price-Level Changes in Financial Statements (New York, 1974), p. 3.

[21]Arthur Andersen & Co.: *Executive News Briefs* (Vol. 2, No. 7, May 1974), p. 2.

## Other CPAs

### The New York State Society of Certified Public Accountants

. . . recommend that *additional research into* matters of *usefulness* and problems of *implementation* be undertaken prior to the issuance of an accounting standard requiring price-level adjusted financial statements as supplementary information.

Our general position, *assuming* a *standard* is *issued without* additional *research,* is (1) Price-level adjusted financial statement *should be mandatory supplementary information* for all reporting entities. (2) The techniques described in *APB Statement No. 3* should be adopted as the implementation guideline.[22]

It is evident from the above responses that the interested parties are not in substantial agreement concerning price-level adjustments. Frequent arguments that price-level adjusted statements are an extension of historical-dollar statements and as such have the same limitations inherent in historical cost concepts deserve considerable consideration. The argument that price level adjusted historical-dollar financial statements will further confuse users of financial information cannot be ignored. The lack of agreement on one specific index that is best in implementing a general price-level adjustment cannot help to remove misinterpretations of price-level adjusted statements. Since *Accounting Principles Board Statement No. 3* (AICPA, 1969) recommended price-level adjusted financial statements to be disclosed as supplementary information, there has been no significant acceptance and implementation of this recommendation by industry.[23] The ever-present questioning of the usefulness and meaningfulness of price-level adjusted statements to users of financial information by accounting firms, businesses, and the academic community, cannot and should not be ignored. It is certainly true at the present time that general price-level adjusted financial statements are not a panacea for the imperfections and limitations of traditional historical-dollar financial statements.

## AN EXPOSURE DRAFT

On December 31, 1974, the Financial Accounting Standards Board issued an exposure draft entitled, "Financial Reporting in Units of General Purchasing Power" which incorporated many of the viewpoints set forth in the preceding paragraphs.[24] The FASB exposure draft concluded that general price level adjusted statements should be a

---

[22]The New York State Society of Certified Public Accountants: Position Paper (April 8, 1974) submitted to The Financial Accounting Standards Board related to its Discussion Memorandum on Reporting the Effects of General Price-Level Changes in Financial Statements, p. 1.

[23]Accounting Principles Board: *APB Statement No. 3*, "Financial Statements Restated for General Price-Level Changes" (New York: AICPA, 1969).

[24]Financial Accounting Standards Board: *Financial Reporting in Units of General Purchasing Power* (Stamford, Conn.: FASB, 1974).

*mandatory* reporting requirement. Other significant conclusions included the following:

1. General price level information need not be reported for interim periods.

2. General price level restatements should be comprehensive in scope and should encompass all financial statement items.

3. The Gross National Product Implicit Deflator shall be the index used in preparing restatements.

4. General price level information should be stated in terms of the most recent balance sheet date.

5. The net gain or loss of general purchasing power that results from holding monetary assets and liabilities shall be included in determining net income in units of general purchasing power.

6. Gains or losses of general purchasing power that result from monetary stock-holders' equity items, for example, preferred stock that is carried in the balance sheet at an amount equal to its fixed liquidation or redemption price, shall be charged or credited directly to common stock-holders' equity in the general purchasing power financial statements.

7. The presentation of general purchasing power information shall include an explanation of the basis of preparation of the information and what it presents.

8. The statement would be effective for fiscal years beginning on or after January 1, 1976.

Comments on the exposure draft are due by September 30, 1975. The rather lengthy exposure period implies some apprehension as to whether the proposed statement might not require significant revision.


## CONCLUSION

The accounting profession in the United States is currently considering the question of whether price level adjusted financial statements should be a mandatory disclosure requirement. Major arguments for and against, and opinions from industry, public accounting, and the academic communities have been presented. Regardless of national boundaries, the single most important criterion to use in evaluating whether to modify traditional historical-dollar financial statements should be based upon the primacy of users' needs. The basic objective of financial disclosure should be to provide information *most* useful for making economic decisions.


## QUESTIONS

1. What is the generally accepted valuation basis within the United States, and what are its merits?

2. What are price-level adjusted statements? How do they differ from historical-cost valued statements or current-value statements?

3. What evidence do the authors report that is useful in answering the question

that they raise: "whether or not financial information prepared utilizing the stable dollar-measuring-unit assumption is more helpful in predicting future cash flows than price-level adjusted statements?"

4. What do the degree and extent of inflation have to do with a possible requirement that general price-level adjusted statements be prepared?

### SELECTED BIBLIOGRAPHY

Davidson, Sidney S., and Roman Weil, "Inflation Accounting: What Will General Price Level Adjusted Income Statements Show?" *Financial Analysts Journal*, Jan.-Feb. 1975, pp. 27-31, 70-84.

Moonitz, Maurice, "Restating the Price-Level Problem," *CA Magazine*, July 1974, pp. 27-31.

Stickney, Clyde P., and David O. Green, "No Price Level Adjusted Statements, Please (Pleas)," *The CPA Journal*, January 1974, pp. 25-30.

Zlatkovich, Charles, "Accounting under Inflation and Its Implications for Management," *Cost and Management*, March-April 1975, pp. 7-16.

# 70
## SEC PROPOSES ACCOUNTING-RULE CHANGES
## TO DISCLOSE EFFECTS OF INFLATION ON FIRMS*
Wall Street Journal

The Securities and Exchange Commission proposed changes in its accounting rules aimed at helping investors better understand how inflation is affecting the financial strength of publicly held corporations.

The changes would make companies account for the toll that inflation is taking on the cost of replacing inventories, materials, machinery and other assets.

The commission acknowledged that developing the accounting procedures would be difficult because many companies have little experience in the field and only sketchy information is available on inflationary impact.

"Because of the significance" of the proposal, the SEC said it will allow an unusually long period for public comment—through Jan. 31, 1976. This means any final rule isn't likely until mid-1976 at the earliest.

Under the proposal, publicly held companies would be required to disclose in footnotes to their financial statements:

Current replacement cost of inventories as of the close of the fiscal year. If current

*From the *Wall Street Journal*, Aug. 22, 1975, p. 3. Reprinted by permission of the publisher.

replacement costs exceed "net realizable value," the amount of the excess cost would have to be shown.

What the approximate cost of sales would have been for the two most recent fiscal years if it had been based on the current replacement cost of goods and services sold, as reckoned at the time the sales were made.

The estimated current actual cost of machinery, raw materials and other facets of "productive capacity" and the current net replacement cost, reflecting depreciation, depletion and amortization of assets at the end of each fiscal year. Such figures would show, for example, the extent to which total depreciation is failing to keep up with the rising price of capital goods.

The amount of depreciation, depletion and amortization that would have been accrued if the company had figured them on the basis of current replacement cost of productive capacity.

The commission first expressed concern in January 1974 that traditional accounting procedures—usually based on "historical" costs unadjusted for subsequent increases—might be concealing the impact of inflation on corporate fortunes. At that time, the SEC urged publicly held companies to make "supplemental disclosure" of "inventory profits," defined as the difference between the historical cost of goods sold and the current replacement cost of such goods at the time of sale.

But the commission said it has seen "very little response" to this suggestion in communications from companies to their shareholders. It also hasn't observed publicly held companies making any systematic effort "to quantify the effect of changing current costs on the economics of a registrant's business," it added.

The commission acknowledged that compliance with its proposed rules would require "estimates and judgments" to a much greater degree than is demanded for conventional financial reporting. One major difficulty for accountants will be deciding what price indices apply to various segments of the production cycle. "At the present, there isn't any generally available set of indices which appear useful to all entities," the commission noted.

Because of the imprecision expected in such inflation-impact footnotes, the commission said that it's weighing whether to label such accounting "unaudited." It also asked for comment on whether inflation reports should be required only from companies of a certain size—those with annual sales or assets above $50 million, for example.

## QUESTIONS

1. Accountants are talking now about a new inventory accounting method for the stagflation era: FISH (first in, still here). Comment.

2. The chief accountant of the SEC, John C. Burton, has referred to financial statements adjusted for general price-level changes as "PuPu" accounting. Why do you think he has done this?

3. What are the practical problems with the SEC proposal?

4. What is the difference between price-level adjusted accounting (see Selection 69) and current replacement costs?

# 71
# PUCO RATE PLAN GAINS SUPPORT*

Ann Tomlinson

Representatives from statewide consumer groups told Public Utilities Commission of Ohio (PUCO) officials Tuesday they approved of PUCO's call for repeal of Ohio's present rate making formula.

The present system, "replacement cost new less depreciation" (RCNLD), is based on what utility land and equipment would cost to replace at today's prices minus depreciation, according to David C. Sweet, one of three PUCO commissioners. He recommended that RCNLD be replaced with the original cost system, which values the property at what it cost to build.

Sweet said the original cost system could save the average family of four as much as $400 annually in utility bills because it would reduce the utilities' return on invested capital to 14 per cent.

Utility companies earn "$1.2 billion over what would be considered fair," said Sally W. Bloomfield, a PUCO commissioner. "We picked 14 per cent because our financial people told us that was a reasonable rate of return."

Sweet said 73.3 per cent of the average utility bill goes for operating costs, and the original cost system could help reduce these charges.

He urged consumers to concern themselves with the operating costs rather than the fixed costs which comprise only 26.7 per cent of the utility bill.

Sweet said the original cost system is used now in about 30 other states.

Luther Heckman, chairman of PUCO, said he thought the fair value system should be studied before any definite plans are made to adopt the original cost system.

"RCNLD provides an inflationary rate base. The original cost system provides too small of a rate of return. It's deflationary. We need to determine what the rate base really is," Heckman said. "I haven't advocated RCNLD because I want to find what the fair value is."

Patrick Nelson, a representative of the Energy Consumer League of Springfield, said consumers are looking to PUCO for help in reducing fuel bills.

## QUESTIONS

1. What is the difference between RCNLD and original cost?
2. What is the fair value system?
3. What valuation system do you recommend for PUCO, and why?

*From *The Lantern*, Aug. 14, 1975, p. 3. Reprinted by permission of the publisher.

# Part 4
# Management Planning
# and Control

# 72
## LOOKING BACK*
Kenneth H. Bergstrom

The management accountant today is an accepted member of the team. His contribution in helping management to hold down costs and in planning the most feasible, least costly ways of doing business is indispensable in the modern, highly competitive business environment. Management expects—and demands—that its accounting staff show it how to reduce costs and improve profits.

But it wasn't always that way. When I first started working almost 50 years ago we accountants had to fight every step of the way to get our ideas across and in order to be heard by management. It was an exciting time to live as an emerging discipline was being refined from day to day right on the production line. I can remember, for example, how the study group sessions of the Worcester Chapter in the forties fairly crackled with ideas as cost accounting discussions went on for three to four hours a night.

Fortunately, my experience in business ranged across a wide spectrum of disciplines, and each experience tended to reinforce and cross-fertilize what I had learned earlier. I started out in cost accounting, went into systems and procedures design and installation, later worked as an industrial engineer and production manager and then took advantage of this rich cumulative experience to become a consultant.

To give some form and shape to these experiences, I have arbitrarily divided the last four decades into four periods. Some of the major characteristics of the periods in an accounting sense are:

1930-39 Mostly manual operations; Depression period, overhead kept low.
1940-49 Mechanical calculators, posting machines, punched card methods. World War II period; Cost control required.
1950-59 Computer development; Korean War.
1960-70 Vietnam War period. Cost less important than production; inflation.

During the 30's and 40's we concentrated principally on the development of meaningful cost accounting procedures and reliable product costs. This effort contributed to more consistent and uniform costing practices in industry. The cost elements: material, labor, overhead, had to be defined and methods developed to charge costs to products equitably. Many complicated problems had to be solved, including:

How do we set up product cost centers to accumulate costs?
What method(s) should be used to distribute factory overhead costs?
How should administrative and selling costs be charged to products?
What volume level should be used? Projected sales? Percentage of plant capacity? Past experience?

*From *Management Accounting*, March 1974, pp. 47—50. Reprinted by permission of the publisher.

## OVERHEAD—A DIRTY WORD

On joining the accounting staff of Tyer Rubber Co., in Andover, Mass., I found the accounting system adequate only for financial reporting purposes. The monthly and quarterly profit and loss and balance sheets were the only accounting management information reports. When I prepared my first quarterly report, the general manager wanted to see it as soon as it was completed. Proudly, I gave him the statements. To my chagrin he tore off the bottom line and walked into the director's meeting.

Of course, management has grown in financial sophistication to the point such arbitrary amputation of financial reports would not be tolerated today. One must keep in mind, however, back in the old days management was often by the "seat of the pants." The reams of computer-produced data which is a commonplace today were simply not available then. Moreover, many of the accounting techniques and procedures had not been developed.

The year 1930 marked the beginning of the Depression years. Overhead was a dirty word to management. Every element of burden was challenged from a pay-off basis. Proposed additional overhead required to operate a factory ledger and develop reliable unit product costs met with management refusals on the grounds that "competition sets selling prices, so why incur overhead to decrease profits or increase losses?" Given the recession, we had no alternative other than to meet or be below competitive selling prices.

We in accounting persisted. We all knew the importance of cost reduction: our task consisted in showing management just how it could be done. The largest element of cost was in the direct costs—materials and labor. Why not tackle them?

During that era the "hot" subject was work simplification. As members of the Industrial Engineers' Boston Chapter, some other employees and I attended study courses held on the subject. Then we gave company foremen and other key men the course in ten evening sessions. Next we went to work in the factory to reduce direct costs through methods improvements. A change in the method of "curing" chemicals saved approximately $50,000 a year; a multiple die method enabled us to produce gaskets at a profit, not a loss. Within nine months, direct costs were reduced 15 percent because of methods improvements which involved little or no capital investments—all because many people asked "why."

Similarly, cost analysis studies indicated that excess cost variances were caused by too many changes in styles in the production of waterproof footwear. We had to determine the best possible scheduling giving proper consideration to the delivery promise to customers, longest possible run on similar styles and colors, and direct labor effort.

Using a little Yankee ingenuity, we developed a new order system which we could also use for production control. It was B.C. (Before Computers) so we had to make-do with what was available. We borrowed some addressograph equipment and plates discarded by the sales department and since a large style and size label had to be prepared and attached to each case, it seemed logical to make extra copies for production control purposes. Then we proceeded to print material cutting room requirements on the right side of the making ticket, and style and size data on the left side.

As a result, the direct labor savings in the cutting room payroll alone was 25 percent; in the mill room, 10 percent, and in the making room, 12 percent. The principal reasons were longer runs by style and colors and elimination of changeover costs.

Management was alarmed at first because it seemed the overhead rate had increased! Closer analysis, however, enabled us to demonstrate to management that overhead dollars had not increased. Instead, the base figure, the direct labor costs had decreased.

All of these improvements did not come easy. We had to persuade management that they would work. The view then seemed to be that accountants were necessary overhead evils. We had to gain the confidence of management through accomplishments which required extensive shirtsleeve teamwork with operating people throughout the company.

Once the cost reductions were achieved, management gave us a budget for a good cost system and planning functions. We installed a "predetermined cost system," which later became known as a standard cost system. Labor dollar variance reports were issued to foremen weekly.

One report showed a negative variance of 40 percent in a major department; the underlying reality of accounting figures was made quite clear to this accountant when the department's big foreman marched into the office and threatened my scalp! After everybody had cooled off we delved into the reason why. An extensive analysis indicated that conditions which could be corrected accounted for about half the excess and the balance was due to accounting reasons.

## PRICE FREEZES AND FERMENT

During the Forties, World War II price freezes presented us with a whole new set of problems. It was the decade in which I was most active in NAA, serving in several directorates and finally as president of the Worcester Chapter, in 1947-48.

The entire cost accounting field was in ferment. As I remember, the chapter study group sessions were highly stimulating. Accounting theories and their practical applications frequently clashed. The college professors who served as session leaders were put on their mettle by those of us actually working in industry. Work simplification studies were extending into clerical and accounting fields, and we no longer accepted the traditional accounting methods if we found we could do the same task equally as well by less costly methods.

By contrast with the present, and recent years, we still had to work on cost reduction if we wanted to survive and grow. We couldn't continuously raise selling prices. The computer wasn't invented so we couldn't blindly fall back on a miraculous cureall for everything. We started with one fundamental: there must be a purpose for every effort and the objective must be worth the cost. The Worcester Chapter group had members from several different types of manufacturers, so right from the outset we realized that identical accounting methods were not universally applicable all over. The important thing was to properly diagnose the problem and then apply the simplest and most effective solution.

Some of the benefits to the company which came about, in part, because of the contributions gained from the study group included: a ledger-less accounts receivable system which reduced our clerical costs 50 percent; a tied-in general accounting and cost system which provided all features of the direct cost method, effective standard costs, job costs for specific large orders and full absorption costs; a simplified payroll system, and a sales analysis by comptometer peg board method at a cost no greater than the key punch operation on tab cards.

The late forties and early fifties comprised the systems and procedures phase of my career. As director of systems and procedures for the Yale & Towne Mfg. Co., Philadelphia Division, I continued to attend meetings of NAA and at the same time joined the Systems and Procedures Association.

Management procedures and data processing technology were growing at a faster rate. Computers loomed just over the horizon but we still clung to the basic principle that all clerical effort must have sufficient "payoff." Moving one step at a time to keep management's full backing, we first installed production control procedures on one product line, supported by a sales schedule, engineering department work loading, procurement lead time and parts manufacturing and assembly time tables. Nine months of the new procedure gave the company the desired payoff in a greater number of customer order deliveries on time and a rise in industry sales and shipments from 35 percent to 52 percent. What's more, clerical operation costs did not increase.

The new data processing technology came into bloom during the Sixties. This period comprised the years in which I did consulting before finally retiring last year. It was particularly gratifying after struggling with manual systems early in the century to install electronic data processing systems at a corporation in Boston. Conceptual procedures and backup hardware for management information, control and planning systems had been revolutionized in the span of a lifetime and yet the basic principles that guided the early accountants laboring in the industrial vineyards still apply.

## ACCOUNTING

. . . Ideally, my job changes permitted me to supplement accounting knowledge with that of related fields. I was able to use each job assignment as a building block leading to increased responsibilities. The skills demanded by each task differed considerably.

The *auditor,* for example, like a detective, must be able to detect errors of commission and omission. Auditing requires endless patience with details. Not only must the *cost accountant,* like the auditor, be accurate with detailed figures but he must understand manufacturing operations and organization relationships. Moving up to the *controller* slot demands even greater knowledge of overall operations, including the functions of sales, manufacturing, engineering, and administration departments. The controller especially needs selling ability to carry out his responsibilities.

Innovation and resourcefulness are called for in carrying out the responsibilities of the *industrial engineer*. But experience in this function carries over into similar work in *systems and procedures* which is industrial engineering applied to management information and data processing procedure.

The *production manager* must have great fortitude—all the mistakes of the whole company show up in his area. I realized this when I moved from director of systems and procedures to operate the system I had installed. Finally, the *management consultant* must be diplomatic and quick to find a "handle" to the problem even though he labors under the handicap of having less knowledge of company operations than an employee.

The old problems are still with us in a different form. As we read about the energy shortage and the need to conserve the earth's resources, the economic solution comes ultimately down to cost control, cost analysis and the figuring of trade-off benefits at the corporate level. Given the projected era of shortage economies, the skills and experience of the accountant will continue to be needed.

Standing on the foundation of methods, procedures and techniques, tediously developed and tested in the first five decades of this century, the management accountant can—and should—take the lead in providing all levels of management with practical and usable information. He must encourage operating people to contribute from their particular know-how. Above all, he must keep certain questions in mind in approaching every problem: What information do we really need? Are we getting more data than we can use? Is it timely? Is it worth the cost? And, of course, the most important of them all—Why?

## QUESTIONS

1. What are the differences between the duties of an auditor, a cost accountant, a controller, an industrial engineer, a production manager, a management accountant, and a management consultant?

2. Arrange the following items in the historical order in which Mr. Bergstrom took them up in his career: electronic data processing, direct costs, product cost centers, standard cost system, and predetermined cost system.

3. In general, how does a cost accountant arrive at a price to charge for a given item? What are criticisms of this approach?

4. Under what circumstances might it be advisable for a firm to set the price of a product at less than its average cost?

# 73

## THE HARDSHIP OF ACCOUNTING*
Robert Frost

Never ask of money spent
Where the spender thinks it went
Nobody was ever meant
To remember or invent
What he did with every cent.

# 74

## THE NATURE OF INFORMATION AND INFORMATION SYSTEMS†
Gerald A. Feltham

### INFORMATION AND DATA

"Data" sometimes refers to signs or signals generated as a result of direct observation of events or states. . . .

"Information" is often defined as the useful knowledge obtained from the data received and, therefore, is dependent upon the person who receives the data and the decisions he will make. . . .

The problem with many definitions of data and information is that certain signs and signals are excluded even though they are pertinent to the discussion. If data include only facts based on direct observation, then they do not include the results of mathematical decision models and the signs and characters which represent an individual's beliefs, e.g., a department head's estimate of expenses for the coming year. However, these signs are often recorded and transmitted to decision makers; it seems reasonable to refer to them as data. . . .

. . . "Data" refer to signs and characters generated by a person or a machine, provided these signs and characters have a meaning which is understood by the person who determined how they would be generated.

The above information definition excludes signs and characters which add to the decision maker's knowledge if this knowledge is not used in making any decisions. Therefore, the decision process must be specified before any particular sign or charac-

*From *Complete Poems of Robert Frost*, Holt, Rinehart & Winston, Inc., New York, 1964. Reprinted by permission of the publisher.

†Excerpted from G. A. Feltham, *Information Evaluation*, Studies in Accounting Research No. 5, American Accounting Association, 1972, pp. 7—19. Reprinted by permission of publisher.

ter can be designated as information; these decisions may be far in the future. In this study information refers to the *meaning* derived from data provided the knowledge of the person receiving those data is changed. Hence, whether certain data provide information depends on the state of the receiver at the time the data are received. In a decision theoretic context, knowledge is represented by the person's probability distribution over the events that may have occurred in the past and those that may occur in the future—data are information if their receipt results in a change in the receiver's probability distribution.

An interesting aspect of this definition of information is that "misinformation" is information. The definition says nothing about accuracy, reliability, etc.

The term "useful information" is no longer redundant; information does not imply usefulness. "Useful" is merely one of a number of the characteristics which may be attributed to various information. . . .

"Regardless of the manner in which information is viewed, its function is to reduce the amount or range of uncertainty under which decisions are made." The firm's expected payoff is usually increased if the uncertainty with respect to future events is decreased. Future events cannot be directly observed, but probability distributions over these events depend upon the decision maker's knowledge about the past. Therefore, reductions in the uncertainty with respect to past events usually reduces the uncertainty with respect to future events.

The entropy measure of statistical communication theory provides a measure of the reduction in uncertainty resulting from a signal from a given source. It . . . is often referred to as the amount of information.

## THE INFORMATION SYSTEM

The previous section considered the nature of data and information; this section considers the nature of the system which handles and produces data and information. The discussion is restricted to the formal information system and, therefore, deals only with recorded symbols; it does not handle verbal communication.

The following discussion considers the general processes which are included in the information system; the discussion does not consider the specific elements of the physical structure and techniques. However, use of the framework developed in this study requires an analysis of the specific elements.

The basic elements of an information system . . . are classified as data collection, data processing, data storage and retrieval, and data transmission.

Operationally, a particular process may be performed by several physical units or one physical unit may perform several processes. Furthermore, a physical unit may perform both informational and noninformational tasks.

. . . A major problem in specifying the limits of the information system . . . is . . . separating the information system from the decision making process. The decision maker and his staff often process information received prior to making a decision; it is difficult to distinguish this processing from "data processing." A consistent distinction can be achieved if all processing is included in data processing, but this leads to the inclusion of many activities which are usually in the domain of the decision maker. Therefore, the distinction is left somewhat vague.

## DATA COLLECTION

The mere observation of events is not sufficient; the data collection unit also records (using symbols) descriptions of some of the characteristics of some of these events. The analysis focuses on accounting information systems and, therefore, most descriptions consist of the measurement of some characteristic of the chosen event. Measurements and recording measurements are the key tasks assigned to data collection units.

The actual data collected depend on the characteristics of the men and machines used in the process, their location, and the way in which they are programmed to carry out their tasks.

As indicated by the first and second elements, the purpose of the information system must be considered in order to determine the basic data that should be collected. That is, determining what should be measured requires full awareness of the kind of output desired from the information system. This requires knowledge of the objectives of the firm and how they are to be achieved.

After the purpose of the measurement has been established, consideration is given to *what* is to be measured and *how* it is to be measured. . . . "What is to be measured" refers to both the events and the particular characteristics of those events that are to be described—an event is never "completely" described. . . .

Essentially, measurement is the assignment of a number, according to some rule, to the characteristic of the event being described.

There are many characteristics for which suitable techniques of measurement have not been developed. The various disciplines are constantly attempting to extend the boundaries of measurable characteristics and the level of scale which may be used in measuring a particular characteristic.

When selecting the characteristic to be measured and the scale to be used, the measurer should specify carefully *what* is being measured and *how* this measurement is to be performed.

Because standards are established and a number is used to describe a particular characteristic, a false sense of precision is often generated by measurements. Decision makers should realize that measurements are not one hundred per cent accurate; they almost always contain some error.

Since measurements should be made with the user in mind, a conflict develops when more than one user is interested in a particular measurement.

## DATA PROCESSING

Recorded observations may be immediately useful to a decision maker, but most raw descriptions must be "processed" in order to obtain data which provide useful information. "The Data Processing Component is the heart of the information system. It forges raw data into usable information. . . ."

The objectives of the firm, and the information useful in attaining these objectives, must be considered when determining the processing to be performed. This establishes the desired outputs. The outputs are dependent on both the processing and the inputs. Therefore, consideration must be given to the data which are, or can be made, available to the processing component. Once the type of inputs and processing has been determined, consideration can be given to the people, equipment, and programming necessary to carry out the processing.

The most common types of processing in accounting are classification and aggregation. Classification is the categorization of events according to sets of characteristics. Aggregation is the addition of the numerical descriptions of all events in a given category.

Another form of data processing is the calculation of various statistics such as the mean, variance, or mode. Also, the totals of various categories may be compared by using differences and ratios. More complex processing involves the use of mathematical or statistical models such as linear programs or regression analyses. In these cases the nature of the output may be entirely different from the nature of the input.

## DATA STORAGE AND RETRIEVAL

The reason for storing particular data is the belief that there is some chance that these data will be useful in making some future decision. This results in large amounts of data being stored "unnecessarily" in the sense that the data are never used. "Unnecessary" data storage cannot be eliminated; the decision to store must be made *ex ante* and should be based on a comparison of the costs of storing data with their *expected* value.

The usefulness of stored data is limited by the fact that decisions are based on expectations of the future; old information often has limited use in predicting the future. On the other hand, data not stored may be lost forever. Other data and the memories of those involved permit approximation of the data at a later date, but it will only be an approximation.

Processing data before storage often reduces the amount of processing that can be done later and, thus, reduces the information that can be obtained later. This loss must be compared with the fact that the cost of processing the input and storing the output may be less than the cost of storing the input and performing the processing later.

## DATA TRANSMISSION

Data transmission takes place among all the elements of the information system and between the information system and the decision makers. Decisions are required to determine *what* is sent, *to whom* it is sent, and *how* it is sent.

"What" involves more than the selection of particular data: there must also be a selection of the method of expressing those data. The results of measurement and processing must be described and different methods of presentation convey different meanings to the users. The user's perception should be considered; his actions may be affected by his perceptions of the data received and the outcome of these actions is important in evaluating changes in the information system.

"To whom" refers to the selection of the data recipients and the route by which the data are sent. Obviously, the person or department whose needs gave rise to the data will receive them. In addition, the data should be sent to any person to whom the expected value is greater than the transmission cost.

Data may be routed through a number of users. The selection of the route must consider that the meaning originally conveyed by the data may be distorted as the data pass through various individuals.

"How" data are sent refers to the physical method of transmission. The methods of transmission vary from the personal carrying of a report to the electronic communication between computers. The medium selected depends on the relative cost, speed, and accuracy of the alternatives available.

The questions "What?", "To Whom?", and "How?" apply to the transmission of data to both internal and external users.

## THE ACTION SYSTEM

The components of the firm which determine the value of the data produced are considered below. The links between the data produced and the firm's payoff are the decisions which use the information resulting from that data, and the actions resulting from those decisions.

### Decision Making

The evaluation of any information system change which affects the data produced must consider the way in which the decision maker uses the resulting information. Thus, consideration should be given to the decision models which are used or which might be used if different data are made available.

Analysis of the decision models used by any particular decision maker is not an easy task. Operations research has developed a number of formal decision models, but they have received only limited implementation. Instead, intuition, rule of thumb, and *ad hoc* analyses are the main bases for decisions in the present business world. It is extremely difficult to determine how the decision is actually made, and, particularly, to sufficiently understand the decision process so that the results of changes in data can be predicted.

The decision maker's choice depends on the alternatives of which he is aware and the expected results of the actions related to those alternatives. Information generates alternatives and supplies descriptions of events and states which may be useful in evaluating given alternatives. Accounting information is mainly concerned with the latter.

Both the person making a decision and the type of decision model he uses must be ascertained if an efficient information system is to be developed. Failure to do this may result in data being sent to those who have little or no use for them or not being sent to those who need them. The former is detrimental if the receiver wastes time considering useless information or there is a cost of sending the data to him.

### Implementation

Decision making does not end the process; the decisions must be implemented. Implementation requires effort.

. . . Implemented actions are not necessarily the same as those selected by the decision maker. The actions resulting from a decision are affected by the motivation, perception, training, and knowledge of the people who receive the decisions and take action on them. These factors should be considered in predicting the events which will result from a particular decision.

## QUESTIONS

1. What is the difference between data and information?
2. Why must the decision process be specified before any particular sign or character can be designated as information?
3. Define the basic elements of an information system?
4. "Since measurements should be made with the user in mind, a conflict develops when more than one user is interested in a particular measurement." Explain.
5. What are classification and aggregation in accounting?
6. If an efficient information system is to be developed, why must both the decision maker and the decision model be known?
7. Illustrate why the actions intended by a decision maker do not always occur?

## SELECTED BIBLIOGRAPHY

Camman, Cortlandt, and David A. Nadler, "Fit Control Systems to Your Managerial Style," *Harvard Business Review*, January-February 1976, pp. 65-72.

Howitt, A. W., "Information Needs of Management," *Management Accounting*, November 1972, pp. 350-352.

# 75
# TYPES OF INFORMATION SUPPLIED BY MANAGEMENT ACCOUNTING*

Charles T. Horngren

EDITORS' NOTE: The following excerpt is from the prize-winning paper "Choosing Accounting Practices for Reporting to Management." The ideas in the section reprinted, while not original with Professor Horngren, have received much attention since his article appeared.

What information should the management accountant supply? The types of information needed have been neatly described by Simon *et al.* as a result of their study of

*Excerpt from "Choosing Accounting Practices for Reporting to Management," *NAA Bulletin* (now *Management Accounting*), September 1962, pp. 3–15. Reprinted by permission of the publisher.

seven large companies with geographically dispersed operations. The approach of the Simon research team would probably be fruitful in any company:

> By observation of the actual decision-making process, specific types of data needs were identified at particular organization levels—the vice presidential level, the level of the factory manager, and the level of the factory head, for example—each involving quite distinct problems of communication for the accounting department.[1]

The research team found that three types of information, each serving a different purpose, often at various management levels, raise and help answer three basic questions:

1. Score-card questions: "Am I doing well or badly?"
2. Attention-directing questions: "What problems should I look into?"
3. Problem-solving questions: "Of the several ways of doing the job, which is the best?"

Score-card and attention-directing uses of data are closely related. The same data may serve a score-card function for a foreman and an attention-directing function for his superior. For example, many accounting systems provide performance reports through which actual results are compared to predetermined budgets or standards. Such a performance report often helps answer score-card questions and attention-directing questions simultaneously.

Furthermore, the "actual results" collected can help fulfill not only control purposes but also the traditional needs of financial accounting. The answering of score-card questions, which mainly involves collection, classification, and reporting, is the task that has predominated in the day-to-day effort of the accounting function.

Problem-solving data may be used to help in special nonrecurring decisions and long-range planning. Examples include make-or-buy, equipment replacement, adding or dropping products, etc. These decisions often require expert advice from specialists such as industrial engineers, budgetary accountants, statisticians, and others.

## MANAGEMENT ACCOUNTING AND THE OVERALL INFORMATION SYSTEM

These three uses of data may be related to the broad purposes of the accounting system. The business information system of the future should be a single, multi-purpose system with a highly-selective reporting scheme. It will be tightly integrated and will serve three main purposes: (1) routine reporting on financial results, oriented primarily for external parties (scorekeeping); (2) routine reporting to management, primarily for planning and controlling current operations (score-keeping and attention-directing); and (3) special reporting to management, primarily for long-range planning and non-

[1]H. A. Simon, *Administrative Behavior* (2nd ed.; New York: The Macmillan Company, 1957), p. 20. For the complete study see H. A. Simon, H. Guetzkow, G. Kozmetsky, and G. Tyndall, *Centralization vs. Decentralization in Organizing the Controller's Department* (New York: Controllership Foundation, Inc. 1954). This perceptive study is much broader than its title implies.

recurring decisions (problem-solving). Although such a system can probably be designed in a self-contained, integrated manner to serve routine purposes simultaneously, its special decision function will always entail much data that will not lie within the system.

## USE OF DATA AND ORGANIZATION OF THE ACCOUNTANT'S WORK

The Simon study also emphasized that ideally the management accountant's staff should have its three distinct functions manned by full-time accountants: (1) score-keepers, who compile routine data and keep the information system running smoothly; (2) attention-directors, who attempt to understand operating management's viewpoint most fully and who spotlight, interpret, and explain those operating areas that are most in need of attention; and (3) problem-solvers, who search for alternatives, study the probable consequences, and help management follow an objective approach to special decisions.

If one accountant bears responsibility for more than one of these three functions, his energies are prone to be directed to (1), then to (2), and finally to (3). If this occurs, his two foremost values, as far as management is concerned, are likely to be dissipated.[2]

## QUESTIONS

1. What impact on an accountant's work is the increasing use of data-processing equipment, particularly computers, likely to have?

2. "If one accountant bears responsibility for more than one of these three functions, his energies are prone to be directed to (1) (score-keeping), then to (2) (attention-directing), and finally to (3) (problem-solving)." What support do you find for this statement?

## SELECTED BIBLIOGRAPHY

O'Brien, J. A., "Do Accountants Make Good Managers?" *The Australian Accountant,* June 1974, pp. 272-274.

[2]Simon, et al., op. cit., p. 5.

# 76

## CLASSIFICATION OF BUSINESS ACTIVITIES*
Robert N. Anthony

### STRATEGIC PLANNING

To start with, we found it easy to identify two rather different types of planning activities in an organization. One is the type of planning . . . associated with the control process, an activity related to the ongoing administration of the organization. The other type is identified by terms such as policy formulation, goal setting, and top management planning. The thought processes in each of these types of planning are similar, but in most other respects the two types are so different that almost no important generalizations apply to both of them.

We identified this latter planning activity as the first of our main categories and labeled it *strategic planning.* The definition we suggest is as follows:

*Strategic planning* is the process of deciding on objectives of the organization, on changes in these objectives, on the resources used to attain these objectives, and on the policies that are to govern the acquisition, use, and disposition of these resources.

"Objectives" are what the organization wishes to accomplish (in military parlance, the "mission"), and "policies" are guidelines that are to be used in the choice of the most appropriate course of action for accomplishing the objectives.

The word "strategy" is used here in its usual sense of combining and employing resources. It connotes big plans, important plans, plans with major consequences. Some students of management restrict the word strategy to those plans that are made in response to a competitor's action or in anticipation of his probable reaction, but there appears to be no particular reason for making such a restriction, and the word is not used here in this limited sense. Others draw a distinction between strategy and "grand" strategy, but again, there seems to be no valid reason to set up separate categories. . . .

### MANAGEMENT CONTROL

Whereas strategic planning is one type of planning, there is another type that is associated with the ongoing administration of the enterprise, but, as already pointed out, this other type is so closely associated with control activities that setting it up as a separate main category would be artificial. For our second main category, therefore, we use a concept that combines both planning and control. As a label for this concept, we use "management control."

This label has the obvious weakness of not mentioning planning. The obvious solution, to use "management planning and control," seems unnecessarily cumbersome,

---

*Excerpt from *Planning and Control Systems: A Framework for Analysis*, Division of Research, Harvard Business School, Boston, 1965, pp. 15–19. Reprinted by permission of the publisher and the author.

and the alternative of coining a new term seemed undesirable for reasons to be discussed. . . . Furthermore, there seems to be increasing use of the term management control to refer to the same combination of planning and control activities that we have in mind. The definition we suggest is as follows:

*Management control* is the process by which managers assure that resources are obtained and used effectively and efficiently in the accomplishment of the organization's objectives.

This definition is intended to convey three key ideas. First, the process involves managers, that is, people who get things done by working with other people. Second, the process takes place within a context of objectives and policies that have been arrived at in the strategic planning process. Third, the criteria relevant for judging the actions taken in this process are effectiveness and efficiency. . . .

## OPERATIONAL CONTROL

At one time, we thought that strategic planning and management control should be the two main topics of our framework. It became apparent, however, that many of the generalizations that are relevant for management control do not work well for a certain class of the organization's activities, and that there are generalizations applicable to this class that are invalid for other activities. It also is apparent that mistakes with serious practical consequences have been made when techniques and generalizations found valid for one class of activities have been applied to the other. We therefore saw the need for a third main topic.

We groped for the most useful way of describing this third topic so as to differentiate it from management control, but even now are by no means satisfied with the results. One possibility was to draw a line between activities that required the use of judgment and those that could be completely governed by formal decision rules. We referred to these as nonprogrammed and programmed activities. However, this distinction eventually seemed to be less useful than a slightly different one, one that is based on the distinction between the activities properly referred to as management and activities that relate to the performance of specified tasks. We call the latter *operational control* and define it as follows:

*Operational control* is the process of assuring that specific tasks are carried out effectively and efficiently.

This definition is somewhat vague. It intends to convey the idea that operational control is to be distinguished from management control in at least the following key ways: (1) Operational control is concerned with tasks (e.g., manufacturing Job No. 5687; ordering 500 units of Item 84261), whereas management control is concerned with individuals, that is, managers. (2) The tasks to which operational control relates are specified, so that little or no judgment is required as to what is to be done; the activities to which management control relates are not specified, and management decides what is to be done within the general constraints of the strategic plans. In operational control, the focus is on execution; in management control it is on both planning and execution. . . .

## CLASSIFICATION OF BUSINESS ACTIVITIES

The three processes described briefly in the preceding paragraphs are the main categories of our framework. . . . Exhibit 1 is given as a preliminary device for this purpose. It classifies certain planning and control activities of a business organization under our three main categories. Note that the activities listed under strategic planning are almost entirely planning activities, that those listed under management control are a mixture of both planning and control, and that those listed under operational control are almost entirely control activities.

## QUESTIONS

1. Define the following terms: strategic planning, strategy, objectives, policies, management control, effectiveness, efficiency, and operational control.

2. The activities of a business are often considered for accounting purposes to be production, distribution, and administration. Why do you think Anthony's classi-

**Exhibit 1   Examples of Activities in a Business Organization Included in Major Framework Headings**

| STRATEGIC PLANNING | MANAGEMENT CONTROL | OPERATIONAL CONTROL |
|---|---|---|
| Choosing company objectives | Formulating budgets | |
| Planning the organization | Planning staff levels | Controlling hiring |
| Setting personnel policies | Formulating personnel practices | Implementing policies |
| Setting financial policies | Working capital planning | Controlling credit extension |
| Setting marketing policies | Formulating advertising programs | Controlling placement of advertisements |
| Setting research policies | Deciding on research projects | |
| Choosing new product lines | Choosing product improvements | |
| Acquiring a new division | Deciding on plant rearrangement | Scheduling production |
| Deciding on non-routine capital expenditures | Deciding on routine capital expenditures | |
| | Formulating decision rules for operational control | Controlling inventory |
| | Measuring, appraising, and improving management performance | Measuring, appraising, and improving workers' efficiency |

fication will be more or less helpful to managers than the conventional one? To accountants?

3. If accounting followed this classification, what specific changes would be required?

## SELECTED BIBLIOGRAPHY

Goetz, Billy E., "The Management of Objectives," *Management Accounting*, August 1973, pp. 35-38.

# 77
## BATTLE OF THE BASKETS*
Richard Armour

Here's a battle that I wage
   Each day, and never win:
To pile more papers in my "Out"
   Than others pile in "In."
The battle starts at nine A.M.
   Amidst a frightful din
Of clacking keys and clicking heels
   That strive to fill my "In."
Till noon and past, with flitting eye,
   Quick hand, and jutting chin,
I thread the ins and outs of "Out,"
   The outs and ins of "In."
By five P.M. I'm glassy-eyed,
   My nerves are frayed and thin,
But everything is piled in "Out,"
   And, likewise, out of "In."
But victory is not yet mine:
   I find, to my chagrin,
That as my "Out" is emptied out
   A lot more "In" comes in.
"It is too late," I sadly sigh,
   "Too late, now, to begin,"
And so I put my hat on and
   Once more go out—all in.

*From "A Satirist Looks at the World," 2d Annual Wm. McInally Memorial Lecture, Graduate School of Business, University of Michigan, 1967. Reprinted by permission of the publisher.

# 78

## CLASSIFICATION OF COST DISTINCTIONS*
Joel Dean

| DICHOTOMY | | BASIS OF DISTINCTION |
|---|---|---|
| 1. Opportunity costs | Outlay costs | Nature of the sacrifice |
| 2. Past costs | Future costs | Degree of anticipation |
| 3. Short-run costs | Long-run costs | Degree of adaptation to present output |
| 4. Variable costs | Constant costs | Degree of variation with output rate |
| 5. Traceable costs | Common costs | Traceability to unit of operations |
| 6. Out-of-pocket costs | Book costs | Immediacy of expenditure |
| 7. Incremental costs | Sunk costs | Relation to added activity |
| 8. Escapable costs | Unavoidable costs | Relation to retrenchment |
| 9. Controllable costs | Non-controllable costs | Controllability |
| 10. Replacement costs | Historical costs | Timing of valuation |

EDITORS' NOTE: In his book, Professor Dean explains that the distinctions in this table are basically of two different kinds. In one, he views costs from an accounting as contrasted with an economic viewpoint—included here are numbers 1, 2, 3, and 10. In the other kind of distinction, he divides total aggregate accounting costs in various ways—included here are numbers 4, 5, 6, 7, 8, and 9. Thus *costs,* including *accounting costs,* do not mean the same thing in all circumstances. Quite the contrary: the appropriate cost concept will depend upon what is relevant to the kind of decision to be made.

## QUESTIONS

1. Show how all Professor Dean's dichotomies might be utilized in a single managerial decision.

2. What are some other cost dichotomies that are extensively utilized in accounting? That might be utilized?

---

*Excerpt from *Managerial Economics*, Englewood Cliffs, N.J., Prentice-Hall, Inc., 1951. Reprinted by permission of the publisher.

# 79
# THE BENEFITS OF DIRECT COSTING*
Richard W. Swalley

In 1936, Jonathan Harris, a controller, was questioned by the president of his company as to why the company's profits showed a drop of $20,000 from the previous month while sales showed an increase of over $100,000.[1] It was then, and is now, a *bona-fide* question. In response to the question, he devised a system of cost accounting which would show profits as a function of sales—something which absorption costing, the method then in use, did not do. He had come to realize that the reason for the incongruity between sales and profits centered on the absorption or full-costing method of cost allocation which was (and still is) considered the "ultimate" method of calculating product costs. Ever since, his direct-costing proposal has been one of the most controversial issues within, and without, the accounting profession.

It is certain that even today there are presidents who don't quite comprehend the concept of absorption costing. They know that variances from standard are generated, but they don't know how much of any variance is being charged or credited to cost of sales and how much is being deferred. Not many of them really know that direct costing would be of real value in alleviating this situation. Not many of them know that they would understand variances (which in some cases now frighten them) generated under a direct-costing system and, in all probability, they unknowingly are waiting for the accounting profession to accept Harris' direct-costing system.

The controversy over direct costing includes but is in no way limited to the following questions:

1. What effect does direct costing have on internal and external reporting?

2. How does the delineation of costs into period and product costs coincide with the matching concept which is paramount in income determination and asset valuation?

3. Will the Securities and Exchange Commission and the Internal Revenue Service accept statements based on the direct costing method?[2]

Before attempting to answer these questions, it would perhaps be wise to review briefly absorption and direct costing and point out the major differences. One of the major differences is essentially concerned with the amount of fixed overhead that is apportioned to the inventory account.

## ABSORPTION COSTING

Absorption or full costing calls for the accountant to calculate standards for all the products produced within a definite period of time by allocating total costs, regard-

---

*From *Management Accounting*, September 1974, pp. 13–16. Reprinted by permission of the publisher.

[1]Jonathan N. Harris, "What Did We Earn Last Month?" *NAA Bulletin*, January 1936, p. 501.

[2]See A. N. Davidson's "Acceptance of Direct Costing," *Management Accounting*, March 1970.

less of the fixed or variable nature of those costs. The standards are set using normal operating capacity as a basis for spreading the fixed costs. Variances which are generated from operating under or over this capacity can be charged in total to cost of sales or they may be apportioned between cost of sales and the inventories. Thus, under absorption costing, when production exceeds sales, the ending inventory value is greater than the beginning inventory value. Consequently, the cost of sales, after adjustments for variations from standard, will be reduced by the amount of increased fixed or period costs allocated to the larger ending inventory. When sales exceed production, the reverse is naturally true. Generally speaking, income appears to be increased during periods when finished goods inventories are increased, and decreased when finished goods inventories are decreased. Under absorption costing, the income concept is rather ambiguous; wide swings in inventory levels without corresponding sales can affect the income reported.

It is easy to see that under absorption costing management can manipulate profits to a degree. A stepped-up production schedule in certain months can aid profits in those months. Should the year be coming to an end with an almost-but-not-certain budgeted income picture developing, steps can be taken, production-wise, to generate the budgeted income. This might satisfy the current year's management, and even provide it with a bonus, but at the expense of next year's management.

Other disadvantages of absorption costing include the fact that information is not easily obtained for break-even analysis, and there is no readily adaptable tool for budgetary control of fixed expenses.[3] As a result of including fixed period costs in standard overhead rates, management is forced to prepare supplementary reports to perform such functions as pricing and control.

## DIRECT COSTING

A direct-costing system overcomes most of the disadvantages normally related to absorption costing. Direct costing is based on the incontrovertible fact that some costs are attributable to a particular time period while other costs are dependent on the volume produced.

Fixed or period costs are shown in total as an expense in the year in which they are incurred. Variable costs are shown as costs of sales relative to the number of units sold or as an inventory valuation relative to the number of units on hand at the end of the year. Direct costing facilitates incremental profit analysis and recording of income based on sales by removing from income determination the effect of inventory fluctuations.[4] In addition, the calculation of standards are simplified by eliminating the need to consider fixed factory overhead. This does away with the controversy of what is "normal" plant capacity in setting standards and the subsequent under or over-absorbed overhead related with those standards.[5] It does, however, require strong

[3] Waldo W. Neikirk, "How Direct Costing Can Work for Management," *NAA Bulletin*, January 1951, pp. 524–525.

[4] James M. Fremgen, "The Direct Costing Controversy—An Identification of Issues," *Accounting Review*, January 1964, pp. 44–45.

[5] Harris, op. cit., pp. 508–509.

and effective definitions of what costs are to be considered product costs. It also requires very good reasons for expensing period costs in the year in which they are incurred.

Under the direct-costing concept, fixed or period costs are generally considered to include all costs necessary to provide and maintain a specific capacity to produce. Changes in that capacity occur only in the long range as a direct result of top management's decisions to alter the capacity to produce. The fixed or period costs include depreciation, property taxes, insurance, salaries of factory superintendent and his staff, and other costs not directly affected by the volume of production.[6] The concept of fixed, period costs is a total concept in that the fixed costs are to be completely absorbed by revenues generated in the year in which they are incurred. They should not become part of standard unit costs (unless they are treated in some way as a special standard amount easily separated from the whole and used only as a guide for pricing). They should be shown in total on the statements in a separate category clearly labeled as period or fixed costs.

It follows then that product costs must be the remaining costs. These will consist of prime costs (direct labor and direct materials) and variable overhead expenses. They do fluctuate directly with the volume produced. At zero level of production these costs will be, by definition, zero, and will increase as a linear function of production.

## COST ALLOCATION

The controversy between absorption costing and direct costing centers around the impact of fixed or period costs on the financial statements of the firm. The systematic allocation of overhead expenses is absolutely necessary so that more realistic and more accurate information can be provided to management. With the absorption-costing system, much time is utilized in carrying out the fixed-cost allocations—time that could be utilized much more efficiently on other problems and in securing more practical information for users of statements. Direct costing with its separation of costs into fixed and variable elements eliminates much of this problem.

Depreciation, for example, is allocated to various periods. However, of all the methods available for allocating this value, only one, the unit-of-production method, attempts in any way to tie the depletion of fixed-asset value to the goods actually produced. All other methods, in reality, consider depreciation as a reduction in value due to the lapse of time. Since time is the basis for determining the depreciation in a specific period, it does not seem logical that any portion of that depreciation should be re-allocated to another time period. Although improbable, it is possible for this amount, so allocated, to remain as an asset in the form of inventory for a year or more after the original write-off took place. It is possible for a depreciated portion of a fixed asset to wind up on the balance sheet as a current asset, thereby increasing working capital. With direct costing, period and product costs are combined in a logical manner to avoid the problems of this form of cost allocation.

[6]Neikirk, op. cit., pp. 526–527.

## DIRECT COSTING AND INTERNAL REPORTS

With direct costing, cash flow analysis and working capital analysis would be benefited. Cash requirements could be projected directly in relation to volume changes and anticipated capital expenditures. The statement of source and application of working capital, which is essential to planning the growth of any business, could be made more meaningful to readers by depleting from it that amount of depreciation which appears in both the working capital section and as a source of funds. Claiming depreciation as working capital and a source of funds is clearly a stretch of the accountant's wildest imagination and is justified only because it is a necessary manipulation of the figures to reconcile with reality.

In addition, direct costing facilitates the computation of flexible budgets through defining period and product costs. The variable costs of each individual product thus become its standard costs. At any level of production or sales, total costs can be automatically predicted simply by multiplying units by variable costs per unit and adding the period costs.[7] This flexibility is also a necessary aid in logical long-range planning. For example, since no fixed costs will be included in unit costs, product costs can be estimated according to historical economic indicators.[8] Period or fixed costs are treated in total. Budgets and forecasts would be more accurate because future income will have a direct relationship with future sales. It follows also that break-even analysis is an easily generated by-product of a direct-costing system, and the merits of break-even analysis are not controversial.

There is, however, the fear of price cutting in some product areas for competitive reasons. If attention is focused completely on variable costs, a firm could conceivably cause its own failure. But it is doubtful that the judgment and insight of most product managers would permit this to happen. It is equally doubtful that standards based on variable costs would so confuse a product pricing manager that he would not take into account all costs and a margin of acceptable profit. Prices on most commodities are determined by other factors, the most important of which is what the market will bear. If a product cannot contribute anything to covering fixed costs, that product should be dropped from the line. It is of no value.

A much better presentation to product pricing management is made by supplying them with the variable costs of all products they are expected to sell, the total fixed costs they are required to cover, and the total profit they are required to generate, and let them decide, based on market conditions, what prices are to be used. In this way the parameters for pricing are automatically set. How the fixed costs are to be covered is left to the responsible individuals (price administrators) who work closely with the product managers. With clear-cut records of competitive price structures, they are certainly better equipped to coordinate accounting with marketing. Subsequent records, generated under a direct-costing system, supply even more timely information for future comparisons of projections without recourse to extensive calculations.

[7]Ibid., p. 529.

[8]Wilmer Wright, "Why Direct Costing Is Rapidly Gaining Acceptance," *The Journal of Accountancy*, July 1962, pp. 41–42.

An illustration by Clem N. Kohl of the impact of fixed costs on the extension of credit by the credit manager is an interesting one. He points out that a wise credit man is aware that the only dollars really lost when an account goes bad are the dollars necessary to replace the items sold. And the only dollars needed to replace the items sold are the variable dollars, since the fixed-cost dollars are expended anyway you look at it. By having an awareness of this difference between fixed and variable costs, ". . . the credit manager has his foot on the gas instead of on the brake."[9]

## DIRECT COSTING AND EXTERNAL REPORTS

External reports are the published reports and they represent management to the stockholders, government, potential investors, and the general public. These are the reports which the public accounting profession certifies as a fair representation of the company's operations in conformity with generally accepted accounting principles consistently applied. They also become the basis for countless financial decisions. The general acceptance of these reports naturally depends upon their usefulness. However, before we consider the question of usefulness, we should first consider the accounting principles involved in the direct-costing controversy. These principles center around the matching concept and inventory valuation for more accurate income determination.

### The Matching Concept

The focal point of the matching concept is, of course, the proper matching of revenues with relevant costs in the proper period to produce accurate income determination. Fixed costs are costs of providing the capacity to produce within a definite time period, and they expire with time, regardless of the extent to which the facilities are actually utilized.[10] Therefore, supporters of direct costing quite generally agree that fixed or period costs cannot logically be re-allocated to inventory to be treated as an expense in any other period than the one in which the cost has actually expired. Another inconsistency exists when the depreciation of a building is shared evenly by manufacturing and selling and administration. The portion allocated to the latter departments will in total be treated as a period cost under absorption costing. However, only if sales equal production will absorption costing permit this to be done in the manufacturing department. In manufacturing it becomes a product cost and subsequently part of inventory.[11]

Research and development costs are in many cases also allocated to other manufacturing departments and subsequently become part of inventory. Logically, they are

[9]Clem N. Kohl, "What Is Wrong with Most Profit and Loss Statements?" *NAA Bulletin*, July 1937, pp. 1214–1215.

[10]Herman C. Heiser, "What Can We Expect of Direct Costing as a Basis for Internal and External Reporting?" *NAA Bulletin*, July 1953.

[11]Robert E. Seiler, "Improvements in External Reporting by Use of Direct Costing," *Accounting Review*, January 1959, p. 64.

period costs because of their on-going nature. The products being developed are not part of current inventory. Since it is not known whether a product will even result from current expenditures, capitalization seems unjustified. The only fair alternative is to write them off as period expenses and avoid a definite mismatching of costs and revenues.

### Inventory Valuation

The end result of any costing technique is to record the proper income determination through properly and accurately valuing the assets on hand at the end of the period. They become a "resting place" for dollars before being transferred to the income statement.[12] Horngren and Sorter consider costs to be assets ". . . if they can justifiably be carried forward to the future, if they bear revenue-producing power, if they are beneficial to future operations."[13] Being beneficial to future operations is defined as possessing "service potential" and the critical test of service potential is whether or not a future cost is avoided by incurring that cost now. The major test for placing an item on the balance sheet then becomes a determination of whether or not the item will be of "future benefit."[14] Since inventories valued on the basis of variable costs would reflect the amount of working capital tied up in unsold products, there would be a definite "future benefit" in the variable costs.[15]

Conservatism has dictated the acceptance of "cost or market, whichever is lower" as a highly respected inventory valuation method. It is based on the theory that losses should be recognized as they are realized—in the year in which they are realized. This is considered necessary to provide the readers of the statements with an accurate accounting of the income and the true value of the assets. However, when a period cost is expended within a period, it is gone—forever. There is no possible way it can be regained. This is not true with the "cost or market, whichever is lower" concept. Except for obsolete material, there is always the possibility that the market will respond favorably in the subsequent period affording a greater than normal profit in that period.

Total acceptance and full utilization of direct costing might obviate the need for the "cost or market, whichever is lower" concept of inventory valuation. This seems to be a logical conclusion since any product whose market value has fallen below the variable costs of production must be considered obsolete. The removal of cost or market inventory valuation could, in no small way, aid in providing understanding and usefulness to those who read and compare balance sheets.

It is logical in that all costs directly involved in producing a particular item be attached to that item. The valuation should not be burdened with period expenses

---

[12]Robert B. Wetnight, "Direct Costing Passes the 'Future Benefit' Test," *NAA Bulletin*, August 1958, p. 83.

[13]Charles T. Horngren and George H. Sorter, "Direct Costing for External Reporting," *Accounting Review*, January 1961, pp. 85—86.

[14]Wetnight, op. cit., p. 83.

[15]John R. E. Parker, "Give Consideration to Direct Costing for External Reporting," *NAA Bulletin*, October 1963, p. 4.

assigned to product costs on a basis which may or may not be justified. The value of the inventory should be defined as the amount of money actually spent in the particular period, and will not have to be spent in the next period in order to acquire a like asset. It is measurable because it is based on the logic that only those incremental costs necessary to produce the asset in a previous period are included in the asset.

### External Reporting

Most current writers agree that behind the basic ethics fostered by the accounting profession is the fundamental objective of fairness. That is, the accountant is faced with the responsibility of presenting to management, creditors, present and potential stockholders, the Internal Revenue Service, labor, and society a picture of a firm that is just and equitable. Attempting to prepare "fair" statements requires a judgment to be made by the accountant—a judgment that is not an easy task to make. Each accountant makes a choice of how best the firm should be represented.

In 1939, Kenneth MacNeal attempted to show the accounting profession through his proposed "truthful balance sheet" and "truthful profit and loss statement" that it was not fulfilling its obligations to society by not reporting unrealized gains. He felt that marketable assets should be valued at market price, non-marketable reproducible assets should be valued at replacement cost, and occasional non-marketable, non-reproducible assets should be valued at original cost.[16] The unrealized profits from these valuations would then be shown in a separate section in the income statement.

The point he was stressing was that readers of statements were not getting an accurate picture of the firm. Land valued at cost, plant and equipment recorded at cost less depreciation, and investments listed at "cost or market, whichever is lower," even in 1939 did not present an accurate balance sheet to readers. In most instances they were valued way below true market value.

This is still the case today. Full disclosure dictates that true values be supplied the readers. Because the true values are not in the accounts, the balance sheet and income statements are far from a true and "fair" picture of actual happenings. They are not in tune with reality. MacNeal's theory could, in a sense, justify the writing-off of period costs in the period in which they were actually incurred. By doing so, the stockholders of a period other than the one in which the expenses were actually incurred would not lose from re-allocating those expenses. Potential stockholders as well as other interested parties would not be completely unaware that they could suffer financially.

### CONCLUSION

There are many accounting procedures in use which lead to confused, meaningless and even misleading information to readers of financial statements. Among these is the concept of absorption of full costing which will probably continue to be used by

---

[16]Kenneth MacNeal, *Truth in Accounting*, University of Pennsylvania Press, Philadelphia, Pa., 1939, pp. 189–190.

most firms for one or more reasons. But if the reasons are attacked individually, many of them actually provide a basis for a change to direct costing.

It is up to the accounting profession itself to foster new traditions and customs to replace the old, and to provide understanding of new accounting principles. Given the proper and deserved sanction by all existing professional accounting societies, direct costing can provide less confusing and more meaningful statements for internal and external readers. It is up to the accounting profession also, to determine if the Securities and Exchange Commission and the Internal Revenue Service will accept the direct-costing technique of reporting.

## QUESTIONS

1. What is the difference between absorption or full costing and direct costing?
2. How does a direct-costing system overcome most of the disadvantages usually associated with absorption costing?
3. What is MacNeal's theory?

## SELECTED BIBLIOGRAPHY

Stutler, Don C., "Cost Accounting for Sand Castings," *Management Accounting,* April 1972, pp. 27-30.

# 80

## MANAGEMENT ACCOUNTING
## Where Are We?*
Charles T. Horngren

This paper presents some personal reactions to the evolution of management and cost accounting. My perspective is always changing, so this critique will undoubtedly continue to be modified as the years unfold.

## THE DEVELOPMENT OF MANAGEMENT ACCOUNTING COURSES

The field of management accounting has come a long distance since I first learned accounting during the late 1940s. My early schooling in accounting was like that of thousands of other students—a heavy emphasis on public accounting and the pro-

*From *Management Accounting and Control*, William S. Albrecht, ed., Proceedings of the Robert Beyer Symposium at the University of Wisconsin—Madison, May 8—9, 1975, privately printed June 1, 1975, pp. 9—26. Reprinted by permission of the publisher and the author.

duction of accounting data for external purposes. Uses of accounting data internally were given little attention in textbooks and in classes. At that time (1949), there were almost zero courses in management accounting as it is known today.

When I was an undergraduate student, the cost accounting courses and textbooks were largely concerned with how systems could trace costs to products and services for income statements and balance sheets. In an exaggerated sense, the cost accountant's main mission might have been depicted as the pursuit of absolute truth,[1] where truth was defined in terms of getting as accurate or precise costs as possible. Indeed, some "advanced" cost accounting courses were largely concerned with how to track costs in complex production settings (e.g., three or four processes with varying spoilage, shrinkage, and waste in each process).

The absolute truth approach is more accurately labeled as the historical communication approach. The approach aims at producing a unique set of historical information for all purposes. The objective is to use measurement rules that supply unambiguous information in the sense that only one measurement system is acceptable. The user can then supply his or her own adjustments as desired.

This unique historical data phenomenon had a narrowing impact on impressionable students. For example, when I began teaching management accounting in 1953, I encountered several students who (like me) initially resisted the idea that historical costs or book values might be safely ignored in some decision situations. The absolutist phenomenon also hobbled students' ability to see the potential of direct costing or contribution reporting. Inevitably, the students with heavy previous training in accounting offered the strongest opposition. Somehow these ideas were heretical because they challenged a measure that was perceived as a unique and unalterable truth.

During the 1950s, new courses in management accounting were begun in several schools. These courses were required in many MBA programs. During the 1960s and 1970s, management accounting courses have also tended to become required courses in undergraduate programs. Meanwhile, the cost accounting courses were taking on a much heavier management accounting flavor. (This paper will use "management accounting" to encompass all courses and accounting research that stress internal uses of accounting data.)

Consider why management accounting started to flourish. It remedied many defects, including the preoccupation with finding "the" unique cost. The most refreshing contribution of management accounting has been its focus on the potential uses of decisions that might be affected by the accounting data. The theme of "different costs for different purposes" was stressed—a preoccupation with finding conditional truth. This conditional truth theme has been labeled as the user decision model approach. Decision models are assumed for output levels, investments, and other purposes. Deductive reasoning is used to isolate and measure relevant data. Thus, accounting became more complex, more fascinating, and more responsive to students' perceived future roles.

---

[1] J. Demski, G. Feltham, C. Horngren, R. Jaedicke, *A Conceptual Approach to Cost Determination* (Ames, Iowa: Iowa State University Press, 1976), Chapter 1, pp. 2–3. Also see Report of the Committee on Concepts and Standards—Internal Planning and Control, *The Accounting Review*, (Supplement to Vol. XLIX, 1974), pp. 79–81. Also see Yuji Ijiri, *Theory of Accounting Measurement* (Sarasota, Florida: American Accounting Association, 1975), pp. 30–33.

After all, only a slim percentage of students in accounting courses become lifelong career specialists in auditing or income taxes. Instead, the large percentage become managers or accountants who serve managers.

As I have taught various courses in management accounting through the years, I have been increasingly troubled by its decision model approach. It has too much of an *ad hoc,* or "let's solve this case" flavor that I find unsatisfying. There is no unity, no common element beyond the caveat that each situation "requires" different costs.

I started casting about a more robust conceptual framework that I could apply serenely in this variety of decision settings. My present views are slightly more comforting, but my quest for the grail has failed. My search for a framework will continue, but it will be a look for modest improvements in my slippery grasp on an openended subject. My current perceptions are an amalgamation of much influential thinking done by many individuals, too many to name without overlooking somebody. I have tested these perceptions with my classes, so let me test them with you.

## FOCUS ON DECISIONS

As most of us can testify, our individual approaches to professional problems are frequently affected by our readings and by our conversations with colleagues. The authors who recently have influenced me the most have been my colleagues, Joel Demski and Gerald Feltham.[2] They approach these issues with more rigor and abstraction than I can muster. They also may cringe at my simplifications of their ideas. But our general philosophy is similar.

The Demski-Feltham approach has been called information analysis or information evaluation; it might also be dubbed as the "costly truth" approach (as contrasted with the "true cost" approach). They fundamentally regard management accounting as being concerned with how accounting data facilitate rational economic choices by internal decision makers. Their framework focuses on the roles of the decision maker and the accountant. The decision maker selects an action in a specific situation. The accountant provides information to facilitate the decision maker's choice. Of course, the two roles may be performed by the same individual, different individuals, or a group.[3]

---

[2]See Joel S. Demski, *Information Analysis* (Reading, Mass.: Addison-Wesley Publishing Co. Inc., 1972) and Gerald A. Feltham, *Information Evaluation* (Sarasota, Fla.: American Accounting Association, 1972). The Demski-Feltham approach has influenced the American Accounting Association committee reports on management accounting. For example, see *The Accounting Review Supplements* for 1972, pp. 317–335; 1973, pp. 234–235; and 1974, pp. 79–99. Demski and Feltham have been heavily influenced by the publications of Kenneth Arrow and Jacob Marschak.

[3]Ijiri, op. cit., p. 45, favors another approach, the *information control approach.* He states: "In a fourth method which we propose here, the same relationship is observed but is shifted to one level higher. A systems designer will now foresee all optimization behavior of accountants under each alternative rule. He will then select the one method most suitable for achieving the overall goal of the system. We may call this the *information control approach*, since one of the purposes of issuing rules is to control information processing systems by eliminating much of the discretionary activity of accountants." Ijiri also (pp. 32–33) stresses *accountability* as what distinguishes accounting from other information systems.

The costly truth approach emphasizes a method of analysis that explicitly regards the accountant as a decision maker. He (or she) must identify the information alternatives, evaluate them in terms of some set of objectives, deal with the existence of uncertainty, and choose the most desirable alternative. The information evaluation method can be plainly called a cost-benefit method whereby the accountant predicts the relationships among the accounting system, the decision maker's choice process, the selected action, and the resulting consequences. The central thrust is expressed by the question: In a world of uncertainty, how much are you willing to pay for one information system versus another? What system are you willing to buy?

## ACCOUNTING INFORMATION AS AN ECONOMIC GOOD

Information is a commodity. Measurement consumes resources. Kenneth Arrow has commented: "... in organizational control, as in automobiles, cuisine, and every other commodity, the benefits of improved quality [of information] must always be compared with their costs."[4]

Accounting data are economic goods (just like cuisine and smog control devices) obtainable at various costs. The manager, therefore, buys accounting data as well as other data. Ideally, we should evaluate various types of information in terms of whether the action choices will be affected by the information in question. For example, if the information will not affect the action choice, it is valueless. On the other hand, if the information will lead the manager to a better action choice, then its value is measurable in terms of the increase in net benefit (e.g., net profit after deducting the costs of getting the information) obtained with the information as compared to the net benefit obtained without the information. In its most simplified sense, we have described a cost-benefit approach to management accounting issues. The cost of acquiring accounting information includes compilation, processing, and education, which can be enormously expensive.

Consider how the economist approaches the question of buying commodities like butter or internal accounting information. Do we see economics textbooks that tell us how much or what quality of butter the consumer needs? No. The economist tells us about the conditions of optimality (e.g., for the consumer to be in equilibrium, the marginal utility of the last dollar spent on each commodity must be equal). In contrast, the accounting literature is more doctrinaire; it is far more willing to tell you how much or what quality butter or accounting to consume. The primary implication of the economist's approach to information is almost philosophical. It is a rejection of both the unique truth and the conditional truth philosophies in favor of the cost-benefit philosophy. The foregoing examples may be trivial, but the cost-benefit approach to information is not trivial.

To see how my views have been reshaped, I reread my thirteen-year old "perspective" article, "Choosing Accounting Practices for Reporting to Management" (NAA Bulletin, September, 1962, pp. 3-15 [see Selection 75, pp. 239-241]). That article

---

[4]Kenneth J. Arrow, "Control in Large Organizations," *Management Science*, Vol. 10, No. 3 (April, 1964), p. 401.

summarized a few existing ideas that I continue to emphasize, particularly the idea of gathering relevant data for particular purposes and the idea of motivation in harmony with organizational goals. That article also contained phrasing that I want to disown, such as: "the information needed" and the major sub-title, "relevant information—the basic need." The major weakness of the article was probably its failure to give cost-benefit analysis the prominence it merits.

Even though these cost-benefit decisions are most often made implicitly (sometimes as a rationalization of a decision *ex post*), the underlying philosophy here should not be overlooked. For example, in many places we see opinions about what data are "needed" for making assorted decisions with only passing reference (at most) to the associated "costs" and "benefits."

My distaste for thinking in terms of data "needs" is not a semantic quibble. On the contrary, it is a basic criticism of academic thought and accounting theories that are often incomplete and hence inapplicable. How can we conclude whether accounting data (or perfectly clean air) are "needed" *per se*? Accounting data are economic goods. Many alternatives exist, and choosing one over another is just one more type of decision that must somehow be made.

To illustrate this point, you may encounter arguments from time to time that one way is better than a second way of computing the cost of a product. The first way is "needed" because it provides a "more accurate" or a "truer" approximation of "economic reality." The cost-benefit approach to such an issue does not use "need" or "truth" or "accuracy" as the fundamental method of resolving the dispute. Instead, its method is to ask whether the decisions affected by these costs will differ if the first way is used rather than the second way. The direct costing-absorption costing controversy is an example. More specifically, my preferred way for settling arguments about direct costing versus absorption costing for internal purposes is to predict how each method or system will affect volume, mix, pricing, investment and other decisions in a particular organization. If the decisions will be unaffected, then the less costly alternative is preferable. If the decisions will be affected differently, then the preferable alternative is that which is expected to produce the most net benefit. Management accounting choices are inherently contextual; sweeping generalizations across contexts are alien to the cost-benefit philosophy. For instance, a cost-benefit adherent would refrain from making a generalization such as "direct costing is better than absorption costing."

The cost-benefit approach is especially attractive to me because it provides a starting point for tackling virtually all accounting issues. Furthermore, it can be subsumed under a rich theoretical structure of information economics,[5] which is the application of microeconomic theory to questions of purchasing information. Also, it has practical appeal because accountants, managers, and students find its central ideas easy to accept.

---

[5]For a description of the theory, and the works in economics from which it sprung, see Demski, op. cit., and Feltham, op. cit., and the ample references therein.

## CRITICISMS OF COST-BENEFIT APPROACH

Some critics may claim that there is nothing new here, that cost-benefit analysis has been important in accountants' thinking for years.[6] Perhaps, but too often it has been implicit and too often it has been an "implementation" or "practical" aspect or criterion—not the dominant, central theoretical thrust.

Cost-benefit analysis is anchored to a rationalistic view of organizations, a view that has been assailed by many as being far too simplified and abstract.[7] The information economist will defend the rationalistic view as follows:

> There is no intention of denying that non-rational factors, sociological and psychological, are of utmost importance in the study and development of organizations. But a rational point of view is also needed, and indeed much of the value of studies in group dynamics will only be properly realized in the context of rational design of organizations.[8]

This audience consists of practitioners and academicians. Practitioners may respond to my focus on cost-benefit analysis by gloating, "That's what I've been using throughout my career. It's about time you professors recognize that we've been operating as sub rosa information economists." Nevertheless, until recently the practitioners' official literature has rarely cited cost-benefit analysis as a major means of resolving issues.[9]

Academicians may have a ho-hum response to my focus on cost-benefit analysis. After all, the information economics model and its cost-benefit simplifications are too hopelessly broad, normative, theoretical, and nondescriptive to be useful template to lay over the discipline of management accounting.

A similar criticism was leveled against the notion or concept of relevance, when it was advanced as a starting point for developing the decision model approach to man-

---

[6] For example, Robert T. Sprouse, reporter, *The Measurement of Property, Plant and Equipment in Financial Statements*, Accounting Round Table, April 29-30, 1963 (Boston: Harvard Business School, 1964), p. 22, cited feasibility along with usefulness and objectivity as the three major criteria for the general acceptance of an accounting principle or practice: "In order to merit serious consideration, valuation bases must be capable of practicable and economic implementation . . . Similarly, proposals are unacceptable that are possible of attainment but only at a cost that is clearly disproportionate to any additional benefits relative to less costly alternatives."

[7] Many alternative models have been championed. For example, Michael D. Cohen, James G. March, and Johan P. Olsen, "A Garbage Can Model of Organizational Choice," *Administrative Science Quarterly*, Vol. 17, No. 1 (March, 1972), suggest that some "organizations can be viewed for some purposes as collections of choices looking for problems, issues and feelings looking for decision situations in which they might be aired, solutions looking for issues to which they might be an answer, and decision makers looking for workers."

[8] Arrow, op. cit., p. 399.

[9] During the 1970s the Securities and Exchange Commission and the Financial Accounting Standards Board have explicitly recognized the importance of cost-benefit analysis as one consideration in their decisions. Still, the Trueblood Study Group, *Objectives of Financial Statements* (New York: American Institute of Certified Public Accountants, 1973), gave scant attention to the cost-benefit approach.

agement accounting during the 1950s. A committee of the American Accounting Association observed:

> There is a temptation to dispense with the whole question concerning concepts underlying internal reports by saying that the only concept of general applicability in this area is the concept of relevance. That is, what is good or bad accounting is decided fundamentally by the usefulness of the result in meeting specific management problems. While this is true of internal reporting, such a general statement hardly justifies stature as an underlying concept. It does not provide guidance to accountants regarding methods to follow nor does it assist users in the interpretation of internal reports. When used with this meaning, the term relevance is more a statement of the problem rather than a solution to it.[10]

Whether you call it a concept, a principle, an insight, or a hackneyed expression, the idea of relevance had immense impact on our literature and our courses of the 1960s and 1970s. Relevance had been lurking in the wings for years,[11] but until it was stressed by a few individuals, it had little effect on curricula or on settling accounting controversies.

Similarly, cost-benefit analysis has been in the woodwork for years.[12] If it offends you to call it a theory, then call it a state of mind. Along with the idea of relevance, it offers a focus for the 1970s that may help explain and improve management accounting.

## EXAMPLE OF APPLYING COST-BENEFIT ANALYSIS

Consider the application of cost-benefit analysis by a control systems designer, who may be an accountant, a manager, or both. A troublesome problem in both internal and external accounting has been asset valuation for performance measurement. Among the alternatives are historical costs, historical costs restated for a general price index, and some version of current value. The accounting literature is replete with exhortations about the infirmities of historical costs and the virtues of one or more of the alternatives.

Ten years ago my criterion for choosing was: which measurement was most directly relevant to decisions? Obviously, I thought, the manager "needs" something beyond historical costs. A web of impeccable logic can be spun that will demonstrate the conceptual superiority (usually under conditions of certainty) of some version of current or future values for decisions.

Although the relevance criterion is appealing, it is not sufficient. Most important, we should recognize that the basic job of accounting systems is to supply information.

---

[10]Report of the 1961 Managerial Accounting Committee, *The Accounting Review*, Vol. XXXVII, No. 3 (July, 1962), p. 536.

[11]J. M. Clark, *Economics of Overhead Costs* (Chicago: University of Chicago Press, 1923), Chapter 9.

[12]An *early* citation would be appropriate, but my limited search of the literature has produced none.

Furthermore, the system is only one source of information. The issue of comparative advantage must be faced. The acceptance or rejection of historical cost, when compared to some version of current value, would depend on the costs of each alternative set of information in light of the perceived benefits that might arise from better economic decisions, as well as on what competing sources of information are available.

Given the defects of historical cost, why do organizations continue to use it for evaluating performance of the company as a whole and its subunits? There are several reasons. Some seem unjustifiable, while others make sense. Ignorance has been cited as a likely reason. But I have not encountered a convincing argument as to why this supposed ignorance persists. The routine use of some alternative value entails an extra cost of compiling data. The manager (and some investors) want *routine* data essentially as clues for deciding whether and how to seek (buy) more information. The constraints of generally accepted accounting principles are not as dominant for internal purposes. Still, most managers have regarded historical costs as good enough for such purposes.[13] Major internal decisions to invest or disinvest are not routine decisions. From the viewpoint of the systems designer, it may be more economical to get replacement and net realizable values by conducting special studies as desired rather than by routine recording.

The implications from practice are clear. The use of "defective" data such as historical costs may often make both conceptual and practical sense—even though advocates of the user decision model approach find the idea difficult to swallow. Although current values may indeed be more relevant and even more objective, they still may not be preferable to historical costs if the latter are less costly to compile and will lead to the same decisions.

The advocates of a multiple value or fair value system bear the burden of demonstrating its superiority over historical cost. To my knowledge, the advocates have had few successes in convincing management of its advantages for the internal routine evaluation of performance. This would be the first step in showing that a current value framework can be implemented successfully.

## TWO SETS OF ACCOUNTING PRINCIPLES

An example from the area of external reporting also may clarify or reinforce my major point. For years, many CPAs have complained that several Accounting Principles Board requirements are often too costly for smaller clients. For instance, the computations of earnings per share statistics and the preparation of a statement of changes in financial position, may be onerous burdens with negative benefit.[14] Also

---

[13]John J. Mauriel and Robert N. Anthony, "Misevaluation of Investment Center Performance," *Harvard Business Review*, Vol. 44, No. 2, summarize the practices of 2,658 companies. Only three percent of the companies used some measure that departs from historical cost, such as insurance value or appraisal value.

[14]On March 31, 1975, the AICPA's Accounting Standards Division issued a neutral discussion paper on the application of generally accepted accounting principles to smaller and/or closely-held businesses.

imagine the possible new burden of adjusting the financial statements for the changes in the general price level.

The replies to these complaints have consistently stated that society should not have a separate set of accounting principles for large organizations and a different set for small organizations. I tended to agree with that position, primarily because I had a knee-jerk reaction as a professor who preferred a universal set for all.

Now I think of this issue in terms of cost-benefit analysis. That is, as organization by organization is examined, there may be convincing reasons in terms of cost-benefit analysis against using the same financial accounting standards for many small organizations.

Does this mean that we would have chaos? No, but it might mean giving a more careful consideration to these complaints of the smaller organizations. Of course, boards like the APB or FASB may still reach the same conclusions in favor of a single set of financial accounting standards. But I would feel more comfortable if those conclusions were framed in terms of the net benefits to society compared with the net cost to individual organizations. That is, the net benefit to society as a whole must be perceived as exceeding the net costs suffered by many organizations from compiling useless data. In a sense then, the smaller organizations are being taxed in the interests of more uniform accounting.

## BEHAVIORAL PROBLEMS AND MANAGEMENT ACCOUNTING

Cost-benefit analysis is most highly developed in relatively abstract, single-person decision situations. Although cost-benefit analysis provides a pervasive general state of mind for judging accounting systems, there still is no tightly-knit framework that gives operational guidance to systems design in the multi-person situations found in complex organizations. Information economics, behavioral science, and welfare economics are applicable to a multi-person setting, but all are better at identifying problems than at supplying operational methods of analysis or solutions. In short, the challenge to cost-benefit analysis is to make it more operational in multi-person settings.

Of course, many unsolved problems exist in management accounting, particularly in complex situations. When I teach my classes, I feel obliged to stress some dimensions of the multi-person problems even though I have no pat answers or even a systematic method for solving the problems. Therefore, my teaching has a strong behavioral focus.

Unfortunately, many management accounting teachers skim or dodge "the behavioral stuff" entirely because it is too messy and too intractable for discussing in a classroom. But I am convinced that students should get a steady exposure to the behavioral implications of the choices of accounting data and systems. A major objective of a management accounting course should be to give students an overview of the important *problems* in the area, even though universal methods of solution are undiscovered or will never be discovered. A comparative advantage of education is to create an awareness of widespread problems that the students are likely to encounter. Unless students are placed on the alert, they will be ill-equipped and will be less likely to see the major behavioral problems that should be identified before choosing a particular accounting system.

In my courses, I have tended to stress the problems of obtaining goal congruence and incentive, which can be wrapped together in one word, *motivation*. Psychologists have defined motivation as the perception of some want or goal together with the resulting drive toward achieving the want. Many authors in the 1950s and 1960s stressed the link between these seemingly foreign ideas of motivation and the design of management accounting systems.[15]

The difference between goal congruence and incentive deserves elaboration. Goal congruence is having two or more persons *aiming* toward the same objective, while incentive is a *striving* toward the given objective, whatever it may be. For example, if you want a subordinate to move through a doorway, you want a measure or a system that will aim him or her accordingly. But you probably do not want the subordinate to take baby steps toward the doorway. You want him or her to *move*—the quicker, the better. So goal congruence and incentive are intertwined, yet they are separable characteristics that warrant attention when appraising or designing a control system.

The distinction between goal congruence and incentive might be clarified by an additional example. Division managers may accept top management goals as their personal goals regarding sales, costs, quality control, research, or other items. So goal congruence may exist. But the incentive problem still remains. A major means of providing incentive is the evaluation of performance. Clearly, the manager is influenced by how his or her performance is appraised. The choices of the content, format, timing, and circulation of performance reports are heavily affected by their probable influence on incentives. For instance, top managers may want to predict the incentive effects of alternative accounting measures of performance (e.g., profit centers, cost centers, cost allocations, human resource accounting, replacement costs).[16]

A summary of my general approach to teaching complex cases in management accounting follows. The task of the formal control system is to help provide goal congruence and incentive through the use of technical tools (e.g., budgets, standards, formal measures of performance) that provide information and feedback. The systems designer usually considers various technical proposals (usually at the margin) in a cost-

---

[15]An early effort was R. N. Anthony, "Cost Concepts for Control," *Accounting Review* (April, 1957), p. 234. Anthony has suggested that a control technique can be judged in two ways: by the *direction* and by the *strength* of its motivation. See his *Management Accounting* (rev. ed.; Homewood, Ill.: Richard D. Irwin, Inc., 1960), p. 317. As far as I can determine, Anthony was the first to introduce the now-popular term, goal congruence, to the accounting literature. See p. 362 of the third edition of his *Management Accounting*, 1964.

[16]There is little theory or research available regarding the relationships between management incentives and the evaluation of performance. Arrow, op. cit., p. 400, observes: "There are (at least) two problems in devising incentive systems: (1) an effective incentive system creates new demands for information; the reward is a function of performance, so top management must have a way of measuring performance. (2) Even if the [performance] index is appropriate, the relationship between the reward and the index remains to be determined." Also see E. E. Lawler, *Pay and Organizational Effectiveness* (New York: McGraw-Hill, Inc., 1971). For an overview of accounting and behavior, see Anthony Hopwood, *Accounting and Human Behavior* (London: Haymarket Publishing Limited, distributed by Prentice-Hall International, 1974).

benefit sense. Will the new data or configurations promote a net benefit of more congruence and incentive?

Keep in mind that the approach applies a cost-benefit framework—as a fundamental approach, not as an after-thought. Accounting data and control systems are economic goods. The application occurs in a multi-person setting in a world of uncertainty, so obviously the choices are not easy to justify in comfortable quantitative terms. Generalizations are especially perilous, so we should concentrate on the identification of the key problems and on the *method* for making the hard choices, not on prescriptions that represent widespread solutions. Because definitive answers seem hard to isolate, this approach will never satisfy absolutists or teachers and students who avoid the challenge of pinpointing central problems in untidy situations.

## EXPLAINING THE EVOLUTION OF SYSTEMS

The application of cost-benefit analysis and the identification of problems of goal congruence and incentives provide an explanation for the evolution of management accounting systems in many organizations. The sequence frequently is:

1. Physical observation
2. Historical records
3. Static budgets
4. Flexible budgets and standards
5. Profit centers and investment centers

As the sequence occurs, the system tends to become more elaborate and costly because the earlier facets of the system are often retained.

A scenario may occur as follows. A proprietor (or two partners like Hewlett and Packard) may begin a modest enterprise in a garage. The manager's physical observations may provide the sole planning and control system for a day or two. But the simple tracking of cash will require a modicum of historical records. Furthermore, no formal cost-benefit analysis is necessary to convince the manager that sufficient documentation be kept to satisfy the Internal Revenue Service; the benefits are keeping the business as a going concern and staying out of jail.

Historical records may be compared from year to year as a basis for evaluating performance and planning. But many managers find that investing in a formal budgeting system is a cost-effective way to compel planning, promote goal congruence, and improve incentive. Managers often begin budgeting with relatively simple static budgets and, as the net benefits seem apparent, gradually develop flexible budgets and standards.

The incentive criterion is a major justification for taking the next step into some kind of profit center or investment center. Cost centers with flexible budgets and standards have sometimes been found wanting. For instance, some cost center managers have focused on meeting a budget and on keeping costs under control—and nothing more. When the cost centers are transformed into profit centers, managers may continue to care about costs, but they may give new attention to production schedules, and important marketing factors. Top managers have sometimes found that pep talks and cajoling do not get subordinates to accept top management goals. But giving profit responsibility works better because it crystallizes goals and provides better incentives. That is, goal congruence may exist in a vague, half-hearted fashion but profit centers provide the formal system that is so often the most persuasive means of communicating top management's goals and boosting incentives.

Professors and managers can spend hours delineating the weaknesses of profit centers and transfer pricing schemes, especially when the managers have little local autonomy. Nevertheless, despite their manifold defects, profit centers may often be the most cost effective way to obtain the desired goal congruence and incentives.[17]

In addition to the questions of using profit centers or cost centers, other accounting issues may be assessed by using the approach advocated here. For example, more detailed or elaborate overhead rates usually are developed in a cost-benefit framework. The key question is not which is the most accurate cost allocation. Rather, it is how much accuracy is justified by potential uses.

Another much-publicized development is human resources accounting. Much of the literature focuses on whether human resources can qualify in an accounting framework as assets and on how they should be valued. To me, the attractions of human resource accounting must focus on whether this more costly system will have the desired impact on decisions.[18] I hope that such evaluations of these human resource experiments are forthcoming soon.

Above all, the cost-benefit theme dominates the evolution of systems. When somebody's money is at stake, accounting systems get renewed attention. For example, the current boom in the installation of cost accounting systems in the health services industry is primarily explained by the growth of government-sponsored health care programs. To get reimbursed by government agencies, the health care institutions often have to use cost accounting to justify their claims. The net benefit of cost accounting has rapidly become obvious throughout an entire industry.

My illustrations here have pointed to cost-benefit analysis as being a major explanation of the evolution of management accounting systems. Practitioners and managers have been operating as information economists. A survival of the fittest mechanism may be at work. The "markets" for management accounting information, models, and specialists may be influenced by an invisible hand. In contrast, the existence and survival of financial accounting is often legislated via a quasi-political system.

## SUMMARY AND CONCLUSION

The best accounting measure or system is that which produces the most benefit after deducting the costs of obtaining the data. We should incessantly ask the question:

---

[17]Incidentally, profit centers and decentralization are sometimes erroneously used as if they were synonymous terms. Decentralization is the relative freedom to make decisions. Although it seems strange at first glance, profit centers can be coupled with a highly centralized organization, and cost centers can be coupled with a highly decentralized organization. So the labels of *profit center* and *cost center* can be deceptive as indicators of the degree of decentralization.

[18]An example of this focus is Nabil Elias, "The Effects of Human Asset Statements on the Investment Decision: An Experiment," *Empirical Research in Accounting: Selected Studies*, 1972, pp. 215–240.

How much are you willing to pay for one accounting method or system versus another?

These implicit cost-benefit tradeoffs can be uncovered throughout the evolution of accounting. However, until recently we have given insufficient attention to the central importance of explicitly recognizing the choice among accounting alternatives as an economic decision made under conditions of uncertainty.

Some predictions are usually a part of this kind of paper, so I offer some at absolutely no incremental cost to you. Keep in mind that they are worth their cost.

Management accounting evolved from an absolute truth (numerical) emphasis to a conditional truth (contextual) emphasis. Currently, much attention is being given to the question of whether a cost-benefit (analytical) emphasis will be productive. The next step will probably be a stronger multi-person (behavioral) emphasis.[19]

The cost-benefit approach does not take us very far when we try to apply it in the multi-person setting of large organizations. The application of welfare economics and behavioral science holds some promise. However, the vast complexity of the subject matter defies any convincing synthesis. Still, I think progress is evident. Despite the absence of a tightly-knit operational framework, management accounting, which is still in its infancy, has become an increasingly strong part of accounting curricula and accounting research.

Management accounting courses and textbooks will probably encompass more of the approach of information evaluation and cost-benefit analysis as a general philosophy or point of view. If this occurs, it will be another illustration of how research—which is frequently highly abstract—eventually affects curricula.

The challenge facing the cost-benefit researchers is how to extend their method of analysis from single-person decision situations to multi-person situations. You can make your own predictions of their likelihood of success.

Of course, as the information economists and their advocates in accounting ease into the multi-person scene, they inevitably must contend, by definition, with complicated behavioral ramifications. Similarly, as management accounting curricula and research push beyond the rudiments of highly simplified situations, they face intricate behavioral problems. So our improvements in management accounting will primarily depend on how we embed behavioral accounting in our thinking.

I have taken no polls, and I have compiled only scattered, cocktail party evidence. Nevertheless, my hypothesis is that the teachers of management accounting are divided into two polar camps regarding the importance of behavioral considerations, a small camp that gives hearty attention to them and a large camp that almost ignores them. Furthermore, my weaker hypothesis is that the practitioners have an even smaller camp that gives attention to behavioral considerations. If these hypotheses are valid, our next step is probably to persuade teachers to give some serious attention to behavioral implications in their management accounting courses.

---

[19]Accounting researchers are conducting research on human information processing that often can be linked with cost-benefit analysis. Some of this work has been influenced by M. J. Driver and S. Streufort, "Integrative Complexity: An Approach to Individuals and Groups as Information-Processing Systems," *Administrative Science Quarterly*, Vol. 14, No. 2 (June, 1969), pp. 272–285.

Although management accounting has thrived during the past twenty years continued progress will depend on whether researchers and teachers can improve our methods for analyzing multi-person situations. As a minimum, I hope that we can identify the major problems more clearly. To do so, the behavioral implications (such as effects on goal congruence and incentives) of our choices of accounting systems deserve front and center attention. Above all, management accountants should communicate the central role of the behavioral problems in management accounting to students, managers, and other interested persons—at least to the extent that individuals become highly sensitive to the idea that accounting may be as closely related to the behavioral sciences as to economics and the decision sciences.

## QUESTIONS

1. What is the historical communications approach?
2. What is the difference between cost accounting and management accounting?
3. Contrast the "costly truth" approach with the "true cost" approach.
4. According to Ijiri, what distinguishes accounting from other informations systemps? Explain.
5. What are the merits and the criticisms of the cost-benefit approach?
6. Why do organizations continue to use historical cost for evaluation performance?
7. What does a multiperson emphasis mean?
8. Define the following terms: transfer pricing, goal congruence, flexible budget, cost center, profit center, and "net cost to an individual organization."

## SELECTED BIBLIOGRAPHY

"Accounting Management for Small Industrial Firms," *The Accountant's Magazine,* September 1973, pp. 490-491.

Goodlad, S.B., "The Importance of Management Accounting," *The Australian Accountant,* April 1975, pp. 170-172.

# 81
# IF YOU WANT A SURE THING*
Telly  Savalas

If you want a sure thing
Become an accountant

*Quoted from television program, "Kojak."

# 82

## ACCOUNTING IN ITS ULTIMATE APPLICATION*
Richard  Cornuelle

Business could not work without accounting. Double-entry bookkeeping, conceived centuries ago by a forgotten Catholic priest, probably had much more to do with the blossoming of business than any other single innovation. . . . When accounting is carried to its ultimate application, when every employee is a hypothetical profit center, then everyone can function exactly as the boss himself functions.

# 83

## A CONTROLLER IN A TURNAROUND†
Craig  E.  Wood

Maysteel Corporation, a $20,000,000 manufacturer of sheet metal fabrications and hose reels, located in Mayville, Wisconsin, experienced a decline in sales and profit from above average earnings in 1966, to a loss in 1971. At the end of 1971 the President, Directors of Marketing and Manufacturing all reached retirement age. Richard Gillis, who after several recent successes had a reputation as a Turnaround Manager, was brought in as President.

During the last three years Maysteel has been "turned around." In 1974 sales doubled their 1971 level and profits were above the industry average. This turnaround was not a short-term paper effort but a bona fide change in the basic elements which make a company profitable over the long term.

### WHERE DOES A CORPORATE CONTROLLER FIT IN A TURNAROUND?

What is required from, and what can be contributed by, a controller in a turnaround effort in a $20,000,000 manufacturing firm?

Mr. Gillis brought me to Maysteel early in 1972 as Controller to take over the financial function and help turn the company around. Over the past three years I've tried to accomplish the following six objectives:

*Excerpt from Richard Cornuelle, *De-managing America,* New York, Random House, 1975, p. 100. Reprinted by permission of the publisher.

†From *Wisconsin CPA,* June 1975, cover and pp. 2 and 9. Reprinted by permission of the publisher.

1. Cut expenses.

2. Identify values being supplied to the customer and monitor cost estimating and pricing.

3. Establish and monitor a capital expenditure program.

4. Develop budgets and continually forecast financial position out 12 months.

5. Develop and monitor a computer program.

6. Monitor the entire company's operations and recommend changes.

First objective was to cut expenses. The initial problem in cost reduction is cost identification—you can't reduce a cost until you identify it, identify who actually controls it and go through a cause and effect analysis to see what would happen if you stopped it entirely or reduced it. After a few months the following changes were made: (1) initiated a new, definitive written chart of accounts; (2) established 60 machine centers, 15 manufacturing departments and 10 office departments; (3) assigned a supervisor to each department and established cost responsibility—defined exactly what costs they were responsible for; and (4) developed a more informative set of financial statements from the department level to the consolidated level.

We have established a full time position—*cost reduction coordinator*—who reports to the President and is responsible for (1) making sure cost reduction goals are set, (2) keeping track of all projects and developing potential projects and (3) making sure responsibilities are assigned, meetings held and decisions made at higher levels, if a stalemate is met. The key point is that this position must be full time!! If not full time his duties get pushed aside! Even though we are only 600 people we feel there is a huge payoff during the next 2-3 years for such a position. We have saved many thousands of dollars on many projects, but many more potential, lucrative ideas went unexplored or uncompleted because of this lack of full time attention.

The second objective, identifying value supplied to the customer and monitoring cost estimating and pricing, has been the most rewarding of the objectives! The existing cost system was manual; used one overall, full absorbed factory burden rate; had a 10% material shrink each year; and was job cost-oriented with closeouts being costed, *behind the fact*, from 2-6 months after shipment. There were many errors and both the older employees and the new ones had little confidence in the system. This lack of confidence and lack of discipline led to a factoring up or down by almost everyone, which also decreased the confidence in, and effectiveness of, the system. This practice had, unfortunately gone on for 15 years, and had become a way of life. The distrust of the product costs was from top to bottom. This distrust resulted in poor decisions and sometimes even worse than that—*no decisions*. I discovered early that the people who needed product cost data were going to too low a level to get it—to people who could not judge what data were needed or the useability of the information. I instructed my people to question the intended use before supplying information and refer the requestor to me if there was any doubt.

The complaint that we did not have good costs is not unique. Usually this kind of complaint comes from someone who is not familiar with what costs mean and how to use them. Much of the distrust of product costs can be done away with by education and making the requestors channel their requests to a qualified person who can evaluate and supply their needs. Many improvements were needed in Maysteel's product cost system, but, perhaps there was as much work to be done on the users!

Two methods commonly followed for establishing selling prices are "cost plus a profit" and "what the market will bear." What method do you follow to establish cost estimates for pricing when your facilities are 15 years behind the times and your methods and labor efficiency are lower than your competitors? Following a cost estimating/pricing system based upon "present actual cost" plus a profit would have been disastrous. In order to arrive at competitive selling prices on major jobs we drew upon Manufacturing Engineering's extremely good industry knowledge to determine what our costs should be. I would review the estimated full absorbed actual product costs and develop an out-of-pocket cost. Then Manufacturing Engineering would factor the estimated actual full absorbed cost to a competitive, industry-wide full absorbed cost, by replacing our non-competitive operational costs with those which could be expected using modern, efficient equipment and methods.

We used the information developed in this way in directing our capital expenditure program. We would not quote a job on this basis if we did not intend to bring in the needed, modern equipment in the next one to two years and would not take it even then, if the selling price would not at least cover out-of-pocket costs. The smaller jobs quoted using only the current actual, inefficient costs, resulted in us finding our position in the market place on a contribution basis. We also discovered that for the last few years, Maysteel had become lax in increasing prices. A few large volume products were discovered which were being sold at out-of-pocket costs when their fair value to the customer was 25-30% above this!

Closely related to identifying value being supplied the customer is monitoring the cost estimating and pricing functions. Changes made and discipline installed in this area probably resulted in 50% of our profits in 1973 and 1974! I cannot over-emphasize how important it is for a Controller to get involved in these formulas and procedures and make sure they are mathematically correct, actually fit the company's operations and are being followed to the letter!

The third objective was to develop a Capital Expenditure Program. For about 10 years or more prior to 1972 only the minimum capital expenditures for equipment had been made. Although it normally takes from 6 months to a year to develop, install and effectively utilize a capital expenditure program even in a small company the size of Maysteel—we needed one immediately. Development, education and follow-up had to be on a "total immersion" basis and there was little time for soft-selling the program to its users. We use a simple "payback" and "rate of return" for small projects and a refined "discounted cash flow" method on large projects.

The fourth objective was to develop budgets and continually forecast the P&L and Balance Sheet out one year. At the start of 1973 I worked up a 1973 budget with each departmental supervisor for the 13 periods in 1973. At the end of each period the departmental supervisors would explain any account with a plus or minus year-to-date variance of over $500.

In 1973 and 1974 we prepared a total of 6 budgets. These budgets were developed using a blend of what we would like to happen and what we thought would happen. If there isn't "task" in a budget the interest declines—especially in the early stages of developing budgets and more importantly in a turnaround. I would also continuously forecast a P&L and Balance Sheet out 12 months to what results I actually expected. These periodic, realistic forecasts were needed to properly assess and guide the turnaround. We thus had developed a system around the needs of a turnaround which exactly fit the needs of the extreme fluctuation in costs and shipments experienced in late 1973 and 1974. Before these most unusual conditions hit us we were able to react quickly and took full advantage of the opportunities.

The fifth objective was to bring in a computer and improve our information systems. I developed a program to:

1. Bring a consulting firm to help us develop a data base.
2. Bring in our IBM System No. 3.
3. Buy accounts payable and receivable packages.
4. Develop in house the general ledger and budget programs.

We went thru the popular program of establishing an implementation team made of representatives from each functional area, to develop a data base. I am a believer in standard packaged programs because of the time saved and the folly of thinking we are unique in our needs.

The sixth objective was to monitor the entire company's operations and recommend changes. President Gillis expects the Controller not only to "keep score" but also to "recommend plays" to both the players and the coach. He expects me to determine what we can and cannot afford.

There are still problems to be solved at Maysteel but a lasting turnaround has been achieved. The requirements for a successful turnaround are many, but one of them is at least 2 or 3 years of the same management. Most companies can be quickly turned around on paper or by making excessive, temporary cuts in heads and quality, but a lasting turnaround takes continuity!

A turnaround also requires that you "control your universe" and make all the decisions. You can't have a corporate office second-guessing you or forcing you to play games on paper to improve short term profits. You also need ample resources and most important, optimism, dedication and a "do it today" philosophy.

## QUESTIONS

1. What is a cost reduction coordinator?
2. Explain how the controller at Maysteel was able to "identify values being supplied to the customer" and to monitor cost estimating and pricing.
3. Assess Mr. Wood's function at the Maysteel Corporation in view of the types of responsibilities that an accountant has (according to Professor Horngren in Selection 75).

# 84
# THE DOOMSDAY MAN*
Bill Paul

He is only the assistant vice president, budget planning, but his work commands the attention of Congress, the Ford administration and such giant corporations as General Motors and U.S. Steel.

He is Ernest R. Varalli, the man who regularly forecasts when the Penn Central railroad next will run out of cash. He also advises the railroad's court-appointed trustees what alternatives they have to closing down the system—a move that would close the doors of GM and others within a matter of days and measurably worsen the recession within a week or two.

There has never been a job quite like Mr. Varalli's, but then there has never been a company like the Penn Central. In reorganization proceedings under federal bankruptcy laws since June 1970, the Penn Central gave up trying to reorganize as a private concern back in 1973. When a company can't be reorganized, it normally is liquidated, and the creditors are paid off. But because the country's shippers can't do without the Penn Central, the railroad is kept alive through artificial means—mostly by injections of government aid, with Mr. Varalli prescribing the needed dosage.

Mr. Varalli is the key man in the trustees' strategy to dramatize publicly the railroad's financial plight by pinpointing the exact time when the cash will run out. "Ernie is Penn Central's doomsday man," says one government attorney who is close to the situation. "His job is to predict when the sky will fall."

## THE LATEST PREDICTION

Mr. Varalli's latest prediction is that without millions of dollars more in emergency government aid, the Penn Central will be forced to stop accepting freight shipments about Feb. 14 in anticipation of a complete shutdown—probably including passenger operations—by the end of February. The Ford administration has bought that forecast—but not before sending auditors to Philadelphia on five separate occasions to check Mr. Varalli's figures. One of these inspections was a Sunday visit that Mr. Varalli was told about by phone only the night before.

Last week, the Senate, acting on the administration's recommendation, voted to give $275 million more to ailing Northeast railroads, with almost all of it earmarked for the Penn Central. Still, Mr. Varalli and the trustees can expect another rough time today when the House Commerce Committee begins two days of public hearings on the aid package. Rep. John D. Dingell, a Michigan Democrat, has publicly urged his fellow committee members not to be "stampeded" into approving the fund request, adding that the Penn Central employed "scare tactics" to get its bill through the Senate.

*From the *Wall Street Journal,* Feb. 4, 1975, pp. 1 and 19. Reprinted by permission of the publisher.

During the hearings, Mr. Varalli will sit at the witness table along with trustee Robert W. Blanchette and the trustees' attorneys. Mr. Varalli will have with him a four-inch thick black notebook that he calls the "Varalli Bible," which contains every figure imaginable on the Penn Central railroad. "Sure, there are people who don't believe me," Mr. Varalli says, "but they've never come up with figures better than mine. The moment a guy can prove I'm wrong, I'll recommend to the trustees that he have my job."

Chances are that after the hearings, the 43-year-old Mr. Varalli will retreat to his home in rural Chadds Ford, Pa., and try to forget it all with a glass of chianti and a good cigar. While "I thrive on always having my neck on the line," he also admits that "if you let this job get to your gut, you're dead."

## WHERE'S THE CASH GOING?

Mr. Varalli has been making his cash forecasts since 1969 when Jonathan O'Herron, who was then the new vice president for accounting, brought him in from a real-estate development firm to "find out where the cash was going," as Mr. Varalli puts it. This was less than a year before the railroad filed for reorganization, and Mr. Varalli remembers that he was "flabbergasted" by the figures he found.

(David C. Bevan, then the railroad's vice president and chief financial officer, and others were later accused of defrauding the Penn Central and its creditors during that period. Mr. Bevan is still fighting those charges, which were brought by both creditors and the Securities and Exchange Commission.)

Even though Mr. Varalli and his figures are well-nigh indispensable, he still earns less than $40,000 a year—one of the consequences of working for a penniless company. As a doomsayer, he also knows that it is best for him to keep as low a profile as possible. Tucked away in a corner office in the Penn Central's headquarters building, Mr. Varalli doesn't even have a nameplate on his door. "I'm a loner," he says. "Nobody knows my face."

## CROSS-EXAMINING THE FIGURES

Still, Mr. Varalli says that he finds his job rewarding. "Some guys need an office with 15 windows," he says, but his ego is massaged in another way: "I love it when my numbers stand up under cross-examination." Mr. Blanchette, the trustee, adds: "Ernie's just great. Everytime we have a crisis, he gets cranked up with the figures. And he's always right."

Mr. Varalli now reports to Norman J. Hull, vice president and controller. Mr. Hull, whose salary is $51,000 a year, handles all current financial matters of the $2.2 billion transportation company, leaving his assistant to forecast both immediate cash needs and the railroad's long-range budget—on the assumption that the railroad will survive. More often than not, however, Mr. Varalli deals directly with the trustees and Penn Central President Jervis Langdon. That way, Mr. Hull says, "nothing gets lost in the translation."

Mr. Varalli's forecasts are based on a multitude of figures—and a great deal of intuition. Especially important to Mr. Varalli are projections of fuel cost, wages, payroll taxes, maintenance expenditures, tariffs and, of course, expected traffic volumes of coal, steel, autos and other goods hauled by the railroad.

Mr. Varalli gets his figures not only from his own staff—which includes a full-time corporate economist—but also from various industry experts across the country and as many business publications as he can absorb. That part of the job is easy. The tough part comes when, say, there's a coal strike or when the economy slumps unexpectedly, as it did late last year. Then Mr. Varalli must gauge for himself how these events will affect the railroad's operations.

When automobile manufacturers announced their rebate program a few weeks ago, Mr. Varalli had to decide how much this might spur new-car shipments out of Detroit—a significant portion of the Penn Central's total freight business. Mr. Varalli says that he is "leery" about predicting any increase in shipments. "I think people will rush to buy cars being discounted, but when the discounts stop, people won't be too anxious to order more from Detroit," he says.

Mr. Varalli admits there is one number that he finds extremely difficult to predict— the amount of money taken in daily under accounts receivable. On a "normal" day, the figure should be about $8 million. But Mr. Varalli says that it takes only a small abnormality such as a snowstorm holding up the mail in one section of the country to throw that figure way off. "I have to watch it like a hawk," Mr. Varalli says. An $8 million fluctuation in the railroad's cash on hand could be the difference in meeting one week's payroll.

## THREE TECHNIQUES

The Penn Central runs into its most severe cash problems in the first and third quarters, which are traditionally low-volume periods. When the situation looks hopeless, Mr. Varalli turns to his "cash-management techniques."

Technique No. 1 is to delay paying the next installment on locomotives and other equipment either owned or leased by the railroad. This often gives the Penn Central anywhere from three to 30 days more to pay bills that usually total about $10 million to $20 million.

When delays aren't enough, technique No. 2 is to persuade Amtrak and other governmental authorities that subsidize various Penn Central passenger operations to speed up their payments to the Penn Central. Amtrak is good for $10 million to $12 million a month, while the Metropolitan Transportation Authority in New York and the Connecticut Transportation Authority together pay $11 million to $13 million every quarter.

In the past, a third technique was to have the railroad's trustees ask the judge in charge of the Penn Central's reorganization to approve either selling some assets or getting a loan from or guaranteed by, the government. (No bank would lend money to the Penn Central without a federal guarantee.) But about two years ago, federal Judge John P. Fullam decided that creditors' constitutional rights were being violated by these sales and borrowings, which diminish the value of the assets to which they laid claim. So the judge in effect put a stop to such procedures, leaving Mr. Varalli with little choice but to recommend that the trustees ask for outright government grants.

## A TYPICAL DAY

Mr. Varalli spends his days reacting to one piece of bad news after another. One day last week, for example, Mr. Varalli was greeted by word of a wildcat strike on the Burlington Northern railroad. As usual, his job was to figure out what effect that might have on the Penn Central, which connects with the Burlington. He and his staff spent nearly half a day assembling and computing figures, but before they finally pinpointed the dollars-and-cents impact, the strike abruptly was called off.

While that was going on, Mr. Varalli conferred with Mr. Langdon, the president, who told Mr. Varalli that the MTA-CTA prepayment that the Penn Central is counting on might not be received early after all, and that Mr. Varalli may have to revamp his projected February figures.

Mr. Varalli returned to his office in time to field two calls from officials of the federal Railroad Administration who were reviewing the Penn Central's anticipated cash balances on certain days in February. Once again, Mr. Varalli says, "the government was looking for something I might have missed." They didn't find it.

Getting back to the potential problem raised by Mr. Langdon, Mr. Varalli spent some time examining the projections of coal-shipment volume that the railroad's marketing specialists regularly submit, as well as expected volume of other major types of shipments. He found nothing that would make him change his forecasts. He turned next to the daily accounts-receivable number, and found for a change that it was about the $8 million that his projections said it should be.

That done, he found himself with a rare spare moment. He picked up a questionnaire that a business publication had mailed to its subscribers. The last question read: "How will your business do in 1975?"

Mr. Varalli smiled.

## QUESTIONS

1. What are the responsibilities of "the doomsday man?"

2. Review Mr. Varalli's function at Penn Central in view of the types of responsibilities that an accountant has (according to Professor Horngren in Selection 75).

3. Can an organization be profitable and still not have sufficient cash on hand to pay its current bills? Why?

## SELECTED BIBLIOGRAPHY

Northrup, Bowen, "The Liquidator," *Wall Street Journal*, Mar. 20, 1975, pp. 1 and 15.

# 85

## THE BIG SEARCH FOR CONTROLLERS*
John M. Healy

Historically, the corporate controller has been an also-ran in the scramble for salary increases, perquisites, prestige and other privileges. But now he seems to be moving ahead in the ranks. What with skyrocketing costs, complex tax laws, numerous government requirements and a host of other problems, the controller is being asked to take on an increasing number of important long-range financial jobs he never handled before.

Yet ask what the market is like for controllers and invariably the answer is negative. "It's not good," flatly states John Laguzza, vice president of F. R. Schwab & Associates.

But not for the usual reason—no jobs. There are plenty of jobs. There are, however, few controllers—at least the kind that companies are looking for. While there have always been controllers with technical skills available, few have the analytical and communication expertise now in demand. "Corporations are being very selective," Laguzza says. "They want sophisticated, informed controllers, not custodial accountants who only keep house."

The controller in demand now is a kind of modern-day Copernicus, capable of adding up the little numbers and then putting them together to get the overall picture. The new controller is expected to handle everything from financial systems and cash-flow analyses to budget planning and forecasting. Moreover, he must be able to communicate with top management, write, be extroverted and people-oriented. The kind of controller companies want has a CPA or MBA—or both—and around ten years of experience, five with a public accounting firm and five more at a company. Unfortunately, the relatively few controllers who possess all the credentials are mostly to be found at companies that are sophisticated in the financial area, which makes it difficult to lure them away.

In smaller companies, the controller is generally being assigned more duties, such as auditing, cash flow and management information systems, in order to improve the company's control function. In larger, more financially sophisticated companies, the tendency is to split off these functions, assigning them to various controllers, and appointing one high-level controller to oversee the whole operation.

Exemplary of the new breed is Martin V. Alonzo, vice president and controller at Amax, Inc. Alonzo spends about 70% of his time on long-range planning, business and profit planning, forecasting and evaluation and analysis of his company's operations. The EDP, accounting and auditing operations all report to him. Alonzo considers himself "more of a business executive." As he puts it, "The controller must rise above technicianship and be alert to the business and political environment."

The search for sophisticated controllers, of course, reflects top management's growing need for high-level problem-solvers in cutting costs and deciding how to utilize assets. Like Alonzo of Amax, many controllers are now reporting directly to

*From "Executive Ledger," **Dun's Review**, April 1975, p. 95. Reprinted by permission of the publisher.

their chief executives. And in one East Coast billion-dollar company, controllers have been made the Number Two executive in each operating group. "The role of the controller as an adviser is increasingly needed," says President Lester Korn of consulting firm Korn/Ferry International, "and this trend will continue. Companies want executives who understand and can communicate the impact of numbers on the corporation's future."

The demand for controllers is not limited to any one industry, but they are most urgently needed by manufacturing companies, according to President Frank R. Beaudine of Chicago-based consulting firm Eastman & Beaudine. "Where manufacturing costs are an important segment of overall costs, there is an emphasis on the need for controllers," says Beaudine. Aerospace, leisure-time and government-regulated companies are also looking hard for controllers.

While more responsibilities are being heaped on the controller, his paycheck—and status—are just beginning to inch upward. Controllers, for the most part are the poorest paid of all financial executives. In a medium-sized company, controllers' salaries range from $35,000 to $45,000, says George Craighead, a partner in consulting firm William H. Clark Associates. "It's a rare controller who makes in excess of $50,000," Craighead goes on. "He usually is on a par with plant managers."

But as controllers come to be regarded as future chief financial officers, as is already beginning to happen, salaries are expected to rise substantially. One billion-dollar petroleum company, for example, recently offered $100,000 for a top-notch controller. And recruiters expect salaries in general to move forward. "As the real importance of the controller's contribution is understood, his salary will increase," says Frank Beaudine. "And with the shortage, the bidding goes up. Not long ago, it would have been inconceivable to me to search for a $100,000 controller for a $500-million company."

Not only are salaries rising, but perquisites and bonuses and other "front-end" compensation are being offered. Some controllers are being enticed to switch companies by severance or termination agreements that protect them financially. What this all means, of course, is greater mobility for controllers who have the skills needed.

## QUESTIONS

1. What is a controller?
2. What are the skills that are most difficult to find in controllers?

## SELECTED BIBLIOGRAPHY

Kilvington, Kenneth W., "The Management Accountant: A British Study," *Management Accounting,* May 1975, pp. 32–38.

Trethowan, J. C., "The Making of a Manager," *The Australian Accountant,* June 1975, pp. 284–296.

# 86
## BUSINESS PLANNING AT 3M*
Donald E. Garretson

Twenty-five years or so ago, when 3M was headquartered down near East Seventh Street in St. Paul, there was a table in our cafeteria—a corner table it was—that was by common consent reserved for management. Oh, anybody could sit there—and many a new employee did on his first day—but it could not escape him, if he did, that what went on at that table was quite extraordinary, and he probably would seek out more common place company next time.

That table was where William McKnight and Archibald Bush and Herbert P. "Herb" Buetow and Clarence B. "Sandy" Sampair and many of the other grand old men of 3M sat and talked business. I used to hear stories of hunting and fishing—and even an occasional bit of ribald humor—as I walked by that luncheon table. But I also heard a lot of "shop talk" and I saw them jotting figures on their paper place mats, often picking up their rough notes as they left to continue their thought processes and discussions in their offices. A lot of "business planning" went on at that table and it must have been awfully good planning, over the soup and the hamburger and the second or third cup of coffee.

The planning that was done in those early years was very good, and it's a tough act to follow, but the point I want to make is simply this: First, it's not the form or the formality of the business planning that's important; and second, the value of business planning is not in the sophistication of the process but in its success.

The truth of the matter is that business planning hasn't really changed all that much over the years. Surely, the technological breakthrough in data processing has sped up the assembly and retrieval of facts and figures, but however useful this has been, the information we need today is pretty much the same type of information we needed 20 or 30 years ago. The "buzz" words of business have changed, but the actions they describe aren't necessarily different; although they are, admittedly, more complex in the larger, worldwide organization we have become. More people are involved, and their efforts are more consciously applied to the planning process, but the basic principles remain the same.

One reason this is true at 3M is that our company was in the vanguard of companies that learned to plan their operations. Recently, a newspaper story about Cyril P. "Cy" Pesek, a 3M executive who had a major role in bringing the new St. Paul Civic Center into being, told how 3M's President, back in 1944, enticed Cy to join 3M by telling him that we would need one billion dollars of new plants, offices, and equipment over the next 25 years to support our growth. Cy admits he didn't fully believe it, but he was sufficiently intrigued and excited about that kind of planning to leave his lucrative architectural practice and become 3M's chief engineer. And the promises made to him, the challenges offered, have long since been exceeded. Through careful long-range

*From *Management Accounting,* November 1974, pp. 33–37. Reprinted by permission of the publisher.

planning, 3M was able to budget wisely for the construction of plants and offices, and for the research and development. The new business planning and the international expansion kept it in the forefront of growth companies, especially in the years after World War II.

Although we are a multi-billion dollar corporation, we are accustomed to thinking small. We're vertically organized into over 40 divisions and departments, and many more subsidiaries, each of which is run like a small company of its own. Each has its own top man, and he has a staff of production, marketing, and technical people. None of us can visualize two billion dollars in sales—but we can visualize, and get pretty excited about, a lot of $1,000 and $2,000 orders. So, the methods of planning that evolved when our company was young have not been outgrown—even though a lot more people are now in the act. And, there is surely a lot more planning going on today, by a lot more people, than ever was true before.

## WHAT BUSINESS PLANNING IS NOT

It would be customary at this point to offer a definition of business planning. But any single definition would have to be so broad that it would be practically valueless. Maybe it's easier, for our purposes at least, to start by telling you some of the things that I think business planning is not.

First of all, it's not forecasting. It's not merely a predictive exercise—it is, instead, action oriented. It's not a guess as to what will happen, but a decision about what we want to happen, and especially how we will go about making it happen.

Additionally, business planning is not just fiscal budgeting. Budgeting, like forecasting, is oriented to the future, but it does get into control. It injects a bit of action or organizational direction—it adds numerical units. Nevertheless, it is not the key product of the planning process, for again it omits the human element, the organizational assignment, and commitments to do the job.

Also, business planning is not a specialized, isolated function. There may be a few individuals, or even departments, bearing titles that include the word "planning" but they don't—indeed they cannot—do the job of business planning for an entire organization. They are at most the catalysts that start or enhance the planning activity. The active ingredients are all of the operating and staff people in the organization.

Finally, planning is not like one of 3M's Travel-aid road maps you've seen in filling stations across the land. Those maps tell you not only what road you'll travel, but what you'll see and where you can eat, sleep, or sight-see on the journey. Those maps are the reports of someone who has traveled that way before, and he tells you what you'll find and how your trip can be made easier and more enjoyable.

## WHAT BUSINESS PLANNING IS

Planning is more like the crude maps of the early western settlers of this country. They were full of unknowns, subject to constant revision, but they still showed the goals or objectives as best they could be visualized in the light of the knowledge and abilities then existing.

I'm not sure whether that is a good analogy or not, but let me focus on two words I just used—goals and objectives. These words separate planning from forecasting and budgeting. They are the start of the planning process, whether done unconsciously at a luncheon table or consciously in a formal management conference.

## WHAT ARE BUSINESS GOALS?

In many remarks to company groups, I've heard a single word—"growth"—given as the 3M goal. And I've sometimes refined that in my presentations to company groups as "profitable growth"—for growth without profit is obviously pointless. But even that statement is inadequate, for it is silent as to some relevant questions: "How fast a growth?" "At what cost are 'growth' or 'profit' desirable?" With what standards of concern for public interest or quality or safety of products will we pursue this growth?" And so on. The shorthand phrase of "profitable growth" is quite inadequate for motivating people or stimulating organizational pride. But it has to be refined and defined if it is to constitute the foundation for a business plan.

This process of refining and defining corporate objectives is the basis for future planning—but it starts with a long hard look at the past and present. It starts with a critical evaluation, or inventory, of resources, and leads then to the setting of goals which are achievable in the light of those resources. Finally, it involves setting a timetable for achieving those goals—with full consideration of the missing resources which must be acquired or developed in the interim.

Under resources, I include such things as the competence of the management team and of the lower levels of supervisions and even of general employees. Usually, this means the existing "team" but it may involve, in certain circumstances, new management which has become involved or can be acquired.

By resources, I also mean the productive capacity of the plants and the strength of the marketing or distribution system. We could go on and on about the inventory of internal resources, both financial and non-financial, which must enter into the setting of goals. But there are also external factors.

External factors include what your shareholders expect. This is revealed in part by objective measures. Your price-earnings ratio, for example, reveals in part the future expectation of investors. It is also measured, more subjectively, by security analysts as they describe or categorize your company in their reports. For example, a "blue-chip" is different from a "growth" stock and a "utility" is different from a "high technology manufacturer." A business plan which involves a dramatic change from one to another of these external expectations must, at the very least, consider the serious consequences of such a change.

External factors also include your customers' views, and those of the community, about your products and your business practices: quality, price, integrity, reliability, viability, etc.

Finally, external factors include the changing business climate. I'm speaking not only about the economy but about the constant changes in laws and regulations and public attitudes. These are many and varied, and they differ in each of the 37 countries in which 3M has its plants and offices. These external factors must affect the corporate goals. But remember this: they often provide business opportunities, not roadblocks, for achieving corporate objectives.

This appraisal of the factors that influence the setting of business goals suggests that planning is solely a top management activity. That isn't the case. Planning involves inputs from many sources, including the more junior levels of the organization.

## LONG-RANGE PLANNING AT 3M

I'm sure you can understand that I cannot reveal our company's specific goals and objectives, or its specific plans. However, I will say this much about the company's overall objectives: they are probably not as formal and precisely articulated as you might expect. They begin with management. Our management has, in general, had long service with the company. We train people on the job and promote from within. Over the years, the management team has developed a unified set of standards which, when coupled with its dedication to "profitable growth," constitutes company goals.

You can tell from the financial statements in our Annual Report what kind of fiscal goals we set for ourselves in terms of return on sales, return on stockholders' investment and growth rate. Other standards are accepted more as tradition than as goals. Examples would be our interest in uniquely useful products for which the customer will pay a premium price, and products where our technology or patent position or research will avoid a flood of "me too" competition.

These standards or objectives are so ingrained that they are re-communicated mainly in terms of change. For example, President Ray Herzog has recently set a new goal for how fast the company should grow. He set this new goal with full regard for the impact this growth will have on both our human and fiscal resources. This has been communicated to the operating and staff groups in management conferences and group review meetings. But it is understood by all, that our other standards are unchanged.

In addition to the corporate standards just described, management has provided general operating targets for each of our operating divisions, relative to the industries each is in. These individual targets may be above or below the overall corporate goal for growth and profitability, but they are gauged to maximize each division's contribution to the corporate goals.

The profit target for each division is stated in terms of a percentage of sales and sometimes also as a percentage of earnings on the division's invested capital. It is both long-range and long-standing. It is not changed simply because it is not met or, alternatively, because it is exceeded for several years. However, it may be adjusted as marketing conditions change, as new products are introduced, or as major research efforts hit pay dirt. It takes a major and permanent change in the division's environment to warrant a target change. So when a division general manager or the managing director of any 3M company, anywhere in the world, sits down with his staff to develop a revised business plan for his division or company, he has the target always before him. How he hits it is more or less up to him. But there can be no doubt what is expected of him in the overall growth of his unit and its percentage of profits to sales.

## THE BUSINESS PLAN

The business plan for each division takes the form, each fall, of a 10 to 12 page document. This report redefines the goals of the division, evaluates its strengths and weaknesses in the current year, provides a general statement of objectives for the coming year (expressed in terms both of numeric and non-numeric goals) with a description of how these objectives are expected to be met, and concludes with a detailed five-year business forecast.

The document also contains a three-year backward look at performance, which can be, and is, easily compared with the projections made in those years. This is the credibility measure.

The detail presented in the business plan will vary, but it will certainly contain sections on such things as marketing, production, and technical plans.

Marketing strategy might include such details as: planned entry into new markets, timetables for product introductions, upcoming advertising and sales promotion campaigns, proposed pricing (including comparison with the industry), effect of price variations, and a schedule of proposed changes.

Production strategy may be outlined in detail, including: present and future production capacity details by plant, plant expansion and new equipment needs, raw materials availability and projections of their cost, future opportunities (such as inside manufacturing of components presently purchased).

Technical strategy may be discussed, including: a report on present research and development, improvement of existing products, technological innovations in industries served, technical staff or facility acquisitions, quality improvements, evaluation of new markets, new laws, new consumer concerns, and how our technology and experience can be applied most profitably in light of these changes.

Other matters which may be covered in the business plan are: outside business opportunities such as acquisitions and licensing agreements, staff levels and productivity projections for a five-year period, and introduction of United States products to international markets and vice versa.

The report will cover some or all of these, and whatever else the managers consider important to their particular business. The report is as personal and distinctive as any other aspect of divisional management. Only a few basic numeric reports are expected to be in a standard format. This standardization is imposed partly to speed up the understanding by the readers, partly to ensure coverage of all key matters, and partly to facilitate the consolidation of the data into groups and eventually, the overall company report.

Preparation of individual business plans and forecasts begins in late summer and follows the company's pyramidal organization. Planning starts at the top with an evaluation of capabilities and environment, and the definition of goals. These are communicated downward and the broad contributions expected of each group to these goals are discussed. Detailed planning then works up through narrowing layers of supervisors, managers, and executives. At each major level within a division, and later at the group level, and the corporate level, competing claims for budget dollars are refereed and balanced.

This is a two-way process with flow of ideas and objectives both up and down the ladder as feedback is generated. It all pivots around the general manager, whose job it is to convince both top management and his own staff of the short and long-range viability of the plan, and the propriety of its contribution to achieving the company's overall goals.

This entire procedure may appear to be awfully time-consuming, but it has the incalculable advantage of involving people at all levels of the corporate and divisional structure. As you may have heard us say, and we mean it, "People count here." Our philosophy is that planning, to be effective, must mobilize all the forces which will be called upon to administer or carry out the plan once it is made and approved.

Planning makes people think—about goals and about problems. It starts them talking, sharing ideas, communicating goals. It makes them stand back from today's routine tasks and problems to take a hard look at longer-range goals and problems. Not the least important, it helps individuals see their work assignments, and even their own career plans, more clearly. The input received from experts at all levels of our organization, right down there where the work is done, is of tremendous value in setting or reappraising the goals realistically.

## BRINGING IT ALL TOGETHER

It all comes together in the Management Committee Room on the 14th floor of our big headquarters building at 3M Center. And it comes together pretty fast, during the fall of each year when the Management Committee meets to evaluate the business plans of each of 3M's eight product groups and their many operating divisions, subsidiaries, and departments. This is when the "go or no go" decisions are made. The Wall Street Journal once described these meetings as the division manager's "moment of truth."

The Management Committee consists of President Ray Herzog, nine group vice presidents (eight are responsible for product divisions, one for international operations) and the vice presidents of such departments as finance, research and development, engineering, manufacturing, purchasing, legal affairs, public affairs and personnel relations.

It's really a pleasure to sit in on these meetings and watch the pros at work. Believe me, they cut through to the essentials of those plans in record time.

Individual sessions are held for each operating group, which may cover from two to six divisions or subsidiaries and perhaps also one or more departments or projects which have not yet reached divisional status. Each group is given as much time as it wants, often a full day.

The group vice president introduces his division managers, who are asked, one by one, to summarize their plans, which they and their associates do in very short order. They don't read their reports. Instead, they highlight what they feel is important. They may unveil new products, or show organization charts, or preview their advertising programs. They may use slides or films or "show and tell" demonstrations. It's up to them. Their only charge is to tell their story and sell their plan.

When all the plans have been presented, the managers and their staff people are asked to leave the room while their proposals are considered.

After they have left, President Herzog makes a round of the table, asking for each committee member's comments or criticisms about any of the plans. When all the forecasts have been evaluated in this way, the general managers and their key associates are asked to rejoin the committee and are given an opportunity to hear any criticisms or doubts which have been expressed, or perhaps to answer questions. Their plans will then be approved as submitted, as modified, or—in less frequent instances—sent back to the drawing board for major revisions.

So you see, it is indeed a "moment of truth." And just as in the bullring, where I believe that expression originates, the better trained the fighter and the more involved the cadre of supporters, the less his chance of being gored.

Out of this single once-a-year meeting for each group comes approval not only of the business plan for the group and for each division within it, but also approval of the budget forecast on which each division and group will operate during the year ahead.

I should point out here, incidentally, that those budget forecasts are not appropriations. The divisions are not given a basket of money that they can spend regardless of sales and profit performance. They are expected to adjust spending, and to produce their promised profits, even though external factors may change drastically as the new year unwinds.

This year's results, after all, will be included in their next year's report! This will be the measure, in part, of the credibility of the following year's plan.

The final stage of our planning is to pull all of these divisional and group plans, as modified, into one overall corporate plan. This, together with the five-year forecasts of source and application of funds, is the subject of a final Management Committee meeting in December. It's later covered more briefly with the Board.

Subsequent meetings of the Management Committee throughout the year tend to be more concerned with review of progress, consideration of new problems, and similar matters. In other words, the meetings I've described are primarily planning sessions with some review and some educational or background aspects. Other meetings during the year are more concerned with review and control, and backgrounding for the members, though planning is never completely absent from them either.


## SUMMARY

To make my main points clear, let me summarize:

A business plan is not simply a forecast or a budget, but is a blueprint for action to achieve pre-determined business goals.

The business goals can be established only after a careful appraisal of the resources available or obtainable, and the external factors which may impede or create opportunities for the organization to achieve these goals.

The plan must contain clear guidelines for the utilization and allocation of all of the human and financial resources available to the organization—and how (and when) other needed resources will be obtained.

The plan must involve the total organization, in the preparation of the plan and in the commitment to carry it out.

Finally, there must be an ongoing review and control, a plan for follow-through, to see that the total planning program is monitored, and that actions, or even the plan, are quickly adjusted to reflect new factors.

I can offer no special plea or evidence that our approach in this year . . . is "right," or even effective. The success of 3M's earlier planning, in part over the lunch table of our old cafeteria, is evident. The success—or failure—of our current approach to business planning will become evident only with the passage of time.

## QUESTIONS

1. What are the fiscal goals for a company? Where are they reported?
2. What are business goals?
3. What is a "profit target" for a 3M division?
4. How are the usual financial statements different from budgeted statements?
5. What is the business plan for a 3M division?

## SELECTED BIBLIOGRAPHY

Fagerberg, Dixon, Jr., "Unmeasured Costs," *Management Accounting*, February 1974, pp. 29-32.

Gambling, Trevor, "Negotiation of Budgets," *The Chartered Accountant in Australia,* August 1973, pp. 20-26.

May, Paul A., "The Budgeting Process," *Management Accounting*, January 1973, pp. 19-23, 25.

Schiff, Michael, and Arie Y. Lewin, "Where Traditional Budgeting Fails," *Financial Executive*, May 1968, pp. 50-62.

# 87

## ACCOUNTING AS A PROCESS OF MAPPING*
David Solomons

In thinking about the fundamental accounting concept, I have found it helpful to think of accounting as a process of mapping. It is as if the accountant is drawing a financial map which bears no resemblance whatsoever to the figures on the page but yet the figures on the page represent the terrain which he is mapping.

# 88

## ACCOUNTING AND OPERATIONS RESEARCH†
Iain W. Symon

### INTRODUCTION

Occasionally, it is a useful exercise for a profession to examine its boundaries, like a jealous landowner who has lost his title deeds. Accountancy has no title deeds and is subject to a continuous process of development; but like some landowners the accountant has unruly neighbours, and there are always areas, even fairly close to his home, that are in dispute. One of these is certainly the field of quantitative business analysis, where mathematicians and statisticians have evolved techniques that have an important contribution to make towards business efficiency. Statistics, a few years ago a subject tolerated rather than studied by apprentices and articled clerks, is now claiming a more important place in the accountancy subject hierarchy, but the really interesting change has been in studies variously entitled "Quantitative Techniques", "Management Mathematics" or "Operations Research". These are not, of course, exactly synonymous terms, but there is an understandable vagueness of ideas, even amongst the best-informed accountants, about the use, definition, and content of such subjects. Most accountants would agree that they should know something about Operations Research, but they are repelled by its mathematical content and, if they are chartered accountants, could be excused for feeling that they have far more urgent tasks to think about, like the latest taxation changes or accounting standards. The aim of this paper is not to describe such techniques in detail so that accountant readers may now feel fully informed—this has been done already by a number of authors—but

*Excerpt from T. J. Burns (ed.), *Accounting in Transition: Oral Histories of Recent U.S. Experience,* College of Administrative Science, Ohio State University Press, 1974, p. 161. Reprinted by permission of the publisher.

†From *The Accountant's Magazine,* December 1974, pp. 480—483. Reprinted by permission of the publisher.

rather to throw light on the relative importance of operations research and accounting, the problems of interaction, the potential misunderstandings, the problems of status, and the ways in which the accountant could well adapt his skill to meet the needs of, and to use, operations research.

## DEFINING OPERATIONS RESEARCH AND ACCOUNTING

Operations Research is a branch of quantitative analysis involving the clarification of decision making issues by the creation of simplified situation models. While it uses certain identifiable techniques, it is not simply a group of mathematical tools from which one selects the most apt for a particular problem. It combines scientific methods with the products of various other engineering, accounting, and social skills; and it can be differentiated from work-study by its emphasis on the abstract and strategic, retaining a wide frame of reference to ensure overall optimisation.

Such definitions and descriptions would seem academically pretentious if it were not true that operations research has had considerable successes, sometimes spectacular ones. It seems likely that the predictive powers of OR have fulfilled a need not being met by accounting. Accountants have often been accused of producing information about the past, while being unwilling to commit themselves on the future. The OR specialist, by a scientific evaluation of probabilities, has shown that the future can be analysed and managed. Yet both professions are model-makers; a profit and loss account and balance sheet make up an elegant financial model of an organisation. Unfortunately, elegance can be deceptive, and the accountancy institutes have recently been looking "through a glass darkly" at their conventional methods. This is a position not yet attained by OR because the methods and approaches have never become conventional, and because there is continuous pressure to improve. The average operations researcher is young, probably below thirty, with a recent qualification in mathematics or engineering; he is unlikely to accept conventions without question.

Perhaps surprisingly, accounting is itself difficult to define. There are accepted areas like auditing, that are clearly part of the accounting province, but outlying areas like finance, commercial law, business economics, and taxation are shared with other disciplines, while corporate planning, marketing, business organisation, and electronic data processing may be considered by some as extra-territorial. Standard definitions of accounting, which emphasise the recording and summarising of financial data, scarcely do justice to its range of functions. It is not surprising that there is not just one accountancy institute or even one type of institute; and there is more than one way of training and educating accountants. However, where a long-established profession with such wide interests meets a vigorous new management skill there are bound to be problems of overlap and status.

## PROBLEMS OF STATUS AND ATTITUDE

For the time being, accountants have nearly every advantage. They are generally older, and are part of an established hierarchy with a tradition of coming out at the top. They have their own esoteric language, and, by taking themselves seriously, have become respectable. The supply of qualified accountants has been limited by a long training period and a demanding examination system, and they have certain exclusive rights. They are institutionalised, professionalised, disciplined and reserved.

There is also evidence that the accountant is more likely than some to be understood by the upper levels of management. Many directors have had formal accountancy education, and, although they may have ceased to act as accountants, they still have an affinity with the accountant. For example, throughout John Copeman's book on "The Chief Executive" (1971—Leviathan House), there are constant reminders that success in business involves a numerical skill in the money game, and a grasp of accounting concepts. Directors look for profitability, and accounting information is still the best medium for routine reporting and control. Those in charge of industry are likely to feel that they can rely heavily on the skills and integrity of the accountant, whatever the nature of his activity. On the other hand, it appears that they are rather more vague on the skills and responsibilities of their operations research men. A survey by L. M. Bennie—"The Impact of Quantitative Techniques on Accountants and Accountancy Systems" (Heriot-Watt University), showed that most firms claiming to use OR were not in fact using it or were using it to a limited extent only. The problem may be that much of OR consists of laboratory trials rather than operational applications; or that some of the work is done by external consultants, and has no familiar routine. In any case, the rather esoteric mathematics often characteristic of OR does not normally constitute part of top management training at any point in their careers, nor do directors need to understand the calculations to observe their results. Thus there may be a tendency to regard operations research as a specialised skill not open to any extent to the outsider, and this attitude seems to be encouraged rather than discouraged by OR men themselves; their literature is often very abstract and incomprehensible to the non-mathematician.

These differences in the attitude of top management towards accountants and OR personnel may seem tenuous, but it is almost certain that they are noticed by the people concerned. For example, Professor Moore observes—

> The basic aim of operational research is to improve on some situation. Hence unless a solution is implemented, little is achieved. There is a fantastic mobility amongst operational research workers. With this mobility has grown an impression that one of the causes of the movement is the difficulty operational research workers have found in getting solutions implemented, with the consequent feeling that the grass is greener in the next field. The solutions they provide may be improvements, but the organization prefers its present ways as being more comfortable for all concerned.

("Basic Operational Research", page 157)

Accountants are subject to stress and frustration also, but their position is much more established, and they do not need to prove themselves by continuous embarkation on new projects. In many organisations they are the people who operate the "present ways" that are "more comfortable for all concerned". They are often key figures in the implementation of routines suggested by operations research.

As far as academic status is concerned, the operations researchers are in a comparatively favourable position. Normal entry to this sphere of activity is, according to a survey done by Eilon, Haugh and Betts (published in OR Quarterly, June 1969), by graduating from a university, with a mathematical or engineering background. On the technical side of industrial production, it is thus only lack of experience that may handicap the OR man compared with the accountant, a disadvantage that would disappear after a few years. While accountancy has a long history as a skill, it is only during the last ten years or so that, in U.K. at least, it has achieved respectability in academic institutions, and it is still doubtfully regarded by those who judge a field of study on its intellectual content. Accountancy institutes have been unwilling to make graduation an essential entry pre-requisite, although the Scottish Institute has gone most of the way towards this. There is still a strong prejudice in favour of teaching accountancy "on the job", so that abstract thinking, knowledge of principles and history, and grasp of social and economic background have not developed as they should. The resulting differences in attitudes between the OR man and the accountant may well have contributed to misunderstanding, since all professional people have a vested interest in maintaining the image and status of their training. The answers obtained by Bennie indicated that, although each side thought that its relations with the other were good, there were significant differences on the contributions made by each to the other's functions, with the OR people being particularly critical of the amount of help in the form of information and co-operation obtained.

Joint action between the two spheres of activity seems very desirable, not just at the level of the company or firm, but also at the level of the parent bodies. Some efforts along these lines have already been made; for example, a working party was set up in 1966 by the Operational Research Society and the Institute of Cost and Works Accountants (as it was then) to establish the fundamentals of project cost control, and a book was published on their work in 1969. ("Project Cost Control Using Net-works.") Problems of status and mutual comprehension should, to some extent, be resolved by such contacts. To quote Professor Moore again—

> Movement towards this "mutual understanding" relationship and away from the "separate function" relationship can take place only slowly and has not yet occurred to any significant extent in the vast bulk of organisations. To achieve it requires a sequence of events:—
>
> (a) Progress towards the communication and persuasion types of relationship
> (b) Re-appraisal of the power differential between the researcher and the manager
> (c) An increase in the consensus of opinion as to the value of mutual co-operation
> (d) A growth in mutual respect.

("Basic Operational Research", page 159)

While this statement refers to managers as a whole rather than to accountants, the remarks are obviously valid when applied to the latter. There is an area of co-operation which should prove well worth cultivating, for extra profits in a narrow sense, for the sake of accountancy on a wider view, and for the efficient use of human resources in the widest—and best—sense.

## WHAT THE ACCOUNTANT CAN DO (AND WHY HE SHOULD DO IT)

To understand where accounting fits in with OR, one must identify the aims and procedures of OR, as well as its techniques.

Essentially OR tends to work in "one-off" projects, i.e., by a series of special investigations on specific problems. This contrasts with accounting, where the task is often of a repetitive and continuous nature; but there are occasions when unique accounting problems are encountered, e.g., a particular capital investment project, and it is in these cases that some of the most important mutual contributions are possible. (Several examples of this are described in OR literature, one of the best full-length books being Fred Hanssmann's "Operations Research Techniques for Capital Investment" (John Wiley and Sons, Inc.; published 1968).) However, this ad hoc nature of operations research means that new information has to be gathered or that existing and available data must be reconsidered. Such information is not only in measurable or monetary form. It may be necessary to bring under scrutiny the unquantifiable and the probabilistic, and the solution must be adjusted accordingly. The average accountant is not comfortable in such a situation, because objectivity and measurability are stock characteristics of his labours. However, the provision of unusual or subjective information must be part of his contribution to OR investigations, and he must be prepared to overcome at least four, perhaps subconscious, prejudices:—

(a) an unwillingness to accept that generally applicable accounting procedures may not fit particular situations and may produce wrong decisions in such cases (e.g., overhead cost allocations, choice of cost centres, differentiation between similar functions in differing departments);

(b) a mistrust of statistically-based manipulation of accounting data (e.g., conclusions drawn from sampling rather than from full examination), and of non-measurable assessments;

(c) a dislike for the purely marginal or incremental analysis as opposed to the total or absorption cost approach; and

(d) a feeling that one should err on the side of safety, so that there is always a comforting cushion of reserve to fall back on.

It may be a little unfair to accuse accountants of subconscious urges that they may disown, but all of these predispositions have a desirable side and are founded on sound reasoning about stewardship or financial responsibilities. They are, however, seldom compatible with an operations research approach, and prejudice (a) was particularly criticised some years ago by Stafford Beer in a well-known article. At that time he suggested that some of the problems would have been overcome if OR had preceded accounting, because cost groupings might have been more scientifically made and there would have been greater consciousness of the need to reflect spreads of possible performances by statistical means. He also suggested that the accountant should consider opportunity cost as a basis for valuation, an approach which would be more compatible with OR technqiues such as theory of games or linear programming. The accountant should also be willing to set standards for costing purposes by utilising OR models which can optimise performance in given situations. All these would require a fundamental adjustment of accounting conventions, and it could be suggested that, however desirable such changes in principle, returns might not be worth the extra effort and cost. A cheap, slightly vulnerable system that works may be superior to one that is expensive and sophisticated. It is comforting to observe that John Argenti examines each OR technique from the point of view of returns to cost and points out those that are too expensive in relation to their achievements (John Argenti—"Management Techniques"—Allen & Unwin, 1969). The points discussed in this present paper are made with this in mind; techniques for greater efficiency must themselves be financially efficient.

Overhead charges are particularly controversial and awkward to deal with. They *are* costs, and they must be covered before profit is made. But where they are inevitable, or already incurred irrespective of a decision to be taken, they cannot affect that decision. Thus, an OR model does not involve overheads as costs because it only examines the causes and effects of a particular situation given a background environment that includes overhead-costed facilities; such is the standard viewpoint of the writers on OR, who also emphasise that such costs should be replaced by the wider, sometimes immeasurable, costs and benefits connected with a decision.

Nevertheless, the exclusion of overheads for OR purposes should be closely examined by the accountant in respect of each project, for the following reasons:—

(a) The decision to go ahead with a particular project following an analysis of strictly incremental costs and benefits may result in liability for an overhead charge at a later point in time. For example, if an existing building is going to be used to house a certain line of production, but that building requires to be replaced before the ultimate item is produced from that line, then the cost of the building, essentially an overhead in the short run, will become an incremental cost in the foreseeable future. Similar situations may occur with any costs incurred by indivisibilities or scale economies, including equipment, skilled labour, technical and administrative facilities, and ancillary services.

(b) The reason underlying the charging of overheads to particular productive functions is that they are incremental or direct costs to all such functions taken together. To a particular function or project in isolation, they are irrelevant. But the presence or absence of a project at any moment or period of time may exclude the possibility of running another project, due to some resource limitation. If, for example, a building company has an administrative framework which incurs overheads, and can handle three contracts of average size in a period of a year, then increased spending to cut time spent on the contracts and allow four to be tackled instead of three can be offset against a month's overheads for each existing contract. If the reduction in time taken on each contract has been achieved by a PERT/cost study, where reduction of time along the critical path is "purchased" by incurring more direct costs, a *net gain* may be achieved by this saving of overheads. This may reflect the more general characteristic of overheads that they are time-costs, being the cost of time taken or time elapsed; this is clearly seen when we extend the accounting period or planning horizon, when more and more overheads take on the appearance of direct costs.

Thus, while OR analysis may not incude overheads, it may be necessary to examine such costs, and to allocate an element of overheads on a time elapsed basis, perhaps in the form of interest.

Factors which are inherently immeasurable are, of course, as little subject to OR analysis as they are to accounting. Nevertheless, OR techniques can bring the unquantifiable aspects of a situation into sharper prominence by identifying and isolating the areas in question, and thus allow subjective judgments to be applied by the decision-maker. It must be understood that neither accountants nor OR specialists are final decision-makers; they are both there as information providers and analysts. Even in an uncertain situation, or one spiked with intangibles, they can apply their logic to what is available, leaving the remainder for the final decision-maker; since the operations researcher uses probability measures, his information is frequently more useful than that of the accountant, and can allow for a greater number of alternatives, but there does not seem to be any reason why the accountant should not adopt a similar "stochastic" (i.e., involving probability assessments) approach to his own data. Probability weightings are already being applied in some discounted cash flow calculations, and the technique should be of much wider application. Of the prejudices previously mentioned, this would have most impact on (b) and (d), but it would bring accountants into a wide field of possibilities for future-oriented information. The concept of prudence in accounting has been a very rough and ready tool, allowing for uncertainty by taking the blackest outlook, and, in the absence of well-developed decision theories, has proved effective if at times imperfect. The steps to better procedures would be, firstly, to develop greater use of statistical analysis of past data to allow projection of performance, followed by the use of probability measures; this would allow continuous control of accounting variables in the same way as quality control charts are used for manufacturing production. Such systems are obviously already operated in the form of variance reporting in standard and budgetary costing, but with the wider availability of computer facilities, better communications and filing, accountants could well consider further refinements in the field of early-warning systems. On these matters, operational research projects could contribute a lot, especially in information flows, stochastic modelling and simulations, and adaptive control, as well as in the more traditional statistical methods (e.g., forecasting, regression, analysis of variance, sequential analysis, quality control).

Apart from incremental and marginal costing methods, opportunity cost details are often part of an operations research approach. "Opportunity cost" has been a stylish term in economic and accounting literature for a long time, and is not such an academic ogre as it must sometimes seem. It expresses the simple point that, when you make a decision between two courses, the alternative ruled out is a foregone opportunity and any potential benefits thus lost must be considered as part of the cost of the course actually taken. The most obvious situation where this arises in accounting is in process costing, and can be seen from two points of view:—

(a) Looking back from a later process stage to an earlier one, the opportunity value at the point of transfer can be regarded as the proceeds that could have been obtained if the items passing between the stages had been sold or used elsewhere.

(b) Looking from the earlier stage, the opportunity value of output is the proceeds that could have been obtained by selling (or using elsewhere) instead of passing the production to the next process.

Such procedures for valuation of inputs and outputs at each stage allow for allocation of profits or losses to individual stages, and they can then be treated in isolation for operational research purposes. The "opportunity value" gives us a basis for valuation identical to that used by accountancy income theorists (e.g., Edwards and Bell, in "The Theory of Measurement of Business Income" (1961), define opportunity cost valuation as the current exit price of an asset in its present form), and this is consistent with opportunity cost as defined by management scientists (e.g., Martin Starr, in "Management: A Modern Approach" (1971) defines opportunity cost as "the difference between the outcome that would result if a specific strategy is chosen and the best outcome that could have been obtained under the circumstances"). If, say, Process A and Process B are applied in sequence to the raw materials entering A, then if a unit of production passing from A to B has accumulated £8 of costs and could have been sold in its current form with net proceeds of £10, historic costs of £8 *and* opportunity costs of £2 must be considered as chargeable to process B for its unit input. Unit opportunity costs of £2 have been incurred and opportunity value is £10. This kind of calculation seems more relevant than historic cost for operational research purposes, being usable for optimising production patterns and policies. The possible complexities are very great, and there are obvious applications in production-line costing, transportation and location studies, and divisional performance measurements.

So far, the discussion has referred mainly to the adaptation of attitudes and techniques. But the accountant is in an important position for ensuring success or failure in implementation and control of changes suggested by OR studies. For efficient functioning in this direction, the actions of accountants in four fields are probably crucial:—

(a) filing and gathering of information about performances;
(b) following-up, testing and adapting routines;
(c) allocation of electronic data processing facilities; and
(d) understanding of methods and implications of OR.

There is no point in an accounting department holding information about an organisation that duplicates, parallels, or competes with, the data used by operations researchers. It is not valid to argue that their records are on a different basis or are inconsistent; there seems no reason to doubt that they can be made consistent and interlocking, and it is obviously better to present guidance for decision-making in a coherently unified fashion. Such involvement of accounting with OR seemed to be acceptable and, indeed, anticipated by both parties in Bennie's survey. A by-product of such close liaison follows from the fact that the OR man is often better trained in the design of information storage and retrieval systems than the accountant, so that he can provide a service in the design and operation of information systems. In turn, the accounting routines can be used for control and follow-up of OR schemes, releasing the operations research staff for further work. Both parties can utilise computers for storage and processing, and, with the high cost of computer time, cost-consciousness is necessary. Lastly, the accountant should have some understanding of operational research methods, so that he can identify potential areas of application, judge the significance of results, and deal sympathetically with success or failure of experiments. To this end, it is not necessary or desirable that accounting educators should instil vast quantities of OR into the minds of trainees, but that future accountants should be familiar with terms, mathematical principles, procedures, information requirements, and general fields of application. Accountants have no time to carry out painstaking operational research, but they should be able to initiate and stimulate projects. In this way, accountants, whether in the management or financial departments, who frequently have a wide yet detailed knowledge of the functional parts of a business, can make a uniquely effective contribution to an operational research group.

## SUMMARY AND CONCLUSIONS

1. Accountants should be aware of the implications and methods of other skills contributing to business success. One of these is Operational (or Operations) Research.

2. There are difficulties of definition and status that can cause friction and inefficiency in areas where accounting and operations research meet. These can be lessened by joint action at various levels.

3. Following the viewpoints expressed in this paper, it is felt that the following areas of accountancy interest could be adjusted to meet the needs of OR specialists:—

(a) The treatment of overheads, cost allocations, and cost centres.

(b) Use of sampling and probability techniques.

(c) More application of incremental and opportunity cost concepts.

(d) Less emphasis on simple conservatism in allowing for uncertainty.

(e) Joint design of information and filing systems.

(f) Use of accounting routines for following-up OR achievements.

(g) Better use of EDP facilities.

(h) Inclusion of operations research methods and possibilities in accounting education.

## QUESTIONS

1. What is operations research?

2. What advantages do accountants have over operations researchers?

3. What are the four "prejudices" that an accountant must overcome in order to be able to contribute to OR investigations?

4. Why should the exclusion of overheads be closely examined for each OR project by the accountant?

5. What is an opportunity cost and its relevance in accounting and operations research?

6. What should an accountant know about operations research?

## SELECTED BIBLIOGRAPHY

Fox, Harold W., "Operational Research Complements Management Accounting," *Management Accounting*, December 1973, pp. 504-506.

McCaskey, Michael B., "Management and Operations Research," *California Management Review*, Winter 1974, p. 13.

# 89

# MODELLING
## Some Implications for Accountants*
Robert H. Chenhall

In recent years the activity of modelling has become increasingly important in the literature of business studies. The purpose of this article is to examine the concept of modelling and indicate its relationship to accounting and financial management.

## THE CONCEPT OF MODEL BUILDING

The concept of model building is often mysterious to many involved in managerial decision-making, and yet a model is no more than a formal representation of notions that the decision maker has about a problem. The construction of a model involves exhibiting, in a manageable form, a set of interrelationships which are thought to represent the essential attributes of a more complex situation.

As the decision-maker builds a model he endeavours to draw the complex strands of his problem into a coherent, logical framework which may then be used for problem analysis. He will specify important factors and discard details which are irrelevant to an understanding of the particular problem. Once evolved, the model may be used to predict and compare outcomes of alternative decisions or strategies. It may also aid organizational control by providing a vehicle for understanding decision problems.[1]

Essentially the purpose of model building is to provide management with the facility for experimental decision-making. By using models to aid policy development it is possible to avoid catastrophic effects that may ensue from trial and error decisions in the real world.

*From *The Australian Accountant*, October 1974, pp. 558–560, 563–564. Reprinted by permission of the publisher.

[1]For a point of view developing the importance of this aspect of models see McRae, see reference (1). However, it is to be noted that the model must also be predictive to ensure verification of the implied understanding of reality.

## THE PROCESS OF MODELLING

Modelling involves an initial process of model formation followed by analysis to prescribe a course of action which may finally be implemented. As interdependencies exist between various parts of an organization many decisions have significant, widespread secondary effects. Consequently it is important that a team of managers drawn from a broad organizational spectrum be involved to some degree in the original process of model formation. It will be argued that the role of accounting specialists is especially important in the model-building team.

The process of model formation can be thought to follow three interacting states. First, qualitative analysis of factors critical to the decision problem, including a statement of objectives. A thorough understanding of the problem in the context of the whole organization is necessary to identify variables that are relevant and causally related.[2] Second, a statement of the problem's elements and limits of the analysis. Finally, the model-building stage will translate the identified logical interrelationships into a mathematical form. This form is necessary to ensure both clarity and precision of manipulation. Elements of the model must be identified as static or dynamic and a time horizon selected. Input and output data requirements will be formulated.[3]

After the model has been formulated a solution is calculated and implemented. The solution will be derived by use of formal mathematics and will generally require application of specialist expertise in mathematics and electronic computers.[4] The latter requirement is necessitated by possible complexity of the model or a large volume of data to be manipulated. Implementation is an important part of modelling and should involve all participating managers. If benefits of model building are to be fully realized, operational managers, whose behaviour is to be affected, must have confidence in the comprehensiveness and merit of the exercise. Wagner [see reference (3)], an expert in operations research, criticizes model building that excludes managers from evaluating the model in terms of their "personalized rationality". He argues that models should be devised so that managers are informed of likely effects of decision strategies that they themselves formulate. He criticizes many modelling exercises claiming that proposed solutions are based on limited data and restricted model formulation. If managers are excluded from model formulation they may be forced to evaluate proposed solutions in the light of considerations omitted from the model. This may involve as much difficulty as the original model-building exercise and defeat the very purpose of modelling.

## THE TEAM APPROACH TO MODEL BUILDING

The success of model building depends on the purposeful interaction of managers each with different perspective and skill but all possessing a belief in reasoned method and a

---

[2]Useful suggestions to aid those inexperienced in this initial stage of model creation may be found in Morris, see reference (2).

[3]Possibly statistical method will aid data formulation. The technique of sensitivity analysis may be used to test the significance of data. Uncontrollable variables may be forecast by analysis of time series.

[4]Operations research provides techniques for solving models drawing on mathematical programming, inventory and production theory, waiting-line theory and computer simulation.

wish to relate such method meaningfully to the task of managerial decision-making. Difficulties may arise through delegating model building to a small, elite group drawn exclusively from various scientific disciplines.[5] These difficulties derive from the possible isolation of a scientist-based team from the operational aspects of implementing suggested solutions to decision problems. Typically, difficulties may arise from over-simplification of model assumptions with the possibility of solutions relating unrealistically to reality, or the model may depend on the existence of data which is never fully available. It is important that operational managers contribute an understanding of objectives and data constraints to the modelling team. Participation of management is also important to ensure adequate recognition of attitudes of individuals influenced by a model's suggested solution. To minimize the possibility of model irrelevance the modelling team should include representatives from functional management affected by the model—for example, production and marketing, as well as technical experts in modelling.[6]

## CONTRIBUTION OF ACCOUNTING AND FINANCIAL MANAGEMENT TO MODEL BUILDING

The contribution of accounting and financial management to a model-building team can be significant. Of the many specialists within a business enterprise, accounting personnel have the greatest opportunity to acquire an understanding or organizational goals, current technological processes, managerial responsibilities, planning and control procedures, possible achievements within the existing planning horizon, and implications to the firm of implementing change.

The ability of accounting staff to describe the structure of a firm and develop an awareness of the operations of many organizational groups will evolve from their central role in the information system which collects and processes data for a wide range of organizational needs, and generates data to aid financial control of the firm. As a consequence of this interaction with organizational groups, accounting is well placed to identify problems which may be solved by use of a formal modelling approach.[7] It is also possible for accounting personnel to observe the interrelationships that exist within both formal and informal organizational structures. They may therefore be aware of employee distrust of modelling activity in general or the use of a particular model.

Perhaps the most direct role of accounting in model building is servicing data requirements of models. It is important that the modelling team is continually aware of availability, format and cost of input data. Accounting staff will have comprehensive knowledge of the firm's formal information system and probably an adequate

[5]A view of using a modelling team drawn from different scientific disciplines is argued in the work of Beer (4).

[6]An idealized list of disciplines relevant to modelling would include production and marketing management, communications, accounting and finance, cybernetics, industrial psychology, applied mathematics, systems analysis and computers as well as those trained in traditional scientific subjects. Clearly, any one modelling team will not possess experts in all these fields.

[7]It is noteworthy that accountancy firms providing management services to their clients can often recognize problems that may benefit from a modelling approach.

understanding of informal communication procedures. It is a function of accounting to ensure that the model-building process is not frustrated by an inflexible information system. Of particular importance is collection and storage of data in a form sufficiently disaggregated to be adaptable to a variety of uses.

A firm's accounting staff will usually have experience in forecasting financial implications of decisions. This activity generates an appreciation of historical trends and relationships which may be useful information for model development. It is also possible that accounting records may provide historical data which could be useful in testing the model. However, it is unlikely that existing accounting records will be usable in their existing form for model building. This is because much of the firm's financial data is based on a set of complicated conventions which if not understood may give rise to inconsistencies and variety in interpretation. It is therefore important that accounting specialists indicate the adequacy of available data and direct the generation of data most relevant to a given modelling task.

It is to be noted that a decision will be required at some stage of model building to stop collecting and refining data. Analysis of sensitivity of the model to changes in accuracy of data will assist in making this decision.[8]

## THE USE OF ESTABLISHED MODELS

The importance of using established models as the basis for modelling is argued by many experienced in scientific management. Rivett [see reference (6)] states "we are concerned with forms of classification which will hasten our understanding of structure and hasten the process of solving the model". Whilst accepting this basic proposition, there is a danger that relying on established models may influence the specification of a model in such a manner that subsequent analysis is irrelevant to the decision problem at hand. The formulation of a given problem to fit a model is not unknown in the practice of modelling.

Several reasons for the importance attached to model classification may be identified. First, creativity in modelling cannot be taught but comes from experience on a team. Teaching of modelling should be directed at developing competence in techniques of quantitative analysis including available solutions for common managerial decision problems. Second, top management will require the modelling team to justify its existence in terms of contribution to the firm's profitability. Application of well-tried models can bring rapid, easily documented results. If rewards from these models are achieved, top management may agree to allocate resources for research into ambitious model building which has less obvious immediate benefits.

Various model classification schemes have been suggested but the following indicate common decision problems for which models[9] have been established:

1. "Allocation problems" exist when a variety of different demands are made on a

---

[8]For a summary of this problem and the use of sensitivity analysis to test the significance of parameter changes in models see Rappaport, reference (5).

[9]See the classification systems of Rivett and Ackoff (7) and Ackoff and Sasieni (8).

given set of resources. The aim of a firm is to maximize (or minimize) an objective such as profit (or cost), whilst operating within available economic, financial and physical resources. The technique of programming is a powerful tool used in solving allocation problems.

2. "Inventory problems" arise when there is a need to balance the costs of holding stock against the costs of holding insufficient stock. The principle may be applied to many situations in which there are idle resources—goods, materials, cash, capital equipment, etc.

3. "Queueing problems" are associated with minimizing costs arising from "waiting lines". The problem involves consideration of entities or "customers" waiting to be served, the location of the server, the waiting procedure of customers known as the queue, and the queue discipline or order of serving. A solution involves minimizing the total costs associated with waiting customers and idle service facilities.

4. "Scheduling and ranking problems" involve deciding the way in which an agreed task should be sequenced. Mathematical analysis has been developed to provide optimal solutions for certain classes of sequencing problems. For example, critical path and network analyses are used to optimally solve sequencing when there are many activities, some of which can only be handled when others are completed.

5. "Replacement and maintenance problems" involve ensuring that productive capacity of the firm is maintained at a planned level. The relevant costs to minimize are those of the initial asset, those of failure, and the replacement and maintenance costs.

6. "Search problems" are characterized by the need to collect information for use in decision-making. Procedures involve designing and selecting samples to investigate such problems as quality control and auditing inspections. Probability sampling is a useful technique in this area.

7. Competitive problems are distinguished by incorporating in analysis of a problem the effect decision-makers have on each other. Model building in competitive situations can be aided by application of the theory of games and statistical decision theory.

It is evident from discussions with practitioners of operations research that allocation and inventory models account for at least half the current industrial applications of established models. These models have also been used in developing solutions to financial problems. The following examples illustrate areas in which research into application of these models have been developed.

The task of budgeting is to allocate resources of a firm in such a way as to achieve given objectives in the most efficient manner. If stated objectives are not attained by a specified budget programme, the programme should be adjusted in ways likely to achieve the objectives. To reformulate plans continually would be a tedious and costly exercise for traditional accounting procedures.[10] Further, the magnitude and direction

[10]Flexible budgeting provides information on planned costs for a selection of activity levels. However, they do not update plans on a continuous basis, nor do they show the effect throughout the firm of changes in its financial characteristics.

of adjustments required to optimize would not be known. Attempts to optimize resource allocation have been developed by applying linear programming to models constructed on the basis of traditional accounting classifications and recording techniques. These models are built by developing a series of equations and inequalities which indicate constraints on a firm's operations as defined by managerial policy and accounting conventions. These constraints are interdependent and must be simultaneously satisfied. They include such items as required minimum cash balances, productive capacity, availability of stocks, market demand, credit and depreciation policy. The objective of models may be maximization of retained earnings, marginal income or contribution, or multiple goals.[11] The models prescribe transaction flows which will bring about financial results that are the best possible for the model.[12]

An important aspect of working capital management is control of a firm's level of current assets. Inventory models have been used to determine the optimum level and replenishment policy for stock and cash. These models recognize that operating and opportunity costs of carrying these assets rise as the quantity increases, but costs of acquiring and holding inadequate amounts fall as the quantity held increases. An Economic Order Quantity (E.O.Q. model) may be used to find an "optimal order size" and "reorder point" that will minimize total inventory costs. A variety of models with different assumptions may be found in the literature: however, many require variables to be highly predictable.

The established model types discussed so far are optimization studies which analytically solve decision problems. In many cases these models cannot be used because of complexity of the problem, lack of a clear objective function, or prohibitive costs of applying the analytical model. The technique of simulation provides an alternative approach which generates solutions that are satisfactory, rather than optimal. Simulation applications evaluate the merits of alternative decisions through experimentation performed on the model. The technique is a powerful aid to the construction and use of models.

It is possible for a computer simulation to trace the simultaneous interaction of elements incorporated in the model. This process assists identification of causal linkages and helps isolate variables significant to the decision problem. The scope of simulation applications is broad, ranging from solving specific financial management problems to studies of firms' information systems and development of overall management control systems. . . .

## CONCLUSION

The purpose of this paper has been to discuss the process of modelling in business enterprises. A distinction was made between model building and the use of established models. It was argued that the relationship of accounting and financial management to

---

[11]These objectives are used in models developed by Ijiri (9), Amey (10), and Jaedicke (11), Ijiri (12) and Charnes and Cooper (13).

[12]A selection of programming applications to problems in financial management may be found in Carsberg (14), and Salking and Kornbluth (15).

both these activities is important. The active involvement of accounting specialists in a model-building team can help ensure successful modelling. Also of interest was the application of established models to areas of accounting and financial management. Whilst these applications may not provide immediate practical alternatives to traditional procedures they do improve the functioning of accounting by developing understanding of the complex task of financial control.

The conclusions of this article have important educational implications for accounting specialists and practitioners of scientific management. If accounting personnel are to fulfil a useful role in a model-building team they should have at least basic competence in the terminology and application of quantitative analysis. This knowledge would provide basic understanding of available modelling techniques and help facilitate communication with specialists in scientific management. The challenge for those trained in quantitative modelling is to understand the possible contribution of operational and functional experts, and the effects of modelling activity on the behaviour of employees.

## REFERENCE WORKS

(1) McRae, T., *Analytical Management*, John Wiley and Sons, 1970, Chapter 2.

(2) Morris, W. T., "On the Art of Modelling", *Management Science*, XIII, August 1967.

(3) Wagner, H. M., "The ABCs of O.R.", *Operations Research*, October 1971.

(4) Beer, S., *Decision and Control*, John Wiley and Sons, London 1966.

(5) Rappaport, A., "Sensitivity Analysis in Decision Making", *Accounting Review*, July 1967.

(6) Rivett, Patrick, *Principles of Model Building*, John Wiley and Sons, 1972. p. 34.

(7) Rivett, B. H. P. and Ackoff, R. L., *A Manager's Guide to O.R.*, John Wiley and Sons, 1963.

(8) Ackoff, R. L. and Sasieni, M. W., *Fundamentals of Operations Research*, John Wiley and Sons, New York 1967.

(9) Ijiri, Y., Levy, F. K. and Lyon, R. C., "A Linear Porgramming Model for Budgeting and Financial Planning", *Journal of Accounting Research,* Autumn 1963.

(10) Amey, L., *The Efficiency of Business Enterprise*, George Allen and Unwin Ltd., London.

(11) Jaedicke, R. J., *Improving Breakeven Analysis by Linear Programming Technique*, N.A.A. Bulletin, March 1961.

(12) Ijiri, Y., *Management Goals and Accounting for Control,* North Holland Publishing Corporation, 1965.

(13) Charnes, A. and Cooper, W. W., *Management Models and Industrial Applications of Linear Programming*, John Wiley and Sons, Inc., 1961.

(14) Carsberg, B. V., *Introduction to Mathematical Programming for Accountants*, Allen and Unwin, 1969.

(15) Salking, G. and Kornbluth, J., *Linear Programming in Financial Planning,* Haymarket Publishing Ltd., 1972.

## QUESTIONS

1. What are the three interacting stages of model formation?
2. Why does Wagner consider "personalized rationality" important?
3. What is the contribution of accounting to model building?
4. List and describe common decision models for which models have been established.

## SELECTED BIBLIOGRAPHY

Krueger, Donald A., "Financial Modeling and 'What If' Budgeting," *Management Accounting*, May 1972, pp. 25-30.

Mepham, M. J., "The Use of Models in Accounting," *The Accountant's Magazine*, June 1972, pp. 282-289.

Precious, J. R., and D. R. Wood, "Corporate Modelling: When Success Can Be a Long-term Forecast," *Accounting and Business Research*, Autumn 1975, pp. 254-272.

# Part 5
# The Rule-making Agencies and Some Issues

# 90

# THE FASB AND ITS ROLE IN THE DEVELOPMENT OF ACCOUNTING PRINCIPLES IN THE UNITED STATES*

Robert L. McKinnell

## INTRODUCTION

Prior to the 1930s the accounting profession made little attempt to establish uniform "principles" to be followed by those preparing financial statements and reports. However, four significant events took place in the United States during the '30s which marked the beginning of the development of accounting principles.

1. In 1932 the AICPA's special committee on development of accounting principles drew up five basic principles to govern the preparation of financial statements. . . . In a letter dated September 22, 1932, to the New York Stock Exchange's Committee on Stock List, the Institute committee recommended that the audit certificates of listed companies should state their financial reports were prepared in accordance with these principles. The Stock Exchange approved the Institute committee's recommendations in general and put them into effect in 1933 with one exception; listed companies did not have to disclose the accounting methods they followed. Instead, in January 1933, the New York Stock Exchange approved two requirements of disclosure for financial statements:[1]

a. Independently audited financial statements had to be filed with listing applications and published annually thereafter.

b. Listed companies had to secure from their auditors and furnish to the Exchange information as to the scope of their audit; the audit of subsidiaries; the auditor's access to essential information; whether the form of the financial statements was such as fairly to present the financial position and results of operations; whether the accounts reflected consistent application of the company's regular accounting system; and whether such system conformed to accepted accounting practices and was not inconsistent with the five broad principles proposed by the Institute committee.

2. In 1933 the Securities Act was enacted by Congress, the intent of which was to protect the purchaser against manipulation, misrepresentation and other fraudulent practices arising through the transaction of securities. The Act required a security to be registered and certain disclosures made before it could be sold to the public.

3. Congress, in 1934, enacted another significant act, the Securities Exchange Act, which required the registration of national securities exchanges, securities listed on exchanges, and brokers and dealers trading in over-the-counter securities markets. The Securities and Exchange Commission (SEC) was also formed as a result of this Act.

*From *Cost and Management*, May-June 1975, pp. 51—53. Reprinted by permission of the publisher.

[1]John L. Carey, *The Rise of the Accounting Profession: From Technician to Professional, 1896-1936,* American Institute of Certified Public Accountants, New York, 1969, p. 177.

4. In 1938, a standing committee on accounting procedure was appointed by the AICPA. This represented the first major effort within the private sector to reduce the number of accounting alternatives for financial reporting purposes.

## ACCOUNTING RESEARCH BULLETINS

Fifty-one Accounting Research Bulletins were issued by the Committee on Accounting Procedure from 1938 to 1959. These bulletins recommended preferred treatment of selected accounting alternatives. Although they were not binding, the SEC, the stock exchanges and the accounting profession to a degree did support them. However, numerous generally accepted accounting principles were still considered appropriate in similar circumstances and this in turn resulted in growing dissatisfaction.

In the latter 1950s the business environment changed with the advent of multi-national corporations, and the resulting alterations in tax laws and financing methods. The AICPA, in an attempt to keep pace with these changes, established the Accounting Principles Board (APB) in 1959.

## ACCOUNTING PRINCIPLES BOARD

The Accounting Principles Board was similar to the Committee on Accounting Procedure which it succeeded. One of the APB's objectives, like the Committee's, was to reduce the number of accounting alternatives for financial reporting purposes. The Board, however, had a more elaborate set of rules governing its procedures. There was also the assumption that the APB would wait until research studies were completed before making specific recommendations on a given subject.

The Council of the AICPA gave the Board authority, like the Committee on Accounting Procedure, to issue its own Opinions. An Opinion required two-thirds approval of the Board before it could be issued. Dissents were also released. The Board's Opinions contained a note, like the Accounting Research Bulletins, to the effect that "the authority of the Opinions rested on their general acceptability and that while it was recognized that general rules might be subject to exception, the burden of justifying departures from the Board's recommendations must be assumed by those who adopted other practices."[2]

The members (18 in the latter years) of the APB were appointed by the president of the AICPA upon approval by the Board of Directors. The appointments were for three years. Members of the APB were also members of AICPA, the majority of which were practicing public accountants.

In the late '60s a great deal of criticism was directed at the APB. This criticism came from various sectors of society and resulted from a number of factors. The accounting profession itself criticized the APB on its ineffectiveness in solving current problems. However, the representatives of the accounting firms on the APB tended to take a company stand when issues of major significance arose. On any particular issue

[2]John L. Carey, *The Rise of the Accounting Profession: From Technician to Professional, 1937-1969,* p. 96.

one would find the representatives of some firms suggesting one acceptable accounting treatment while other representatives suggested another depending on how their firm viewed the issue which often was only a reflection of the accounting treatment they were presently using in the firm. It was virtually impossible for the APB to reflect a united front on any issue. The two-thirds member requirement for adoption of an opinion within the APB usually resulted in a compromise position on an issue to ensure some form of statement release. Heavy criticism also came from industry elements which would be adversely affected by an APB Opinion or who were reluctant to change existing practice. This resulted in lobbying by business interests with Congress to bring pressure to bear on the APB via the Securities and Exchange Commission in the hope the APB would alter its position. The SEC was able to exert subtle pressure on the APB by either an unwillingness to support an APB position or by adopting an alternative requirement for those companies listing on the stock exchange. In fairness to the APB, it should be pointed out that the issues which they were dealing with were highly controversial.

Other areas of criticism could be discussed such as narrow representation on the APB, the length of time required by the APB to respond to current issues or the brush fire response to accounting problems (i.e., continually responding to current issues and immediate problems and subsequently failing to achieve any long-run approach in the accounting area). My concern, however, is not to examine in detail the various aspects of the criticism brought against the APB but merely to highlight its existence.

The APB completed activities on June 30, 1973, having released 31 Opinions since its inception.


## ORIGIN OF THE FINANCIAL ACCOUNTING STANDARDS BOARD

In January 1971 a meeting of top partners from approximately 20 accounting firms was organized by the president of the AICPA. The purpose of this meeting was to evaluate the way in which accounting principles were being formulated. Following this meeting, on April 5, 1971, the American Institute of Certified Public Accountants established a study group (Wheat Study Group), headed by former Securities and Exchange Commissioner Francis M. Wheat, to study the approach used in developing accounting principles and to make recommendations for improving that process. The study group consisted of seven members—three certified public accountants and four representatives from the investment, academic, and business communities. It is interesting to note that four out of seven members of the committee were not CPAs. Thus no one can argue that the committee lacked views of a cross-section of the business community, which was one of the major criticisms of the APB. At the same time a second study group (the Trueblood Committee) chaired by Robert M. Trueblood, Chairman of the Board of Directors of Touche Ross & Company, was formed. This group was to analyze and refine the objectives of financial statements.

The Trueblood study group's report was released in October 1973.[3] The report was not intended as a definitive statement on the objectives of financial statements but rather examined various viewpoints which would have a long-range effect. The report is still being studied by the FASB.

The Wheat study group forwarded its formal report, in March 1972, to the Board of Directors of the AICPA. In April the Board of Directors voted on the recommendations and approved them. This was followed by approval of the AICPA Council in May. The report recommended the establishment of a Financial Accounting Foundation to replace the Accounting Principles Board. Figure 1 depicts the organizational structure explained in the recommendations. Following is a breakdown of the Financial Accounting Foundation and its constituent parts.

## THE FINANCIAL ACCOUNTING FOUNDATION

The Financial Accounting Foundation is an independent (separate from all existing professional bodies) incorporated body.

### 1. The Board of Trustees

The Board of Trustees governs the Foundation and is composed of nine members. The Board of Directors of the AICPA elects eight of these members to serve a three-year term. The members are selected from the following groups:

Four — certified public accountants in public practice;
Two — financial executives;
One — financial analyst;
One — accounting educator.

The latter four members are respectively chosen, one each from lists of names forwarded by the National Association of Accountants, the Financial Executives Institute, the Financial Analysts Federation, and the American Accounting Association. The president of the AICPA is the ninth member of the Board of Trustees serving ex officio during his one-year term as Institute President. The functions of the Board of Trustees include—

(i) appointing members to the Financial Accounting Standards Board;
(ii) appointing members to the Financial Accounting Standards Advisory Council;
(iii) raising and allocating funds for the Foundation;
(iv) reviewing periodically the basic structure, making changes when approved by at least eight trustees.

---

[3] An excellent discussion of this report was done by James D. Edwards, "The Impact of New Dimensions in Financial Reporting—on Management, the Management Accountant and the Auditor," *Cost and Management*, The Society of Industrial Accountants, Hamilton, March-April 1974, Vol. 48, No. 2, pp. 6—18.

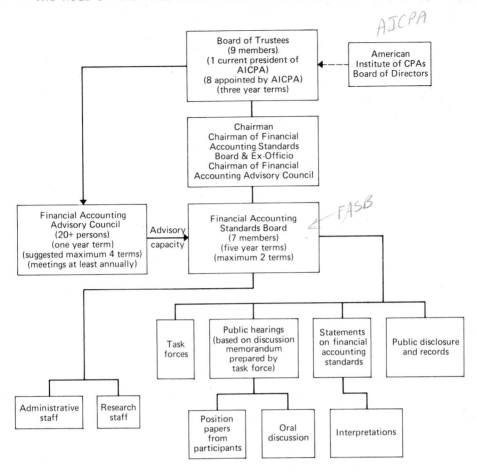

**Figure 1**    Financial accounting foundation organizational structure.

## 2. The Financial Accounting Standards Advisory Council

The Advisory Council is composed of at least 20 members from various occupations serving a non-salaried one-year renewable term, who are familiar with the difficulties of financial reporting. The FASB chairman is also the ex officio chairman of the Advisory Council. The role of the Advisory Council is to comment either collectively or individually on proposed statements of the FASB as well as advising the Board on items to be included in its agenda and the selection and organization of task forces.

## 3. The Financial Accounting Standards Board

The Financial Accounting Standards Board is composed of seven members appointed by the Board of Trustees. Four of the members are to be certified public accountants taken from public practice. The remaining three members, not necessarily CPAs, are expected to be cognizant of the problems of financial reporting. The members serve a five-year term, renewable once. While serving on the FASB they must disassociate themselves from all other business interests. The salary range is from $75,000 to $100,000 a year.

The chairman of the Financial Accounting Standards Board (currently Marshall S. Armstrong) has responsibility for administrative and research staffs. An administrative director and a research director assist him.

The responsibility of the FASB is to issue statements of financial accounting standards and to issue interpretations of the statements when required. The FASB is guided in its approach to setting standards by the By-Laws of the Foundation and the FASB Rules of Procedure. The general approach used in issuing a statement is as follows:

a. Agenda item is selected by the chairman of the FASB based on advice from other Board members, members of the Financial Accounting Standards Advisory Council and suggestions from interested persons and organizations.

b. A task force is then chosen. The chairman of the task force is usually a member of the FASB while its members may include FASB and Advisory Council members and interested persons knowledgeable of issues and the needs of financial statement users or who are experts or have a viewpoint relevant to the project. The task force's responsibility includes—

(i) refining the definition of the problem and its financial accounting and reporting issues,

(ii) determining the nature and extent of necessary research, and

(iii) producing a discussion memorandum.

c. The discussion memorandum is then distributed to interested parties for review. Public hearings are held not less than 30 days, usually 60 days, after the release of the memorandum for the purpose of discussions and receipt of submissions from individuals and groups on the memorandum.

d. An exposure draft of the proposed statement of financial accounting standards is then prepared. Once it receives the support of five of the seven FASB members, it is released to the public for review. The period of public exposure is usually 60 days, but is not to be less than 30 days. The purpose of the public meetings is to provide feedback to the FASB. New arguments both for and against a position may be brought out which might influence the content of the final statement. It also allows the public the opportunity to comment and argue for their own particular position.

e. A draft statement is revised if this is felt necessary based on feedback from the exposure draft. Once five members of FASB agree on a standard, a statement of financial accounting standards is issued.

The FASB may also issue interpretations of statements on financial accounting standards issued by itself as well as on Accounting Research Bulletins and APB Opinions if the need ever arose. An interpretation may be issued if it is first exposed to the Advisory Council for a minimum of 15 days and supported by five members of the FASB. It is not necessary that a public hearing be held on an interpretation prior to issuance as is the case with statements of financial accounting standards.

Accounting Research Bulletins and APB Opinions maintain their present authority except to the degree amended or superseded by statements of the Financial Accounting Standards Board.

## PROGRESS OF FASB

The FASB, as of December 31, 1974, has issued three Statements of Financial Accounting Standards and three Interpretations. The three statements are:

1. "Disclosure of Foreign Currency Translation Information"
   —effective for financial statements reporting results of operations for fiscal periods ending after November 30, 1973, and in financial statements reporting financial position dated after that date.
2. "Accounting for Research and Development Costs"
   —effect for financial statements for fiscal years beginning on or after January 1, 1975.
3. "Reporting Accounting Changes in Interim Financial Statements"
   —an amendment of APB Opinion No. 28
   —effective for accounting changes made in interim periods ending on or after December 31, 1974.

The three interpretations are:

1. "Accounting Changes Related to the Cost of Inventory"
   —an interpretation of APB Opinion No. 20
   —effective July 1, 1974.
2. "Imputing Interest on Debt Arrangements Made under the Federal Bankruptcy Act"
   —an interpretation of APB Opinion No. 21
   —effective for notes issued, modified, altered, or otherwise changed after June 30, 1974, in reorganizations, arrangements or under other provisions of the Federal Bankruptcy Act.
3. "Accounting for the Cost of Pension Plans Subject to the Employee Retirement Income Security Act of 1974"
   —an interpretation of APB Opinion No. 8
   —effective December 31, 1974.

Projects on agenda for the FASB at various states of completion include—

General Price Level Reporting
Accounting for Future Losses—the exposure draft issued for this area was entitled "Accounting for Contingencies"
Accounting for Foreign Currency Translation
Financial Reporting by Segments of a Business Enterprise
Conceptual Framework for Financial Accounting and Reporting: Objectives, Qualitative Characteristics and Information

Accounting for Leases
Criteria for Determining Materiality
Business Combinations

## SUMMARY

This paper has traced the development of accounting principles in the United States from the 1930s to the present. We have briefly examined the Committee on Accounting Procedure, 1938-1959, noting that it issued 51 Accounting Research Bulletins. This committee was followed by the Accounting Principles Board, 1959-1973, which released 31 Opinions. Heavy criticism of the APB resulted in establishment of the Wheat Committee which recommended setting up the Financial Accounting Foundation to replace the APB. We have examined the three parts of the Financial Accounting Foundation, these being the Board of Trustees, the Financial Accounting Advisory Council and the Financial Accounting Standards Board.

One final comment should be made about the work of the FASB. The FASB has taken a great deal of time in issuing its statements to date. Critics of the FASB are focusing on the perceived slowness of this body to respond to current issues. It is very important for the FASB to increase its output within future time periods. Otherwise it will be forced to spend all its time facing current problems leaving no time to deal with future issues. One of the major criticisms of the APB was its brush fire approach to accounting problems; if the FASB is not careful, it will end up in the same predicament.

EDITORS' NOTE: As of January 1976, the FASB had issued 12 statements of standards and 7 interpretations of statements. The FASB has formed a new permanent screening committee on emerging practice problems which will advise the board on actions to be taken on these issues. The 15-member committee will include two FASB members and six members of the AICPA accounting standards executive committee.

## QUESTIONS

1. Define bulletins, opinions, research studies, standards, and interpretations.
2. Compare and contrast this selection and Selection 2.
3. What are the differences between the APB and the FASB?
4. Explain the process for issuing an FASB standard.

## SELECTED BIBLIOGRAPHY

Anreder, Steven S., "By the Numbers? The FASB Goes to Work," *Barron's*, Nov. 18, 1974, pp. 3, 26-30.

Marksbury, Henry, "Portrait of the FASB at Age Two," *The Arthur Young Journal*, Spring 1975, pp. 19-27.

Meyer, Philip E., "The APB's Independence and Its Implications for the FASB," *Journal of Accounting Research*, Spring 1974, pp. 188-196.

Shank, John K., "The Pursuit of Accounting Standards—Whither and Hence," *Journal of Contemporary Business*, Spring 1973, pp. 83-90.

# 91
## FASB PROSPECTS
## A Talk with Marshall S. Armstrong*
Henry C. Marksbury

Many say that the FASB, if it is to operate effectively, must both resolve problems at hand and produce almost immediately major modifications and innovations in accounting standards. Do you agree that the situation is so urgent?

ARMSTRONG: I do.

Do you think this dual mission is feasible? Do you think you can plant and cultivate forests for tomorrow while putting out brush fires?

ARMSTRONG: My answer to both of your questions is a very strong "Yes," but I'd like to spend just a moment explaining it.

While your metaphor describes our working environment accurately, I don't agree with those who maintain that the "brush fires" are the forces of doomsday. On the contrary, I believe that the pressing problems hold some of the answers to long-term solutions.

We gain much knowledge from dealing with the "hot" issues of current practice. Thus, the question becomes one of how to find the most effective solutions both for today's financial accounting needs and for the long term. And the answer, as I see it, is that we *enlist* support. In the nature of our approach to developing financial accounting standards, we stimulate, we learn from, and we draw support from the people whose interests our work serves. What is happening at the FASB has tremendous implications for the business community. And people in business are coming forward readily to contribute to our work.

I should add, however, that to date neither those of us at the FASB nor our general public are currently satisfied with the way in which the brush fires—the so-called emerging practice problems—are being handled. We intend to rectify that situation.

For the past several weeks we have been actively pursuing ways to more efficiently handle the day-to-day emerging accounting issues. Several things are going forward simultaneously: We are carefully examining our own in-house procedures; the American Institute of CPAs is attempting to restructure its Accounting Standards Executive Committee to make it more responsive and helpful to the FASB; and others, including the Financial Executives Institute and the National Association of Accountants, are being requested to provide current assistance to the Board in identifying and aiding in the solution of emerging problems.

It's absolutely essential that the Financial Accounting Standards Board, with the assistance of other responsive organizations, be regarded as the leading force in the private sector to improve and establish financial accounting standards. I'm convinced

*From *The Arthur Young Journal*, Spring 1975, pp. 28–31. Reprinted by permission of the publisher.

that we'll find ways to improve our process to be more effective in dealing with broad, fundamental issues as well as with day-to-day emerging accounting problems before the end of 1975.

## THE SEC: A BOOST, A USEFUL DIALOGUE

There has been much speculation that, if the Board fails, the government—possibly through the SEC—will assume the responsibility for setting financial accounting standards. How would you characterize the FASB's relationship with the SEC?

ARMSTRONG: I would first characterize the FASB's relationship with the SEC as being one of mutual respect concerning the objectives and responsibilities of each organization.

As you know, since its creation about 40 years ago, the SEC has had the power at law to establish accounting standards for those companies that fall under its purview. However, it has always been the policy of the SEC to look to the accounting profession for the improvement and establishment of financial accounting standards. Nevertheless, the SEC's work in the standards-setting area seemed to accelerate starting about mid-1972. This was occasioned to some extent by the hiatus that was created in the private sector during the period the Accounting Principles Board was terminating its activities and the Financial Accounting Standards Board was initiating operation.

We've worked very hard at the FASB to establish a sound working relationship with the SEC—a relationship that has been characterized by a spokesman for the Commission as "a policy of mutual non-surprise."

In December of 1973, the SEC published ASR 150 which, for the first time in its history, made public acknowledgment of its desire to look to a private-sector body for the improvement and establishment of financial accounting standards. That release specifically identified the FASB as the authoritative body in the private sector.

Although the SEC finds it necessary on occasion to improve disclosure in financial reporting for the benefit of investors, there are numerous examples within the past few months that indicate the Commission's willingness to establish a temporary disclosure requirement with the understanding that it will be reconsidered when the FASB pronounces on the subject.

Last June saw a significant "first" with respect to the relationship of the SEC with the private sector's accounting standards-setting body. Four of the five Commissioners and several of their top staff people traveled to Stamford to meet with our full Board and senior staff people. I believe that meeting was most beneficial to both organizations. Operationally, our two organizations go their own ways and that, I think, is as it should be. The seven members of our Board make our decisions and the five members of the Commission reach their own conclusions. However, it's important that we have a continuing dialogue, and that's being accomplished on a very cooperative and mutually satisfactory basis.

Suffice it to say, in my view the relationship between the FASB and the SEC is very good and is improving on a daily basis.

## ORIGINS OF THE FASB:
## "FUTURE SHOCK"

You came to the FASB from more than 30 years in independent public accounting, during which you rose to become managing partner of a regional firm. You served as president of the American Institute of CPAs, and you were for six years a member of the Accounting Principles Board, the predecessor organization to the FASB. To what do you attribute the advent of the FASB? Would you take us back in time to the years leading up to the phasing out of the APB and trace cause and effect? And then tell us why you think the FASB can steer clear of—or resolve—any similar problems it may face?

ARMSTRONG: Please bear in mind that my years on the APB spanned what many regard as its time of trouble, 1963 to 1969, when the going got rough. So I speak with whatever bias, but I also speak as one who took part.

The most important thing, I believe, is that the APB dealt in an objective, timely, and effective manner with numerous issues. But the times were against it. The times were changing, and changing fast. In the mid-sixties, remember, the "go-go" boys came on the scene. It was a period when some people became intent on doing everything possible to make the numbers—the percentages, the ratios—look good. Though they didn't apply to the majority of companies, phrases like "managing earnings" expressed, I think, the need for developing accounting standards which would assure investors that, in comparable situations, earnings data were developed on the basis of consistently applied principles.

I think a strong case can be made that the APB *was* getting that job done. It was addressing itself to such goals. Its opinions were useful and influential. But the times were turbulent. "Future shock" was upon the financial reporting process. What was needed—what the APB didn't have—was public belief in the independence of those charged with the standards-setting responsibility.

In addition, the APB functioned through the part-time efforts of highly qualified but very busy people. And the time had come when the standards-setting process could no longer remain a part-time pursuit. It had become necessary for the standards-setters to have the freedom to concentrate and the depth of commitment possible only through investment of one's full time.

In response to these needs, the FASB was established as a standards-setting body with a full-time staff and a commitment to wholly independent operation. The members and staff of the FASB have severed their relationships with their former firms and employers. Their sole master is the public interest. They have the backing of a well-organized, well-financed foundation. They were selected with great care, and the positions they fill are challenging. In my view, these people are the cream of the crop. With this solid base, I believe that the FASB is in a position to solve the problems that come before us.

"Success" I define simply as so conducting our operations that we enlist the participation and support of the entire business, professional, and financial community—participation in establishing sound accounting and reporting standards, and support in using and implementing those standards. To me, that will be success.

## 1975: TIME OF TESTING

How would you describe the support you are receiving in comparison with the support the business community gave to the APB?

ARMSTRONG: The support of the FASB by people and organizations in the economic community is many times greater than was given the APB. Our resources and our structure—even the form of documentation whereby we expose our views for comment and modification—are designed to elicit input from interested parties. We're certainly encouraged by the way that channel of communication is working. But the toughest test is ahead of us.

What is that test?

ARMSTRONG: Eighteen months ago, we were at the beginning. We were setting up our organization. Now we've arrived at an operational frontier. The test ahead of us—and it will come during 1975—is this: How will those who have taken part in our due process of developing financial accounting standards, as well as others in the business community, react when they find that, after careful consideration, the Board did not go along with their views?

Will the Board's standards at a time like that guide the presentations of financial data of those who dislike as well as those who favor the standards? *That* is the crux of the matter, the test. If the standards are followed by those who don't favor them, we will have passed the test. But if there's a substantial splintering, a refusal by a major portion of the reporting community to adhere to the standards, we won't enhance the reliability and comparability of financial data. Consequently, we would not be able to foster confidence in financial reporting. Such failure would have adverse implications not only for investors but possibly for the economic community as a whole. It would tend to undermine confidence worldwide in financial reporting in the United States.

And the alternative would be government takeover of the standards-setting function?

ARMSTRONG: Presumably—though I'm not personally convinced that that would necessarily result.

## THE GOVERNMENT AS STANDARDS-SETTER

Do you think the standards-setting function should stay in the private sector?

ARMSTRONG: I certainly do. Components of the government are subject—and, in most cases, properly so—to many political pressures. But accounting standards should not be shaped by political or governmental pressures. Decisions about accounting standards should not, for example, be used to "heat up" or "cool down" the economy.

Whatever the past problems have been, I think the potential for undermining investor confidence would be enormous if the treatment of financial reporting data were subject to political pressures or, worse yet, used as an outright tool of some governmental program or policy.

I emphasize that I am not so naive as to think that what we do at the FASB does not have its political aspects. We look very carefully at the political considerations as we evaluate issues and make decisions. Political considerations enter into any situation in which an effort is being made to gain acceptance. Our statements must be capable of practical application, and certainly we must weigh political impact. But that can be done far more effectively outside governmental machinery than within it. Again, independence is the watchword, and I think that, in the most creative sense, we are independent not only of the government but the private sector, too.

But the stern test is still ahead of us. The test of application of standards, adherence to the common purpose, remains to be passed. I am confident that the business community will take the long view and will operate in accordance with FASB-promulgated standards. We'll soon find out.

## DISCLOSURE:
## IN SEARCH OF THE ESSENTIALS

Possibly the most confusing term to the so-called man in the street, the average investor, is the term "disclosure" or "full disclosure." One analyst has advocated that financial statements disclose data that will give "a complete picture, the unimpaired story of a company's earnings, its assets and liabilities." What are the prospects for achieving that goal?

ARMSTRONG: I'm not at all certain that so-called "full disclosure" is an attainable goal or even a definable term. But it is desirable, even imperative, that we go on trying to fathom what "full disclosure" might be at some future time, and what sufficient disclosure is right now. The progress of accounting is linked to developments coming out of efforts to improve, extend, and refine the process of financial reporting. In the private sector, such efforts are now centralized in the work of the FASB.

What would a workaday definition of "sufficient disclosure" be?

ARMSTRONG: I think of it as that degree of disclosure that is necessary to make the financial report not misleading. The objective is, in other words, to present the data that communicate all salient features about a company's operations and financial position. In the late 1960s, even some of those who were referred to as "wheeler-dealers" operated, at least debatably, within generally accepted accounting principles and still managed to obscure one or more of those salient features.

If we're to reach the point where all salient features are visible, are communicated, we have sufficient disclosure. But then the question arises: Disclosure to *whom*? I think it should be stressed at every opportunity that it takes certain skills to attain an informed overview—to say nothing of an in-depth understanding—of the financial status and workings of a business enterprise of any significant size.

Business is complex. Financial reporting is complex. We must try to communicate as much as we can to as many people as we can with the basic commitment of conveying the essentials in appropriate depth and scope.

Accounting standards are a key element in fulfilling that commitment. But, to a great extent, effective financial reporting will always depend somewhat on the judgment, the interpretations, and the empirical reasoning of the people who are involved in the individual company's financial reporting process. These are the minds that know the complete inner workings of a complex business enterprise and that should objectively determine whether or not a "complete picture"—that is, one that is not misleading—is presented.

The role of the FASB is to play a creative part in developing standards and guidelines that will lead to more meaningful and useful financial information relating to these complex business activities.

## A CONCEPTUAL FRAMEWORK: POSSIBLE DREAM?

The FASB is now studying the "conceptual framework for accounting and reporting." The accounting profession has tried to come to grips with this subject numerous times. Most recently, the Trueblood study of the objectives of financial statements attempted to describe a foundation of concepts of financial reporting. But the findings of that study have been the subject of criticism and debate. What are the prospects for the FASB coming up with a workable conceptual framework?

ARMSTRONG: The "framework" project is the most important one we have embarked on. It is basic, and it can lead to improvements throughout the range of accounting theory. We believe we can succeed with it. Before I tell you why, some background might be helpful.

The attempts to come up with such a framework—usable in the sense that it would elicit widespread agreement and acceptance—go back more than forty years. The effort has been made but, by and large, the goal has not been attained.

Despite the criticism, the Trueblood study was, I think, an important step toward the development of a conceptual framework. The study was successful in that it did what it set out to do. It describes a broad, philosophical framework. Criticism of it is usually lodged on grounds of unresolved problems of implementation—an area which the Trueblood group was not asked to explore.

Obviously our project can't be completed overnight. It's a subject that the APB addressed, but one on which it was unable to issue an Opinion. We're well aware of the complexity and importance of the subject—and of the frustrations that previous approaches have met. But I *don't* feel that we're searching for the unattainable truth in accounting—a "holy grail," if you will.

The failure of previous efforts to establish a complete conceptual framework in one fell swoop strongly suggests that such an approach by the FASB would not be successful. Accordingly, the Board has determined to deal with the conceptual-framework project in a number of coordinated steps, with each step progressing from the previous one. Such a process will more than likely result in the issuance of not one but several discussion memoranda and more than one public hearing.

The first discussion memorandum, a consideration of the Trueblood report, has been issued. We are now studying the feedback on the memorandum and from the public hearing. At the same time, we're developing a second discussion memorandum.

This gets ahead of the process, but I think it's quite likely that in the second memorandum we will have begun to expand on the Trueblood material and on our own tentative thoughts about the objectives of financial statements. We quite probably will also be raising some detailed questions about implementation techniques.

So we will go step by step, considering input received from preparers, auditors, and users of financial reports.

We have a parallel experience with a step-by-step approach in the "price-level" project—or, as it's now called, "Financial Reporting in Units of General Purchasing Power." An exposure draft of a proposed accounting standard was issued last December, and we've provided an extensive period of time in which public comment can be communicated to us. Observations are being sought as to whether implementation of the proposed techniques is practicable and whether the resulting information is useful.

To aid us in this effort, more than a hundred companies have agreed to convert their '73-'74 reports in accordance with the proposed standard and the related techniques. That phase of the project is expected to be completed by September of this year.

By this step-by-step process, by enlisting the aid and support of concerned parties, by carefully conducting our research, and by sifting public comment through our thinking, I believe we should be able to arrive at financial accounting standards that are both theoretically sound and capable of practical implementation.

## QUESTIONS

1. How can the FASB-SEC relationship be described as "a policy of mutual non-surprise?"

2. Who were the "go-go" boys in the 1960s? What problems did they cause the accounting profession?

3. What does the term "future shock" mean in relation to accounting?

4. What is the difference between "full disclosure" and "sufficient disclosure?"

5. What are the risks in the FASB's policy for simultaneously solving current problems and establishing accounting standards?

## SELECTED BIBLIOGRAPHY

"A Helping Hand for the FASB," *E&E*, Winter 1974-1975, pp. 26-34.

Sprouse, Robert T., "Establishing Financial Accounting Standards: The Plan and the Performance," *Stanford Lectures in Accounting*, The Price Waterhouse Foundation, 1974.

# 92

## THE HISTORICAL ROLE OF THE SEC IN ACCOUNTING MATTERS*

William O. Douglas

More and more we became involved under the 1933 Act not only in the independence of accountants but in the reach of an accountant's certificate. What is the standard for a complete audit? What about securities listed or assets actually held in escrow? Can footnotes making full disclosure rectify falsehoods in registration statements? What contingent liabilities need be disclosed? When can property received for stock be carried at the par value of the stock? When can capitalization of the excess of total expenses over total income be treated as an asset? Can securities of no apparent value be carried at their face value as an asset, and later be written off against a reserve for losses?

The problem is an ongoing one. In 1973 the SEC proposed a rule that would require a financial statement as to whether more than one accounting principle had been used in the previous two fiscal years, significantly affecting net income. Battle lines have been drawn with the oil industry, as some companies write off the costs of drilling unsuccessful wells immediately as expenses, while others use "full costing." That means that those costs are amortized, year by year, over the life of the producing reserves. A shift from one method to another might produce startling results.

The role of the SEC in accounting matters has an interesting history. In 1936 and 1937 Robert E. Healy and I thought the commission should take the lead in formulating accounting principles as it was empowered to do under the 1933 Act. No one in the commission thought it should abdicate this responsibility. All of us had seen partners even in the best firms walk perilously close to the line both as respects civil and criminal liability. James Landis, in his speech of December 4, 1936, before the Investment Bankers, said that our experience with accountants led us to conclude that the form of financial statements should not be left "to professional responsibility alone," that the SEC had a responsibility to see to it that financial statements were not misleading.

Our chief accountant, Carman G. Blough, stated on December 13, 1937, that immediate SEC action on statements was required, but the commission often did not have time to do the extensive research necessary to formulate the correct accounting principles in a given case. Even though the prevalent practice seemed "improper," the commission (over my dissent and Healy's) often accepted a statement, provided there was in a footnote a "complete disclosure of the questionable matters."

On February 12, 1938, the commission appointed an intra-agency committee to work on "rules prescribing accounting practices and procedures."

Healy's view and mine were reflected in Commission Release No. 4 on April 25, 1938:

---

*From W. O. Douglas, **Go East, Young Man,** New York, Random House, 1974, pp. 274–276. Reprinted by permission of the publisher.

In cases where financial statements filed with this commission pursuant to its rules and regulations under the Securities Act of 1933 or the Securities Exchange Act of 1934 are prepared in accordance with accounting principles for which there is no substantial authoritative support, such financial statements will be presumed to be misleading or inaccurate despite disclosures contained in the certificate of the accountant or in footnotes to the statements provided the matters involved are material. In cases where there is a difference of opinion between the commission and the registrant as to the proper principles of accounting to be followed, disclosure will be accepted in lieu of correction of the financial statements themselves only if the points involved are such that there is substantial authoritative support for the practices followed by the registrant and the position of the commission has not previously been expressed in rules, regulations, or other official releases of the commission, including the published opinions of its chief accountant.

Healy had anticipated that ruling in an address on December 27, 1937, before the American Accounting Association, when he said the commission was undertaking "to express a few standards as to principles which we believe are accepted by a majority of good accountants, especially those who do not assume the role of special pleaders for their more lucrative clients."

One example he gave was preferred stock issued at eighty dollars a share with a par value of forty. On its balance sheet the company showed forty dollars a share for the preferred and ten dollars a share as "paid-in surplus." The company claimed the ten dollars could be used to pay dividends to the common stock. Healy denounced that practice. He listed other cases of like gravity and gave instances where the commission was divided, the majority clearing registration statements, though in Healy's view and in mine they were misleading. It was our contention that "if an earnings statement and a balance sheet reflect the results of improper accounting, they amount to misrepresentative and misleading statements in violation of the Security Act."

Healy said that "the commission will continue its efforts to develop a body of accounting principles through its decisions."

What happened in my time was a common-law development of precedents—case by case. Some principles were established by commission rulings, others by opinions of the chief accountant.

EDITORS' NOTE: Before he was named to the Supreme Court in 1939, Justice Douglas served on the staff of the SEC starting in 1934, became a commissioner in 1936, and became SEC chairman in 1937. Justice Douglas resigned from the court in November 1975 due to illness.

## QUESTIONS

1. Why did Healy denounce the practice of declaring dividends on the basis of "paid-in-surplus?" Defend his position.

2. What is meant by a common-law development of accounting principles? What are the merits and shortcomings of this approach?

3. Why did Justice Douglas object to statements with footnotes containing a "complete disclosure of the questionable matters?"

## SELECTED BIBLIOGRAPHY

Burton, John C., "The SEC and the Changing World of Accounting," *Journal of Contemporary Business*, Spring 1973, pp. 51-64.

# 93
# THE SEC CHIEF ACCOUNTANT
## An Interview*
John C. Burton

Would you summarize the responsibilities of the office of Chief Accountant as you see them?

BURTON: The Chief Accountant's responsibility is to advise the Commission on all accounting matters and that has many dimensions. In the first place, it deals with the problem of disclosure requirements, that is, what requirement should we impose either through Regulation S-X or through our forms. It also contemplates dealing with registrants who have specific accounting problems that move beyond the level where they are handled by the reviewing staff.

The staff in the Division of Corporation Finance review registration statements and '34 Act filings, 10k's and so forth on a primary basis, but sometimes their comments or other things they notice lead into problems which will come to me . . . or sometimes a registrant has an unusual problem which comes directly to me.

For example, if a registrant wants to include appraisal data or present data on a range basis, or something else that's quite innovative, he'll usually start in my office because he knows that's where that type of policy decision will wind up.

Then, in addition, I have a substantial responsibility in the area of communicating to the accounting profession what we are thinking in the accounting area. In that connection I do quite a lot of talking. I guess I give somewhere between 50 and 70 speeches a year and make appearances on panels and other things of that sort. Then I'm also involved as an advisor in connection with the Commission's enforcement activities. Whenever the Commission has an enforcement problem which relates to financial statements, they will generally ask my advice before taking any action. Therefore, I will first work with the Division of Enforcement as a case is being developed and I will secondly advise the Commission on the accounting issues and make recommendations regarding the actions they might take.

*From *Management Accounting,* May 1975, pp. 19–23. Reprinted by permission of the publisher.

Is there any set term for the office of Chief Accountant?

BURTON: I am appointed by the Commission and serve at the pleasure of the Commission so there is no set term. I am the fifth Chief Accountant in the Commission's 40 years. The office hasn't turned over very frequently.

How does the Commission hammer out proposed disclosure regulations?

BURTON: Well, I guess it's done in a number of different ways. In the first place, problems are called to our attention in different ways. Some are received internally through our review of registration statements and other filing documents. Some are called to our attention by individual registrants or by public accountants. Some are called to our attention by analysts. Occasionally they arise out of our enforcement activity. Sometimes it's a combination.

For example, take one of our most significant current proposals—the area of interim financial reporting. This is a problem which was called to our attention initially by a number of analysts who complained that there is not adequate information in regard to interim results. I had a couple of members of my staff serve as a task force to look at this problem. We also asked the Financial Executives Institute for some assistance and their committee on relations with the SEC put together a subcommittee headed by Al [Allan C.] Crane from A.O. Smith Corp., Milwaukee, and that committee gave us some input as to what they thought could be done and what would be difficult. We also heard from various public accounting firms.

This all happened in the stage when we were just thinking about the subject and, of course, one of my beliefs is that as we are thinking about a subject, I like to mention it in speeches and let the world know we're thinking about it so that we can get input from various people as to what can and should be done.

In addition, we had a number of enforcement cases where there were serious deficiencies in the interim reports. But I don't think this was an area that primarily arose out of abuse but rather out of a perceived need on the part of the investment community for better interim data, and, particularly, as the economy moved into a tight liquidity position the annual balance sheet seemed to many people just not to be sufficient.

Interest capitalization, a disclosure regulation which we put out last year, provides a somewhat different example. This problem was primarily called to our attention by two public accounting firms as a result of research which they did using the NAARS system [National Automated Accounting Research System] and also the pressure they felt from clients. They were concerned and we agreed that it appeared there was a danger that a new accounting principle would be adopted more or less by default in the face of high interest rates.

In addition, of course, the staff of my office and the staff of the Division of Corporation Finance are continually talking about disclosure problems. Both have responsibility in that area so that we often talk internally about problems as we see them.

Once a problem is identified, very commonly—and again there is not a single way of doing it—there will be a task force set up which includes representatives of my staff and representatives of the Office of Disclosure Policy in the Division of Corporation

Finance. The task force will start the process of developing possible regulations. In many cases, we conclude that perhaps nothing should be done. In other cases, we develop alternative approaches. We can, of course, exhort, as we did in the case of inventory profits and in the case of business uncertainty at the end of the year. We can propose disclosure rules, which may include amendments to Regulation S-X. There are various approaches we can take, but generally the task force will develop some proposals and the senior staff of the divisions will sit down and talk about the proposals and the areas where they are deficient.

During this period of time, we will also be talking with representatives of the accounting profession and the business community. As we go out and talk in various places we get a number of inputs and, finally, we will get to the point where we are prepared to recommend a proposal to the Commission for publication.

Sometimes some of the Commissioners will be involved earlier. For example, Commissioner Sommer is very frequently involved in disclosure proposals before they reach the stage of getting up to the Commission for action. He will do a lot of talking and discuss various ideas with the staff. Some ideas may be exposed in his public speeches.

If the Commission concludes a proposal is meritorious, they may make some modifications and then will approve it being issued for comment. There is then a comment period that runs 60 to 90 days. The staff reads and evaluates all the comments. In addition, the Commission's legal assistants read them all the comments. Some of the commissioners will read them all; some will read some of them. The staff summarizes the comments, indicates its responses and then recommends a final rule for adoption. Then presumably, it's adopted.

Do you hold public hearings on any of these issues?

BURTON: In some cases. It's not common, but, for example, on the subject of forecasts we held hearings. We are going to hold hearings on the subject of going private.

How big is the staff of the Chief Accountant?

BURTON: At the present time the staff of the Chief Accountant is 12 professionals. We are authorized to add one more this year so it'll be up to 13 professionals and four administrative. This group is basically policy oriented. In addition there are about 65 accountants in the Division of Corporation Finance who review registration statements and filings. I have what could be called staff authority for all accountants in the Commission because I have responsibility for accounting policies of the Commission. Nationwide there are between 100 and 125 accountants in the Commission.

How would you characterize the nature of the disclosure regulations since you've been Chief Accountant? Is there one single objective or is there a series of objectives on the part of the Commission?

BURTON: I think the objective is to give investors more analytically-oriented information so that they can develop a better understanding in depth of what is going on, while at the same time putting upon management a responsibility to provide the average investor a textual analysis of what's going on. We have adopted a number of disclosure rules in the area of leases, tax expense, analysis of short term borrowing, interest capitalization and a number of others where we have asked for substantially more detailed information, primarily oriented toward the person who wants to devote a lot of time studying the annual report and getting the information out of it. Then, in Accounting Series Release (ASR) No. 159 we have also required a substantial explanation of what is deemed most important by management through the vehicle of what we call management's discussion and analysis of the summary of earnings. I guess I would say if I were to identify the thrust of SEC actions, it's in the direction of what we characterized as differential disclosure, more detailed information for the analyst, for the professional; better summarization for the average investor.

What do you hope will be the long term effects of these disclosure regulations?

BURTON: In a broad sense we hope it will contribute to a more efficient capital market. That's a very broad motherhood-type objective but a very real one in terms of what we are trying to achieve. The way in which we hope that will be achieved is first by giving investors more confidence that they are getting the whole story and second by encouraging the development of better tools of analysis and more responsibility on the part of the professional analyst to understand what's going on. We think that by giving them better data we can encourage them in the direction of doing a better job, thus leading, we hope, to more effective capital markets.

Some corporate officers have stated that disclosure requirements imposed within the last couple of years entail added costs to business in a time of business downturn.

BURTON: I think there's no question they have entailed added costs and we don't deny that. The difficulty is in how you weigh costs and benefits. The business community tends to see the costs, and the benefits are less clear to them because the costs are of an immediate short run nature; the benefits are of a longer term nature associated with a better capital market. As businesses and the market begin to turn up at some point, we will have built a sound basis for continued confidence. I think that our disclosure requirements may involve a substantial one-time cost, but their incremental cost is not very large once they become built into the information system.

Chairman Ray Garrett, Jr., in one speech hails the evolution of the CPA from an examiner of books to a continuous partner in reporting. Isn't this an indication of a lack of confidence in the internal accounting staff?

BURTON: I think the Commission does not have any lack of confidence in the internal accounting staff. I think it believes that professional accountants whose principal professional skill goes to public reporting and measurement, who do it in a large number of companies, and who have a great deal of experience with it are likely to be able to make a significant contribution to the quality of public financial reporting, and therefore, it is appropriate to place upon them a responsibility in this decision. Further, in today's legal environment, it appears that the CPA is perceived as jointly responsible because he gets sued just as much as management does where there are deficiencies. As a practical matter, therefore, it seems to us, he is a partner in the reporting process.

Could you outline the SEC's working relationship with the FASB?

BURTON: I think it's very good. I believe that the objectives of the FASB and the SEC are identical. They are both concerned with better financial reporting and I think our relationships are good. We are in frequent communication. We discuss our problems with each other and I think that we are working well together. For instance, a problem came up from a registrant filing dealing with early extinguishment of debt and how it should be accounted for. We thought it was a problem beyond that one registrant. We had seen it in a number of different cases. The matter was referred to the FASB with a request for prompt action and the FASB took prompt action.

They've also put some of our longer term concerns on their agenda such as interest capitalization, and business combinations. These have been items which we, as well as others, have urged them to put on their agenda. I personally think in the financial reporting world there is more than enough for us all to do. I think, basically, an active SEC is beneficial to the standards board in that it pushes them a little bit, which I believe is useful. As long as this activism is not in different directions from the standards board but is complementary and supportive, it should serve to improve financial reporting.

Do you foresee any time when the SEC would be setting accounting standards?

BURTON: No, I don't believe so. I think that we now have an active role in the broad areas of disclosure and financial reporting, and it comes into accounting in a number of respects, but I see no reason to think that the SEC is going to become the center of accounting principles in the foreseeable future. I think our system which has been one of reliance upon the accounting profession has worked well. Some people have said not fast enough, but I think right now there is evidence it is working pretty rapidly.

What action do you think the Commission will take as to forecasts, if any at all, this year?

BURTON: Well, I would suspect that by the 1st of April we will have published for comment a series of proposed rules and releases which the staff is now actively working on. I would expect that these rules and releases would largely implement the statement of policy that was issued two years ago. They will not, as they are currently being developed, mandate forecasts. They will permit them under certain controlled conditions. They will attempt to provide certain protections to those who forecast as long as they fulfill certain responsibilities. I would guess that the only major change from the statement of policy will be that the proposals will no longer prohibit the association of experts with forecasts. The statement of policy said that there will be no expertising permitted in the forecasts. I think that probably we will allow expertising to the extent people want to, subject again to certain constraints.

You are on record as opposing supplemental general price-level adjusted financial statements. What is your alternative?

BURTON: I think that the article that I wrote in *Business Week* [Nov. 30, 1974] suggested that certain replacement cost data would seem to me to be more meaningful than data based on price-level adjusted historical costs. If you are going to deal with inflation, it seems to me, you have to move away from historical costs—and the general price level adjusted figure is merely an adjusted historical cost figure. I think if we are going to move in the direction of supplemental data, it would be more desirable to move in the direction of replacement cost data rather than general price level adjusted data, although there is something to be said for moving in both directions since they are not mutually exclusive.

I would anticipate that we would put out some proposals for certain replacement cost disclosure and allow comments to be made. This would be in addition to what the FASB is proposing [see Selection 70, pp. 223-224].

Are you particularly concerned about the possible problem of a lack of objectivity insofar as replacement costs are concerned?

BURTON: No, I think it's do-able. I think there is some lack of objectivity but I would guess that estimates there can be made every bit as objectively as estimates that deal with the economic life of assets and things of that sort which are estimated all the time. A number of companies have been doing it for a number of years and they found that it was do-able without undue costs and it provides some useful management information. I've heard from quite a few financial executives who feel that if they have to do something they should at least do something that gives them useful internal data, and the ones that talked to me seem to favor replacement costs. I suppose the other ones just aren't talking to me.

Regarding the proposed amendments to Regulation S-X calling for expanded interim reporting, do you think the requirement for inclusion of selected quarterly data in the notes to the annual financial report will lead to the CPA becoming more and more involved in the production of interim reports and to the actual certification of such reports?

BURTON: I don't believe it will lead to the certification of interim reports. I think it will lead to substantially greater involvement with interim reports and it will be beneficial for the same reason I believe CPA involvement is desirable in other respects. Again, I think it is not so much a question of CPA involvement to check on the management as it is CPA involvement to improve the general quality of interim reporting. I think that with auditor involvement there will be a far greater tendency to develop a better controlled system for interim reporting. There are certainly a number of companies today that make their interim estimates pretty casually and it seems to me desirable that we encourage these companies to develop better controlled systems for interim reporting.

What other areas is the SEC considering that will affect financial and management accounting?

BURTON: I would anticipate that we will do something this year on the subject of pension disclosure in coordination with the FASB. Interim reporting and replacement costs are going to be our two largest projects this year.

## QUESTIONS

1. How do disclosure problems come to the attention of the SEC chief accountant?

2. Elsewhere Dr. Burton has argued that the chief accounting responsibility of the SEC is for disclosure whereas that of the FASB is for measurement. Do you feel that these are overlapping responsibilities? Explain.

3. What are the duties of the SEC chief accountant?

4. Contrast the actions taken by and proposed for the SEC with those taken by and proposed for the FASB (in Selection 91).

# 94

# DEFENSE COST ACCOUNTING WIDENS ITS REACH*
Business Week

The annual report getting the closest scrutiny by accountants this month was issued by a tiny government regulatory agency, the Cost Accounting Standards Board. Although the CASB is not yet widely known to the public, many accountants and businessmen fear that it may one day dictate accounting principles for corporate shareholder reports.

On the surface, the realms of the public accountant and the CASB bureaucrat are poles apart. As the CASB's unpretentious 72-page second annual report to Congress shows, the board was set up in 1970 to create uniformity and consistency in the way companies estimate and account for the costs of producing tanks, planes, and other products under most negotiated defense contracts. CASB rules may be applied to such minutiae as pinpointing the costs of services of senior engineers from those of junior ones. Public accountants, on the other hand, concern themselves with the big picture—whether management's stockholder reports are a "fair" presentation of the financial results of the enterprise.

The board's first two rules, enacted last year, were innocuous enough. "They were motherhood kind of things that said, in effect, don't try to cheat the government," quips one accountant. But the CASB has its eye on bigger game. Recent work projects on depreciation, pension plan costs, and capitalization of assets have moved the CASB into the backyard of the commercial accounting sector. The Financial Accounting Standards Board . . . is delving into similar issues.

## THE COMPLAINTS

"The potential for conflict and confusion is of extreme concern to us," says a controller for a big government equipment supplier. "Just how many different

*From *Business Week,* Sept. 1, 1973, pp. 40 and 44. Reprinted by permission of the publisher.

accounting rules and objectives are we going to be subjected to by these proliferating bodies?" And he complains: "It's getting to the point that, in addition to keeping books for the IRS and books for the shareholders, we'll be keeping another set for the CASB."

But what worries some defense contractors even more is that their carefully guarded cost data may not be kept confidential. Last week, a federal court in Washington ruled against lawyers working for Ralph Nader who sued the CASB to make public certain corporate cost accounting records filed with the board. The companies argue that disclosure would reveal trade secrets and destroy their ability to compete. Though they lost in the lower court, the Nader group is appealing.

The CASB's first rules—particularly one on allocation of home office expenses—are too detailed to suit many corporations. "Some good can come of cost accounting standards," concedes Russell Cooke, director of contract practices for Sperry Rand Corp. "But CASB shouldn't be built with the delicate tracery of a Taj Mahal."

The agency's jurisdiction has also stretched far beyond negotiated defense contracts. The General Services Administration has amended the federal procurement regulations to apply CASB rules to practically all nondefense contracts with the government. Thus, the CASB report notes, an agency advisory committee that is set up to include the Defense Dept., GSA, and the National Aeronautics & Space Administration now also includes representatives from Health, Education & Welfare and the Transportation Dept.

The CASB says that it has no intention of superseding private accounting rule-making groups or bumping heads with the Securities & Exchange Commission, which has ultimate authority to set accounting rules for public companies under the securities acts. But cost accounting is so central to corporate financial record keeping that CASB actions are bound to have an impact on other accounting areas.

## THE CASB'S MAKEUP

Its five-man board represents a cross-section of the government-business fraternity. The chairman is Elmer B. Staats, the Comptroller General. Other members include two practicing accountants—Herman W. Bevis, former senior partner of Price Waterhouse & Co., and Robert K. Mautz, an Ernst & Ernst partner. Also on the board are Charles A. Dana, director of government accounting controls at Raytheon Co., and Robert C. Moot, vice-president of Amtrak and a former Assistant Defense Secretary and the department's controller.

Heading the CASB's day-to-day operations is tough-minded 48-year-old Arthur Schoenhaut, the CASB's executive secretary, former deputy controller of the Atomic Energy Commission. He, like the board, refuses to be pinned down on what the boundaries of the cost accounting field are. And while the CASB wins praises from many for its willingness to take suggestions from outsiders and to keep them informed of its activities, it takes every opportunity to assert its independence.

"Undoubtedly," says Schoenhaut, "one reason the board was created is that the accounting profession ignored the subject of cost accounting. The government stepped into that vacuum."

The vigor with which the board's highly regarded 22-man professional staff delves into sensitive accounting issues creates a continuing tension between the CASB and accountants for defense contracting companies. A current project, for example, involves establishing "objective" standards governing the methods of depreciation that contractors can use. The traditional view is that companies should be able to set their own depreciation policies. So long as they are consistently followed, most policies need only be justified to the IRS.

"The staff looked into it," says Schoenhaut, "and was astonished to find that companies really can't justify the depreciation methods they use. The thing that is really incredible is that many are using one method for tax purposes and another for book purposes with no logic at all."

The question of what kind of accounting companies can use on their own books—from which shareholder reports are developed—seems squarely in the province of the SEC and the private rule-making bodies. While decisions that the CASB reaches on depreciation policies, for example, would only apply to government contracts, smaller companies exclusively engaged in government work might find it too expensive to keep another set of books. They may choose to follow CASB rules in reporting to shareholders, even though it might lead to distortions.

"The board is really too new to have had all that much impact yet," says Donald Trawicki of Touche Ross & Co., who serves on the CPAs' liaison committee to the CASB. But he quickly adds: "It's inevitable that there will be overlapping. The things they do will have implications far beyond what they were set up to do."

## QUESTION OF DETAIL

Already some contractors are being asked by their auditors why they do not keep the same kind of detailed records for their regular books that they have to use to estimate costs of contracts under CASB rules. The question of whether the CASB intended for a contractor's regular books to be kept in the same detail now is under study by the board, and it may soon issue an interpretation of its rules.

"Questions of implementation and interpretation are of real concern to us right now," admits a staff member of the Financial Executives Institute, a private organization of corporate specialists. "Admiral Rickover once said the government could save $2-billion a year by having a CASB. Well, what about the costs of settling the controversies that will arise over CASB pronouncements? I don't think anybody has seen that $2-billion saving yet."

Still, the board's most important impact on business accounting seems likely to come through its influence on basic accounting theories. A central problem that is important, not only to the government but to private accountants and the SEC, is that of "allocation"—the spreading of general and administrative expenses to different products and divisions of a company. The issue has become increasingly important with the rise of complex conglomerate corporations and the advent of SEC rules requiring breakdowns of sales and revenues by major lines of business.

Today, many companies avoid full disclosure by arguing that it is impossible to make allocations of overhead to each business area. John C. Burton, the SEC's chief accountant, says that it is "not inconceivable" that CASB work on the allocation problem might eventually be used by the SEC to obtain fuller disclosure.

While the CASB may some day hold considerable sway over accounting thought, there remains a fundamental difference between objectives. The CASB's task boils down to protecting the government and, some say, saving it money on contracts, while the job of the SEC and the accounting profession's FASB is to protect and enlighten shareholders and investors. And this is the root of the wariness many accountants feel toward the CASB's growing influence. Some complain that the CASB is pushing a "full costing" concept too far. In the case of general and administrative expenses, some of the costs would be allocated to unfinished work and carried into inventory rather than written off immediately. That practice is not permitted for such costs under generally accepted accounting principles in shareholder reports.

## THE PRESSURES

CASB pressure on the accounting profession and private industry will continue to mount. The board has put out a long list of issues that it intends to explore. . . . One subject, capitalization of leased equipment by lessees, which was part of a rule proposal, has been put aside to give the Financial Accounting Standards Board time to deal with it. But the pressure can move both ways. The CASB is under pressure from business to restudy the portion of an existing rule on allocating state and local taxes. Executives say that such a detailed breakdown is impossible or prohibitively expensive and time-consuming to make.

Still, an open confrontation between the CASB and the business community does not seem imminent. And as for the accountants' rulemakers, relations between the FASB and the CASB have been cordial and cooperative. "The staffs interact," Schoenhaut explains, "and everyone understands that it wouldn't serve the public interest to have different rules established unless there was a rational reason."

## QUESTIONS

1. What is the CASB? Why was it set up?

2. Use the depreciation method issue to illustrate how CASB decisions may have an impact on financial statements?

3. What is the overhead allocation issue, and why is it a particularly bothersome one for accountants?

# 95

## AN INTRODUCTION TO THE COST ACCOUNTING STANDARDS BOARD*

Robert K. Mautz

To those who are not familiar with the Cost Accounting Standards Board, a number of questions come readily to mind:

What is the Cost Accounting Standards Board?
What does it do?
How does it operate?
What has it done so far?
What has been the response to its work?
What is it likely to do in the future?

Let me try to respond to each of these questions as best I can. You will appreciate, I am sure, that I respond only for myself and not for other members of the Board or of the staff. Work with the CASB is a new kind of activity for me and a very interesting one. Participating in an effort of this kind from its very inception has opened my eyes to problems and possibilities that I might otherwise never have recognized.

### WHAT IS THE CASB?

The CASB is a five-man Board created by and responsible to the Congress of the United States. Thus, the Board is in the legislative branch of the Federal Government and serves in a limited way as something of an extension of the Congress. It is charged as follows:

The Board shall from time to time promulgate cost-accounting standards designed to achieve uniformity and consistency in the cost-accounting principles followed by defense contractors and subcontractors under Federal contracts.

The Comptroller General of the United States, Mr. Elmer Staats, is by law the Chairman of the Cost Accounting Standards Board, and he appoints the other four members, one of whom is to be representative of industry, one must be appointed from an agency or department of the Federal Government, and two chosen from the accounting profession. Members are appointed for four-year terms and serve on a part-time basis. The Board is adequately funded and has an excellent staff of 22 professionals plus clerical and secretarial help.

The staff is headed by Mr. Arthur Schoenhaut, the Executive Secretary, who is assisted by a general counsel and four project directors. The staff is competent, enthusiastic, and dedicated. A question often raised ... is whether a

*From *The Ohio CPA,* Winter 1974, pp. 36–42. Reprinted by permission of the publisher.

part-time Board can keep up with and control a full-time staff. In my opinion it can and at the present time is doing so. I believe we have successfully worked out in an informal but highly effective way the respective responsibilities of the Board and the staff. Each of us recognizes what these responsibilities are and our operating procedures respect the essential difference between the Board's obligations and those of the staff.

## WHAT DOES THE CASB DO?

As indicated in the quotation above, the Board has a fairly narrow range of responsibility. Its mission is to promulgate cost accounting standards designed to achieve uniformity and consistency in the cost accounting principles followed by defense contractors and subcontractors under Federal contracts. Our assignment is sufficiently specific that we have felt no need to either undertake ourselves or ask others to develop for us a statement of objective or purposes.

Negotiated defense contracts represent a narrow but well-defined portion of the total economic activity in this country. We have neither responsibility nor authority beyond that range. Nevertheless, the full impact of our promulgations may well extend further than provided for in the enabling legislation. Some government agencies have decided that they will rely upon our cost accounting standards for all contracts, defense or civil. Some state governments have suggested that they too may decide to use our standards, and we continually receive comments from contractors to the effect that they hope to avoid "two sets of books." In other words, they would like to be able to use the standards we promulgate for both their government and commercial business. Thus, it seems likely that over time our standards may have a significant impact upon cost accounting generally.

In a sense this is a new activity for the government. For the first time, a governmental body is seriously engaged in the development and promulgation of accounting standards. Other bodies have this power, of course, but few of them have chosen to use it. We have very little alternative. It is our specific assignment and we must get on with it. It is a new activity in another sense also in that for the first time the formerly private preserve of internal accounting rules and regulations has now become subject to outside authoritative requirements. Although a great deal of attention has been given to accounting principles for external financial reporting, almost no previous attention has been given to such internal accounting as cost determinations. We might go one step further. Note that our standards are concerned with contracts rather than with profits for a period. Thus we must focus in on specific cost objectives, the cost of contracts, in a way that general financial accounting has never had to be concerned.

## HOW DOES THE CASB OPERATE?

The Board meets about one day a month, generally for a single day although we have had longer meetings. At a typical meeting, all members of the Board, the Executive Secretary, our legal counsel, and the four project directors will be present. Other members of the research staff will join us when specific subjects with which they are concerned are under discussion. The meeting generally begins with a review by the Executive Secretary of the activities of his people since the last meeting. This includes a report of any special meetings with representatives of professional or industry associations and government agencies, speeches given, meetings attended, and the progress of major research projects now under way.

Any requests for exemptions from our standards will be considered and disposed of. I might say that although we are granted authority by law to exempt contractors from the standards we establish, we are reluctant to do so. We have had requests to exempt certain industries and certain classes of contractors. Our approach has been to refuse to make blanket exemptions with respect to an industry or a group of contractors, or a general exception to a specific standard. We review such requests on a case by case basis and grant exemptions only when we feel that the best interests of the government are so served.

Any proposals by the staff to undertake a new research project will come before the Board for a decision. We will hear reports on research in progress and will review data that have been collected by previous research efforts. If the staff has a proposed standard far enough along that it wishes to expose the standard, that proposal will be given adequate attention for the Board to decide whether to expose. Standards previously exposed on which comments have been received will be brought up for review of the comments and suggestions by the Board members for any modification of the draft standard. Because we have now been in operation for something over two years, we may at any meeting have all of these matters before us plus a proposal by the staff for the actual promulgation of a standard—which we look upon as our most significant action. Finally, we will have reports on reactions to standards promulgated previously.

Our meetings are rather informal, although of course we have an agenda and keep careful minutes which are a matter of public record. Some matters lead to lengthy and intense debate among Board members and between Board and staff members. No one feels inhibited in expressing his views, but everyone is expected to defend them with something more than an emotional argument.

## PROCEDURE FOLLOWED IN DEVELOPING STANDARDS

Another way of looking at what we do is to consider the procedure we follow in developing a cost accounting standard. Proposals for introduction of a new subject for study come from the staff in the form of a staff paper presented to the Board. The Board will consider this proposal and either accept or reject the proposal. If approved, the staff then commences research, generally with a library study to determine what materials are already available on the topic and to screen out those which are not particularly useful.

At the same time that the library study is commenced, or shortly thereafter, a number of visits to contractors' plants or offices will be scheduled. Staff members will call upon contractors and engage in intensive discussions with them as to the problems and possibilities of establishing a standard on the topic selected. After a number of such visits and completion of the library study, the staff will attempt to identify the major and subsidiary issues involved in developing a standard on the subject. This identification of issues will serve as the basis for preparing a questionnaire, a discussion outline, or perhaps an interview guide to be used in obtaining additional data from contractors, professional associations of accountants, trade associations, consultants, and others who have indicated an interest in participating in the work of the Board.

On the basis of such information, the staff will draft a standard in as close to what it believes to be final form as possible, and will discuss this draft at length in staff meetings. The staff's draft standard may then be circulated to a limited number of contractors in order to obtain their reaction.

Up to this point, the Board has taken no active part in the research other than to approve the topic for study. At any time, however, the staff feels free to bring to the Board a working paper for discussion purposes and to seek guidance and advice from the Board. On the other hand, unless the staff feels this is necessary, it has the responsibility and the freedom to carry its research forward without specific Board approval of each step in the process.

At some point in time, the staff will feel that it has gone as far as it can with its research and that it has a staff draft of the proposed standard which it would like to expose on a wider basis and in a more formal fashion. At this time, the Executive Secretary will bring the standard to the Board and recommend to the Board that the standard be published in the *Federal Register*. We regard publication in the *Federal Register* as a part of our research procedure. Nevertheless, we also regard it as a very important step and the Board will discuss the proposed standard at some length before approving publication. Approval for publication, however, does not commit the Board members to any specific point of view. Our purpose in this exposure is to get a maximum reaction to the draft from contractors, government representatives, and others.

As you know, the *Federal Register* is distributed widely, but in additon our staff takes the precaution of sending a copy of any issue of the *Register* containing a proposed standard to a lengthy mailing list of companies and people who have indicated an interest in our work and requests them to comment. Our practice is to allow a period of at least 60 days for comment. We have been gratified by the interest shown in our work and the usefulness of the comments received. Some of those who respond do so at length and with great care and we find their statements very useful in pointing out to us aspects of the topic, including illustrations of the proposed standard's impact upon their work, that we might not have considered otherwise.

The staff prepares a memorandum for the Board summarizing the comments received and its evaluation of them. In addition, each member of the Board receives a copy of each letter, and I am confident that each one of us reviews all of these. Based upon the comments received and its evaluation of them, the staff will modify or otherwise revise the standard as necessary and bring it to the Board at a subsequent meeting for further discussion. By this time the Board members will have read the comments as well as the staff summary and we will engage in a lengthy and intensive discussion leading to a decision as to whether we should now promulgate or whether additional research or rewriting of the standard is necessary. Ultimately, of course, we either reject the proposed standard or promulgate it. Promulgation is accomplished through a second publication in the *Federal Register*, this time with a statement to the effect that our intention is to make the standard effective as of a given date.

Accompanying this publication will be a point by point explanation of the Board's reaction to the comments submitted in response to our earlier publication.

Standards so promulgated are transmitted to the Congress where they remain for a period of 60 days of continuous session. Within that 60 days the two Houses of Congress can pass a concurrent resolution stating in substance that the Congress does not favor the proposed standard, rules, or regulations in which case, of course, they would be withdrawn or modified. Once this period passes without comment from Congress, the cost accounting standard has the full force and effect of law and it is then required to be included in negotiated defense contracts over $100,000.

Note that in this process the Board and the staff make every effort to give contractors and others concerned an adequate opportunity to express their views on the subject before us. For myself, I am convinced that the quality of our standards depends directly upon the quality of the research which we perform in developing the standard. We must have maximum interchange with those who will be living with our standards on a day by day basis in order that we can understand their problems and difficulties in meeting our requirements. This does not mean that we will withdraw proposed standards which contractors state they find offensive. Members of Congress and others take a keen interest in our work also, and insist that we demonstrate progress in achieving our assigned purpose. We are in no position to defer to every criticism. Yet failure on our part to be pragmatic in proposing only those standards that actually can be implemented would soon get us heavy criticism. We are engaged in a political process just as is the Congress itself, and we must be concerned with the actual problems of implementation as well as with what someone might view as theoretically sound cost accounting.

## ALTERNATIVE APPROACHES

Two possibilities seem apparent in selecting an overall approach for the kind of effort in which the CASB is engaged. One possibility is to devise, first of all, an overall statement of cost accounting concepts by which we would then be guided in meeting specific problems. In theory, this is something of an ideal approach. The alternative is to turn to specific problems, solving each one of these as best we can with the hope that ultimately, on the basis of our solutions to specific problems, we can extrapolate some overall guiding concepts.

As a matter of fact, our approach is actually somewhere between these two. Early in the life of the Board we spent a good deal of time attempting to establish an overall statement of concepts. In this we had significant help from the National Association of Accountants and others who were working on such a statement. We found that the first steps in developing an overall statement are intellectually exciting, interesting, and easy. When one comes close to the final wording, however, he begins to run into all kinds of difficulties of interpretation. I am confident that if we had continued on that course, striving to prepare an acceptable statement of basis concepts, we would still be involved in attempting to polish up the documents to the point where all could accept it.

We found it necessary, therefore, to turn our attention to specific problems. This is not to say that we have no conceptual foundation for our standards. Indeed we do have an internal document on which we are substantially in agreement and which serves quite well, operationally, as a guide to the solution of most problems. We are not ready to expose it for general comment for two reasons. First, because we would have differences within the Board on some specific statements and, secondly, because we think that we would get questions and criticisms to such an extent that we would be forced to spend far too much of our limited time in responding to such criticism when we should be getting on with the task of devising standards.

We are being very pragmatic about this. We think we have made sufficient progress in agreeing on concepts that we are unlikely to find ourselves in an inconsistent position on any significant subject. At the same time, we see no need to expose ourselves to the risk of criticism by those who would prefer a different statement of concepts. Hopefully, as we gain more experience with our internal statement of concepts, and in implementing it through cost accounting standards, we may be able to develop and publish such a statement. As a partial step in this direction, the Board published in March of 1973 a "Statement of Operating Policies, Procedures & Objectives" which, although not a complete statement of concepts, does give some indication of the fundamentals behind the Board's standards.

## WHAT HAS THE BOARD DONE TO DATE?

Within a year of its appointment, the Board sent to Congress a package which included a proposed contract clause to be included in all negotiated defense contracts, a disclosure statement in the form of a questionnaire requiring contractors to describe the cost accounting practices which they follow in proposing, administering, and settling contracts, and two cost accounting standards. The first standard called for consistency in the cost accounting practices followed in proposing, administering, and settling contracts. The second standard called for the avoidance of double counting in determining the total cost on a government contract, i.e., every item of cost is to be considered either as a direct or as an indirect cost and allocated accordingly so that no contract would be charged directly with its full share of a certain kind of cost and then have allocated to it on an indirect basis additional costs of the same type and for the same purpose.

Since that time, three additional standards have been promulgated:

#403—Allocation of Home Office Expenses to Segments
#404—Capitalization of Tangible Assets
#405—Accounting for Unallowable Costs

These standards have all been accepted by the Congress and are in force. . . . In addition, the Board has on its active agenda possible standards concerning depreciation, standard costs, and the allocation of overhead costs to contracts, accounting for scrap, accounting for pensions, determination of a cost accounting period, accounting for inventory and other subjects.

## WHAT HAS BEEN THE RESPONSE TO THE BOARD'S WORK?

Early opposition to the Board has changed to a relatively graceful acceptance of the inevitable. As mentioned earlier, we have received exceptionally good cooperation from industry and others, and this greatly facilitates the work of the Board. Without question, most contractors would prefer that the Board not exist at all. No doubt some of the government agencies we serve feel about the same way. Others criticize us because we are not moving rapidly enough. Although there is genuine concern and a continuing fear that we may become unduly restrictive in narrowing the range of acceptable cost accounting practices, I think the feeling, on balance, is that we have developed a working relationship with industry and others which at least permits a full exchange of views.

## WHAT WILL THE BOARD DO IN THE FUTURE?

What the future holds for the Board and for industry is the $64 question. Again, I speak only for myself, but I would summarize it something like this. The Cost Accounting Standards Board does exist. The Congress feels that cost accounting standards for negotiated defense contracts are necessary and desirable, so whatever the composition of the Board, such standards will emerge. The present members of the Board accepted their assignments voluntarily and with the thought that they could make an honest contribution to government contracting if they could establish cost accounting standards which were clearly understandable to all concerned. The pressures on the members of the Board are such that they must continue to issue standards, standards that can be applied without working excessive hardships on anyone.

I don't think the Board will do much pioneering in cost accounting theory. Neither do I think it will retreat from its obligations. We are five relatively ordinary, decent human beings with a variety of experience and with a very difficult assignment. If you were in our position, what kind of help would you like to have in the performance of that assignment? If you will give that question a little thought and then act accordingly, and if we will continue to strive to be as responsive as we can, the process of establishing cost accounting standards for negotiated defense contracts should not develop into an intolerable burden for any of us.

EDITORS' NOTE: Since this article was written, the CASB has issued the following additional standards: #406—Cost Accounting Period; #407—Use of Standard Costs for Direct Material and Direct Labor; #408—Accounting for Costs of Compensated Personal Absence; #409—Depreciation of Tangible Capital Assets; #410—Allocation of Business Unit General and Administrative Expense to Cost Objectives; #411—Accounting for Acquisition Costs of Material; and #412—Composition and Measurement of Pension Cost.

As of Summer 1975, the following topics were on the CASB Agenda: (1) allocation of manufacturing, engineering, and comparable overhead; (2) direct materials not incorporated in contract end items; (3) cost of capital; (4) direct and indirect charging; (5) independent research and development and bid and proposal costs; (6) standard costs for service centers and overhead; (7) termination accounting; (8) deferred incentive compensation; (9) other labor-related costs; (10) current-value or price-level accounting; (11) special facilities; and (12) terminology.

## QUESTIONS

1. What does the CASB do?
2. How does the CASB operate?
3. Contrast Dr. Mautz's views on setting rules by the CASB with those of Mr. Armstrong for the FASB (Selection 91).

## SELECTED BIBLIOGRAPHY

Mautz, Robert K., "The Other Accounting Standards Board," *The Journal of Accountancy*, February 1974, pp. 56-59.

Mayer, Harry O., "Cost Accounting Standards," *Management Accounting*, October 1974, pp. 17-20.

Rayburn, Frank R., "The Cost Accounting Standards Board," *The Accountant's Magazine*, August 1975, pp. 273-276.

# 96
# THE WORK AND PURPOSE OF THE INTERNATIONAL ACCOUNTING STANDARDS COMMITTEE*
International Accounting Standards Committee

## THE ORIGINS

The first steps in the development of international accounting standards were taken in 1966 when the President of the Institute of Chartered Accountants in England and Wales visited the United States of America and Canada and obtained the agreement of the Presidents of these two bodies to set up a three-nation study group (Accountants' International Study Group—AISG) to make and publish comparative studies of the accounting problems in the three nations. This study group did good work in the ensuing six years and contributed to greater harmonisation amongst the three countries; but it was recognised, at the time it was set up, that this was no more than the first step in a much larger concept. During this period accountancy bodies in other

*From *The Chartered Accountant in Australia,* February 1975, pp. 4—6. Reprinted by permission of the publisher.

parts of the world indicated that they would like to be associated with work similar to that initiated by AISG.

At the time of the International Congress of Accountants in Sydney in October 1972 it was clear that the mood of the professional bodies was ripe to take a further step forward. In Sydney therefore the United Kingdom bodies involved in AISG proposed to America and Canada that an international committee should be set up in order to formulate international accounting standards. In the surprisingly short period of nine months this came into effect on June 29, 1973, and the leading accountancy bodies in Australia, Canada, France, Germany, Japan, Mexico, Netherlands, United Kingdom and Ireland, and the United States of America committed themselves to this venture as Founder Members.

## FOUNDER MEMBERS AND ASSOCIATE MEMBERS

The Agreement made on June 29, 1973, provides for the admission of Associate Members, namely accountancy bodies of other countries which, if admitted to membership, undertake to adhere in all respects to the objects of IASC and to apply the same disciplinary procedures.

There has been a satisfactory response from accountancy bodies; fifteen have already been admitted as Associates and others have indicated that they will apply for Associate Membership in due course.

## THE OBJECTIVES

The objectives of IASC as set out in paragraph 1 of the Agreement are to formulate and publish in the public interest basic standards to be observed in the presentation of audited accounts and financial statements and to promote their worldwide acceptance and observance. By the same Agreement, the Founder and Associate Members have agreed to support these objectives by undertaking the following obligations:

(a)  to support the standards promulgated by the Committee;

(b)  to use their best endeavours

(i)  to ensure that published accounts comply with these standards or that there is disclosure of the extent to which they do not and to persuade governments, the authorities controlling securities markets and the industrial and business community that published accounts should comply with these standards;

(ii)  to ensure that the auditors satisfy themselves that the accounts comply with these standards. If the accounts do not comply with these standards the audit report should either refer to the disclosure of non-compliance in the accounts, or should state the extent to which they do not comply;

(iii)  to ensure that, as soon as practicable, appropriate action is taken in respect of auditors whose audit reports do not meet the requirements of (ii) above.

(c)  to seek to secure similar general acceptance and observance of these standards internationally.

It is important to observe the degree of authority which attaches to the issue of the definitive International Accounting Standards as and when published. The accounting profession cannot normally impose its views except upon its own members and the task therefore is to persuade by example, leadership and exhortation the classes of persons referred to above to support the standards. In most countries of the world the accounting profession has a prestige and standing which will be of great significance in achieving this task of persuasion. This explains, in this context, the use of the words "to use their best endeavours".

The obligations referred to are in a different category. In order to discharge these obligations, each Founder and Associate Member of IASC must put itself in the position that auditors in its country can be required to comply with the provisions and that appropriate action, which may be of a disciplinary character, can be taken if they do not comply. This is the most important and serious obligation which Founder and Associate Members of IASC have undertaken. Some professional bodies are already, by the terms of their constitutions, able to meet these obligations. In other cases, changes in their constitutions or of the laws prevailing in their countries are first necessary; in these cases they have undertaken to procure the necessary changes as soon as possible. This is the reason for the use of the words "to use their best endeavours".

The difficulty which the professional bodies will encounter in enforcing the standards upon their members should not be underestimated. It will involve an administrative burden which will be costly in time and money. None the less standards are of little value unless they are observed. All the professional bodies who are Founder or Associate Members will need to examine their procedures afresh in the light of the heavy responsibilities they have now undertaken.

The undertaking to formulate international standards was in itself a significant step forward in the history of the accountancy profession. Even more important was the undertaking by the professional bodies to agree to impose sanctions on their members who do not comply with the standards. It is believed that the accountancy profession is the first profession in the world which has undertaken not only to lay down international standards of this character but also to impose them upon its members, including the possibility of disciplinary proceedings.

## BASIC STANDARDS

Within each country, local regulations govern, to a greater or lesser degree, the issue of financial statements. Such local regulations include accounting standards which are promulgated by the regulatory bodies and/or the professional accountancy bodies in the countries concerned. These accounting standards, already published in many countries, differ in form and content. IASC takes cognisance of exposure drafts, or of accounting standards already in issue, on each subject and in the light of such knowledge produces an International Accounting Standard for worldwide acceptance. One of the objects of the formation of IASC was to harmonise as far as possible the diverse accounting standards and accounting policies at present in use in different countries.

In carrying out this task of adaptation of existing standards, and in formulating International Accounting Standards on new subjects, it is the intention of IASC as stated above, to concentrate on basic standards. It will therefore endeavour to confine the International Accounting Standards to essentials and not to make them so complex that they cannot be applied effectively on a worldwide basis. In the years to come it is to be expected that the International Accounting Standards issued by IASC will undergo revision and a greater degree of sophistication may then be appropriate.

## POSSIBLE CONFLICT WITH LOCAL STANDARDS

The International Accounting Standards promulgated by IASC do not override the local regulations, referred to above, which govern the issue of financial statements in a particular country. If the International Accounting Standards issued by IASC conform with local regulations on a particular subject no difficulty arises because the financial statements issued in that country which comply with the local regulations will automatically comply with the International Accounting Standards in respect of that subject. When International Accounting Standards differ from local regulations, the obligations undertaken by the Founder and Associate Members are designed to ensure that the financial statements and/or the auditor's report will indicate in what respects the International Accounting Standards have not been observed.

## THE WORK TO DATE

The programme of work which IASC has set itself is outlined later and every effort will be made to keep the work up to schedule. . . . The first definitive Standard on the Disclosure of Accounting Policies was approved in November 1974. This will be followed by the Standards on Inventories and Consolidated Financial Statements which are expected to be issued in mid and late 1975 respectively; exposure drafts on these two subjects were issued in late 1974.

The time required to undertake the necessary research work, to prepare and obtain the approval of the Committee to an exposure draft, to circulate the exposure draft worldwide, and then to assess the comments received and finally formulate the definitive standard is considerable. A minimum of twenty-four months is required for this purpose.

A point of interest in relation to the programme of work is the nature of the subjects. It will be seen that they have been carefully chosen so as to go to the root of most published accounts. If all these subjects are launched successfully in the next three or four years IASC will have made a major impact on the form and content of financial statements, worldwide.

## LIAISON WITH OTHER BODIES

In October 1974 the General Assembly of the Federation Internationale des Bourses de Valeurs (International Federation of Stock Exchanges) recommended that its member exchanges situated in countries whose professional accountancy bodies are either Founder or Associate Members of IASC should take steps to include in their listing requirements reference to compliance with standards issued by IASC.

In the United Kingdom, The Stock Exchange, London, issued a notice dated October 23, 1974, to the effect that listed companies are expected to prepare their accounts in conformity with International Accounting Standards. When IASC was set up in June 1973 the then Secretary of State of the Department of Trade and Industry promised support from Her Majesty's Government.

A liaison committee has been established comprising the Chairman of the Groupe d'Etudes (Monsieur Andre Reydel), the President of the Union Europeenne des Experts Comptables Economiques et Financiers (Dr. Erwin Pougin) and the Chairman of IASC. This will bring a close liaison with the accountancy bodies which have a

## Programme of Work

| | EXPECTED DATE OF APPROVAL FOR PUBLICATION | | STEERING COMMITTEE MEMBERS |
|---|---|---|---|
| | EXPOSURE DRAFT | DEFINITIVE STANDARD | |
| 1. Disclosure of accounting | January 1974 (issued) | November 1974 (approved) | France Netherlands U.K. and Ireland |
| 2. Inventories in the context of the historical cost system | July 1974 (issued) | July 1975 | Canada Japan Mexico |
| 3. Consolidated financial statements | November 1974 (issued) | October 1975 | Australia Germany U.S.A. |
| 4. Depreciation | April 1975 | April 1976 | Australia Canada France |
| 5. Information to be disclosed in financial statements | April 1975 | April 1976 | Germany Mexico U.K. and Ireland |
| 6. Translation of foreign accounts | July 1975 | July 1976 | Japan Netherlands U.S.A. |
| 7. Inflation accounting | October 1975 | October 1976 | Canada Israel Netherlands U.K. and Ireland |
| 8. Source and application of funds | January 1976 | January 1977 | Australia France South Africa |
| 9. Presentation of the income statement including extraordinary items, prior period adjustments, and accounting changes | April 1976 | April 1977 | Germany Japan U.S.A. |
| 10. Research and development | July 1976 | July 1977 | Canada Mexico New Zealand |

special interest in Europe. It is hoped that the work of IASC may, by reason of this association with the Groupe d'Etudes, be of some assistance to the Commission in Brussels in drafting directives on accounting standards, for example on the subject of Consolidated Financial Statements; it is too early to judge the impact at this stage.

Discussions have been held with the Chairman of the International Association of Financial Executives Institutes (IAFEI) . . . on international accounting standards and methods of financial reporting. As a result arrangements have been made to keep each other informed of activities of mutual interest.

Following the report on multinational companies submitted to the United Nations on May 24, 1974, by The Group of Eminent Persons, in which certain proposals were made for international standardisation of accounting and reporting, discussions have been held between the Secretary of IASC and the Special Assistant to the Under-Secretary General for Economic and Social Affairs at the United Nations. These discussions are continuing with a view to obtaining recognition of the work of IASC by the United Nations.

## CONCLUSION

Provided that the initial enthusiasm and thrust with which IASC was started is continued, its impact in the years to come will be important. It will take perhaps five to ten years before its full effects are recognised but after that they will increase each year. Accounts issued in every important nation of the world will comply with the standards promulgated by IASC or will disclose the extent to which there has been non-compliance. This will itself improve the presentation of accounts issued to the public; more information which is essential to an understanding of the accounts will be made available; there will be an increasing harmony in the accounting standards adopted worldwide; comparisons will be facilitated. Quotations on the Stock Exchanges and Bourses will make compliance with the standards a condition of quotation. Governments will recognise the importance of the standards and, where appropriate, will require compliance with them. In the result, company administration will be improved; auditors will do a better job; users of accounts will have more information; and shareholders and creditors will enjoy a greater degree of security and protection than is at present the case. The reputation of the accountancy profession will be enhanced.

EDITORS' NOTE: For further information on this subject, readers are referred to Selection 130. The ICCAP is to be replaced after a 1977 Munich conference with an International Federation of Accountants (IFA) whose membership will be open to communist countries.

## QUESTIONS

1. Who are the founding member countries of the IASC? Speculate on why these countries rather than others are founding members.

2. What impact does the IASC expect to have on accounting?

3. How are conflicts between international accounting standards and local regulations resolved?

## SELECTED BIBLIOGRAPHY

Cowperthwaite, Gordon H., "Building a Global Federation," *World*, Autumn 1974, pp. 54-55.

# 97
# A CRISIS OVER FULLER DISCLOSURE*
Business Week

The first law for accountants was not compliance with generally accepted accounting principles but, rather, full and fair disclosure, fair presentation and, if principles did not produce this brand of disclosure, accountants could not hide behind the principles but had to go behind them and make whatever disclosures were necessary for full disclosure. In a word, 'present fairly' was a concept separate from 'generally accepted accounting principles,' and the latter did not necessarily result in the former.

When U.S. Court of Appeals Judge Henry J. Friendly wrote those words in his landmark Continental Vending decision in 1969, he set off shock waves that are still shaking the accounting profession. All the ramifications of that statement are yet to be fully tested in the courts, but its message comes through loud and clear: Merely sticking to the rules will not keep an accountant—or his client—out of trouble.

Judge Friendly's interpretation of what it means when a certified public accountant puts his signature to a company's financial statement goes to the heart of the public accountant's problem: He makes his report to the management of the corporate client that hires him, but the statement that he attests to is relied on by others whose interests may be directly opposed to the corporate management—creditors, investors, government policymakers. What management considers fair presentation may be outright deceit from the standpoint of a potential lender or a disgruntled stockholder.

From the accountant's standpoint, he cannot win. Some stockholders, too, particularly the short-term traders, would like the auditor to put the best face on company reports to enhance the market price of the stock. This inherent conflict on disclosure is prompting some frustrated CPAs to insist that financial reports be prepared not just for stockholders, but for prospective investors as well.

The problem is complicated by the enormous complexity of modern business. Companies can operate in a dozen different countries and two dozen different industries. To reduce such complex operations to a simple balance sheet and consolidated income statment—even with supporting tables and pages of detailed

*From *Business Week*, Apr. 22, 1972, pp. 55–60. Reprinted by permission of the publisher.

footnotes—calls for sweeping simplification. It also calls for a high degree of faith in the company's own system of financial reporting and controls. No accounting firm can hope to count the last carton of rivets in the inventory of the Tanzanian subsidiary, and an accounting firm will be careful to put language in its attestation that says it did not. But who pays attention?

## THERE ARE NO PRECISE RULES

This is why the fair disclosure doctrine has thrown the accounting profession into a state of confusion, confrontation, and crisis. Accounting is not a precise body of rules covering every case that comes up. It is a set of general principles—some of them going back to the Middle Ages and the invention of double-entry bookkeeping—applied in the manner that the accountant on a particular job thinks appropriate. Inevitably, it contains a large component of personal judgment. Should a securities firm, for instance, value the securities on its shelves at the price it paid for them or the going market price? Or at liquidation value? A simple question, but the answer may determine whether or not the securities firm goes into default on New York Stock Exchange capital requirements. Naturally, the management will want to value at market when the price has gone up and at cost when the bottom has fallen out. Conservative accounting calls for carrying securities at the lower cost or market, but many CPAs contend that some estimate of long-term value should be made.

The rapid growth of the accounting business has put a new twist on this problem: It is harder and harder to find enough top-level, trained men who can make judgments of the sort that modern accounting demands. The steadily increasing number of corporations listed on one of the stock exchanges (which require an audit by outside accountants), plus the expansion of the accounting firms into new fields, has brought a bonanza in revenues. But it has put a severe strain on auditing manpower. Inevitably, this means a dilution of the total of real accounting talent a firm can command.

Public accounting has become a big business—and a growth business. Recent estimates put total domestic revenues of U.S. accounting firms at $2.5-billion a year. It also is a concentrated business. Eight big firms at the top—known as the Big Eight—together generate at least $1-billion of those revenues. These firms and their dozen or so nearest competitors have seen net billings double in the past five years—fed by a rapid expansion of management services that range from the design of information systems and data processing controls to pension planning and executive recruiting.

At the same time, CPA firms have been aggressively offering their audit, tax, and consulting services to sectors outside the industrial corporate milieu: to federal, state, and local governments, and to banks, insurance companies, hospital and health care agencies, labor unions, trade associations, churches, and universities. Growth has also been rapid in the international arena, with the larger U.S. accounting firms establishing offices of their own in major trading cities overseas, or entering into joint working ventures with large and prestigious British and Canadian CPA firms.

Such rapid growth has set up new potential conflicts. When a firm expands into a new area such as auditing big banks, as Peat, Marwick, Mitchell, Ernst & Ernst, and

Price Waterhouse have done, is there a conflict of interest created because the accountant audits both the bank and some of its corporate borrowers? Since the auditor has to offer an opinion as to the quality of loans in the bank's portfolio, will he reveal inside information obtained by examining the borrower's books?

## PUBLIC DISILLUSIONMENT

In this fast-paced, emotionally charged atmosphere of mergers and acquisitions, increasingly complex tax laws, and brand-new financing devices, accountants are caught more keenly than ever before between the pressures of serving their clients and their traditional public role as independent, objective auditors. Recent efforts within the profession to end some of the major accounting abuses, and to narrow accounting alternatives so that "like things look alike and unlike things look different," have been met with interfirm squabbling among the Big Eight, intense industry opposition, and political pressure from government.

When the CPAs' [former] rule-making Accounting Principles Board finally agreed after 10 years of debate that the investment tax credits could not be flowed through immediately to income, but would have to be spread out over the life of the new assets, corporate executives howled so loudly that Congress, with the Treasury Dept.'s backing, legislated an accounting rule to allow the immediate flow-through. And as more and more questions have arisen about the ability of present accounting principles to deliver full and fair disclosure in financial statements, the public has become disillusioned.

James J. Mahon, a top partner at the Big Eight firm of Coopers & Lybrand, explains the roots of the disillusionment this way: "First, we failed to perceive the growing cleavage between independent ownership and professional management; second, we were slow to recognize the emerging power of the institutional investor in the financial community; third, and perhaps the most important, we did not anticipate the public clamor for exactitude in financial reporting."

As a result, the accounting profession now has a brand of consumerism growing in its own backyard. A barrage of lawsuits by shareholders, creditors, and trustees, and complaints by the SEC have emerged from the drama of the past few years following the spectacular stock price dips, corporate bankruptcies, brokerage house failures, and other misfortunes. Suits against management have become commonplace, but these newer cases have an added dimension: They also include the company's outside accountant.

The complexity of modern business has produced devious and complicated new sets of shenanigans that have sometimes escaped the auditor: complex circular relationships in which a company sells off, at inflated prices, stock or real estate that is doing badly to a friend or officer just before the audit is performed and then later buys it back at the real market value, paying the "buyer" a fee for his service. Or selling a small piece of a large real estate holding at a high price to raise the value of the entire parcel. Or manipulating dividends in subsidiaries to make up for losses in operating income. Or issuing a bewildering variety of debentures with convertible features, warrants, or other "funny money" financing devices. . . .

## THE SEARCH FOR STANDARDS

For example, the [former] APB did not face up to requiring a corporation to consider the potential impact of convertible debentures on earnings per share until 1969, years after James J. Ling, an imaginative pioneer in financial strategy, started using them at Ling-Temco-Vought to acquire companies. And only late [in 1971] did it start probing the off-the-balance sheet financing of jet aircraft and other kinds of leasing devices. . . .

But even with [the FASB] a more responsive full-time board with a wider base of support, a more serious problem remains. When loopholes are closed and detailed rules are drawn up on an issue-by-issue basis, the result often is illogical, arbitrary, and inconsistent.

One source of discontent is APB opinion 17, on accounting for intangible assets or goodwill, issued in 1970. The board could never decide whether to let goodwill pile up as an asset on the balance sheet indefinitely or to insist that it be written off immediately against shareholders' equity. The result was a compromise no one was happy with. Now, the difference between what one company pays for acquiring another business and the net value of those assets—goodwill—must be written off over an arbitrary period of not more than 40 years. But conglomerates and others who piled up huge amounts of goodwill in the 1960s can still carry it unamortized on their books.

What constitutes fair presentation is still largely a matter of professional judgment. No rule can cover every contingency. What has been missing is an over-all, logical accounting framework—a broad set of goals or objectives. . . .

Nowhere are the implications of what is happening being studied more closely than behind the traditional wood-paneled doors or the modern sparkling glass partitions in the home offices of the Big Eight firms: Arthur Andersen; Ernst & Ernst; Haskins & Sells; Coopers & Lybrand; Peat, Marwick, Mitchell; Price Waterhouse; Touche Ross; and Arthur Young. Together, they audit more than 80% of the companies listed on the New York and American stock exchanges.

Just below the Big Eight in size is another group of 15 to 20 well-known national CPA firms. . . .

## THE BIG EIGHT DRAWS FIRE

Because the Big Eight firms audit the books of so many publicly held companies, they have been hit with the major lawsuits and with the publicity when something goes wrong. Arthur Andersen has had to defend its accounting practices in Four Seasons Nursing Homes, King Resources, and Black Watch Farms. Ernst & Ernst is named in the long and messy Westec suit. Haskins & Sells has been sued along with American Express in the wake of the "salad oil scandal" and after the brokerage house failure at Orvis Bros. Coopers was named in Mill Factors, R. Hoc, and Continental Vending. Peat, Marwick has had a score of complaints arising from Penn Central, National Student Marketing, and the recently settled Yale Express fiasco. Price Waterhouse is a defendant in Performance Systems actions. Touche Ross caught fallout from Revenue

Properties. And Arthur Young is involved in suits following troubles at Commonwealth United.

And it has been the Big Eight, too, that have moved the most aggressively into such tangential fields as consulting, often through mergers with smaller, specialized regional and local accounting firms. Like drummers with wagon loads of new wares, most of the big CPA firms are stocking a full line of management advisory services these days. Peat, Marwick will help clients find a new president or top financial officer, or tell top executives they should switch part of their pay into tax shelters. Coopers will help a company set up a new pension plan; Touche Ross and Ernst & Ernst will undertake detailed marketing plan strategy. Arthur Young will help a corporation defend itself against a takeover. .

But accountants are divided over where to draw the line on consulting to avoid conflicts—either in fact or in appearance—with their audit work.

Many Big Eight firms contend that they have provided management advice for clients since they were founded around the turn of the century. But consulting began to emerge as a separate area for CPAs in the mid-1950s and it mushroomed with the rise of the computer and its impact on accounting and records systems. Most firms moved quickly into the design, planning, and control of EDP and management information systems. But they also have picked up more and more of the old-line management consultant's offerings: executive search, pension planning, job evaluation and manpower planning, executive compensation, marketing analysis, organizational studies, and merger and acquisition work.

Most top partners quickly defend this array of services as "meeting client needs." Says Richard T. Baker, managing partner of Ernst & Ernst, a Big Eight firm that has been one of the most active in consulting: "Our attitude has always been that we really weren't giving clients service unless we helped them with their problems."

But for some CPAs, management service is fraught with potential hazards and conflicts. "The profession is going the route of conglomerates," growls Harvey E. Kapnick, Jr., chairman of Arthur Andersen. "They hate for me to say that, but they are." Kapnick is especially critical of executive recruiting, tax shelter, and acturial activities by CPAs. "there is absolutely no reason why we should grow just for the sake of growth," he insists.

Although there have been no major lawsuits involving consulting and auditing conflicts, Kapnick says flatly that "some day this is going to come right down around the neck of the profession." If that happens, accountants might lose all their consulting work, including their biggest, most lucrative non-audit, non-tax service: financial planning and computer control systems. "Somebody's going to say you've got to give up those extra services," Kapnick warns. "That's the risk involved."

In the recruiting area, that risk turns on answering questions like these: Can an auditor be critical of the abilities of a financial executive it recruited for the client? Does the CPA have the credentials to make such a critical appraisal in the first place? Is the financial executive, hired through the offices of the auditor serving as an executive recruiter, likely to fire the firm if it does not perform adequately?

Others argue that the accountant's independence can be maintained through elaborate quality control procedures for both auditing and consulting, and by focusing on consulting's quantitative aspects. Accountants should develop the numbers and present the alternatives, they say, but must insist that the clients make the final decision. Touche Ross, the youngest of the Big Eight firms, has heavily emphasized consulting since it was founded in 1947. Its managing partner, Robert Beyer, says: "If you, in effect, make the decision for management, you've lost your independence."

Most Big Eight partners recognize the inherent dangers in mergers and acquisition work, and they claim that their firms stop short of recommending actual takeovers or setting an appropriate offering price. "Things do go wrong," explains Ralph E. Kent, [former] managing partner of Arthur Young. "What if a company should buy another company at our urging and it turns out to be a dog? Then there certainly would be the appearance of an unwillingness on our part to be able to say at the next audit: 'By the way, that was a lousy acquisition you made, and now we want to write it off.' " . . .

## MORE ACTION FROM THE SEC

There is ample evidence to suggest that the SEC will be taking a more active role in other accounting areas as well. Under the Securities Act of 1934, the SEC is empowered to establish and enforce accounting rules. In practice, however, it has allowed the accounting profession to come up with appropriate standards. The SEC retains the ultimate enforcement power, and most accountants assert that the commission is the only body that can effectively enforce the rules. . . .

In the final analysis, despite all of the detailed rules and no matter how carefully an accountant's legal and social responsibilities and liabilities are defined, the ultimate quality of the financial statements, the fairness of their presentation, and their usefulness to the investor turns on the competence and independence of the individual professional auditor.

One thoughtful CPA looks at the role of the independent certified public accountant this way: "Accountants are too worried about service to the client. Most times they're too friendly with the client. I think there's simply got to be a mild adversary relationship there." And in that kind of critical relationship lies the public's best guarantee of full and fair disclosure.

EDITORS' NOTE: The chart that appeared with this article is Selection 23.

## QUESTIONS

1. What are the implications of Judge Henry J. Friendly's decision in the Continental Vending case in 1969?

2. What kind of problems have accompanied the rapid growth of the accounting business?

3. What has been the major basis for the discontent with APB Opinion 17?

4. Why is the management services function of public accounting firms one that is at least a potentially hazardous and conflictful one?

## SELECTED BIBLIOGRAPHY

Malloy, John M., J. Timothy Sale, and Eugene Willis, "Interim Financial Reporting," *The Ohio CPA*, Spring 1975, pp. 61-69.

Meonske, Norman R., "Accounting for Retail Land Sales," *The Ohio CPA*, Winter 1973, pp. 12-24.

Nelson, Carl L., "The Case for Decent Disclosure," *CA Magazine*, March, 1975, pp. 35-38.

Randall, Robert F., "Finally—Inflation Accounting," *Management Accounting*, November 1974, pp. 57-59.

Retz, David J., "Business Combinations: Pooling or Purchase?" *Management Accounting*, February 1973, pp. 45-46, 50.

# 98

# SETTING STANDARDS FOR SEGMENT REPORTING*

George C. Watt

Seven years ago, the Accounting Principles Board issued an advisory statement about segment reporting. At that time—as well as in subsequent years when I served on the APB—I was concerned about this important unresolved issue. I am still concerned. . . .

Since the APB issued its statement in 1967, two agencies of the federal government have gotten involved. The Securities and Exchange Commission has imposed narrow line-of-business reporting requirements on all registrants, reaching down to product lines. And the Federal Trade Commission has begun gathering detailed line-of-business data from corporations having substantial domestic manufacturing revenues based on the Standard Industrial Classification Code.

Against this background of growing government involvement, the APB's successor, the Financial Accounting Standards Board, has moved swiftly toward setting standards in this area. Only a few months ago, the FASB issued a discussion memorandum entitled "Financial Reporting for Segments of a Business Enterprise" and asked for comments. Price Waterhouse responded with a paper that outlined our firm's position on issues posed by the FASB.

In our paper, we stated our belief that information concerning segments of a diversified enterprise *should* be included in financial statements for a fair presentation of the results of operations. Why?

Many industries have characteristics that do not necessarily follow the trends of the economy. Individual markets—consumer, industrial, government—have individual sensitivities to changes in the general economy. At times, the principal products and

*From *Price Waterhouse Review*, Fall 1974, pp. 30—31. Reprinted by permission of the publisher.

services of many companies may attain and lose popularity contrary to the trend in their industry in general.

Segmented information permits the investor to assess external influences on specific segments of a corporation. For example, at any given time, a particular industry may appear to have a potential for high profits or a possibility of declining profits or increased government regulation. We know that organizations and product mixes are so complex that comparing segment information with that of other companies in similar activities may not be valid. Nevertheless, we believe comparative segment information is useful in indicating trends of a segment within a reporting company and the types of market risks to which the company is exposed.

Revenue and "profit contribution" of clearly separable, broadly defined industries or services should be presented for each major segment. What about common costs? We believe there should be no allocation of costs that are not objectively traceable, such as corporate general and administrative expenses, general research, institutional advertising, interest (except sales finance activities), and income taxes. We see little need for a complete or condensed segment income statement.

Each segment presented should be supplemented by disclosure of the names of the principal products or services. And, if they are not apparent from the product or service names, the market or markets in which they are sold should be disclosed, along with some indication of volume in the different markets. We believe information of this type is objectively determinable and would be meaningful to investors. However, if segments are too narrowly defined or further subdivided by geographical regions or product lines, the detailed disclosures might in some cases be valuable to competitors and harmful to the company. What's more, this information would probably require such arbitrary assumptions that the results would be of questionable value to shareholders.

There is little doubt that the single most pressing problem for the FASB is to develop a workable definition of a segment. The matter of disclosure of financial information by geographical areas is an entirely different subject—that is, quantifying risk of loss of assets, production facilities, or markets. Such information should not be included in a statement on segment reporting.

In our position paper, we conclude that the FASB should (1) specify a basis of segmentation and (2) define the significance of a segment by guidelines related to revenue, not to profit or loss.

## QUESTIONS

1. What is segment reporting?
2. What problems exist with specifying a segment?
3. Contrast Mr. Watt's position in regard to allocation with that presented by the CASB (in Selection 94).

# 99

## FIGHTING THE F.T.C. DOWN TO THE BOTTOM LINE*
David Burnham

A fierce battle between big business and the Federal Trade Commission is continuing right down to the wire.

At issue is the F.T.C.'s requirement that, starting Jan. 1, several hundred designated companies, all of them big, must submit detailed "line-of-business" reports on how they make their profits and how they spend their money on research and advertising.

The commission's original proposal has already been watered down under withering pressure from the business community, and a dozen of the companies involved are raising the ironic argument that the data will be "utterly meaningless" precisely because the F.T.C. did give in to the pressure.

Ever since the commission first proposed it, more than three years ago, the program has been the subject of a determined industry lobbying effort.

More than 200 of the 345 subject companies have formally requested the F.T.C. to abandon it. Their arguments: It will be too costly for individual business, it will not help the Government and it will give competitors confidential information.

Supporters of the program, however, argue that the profits and expenses of individual lines of business have been increasingly obscured in recent years as many companies have moved to diversify their product lines. They argue that this injures the economy by making it more difficult for investors to know where to invest their money, and for the Government to know if and where windfall profits are being realized.

In addition to helping trust busters pinpoint the best possible targets, the program also could affect legislation. If the line-of-business data showed, for example, that the average pharmaceutical company was spending far more money on sales and promotion than on research and development, remedial regulations might be proposed.

The names of the companies that must report have not been made public by this commission on grounds that the object of the program is to develop aggregate figures, not individual company data.

The *New York Times* has compiled a list of almost three-quarters of them, partly based on names gathered by an industry organization involved in the compaign to kill the program, and partly on the names of the 216 companies who asked the commission to abandon the program. The latter list was made available to Consumers Union, but only after it threatened to bring suit against the commission under the Freedom of Information Act.

Most of the known companies are on Fortune Magazine's list of the 500 largest industrial outfits in the country. From the F.T.C.'s point of view, they provide a representative selection of companies—some giant, some medium-sized—in major industry groups, such as oil, chemicals, publishing, automobiles, trucking, railroads and aircraft.

*From the **New York Times**, December 1974, pp. C1 and 4. Reprinted by permission of the publisher.

Since the F.T.C. sent the forms out to the 345 companies last summer, the brunt of the legal counter offensive on the program has been borne by 12 companies: the Aluminum Company of America, Armco Steel, Coca Cola, duPont, General Electric, General Motors, Goodrich, International Harvester, International Paper, Kraftco, Owens-Illinois and Union Carbide.

The central architect of the corporate argument has been Ira M. Millstein, a partner in the New York law firm of Weil, Gotshal and Manges.

Mr. Millstein wrote in a Nov. 15 memorandum that once the companies demonstrated that it was "impossible" to directly compare information derived from different companies, the F.T.C. "staff—instead of continuing to strive for comparability—totally abandoned the notion."

The commission staff, Mr. Millstein continued, "in an effort to get something, anything, on segments, told each company, virtually, 'Do what you can—anything you can.' "

By adopting this strategy, Mr. Millstein said, "it is true that the commission may now get numbers dealing with segments—but, those numbers will be so totally different in concept, origin and quality that to talk about aggregating and comparing them is utterly senseless, if not simply disingenuous."

While arguing that the information could not be averaged or aggregated for any useful purpose by the Government, however, the memorandum said potential business competitors would be able to take the averages and gain secret information about individual companies through sophisticated statistical studies.

Mark Silbergeld, an attorney in the Washington office of Consumers Union, said the argument of the corporations was inconsistent. "They can't have it both ways," he said. "They say the information is so good that it will let potential competitors get confidential information, but that on the other hand it will be so incomplete that it will be useless to the Government."

Mr. Silbergeld added, however, that in his view Mr. Millstein's analysis was partly correct.

"The commission has given in to business too much and the data is not as good as it should be. His memorandum will provide the F.T.C. and Congress an excellent blueprint on how to improve the program," Mr. Silbergeld said.

The Consumers Union lawyer noted that, judging from the names of the companies which have received the line-of-business form, it would seem that the commission had decided not to survey just the largest manufacturers in the major industries.

"We only have about two-thirds of those who have been asked to respond, but this sample suggests that the commission has decided to survey such areas as publishing, textiles, clothing, food and drugs and hospital supplies," he said.

In the publishing area, for example, the incomplete sample showed that those requested to file a line-of-business form included The New York Times, the Times Mirror, Time Inc., the Tribune Company, Gannett, Macmillan and Western Publishing.

Under the F.T.C. program, the companies are scheduled to begin filing their completed forms within the next month. The first reports due are those which cover a company's fiscal year which ended last June 30 or during the preceding 12 months.

The commission is expected to issue its final reply to motions to kill the program within the next few weeks.

The legal battle, however, probably will not end with the F.T.C.'s decision. One way or another, the question of whether the commission has the authority to require corporations to file line-of-business information will go before the Federal courts.

A courtroom ending would be fitting with the whole history of the reporting program. It has been a tremendous tangle from the start.

It began as a commission proposal in late 1970 to canvass all of the Fortune 500. This idea was squelched by the Office of Management and Budget, which has the final power of review over all Federal reporting requirements. That led, in turn, to the O.M.B. being stripped of its authority.

Senate liberals tacked an amendment onto the Alaska pipeline bill transferring the O.M.B.'s review power to the General Accounting Office. The Administration opposed the transfer but wanted the pipeline, so President Nixon signed the bill.

The G.A.O. subsequently approved the F.T.C. program, but said that the problem of definition concerning such matters as transfer costs "will make the initial responses unreliable, at best, in our judgment." It also estimated that the reporting paperwork would cost businesses substantially more than the F.T.C. had said.

The final tangle—before the present one—was over the F.T.C.'s budget. The Senate voted funds for a survey of 500 companies. The House version allowed for only 250. The end was a compromise which, ironically, wound up as President Nixon's last veto, because it was attached to a farm bill that he opposed.

## QUESTIONS

1. What is the nature of the conflict over "line-of-business" reporting between the FTC and several hundred companies?

2. Apply a "cost-benefit" approach to this problem. EDITORS' HINT: This means try to estimate the costs and the benefits associated with this program not only for individual companies and individual investors but for all society.

3. Explain the relationship between this issue and segment reporting (Selection 98) and the allocation problem (Selection 94).

## SELECTED BIBLIOGRAPHY

Baumler, J. V., "Line-of-Business Reporting: A Legal Basis," *Cleveland State Law Review*, Spring 1975, pp. 215-222.

# 100

## SIGNIFICANCE OF FORECASTS TO MEANINGFUL FINANCIAL DISCLOSURE*

Thomas L. Stober

### THE CONTROVERSY

Possibly the most controversial subject in accounting today is the question of reporting forecasted information. Presently, the American Institute of Certified Public Accountants' Code of Professional Ethics prohibits accountants from attesting to forecasts with the directive: "A member or associate shall not permit his name to be used in conjunction with any forecast of the results of future transactions in a manner which may lead to the belief that the member or associate vouches for the accuracy of the forecast."[1] The American Accounting Association provides an underlying reason for such a position in their Statement of Basic Accounting Theory by noting "Accountants generally refrain from reporting budgets relating to future periods to external users on the grounds that the information is not sufficiently verifiable, although it might be highly relevant to external users needs."[2]

However, in early February 1973, the Securities and Exchange Commission announced that it would no longer ban forecasted information in the statements of companies issued under federal securities laws. Disclosure was made optional, not mandatory, provided forecasted data was not made available to any parties as "inside information." The SEC also determined that at this time, forecasts were not to be independently audited.

But why was such a move made toward disclosure of forecasts? What information do they contain for members of the financial community? The purpose of this paper is to assess the significance of forecasts to the external users of financial statements and determine how meaningful disclosure of forecasts can be made.

### BENEFITS TO SHAREHOLDERS

Shareholders make two major types of decisions related to the stock of a particular company. The first type is a market oriented decision—to buy, sell, or hold shares of stock. The second type of decision is made when the shareholder has some opportunity to exercise control over the company's management (for example, in a proxy fight). Presumably then, for financial information to be significant, it must relate to these decisions.

*From *Beta Alpha Psi Newsletter,* Fall 1973, pp. 2, 4, and 6—7. Reprinted by permission of the publisher.

[1]Willingham, John J., Charles H. Smith, and Martain E. Taylor, "Should the CPA's Opinion Be Extended to Include Forecasts?" *Financial Executive,* v. 38, Sept. 1970, p. 80. Quoted from AICPA, "Code of Professional Ethics" (1967).

[2]Ibid., p. 88, quoted from AAA Committee to Prepare a Statement of Basic Accounting Theory, "A Statement of Basic Accounting Theory" (1966).

Revsine has proposed that information relevant to the market oriented decision must be an indicator of either (1) future distribution flows or (2) the market price of the stock held. Furthermore, if misleading information increases the market price of the stock beyond what would be expected given the distributional flows and the risk involved, the market will begin discounting such information and the second condition reduces to the first. Therefore, income is a relevant object for prediction if it is a good reflection of future distributions to stockholders. But the empirical evidence available does not correlate income with operating distributions, so, from a theoretical standpoint, it would seem that forecasts have little relevance to investors. It must be noted that the same argument could be leveled at using current net income to predict these future distributional flows.

Evidence is available, however, to support the position that forecasted earnings are currently being used in investors' decisions despite their theoretical shortcomings. A survey conducted by the National Investor Relations Institute cited that 69% of the companies surveyed gave "ball park range" guidance to investment analysts regarding forecasted information.[3] Casey of the SEC remarks that "After all, analysts make such projections and make research reports on that basis, management estimates do circulate, and trading values do relate to earnings estimates more than anything else."[4]

The fact that forecasts are currently circulated as inside information, not available to all investors on an equal basis, provides the main impetus for disclosure of forecasts in financial statements.

The second type of shareholder decision mentioned previously is the management efficiency decision. Here, forecasts provide the basis for evaluation of actual results with what should have been attained. Perhaps a valid criticism of disclosing forecasted information is that shareholders would be too quick to criticize on the basis of the difference between actual and projected results, while management considers the sources of the deviations more important than the deviations alone. The reconciliation of differences between forecasted and actual results would have to be made in terms of controllable and noncontrollable factors. Notice that this could work to management's advantage if poor results could be attributed to factors that could not have been anticipated or controlled by management, provided their course of action was the best possible in that circumstance.

## BENEFITS TO OTHER EXTERNAL USERS

Benefits of forecasted information could accrue to other external users of financial statements besides shareholders. Bond holders and lending institutions are primarily interested in a company's debt paying ability. A projected statement of changes in financial position would be of value in determining the relative security of debt. Projected earnings would also provide information to employees in collective bargaining situations involving the "ability to pay." If governmental source data were

[3]Schnellhardt, Timothy D., "Despite Wide Protests, SEC Moves Closer to Allowing Forecasts in Firms Reports," *The Wall Street Journal*, Nov. 20, 1972, p. 3.

[4]Ibid.

collected from forecasted information, presumably governmental agencies would have an improved basis for making decisions with future economic consequences.

## CORPORATE OBJECTIONS TO DISCLOSURE

A study by Skousen, Sharp, and Tolman revealed that a large number of corporate financial executives were confident in the accuracy of their budgetary data but the majority of those interviewed resisted disclosure. The responses to the study questionnaire seemed to indicate that management felt any information regarding the assumptions used in forecast preparation would be useful to its competitors. Yet, for forecast data to have any real meaning, these assumptions must be disclosed.

However, Mitchell points out that most companies voluntarily disclose strategic information in their annual reports, especially information dealing with large scale changes in operations. Also, disclosure provides a reciprocal opportunity to gain insight into a competitor's operation, particularly if disclosure is mandatory. Even if strategic assumptions were not disclosed, companies could provide their assumptions regarding their particular industry and the economy as a whole, which the investor could then compare with his own expectations.

## ANALYTIC CAPABILITIES OF EXTERNAL USERS

In the study by Skousen, Sharp, and Tolman, CPAs, professional analysts, and financial executives were of the consensus that the average investor lacked the sophistication to use forecasted information properly. The underlying reason was that unsophisticated investors might be misled by forecasts because of the reliability attached to the financial statements, failing to recognize the assumptions inherent in the budgets presented or that budgets are subject to revision over time. Such action could lead to an adverse investor reaction when the forecasted plans do not materialize, and a lessening of confidence in reported financial statements. This would suggest that forecasts should be clearly differentiated from historical data, and updated periodically. In addition, budgeted figures compared to actual results over a period of years would produce some basis for the investor community to draw its own conclusions about the reliability of a company's forecasts.

## MATERIALITY—THE MEANINGFUL RANGE

The reliability of forecast data cannot be measured in absolute terms. Rather, the reliability of such data must be expressed relative to the materiality of the item under consideration. The AAA has defined materiality of an item as "reason to believe that knowledge of it would influence the decision of an uninformed investor."[5]

---

[5]Daily, R. Austin, "Feasibility of Reporting Forecasted Information," *The Accounting Review,* v. 46, Oct. 1971, pp. 686–92. Quoted from Committee on Concepts and Standards Underlying Corporate Financial Statements, "Accounting and Reporting Standards for Corporate Financial Statements 1957 Revision," *The Accounting Review*, Oct. 1957, p. 543.

Bernstein has conducted an empirical study of practicing accountants which revealed that 10%–15% of net income is the "border zone" between materiality and non-materiality. Daily provides empirical evidence from 12 firms in five different industries that only 10% of those interviewed had differences in forecasted and actual revenue exceeding 10%. Two-thirds of those responding had differences between forecasted and actual net income of less than 15%. This evidence seems to support the position that most forecast errors would not materially affect the investor's decision process.

However, others disagree. Elgers and Clark feel that net income is much more sensitive to changes in revenues. This might point out a need for several forecasts given different levels of sales revenue.

## REGRESSION ANALYSIS—A FORECASTING METHOD

Regression analysis is a technique used to explain the movement of one variable relative to changes in other variables over time. The variable explained (the dependent variable) could be sales or possibly various expenses, although accountants have developed other techniques to explain the cost behavior of the firm. The objective of regression analysis is, then, to obtain a cause-effect relationship between the independent and dependent variables. While interrelationships are admittedly possible, the true test of a regression model is how well it predicts over several periods.

The probability of a period forecast being a reasonable estimate of the actual is indicated by the standard error of the estimate $S_e$. Two-thirds of all the estimates produced by the model are assumed to lie inside of $1S_e$ of the actual and 95% of the estimates produced by the model are thought to be within $2S_e$ of the actual. This statistic is, then, a measure of the reliability of the estimation procedure, although it must be noted that the standard error is based on historical data only and would be presumed to be somewhat greater for forecast data.

Relating this reliability estimate to the concept of materiality, a probability can be assigned to the size of the confidence interval around net income which is thought to be material to investors' decisions. This would normalize the forecaster's reliability estimate to our hypothetical investment decision model.

Parker and Segura provide empirical evidence for the predictive ability of regression analysis with regression estimates of sales and net income compared with actual values and values extrapolated from historical sales and net income figures for an actual firm in the home furnishings industry.

Their conclusions are that predictions based on regression analysis are in both cases superior to those based on the extrapolation of historical values, and are sufficiently reliable to merit their inclusion in financial statements.

## AUDIT OF FORECASTED FINANCIAL INFORMATION

Would the audit of forecast data serve a useful function? The answer may lie in British experience with financial forecasts. In the United Kingdom, audits are required on forecasts issued in connection with takeover attempts. In a recent survey, Carmichael found that the British feel the audit of forecast data provides the necessary objective viewpoint, where before audits of forecast data were required, financial forecasts contained too much of management's optimism.

CPAs surveyed by Skousen, Sharp, and Tolman indicated that they felt accountants could devise auditing procedures to quantitatively attest to the validity of forecasts, but not qualitatively. That is, the method and the mathematical computations would be under scrutiny, not the reliability of the predictions made. The CPAs surveyed also felt that it would be necessary to spell out the underlying assumptions in detail. Mitchell goes one step further in proposing that the auditor make some judgment as to the realism of the assumptions made and the validity of the prediction based on trend analysis.

Ijiri formalizes these views in two standards for auditing forecasts: internal and external consistency. Internal consistency requires that generally accepted accounting principles be used for forecasted and actual statements and that the predictions made must fall within the limits of the productive capabilities of the firm. External consistency is that the forecasts must be reasonable in terms of reported economic trends for a particular industry or the economy as a whole.

The SEC has decided against the audit of forecast data because generally accepted forecasting principles were not available. If generally accepted forecasting principles did become available, the SEC said it would reconsider its position.

## LIABILITY

Liability for an inaccurate forecast is possibly the most significant question to be answered. British experience is not applicable here, because in the United Kingdom there are no class action suits, contingent fee arrangements, or securities acts like the 1933 and 1934 acts. As a result, British auditors rarely get sued.

Under common law, a fraudulent misstatement of opinion (made intentionally or by gross negligence) may result in legal action. The landmark case in this area may be the Monsanto Chemical case decided in October 1971. The decision indicated there was no liability where forecasts were carefully prepared if they later became inaccurate because of unforeseen circumstances.

Under the securities laws, liability exists for a material misstatement or omission of fact. The obvious question is, are forecasts fact or opinion? The SEC has indicated they support the latter view. In their statement after the forecast hearings, the SEC also indicated they would seek appropriate legislation to the effect that a forecast is not to be construed as a promise.

## CONCLUSION

In conclusion, there is little doubt that forecasts could provide relevant information to external users of financial statements, evidenced primarily by the use of forecasts as inside information today. That forecasts are not completely verifiable is not sufficient reason to exclude them from financial reporting. It is important to note that accountants attest to the validity of estimates every day—for example, the estimate of usable life made in the depreciation of assets. It is my conclusion that forecasts can be prepared accurately enough to conform to the expectations of investors with regard to the materiality concept advanced here. If an audit is desired, the audit of forecasted information should be made under the standards of internal and external consistency, with the assumptions stated and the procedural elements checked for accuracy. The liability for inaccurate forecasts should not be significant, especially if the SEC drafts appropriate legislation to protect issuers.

## BIBLIOGRAPHY

Birnberg, Jacob G., and Nicholas Dopuch. "A Conceptual Approach to the Framework for Disclosure," *Journal of Accountancy*, v. 115, February 1963, pp. 57-63.

Carmichael, Douglas R. "Reporting on Forecasts, a U.K. Perspective," Graduate School of Management, University of California, Los Angeles, August 1972.

Cooper, W. W., N. Dopuch and T. F. Keller. "Budgetary Disclosure and Other Suggestions for Improving Accounting Reports," *The Accounting Review*, v. 43, October 1968, pp. 640-8.

Daily, R. Austin. "Feasibility of Reporting Forecasted Information," *The Accounting Review*, v. 46, October 1971, pp. 686-92.

Elgers, Pieter, and John J. Clark. "Inclusion of Budgets in Financial Reports: Investor Needs v. Management Disclosure," *Accounting and Business Research*, v. 3, Winter 1972, pp. 53-61.

Greenball, M. N. "Predictive-Ability Criterion: Its Relevance in Evaluating Accounting Data," *Abacus*, v. 7, June 1971, pp. 1-7.

Guy, Dan M. "Auditing Projected Financial Statements," *Management Accounting*, v. 53, November 1972, pp. 33-37.

Ijiri, Y. "On Budgeting Principles and Budget-Auditing Standards," *The Accounting Review*, v. 43, October 1968, pp. 662-7.

Mitchell, Charles L. "Disclosure of Budgeted Financial Statements," *Canadian Chartered Accountant*, v. 95, November 1969, pp. 326-30.

"NAA Testifies on Forecasts," *Management Accounting*, v. 51, February 1973, pp. 53-54.

Parker, George, and Edilberto L. Segura. "How to Get a Better Forecast," *Harvard Business Review*, v. 49, March-April, p. 99.

Peterson, William A. "Significance of Prospective Income Data," *The Accounting Review*, v. 41, April 1966, pp. 275-82.

Reiling, Henry, and John Burton. "Financial Statements: Signposts As Well As Milestones," *Harvard Business Review*, v. 50, November-December 1972, pp. 50-54.

Revsine, Lawrence. "Predictive Ability Market Prices and Operating Flows," *The Accounting Review*, v. 46, July 1971, pp. 480-9.

Schnellhardt, Timothy D. "Despite Wide Protests, SEC Moves Closer to Allowing Forecasts in Firms Reports," *The Wall Street Journal*, November 20, 1972, p. 3.

Skousen, K. F., R. A. Sharp and R. K. Tolman. "Corporate Disclosure of Budgetary Data," *Journal of Accountancy*, v. 133, May 1972, pp. 50-7.

"Statement by the Commission on the Disclosure of Projections of Future Economic Performance," Securities and Exchange Commission, 1973.

Summers, Edward L. "Opportunity Costs for Planning, Control and Financial Reporting," *Budgeting*, v. 15, January-February 1967, pp. 6-9.

Willingham, John J., Charles H. Smith and Martin E. Taylor. "Should the CPA's Opinion Be Extended to Include Forecasts?" *Financial Executive*, v. 38, September 1970, p. 80.

EDITORS' NOTE: This paper won the national Beta Alpha Psi Manuscript Contest in 1973. Beta Alpha Psi is a scholastic and professional fraternity for university students majoring in accounting; it has over 100 chapters. When Mr. Stober wrote this paper, he was a 20-year-old junior student majoring in accounting in the honors program at Ohio State University and a member of that university's Beta Alpha Psi Chapter.

## QUESTIONS

1. What decisions do investors make about the stock of a particular company, and of what benefit might forecasts be to investors?

2. What is forecasted information?

3. How might other external users of financial statements benefit from availability of forecasted information?

4. Compare predictions based on regression analysis with those based on extrapolations of historical values.

5. Evaluate the analytic capabilities of external users, materiality, auditing, and liability issues in this controversy.

# 101

## SEC PROPOSES FIRMS REPORT TO AGENCY PROFIT FORECASTS GIVEN TO ANALYSTS, PRESS*
Wall Street Journal

The Securities and Exchange Commission proposed that corporations be required to report to the agency any profit forecasts they give to securities analysts or financial reporters.

The proposal, which adds detail to a policy decision made two years ago, doesn't require corporations to forecast their earnings. But the many corporations that make such projections, either in response to questions from analysts and reporters during

*From the *Wall Street Journal,* Apr. 29, 1975, p. 2. Reprinted by permission of the publisher.

interviews or at securities analysts' meetings, would have to comply with a new set of public reporting requirements.

Current SEC rules bar corporations from including projections in SEC filings, but few other standards apply, although a company could be prosecuted under the SEC's antifraud rules if the agency believed that a company was issuing false projections to influence the price of its stock.

## COULD HAVE BROAD IMPACT

Thus, the new standards, if adopted, could have a broad impact on the frequency and content of corporate earnings forecasts. The proposed rules will "make people sit down and think" before making a projection, no matter how casual, an SEC official asserted. These forecasts play an important role in investment decisions.

For this reason the agency adopted a broad definition of what constitutes a projection. It both includes "future revenues, sales, net income or earnings per share" expressed as a specific amount, range of amounts or in percentage terms, and covers assertions that a figure is "in the ball park," "attainable," or "on target," the SEC said.

Under the proposal, a corporation would have to report a forecast to the SEC within 10 days of making the projection and disclose:

"The circumstances in which the projection was furnished, including the date it was furnished and the manner in which it was communicated."

The time period covered by the projection and the assumptions behind it, along with a statement cautioning "that there can be no assurance that the projection will be achieved since its ultimate achievement is dependent upon the occurrence of the specified assumptions."

## POSSIBLE SECOND REPORT

In addition, the company would have to file a second report if it concludes that a previous projection doesn't stand any longer, and give either a new projection and the reason for the change, or an explanation of why it can't make a new projection. It would also have to file a report if it decides to stop making projections, giving its reasons for the new policy.

These disclosures would have to be made on a so-called Form 8-K, which companies must file to report lawsuits, new financing agreements and other important events. Generally, 8-K reports needn't be filed until the tenth day of the month following the event, but a report of a projection would have to be filed sooner, within 10 days of the forecast.

This reflects the SEC's conclusion that "management's assessment of company's future performance is information of significant importance to the investor" and that the projection, along with the assumptions behind it, should be made available quickly.

The proposal applies to any projection, except those made in the course of discussions to arrange private financing, underwriting agreements or mergers. Certain projections made to government agencies also would remain private.

Along with reporting a projection in an 8-K report, companies making projections would also have to disclose them in annual reports to shareholders, 10-K annual reports filed with the SEC and registration statements companies must file when they sell securities to the public.

## WHAT PLAN REQUIRES

Under the proposal, annual reports and registration statements would have to include projections made during the past year and a comparison with actual results for the period. Any company that made a projection in the year covered by the annual report would also be required to make a projection for at least the first six months of the next year or to explain why it decided to stop making projections.

Realizing that certain companies may shy away from making projections for fear of running afoul of the SEC's antifraud standards if the forecast later turns out to be wrong, the agency said companies would be protected from antifraud liability if certain standards are met.

To qualify for this so-called "safe harbor" provision, a company would have to show that it has:

Been subject to and complied with the SEC's reporting requirements for at least three years. (More than 10,000 publicly held companies are currently covered by these requirements.)

Prepared corporate budgets for internal use for the last three fiscal years.

Prepared and reviewed the projection and the assumptions on which it's based "with reasonable care."

Richard Rowe, associate director of the SEC's Division of Corporation Finance, said the proposals "should encourage those who can meet the safe harbor rule to make projections," but he conceded that the proposals "may discourage other companies from making projections."

The SEC doesn't know how many companies make projections in an average year, but some estimates run into the thousands. Several years ago the agency said that in November 1972 alone, the *Wall Street Journal* carried 153 reports of forecasts by corporate managers.

Under the proposal, if any projection is reviewed by anyone outside of the company, such as an accountant or a lawyer, the company must disclose the person's relationship to the company, his qualifications and the scope of the review.

This is a change from the SEC's first announcement in 1973. Initially, the agency said it wouldn't allow a third party to certify a projection.

The latest proposal also drops a requirement that a company must have a history of earnings before it can report a projection and deletes an earlier conclusion that projections should be updated on a regular basis.

In addition, the agency added to its proposal a requirement that has nothing to do with forecasts. It proposed that companies report any change of control of the corporation within 10 days of the change, rather than waiting to file within the first 10 days of the following month, as is the previous requirement. In part, this proposed acceleration reflects the growing congressional interest in increasing public awareness of changes in corporate control, particularly where foreign take-overs are involved.

The agency asked for public comment on the proposals by June 30.

## QUESTIONS

1. What are the essential features of the SEC proposal?
2. What impact would the proposal have?

## SELECTED BIBLIOGRAPHY

Bacon, K. H., "Forecast Flight," *Wall Street Journal*, Dec. 1, 1975, pp. 1, 11.

National Accounting Association, "NAA Testifies on Forecasts," *Management Accounting*, February 1973, pp. 53-54.

# 102
## EXECUTORY CONTRACTS*
American Accounting Association

Accounting at present recognizes most market transactions involving goods, services, or money as one of the elements of the transaction. Present accounting also generally ignores, except in special circumstances, transactions involving an exchange of a promise for a promise. Leases, purchase commitments, executive and other labor contracts are generally denied recognition until the services or goods specified in the contract are either used, delivered, or paid for.

Many of these contracts meet the standards of verifiability, freedom from bias, and quantifiability at least as well as other reported events.

Generally a contract specifies amounts that allow verification and quantification. For contracts of long duration, a valuation problem in terms of present values exists, but this problem is no greater than in other problems involving accounting judgment, such as estimation of collectibility of receivables. These contracts do not appear to contain any biases. The only reason for exclusion, where the other standards are met, must be based on relevance. The committee feels that short-term contracts or contracts that are essentially renewed periodically in equal amounts may justifiably be ignored on the grounds that information about such comitments does not possess sufficient relevance to justify inclusion in accounting reports. Perhaps a better way of stating the above conclusion is that in such cases deferring recognition of such events

*Excerpt from *A Statement of Basic Accounting Theory*, AAA, 1966, pp. 7-10, 32-33. Reprinted by permission of the publisher.

until the services or goods are used or delivered does not do much harm. This, however, cannot be said about contracts extending over long periods that are material or that are not repetitive. Information about such contracts is clearly relevant to a host of decisions involving stewardship, changes in management, credit extension, and investment decisions. Recording of these events would also result in greater uniformity of reporting essentially similar events where the only difference lies in the form of obligation assumed. There, the committee recommends the reporting of all long-term leases, material and non-repetitive purchase commitments, pension plans, and executive compensation contracts including stock options or deferred payments and the like in dollar terms in the regular framework of the statements.

This does not imply that all useful accounting information must be incorporated in the double-entry structure; at the same time, maximizing what is recorded in that system is a useful means of avoiding errors of omission in reporting of relevant information.

### QUESTION

1. Of the various kinds of executory contracts that the AAA recommends should be booked, do you think there are any that accountants would have more difficulty in recording than the others? If so, which and why?

# 103
## FOES OF LEASE-ACCOUNTING CHANGES FAIL TO CONVINCE STANDARDS BOARD OF DANGERS*
Frederick Andrews

Maybe the controversy over new rules for lease accounting won't be as tough as it's cracked up to be.

That was the impression left by four days of public hearings last week before the Financial Accounting Standards Board, which has in mind a thorough revamping of lease accounting. By far the hottest issue is whether lessees must include their extended commitments to pay lease rentals in their balance sheets as a form of long-term debt. Few companies do at present, and lessees vigorously resist the idea.

Lessees contend that requiring them to show lease commitments as debt would hurt their credit, inflate their financial costs and damage the economy. But at the hearings, they seemed unable to make a persuasive case that sophisticated lenders and investors haven't already taken lease obligations into account.

*From the *Wall Street Journal*, Nov. 25, 1974, p. 5. Reprinted by permission of the publisher.

Leasing has mushroomed into an enormous business and a routine means of industrial financing. By one estimate, some $50 billion of equipment is leased—much of it such "big ticket" items as oil tankers, computers, airliners, nuclear fuel cores and entire plants. One prominent appeal of leasing has been "off balance sheet" financing: All that appears about the lease in the lessee's financial results is the annual rental payment (though more lease data is given in footnotes to the statements).

## CONSENUS REACHED

The hearings last week reflected a consensus among accountants that most long-term, noncancelable leases amount to installment purchases and should be accounted for as such. Tough accountants differ on the details, such leases would be "capitalized"—treated as assets and charged off over their useful lives.

Lessees not only object to carrying the lease liability as long-term debt. They also object because capitalizing the lease commitment will likely cut a lessee's earnings. That's true because instead of a rental payment, the annual charge against the lessee's earnings reflects both depreciation of the "asset" and imputed interest on the installment "debt." In the early years of a lease, the sum of these two charges exceeds the actual rental payment.

Those who oppose changing lease accounting usually base their claims on economic grounds, rather than accounting theory. At the hearings there were frequent predictions of dire impact. Robert O. Whitman, speaking for the Financial Executives Institute, an influential industry group, contended that the accounting changes would conflict with the nation's goals of combating inflation, fighting unemployment, protecting the environment and seeking energy self-sufficiency.

Capitalizing leases would cause "serious financial difficultues" for many lessees, Mr. Whitman said. For some lessees, it would mean a default under existing loan-indenture agreements, which place restrictions on incurring new debt. Mr. Whitman said this could make it impossible to raise new debt and, in fact, require companies to issue new stock, further depressing stock markets. Another speaker predicted that capitalizing leases would add $4 billion a year to industry's financing costs.

On balance, however, the opponents appeared unable to make a strong case that capitalizing leases would cause economic havoc. In rebuttal, many speakers testified that leases are well known, and that lenders, analysts and other key parties—such as the agencies that rate bond issues for credit-worthiness—already take lease obligations into account in setting credit terms. Indeed, more recent indenture agreements limit lease obligations as well as outright debt, speakers said.

"No matter what standard (the board sets), the United States of America won't incur a depression," declared Michael Jayson of the New York Stock Exchange, a proponent of capitalizing long-term leases. "The people in the know are aware of (leases) now."

## BOARD HELPED BY SEC

In that regard, the standards board is benefiting from an earlier move by the Securities and Exchange Commission, often typecast as an impatient rival, goading the board on.

A year ago the SEC imposed an interim requirement that companies disclose in footnotes the "present value" of long-term lease commitments and estimate how capitalizing those commitments would have affected earnings. (A "present value" computation reflects the fact that a sum received today is more valuable than the same sum received in several years because it could be invested in the interim. Thus sums due or payable in years to come are discounted to get their present equivalent.)

The SEC move has turned out to be a sleeper. It tends to deflate the arguments of those who predict dire consequences if leases are capitalized. It bolsters the proponents' argument that capital markets already know about lease obligations and have reacted to them. A change to capitalizing leases would merely move the data from footnotes to the balance sheet itself, some speakers said.

Thus the question of impact tended to narrow to the actual wording of indenture agreements, and whether counting leases as debt would force the renegotiation of such agreements, as some speakers predicted. Other speakers suggested the standards board might finesse that problem by a careful choice of labels or by keeping the lease commitments separate from outright debt in the balance sheet. Still others predicted a period of confusion in which lawyers would be leery of giving opinions on whether lease commitments were what the indentures meant by debt.

As yet, the standards board hasn't taken any position, though the weight of accounting opinion favors capitalizing most long-term leases. Under its procedures, the standards board will next propose an "exposure draft," which it may adopt as binding accounting rules following a period of public comment.

## FIRST ISSUE OF BOARD

The leasing issue is generally regarded as the first clear confrontation for the standards board, which was formed last year as the private sector's top rule-making body in accounting matters. The standards board's predecessor, the Accounting Principles Board, found lessee accounting too hot to handle.

There seems little doubt that those opposed to capitalizing leases will seek to bring Congress into the controversy, as they did when the issue was before the Accounting Principles Board. This is one reason why the arguments over economic impact, rather than accounting theory, may be decisive.

According to John C. Burton, SEC chief accountant, the pressures in Washington have already begun. "Those opposed (to lease capitalization) sense that they have lost the battle in the accounting profession, and they are now looking to Congress," Mr. Burton said in a speech last week. It's important that the standards board "be prepared to make a case to Congress," he added.

## QUESTION

1. Why did the foes of lease-accounting changes fail to convince the FASB?

## SELECTED BIBLIOGRAPHY

Watt, George C., "Setting Standards for Reporting Lease Transactions," *Price Waterhouse Review*, 1975, no. 1, pp. 29 and 31.

# 104

# ACCOUNTING BOARD PROPOSES NEW RULES IN CONTROVERSIAL AREA OF LEASE REPORTING*
Wall Street Journal

One of the accounting profession's longest-running controversies—reporting on leases—is moving into its final stages.

In the face of stiff opposition from many corporate financial officers, the Financial Accounting Standards Board, the profession's rule-making body, proposed a new set of accounting rules for lessors and lessees. Although the proposal covers a broad variety of issues, the most controversial one involves balance-sheet accounting for companies that lease property, including such things as jet aircraft, computers, heavy equipment and entire factories.

The subject is a complex one and the proposed ruling is highly technical, but analysts said it appears likely the ruling would require many more companies to report lease obligations as liabilities on their balance sheets than currently do so. Some industry analysts fear the additional reporting will appear to increase corporate debt, with adverse effects on the stock market's valuation of corporate stock and on loan agreements, which frequently specify maintenance of specific debt-to-equity ratios.

The proposed "statement" was released in the form of an exposure draft, which is subject to change. Comments on the draft will be taken until next Oct. 31, and then the accounting board will issue a final ruling. This ruling will then come under the profession's code of ethics and, in effect, be binding on auditing firms.

## ARGUED FOR YEARS

The accounting profession and corporate financial executives have argued about lease accounting for years. Essentially, the problem is how to report on transactions that combine elements of a sale of property, borrowed money and a form of installment payments. The question is: When and under what terms are the benefits and risks of the property's ownership transferred? Because of the complex variety of leases, the

*From the *Wall Street Journal*, Aug. 29, 1975, p. 8. Reprinted by permission of the publisher.

answer is often unclear. The same piece of equipment can be accounted for one way by the lessee and another way by the lessor.

As a result, the board's announcement noted, "inconsistencies remain in lease-accounting practices along with differences of opinion as to what should be done about them."

While the accountants debated the issues, lease financing has grown rapidly over the years. One of its attractive features for many companies, a feature that would be curtailed under the proposed ruling, is that it permits "off balance sheet" financing. That is, a company can acquire the use of property without showing it as an asset and without reporting the "liability" that otherwise would be incurred for payment.

The board said it is estimated that more than $11 billion of new equipment was leased in 1974 and that by the end of 1975 equipment on lease will total $100 billion. As the industry has grown, the accounting profession and the Securities and Exchange Commission have been pushing for better rules. The SEC, for example, in 1973 began requiring footnote disclosure of lease obligations. The accounting board has held numerous public hearings on the subject of its proposed draft.

## LEVERAGED LEASES

Under the proposed rule, the same basic reporting criteria would apply to both lessors and lessees. Separate accounting and reporting requirements are proposed for leveraged leases, which are leases in which the cost of the leased property is financed through long-term debt.

The key controversial proposal would apply to so-called "capital leases." The lessee would have to show this equipment on the balance sheet as an asset, and the obligation to make rental payments would be shown as a liability.

A lease would be classified as a capital lease if it meets any one of five criteria: The lease transfers title to the property to the lessee by the end of the lease term; the lease contains an option to purchase the property at a bargain price; the lease term is equal to 75% or more of the estimated economic life of the property; it is estimated that by the end of the lease the property's fair value will be less than 25% of what it was at the beginning, or, finally the property has a special purpose for the lessee and wouldn't be readily resaleable to another user.

If a lease doesn't meet any of the five criteria, it would be classified as an operating lease and wouldn't appear on the balance sheet.

The proposed ruling also provides for disclosure of lease obligations, including much information already required under existing rules.

## QUESTIONS

1. What changes in lease-accounting have been enacted?
2. What are the criteria for capitalizing a lease?

# 105

## TO CAPITALIZE OR NOT TO CAPITALIZE, THAT IS THE QUESTION*

Forbes

Suppose a company is free of long-term debt. Does that mean that the company is in good financial shape? Not necessarily. The company may be loaded down with long-term leases, which can be as much of an obligation and a burden as actual debt.

In the old days, leasing chiefly affected retailing companies, which frequently leased their premises. But over the past decade, leasing has grown in popularity as a means of off-balance-sheet financing. Instead of borrowing money to buy an airplane, a computer or a nuclear core, the company leases it.

Tight money and the ability to pass on the investment tax credit gave the practice a big boost. Leasing, of course, involves lease payments rather than straight interest and amortization, but the lease payments contain an interest rate factor; the lessor, after all, must make a profit on the money he invested in the property. By passing the investment tax credit on to the lessor, however, the people who actually used the property often were able to get a lower rate of interest; the lessor took part of his return in the form of the tax credit.

Obviously, business loves leasing. Today, a ball-park estimate puts the capitalized value of all leases outstanding in the U.S. at around $80 billion, and in 1974 alone leases outstanding grew by over $10 billion.

However, the Financial Accounting Standards Board is working on drafting an opinion that could force companies to capitalize a substantial portion of the value of outstanding leases and report them on the balance sheet.

If the accountants decide that *all* or most leases should be capitalized, certain industries would be greatly affected. Take airlines: According to its latest balance sheet, UAL Inc. had long-term debt of $936 million. UAL had over $700 million in equity capital. Therefore, UAL's debt-to-equity ratio was a high but manageable 1.34-to-1. But UAL also is obligated under leases, chiefly for airplanes and terminals, which cost it $112 million in 1973; the capitalized value of these leases was $815 million. Add that to the debt, and UAL's obligations mount to $1.75 billion, and the debt-to-equity ratio climbs to 2.4-to-1. American Airlines, TWA and Pan American also are loaded with leases.

The airlines are not alone. The railroads also do a huge amount of equipment leasing, and many hotel and motel chains lease their facilities. All retail chains, of course, lease the bulk of their retail premises and warehouses. Increasingly, utilities have turned to leasing, as it has become harder for them to borrow money.

With the 1973 annual reports, companies began disclosing the capitalized amount of lease obligations in the footnotes to their financial statements. This was a result of

*From "The Numbers Game," *Forbes*, Jan. 15, 1975, pp. 42–43. Reprinted by permission of the publisher.

an interim-disclosure requirement demanded by the Securities & Exchange Commission. But the SEC's activist chief accountant, John C. (Sandy) Burton, is determined to go further.

"Lease accounting," Burton complains, "is one of the most spectacular sources of the accountant's lack of credibility." Burton regards it as reprehensible for a company to use leasing as a means of dressing up its balance sheet, and for the accountants to go along.

Of course, there are all kinds of leases. There are two major ways to categorize them. Financing leases are typically long-term, 30-to-40 year leases on buildings or shopping centers and typically noncancellable. The other major kind of lease is the operating lease, where the lessee gets only temporary (usually less than a year) use of the asset. Here, the lessor is still clearly the owner of the asset. An example would be the rental of an auto for a short period.

Sandy Burton and a number of other accountants say, at the very least, capitalize all financing leases that result in the acquisition of the asset. Burton's criteria for what constitutes an acquisition are very broad.

As is nearly always the case with this type of reform, it inevitably involves stepping on some toes.

The supermarket chains are worried. "Look at Safeway," says one supermarket executive. "They could have to capitalize lease commitments with a present value of $777 million. Think what this would do to their balance sheet, with only $129 million in long-term debt."

Karl Ziebarth, treasurer of the Missouri-Kansas-Texas Railroad, makes this point against compulsory lease capitalization: "We would not have been able to rehabilitate this railroad, considering our weak balance sheet, had we been required to capitalize the leases."

UAL, whose already big debt load would be almost doubled if it had to capitalize all its financing leases, takes a middle position on the controversy. It reluctantly would go along with capitalization of equipment, but argues that it should not be required to capitalize leases for terminal facilities, where the airline frequently has no choice in leasing.

## PROBLEMS GALORE

Russell Fraser, the head of credit rating at Standard & Poor's, points up another difficulty: "For some companies, capitalization could play havoc with their indenture agreements. It might put them in technical violation of debt covenants." Fraser is against capitalization: "Too arbitrary and too complicated for a balance sheet," he says. He prefers more disclosure in the footnotes.

AT&T has relatively few leases, but its assistant controller has some strong feelings on the subject. Says AT&T's Warren W. Brown, "While we agree with the theory of capitalizing leases that are purchases or in substance debt, we feel that it would be prudent to put off capitalization for a few years." Why delay? "It's like switching over from the U.S. measurement system to the metric system. There would be lots of confusion. After all, you are moving from no figure on the balance sheet to a very large present value calculation."

Another major reason that Brown feels the change should not take place overnight, is that the switchover might distort earnings comparisons for some companies. It works like this: A lease generally is set up so that the charge is the same each year over its life—a level payment system of depreciation and interest. But when equipment is purchased outright with borrowed money, the cost tends to be heavier in the early years. Reason: As the balance of the loan declines, the interest cost goes down.

What this means is that rapidly expanding companies doing a great deal of leasing tend to have an earnings advantage over companies that prefer to buy outright. "But if the leases are capitalized," says Brown, "the present value calculation of the cost of the leases will tend to reduce earnings. This is what many are worried about even though they talk balance sheet and debt ratios."

AT&T-man Brown has a point. Had Safeway capitalized its lease costs last year, its earnings would have been reduced by 7%. Levitz Furniture's earnings would have dropped 22%. UAL's 15%, Kresge's 5%.

W.T. Grant's 1973 earnings, already much weakened, would have been hit harder still. Grant's is a good case in point. Few realized how precarious its situation had become: After all, as recently as early 1974 it had $330 million in equity capital and only $220 million in long-term debt. What Grant didn't show in its annual report but did in its 10-K report was that it also had $458 million worth of the present value of lease liabilities.

Some, however, argue that unlike debt, many long-term financing leases possess an indeterminate liability. Thus they say putting a capitalized value on the balance sheet could prove misleading. Better to put them in a detailed footonte. Only when a lease is really debt should it be capitalized.

There are several gray areas. The FASB will also have to decide whether to use capitalization techniques on all leases or only on leases that are really purchases. Further difficulties arise in determining how to calculate interest components in leases.

The lessor also poses some accounting problems. Most stem from the more recent upsurge in the use of leveraged leasing. Such leases involve three parties, a lessee, a lender and a lessor. The purpose: Most of the capital is provided by an institutional lender so that the lessor can obtain tax-sheltered income. This in turn enables him to charge the lessee an attractive rental. One of the accounting problems relates to the timing of recording income on the transaction, which has an impact on the lessor's earnings.

Despite all the complexities, Burton is adamant. If the FASB fails to act, he says, "then the SEC will. At a minimum, capitalization of leases that are primarily financing devices to permit acquisition should be required—and retroactively."

None of this will make life any easier for accountants. But that's what the accountants are supposed to be paid for: to go to great pains to be certain stockholders get a fair and accurate picture.

## QUESTIONS

1. What are the potential costs and benefits of capitalizing all or most leases?
2. What is the distinction between a financing lease and an operating lease?

# 106

## PENSIONS
## Reporting . . . under ERISA*
Ernest L. Hicks

Late in the summer of 1974, when the lawgivers on the Potomac enacted a new pension reform law that immediately was dubbed ERISA, they added copiously to the burdens of employers. However much employees may have gained in retirement income security, the financial executives of their employers are slogging—along with legal, actuarial, accounting, tax and investment advisers—through a mire of uncertainty as they gear themselves to comply with legal provisions whose intent, in many crucial respects, is obscure. . . .

This article . . . raises many questions and gives few answers. . . .

### EFFECTS FOR EMPLOYERS

The financial effects of ERISA overlap its effects on administrative aspects of an employer's activities, such as benefit practices and other elements of compensation, not to mention the special effects—of crucial concern to individual executives—of the fiduciary responsibility provisions. Consequently, financial and accounting executives must work closely with other corporate executives and professional advisers. . . .

Among the most significant considerations for the financial executive is the added expense ERISA may generate. For some employers, meeting the new rules on participation, coverage, vesting, funding and the form of benefit payments will be burdensome. Financial executives will want to factor cost increases into the employer's planning, with regard to both earnings and requirements for cash. It may be necessary to disclose the expected cost in the employer's financial statements.

But, however costly the required changes, making them may in the end prove the less expensive route. Failure to comply with the new requirements may jeopardize the deductibility for tax purposes of plan contributions or result in assessment of an excise tax.

### ACCOUNTING PRINCIPLES

The enactment of ERISA has not brought about any changes in the principles of accounting for pension cost. The principles applicable at present are expressed in Opinion No. 8 of the APB, "Accounting for the Cost of Pension Plans" (1966). An Interpretation of this (No. 3, "Accounting for the Cost of Pension Plans Subject to the Employee Retirement Income Security Act of 1974) was issued by the FASB in December 1974. In that publication, the FASB addressed the questions and provided the answers—both of which, for the sake of brevity, I have paraphrased—that follow.

*From *Financial Executive,* July 1975, pp. 17—23. Reprinted by permission of the publisher.

QUESTION: Will any of the provisions of the new law make it necessary for an employer to show unfunded prior-service cost or part of that cost as a liability?

FASB: In general, no, but there are two exceptions: the amount currently required to be funded and the amount of a liability imposed by the Act in the case of a plan that has been terminated or is about to be terminated.

QUESTION: When should an employer begin to recognize in its income statements any increases in pension cost expected to result from complying with ERISA?

FASB: Subsequent to the date when a plan becomes subject to the Act's requirements.

QUESTION: Will amortization of unfunded prior-service cost become mandatory for accounting purposes (because under the new law, the minimum funding standard specifies funding of prior-service cost and actuarial gains and losses over a specified period)?

FASB: Pension cost for financial accounting purposes is not necessarily determined by pension funding. Therefore, the Act does not require any change in paragraph 17 of APB No. 8, which sets upper and lower limits for annual pension cost.

QUESTION: Should the notes to an employer's financial statements include information describing the future effects, or potential future effects, of the enactment of ERISA?

FASB: If it appears likely that complying with the Act will have a significant effect on pension expense, funding of pension cost or the unfunded cost of vested benefits, that fact and an estimate of the effect should be disclosed. If an estimate cannot be furnished, an explanation should be provided.

In its Interpretation No. 3, the FASB announced that it has placed the overall subject of pension accounting on its technical agenda. . . .

## EFFECTS FOR BENEFIT PLANS

Duties of disclosure and reporting fall on the administrator of a plan, who may be a person so designated or the plan's sponsor, who in turn may be the employer, a labor union or a joint employer-union board or committee. The administrator must furnish specified information to participants and beneficiaries and must file specified information with the Secretary of Labor, and, because of amendments to the Internal Revenue Code, with the Secretary of the Treasury.

### Annual Report

This must be sent to the Secretary of Labor. Excerpts are to be furnished to participants and beneficiaries. The reporting requirements differ for employee welfare plans and pension plans, and it's expected that regulations will make for more differences by modifying requirements for welfare and small pension plans.

Two components of the annual report now claim our attention: (1) a set of financial statements (including notes), and a series of schedules whose content is prescribed by the Act. These are to be accompanied by an opinion of an "independent qualified public accountant," as to whether the information is "presented fairly in conformity with generally accepted accounting principles applied on a basis consistent with that of the preceding year." (2) An actuarial statement, accompanied by a report by an "enrolled actuary" expressing his opinion concerning the information.

The Secretary of Labor may reject an annual report "if he determines that there is any material qualification . . . in an opinion submitted by an accountant or actuary."

The excerpts from the annual report to be furnished to participants consist of:

A schedule showing the assets and liabilities of the plan aggregated by categories and valued at market and the same data for the end of the previous fiscal year of the plan.

A statement of receipts and disbursements during the preceding twelve-month period aggregated by general sources and applications.

Such other material as is necessary to fairly summarize the annual report.

The Act requires the plan's auditor to issue a separate report, filed as part of the annual report to the Secretary of Labor, with respect to this information.

For a plan that reports on the basis of a calendar year, the requirements to file and to make excerpts of the report available to participants apply for the calendar year 1975; thus, the first audited report will not be due until about the middle of 1976. For a plan whose reporting year straddles December 31, 1974, the Secretary of Labor may postpone the due date by regulation. The Secretary has issued, but not adopted, a proposed regulation which would make the reporting requirement effective for plan fiscal years beginning after January 1, 1975.

## ANSWERS, ANYONE?

. . . Financial executives, with their auditors, actuaries and other advisers, should now be planning ways to meet the new requirements. This may be difficult at best because at every step questions are encountered for which there are no clear-cut answers. . . .

### Accounting Questions

Presumably, these will be answered by the FASB, which is proceeding with a project on the accounting and reporting implications of employee benefit plans and has appointed a task force to assist it.

In prescribing the content of an auditor's opinion, ERISA implies that the financial statements required to be included in an administrator's annual report to the Secretary of Labor are to be presented in conformity with generally accepted accounting principles. Several accounting questions are discussed below; present practice on all, except the first, varies.

**Statements of What?**   In the past, financial statements having to do with pension plans have almost always been designated as statements of the "fund" or the "trust." ERISA suggests that the statements to be filed are those of the "plan." Are the terms "fund," "trust" and "plan" to be used interchangeably? If not, do the GAAP for the financial statements of a pension fund or trust differ from those for the statements of a pension plan?

**Cash vs. Accrual Basis**   The proposition that cash-basis statements—for whatever manner of entity—are not in conformity with GAAP may long since have reached the status of folklore in accounting. A health and welfare audit guide, issued by the AICPA in 1972, specified use of the accrual basis, as did the exposure draft of a pension audit guide released in 1973. On the other hand, financial statements of many pension funds are prepared on the cash basis at present.

**Basis for Stating Securities**   The health and welfare audit guide specified cost as the basis for stating securities. The exposure draft of a pension guide specified market. Should the basis be the same for all types of plan? On a different note, it is interesting to observe that ERISA implies that GAAP are to be the basis for presenting the financial statements and schedules required to be included in the annual report to the Secretary of Labor and also calls for including in that report a schedule in which assets are "valued at their current value." One could use the contrast to support a conclusion that ERISA expresses any of three divergent understandings: that cost is GAAP, that market is GAAP or that there is a choice.

**Market below Cost**   If cost is to be the basis for stating securities, there is a further question: What effect should be given, either in a plan's financial statements or in an auditor's report, to declining market values of pension fund investments?

**Actuarial Information**   What actuarial information, if any, should appear in the financial statements of a defined-benefit pension plan? Should the actuarial value of vested benefits, or the prior-service cost, appear as a liability of a pension fund? Are participants creditors? Or is their interest analogous to an equity interest? In the latter event, should the actuarial values appear in a note?

## ERISA WONDER-WORLD

When they pass through the door marked "ERISA," financial executives enter a wonder-world of novel requirements imposed by marvelously intricate legislation. [But] ... financial executives are a tough breed; they'd rather spend their time and energies arming themselves to deal with a job than complaining of its problems.

EDITORS' NOTE: ERISA stands for Employee Retirement Income Security Act of 1974. FASB Interpretation No. 3 (December 1974) was issued on the ERISA.

## QUESTIONS

1. What is the distinction between pension costs for financial statements and pension funding?

2. What is the difference between cash-basis and accrual-basis statements for pension funds?

3. Check Accounting Principles Board Opinion no. 8 (or your textbook) for the upper and lower limits for annual pension cost.

4. Define the following terms: actuarial information for a defined-benefit pension plan, unfunded prior-service cost, APB Opinion no. 8, and FASB Interpretation no. 3.

5. What are the principal accounting requirements of ERISA?

## SELECTED BIBLIOGRAPHY

Kleber, Louis C., " The Implications of Pension Reform," *World*, Autumn 1974, pp. 20-27.

# 107
# TAX ALLOCATION
## A Debate*
Sidney Davidson, Maurice Moonitz, and Carl Nelson

EDITORS' NOTE: The three professors engaged in the following debate for the Omicron Chapter of Beta Alpha Psi, the accounting scholastic and professional fraternity, at Ohio State University.

PROFESSOR NELSON: The APB supposedly solved the problem of deferred taxes by APB No. 11 which affected all the years starting after 1967. Those who have delved into accounting history know this was the culmination of previous statements by the APB and its predecessor committee on Accounting Procedure on the subject of allocating income taxes. The purpose of APB No. 11 was to cover the accounting for income taxes in those circumstances in which there were timing differences between the income tax return and the income statement. Those cases were either where a deduction on the income statement preceded one on the income tax return or the revenue appeared on the income statement prior to being reported as gross income on the income tax return or the reverse. This opinion provided that when there were timing differences that the income tax expense be calculated on the income reported on the income statement rather than on that appearing on the tax return. I am using the term "income tax expense" with full. knowledge that this will raise some

*Reprinted with permission of Omicron Chapter, Beta Alphi Psi, Ohio State University, November 1970.

disagreement as to that classification from some here including the three participants in the debate. The opinion required tax allocation as the application of the accrual principle to the accounting for income taxes. It went further and said that the balance sheet item that results from the deferring and normalization of the income tax should appear as a deferred credit or debit as the case may be. It would not be a liability and it would not be an asset. As a result there was to be no discounting; no consideration to be given to the passage of time or the existence of an interest rate above 0. There would be also no adjustment in the balance sheet figure as a result of a change in tax rates.

When you get one professor to consider APB 11 or any other pronouncement of the Accounting Principles Board obviously he is not going to agree with it. When you get two professors this makes it squared that they are not going to agree and if you have two professors the probability is also very high that they will disagree about their disagreement. However, we do have an unusual situation in that Professors Davidson and Moonitz agree on some things. If there is to be any tax allocation on the balance sheet, they agree the item should not be a deferred credit but instead should be classified as a liability. They also agree that this liability ought not to be measured at its face amount but rather there should be consideration of the fact that present dollars are not equal to future dollars and therefore a discounting process occurs. Neither debator has considered the question as to the discount rate however. On the other hand, there isn't complete agreement as to the extent that income tax allocation is desirable. They do agree that in those cases where the item appears on the income tax return in year 1 and it will appear on the other statement in the year 2 there should be allocations. They do agree that in case of a war, since in the past Congress has permitted a five-year write-off of plant even though the actual life might be much greater, tax deferral or tax normalization is desirable. In another situation if a company is going to eliminate a division and as a result of it recognizes a loss in 1975 that will be deductible in the tax return in 1976 or 1977 when the division is actually disposed, they agree on tax allocation. In another situation if a company that has a single depreciable asset, for instance, a building they agree that tax deferral is desirable. This still leaves a considerable area of disagreement. They do not agree that in the case of the typical normal manufacturing firm that is expected to grow that tax normalization would be desirable. Also in the case of the firm selling goods on the installment plan (or a revolving credit plan) which recognizes revenue at the time of sale but reports the gross income on the tax return at the time the amounts are collected, they do not agree as to whether there ought to be normalization. The debate will start with a statement against tax allocation by Dean Davidson, second, there will be a statement in favor of tax allocation by Professor Moonitz.

DEAN DAVIDSON: All I have to say could be summarized in three brief sentences. My view on deferred taxes could be summed in what I think are three attributes of accountants: 1) accountants possess and exert judgment and courage; 2) accountants do not attempt to do the impossible or the illogical; and 3) accountants do continually assess probabilities. If you accept those three sentences perhaps I should sit down; if you don't maybe I should expand on them a bit.

First, accountants possess and exert judgment and courage. APB Opinion No. 11 simplifies the situation greatly. Whenever there is a timing difference (i.e. whenever an item of expense or revenue appears earlier or later on the tax return than it does the financial statements) APB Opinion No. 11 requires that the firm must recognize a deferred tax debit or the deferred tax credit. It is all very simple in terms of computation for anyone who is capable of determining the amount of the difference and multiplying it by the appropriate tax rate. All accountants will come up with the same answer; all firms will be treated the same way whether their economic circumstances are similar or not. If accountants do possess judgment and courage, they should instead inquire into the firm's economic circumstances for each of its plants and treat like situations similarly and different situations differently. Naturally, this will produce some areas of uncertainty and some differences in interpretation among accountants who apply their best judgment. But under the APB No. 11, the comprehensive allocation view, the view that I assume Professor Moonitz is going to defend, all firms would be treated exactly the same; that is, all would have to recognize deferred taxes whether justified by economic circumstances or not. My view on this, recognizing the problems, the imperfections, the limitations, is that we should not allocate in all cases but only in those where we feel it is justified. My feeling here is summed up by one of the more apt remarks of Lord Keynes where he said that in general he would rather be vaguely right than precisely wrong. The comprehensive allocation procedure would provide a great degree of precision but also insures error in a large number of cases. I think we should prefer to be a little bit wrong in some cases in order to achieve this greater realism in most cases.

Accountants do not attempt to do the impossible or the illogical. We must recognize that income for any kind of enterprise typically results from a successful blending of a variety of economic resources, all of which are necessary to achieve the desired profitable result. Any effort to allocate income to specific assets is likely to be fruitless or misleading; the joint cost and joint revenue situation for the firm applies to all of its assets and any attempt to determine the income resulting from each of the assets is as likely to be at best meaningless and at worst downright misleading. In the usual case, income can only be associated with the firm as a whole, or with a distinct operating division which is virtually a separate firm. If this is the case, income taxes which are simply a rate applied to the income can only be associated with the firm as a whole and not with any individual asset. We do not pay income taxes on income resulting from an asset but on the final taxable income that emerges from the firm as a whole. Consequently accountants, it seems to me, do not attempt to do the impossible or illogical of subdividing the income of the firm into the income of individual assets but instead deal only with the income of the firm as a whole.

My third contention is that accountants do continually assess probabilities. This is true in most areas of accounting. In fact whenever we show assets other than cash on the balance sheet, it is because we have gone through some Bayesian analysis that suggests that there is a strong probability that future benefits will be conferred upon the firm by these assets. This is the meaningful definition of an asset. This is why we do not expense all of our purchases if there are some physical goods left on hand because we feel there is a probability that these can be disposed of in the future. All accounting, whether recognition of assets or failure to expense all expenditures, is based upon the accountant's subjective estimate of market conditions and the plants and the firms. Similarly it seems to me that this should be the basis for our deciding whether we want to recognize a deferred tax liability for the firm, when we want to recognize a tax expense which differs from the tax accrued. This has been demonstrated in ways that are familiar to all of you. If we take one case that I think is most conspicuous, that both Professor Moonitz and I have agreed to focus on, the depreciation case in which it has been demonstrated both arithmetically and mathematically that for a firm that has a stable or growing investment function the accelerated depreciation claimed on the tax return will be equal to or greater than the straight-line depreciation shown on the financial statement. As long as the investment function of the firm grows or is stable, its tax return depreciation will be equal to or greater than its financial statement depreciation. I suggest that the accountant exercising his judgment and his courage must apply his probabilistic approach to the question of what is likely to be the investment policy of the future. In the cases of the firm possessing the single asset with no intention of replacing it, it is clear that in the latter portion of the life of that asset the depreciation on the tax return will be less than the depreciation on the financial statements and there is, if you like, a borrowing of tax deductions until later years. In the case of the five year emergency amortization Professor Nelson spoke about, if the Congress says that the right to make accelerated depreciation applies only on this one batch of assets and not to later ones or if we feel that the Congress is likely to make the depreciation provisions in the tax law more stringent in the future than they are now, there would be a case for the recognition of a deferred tax liability. But if we expect the Congress to continue the present depreciation provisions of the tax law and if we expect the firm's investment function to be roughly constant or growing, there is no future obligation and no additional expense to be recognized.

Concerning the first of these two qualifications, whether Congress might be expected to make the depreciation laws more stringent, none of us possesses the power of prophecy. If we review the past history of depreciation provisions in the tax laws, we find that there has been an unbroken series of efforts to liberalize rather than to tighten the depreciation provisions. I predict too that before the 1972 election we are likely to see enactments with regard to depreciation which will shorten permissible service lives (as expressed in the guide lines) or will result in some exotic thing like a triple declining balance method. But again each accountant must make this estimate on his own. If he chooses to disregard our recent history, he may feel that depreciation provisions of the tax law will become more stringent and so he might choose to recognize a deferred tax expense or a deferred tax obligation.

The accountant must also make his own estimate about the investment policy of the firm. If a firm has exhibited a regular policy of steady investment and if their long range planning indicates that this policy of reasonable steady investment will be continued, the accountant again must decide whether he will be guided by this evidence or whether he will shut his eyes to economic reality and say that any investment that hasn't already been made will never be made. In many of our public utilities, in fact every one that I have had any association with, they have planned their investment expenditures until the next millennium. I have yet to see a utility which does not plan a reasonably steady growth pattern of expenditures extending till the year 2000. (Really, I guess the next millennium starts 2001 not 2000 because there was no year 0. We went from BC to 1 AD and so most of the utilities will have to extend their planning one more year before they can promise there will be no diminution of their planned investment expenditures in this millennium.) Whether for the year 2000 or 2001, it seems to be reasonably sufficient to suggest that where we do see a steady investment pattern extending that far into the future, to recognize that deferred tax obligations that will not be paid over the next forty years or so would seem to be a futile and useless sort of act. We have seen this from the work of Professor J. L. Livingston, Professor William Voss and others. But even where there are reasonable variations of the investment pattern, we are dealing with such a large group of assets that there is virtually no likelihood of any reversals of this path. So I am left with my view that accountants do possess the courage and judgment to assess situations and that they are not convinced by illogical exercises that seek to relate income to individual assets but instead will be guided by the probabilities of what is likely to be the investment pattern in the future. With these views prevailing, in a very large portion of the cases, deferred taxes would not be recognized.

PROFESSOR MOONITZ: Following the example of my opponent, let me quote the eminent Lord Keynes who once said about an eminent fellow economist: "Alfred Marshall was too anxious to do good." I suspect he would say the same thing about Professor Davidson. He has failed to consider the accounting issues involved in his anxiety to do something with the results of certain calculations and to take care of the awful problems practitioners face in preparing financial statements. When the OSU football team takes a licking, Woody Hayes puts them back to blocking and tackling. So why don't we go back to basics too? Incidentally, I am not going to try to provide a defense of APB No. 11. Professor Davidson has tried to maneuver me into that position. He is unsuccessful because as you will recall in the stipulations stated by the moderator we did agree that if there is anything at all to these deferred taxes, they constitute a liability, which is not the position taken in APB Opinion No. 11 (which claims it is a deferred credit). So let's put that aside. I prefer the terms Professor Homer Black of Florida State University uses in his AICPA research study: postponed and prepaid income taxes.

One of the interesting things about the various discussions on tax allocation is how hard it is to get those who don't like tax allocation to accept accrual accounting. In this situation, practitioners, although kicking and screaming, have come to accept tax allocation. But Professor Davidson is attempting to avoid entering the accrual citadel in which accountants have lived for some time. He wants us to stay in a cash-based world. The cornerstone of accounting, however, and the position I would defend here is to adopt a consistent point of view in our analysis of the tax allocation situation.

In the first place, I think it is clear what is meant by accrual accounting as it exists at the present time. We restrict our accounting to events and transactions that have occurred and the consequences of those particular events. We have not yet adopted proposals to bring budgeted figures into financial reporting, although intellectually I am sympathetic toward that development. Consequently we are not talking about forecasts, projections of cash flows, budget position a year or five years from now or in the year 2000. We are not yet to that state. We are talking about accounting as we know it now and of necessity are restricted to transactions that have occurred and the consequences of those events. I certainly agree that assets relate to the future but this futurity is a consequence of something that has already happened. We do recognize "the future" with an asset that has been acquired next month, next year, five years from now, or fifty years from now. We don't do that yet. Perhaps sometime we will, but at this time and in this place I am certainly not advocating it. So we should restrict ourselves to events that have occurred, and rule out the invocation of future purchases of plant as a basis of undercutting the attempt to show postponed prepaid taxes.

This leaves us with what I think is the rollover argument. If we look at the present complement of plant on which the firm is taking accelerated depreciation for tax returns and straight-line per books, we can see precisely at what point of time in the future the deduction, per tax return, will be less than the deduction in the books for this particular complement of assets. This is the basis on which the argument in favor of a postponed income tax credit rests. For convenience, we can talk about a case in which there was a postponement of tax and a credit balance as a result of this procedure. Logically the same applies to a debit balance. If we adhere to this consistent argument we must take the same position we take whenever accrual accounting is involved. If we recognize revenues on an accrual basis, we cannot, when we come to the pretax figure, adopt the government's position with respect to the revenues and expenses. I think it follows as a result of our accrual accounting that we have to calculate the tax on the basis of the items recognized in our accrual accounting and that will in fact enter into the tax return of some future period or periods. This leads to a slogan which conveys the essence of what I mean, namely, "let the tax follow the income." In order to deny the postponed tax you have to deny the reality of everything else you have reported in the financial statements.

Now, I will agree, that there will not be a postponed tax if two conditions exist. *First*, if you are willing to assert or believe that Congress will repeal the provisions of the Internal Revenue Code applicable to your particular operation, then clearly there is no sense talking about a postponed tax. If there is to be no tax in the future, no postponement is required. I think most of us are unlikely to accept that premise. *Second*, if you are willing to assert that your particular operation will not show any taxable income at any time in the future then clearly there will not be any postponed income tax effect. Historically, this seems to be the case of the railroads in this country. For your firm, however, I would insist that you say this explicitly before agreeing that there is no postponed tax. If this company, without a future, will not show any profits, it should follow through on these consequences and reduce its asset total. Otherwise you will have overstated the owners' equity by a considerable amount. If there is no postponed tax, it has to be a result of these two rigorous conditions, either one or both of these things.

A further consequence follows, if we visualize the balance sheet which results if we do not show the tax effect of accelerated depreciation on the tax return and straight-line on the books. Retained earnings will be overstated. The reader of a financial statement is entitled to assume that all of the reported earnings are "after tax." All retained earnings are considered to be "after taxes" unless you tell the reader explicitly that this is not true. If you tell him that this is not true, you have to tell him the extent to which those earnings may be overstated because of the loss of tax deductability of the plant. If you tell him, you have to give him the figures on the basis of which he can calculate the amount of the postponed tax. If you do that you might as well put in the "equity of the government" in this particular enterprise. You see I am arguing basically in terms of the statement of financial position in which you report the assets and the liabilities in which the owners have an equity. You have to be careful not to overstate that equity, within the framework of the rules adopted by accountants. I am a little bit jittery about invoking things outside this set framework.

One point on Professor Davidson's examples: one can clearly demonstrate that after a certain point the magnitude of the postponed tax liability will not change by very much. It will reach a plateau. But even after that point is reached the magnitude of the proposed tax is of significance in assessing the relative size of the business and the relationship to other equities in the business. Before that point is reached, however, the growth in the stock of depreciable assets will make a difference in the reported income, year by year. This is the part of the pattern of the company's history that is glossed over by those like Professor Davidson who emphasize the lack of change in the calculated magnitude of the difference between the two different depreciation calculations (tax versus book). They continually overlook the distorting effect of their procedure. In the world of change that you and I live, where business firms do expand and do contract, I think it is extraordinarily important to know whether or not businesses are changing, expanding or contracting, and the effect of these changes, at least approximately, on their financial statements.

PROFESSOR DAVIDSON: Professor Moonitz's chief complaint seems to be that I come only to do good. I am reminded of James Michener's comment about the Hawaiian missionaries who came to Hawaii to do good and did well. And it does seem, regardless of my motivation, that we will have done well for readers of financial statements by answering the question of whether they do reflect economic realism. As a matter of fact I'd be inclined to give even greater weight to economic realism than I would to maintaining the accrual citadel. But I am perfectly willing to move to his point as well. I must confess my sins to you, however, since I do not consider the question of whether this jibes with the views of Pacioli expressed so well some 500 years ago to really be the paramount question. I'd much rather ask whether the financial statement jibes with the views of individuals who are seeking realistic information about today's business firms. But if we were to retreat to the citadel of the accrual system, recollect that Professor Moonitz said that we deal only with transactions that have occurred but nevertheless in deciding on whether assets have value we do look to see what will happen in the future. I find it incomprehensible to say that if we are going to sell something that we now own we are only looking to past transactions that have occurred. If we are to use plant that we bought sometime ago, we'll use it in the future. It seems to me that under the accrual system we are continually assessing the probabilities of what the future holds for us rather than trying to narrow the number of cases. We should try to take a realistic view of what the future holds if we are to do our job effectively; we ought to try to expand out efforts to inquire into what is the future of the firm for which we are accounting. Professor Moonitz says we should be guided by a phrase, "let the tax follow the income" I suggest that if the tax follows the income by something more than a half century that it really doesn't have a great deal of relevance for our current accounting.

PROFESSOR MOONITZ: It is hard to rebut someone who utters such profound truths as Professor Davidson just did. I probably should agree and sit down. If you can demonstrate that there will be no rollover for 50 years, I would agree by applying discounting procedures to the magnitude 50 years away. I would come out with an amount so small that it would be negligible. I think I remember something about 6% interest compounded annually doubling in about 12 years. This means that if we look at one dollar due 12 years away it is worth 50 cents now. This means that 12 years prior to its due date, the amount is one-half; 24 years before it is due, $\frac{1}{4}$ of the amount; 36 years, one-eighth; 48 years, $\frac{1}{32}$ and for 60 years, we get about $\frac{1}{16}$ or 3%. At rates of interest over 6% obviously we will get even less. So in a particular case if you can demonstrate on this roll-over basis that the amount will not be paid in 50 years, I will agree that in our current financial statements we have nothing to worry about. but the relevance relates directly to the time dimension. If you stretch it out far enough the discounting process will make it disappear. This happens in depreciation calculations, aside from tax effects, as we all know. I recall Professor Eric Kohler telling about when he was controller of TVA back in the late 30's. During one of his early reports to Congress, he was asked why there was no depreciation for the TVA dams. His rebuttal I thought was irrefutable, and yet he did not refute depreciation accounting. He replied that the engineers estimated the dams will last not less than 500 nor more than 2000 years. He said to Congress, if you will tell us what the depreciation rate should be, we would be very happy to use it. That was the end of that argument. If under these similar circumstances you can demonstrate that there will not be any payments for not less than 50 or 500 or more than 2000 years, I'll go along with you. But I don't think you can.

## QUESTIONS

1. What is tax allocation? Illustrate.
2. What is the position of Accounting Principles Board Opinion No. 11 on tax allocation?
3. What arguments does Professor (at that time Dean) Davidson make against tax allocation?
4. What arguments does Professor Moonitz make for tax allocation?
5. Who do you think won the debate, and why?

## SELECTED BIBLIOGRAPHY

"Court Allows Disney Investment Tax Credit on Film-making Cost; Broad Effect Seen," *The Wall Street Journal*, June 4, 1973, p. 7.

# 108

## FRANCHISING REVISITED*

Herbert Hartley and Donald L. LoFranco

### THE GROWTH OF FRANCHISING

In the past few years, "franchising" has become almost a household word, and to some it would appear to be a phenomenon of the jet age. Street corners, magazines and even courtrooms have seen their share of the action. Anyone who has a name, or a reputation of some sort, seems to be trying to capitalize on it—not always with great success. What one must bear in mind however, amid all the excitement, is that franchising is not new—it is here to stay—and there are many illustrations of extremely successful franchising operations. If you think of franchising dealing mainly with the fast food business, here are some other popular examples:

automobile sales, rentals and service
automotive and hardware stores
beauty salons
bookkeeping services
candy and ice cream stores
car washes and equipment
correspondence schools
cosmetics
credit and collection services
dance schools
doughnut shops
employment and personnel agencies
grocery stores
gymnasiums
health aids and services
laundry and cleaning
men's and women's clothing shops
sports and recreation
tax services
travel agencies

Gasoline stations are among the oldest and most successful franchising operations. Although company operated gas bars are now appearing, the basic franchised operations are examples of demonstrated success.

Among the newer franchising operations are hotels and motels. It would appear that they compare very favourably with some of the older hotels to which we have become accustomed. Today, a person or a group with the ability and the funds

*From *Canadian Chartered Accountant,* April 1973, pp. 46–50. Reprinted by permission of the publisher.

available to invest in a hotel is franchised and, in return supplied with expert advice on how and where to build the hotel and how to operate it. For this an initial fee is paid, as well as an annual royalty, usually based on volume of business. True, the franchisor makes a profit, but the franchisee is in a business of his own and receives expert advice on its operation. The better he operates it, the more profit he makes. Usually, he can, at any time, sell his franchise to another suitable operator. While there is obviously room for many different methods of hotel operation, this kind offers many advantages to the travelling public and to free enterprise.

A survey and report prepared and published last year by the United States Department of Commerce, "Franchising in the Economy," revealed that franchising has grown so dramatically that it is now a major economic force. It has, indeed, displaced some small, independent businessmen, but it has stimulated a revival in small business operations in general. The report summarized its survey with the following information:

|  | 1971 (ESTIMATED) | 1969 | INCREASE |
|---|---|---|---|
| Sales of all kinds of franchising establishments | $131.6 billion | $119.5 billion | 10.1% |
| Number of establishments | 407,000 | 384,000 | 6% |

The survey also indicated that the recreation, entertainment and travel categories of franchising establishments are estimated to have made the largest increase in sales between 1969 and 1971. In two years this has increased from $48.3 million to $103.5 million—an increase of 114%.

## METHODS OF OPERATION

One authority on franchising said, "if it is eatable, drinkable, wearable or thinkable, it is franchiseable."[1] With this in mind, it is easy to imagine that the methods of operation are of vast proportions. Generally, the franchisor owns, or has exclusive rights to, trademarks, names, patents, etc., which his franchisees are authorized to use. There is considerable variation in the nature and extent of the services rendered by the franchisor with the initial sale of the franchise, and with those that continue after operations commence.

### Initial Fees

It is interesting to analyze the main sources of the franchisor's revenues. Obviously, one of the main sources has been "initial fees" and this subject has received

[1]Thomas L. Holden and Olden J. Hoover, "Accountants Stand on Franchise Reporting," *World*, Summer 1970.

considerable comment. Although there may be no common basis for comparing the selling price of franchises, the price range can vary tremendously from, say, $10,000 to well over $100,000 in the same line of business. One company requires franchise fees to be payable upon the granting of the franchise, while another is satisfied with a collection period ranging up to 20 years. This raises the question of whether the size of the initial franchise fee, and the period over which it is collected, should govern the method of accounting. It also raises the question as to whether initial franchise fees are always what they purport to be. Is a large initial franchise fee and a low annual charge the same as a small initial franchise fee and a higher annual charge? Realistically speaking, the company with proven valuable franchises to sell will charge more as the value of the franchises (as demonstrated by successful operations) increases.

### Opening Fees

Companies sometimes charge a separate fee for services rendered in connection with an opening of a franchised outlet and on the job training of employees. Other companies do not make a separate charge for this service, but presumably it is included in the initial franchise fee.

## FRANCHISE COMMISSION

A franchise commission is often referred to as the royalty which the franchisee must pay to the franchisor during the term of the contract. The royalty payment is a major incentive for both parties. Because the franchisor's earnings are dependent on the sales by the franchisee, both have the common goal of increased sales. Most franchisors charge this royalty commission, but they vary from franchise to franchise, particularly between different industries. Again, the franchisor who has charged a small initial fee may charge a larger commission.

## ADVERTISING

Franchise agreements usually provide for an advertising charge to cover national advertising and, in some cases, local advertising. National cooperative advertising programs are administered by the franchisors on behalf of the operators. Carrying out programs on this basis ensures that both the franchisor and the franchisee may avail themselves of an organized, uniform, high-calibre advertising program at reasonable cost.

## MATERIALS AND SUPPLIES

Sales of materials and supplies to franchisees are another source of income. Since quality control is an important aspect of franchising, the franchisor under certain circumstances finds it necessary to sell his goods directly to the franchisee. The selling price would normally include a profit. Because of the purchasing power of the franchisor, it would probably be difficult for the franchisee to match the quality and price with those from another source, but this may not always be the case.

Some franchisors use another approach to quality control. Rather than become involved in stock control, purchasing, receiving, shipping and billing, arrangements are made with selected suppliers to ship the goods directly to the operators. Suppliers then send the franchisor a commission in consideration for directing the sales to them. Prices and quality are generally arranged beforehand to ensure that the operator is receiving the appropriate value. Operations are inspected on a frequent, regular basis and the quality of material and supplies is closely examined at this time.

## LEASING LAND, BUILDINGS AND EQUIPMENT

Some franchisors lease real estate and/or equipment to operators and rental charges are usually determined by the franchisor on the basis of his actual and imputed costs.

Leasing offers the franchisor certain inherent advantages. Of primary importance is the control over the assets and, accordingly, the operation. Of secondary importance are the leasing profits and the unrecorded and unrealized gain in the value of the real property. This is particularly evident from the recent inflationary real estate price trends. Many franchisors who have acquired property in key merchandising locations over the past ten years continue to maintain these properties on their records at historical costs. Liquidation of these assets would result in sizable profits on disposals.

Some franchisors lease from the property owners and in turn sublet the premises to a franchisee. Usually a profit is made on this type of leasing operation and control over the property is maintained by the franchisor until termination of the lease. The purchasing of real estate is obviously the more desirable method to perpetuate franchising. Nevertheless, budgets, projected cash flow, funds availability and economic conditions are management's major considerations prior to embarking on a series of real estate acquisitions.

## SIGN RENTALS

The renting of signs to operators who own their establishments, or lease directly from the property owners, serves as a control over the operations. Profits from sign rental operations are earned on a minimum capital outlay. In actual fact, these profits represent the combination of sign rental profits and a premium charge for trade-mark usage.

Sign maintenance is usually the responsibility of the franchisor. In the event that the franchise agreement is prematurely terminated, the franchisor need only remove the signs identifying the franchise.

## COMPANY OPERATED LOCATIONS

The progressive franchisor is interested in maintaining a number of company operated locations for several reasons. These operations:

may serve as training grounds for new operators;
may be considered as inventory awaiting sale;

may be treated as experimental locations for testing new products and techniques;

would serve to establish by geographical distribution a reputation in virgin territories and expose the public to the products or services;

if profitable, could be important source of revenue to the franchisor.

## PROBLEMS FOR THE ACCOUNTANT

All of the above is of vital interest to both the franchisor and franchisee, as well as to their accountants.

## INITIAL FRANCHISE FEES

The most troublesome problem is the sale of franchises and the accounting for initial franchise fees.

A review of certain prospectuses of U.S. and Canadian companies indicates that many companies were at one time accounting for the sales of franchises on the basis of immediate recognition of full revenue. The Securities and Exchange Commission and some major accounting firms were naturally concerned about this practice. Stocks of franchising companies were at that time selling for high earnings multiples and doubts were arising as to whether or not the revenue had actually been earned by the company.

In addition to this, leasing losses may give rise to scepticism as to the validity of taking the entire franchise fee into income. A leasing loss may be considered an expense to earn the franchise fee. Therefore if this theory is accepted, the known losses to be incurred over the life of the franchise should be deducted from the initial franchise fee. This is illustrated below in comparative hypothetical situations:

| | $ | $ |
|---|---|---|
| Annual Income | | |
|     Real estate and equipment rental | 10,000 | 6,000 |
| Annual Expenses | | |
|     Mortgage interest | 3,000 | 3,000 |
|     Imputed interest on equity in real estate and equipment | 1,000 | 1,000 |
|     Interest on equipment contracts | 1,000 | 1,000 |
|     Depreciation on building and equipment (straight-line basis) | 1,000 | 1,000 |
|     Property taxes | 500 | 500 |
|     Maintenance costs | 500 | 500 |
| | 7,000 | 7,000 |
| Estimated Annual Profit (Loss) on Leasing | 3,000 | (1,000) |
| Selling price of franchise for a ten-year period | 30,000 | 30,000 |
| Leasing loss to be absorbed over the life of the franchise | – | 10,000 |
| Adjusted selling price of franchise (giving recognition to leasing loss) | 30,000 | 20,000 |

Under circumstances where a continuing fee, be it rent or something else, appears to be inadequate to cover the cost and a reasonable profit on the continuing services to be provided by the franchisor, some or all of the initial franchise fee should perhaps be deferred and amortized over the life of the franchise.

It has been suggested that in view of the complexity of franchise agreements and problems of collection, initial fees should be accounted for as received in cash. Undoubtedly, there is a simple appeal to this basis of accounting, but it is argued that it has all the weaknesses of the cash basis for accounting, which has been rejected elsewhere.

Another suggestion is that the initial fee should be taken into income over the life of the franchise. Here, again, those who resist this would point out that normally there are other means of compensating the franchisor over the franchise period, such as commissions and rents, etc., and that there is no direct relationship between the initial fee and the life of the agreement.

In most of these discussions some reference is usually made to Accounting Research Bulletin No. 43, of the American Institute of Certified Public Accountants, which states that:

> Profit is to be deemed to be realized when a sale in the ordinary course of business is effected, unless the circumstances are such that the collection of the sale price is not reasonably assured.

The Accounting Principles Board recognizes however, that receivables may be collected over a lengthy period of time and, because of existing conditions, there might be no reasonable basis for estimating their collectibility. Inexperienced operators with little or no financial investment, apart from a small down payment, and whose main source of revenue will come from a franchise in an unproven location, create a rather pessimistic forecast as to the collectibility of receivables. Situations could arise whereby a franchisor acting within the terms of the franchise agreement may be forced to cancel the contract. When such an event occurs, a court of law may conclude that the franchisee, in surrendering the franchise, has the "right of set-off" against the franchisor for the unpaid balance. Consequently, an intangible asset of questionable value replaces the receivables in the hands of the franchisor.

Under such circumstances, the Accounting Principles Board suggests that either the cost recovery method or installment method of accounting may be used. Under both methods the proceeds collected measure revenue.

On balance, the best advice appears to be that revenues should ordinarily be accounted for at the time a transaction is completed, with appropriate provision for uncollectible accounts. The use of the installment or cost recovery methods would be exceptions to this.

Before recognizing a profit, each franchise agreement should be reviewed by the accountant to determine the circumstances preceding potential refunds to the franchisee. Also potential future costs of obligations and services by the franchisor must be carefully evaluated.

Similarly, notes receivable at little or no interest rate should perhaps be discounted to present value and revenue recognition from the franchise should be adjusted accordingly.

Assuming that no such problems are encountered, here are some general criteria, which to date have been used with success in determining the initial recognition of income from the sale of the franchises:

(a) All documentation including the franchise agreement, notes receivable and any security will have been properly completed and lodged with the franchisor.

(b) The agreed down-payment will have been significant and paid to the franchisor.

(c) There will be no circumstances under which the franchisor is obliged to repurchase the franchise rights.

(d) Possession of the franchise location will have been taken by the franchisee and he must have commenced operation as evidenced by operating returns including the receipt of commissions, etc.

(e) Substantially all the initial services of the franchisor will have been performed.

(f) An adequate provision for doubtful accounts should be made. The initial provision would of necessity be based on experience and an annual review and adjustment would be planned. This would include plotting sales trends and matching break-even points with actual performance and payment histories. A successful franchisee is the most important element in the collection of unpaid balances of franchise sales.

These criteria may suffer from simplicity. There has been heated writing on the subject, particularly in the United States. . . .

### Sources of Income and Related Costs

Gross revenue figures set forth in financial statements of franchising companies very often contain several major sources of revenue. Revenue generated through the operation of retail outlets is certainly different from that derived from the sale of franchises or from the leasing of premises. A single revenue source, such as franchise sales, can have such a significant effect on net profits and earnings per share, that it is essential that the readers be made aware of the amounts relating to the different types of income, so that earnings may be assessed more intelligently. Insofar as it is possible, costs as well as revenues for each segment of the business should be distinguishable.

The recommendations of the accounting and auditing research committee of the Canadian Institute of Chartered Accountants have encouraged the provision of such segmented information to shareholders and others.

In order to match revenue and expense as it applies to initial franchise fees, the franchisor should accumulate, in the accounts, costs by franchise location. As these are sold and revenue taken up, the corresponding costs should be charged against income. Costs not directly related to specific revenue producing transactions, including fixed costs, should of course be expensed as incurred.

### REPURCHASE OF FRANCHISES

The repurchase of franchises has in the past presented some problems, but this need not be so. The repurchase of a profitable franchise can be the result of a sound business decision. The question is whether the transaction is an adjustment or a cancellation of a previous sale, or whether it is in fact the purchase of an asset for the earning of greater income. Usually a review of the facts will disclose the required information.

If the franchisor refunds the consideration received, the original sale should be cancelled, which would result in a reduction of current revenue. If franchise rights are repossessed, but no refund is made, the transaction should not be regarded as the cancellation of the sale. A franchisor acquiring the business of an operating franchisee should normally account for the transaction as a "purchase" according to the rules of business combinations.

## AREA FRANCHISES

So far, we have dealt largely with the sale of single-establishment franchises. Fees relating to the sale of area franchises (i.e. geographical territories) can be significant and may pose additional accounting problems. It is suggested, however, that the same principles are involved and that the substance of the franchise agreement may well indicate the most appropriate method by which income should be recognized in the accounts.

## RELATIVE SIGNIFICANCE OF TRANSACTIONS

A large well-established organization, operating numerous locations itself, may also sell franchises for modest amounts, or occasionally sell a single area franchise to a franchisee of substance for a very large amount. The economics and relative significance of these transactions for a large organization, as opposed to a small one, may influence the acceptance of the accounting methods used. This of course is not new to accountants, but illustrates the difficulty in endeavouring to provide hard and fast accounting rules for a whole industry.

## CONCLUSION

Franchising has been a troubled industry. . . .

When the complexities of franchising are stripped away and the true facts of each situation are known, it is not difficult to apply appropriate accounting principles. The challenge to the profession, as it has been in most new industries and special situations, is to avoid being hampered by hard and fast technical rules which do not apply in every case, and to be flexible and knowledgeable enough to present a fair view of the operation. Franchisors are subject to the same accounting standards and disciplines as are other industries.

EDITORS' NOTE: The AICPA has published guidelines on accounting for franchise fee revenue that emphasize essentially the same conclusions as this article.

QUESTIONS

1. Illustrate the following quotation, "if it is eatable, drinkable, wearable or thinkable, it is franchisable."

2. In franchising, why does the most troublesome accounting problem concern the sale of franchises and the initial franchise fee?

3. What accounting problem can develop with the repurchase of franchises?

# 109

## ACCOUNTING FOR MULTINATIONALS*

Gerhard G. Mueller

The growth of multinational (or international, transnational or possibly global) business during the last two-and-a-half decades ranks near the top of new business developments—comparable with, let us say, the electronic computer revolution.

Basically, a multinational company is one which conducts a significant portion of its total business across national borders and/or raises long-term capital wherever in the world it is available. But the *intensity* of multinational business activities can be expressed in terms of several variables. Six hundred and fifty of the world's industrial companies have annual sales in excess of $300 [million] (measured on the basis of 1971 turnover).

The multinational company has been studied as a competitor of the nation-state, as a factor in world economic development, and quite often as an object of national policy changes. But however it is analysed or classified, the multinational company has gained economic, social and political significance of major proportions.

Hence it is not surprising to find that the meteoric rise of the multinational company after World War II has produced, among other things, some new accounting developments.

Accounting's responses to its environment have, of course, been as diverse as the environment itself. The accounting needs of a centrally-controlled economy like that of the Soviet Union are quite different from those found in an administered market economy. Similarly, accounting in a developing country has functions which are different from those in a highly developed country. This manifests itself in different accounting standards and practices between different environments. If one has a broad social science view of accounting, environment-related differences in accounting seem perfectly logical.

Yet this is exactly the point where the growth of the multinational company has caused a problem. Because of its nature and role in society, accounting has developed

*From *Accountancy*, July 1975, pp. 70–75. Reprinted by permission of the publisher and author.

with strong national accents. It is built into the various national companies laws; it is developed and applied by national groups of professional accountants; and it serves in national systems which may or may not be similar in a cultural or social sense.

In sum, accounting is a very nationalistically orientated discipline, very much like law. This is understandable, and environmentally rather desirable. But it is almost the antithesis of the spirit and style of the multinational company.

Multinational companies—at least those that are predominantly host-country orientated—are eager to lose a strict national identity in favour of multinational acceptance in many different countries. For instance, Philips of the Netherlands feels best if Germans see it as a German enterprise, Australians as an Australian company and US citizens as a US corporation. Multiplicity is the key characteristic of the multinational company.

But this same company has difficulty in existing with multiplicity in accounting. It cannot plan and control its operations under dozens of different national accounting viewpoints. It must somehow achieve a unified consolidated financial report despite the fact that its business operations may well be transacted in 100 or more different national currencies.

Also it cannot, at one and the same time, apply several dozen different national financial accounting standards and procedures. It must somehow find a way to present its financial affairs to outsiders so that they can be read and understood by investors, financial communities, other business firms, government agencies and the business public at large in many different national environments.

Thus, we have a conflict of fairly major proportions—on the one hand, the multinational company seeking to transcend strictly national visibility and practices; and on the other hand, an accounting discipline deeply anchored in exactly the type of constraints which the multinational enterprise is seeking to avoid, or at least minimise.

The full impact of multinational company growth on accounting theory and practice, as well as accounting research and education, is still indeterminate. As far as theory is concerned, the available literature is limited to a few books, a few sections in accounting and finance handbooks and some two or three dozen PhD dissertations.

As for practice-related efforts, these have produced a rather huge descriptive periodical and brochure-type literature which lists and sometimes classifies accounting and financial reporting standards and practices found in individual countries. Most recently, this literature has become comparative in nature.[1]

Actual practice, as observable in internal company reports, annual reports to shareholders or prospectuses underlying new issues of securities, reflects divergent national viewpoints tempered with *ad hoc* adaptations toward the needs of the multinational company. For instance, multinational companies based in Sweden have begun to make available, together with English-language translations of their annual reports, little booklets explaining Swedish accounting principles to Anglo-Saxon readers.

---

[1] For example, *Accounting Principles and Reporting Practices—A Survey in 38 Countries,* New York: Price Waterhouse International, 1973.

On the research and education front, international accounting matters are also receiving increasing attention. For instance, many professional accounting rule-making bodies across the world are studying, or recently have studied, international accounting questions with a view toward eventual standard-setting. The Financial Accounting Standards Board . . . gave the question of foreign currency translation top priority among its research projects.

In March 1975, the FASB issued an Accounting Standard proposing new rules of foreign currency translation requiring what it calls 'the temporal method'—and is simply the British 'historic rate' method under another name. Under this proposed Accounting Standard, the 'closing rate' method of conversion, to which most British companies have moved in recent years, will be unacceptable. This will mean that, for a time at least, British and American accounting are out of step.

The flurry of related activity in accounting education is also unmistakable. For some 10 years now, the American Accounting Association has annually appointed a committee to explore a particular phase of the overall international accounting problem.

The International Accounting Standards Committee came into existence on 29 June 1973, and has issued its first Standard 'Disclosure of Accounting Policies'. Management development programmes, particularly in Europe, increasingly include material concerned with accounting for the multinational firm. Taken together, these various activities support the conclusion that new accounting developments of an international nature can be expected routinely during the near future.

Professor G. M. Scott of the University of Texas has recently categorised *internal* accounting problems of the multinational company into the following six areas: (a) taxation; (b) currency translation; (c) transfer pricing; (d) financial planning; (e) performance evaluation; and (f) information systems.[2]

## TAXATION

Different countries, of course, have fundamentally different tax systems. These differences manifest themselves in different types of taxes (eg, income taxes, purchase taxes, and turnover taxes with the value added tax being a special variation of the latter); in different tax rates (eg, income tax rates are zero in the Bahamas and the Bermudas, 15% in Hong Kong, 25% to 30% in Switzerland, 48% in the US, 50% in Canada, 53.5% in Israel, 55% in India, and 60% in Sri Lanka[3]); in different tax bases (eg, certain types of income go completely tax-free in one country, but are taxed to the extent of the full normal rate in another country); and in special tax provisions applicable to international operations which sometimes penalise and sometimes benefit multinational companies (eg, bilateral tax treaties between countries, border taxes like tariffs, and tax holidays on some new investments).

---

[2]*An Introduction to Financial Control and Reporting in Multinational Enterprises.* Studies in International Business No. 1 Austin: The University of Texas, 1973.

[3]Board of Inland Revenue Foreign Intelligence Section, 'Overseas Company Tax Rates.' *Accountant,* vol 168, no. 5121, pp. 177—182.

Taxation has an all-pervasive impact on aspects of international operations: where to invest, how to market, what transfer prices to charge, what form of organisation to utilise, where and when to shift production locations, how to finance, etc. The prevailing point of view among multinational company managements is that careful and systematic tax planning and accounting, supervised by international taxation specialists, will yield significant tax savings in international operations.

The problem in this area is primarily one of huge complexity, constantly changing rules and regulations in individual countries, and a massive information retrieval system. Effective international tax planning and accounting is still a major bottleneck for many multinational companies.

## FOREIGN CURRENCY TRANSLATION

For various management and investment purposes, the multinational company must prepare budgets, many internal management reports and, ultimately, its published financial statements in terms of one national currency unit. One simply cannot add Australian, Canadian, New Zealand and United States dollars arithmetically and get a sum that has any meaning at all.

Hence the multinational company has two specific problems: (a) choice of a reference currency, as it is sometimes called, and (b) translating accounting data back and forth from one currency to another.

Arguments have been made to suggest that the reference currency ought to be the one in which the majority of a company's actual transactions are conducted, the one with which top management is most familiar, or the one in which dividends are paid to shareholders. In practice, most multinational companies choose as their reference currency the money unit of the country in which the company is incorporated or has its legal domicile. By and large, this is a workable convention, even though it causes some special problems—for instance, in the petroleum industry, where most crude oil contracts and agreements are expressed in terms of US dollars irrespective of a company's legal domicile.

The foreign currency translation problem is considerably thornier. Firstly, translation is often confused with conversion. By convention, accountants think of conversion when an actual money unit is directly exchanged for another. A French tourist arriving at the Wentworth Hotel, in Sydney, 'converts' French francs into Australian dollars to meet his expenses while in Sydney. On the other hand, 'translation' is only a paper process. It takes existing account balances in one currency and translates or restates them into another currency.

Thus, the accounts of a British Petroleum Company affiliate in Australia are originally stated in terms of Australian dollars, reflecting the Australian financial position and results of operations. But the parent company in the UK, for reasons already mentioned, requires that these accounts be translated into pounds sterling. On paper only, they must appear as sterling expressions, so that they can be integrated in further information-generating processes or be better understood by foreign readers.

Several key questions mark this translation process:

1. At which rate should the translation occur, since actual foreign exchange dealings take place at many different and changing rates? The tourist at the Wentworth receives a considerably worse rate than a large French company would be able to obtain in making a long-term investment in Australia.

2. Should all financial items be translated at the same rate? If a current or daily rate were so used, one would have to look at all business transactions from an extremely short-term or cash point of view, and abstract from the fact that many companies make rather permanent international investments and constantly reinvest earnings achieved abroad without any intention of ever remitting them in the form of dividends (cash) to the parent company.

3. How should one account for translation differences? For instance, if a US company had borrowed the equivalent of US $50 [million] in Germany, and early in 1973 the exchange value of the US dollar *vis-à-vis* the Deutsche mark fell approximately 15%, the US company would need eventually 15% more dollars to liquidate its German mark debt. But prior to actual liquidation of the debt, the 'difference' is a paper difference only. Should it be shown as a loss on the US company's financial statements? If so, should it be amortised, let us say, over the time during which such debt is outstanding? Should the difference be shown in the profit and loss account, or should it be subtracted from a capital reserve of some type?

Many formal proposals have been made on how the translation of foreign currencies in accounts should be accomplished and reported. None of these proposals has been generally accepted. Actual foreign currency exchange (ie conversion) rates are current market prices, and therefore, at least to the extent that they represent the free interplay of markets, representative of current economic values. It is conceptually impossible to apply such value indicators to historical cost amounts and achieve intelligible results. Combinations of national price-level adjustments and foreign exchange rate translations don't seem to fit the bill either. Hence significant diversity marks foreign currency translation procedures presently employed by multinational companies.

## MULTINATIONAL TRANSFER PRICING

In a domestic setting, transfer pricing between dependent branches, divisions or affiliated companies is used to facilitate the control and evaluation of operations and to motivate divisional managers toward corporate-wide goals. Some perceived equity between managers of profit or investment centres is usually an overriding consideration in domestic transfer price setting.

Even though some theoretical approaches to this problem are available, the prevailing state of the art (ie difficulty with measurement problems) has made their adaptation to real-world business practice all but impossible. Here we have another area where *ad hoc* solutions prevail in the everyday life of business companies.

The problem is accentuated in the multinational company. Multinational companies typically transfer greater proportions of their total output between related companies than do domestic companies—approximately 40% of all international trade is thought to be transfers between related companies.

One author[4] has stated the dilemma in the following terms: 'The lack of an approach to transfer pricing which is compatible with the mode of operations of multinational companies must be counted as one of the major management technology roadblocks preventing multinational companies from moving as far toward global co-ordination as they would like.'

A problem within the area of multinational transfer pricing is taxation. Since a tax collector sits at each end of goods and services transferred by multinational companies, there is an inherent conflict between sovereign governments about shifting the incidence of taxation from one country to the next.

If a Toyota car, manufactured and assembled in Japan, were exported to Australia at a very high transfer price, the profit from manufacture and sale of that car would accrue totally in Japan and allow the Japanese government to tax it in its entirety. This might not please Australian authorities, since the sale occurred there. Presumably part of the profit should be attributed to the sales transaction, and therefore be taxable in Australia.

Aside from tax problems, the multinational company must consider multinational cash movements and managerial decision-making among many other lesser factors when it sets its international pricing system. In the cash area, we have situations where one might actually be able to repatriate some profits or investments from a country despite, let us say, stringent foreign exchange controls to the contrary. If one can set transfer prices high enough, some margin of cash is 'returned' each time a transaction with that country is undertaken.

With regard to managerial decision-making, one need only think of make-or-buy decisions to appreciate how crucial it is that headquarters management has reliable cost and revenue information which is not influenced by exogenous transfer price considerations. Every purchase of local goods and services, and every employment of a local human resource, may represent a sub-optimal decision if the multinational pricing system within a group of affiliated companies is not fully effective. Much additional research and experimentation are needed if progress is to be made with this problem.

## FINANCIAL PLANNING

Multinational financial planning has been characterised as a 'mission impossible'. While the financial planning processes at home are conceptually similar to multinational planning processes, the latter are vastly more difficult to execute because multinational business objectives are typically quite different. There is not only a much greater number of variables which must be brought to bear, but also language and intercultural factors generally tend to inhibit effective planning procedures across national borders.

---

[4]G. M. Scott, '. . . Control and Reporting in Multinational Enterprises,' p. 62.

As a simple example, an international hotel company might typically have as its main domestic objectives: (a) maximisation of property values of hotel sites for long-term gains; (b) emphasis on equity interests for the same reason; and (c) emphasis on conference services.

For its operations abroad, the same company may have these objectives: (a) minimisation of property values in certain countries; transfer of maximum profits to others; (b) minimisation of equity interests abroad; and (c) emphasis on tourist services.

One particularly onerous profit-planning problem relates to the organisational form of the multinational enterprise. In strictly domestic operations, there is usually a strong orientation toward short-term planning *by* profit or investment centres *for* profit or investment centres. A clear tendency toward a decentralised form of organisation exists here. In contrast, the multinational company can realise its comparative advantage and achieve many of its objectives only if it co-ordinates closely on a world-wide basis. This assumes a fairly centralised form of organisation, and thus almost immediately a planning conflict and dichotomy of approaches.

Long-term or investment planning poses questions of its own. Because of all types of local or national constraints, the multinational company cannot always apply the least expensive capital to the most rewarding investment project. For instance, the availability of local capital may be fairly dependent upon political desirability of a planned project or the amount of local equity participation that is to be made available rather than upon strict economic considerations.

It is also especially difficult in international situations to measure return on investments and assign the costs of long-term capital to individual projects or countries. Yet in financial planning—particularly in budgeting procedures—multinational companies seem to be making steady progress. Professor G. M. Scott[5] observes: 'It is likely that this aspect of management technology in multinational companies is developing as fast as, or faster than, any other.'

## MULTINATIONAL PERFORMANCE EVALUATION

In the typical domestic case, company operations are divided into profit or investment centres which, in turn, allows the use of various financial ratios, especially rate of return ratios, to be employed as indices of managerial performance. In the multinational company, this possibility is often obstructed because global coordination of investments, taxes, transfer prices and other managerial business procedures obscures cleavages between operating entities and therefore between the profit or investment centres. In multinational companies, headquarters management tend to make the major decisions which affect profitability of individual units.

Moreover, multinational managers are encouraged to make decisions which may benefit a unit other than their own, if this contributes to increased benefit for the total system on a global basis. Thus performance evaluation is a difficult problem in multinational companies. Local requirements often influence local operations and thus

[5]G. M. Scott, '. . . Control and Reporting in Multinational Enterprises,' p. 68.

become difficult to measure on a comparable basis between countries or geographic regions.

## INFORMATION SYSTEMS

A number of factors contribute to the general condition that multinational companies need sophisticated information as a basis for managing themselves. Distance is one such factor. Here, information must become a substitute for relatively frequent personal contacts between managers operating in local environments and headquarters managers.

A second factor is the great diversity of external conditions which must be considered in multinational decision-making. This refers to legal, political, social and cultural factors that bear upon business decision-making. Included are also economic data such as actions of competitors, tax developments, local money sources and interest rates, raw materials sources and prices, and the like.

A third factor is feedback requirements. An operation halfway round the globe is more easily neglected than one only a few miles away. In multinational settings it is particularly important that all points of operation be provided systematically with timely and relevant information between different points in the system (ie lateral information demands).

Business information traditionally flows upwards or downwards in organisational hierarchies. Lateral information flows, such as between Far Eastern subsidiaries of a multinational company based in Europe, are potentially as important as information flowing to and from company headquarters. In conclusion, the multinational company needs more, and in part different, business information than its domestic counterparts.

The annual end product of the various accounting processes within the multinational company is a set of consolidated financial statements prepared for the company and all of its subsidiaries and affiliates. We have already discussed the foreign currency translation problem which must be resolved before financial statement consolidation procedures can be undertaken. There are, however, at least three further critical problems.

The first of these problems relates to the consolidation process itself. It involves the realisation, already pointed out, that financial accounting standards and practices have developed on different national levels and therefore differ from country to country—sometimes substantially. Where local laws require that local accounting rules and regulations be observed by local companies, which in turn are subsidiaries of multinational companies, a process of adjustment and restatement has to take place before the various subsidiaries can be consolidated with the parent company's financial statements.

Put differently, statements prepared on a replacement value basis cannot be consolidated with statements prepared on a transaction cost basis. The eventual consolidated statements will have a domicile in terms of a specific country and that country's accounting standards and practices. All statements prepared from other viewpoints or on the basis of other underlying principles must first be restated or adjusted to be eligible for consolidation.

The second external financial reporting problem faced by multinational companies relates to disclosure. In case of a huge multinational company, financial statement consolidation probably hides enough facts and relationships to offset partially the benefits of consolidation. Hence, arrays of informative financial disclosures are a 'must' if consolidated financial statements of multinational companies are to be understood reasonably well. The following is a brief and by no means exhaustive list of absolutely necessary disclosure:

1. A specific statement of the national accounting principles on the basis of which the consolidated financial statements have been prepared (eg 'in conformity with accounting principles generally accepted in Germany').

2. Specification of the consolidation practices employed—especially any exclusions from consolidation and the reasons therefor.

3. Clear description of the foreign currency translation methods used and the disposition made of translation adjustments or differences.

4. Analysis of key financial variables like sales, net income from operations, net assets, and the like, according to geographic dispersal; especially dichotomies like domestic/international, developed/underdeveloped areas, and private/non-private business.

5. Consolidated funds flow analysis, with an elaboration by management of the direction of new multinational investments and/or disinvestments.

6. Analysis of international sources of long-term capital, including interest and dividend requirements in what currencies and listings of securities on what stock exchanges.

The third problem is resolved the least. It involves making published financial reports available to interested parties in third, fourth and 'enth' countries. In other words, an Australian investor who has acquired securities in a large Swiss-based multinational company ought to receive and be able to understand periodic financial reports of that company.

But here the thornier question relates to accounting data. If, let us say, the statements are prepared according to Swiss accounting principles, their meaning is likely to be misunderstood in Australia. On the other hand, it is not clear that it is feasible to restate (ie transliterate) the completed and published statements from a Swiss base to an Australian base.

If one could restate the statements of multinational companies from one set of accounting standards and practices to another, one might then have as many as 20 or 30 simultaneous sets of financial statements for the same company—each expressed on the basis of a different set of national accounting principles and each showing different amounts for such figures as working capital, total assets, and net income.

To date, little progress has been made on this rather pervasive question of transnational financial reporting. It joins the multinational managerial accounting problems described earlier in a demand for much closer interface between the multinational company and the theory and practice of accounting.

## QUESTIONS

1. What is the key characteristic of the multinational company, and why does it cause accounting problems?

2. What are the chief internal accounting problems of the multinational company in regard to the following accounting areas: taxation, currency translation, transfer pricing, financial planning, performance evaluation, and information systems?

3. What are three external financial reporting problems of multinational companies?

# Part 6
# Financial Statements
# and Their Users

# 110

## UNITED STATES
## Objectives of Financial Statements*
George M. Scott

Accountants the world around have not adequately specified the fundamental assumptions and philosophy underlying our financial reporting processes. We have been remiss, for example, in not specifying the objectives of financial reporting. Partly as a consequence of the failure to agree on these objectives, there is no benchmark against which to test the utility of our financial reporting practices, and financial statements often seem to become an end in themselves rather than a means to an end.

The ever more sophisticated US investors and financial analysts, along with others interested, have served notice that accounting statements do not adequately serve them, and that they are placing decreasing reliance on these statements. Public statements by company officials, *ad hoc* financial statements, special forecasts prepared within the investment community, and information from within the company are increasingly being used instead of accountants' statements. Small investors without extensive and systematic access to these non-accounting sources suffer an especial hardship when the accounting statements do not satisfy their information needs.

This perceived lack of utility associated with accounting financial statements has not gone unnoticed by the accounting profession; indeed, it could not, since the investment community loudly calls for accounting reforms to provide better information. The American Institute of CPAs took two simultaneous steps in April 1971 to this end—it appointed the Wheat Committee and the Trueblood Committee (each known by its chairman's name). The Wheat Committee's recommendations have resulted in the establishment of the Financial Accounting Standards Board (FASB), examined in this journal in October by Professor Lee Seidler. In October 1973 the Trueblood Committee (the Study Group on the Objectives of Financial Statements) rendered its seventy-page report on Objectives, which is published by the American Institute of CPAs. The main body of the report consists of a series of arguments, each followed by a statement of a recommended objective which is based on and supported by the preceding arguments.

While other studies by professional bodies have been directly or tangentially concerned with objectives, the Trueblood report has a pragmatic and authoritative mien which makes it likely to have a significantly greater impact than preceding studies. Although its recommendations will not be officially accepted or rejected by the profession, they can be expected to carry heavy weight in the deliberations of the FASB and others who will determine US accounting principles.

Several criticisms of financial accounting in the US are set forth in the report and are apparently perceived by the Committee as valid criticisms. These criticisms suggest

*From *The Accountant's Magazine,* December 1973, pp. 669–670. Reprinted by permission of the publisher.

manner

CRITICS

the flavour of the report and are summarised by such statements as "Accountants have considered themselves primarily historians, not prophets.", "Historical costs of resources and obligations only coincidentally reflect their current values.", "When like things are not reported alike, users of financial statements have difficulty comparing competing economic opportunities." and "Assertions have been made that financial statements do not provide sufficient information about the liquidity and cash flows of an enterprise."

The one basic objective of financial statements is set forth by the report as ". . . to provide information useful for making economic decisions.", an objective which should surprise no one. The report goes on to note that "This basic accounting objective requires that every accounting objective, standard, principle, procedure and practice should serve users' needs". With respect to users the report notes the following:

> An objective of financial statements is to serve primarily those users who have limited authority, ability, or resources to obtain information and who rely on financial statements as their principal source of information about an enterprise's economic activities.

The report places direct emphasis on "predicting, comparing and evaluating" as functions of financial statements in two of the three of its objectives statements which follow, and these considerations are implicit in the third:

OBJECTIVES

> An objective of financial statements is to provide information useful to investors and creditors for predicting, comparing, and evaluating potential cash flows to them in terms of amount, timing and related uncertainty.

> An objective of financial statements is to provide factual and interpretative information to users about transactions and other events which is useful for predicting, comparing, and evaluating enterprise earning power. Basic underlying assumptions with respect to matters subject to interpretation, evaluation, prediction, or estimation should be disclosed.

> An objective of financial statements is to supply information useful in judging management's ability to utilise enterprise resources effectively in achieving the primary enterprise goal.

The predictive functions become much more explicit in the following objectives statement:

> An objective of financial statements is to provide information useful for the predictive process. Financial forecasts should be provided when they will enhance the reliability of users' predictions.

With respect to financial statements the report recommends the following, while at the same time further emphasising the predictive, comparative and evaluative aspects of financial reporting:

> An objective is to provide a statement of financial position useful for predicting, comparing, and evaluating enterprise earning power. This statement should provide

information concerning enterprise transactions and other events that are part of incomplete earnings cycles. Current values should also be reported when they differ significantly from historical cost. Assets and liabilities should be grouped or segregated by the relative uncertainty of the amount and timing of prospective realisation or liquidation.

An objective is to provide a statement of periodic earnings useful for predicting, comparing, and evaluating enterprise earning power. . . .

An objective is to provide a statement of financial activities useful for predicting, comparing and evaluating enterprise earnings power. This statement should report mainly on factual aspects of enterprise transactions having or expected to have significant cash consequences. This statement should report data that requires minimal judgment and interpretation by the preparer.

Thus, both expected and unexpected recommendations can be seen to be contained in the report. While user needs are paramount, the user with limited additional information sources is singled out as being the primary user to be served by financial statements. Emphasis is predictably placed on earning power, but cash flow reporting and evaluation appear to be accorded a position of co-equal importance by the report; this cash orientation is indicated in the report in two major ways. First, the financial position and earnings statements themselves are recommended to have a cash orientation, as exemplified by the statement that ". . . information about transactions and events . . . should be stated in terms of actual or prospective cash impact and should facilitate comparisons". Second, the third recommended financial statement is a quasi-cash flow statement, which by implication downgrades the importance of the net working capital funds flow statement which has come increasingly into use in the US. Transactions that establish highly probable future cash flows—such as purchase commitments, lines of credit and sales order backlogs—are recommended to be a part of this financial activities statement, and the statement is not necessarily expected to articulate with the other two statements.

The report provides further impetus to modest movements in the US towards current value accounting, while at the same time its statements on this topic are not strong ones. Uncertainty is accorded explicit cognisance by a suggestion that assets and liabilities be grouped according to degree of uncertainty. The triple criteria of providing information for predictive, comparative and evaluative purposes are pervasive throughout the report and, coupled with identification of the primary user, provide the most authoritative and reasonably explicit objectives and focus for financial reporting to date in the US; the statement that an objective of financial statements is to provide information useful for the predictive process will certainly serve to move the very reluctant US accounting community toward the acceptance of financial forecasts as a part of our responsibilities.

Other matters briefly examined in the report, but not mentioned in this news article, include consideration of the objectives of reporting for government and not-for-profit organisations and reporting on the social impact of an enterprise.

Overall, the report serves to clarify the objectives of financial reporting in the complex business and investment environment of the US and provides a great deal of needed direction for the establishment of accounting standards and principles.

## QUESTIONS

1. What did the Trueblood and Wheat Committees accomplish?

2. What criticisms of financial accounting in the United States were made by the Trueblood Committee?

3. What is the one basic objective of financial statements as reported by the Trueblood Committee?

4. What three functions of financial statements are emphasized in the Trueblood Report? Define each function.

5. What three statements are recommended by the Trueblood Report?

6. Which concept of fund was recommended for statement purposes in the report? Why?

7. What support for financial forecasts is provided by the report?

## SELECTED BIBLIOGRAPHY

Chambers, R. J., "Many Curiosities," *CA Magazine*, December 1973, pp. 19-20.

Mautz, Robert K., "A Significant Shift in Emphasis," *CA Magazine*, December 1973, pp. 17-19.

Skinner, Ross M., "Brave New Beginning or Dead End," *CA Magazine*, December 1973, pp. 12-15.

Sorter, George H., "Objectives of Financial Statements: An Inside View," *CA Magazine*, November 1973, pp. 30-33.

Stamp, Edward, "A Curate's Egg," *CA Magazine*, December 1973, pp. 15-17.

# 111

## OBJECTIVES OF FINANCIAL STATEMENTS
## Some Managerial Questions*

James Don Edwards and Carl S. Warren

On June 6, 1974, the Financial Accounting Standards Board (FASB) issued a discussion memorandum concerned with objectives of financial statements and qualitative characteristics of financial reporting. This memorandum raises several questions about the objectives of financial statements which, in turn, relate directly to

*From *Cost and Management,* January-February 1975, pp. 46—49. Reprinted by permission of the publisher.

**Table 1    Objectives of Financial Statements**

1. The basic objective of financial statements is to provide information useful for making economic decisions.

2. An objective of financial statements is to serve primarily those users who have limited authority, ability, or resources to obtain information and who rely on financial statements as their principal source of information about an enterprise's economic activities.

3. An objective of financial statements is to provide information useful to investors and creditors for predicting, comparing, and evaluating potential cash flows to them in terms of amount, timing, and related uncertainty.

4. An objective of financial statements is to provide users with information for predicting, comparing, and evaluating enterprise earning power.

5. An objective of financial statements is to supply information useful in judging management's ability to utilize enterprise resources effectively in achieving the primary enterprise goal.

6. An objective of financial statements is to provide factual and interpretive information about transactions and other events which is useful for predicting, comparing, and evaluating enterprise earning power. Basic underlying assumptions with respect to matters subject to interpretation, evaluation, prediction, or estimation should be disclosed.

7. An objective is to provide a statement of financial position useful for predicting, comparing, and evaluating enterprise earning power. This statement should provide information concerning enterprise transactions and other events that are part of incomplete earnings cycles. Current values should also be reported when they differ significantly from historical cost. Assets and liabilities should be grouped or segregated by the relative uncertainty of the amount and timing of prospective realization or liquidation.

8. An objective is to provide a statement of periodic earnings useful for predicting, comparing, and evaluating enterprise earning power. The net result of completed earnings cycles and enterprise activities resulting in recognizable progress toward completion of incomplete cycles should be reported. Changes in the values reflected in successive statements of financial position should also be reported, but separately, since they differ in terms of their certainty of realization.

9. An objective is to provide a statement of financial activities useful for predicting, comparing, and evaluating enterprise earning power. This statement should report mainly on factual aspects of enterprise transactions having or expected to have significant cash consequences. This statement should report data that require minimal judgment and interpretation by the preparer.

10. An objective of financial statements is to provide information useful for the predictive process. Financial forecasts should be provided when they will enhance the reliability of users' predictions.

11. An objective of financial statements for governmental and not-for-profit organizations is to provide information useful for evaluating the effectiveness of the management of resources in achieving the organization's goals. Performance measures should be quantified in terms of identified goals.

### Table 1    Objectives of Financial Statements (Continued)

12. An objective of financial statements is to report on those activities of the enterprise affecting society which can be determined and described or measured and which are important to the role of the enterprise in its social environment.

managerial accounting. The purpose of this article is to set forth some of the major issues raised in the AICPA memorandum, briefly comment on these questions, and raise some additional issues concerning the objectives of financial statements as related to managerial accounting. In doing so, hopefully this article will stimulate additional thought and response as to the role of the managerial accountant in determining objectives of financial reporting.

The Objectives Study specified twelve "objectives" and seven "qualitative" characteristics of financial reporting as shown in Tables 1 and 2. In considering the Objectives Study, the FASB discussion memorandum addressed itself to four *general* questions:[1]

Which, if any, of the objectives and qualitative characteristics set forth in the *Report of the Study Group on the Objectives of Financial Statements* should the FASB adopt at this time?

Which, if any, objectives and qualitative characteristics should the FASB subject further to study and consideration before deciding whether to adopt?

Should the FASB defer further consideration of any of the objectives and qualitative characteristics set forth in the *Report of the Study Group on the Objectives of Financial Statements*? If so, which?

Are there objectives or qualitative characteristics other than those set forth in the *Report of the Study Group on the Objectives of Financial Statements* that the FASB should consider?

Each of the twelve objectives and seven qualitative characteristics was examined in the light of these four general questions.

[1]Financial Accounting Standards Board, *FASB Discussion Memorandum:* "Conceptual Framework for Accounting and Reporting: Consideration of the Report of the Study Group on the Objectives of Financial Statements" (Stamford, Conn., FASB, 1974), pp. 2–3.

### Table 2    Qualitative Characteristics

Relevance and materiality
Form and substance
Reliability
Freedom from bias
Comparability
Consistency
Understandability

From a managerial accounting viewpoint, the first question of major concern dealt with the specification of what information should be provided by financial statements versus other types of information which should be reported through different communicative media. From both a preparer and user standpoint the managerial accountant is perhaps best qualified to make this judgment. This judgment must be made in the light of the potential benefits to the users of financial information of releasing the information in a particular medium versus the associated costs. The managerial accountant is perhaps best able to measure the costs of releasing information. For example, what are the costs of releasing information in the annual report versus releasing the same information in a financial newspaper? Is there a significant difference? In arriving at such estimates, opportunity costs (effect on competitors, etc.) as well as out-of-pocket costs must be considered. Measurement of the associated benefits of releasing information is exceedingly difficult to estimate. However, in deciding what information to provide for top executive decision-making, managerial accountants must deal with this problem on a day-to-day basis. Managerial accounting expertise in this area of how much and what information to provide would be a valuable input in resolving the financial accounting dilemma of determining how much and what information to provide to investors (external users of accounting data). For example, should financial forecasts be presented in annual reports or should they be presented only in financial newspapers? What are the costs of presenting this information? How do we measure the potential benefits to investors of presenting financial forecasts? Managerial accountants can provide valuable answers to these and similar types of questions.

One of the major objectives set forth by the AICPA Study Group implies that "financial statements should serve primarily those users who have limited authority, ability, or resources to obtain information and who rely on financial statements as their principal source of information about an enterprise's economic activities." The discussion memorandum raises the question of what basis should be used to determine this primary audience of financial statements users. That is, which user group should management, as the preparer of financial statements, be most concerned with (stockholders, creditors, financial analysts, etc.)? Creditors and financial analysts have relatively more ability, resources, and authority to demand and analyze financial information than do stockholders. Given the above objective, this implies that management should be primarily concerned with reporting to stockholders in annual reports. Is this the current orientation of financial reporting? In addition, this objective, from a managerial accounting viewpoint, relegates management, *as a user of financial statements*, to a relatively low status because of management's ready access to enterprise information. Is this low consideration to management's use of financial statements warranted? Does management use financial statement information extensively in its decision-making processes? Also, given the costs of gathering information, the assumption that management has ready access to all enterprise information may not be a valid one. Answers to these questions must entail analyses of information uses of management and primarily, management's use of financial statements. Again managerial accountants can provide valuable insights.

The Objectives Study placed a great deal of emphasis on past, present, and prospective cash flows. This objective implicitly assumes that "the principal goal of a commerical enterprise is to maximize cash return to owners; its management is accountable for progress toward this goal." A logical question is whether the maximization of cash flows is the goal of most enterprises? Other alternative goals could include growth of the enterprise, continuity of enterprise life, maximization of the share of the market within an industry, and stability of enterprise earnings. In addition, even if one does accept the maximization of cash flows as an established goal, there is a possible conflict between emphasizing cash flows versus accounting earnings as reflected in current income statements. The maximization of accounting earnings will not always lead to the maximization of cash flows. This could mean that we may move more towards cash accounting or more likely, towards a modified accrual/cash accounting basis. This would obviously entail some dramatic changes in current reporting practices. However, these possible changes are dependent upon (1) the maximization of cash flows as an enterprise goal and (2) whether a material inconsistency exists between the goals of maximization of cash flows and accounting earnings. Management and managerial accountants can give us significant insights into these questions.

The prior paragraph raised the question of enterprise goals. The answer to that question will have significant ramifications for management and managerial accountants in that management must be evaluated in relation to enterprise goals. Hence, if the maximization of cash flows is established as "the" goal and the financial reports are properly adjusted, shareholders will logically use cash flows to evaluate management's performance. Will this have serious short and long-run implications for operating management? Will significant decision-making policies undergo revision in view of a switch from an accounting earnings emphasis to a cash flow emphasis? A more general question along this line is: Should financial statements be used to evaluate management at all? If so, are current reporting procedures adequate? If not, what other alternative evaluation schemes are available?

The Objectives Study recommended the reporting of current values, and the grouping of assets and liabilities by the relative uncertainty of their realization or liquidation. For which items should current values be reported? From the user and preparer standpoint, managerial accountants should have valuable input to contribute in answering this question. For example, the cost of gathering current values for fixed assets might be prohibitive when viewed from a cost/benefit standpoint. In addition, it would be of significant import to isolate whether top management requests and uses information on current values. If this information is used, what meaning does a manager attach to changes in current values? Should these changes be used in evaluating the effectiveness of management? For example, assume that the liquidation value of a depreciable asset increases by $200 over last year. Since this gain can be associated with a managerial decision (to retain the machine), it could be interpreted as reflecting favorably on management's overall performance. The grouping of assets and liabilities by the relative uncertainty of their realization or liquidation also raises several questions such as: (1) How does management currently assess uncertainty? Would it be reasonable to provide management's assessment of uncertainties in the form of supplemental financial information? If so, in what form would this information be presented?

The Objectives Report recommended the reporting of a new financial statement—the "Statement of Financial Activities." Given the assumed goal of maximization of cash flows, this statement can be viewed as a first step in modifying traditional accounting reports (strictly accrual basis) more towards a cash flow concept.

This statement would report factual aspects of enterprise transactions having or expected to have significant cash consequences. The Report specifically mentioned sales backlogs and purchase commitments. What other types of information would be of interest to financial statement readers? What similar types of information have managerial implications of disclosing such data? (Could these data be used by competitors to gain unfair advantages?)

"Financial forecasts should be provided when they will enhance the reliability of users' predicitons." Related to this Study Group objective is the question: Are most management information systems capable of generating reliable forecasts? How should the accuracy and uncertainty surrounding forecasts be presented in financial statements? How do top executives currently evaluate the accuracy and uncertainty of forecasts?

Finally, the Objectives Report set forth seven qualitative characteristics of reporting that information in financial statements should possess in order to satisfy users' needs. These characteristics are given in Table 2. From a managerial accounting viewpoint, are these attributes adequate? If so, how are these characteristics incorporated into managerial accounting reports? If not, what modifications should be made to these characteristics?

## CONCLUSION

Obviously, we have asked far more questions than we have attempted to answer. Such was our intention in illustrating the potential effects the establishment of a uniform set of objectives may have on the managerial accountant and the executive manager. Hopefully, along the way we have stimulated some thought as to the valuable role the executive manager and the managerial accountant could play in the establishment of a meaningful set of financial statement objectives.

## QUESTIONS

1. Write a paragraph (or two) summarizing the twelve objectives of financial statements in the Trueblood Report.

2. Define each of the seven qualitative characteristics of financial reporting that were identified by the Trueblood Committee.

3. If you were a manager, identify which of the twelve objectives you would be in favor of having the FASB adopt, and state why.

4. If you were an accountant, specify which objective (or objectives) you might be against adopting now, and give possible reasons for your position.

5. What is a statement of financial activities?

# 112

## FINANCIAL STATEMENTS
### Corporations, Users and the Profession*

Richard M. Cyert and Yuji Ijiri

Financial statements are not just statements reporting on the financial activities and financial status of a corporation. They are a product of mutual interactions of three parties: corporations, users of financial statements, and the accounting profession.

Corporations are not only the subjects whose status and activities are reported in financial statements; they are also the sole suppliers of financial statements. Without actions by corporations there is no way for an outsider to prepare financial statements with a satisfactory degree of reliability. This feature of self-assessment—namely, a corporation's assessing and reporting its own financial status and performance—has a significant implication to the institutional structure that surrounds financial statements, as we shall elaborate on later.

By users—the second party that is intimately related to financial statements—we mean not only past, present, and future shareholders and creditors but also financial analysts, governmental agencies, and the public in general.

The third party is the accounting profession (or simply the profession), by which we mean not only individual accountants and auditors but also the system that influences the activities of accountants and auditors. The role of the profession is to improve the reliability of the contents of financial statements.

The interests of these three parties interact as shown in Diagram 1. In the diagram, Circle C represents a set of information that the corporation agrees to report in financial statements (voluntarily or because of requirements). Circle U represents a set of information that the users want to see reported in financial statements because this information may be useful for their decision making. And Circle P represents a set of information for which the profession has developed a way to verify and has agreed to attest.

Area I is a happy intersection where the corporation agrees to disclose, where the users find the information useful, and where the profession agrees to attest. If all areas were like this, i.e., if all three circles coincided, objectives of financial statements would not have been presented as an issue, let alone their implementation. The fact is that there are relatively large areas of discrepancies among these three circles together because only Area I is implementable under the present institutional arrangement, while the other areas have some difficulties in implementation. The nature of the obstacles differs depending upon the areas, and so it may be worthwhile for us to explore each area separately.

Area II represents a set of information which the corporation agrees to disclose and the users consider to be useful, but for which the profession has not been able to

*Excerpt from "Problems of Implementing the Trueblood Objectives Report," *Studies on Financial Accounting Objectives: 1974 Journal of Accounting Research,* pp. 29–32. Reprinted by permission of the publishers.

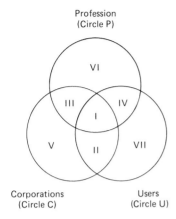

Profession
(Circle P)

Corporations
(Circle C)

Users
(Circle U)

**Diagram 1**

develop technology for attestation because, for example, the item may be too subjective. Financial forecasts are good examples. Many corporations have been providing financial forecasts to investors in their annual reports or through other media and investors and financial analysts have found them to be useful.[1] However, so far the profession has not been able to come up with a system that will insure a satisfactory degree of reliability. This does not mean that the profession cannot develop such a system. In fact, there is a good possibility that it will.[2] Nevertheless, until this groundwork is completed, such pieces of information should be clearly separated from those in the present financial statements for which the profession is willing to attest.

Area III is a set of information which the corporation is willing to provide and the profession is willing to attest for but which the users find useless for their decision making. It tends to disappear quickly. For example, the last three digits of financial data in the millions or billions are of almost no use to users even if the corporation is willing to provide and the profession is willing to attest. The same is true with minor accounts, such as petty cash and accrued payroll taxes, although it is certainly conceivable that for some unusual uses of financial statements they might provide useful information.

[1] The Securities and Exchange Commission decided in 1973 to treat earnings forecasts as important enough events to require equitable dissemination by means of filing with SEC. This is a good evidence that corporate financial forecasts have been accepted by investors and financial analysts as being quite useful.

[2] See the discussions on generally accepted forecasting principles in Yuji Ijiri, "Improving Reliability of Publicly Reported Corporate Financial Forecasts," in *Public Reporting of Corporate Financial Forecasts,* Prem Prakash and Alfred Rappaport, eds. (Chicago: Commerce Clearing House, Inc., 1974).

Area IV represents a set of information which the users find useful and the profession is willing to attest, but which the corporation does not agree to disclose. Detailed product line reporting, more frequent interior reporting, outstanding sales orders, and other contracts and commitments are typical examples. We are not saying that they should all be disclosed. But at least this represents one of the areas for reconciliation before the objectives can be implemented.

Area V is a set of information that the corporation is willing to disclose; however, not only do the users find it useless but also the profession is unwilling to attest for it. It is almost like a piece of repeated advertising that no one wants to hear and that is too subjective for the profession to attest. This too is an area that quickly disappears when recognized by the corporation.

Area VI is a set of information that the profession is willing to attest but that the users are not interested in and the corporation is not willing to disclose. There will be no demand for the profession's service for information in this area.

Area VII represents a set of information that the users are interested in knowing. However, the corporation has not agreed to disclose it and the profession has not developed a system for attestation. . . .

Given the interests of the three groups, an approach that is not meaningless would be to consider the set of all information that the corporation is willing to disclose and then attempt to make the best use of it and to find ways of attesting. In other words, we fix Circle C and let Circles U and P approach C.

The second approach is to fix Circle P and let Circles C and U approach Circle P. This is not as outrageous an approach as it initially may sound. For example, the users may wish to have unbiased current value data and the corporation may be willing to supply them, but the profession may find it extremely difficult to establish a system under which excessive biases can be eliminated. The users can accept minor biases but unless they have some assurance that excessive biases can be eliminated they do not want the data. The profession states that it is willing to attest general price-level adjusted financial statements. The users and the corporation may, in such cases, accept general price-level adjusted financial statements as a rough approximation to current values,[3] even if they all are aware of the conceptual and practical differences between the two.

The third approach is to fix Circle U and let Circles C and P approach it. . . .

This is a logical, if not a unique, approach since in many user-corporate relationships the corporation is *accountable* to the users for its activities. If the users are in a position to demand information from the corporation based on a contractual or statutory relationship between them, it makes sense to define what Circle U is and then attempt to move Circle C toward it. Furthermore, in the interaction of the three groups, the profession's purpose is to help keep a smooth flow of information from the corporation to the users. Hence, Circle P is clearly subordinate to Circles C and U. Thus, it is perhaps the most practical way to state as objectives the need to move Circles C and P toward the goal of a newly defined Circle U.

---

[3]They are exactly the same as current value statements if all prices move up or down in the same proportion.

## QUESTIONS

1. Why is it useful to define financial statements as the product of mutual interactions of three parties?

2. Define each of the seven areas in Diagram 1, and give at least one illustration for each area.

3. Of the three approaches given, which one was taken by the Trueblood Committee?

# 113
# RECENT LEGAL DEVELOPMENTS IN THE UNITED STATES*
Michael H. Granof

One of the most significant developments of the past decade in the profession of accountancy in the United States has been the dramatic increase in litigation involving certified public accountants. Explanations for the proliferation of legal actions against public accountants are open to conjecture: the complexity of financial transactions; the use of imaginative accounting principles; the rapid expansion in size of CPA firms and changes in Federal security statutes that make it easier for aggrieved stockholders to recover damages. But at least one consequence of the litigation is clear. Courts have become active particpants in the development of accounting principles and auditing standards—matters previously in the domain of the profession itself.

The trend of recent judicial decisions is exemplified by four cases which have received a great deal of attention in the United States. The cases are of relevance to accountants in other parts of the world not so much for specific rulings on matters of either law or accounting principles, but rather because they are reflective of the general public concern with the process of financial reporting and indicative of the means by which the public, via the courts, can influence standards of corporate disclosure. The purpose of this article is to summarize the cases and to attempt to discern what it is that the courts are telling the United States accounting profession.

## BARCHRIS CONSTRUCTION CORPORATION[1]

The *BarChris* case is particularly significant because it is demonstrative of the strength of the Securities and Exchange Acts of 1933 and 1934 as they pertain to the

---

*From *The Chartered Accountant in Australia,* April 1973, pp. 6–10. Reprinted by permission of the publisher.

[1]*Escott v. BarChris Construction Corporation,* 283 F. Supp. 643 (S.D.N.Y. 1968).

obligations of certified public accountants. The case makes clear both that the courts will expect auditors to live up to the standards promulgated by their profession, and perhaps more significantly, that when they deem that the accounting profession has been lax in making needed changes in accounting principles, they will do so themselves in its stead.

The *Ultramares* case of 1931 had established the common law precedent that an auditor is liable for damages suffered as a result of his ordinary negligence only to his contractual client—not to third parties who might have relied upon his report.[2] He is liable to third parties, the court held, only for losses suffered on account of his fraudulent conduct or his actions so grossly negligent as to sustain an inference of fraud. The Securities and Exchange Acts of 1933 and 1934, while not abolishing the common law precedent of *Ultramares* significantly extended the liability of the auditor. They prescribed that when issuing reports covered by the act, an independent accountant would be held liable to third parties for false statements unless he could show as a matter of defense that "he had after reasonable investigation reasonable ground to believe and did believe . . . that the statements were true."

In the *BarChris* case, holders of the company's convertible debentures sued the corporation itself as well as its officers, directors, underwriters and auditors for filing a registration statement that contained allegedly false and misleading assertions. They charged that both income and net assets were overstated and that the accountants failed to exercise due diligence in their examination of the firm's books and records.

BarChris Construction Corporation was in the business of constructing bowling alleys. Generally the company sold completed structures directly to the ultimate user, requiring the purchaser to make a small downpayment and give an installment note for the balance. BarChris would then discount the note with a factor, and thereby receive in cash all but a small portion of the total contract price shortly after turning the building over to the customer. Alternatively, however, if a customer were not readily available, BarChris might sell a bowling alley to the factor. The factor, in turn, would lease the structure back to either a wholly-owned subsidiary of BarChris or to an outside bowling alley operator.

The Court, after reviewing in detail the balance sheet and income statement in question, concluded that they did, in fact, contain falsities and omissions. Most of the deficiencies could be attributed to the misapplication of existing accounting principles. For example, in applying the percentage of completion method as a means of recognising revenue, the company recorded as 100 per cent. complete a job that was only 75 per cent. complete. But more significantly, the Court found that even where the company had properly employed accounting principles as they were then generally accepted, its disclosure was misleading. BarChris had recorded as revenue proceeds from the "sale" of a bowling alley to the factor who had, in turn, leased it to a wholly-owned subsidiary of BarChris. Under then applicable principles such a "sale-leaseback" could properly be reported as a sale. The Court, however, asserted that BarChris sold the alley to the factor "purely as a financing mechanism". In substance, the Court declared, "it never sold it to any outside interest", and thus it would be

---

[2]*Ultramares v. Touche,* 255 N.Y. 170, 174 N.E. 441 (1931).

misleading to record the transaction as a sale. Subsequent to the audit engagement in question, but prior to the judicial decision, the Accounting Principles Board had issued an opinion on lease transactions which would have precluded recording the transfer of the alley to the factor as a sale.[3] The Court, in effect, however, retroactively applied the new interpretation to the case at hand, and it thereby put accountants on notice that adherence to generally accepted accounting principles will not necessarily be conclusive evidence of adequate financial disclosure.

The case is also important for the warning that the Court issued regarding auditing standards. "Accountants should not be held to a standard higher than that recognised in their profession," the Court emphasised, but at a minimum, it implied, they will have to live up to that standard. In the case being litigated, the Court asserted, the auditor fell short of established criteria. He failed to heed the danger signals that had come to his attention. "He asked questions, he got answers which he considered satisfactory and he did nothing to verify them;" he was "too easily satisfied with glib answers to his inquiries." He went through the motions required by the audit programme but it was clear that he never really understood some of the more complex transactions.

Moreover, although the court expressed reluctance to "second guess" the judgments of the auditors it made plain that it would do so in situations where the accountants were obviously imprudent. Commenting on the sufficiency of a reserve for uncollectable accounts, the judge declared, that he is "well aware that this question of adequate reserves must be determined in the light of the facts as they existed at the time, not as they later developed." Nevertheless he indicated his belief "that [the auditor's] judgment was clearly wrong," and the firm's bad debt expense was understated.

## CONTINENTAL VENDING[4]

More than any other legal action the *Continental Vending* case shattered the complacency of the accounting profession. Three certified public accountants, each a partner or senior associate of a large, international firm, were convicted of *criminal* charges stemming from their involvement in the audit of Continental Vending Company. The three were found guilty of conspiring to violate both Federal securities statutes and the United States Code by knowingly drawing up and certifying a false and misleading financial statement and by using the mails to distribute such statement.

In essence, the case revolves around transactions between Continental Vending Company and its affiliate, Valley Commercial Corporation. The leading shareholder in both firms was the president and chief executive officer of Continental Vending, who owned approximately 25 per cent. of the stock of each company. Continental Vending Company made substantial loans to Valley Commercial Corporation, and Valley, in turn, made substantial advances to its leading shareholder, the president of Continental

[3]Accounting Principles Board Opinion No. 5, *Reporting of Leases in Financial Statements of Lessee.*

[4]*U.S. v. Simon,* 425 F. 2d (2d Cir. 1969), cert. denied, 400 U.S. 827 (1970).

Vending. The president, it was alleged, used Valley Commerical as a conduit through which to transfer funds to support personal stockmarket transactions. The principal charge in the case was that the financial reports of Continental Vending failed to disclose the loans to the president by its affiliate, Valley Commercial. The defendant CPAs conceded that they knew of the loans, but they maintained that under generally accepted accounting principles and auditing procedures they were under no obligation to either investigate or disclose what Valley Commerical, an unconsolidated affiliate, did with the proceeds of the loans from Continental Vending.

The three defendants were found guilty by a twelve man jury and an appellate court upheld the conviction. The United States Supreme Court denied certiorari.

The appellate court, which delivered the key opinion, recognised that the mere fact that a company has made advances to an affiliate does not ordinarily impose a duty on the auditor to investigate or disclose what such affiliate has done with the proceeds. The Court took judicial notice of the battery of well-recognised CPAs who testified that the defendants had adhered to generally accepted accounting principles. But it nevertheless rejected defense arguments by asserting:

> Generally accepted accounting principles instruct an accountant what to do in the usual case where he has no reason to doubt that the affairs of the corporation are being honestly conducted. Once he has reason to believe that this basic assumption is false, an entirely different situation confronts him.
>
> If certification does not at least imply that the corporation has not been looted by insiders so far as the accountants know, or, if it has been, that the diversion has been made good beyond per-adventure (or adequately reserved against) and effective steps taken to prevent a recurrence, it would mean nothing, and the reliance placed on it by the public would be a snare and a delusion.

The critical test of whether the statements are not misleading, the court emphasised, is not whether they conform to generally accepted accounting principles, but rather, whether they are fair. And the ultimate test of fairness, the Court made clear, would be made by laymen (i.e., jurors), not professional accountants or financial experts. The Court did not, however, assert that generally accepted accounting principles would be ignored in evaluating the fairness of financial reports. It strongly implied that conformance to specific rules or guidelines established by the profession would ordinarily constitute sufficient evidence that the auditor had adhered to the standards of his profession. But in the absence of such rules or guidelines, as in the case at hand, the court would make the necessary judgments.

## YALE EXPRESS[5]

Both the *Yale Express* case and the *1136 Tenants' Corporation* case (discussed below) pertain to accounting services in addition to audits. In each of the two cases the courts

---

[5]*Fischer v. Kletz,* 266 F. Supp. 180 (S.D.N.Y. 1967). A commentary for businessmen on the Yale Express case can be read in *Fortune* (Vol. 72, Nov., 1965) pp. 144–9, 226, 228, 230, 235–6. "Big Skid at Yale Express", by Richard J. Whalen.

extended standards of disclosure associated with audit services to either consulting or "write-up" (bookkeeping) services.

The *Yale Express* case resulted from the bankruptcy of Yale Express System, Incorporated, a publicly held transportation concern. Plaintiffs, who were stockholders in the financially troubled company, charged that they were deceived by the firm's auditor who failed to reveal material irregularities in the financial reports that it had discovered subsequent to the completion of its audit. Early in 1964, the defendant CPA firm undertook the audit of the company's year-ended December 31, 1963 financial statements. It completed its field work by March 31, 1964 and issued its report to the public and to regulatory authorities. Shortly after the firm completed its audit (the exact sequence of events was a matter of factual dispute) it was engaged by Yale to undertake studies of the company's revenue and expenses. In the course of performing the additional management consulting services the accounting firm discovered that the financial statements to which it had previously attested contained material errors. The defendant discussed its findings with officers of Yale Express, but it delayed disclosing the misstatements to the regulatory authorities until it had completed the special studies in May, 1965, over a year after the original statements had been released.

The defendant's legal entanglements arose, as the Court pointed out, because it wore two hats. The first was that of an independent auditor who owes an obligation to investors, creditors, government agencies and anyone else who might rely on the certified financial reports. The second was that of a management advisor, who is accountable solely to his client. The plaintiffs asserted that since the defendant knew that the financial statements would be relied upon by the public, it had a duty, as soon as it became aware that its original report was false and misleading, to so inform the Securities and Exchange Commission. They based their claim on the common law of deceit and contended that the defendant's silence constituted the equivalent of an affirmative misrepresentation. Defendant, on the other hand, maintained that its duty to the investing public terminated as soon as it released its report. There was no basis either in common or statutory law, it argued, for holding it responsible to reveal information discovered subsequent to the completion of the audit.

The Court held, however, that an accountant's duty of disclosure extends beyond the release of the audit report, and under the circumstances the auditor's silence was sufficient to constitute deceit. Citing several common law cases, the Court declared that "the elements of 'good faith and common honesty' which cover the businessman should also apply to the statutory 'independent public accountant.' " The Court recognised some of the questions that might arise as a result of its decision (e.g., how long does the obligation to disclose information last?; to whom should disclosures be made?; what if the information were obtained from a source other than the client?), but it gave overriding consideration in its decision to the need to protect the investor against misrepresentation by those on whom he relies.[6]

---

[6]The position of the court was eventually codified by the profession in Statement on Auditing Procedure No. 41, *Subsequent Discovery of Facts Existing at the Date of the Auditor's Report.*

## 1136 TENANTS' CORPORATION[7]

The case of *1136 Tenants' Corporation v. Max Rothenberg and Company* addresses itself to the question of responsibility of a CPA for unaudited financial statements. Plaintiff, a co-operative apartment corporation sought damages resulting from the negligent performance of accounting services by the defendant, a firm of CPAs. For a period of approximately eighteen months the defendant had been engaged to perform certain accounting services (the nature of the services is a matter of dispute) for the plaintiff. Arrangements for the engagement were made by a second corporation, the managing agents for the co-operative apartment corporation, through its President.

During the period of its engagement the defendant accounting firm performed "write-up" services relating to the books of the tenant-owned apartment company. In addition, the accounting firm submitted to the plaintiff periodic financial statements. The reports were accompanied by a letter of transmittal which began:

> Pursuant to our engagement, we have reviewed and summarised the statements of your managing agent and other data submitted to us by [the managing agents] pertaining to 1136 Tenants' Corporation

and concluded:

> The following statements [the financial statements and appended schedules] were prepared from the books and records of the Corporation. No independent verifications were undertaken thereon.

The financial statements themselves were marked, "Subject to comments in letter of transmittal."

Shortly after the end of the period covered by the last report of the accountants it was discovered that the president of the managing agency had been reporting as paid certain obligations which, allegedly, had not been paid. Instead it was charged, he had been diverting corporate funds for his own use. The financial statements prepared by the accountant did not reveal the alleged defalcations.

The major question under dispute at the trial was whether the accountant had agreed to perform an audit or whether, even if he had not agreed to perform an audit, he was nevertheless obligated to perform such procedures as would likely have revealed the alleged fraud. The plaintiffs contended that the defendant had agreed to perform an audit. They relied for support on the terms (which are in dispute) of the oral agreement, and they pointed to the accountant's working papers which they claimed clearly reveal that the defendant had, indeed, performed auditing procedures that went beyond the scope of a "write-up". The worksheets in question indicate that the defendant had examined bank statements and invoices, and one worksheet is even entitled, "Missing Invoices". The plaintiffs further asserted that even from the work actually performed the accountant should have been aware that something was amiss. The missing invoices should have provided the clue that the books and records from

[7] *1136 Tenants' Corporation v. Max Rothenberg & Co.* Index 10575/1965, New York County, Trial Term, Part VII (1970).

which he prepared the financial statements were something less than a correct representation of the transactions in which the corporation was engaged.

Defendant, on the other hand, maintained that he never agreed to perform an audit. He cited the letter of transmittal which stated that the statements were prepared from "the books and records of the corporation" and that "no independent verifications were taken thereon." The defendant contended that there is a clear distinction between performing "write-up" work and performing an audit, and if engaged only to do write-up work he was under no obligation to adhere to the standards associated with audits. The fact that he failed to investigate the missing invoices was of no consequence; they were irrelevant to the performance of his write-up work.

The Court held that the defendant was engaged to audit and not merely "write-up" the books. But more significantly, it declared that *"even if* [italics added] defendant was hired to perform only 'write up' services," it is clear beyond dispute that he did become aware that material invoices purportedly paid by [the agent] were missing, and accordingly, had a duty to at least inform plaintiff of this."

The position of the Court is counter to that of the profession which has long recognised a fundamental distinction between audited and unaudited statements. In Statement on Auditing Procedure No. 38 (1967), *Unaudited Financial Statements*, the Committee on Auditing Procedure has declared: "The certified public accountant has no responsibility to apply any auditing procedures to unaudited financial statements." And in an *amicus curiae* brief submitted on behalf of the defendant, the American Institute of Certified Public Accountants and the New York State Society of Certified Public Accountants contended that although certain auditing procedures may be applied to unaudited financial statements, the accountant's responsibility with respect to such statements (over and above his general obligation of exercising due professional care in their preparation) is limited to disclosing matters which have actually come to his attention. Only if he is actually aware that the statements contain discrepancies must he insist that they be disclosed. But he is under no obligation to conduct an examination designed to detect the discrepancies.

Although the case is one of very few that pertains to unaudited financial statements it is clear that the courts have put the CPA on notice that he will be held accountable for his association with them. The extent of his responsibility remains uncertain at this time, but it is obvious that the liability of the CPA is being extended, pronouncements of professional organisations which attempt to limit the scope not withstanding.

## SUMMARY

Courts do not speak with one voice and they direct their opinions to the specific fact situations presented by the cases at hand. Hence it is sometimes difficult to discern with certainty what it is they are trying to communicate to the accounting profession. Nevertheless, when the four cases discussed in this article are analysed in the light of numerous other recent cases, several messages are transmitted with relative clarity.

First, the Courts have made it obvious that accountants will be held to the standards of performance which they, through their professional organisations, have established for themselves. In the United States basic standards of auditing practices have been codified in a series of Statements on Auditing Procedure. Although most of the pronouncements deal with specific auditing problems, others are quite general (e.g. "Due Professional care is to be exercised in the performance of the examination and the preparation of the report;" "Informative disclosures in the financial statements are to be regarded as reasonably adequate unless otherwise stated in the report").[8] Accountants, the Courts have implied, shall be required to adhere to the spirit of the more fundamental standards and exercise the desire of performance and judgment expected of members of a learned profession.

Second, the Courts have warned that the language of the standard shortform unqualified opinion is to be interpreted literally. When the auditor proclaims that "the accompanying financial statements present *fairly*" the financial position of the firm, the investor should properly be able to infer that the reports are indeed free from bias and dishonesty. He should not have to be concerned that the auditor is implying only that the statements are in technical compliance with a complex set of rules called "generally accepted accounting principles." Expert testimony that the reports conform in all particulars to generally accepted accounting principles will be highly persuasive, but by no means conclusive, evidence that they do in fact fairly present the financial position of the company. The utlitmate decision as to whether statements are fair will be made from the perspective of a layman, not that of accountants or financial analysts.

Third, the Courts have let it be known that the independent accountant is in a position of trust and that his primary obligation is to the general public rather than to his client. Thus, the public will expect that any time a certified public accountant is associated with a statement he will reveal all information necessary for fair financial disclosure. It will matter not whether the information required for meaningful disclosure was obtained in the course of his duties as an auditor or during a subsequent engagement as an advisor or "internal" accountant. The public thinks of the independent accountant primarily as an auditor and although it will still be possible for a CPA to provide services other than audits without being held to the standards of an audit, he will have to go to increased lengths to make certain that readers of reports with which he is associated clearly understand the degree of responsibility he is assuming.

### QUESTIONS

1. What accounting reasons are given for the increase in litigation involving CPAs? What nonaccounting reasons might be given that partially explain this situation? EDITORS' HINT: Consider whether other professions have had an increase in litigation and of what significance is the ever-increasing number of individuals trained as lawyers who cannot find positions as lawyers.

2. Contrast the implications of the BarChris case with that of the Ultramares case.

3. What is the significance of the Continental Vending case?

4. What are the implications of the Yale Express and the 1136 Tenants' Corporation cases?

---

[8]Statement on Auditing Procedure No. 33, *Auditing Standards and Procedures.*

5. From your library, secure information about the following cases which have developed subsequent to the writing of this article: Four Seasons Nursing Homes, Westec, National Student Marketing, Penn Central, and Equity Funding.

6. What does the author conclude about the legal implications for accountants that result from these cases?

## SELECTED BIBLIOGRAPHY

Foster, William C., "The Current Financial Reporting Environment," *The CPA Journal*, March 1974, pp. 31-34.

# 114
## CRITERIA*
American Accounting Association

Four basic standards are recommended as providing criteria to be used in evaluating potential accounting information: relevance, verifiability, freedom from bias, and quantifiability. Adherence to some or all of these standards may be partial. As with all standards, exercise of judgment as to the adequacy with which they are met is essential.

*Relevance* is the primary standard and requires that the information must bear upon or be usefully associated with actions it is designed to facilitate or results desired to be produced. Known or assumed informational needs of potential users are of paramount importance in applying this standard.

2 *Verifiability* requires that essentially similar measures or conclusions would be reached if two or more qualified persons examined the same data. It is important because accounting information is commonly used by persons who have limited access to the data. The less the proximity to the data, the greater the desirable degree of verifiability becomes. Verifiability is also important because users of accounting information sometimes have opposing interests. *those who use it*

3 *Freedom from bias* means that facts have been impartially determined and reported. It also means that techniques used in developing data should be free of built-in bias. Biased information may be quite useful and tolerable internally but it is rarely acceptable for external reporting.

4 *Quantifiability* relates to the assignment of numbers to the information being reported. Money is the most common but not the only quantitative measure used by

*Excerpt from *A Statement of Basic Accounting Theory* (Evanston, Ill.: AAA, 1966), p. 7. Reprinted by permission of the publisher.

accountants. When accountants present non-quantitative information in compliance with the other standards they should not imply its measurability. Conversely, when quantitative information is reported without a caveat the accountant must assume responsibility for its measurability.

Five guidelines for communication of accounting information are recommended. They are:

1. Appropriateness to expected use.
2. Disclosure of significant relationships.
3. Inclusion of environmental information.
4. Uniformity of practice within and among entities.
5. Consistency of practices through time.

We recognize that there is some overlap between the four standards and the five guidelines; the latter are important but less fundamental. . . .

## THE STANDARD OF RELEVANCE

For information to meet the standard of relevance, it must bear upon or be usefully associated with the action it is designed to facilitate or the result it is desired to produce. This requires that either the information or the act of communicating it exert influence or have the potential for exerting influence on the designated actions. For this influence to be exerted, the information must be available in a form and at a time for it to be useful.

As there are differing degrees of usefulness, so are there different degrees of relevance for different purposes. For example, the original recorded cost of a building twenty years ago might have been $200,000 and similar buildings might cost $400,000 today. Each item of information has relevance for a particular use. The $200,000 figure has relevance in the calculation of depreciation for income tax purposes under an historical-cost-based income tax system. The $400,000 figure has virtually no relevance for this purpose. To the person considering what price to pay for the building, the $400,000 figure has a high degree of relevance and the $200,000 has virtually no relevance. The original owner of the building who is now contemplating its sale is interested in its sale price and the total financial consequences of such a sale transaction. To him, each item of information has relevance and both items together have greater relevance than either standing alone.

The accounting function should, under many circumstances, provide information with a high degree of relevance to a specific intended use although it may have little relevance to any other. When this is done, care must be taken to disclose the limitations of the information to prevent the possible assumption of universal relevance. To have information used for purposes for which it has no relevance is likely to be worse than having no information at all. Not only may decisions be influenced wrongly, but the user may be diverted from an effort to acquire relevant information.

The standard of relevance is primary among the four recommended standards. Although not sufficient as a sole criterion, it represents a necessary characteristic for all accounting information. None of the other standards has this position of primacy.

Nevertheless, the committee believes that the process of judging accounting information should involve a combined and simultaneous consideration of all four standards. The required degree of adherence to each standard is conditioned by the degree to which the other standards are met. The relative significance of each standard depends upon the nature of the information and its intended use. Both the minimum conformity required with any one of the standards and rates of substitution (trade-off) among the four standards are conditioned by the circumstances.

## QUESTIONS

1. Do you agree that relevance is a more primary standard than the other three? Why?
2. Does the quantifiability standard imply that only information that is quantifiable can be regarded as accounting information?

## SELECTED BIBLIOGRAPHY

Gibbs, George, "Accounting Fundamentals: Guides to Human Judgment," *Accounting and Business Research*, Summer 1973, pp. 205-212.

# 115

# THREE ALTERNATIVES
## Semantic, Decision, or Result Relevance*
Keith Shwayder

Which level of relevance should be used by accountants? The relevance standard defined in the 1966 Statement reads: "For information to meet the standard of relevance, it must bear upon or be usefully associated with the action it is designed to facilitate or the result it is desired to produce. This requires that either the information or the act of communicating it exert influence or have the potential for exerting influence on the designed actions."[1]

There are two possibilities—decision relevance and result relevance. I suggest semantic relevance as a third possibility. The three levels of relevance form a hierarchy: information cannot affect decisions without influencing the impressions of

*Excerpt from "Relevance," *Journal of Accounting Research,* Spring 1968, pp. 86–97. Reprinted by permission of the author and the publisher.

[1]Committee to Prepare a Statement of Basic Accounting Theory, *A Statement of Basic Accounting Theory* (Evanston, Ill.: American Accounting Association, 1966) p. 9.

the user and information cannot affect goal fulfillment without changing the user's decision.

Accountants would prefer a result relevance criterion. If all the goals of the accounting information system could be specified, then a message that did not affect any of these goals would clearly not be important or significant, even if the message changed all kinds of user decisions. A change in accounting methods in a company (say from LIFO to FIFO) may change an investor's expectations and thus induce him to change his portfolio; but if the revised portfolio has the same risk, market performance, and dividend payout as the original portfolio, the investor's goal attainment has not been changed.[2] Indeed, recent work has indicated that some investment decisions may have little effect on portfolio results.[3]

Although it is difficult to test a message's decision relevance, it is more difficult to test goal relevance. To determine decision relevance we must:

1. define the significant set of decisions
2. trace the effect of particular messages on decisions
3. measure changes in decisions.

To determine result relevance we must perform steps 1 through 3 above, and:

4. define the significant set of goals
5. trace the effects of changes in decisions on goal attainment
6. measure changes in goal attainment (especially difficult when there are conflicting goals).

Steps 4 through 6 substantially increase the measurement problem; empirical measurements of result relevance involve the intractable problems of utility measurement and ex post analysis. Although there have been some attempts to measure the decision relevance of accounting messages,[4] I know of no experiments to test the result relevance.

Often semantic relevance can be tested when it is impossible to test decision or result relevance. The chief advantage of semantic relevance is that the decision

---

[2]Assuming that the investor is a rational man.

[3]Fama compared the performance of mutual funds against the general performance of the market (defined as equal amounts of money invested in all the stocks on the New York Stock Exchange). For the period 1950 through 1960, the mutual funds did no better than the "market." This striking result indicates that during the period under study, an unsophisticated investor picking a random selection of stocks on the New York Stock Exchange would have, on the average, performed as well as the professional security analysts working for the mutual funds. Eugene F. Fama, "The Behavior of Stock Market Prices," *The Journal of Business,* XXXVIII (January 1965), 34–105.

[4]See, for example, William Bruns, "A Simulation Study of Alternative Methods of Inventory Valuation" (unpublished Ph.D. dissertation, University of California, Berkeley, 1962), Thomas R. Dyckman, "On the Investment Decision," *The Accounting Review* (April, 1964), pp. 285–95, and Robert E. Jensen, "An Experimental Design for Study of Effects of Accounting Variations in Decision Making," *Journal of Accounting Research*, 4 (Autumn, 1966), pp. 224–38.

environment does not have to be investigated or simulated.[5] However, tests of semantic relevance are less useful than tests of decision relevance—as observed earlier, a message may be semantic relevant but not decision relevant.

These three alternatives can be ranked in terms of operationality and meaningfulness as follows:

| STANDARD | OPERATIONALITY | MEANINGFULNESS |
|---|---|---|
| result relevance | least | most |
| decision relevance | intermediate | intermediate |
| semantic relevance | most | least |

The emphasis in the AAA monograph is clearly on decision relevance. Decision models, for example, are discussed, utility models are not. Relevance often is synonymous with decision relevance. "It is not necessary to know in detail the needs of all the diverse users of accounting information to prepare relevant reports for them for certain classes of information are relevant to many decisions." As mentioned earlier, the Statement's definition allows for result relevance as well as decision relevance but there is no mention of semantic relevance. I advocate its inclusion because it may be the only alternative when the decision environment is very complicated. Since no one of the three standards dominates any other standard in both dimensions of operationality and meaningfulness, accountants will probably have to use all three definitions of relevance. . . .

## QUESTION

1. Which of the three kinds of relevance are considered most operational and meaningful by the AAA and Dr. Shwayder?

---

[5]Sam W. Woolsey, "Development of Criteria to Guide the Accountant in Judging Materiality," *The Journal of Accountancy* (February, 1954), pp. 167–73 and "Judging Materiality in Determining Requirements for Full Disclosure," *The Journal of Accountancy* (December, 1954), pp. 745–50.

# 116

## AGONIZING AUDITORS*

Frederick Andrews

A few years ago, when a U.S. company's Latin American plant was undergoing an important check by local tax authorities, the tax agent in charge flew off for a Miami Beach holiday at the company's expense. The company's independent auditor, a well-known U.S. firm, found out about the junket but didn't raise a fuss.

"We didn't regard our function as policing the perfidy of the tax agent," an auditor involved recalls.

Today, he says, the firm is having second thoughts about such goings-on. The tax agent's junket would trigger an immediate report to the client company's directors. It also might compel a report to creditor banks and others that had relied on the concern's financial statements. (The company was closely held.) If the company's stock was publicly traded, the auditors would have an agonizing decision over whether to require public disclosure of the incident.

A similar reappraisal of auditing procedures undoubtedly is under way at all large accounting firms and especially at the "Big Eight," which dominate auditing of U.S.-based multinationals. Current scandals have made it clear that business transgressions once considered minor can explode into a headline-provoking corporate disaster. Rightly or wrongly, federal regulators seem to expect auditors to "police" their corporate clients.

### PUZZLED PARTNERS

The new pressures puzzle and worry top technical partners at the major auditing firms. Public accountants, while long aware of such activities as bribery and illegal payments, traditionally have ignored the seamy side of business. They haven't considered payoffs germane to their task of rendering an opinion on a company's financial statements. And, confronted with the new pressures, auditors have found it difficult to devise stricter and more workable standards.

Thus far no auditor has been named in the Securities and Exchange Commission's lawsuits against United Brands Co. in connection with its $1,250,000 Honduran bribe and against Gulf Oil Corp., Northrop Corp., Phillips Petroleum Co., Ashland Oil Inc., and American Ship Building Co. over illegal corporate political giving. A deceased partner of Haskins & Sells was named a coconspirator in tax-fraud charges against Minnesota Mining & Manufacturing Co., but not Haskins & Sells itself.

Nevertheless, SEC officials have voiced "disappointment" at how some auditors conducted themselves, and in at least one instance the SEC reportedly came close to charging the auditor. As a minimum, the revelations have been an embarrassing headache

*From the *Wall Street Journal,* June 12, 1975, pp. 1 and 12. Reprinted by permission of the publisher.

for a "blue-chip" firm like Price Waterhouse & Co., the auditor at United Brands and Gulf. Haskins & Sells was fired by 3M, though no evidence tainted the auditing firm. "That was a hell of a price to pay," a partner at a rival Big Eight firm says. "3M is a super client. There aren't many 3Ms around."

Not surprisingly, auditors have become nervous about keeping concealed anything shady. Recently one major U.S. company reluctantly backed out of the sale of a chunk of its business to an oil-rich foreign buyer for more than $100 million because the company's auditor concluded that a multimillion-dollar rake-off would have to be disclosed. For support, the audit firm, without naming names, quietly consulted the SEC staff, which emphatically agreed.

## DETECTION NOT AT ISSUE

But the failure of outside auditors to detect slush funds or payoffs generally isn't at issue. Federal regulators seem convinced that it isn't feasible to audit a $2 billion company for $50,000 items. John C. Burton, SEC chief accountant, says a routine audit will detect an "artfully concealed" payment "only by chance." A modern audit tests a company's financial routines, plus a sampling of transactions; it isn't even close to an item-by-item check.

"If we examined every item over $100,000—which really isn't much for a huge corporation—that would drive our fees skyhigh. There's a real cost-benefit problem here," says Stephen D. Harlan Jr., a top partner at Peat, Marwick, Mitchell & Co., the largest audit firm.

Underlying the problem is the fact that a payoff can be concealed in countless ways. "All you need," says a Big Eight technical expert, "is one advertising agency willing to bill you and call it advertising." Indeed, Kenneth P. Johnson of Coopers & Lybrand is deeply troubled by how fallible audit routines have been shown to be. "Auditors can be fooled," he says, "facts can be hidden from them, and apparently it isn't all that difficult."

In reaction, audit firms are worriedly drafting staff manuals on what to do about illegal or improper payments. Concerning detection, these memos amount to pleas to stay alert. Ultimately, auditors—and client companies—have to rely on normal internal controls, such as requirements that two persons handle cash or sign checks. But while such controls can be stiffened, unfortunately no one has devised a way to impose effective controls on the very top officers, whose rank enables them to override controls. That is why the corporate campaign gifts pose such a problem—they were arranged by chairmen and presidents.

## PROBLEM OF DISCLOSURE

So rather than concerning detection, the current dispute concerns disclosure—what an auditor should do with what he knows. The SEC's Mr. Burton has preached vigorously that an auditor who discovers something illegal must bring it at once before the company's board. If the company fails to act, the auditor must resign and blow the whistle, Mr. Burton says.

That's fine in clear-cut cases, auditors say, but they doubt that many things are that clear-cut. They are wary of being enlisted as policemen of business ethics, expected to make moral judgments for which they aren't any better prepared than anyone else. "Why the auditor?" asks Lee J. Seidler, a New York University accounting professor. "What in four years' undergraduate training in business endows the auditor as a guardian of morals?"

Besides, many, if not most, auditors agree with businessmen who say payoffs are unavoidable in business abroad and sometimes in the U.S. One prominent auditor recalls an audit that turned up a Fifth Avenue jeweler's receipt for $35,000. It covered a bauble for the First Lady of an Asian land, courtesy of a major U.S. company. When challenged, a corporate executive protested, "Oh, come on, you guys know we have to do that to keep on doing business over there." The auditor finds it hard to disagree.

Another reason auditors haven't faced up to shady practices is that their code of procedure provides a convenient out; the idea of "materiality," or the test of whether something matters. Accountants typically weigh a transaction by whether the money involved affects the company's overall financial position, sometimes using rules of thumb like 10% of sales or 5% of profits. By training, auditors use materiality to weed out things. If it's "immaterial," an auditor needn't bother with it. It needn't be disclosed, and it can be put on the books in any convenient way.

In a huge corporation, what is "immaterial" can cover a pile of money. Price Waterhouse, United Brands' auditor, decided that it covered the $1,250,000 bribe paid a Honduran official. Though Price Waterhouse is understood to have played a key role in influencing United Brands to tell the SEC about the bribe, the accounting firm didn't require its disclosure in United Brands' financial statements. Similarly, auditors don't consider the illegal corporate campaign gifts material by traditional standards.

## THE KEY: MATERIALITY

Thus, the controversy over disclosure has become a debate over materiality. SEC people contend that illegal acts by senior management are intrinsically material because of what they convey about a company's integrity. And the SEC's Mr. Burton says auditors must consider not merely the dollar amount of a bribe or payoff but also the financial repercussions of its becoming publicly known. He notes, for example, that paying a bribe may jeopardize extensive holdings in a foreign land.

The SEC has a point, auditors concede. One says. "The president of General Motors could walk off with $2 million without its affecting GM's financial statements, but the public would never sit still for not disclosing that."

Without the familiar dollar yardstick, though, auditors say they're at sea over how to distinguish what matters from what doesn't. And they boggle at being urged to disclose some corporate infraction that's important only because of what might happen if it's disclosed. What about a company that, discovering an unauthorized violation, promptly corrects it? Must the company disclose it, inviting lawsuits and a host of troubles?

Some auditors grumble that the SEC isn't very helpful. "The SEC will never take a public position against disclosure," one audit expert complains. "Rather than making hard judgments, their answer is disclose everything."

Although auditing doctrine doesn't give much advice on how to handle an improper transaction, talks with auditors give an impression of actual practice. When an auditor stumbles over a substantial payoff, the most common reaction is to audit it. Though the auditor may be in a moral quandary, his professional instincts take over. "I've seen receipts for bribes," an experienced auditor says (though he confesses doubt about how much credence to place in them).

As the top technical partner for a Big Eight firm explains, an auditor's first question entirely apart from whether a payoff is legal or illegal in some foreign land, is, "Is it for a bona fide service?" Is the company getting something for the money?

Secondly, he asks, is the money really going where it's supposed to be going, "and not in the pocket of some officer of the U.S. company?" (As another seasoned auditor notes dryly, "There's concern about how sticky this money is.")

## CURIOUS PROBLEMS

The technical man cites an example of just how curious auditing can become. Not long ago, he says, his firm turned up a payment of several million dollars in a European country where the company being audited had never previously sold anything. Apparently, he says, it was purchasing some local friends. The auditors asked the board's audit committee whether the directors had known about and approved the payment. ("You want to make sure it's a conscious decision of the company," an auditor says.)

The directors had approved. Next the auditors requested, and got, an outside law firm's opinion that the payment wasn't illegal. "We're looking to get more guys involved," the technical partner explains. "Accountants aren't the world's ombudsmen. We're looking around for somebody to share the burden."

The auditors also tried to check the financial standing of the supposed recipient of the payment. "And you just can't do it," the technical partner says. "There aren't any Dun & Bradstreets. You can try and find out through banking sources. You'll never get anything in writing." Ultimately, the auditors accepted the payment as a legitimate expense.

Auditors working abroad become ingenious "in figuring a way to do some kind of audit, without giving away the store," says the head of international practice for a Big Eight firm. But the results are rarely satisfactory by U.S. audit standards, he concedes. Just back from Europe, the auditor relates that he and his partners there spent a day-long meeting puzzling over "how to audit the unauditable."

"It's a bit of a nightmare," he says, "for a simple-minded American auditor brought up believing in internal controls and doing the honest thing." Abroad, companies keep two sets of books, tax evasion is common, business abounds with kickbacks and rake-offs. Sometimes, he says, a U.S. firm hasn't any choice but to decline jobs because the audit can't be done to what it considers proper standards.

## QUESTIONS

1. What auditing procedures are auditors and others "agonizing" about?

2. Why should or should not auditors regard themselves as police of social and business ethics on a worldwide basis?

3. How does the auditing test of materiality limit an auditor's responsibility for disclosure?


# 117

# ANNUAL REPORTS ACQUIRE A NEW LOOK*
Lewis D. Gilbert


This spring shareholders will find that their annual reports have a new look.

Thanks to the Securities and Exchange Commission, every annual report is now required to state in its contents that the 10-K report, which is the most extensive financial statement now filed with the commission, is available to any shareholder on request without charge.

The S.E.C., making perhaps its most sweeping changes for annual reports this year, also requires:

1. Financial statements certified for two fiscal years (instead of for one)

2. A five-year summary of operations (none was necessary before)

3. Management assessment of the financial information

4. A brief description of the company's operations and those of its subsidiaries

5. Breakdowns of results by lines of business or classes of product (previously disclosed by most companies only in the 10-K)

6. Identification of each high executive officer and director and their principal occupations

7. Name of the market where the stock is traded with high and low sales prices quarterly for the latest two years. Also dividend data for two years.

What is found in the all-important 10-K? Detailed balance sheet information, for one thing. If the company engages in several lines of business, each group is broken down by sales and earnings. This allows the shareholder to easily see whether any of the business lines are losing money. This information is now also required to be in annual reports. The 10-K also provides data about the purchase of new plant equipment and methods of depreciation.

*From the *New York Times,* Mar. 23, 1975, p. 12, sect. 3. Reprinted by permission of the publisher.

One can also find what state the company is incorporated in, the address of its principal executive offices and the telephone number of those offices. These, perhaps, are small details, but they are also important basic information which many annual reports fail to give.

If an annual report fails to give the cost of research and development or tooling, look for it in the 10-K. Annual reports frequently just summarize litigation facing the corporation, whereas the 10-K provides a great many more details.

An example of the need for the new S.E.C. ruling on 10-K's is in the different ways the increase in accounts receivable was disclosed by the Consolidated Edison Company in its annual report and its 10-K. The 10-K contained the following clear-cut statement:

> During the period January 1, 1968, to December 31, 1972, accounts receivable from electric and gas customers increased from $98.9-million to $227.3-million and at July 31, 1973 were $267.7-million. The company estimates that a substantial portion of this increase is due to deteriorating customer payment patterns. A measure of this deterioration is the age of accounts receivable.

A 10-K will tell much about the competitive position of a company and something of its problems, matters that sometimes are played down in the annual report. It will also provide what some annual reports fail to do—the number of employes the company has, the age of the executive officers and how long they have been in their present posts.

Finally, the 10-K gives the names of subsidiaries and where they are situated, as well as the amount of the parent's ownership. For corporations whose security holdings are a major portion of their income, all of the major stock holdings are listed there. The 10-K for the Loews Corporation shows, for example, that it has blocks of stock in some 163 corporations. The proxy statement, on the other hand, must only list companies in which there is at least a 10 per cent interest.

Naturally there have been some farsighted managements that have been anticipating this trend and have been stating in their annual reports that they would send any shareholder a copy of the 10-K in advance of being required to do so. Some have even been sending out the 10-K in lieu of the annual report.

If the 10-K is incorporated in the annual report management must be careful not to let it become dull and drab. I think the just published Outboard Marine annual report shows that this can be avoided since it is both aesthetically pleasing as well as informative.

Outboard Marine has the usual attractive picture on the cover. The financial highlights take up the inside of the gatefold cover, accompanied by informative charts. The next two pages are devoted to the traditional messages from the chairman and other executives.

The back cover also features a gatefold format similar to the front cover. Here we find a section called "The Year In Review," a list of officers, features and other statistical data. Including the front and back covers the non-10-K section comprises a total of eight pages.

Naturally, this method of combining the 10-K with the annual report results in economies. However, those in management who prefer this sensible approach must weigh these savings against postage costs; sometimes the 10-K is much larger than the 22-page 10-K section for Outboard Marine.

Katy Industries has come up with a sensible approach to this postage problem when it mails its annual reports.

It prints its annual reports in two editions with identical contents. What it does then is simply prepare a limited number of copies on a heavier paper stock for use among professionals. The other edition is printed on thinner paper and meant for general distribution.

But what must not be done is to reduce the size of the footnotes.

A welcome trend in annual reports, and one that will be more evident this year, is a more meaningful breakdown of sales figures. In the past, too many corporations have boasted about their record sales. This is meaningless unless we know how much came from growth and how much came from increased prices due to inflation.

Campbell Soup sets the pace for the right kind of disclosure in its recent annual report. "Approximately one-third of the total increase in the company's sales for fiscal 1974 represented an increase in volume, with price increases accounting for the remaining two-thirds," it said.

More and more reports will devote space to explaining company policies for civic and social betterment. A list of charitable contributions is appropriate, too.

A major weakness of the Campbell Soup report, as well as some other corporate annual reports this past year, was the absence of a breakdown as to how formerly independent companies are now doing under the Campbell banner. This includes such nonsoup brands as Pepperidge Farms and Swanson. It is hoped that the company will someday copy General Mills and Pillsbury in this regard. Many observers believe that sooner or later the S.E.C. will ask for improvement in the 10-K where so-called "one line" businesses are concerned.

There are two basic things a shareholder can look for in the annual report that if present should warn him that the company in which he invested might be in trouble. One is if the report is written in either vague or confusing language, and the other is a "qualified" auditing certificate.

If an annual report starts with a statement like "Last year was a year of transition for the company" it means the company lost money. When the transition is upward, the directors find they no longer need the baffle-gab—they can say it in English.

Since annual reports should really be intended for the layman it is hoped that more corporations will make their balance sheets understandable to the new investor with simple explanations of what individual items mean.

The other common indicator of how a company is doing is its auditing certificate. It is here that the auditors must warn shareholders if there are problems. If the auditing certificate is three paragraphs long, instead of the normal two paragraphs, the shareholder should read with great care. When hedge words such as "subject to" appear, one should read the footnote to which it refers. And when the ominous words "going concern" are used, the auditors are even more worried.

EDITORS' NOTE: Mr. Gilbert is the best-known professional stockholder (professional stock-holders are active in reviewing their investments).

## QUESTIONS

1. What changes has the SEC brought about in annual reports, according to Mr. Gilbert?

2. What is found in the 10-K report filed with the SEC by corporations?

3. What are two things in an annual report that should warn stockholders that the company might be in trouble?

## SELECTED BIBLIOGRAPHY

"Annual Meetings," *Dun's Review*, April 1975, pp. 48-51, 106.

"Management Braces for Annual Meetings," *New York Times*, March 23, 1975, pp. 11-12.

# 118
# A BANKER'S VIEWS*
Walter B. Wriston

EDITORS' NOTE: The following excerpts are from a talk Mr. Wriston gave before Peat, Marwick, Mitchell personnel. Mr. Wriston is one of the world's leading bankers, being chairman and chief executive of the First National City Corporation (New York).

The history of the nation suggests that whenever any segment of society grows large and prominent, it produces a few characters who do something reprehensible or that is viewed as being against the value system of the time. The next step is that the profession or organization involved forms a self-regulating body. Since self-regulating bodies almost inevitably fail to self-regulate, the government takes over the responsibility. It's happened in the securities business, in banking, and now in the automobile industry. . . .

The last couple of self-regulating professions around are accounting and law. And lawyers are in terrible trouble. Any self-regulating group that permits someone like, say, William Kunstler to disrupt the dignity of the American courtroom and doesn't kick him out of the Bar Association is failing the citizenry. And it's not just Kunstler. Look around Washington. A lot of members of the bar, like Agnew and Dean and

*From *World,* Spring 1974, pp. 48—49. Reprinted by permission of the publisher.

Ehrlichman, are also in big trouble. The idea that because you're a member of the bar your moral standards are higher has gone down the drain. It is almost inevitable that the legal profession will be regulated from outside before long. . . .

The accounting profession now stands at one minute to midnight in maintaining its claim to self-regulation. This didn't come about through fraud or through occasional lapses of quality control. The Achilles heel of the accounting profession is that its most influential members can't agree on most things. There is a sense of general frustration with accountants from the business community. It's not that we don't believe the numbers that you produce or that you have occasional lapses; it's simply that you don't agree among yourselves. One firm says, "I'm going to book the investment tax credit this way," and another says, "No, you're not; this is the way." You'd better agree soon or the government is going to do it for you. . . .

The Financial Accounting Standards Board should go a long way in bailing the accounting profession out of this dilemma. It had better because, if it doesn't, the SEC will. In the past two years, the SEC has issued 30 accounting press releases and proposed regulations; the AICPA has issued less than 15. I'm not talking about quality. I'm a night school accountant. But that's a two-to-one ratio. Now, the FASB is a tremendous advance, but it's issued one exposure draft in four months. That's hardly the kind of productivity we need from a national commission. . . .

I'm willing to concede that the issues you face in accounting are terribly complex and that honest men and women have honest differences. But as the proud employee of an organization that filed 3,700 reports last year with the Federal Reserve alone, I don't think I overstate the case to say that your survival depends on your ability to resolve your differences in a timely manner. . . .

The accounting profession still has time but if you don't want to see a future of bookkeepers filling out government forms, it is absolutely essential that the FASB move rapidly. I know how tough that is because you're all skillful, you're all intelligent, you all have theories of how it can be done. The terrible truth is—it doesn't make any difference how you resolve these questions. It's going to help somebody and hurt somebody else. If you have any influence with the FASB, you'll tell them to get busy and issue 30 regulations, most of which you'll disagree with violently. That's fine. As long as you follow them, you'll have a profession. If you don't, you could wind up being an organization of bookkeepers. . . .

When I came into the banking business, we were asset-conscious and we loaned money on that basis. Well, assets give you a warm feeling, but they don't generate cash. The first question I would ask any borrower these days is, 'What is your break-even cash flow?' That's the one thing we can't find out from your audit reports and it's the single most important question we ask. It's important that you figure out a way to present the difference between real cash flow and accrual cash flow. . . .

Your certification and your work is the thin line that stands between most companies and disaster because nobody in senior management, or an outside director, has time to go out and find out the things you report. Now I can just see a group of attorneys and a group of partners sitting around together figuring out how to write a certificate that allows the lowest possible profile from a class action suit. That's the only way you can explain what your certificates say. I understand that because I got sued for $20 million once. I went home and told my wife. It was the best thing that ever happened because she knew it gave me a certain amount of class. So, I understand why these things are hedged. But if you're lending money and you read the thing, you won't lend the money. Put yourself on the other side.

## QUESTIONS

1. What are Mr. Wriston's predictions about self-regulated professions?
2. What does he feel are the information needs of lenders?

# 119
## QUOTH THE BANKER, "WATCH CASH FLOW"*
Herbert S. Bailey, Jr.

Once upon a midnight dreary as I pondered weak and weary
Over many a quaint and curious volume of accounting lore,
Seeking gimmicks (without scruple) to squeeze through
    some new tax loophole,
Suddenly I heard a knock upon my door.
      Only this, and nothing more.

Then I felt a queasy tingling and I heard the cash a-jingling
As a fearsome banker entered whom I'd often seen before.
His face was money-green and in his eyes there could be seen
Dollar-signs that seemed to glitter as he reckoned up the score.
      "Cash flow," the banker said, and nothing more.

I had always thought it fine to show a jet black bottom line,
But the banker sounded a resounding, "No,
Your receivables are high, mounting upward toward the sky;
Write-offs loom. What matters is cash flow."
      He repeated, "Watch cash flow."

Then I tried to tell the story of our lovely inventory
Which, though large, is full of most delightful stuff.
But the banker saw its growth, and with a mighty oath
He waved his arms and shouted, "Stop! Enough!
      Pay the interest, and don't give me any guff!"

*From *Publishers Weekly,* November 1974, p. 34. Reprinted by permission of the publisher.

Next I looked for non-cash items which could add ad infinitum
To replace the ever-outward flow of cash,
But to keep my statement black I'd held depreciation back,
And my banker said that I'd done something rash.
> He quivered, and his teeth began to gnash.

When I asked him for a loan, he responded, with a groan,
That the interest rate would be just prime plus eight,
And to guarantee my purity he'd insist on some security—
All my assets plus the scalp upon my pate.
> Only this, a standard rate.

Though my bottom line is black, I am flat upon my back,
My cash flows out and customers pay slow.
The growth of my receivables is almost unbelievable;
The result is certain—unremitting woe!
And I hear the banker utter an ominous low mutter,
> "Watch cash flow."

## QUESTION

1. Why are bankers so concerned about cash-flow information?


# 120

# THE DATA THAT ANALYSTS WANT MOST*
Corporate Communication Report


From time to time, specific types of corporate data come to the fore as being of
special importance to institutional analysts.

In 1970-71, for instance—in the wake of the credit crunch and the Penn Central
debacle—analysts wanted to know as much as possible about companies' balance
sheets, borrowing arrangements, cash flows, cash requirements and the like.

Today, interest in corporate liquidity has subsided somewhat. But a number of
other items have become matters of great concern:

The anticipated impact of the energy crisis on a company's operations. Penn Siegel
of Drexel Burnham & Co. cites of number of specific items that analysts want to
know: types of energy used, how much, where, sources of supply, types of contracts,

*From *Corporate Communication Report,* December 1973, p. 78. Reprinted by permission of the
publisher.

likelihood that these contracts will be filled, alternate sources of energy, percentage of energy generated from waste materials, potential impact of the energy crisis on markets served, etc. Siegel acknowledges, however, that in many cases the companies themselves haven't been able to come up with all the answers, so there is no way they can tell analysts.

Inventory data. The key point here is the effect of inflation on inventories. J. Kendrick Noble of Auerbach, Pollak & Richardson says that two particularly important items are the accounting treatment of inventories (Fifo, Lifo, etc.) and what the company's inventories consist of. Some analysts are especially worried that lower commodity prices might lead to large inventory writedowns.

"Accounting procedures are very big at the moment," notes Carmine Muratore of Blyth Eastman Dillon. Partly this is tied in with the matter of inventory profits and potential inventory losses. But analysts are anxious to know in general how accounting practices have affected a company's earnings, and by how much.

## QUESTION

1. Why do users want information on the anticipated impact of the energy crisis on a company's operations, inventory data, and accounting procedures?

# 121
# WHAT A FINANCIAL ANALYST WANTS FROM AN ANNUAL REPORT*
David Norr

If there is one word that could sum up what an analyst wants from your annual report, that word is "understanding." Because there are obvious limitations to financial statements—balance sheets, profit and loss statements, and statements of funds are not expected to convey a complete picture—we must go well beyond financial statements and talk about reporting in a larger sense.

Why is it so important that annual reports be understandable? What can the average shareholder be expected to understand? After all, aren't these matters beyond the ken of all but a few professional analysts?

But why should reporting be geared to the few sophisticates? Management has a duty to provide pertinent information to all interested people—owners and potential owners. This duty is not simply to tell the story to get the stock up. It is to provide the marketplace with adequate information so that the stock may sell at an

*From *Financial Executive,* August 1970, pp. 20–23. Reprinted by permission of the publisher.

appropriate level, regardless of whether it is down, up, or unchanged. The point is that free-market forces, irrational as they may appear to you and to me, will influence the stock. Lack of information and understanding should not be a factor in the market.

It is regrettable that all too few investors and analysts are well informed. But the report conducted in March 1969 by former SEC Commissioner Wheat ("Disclosure to Investors—Report and Recommendations to the Securities and Exchange Commission from Disclosure Policy Study") refers to the rise of the financial intermediary—the analyst at a bank, brokerage house, pension fund, mutual fund, or insurance company, who is informed and who operates with the monies of others. The growing institutionalization of the market means a small number of intermediaries advises or handles the funds of many others. These people, operating as fiduciaries, have a need to know what is happening. And they learn what is happening by reading annual reports.

This may be a part of the trend of consumerism. Reporting now goes beyond stewardship; the investor must be recognized as the user of your annual report.

Financial statements are necessarily quite limited in coverage. Because the statements are so limited, legions of analysts telephone or visit with management to get additional information in order to understand fully the company's operations. But much of this information could be included in the annual report. What are some of the things that should be included to make these frequent visits unnecessary?

## TEXT

The elements necessary for understanding vary with each company. It is up to management to provide appropriate text material. For example, even though I have never met the management of Union Camp, the text part of the 1969 annual report is quite informative. The presentation goes well beyond mere accounting.

Every company has individual elements. These elements should be described in the annual report. For example, why not mention in the report that two divisions have a potential capacity for sales of another $120 million rather than wait to tell a visiting analyst? Why not mention in the report that these divisions have 40 per cent fixed costs, now being covered, providing excellent leverage for profits if volume increases? I have long been disappointed at the weak, diluted management presentations before analysts' societies. Why can't a talk or an annual report dwell on the hard economic factors facing a company, the way a good analysis would? Flamboyant language can be eliminated. There is, for example, a spoof which translates "1969 was a year of preparation for the future"—typical annual report language—as "earnings collapsed."

## DIVISIONAL PROFITS

Since divisional sales and contribution to net income may vary widely, divisional earnings are a very significant factor. In my opinion, reporting divisional earnings represents the most important single tool to advance the art of analysis in the post-war era. It is a pleasure to see more companies presenting this information voluntarily in the 1969 annuals. As one looks at the breakdown in the source of earnings in the

Westinghouse annual report, one can only wonder how investment research was conducted without this information in prior years. Although unitary companies need not provide a breakdown, it is most encouraging to see Continental Oil provide profit data for foreign, plastics, plant foods, Canadian, U.S. oil and other North American oil, as well as for the distinctive coal and mineral operations.

No company interested in an accolade for reporting today can omit a profit breakdown.

## VARIANCES

One crucial area—indeed, I find it my best technique of analysis—is an understanding of variances. To what extent were prices increased, wages higher, start-up costs higher? Monsanto has long been outstanding in making this kind of presentation, in quarterlies as well as annuals.

## ADHERENCE TO GAAP

It is a shock to find that some companies ignore generally accepted accounting principles. This is particularly common either in quarterly reports or in the highlights section of the annual report. An all-too-frequent omission is the failure to use fully diluted earnings. For example, one company, in a 12-page quarterly release (adequate space indeed), reported primary earnings without labeling the earnings as primary. Fully diluted figures would have been 14 per cent lower—a material difference. Another company abused the highlights section of the annual report in the same fashion: it called attention to earnings per share without revealing the fully diluted figures, some 15 per cent lower.

There are enough weaknesses in GAAP as they are. Why create new problems? The Wheat report called attention to the many abuses of the highlights section of the annual report, an area for which management is completely responsible. Similarly, the Wheat report also calls for a compulsory quarterly report, to be called 10-Q, because serious abuses have occurred in interim reporting, an area that has been the responsibility of management.

Closely related to this is the problem of the misleading press release—"earnings up 22 per cent"—when it includes extraordinary items and is on a primary share basis.

There is little reason why companies cannot include a brief statement of accounting policies in each annual report. As long as there are substantial variations in depreciation and other accounting policies, descriptive data is necessary to inform readers of these differences.

## MISCELLANEOUS

### Investment Tax Credit

With the change in tax law, it becomes vital to disclose the impact of the investment tax credit in 1969 and the probable influence of the change in the law in 1970 and

1971. It was unfortunate that in prior years many companies failed to state the effect of the credit. This was a bit of vital, bottom-line information.

## Sales Breakdown

... This kind of analysis has grown in popularity. For example, in its 1969 annual report, U.S. Plywood-Champion broke sales down into 17 categories.

## Changes

Management must disclose changes in its estimates or accounting policies. In one case management did not indicate in its annual report that it has taken a 15 per cent writedown (equal to $80 million) on a portfolio of marketable securities. A prospectus issued seven months later revealed the story. Analysts have a much tighter definition of materiality than accountants, since a seemingly small change in absolute numbers may account for a significant portion of the growth in earnings between two years.

## Debt Maturities

In an era of high interest rates, with institutions often seeking equity kickers, a schedule of debt maturities is most valuable for analysis.

## Fully Diluted Earnings

Similarly, it would help if management presented a table showing the impact of dilution from the various issues in order to arrive at fully diluted earnings.

## Statistical Data

Frequently an understanding of operations requires several pages of statistical material. Oil companies and insurance companies have developed statistical supplements, of much use to financial intermediaries, which avoid burdening the annual report reader with such elaborate statistics. The content of these supplements is best left to each company; the concept is very valuable.

## Price Index

In some areas, such as chemicals, an index of realizations is a helpful tool.

## Pension Expense

Year-to-year variations in this figure are often substantial, yet remain unexplained. One company disclosed a 40 per cent drop, $8 million, in pension plan expense without any amplification.

### Research

In some areas, such as drugs, the thrust and direction of research is very useful.

### Supplemental Statement of Funds

Occasionally a second statement of funds covering foreign operations is necessary. This arises when dividends are paid in U.S. dollars, but a significant portion of profits are overseas and are not remitted to the U.S. Variations in the location of capital spending or working capital may also create problems. Of course, this may also be a problem in domestic companies if the parent company earnings are based on consolidated results, but the earning power lies in subsidiaries which do not pay dividends.

### Capital Expenditures Planned

Of course, mention of this should be included in an annual report.

### Backlogs

Where pertinent, this figure should be given for the current year and compared with the backlog for the preceding year.

### Intra-industry Variations

It is to be hoped that other industries will emulate the oil industry, which twice inventoried its accounting principles. Such inventories should produce a rationalization of practices under the aegis of the Accounting Principles Board. For example, the Wheat report disclosed that there were six "adjusted" earnings figures available in one insurance company. Surely rationalization of practices among finance companies would be a most helpful step. But are inventory practices among electronic companies manufacturing semi-conductors comparable? I hope that the next few years will see a genuine attempt to narrow the areas of difference by codifying industry accounting methods. Management should take the lead.

### CONCLUSION

There is much that management can do in an annual report beyond mere accounting. The basic elements are 1) meaningful text information, 2) a discussion of variances, and 3) a table of divisional earnings. Beyond that, the specifics may vary in each situation. All this is designed to make the report understandable. It is the obligation of management to provide information adequate to achieve understanding.

### QUESTIONS

1. What is a financial analyst? How do financial analysts differ from accountants? How are they similar to accountants? To investors and creditors?

2. What are diluted earnings, and how are they computed?

3. If the "understanding" of financial reports could be accomplished to Mr. Norr's complete satisfaction, how would this affect the duties of the financial analyst?

# 122
## HOW TO TALK TO YOUR ANALYST*
Lee Smith

When it comes to handling security analysts, one chief executive who has always kept his company in the front ranks of attention is Dr. Armand Hammer, the much-publicized, colorful chairman of Occidental Petroleum Corp. Yet when Oxy's chief executive spoke to the New York Security Analysts last month, there was none of the old flash and dash.

Instead, after a warm-up joke or two, Dr. Hammer reviewed Oxy's recent past and talked about its future prospects in a dry prose hardly more rhapsodic than that of a 10-K form. And when the analysts started firing away at him with questions, Dr. Hammer frequently left the spotlight to Oxy President Joseph E. Baird and John J. Dorgan, executive vice president for finance.

Were the analysts bored? Not in the least. As one of them had remarked before the meeting, "We are not here for an Elmer Gantry revival."

Clearly, Dr. Hammer still knows how to talk to security analysts, a skill of particular importance for chief executives these days. With the market on the rise, every company has lofty hopes that its stock—probably after years in the doldrums—will be swept up in the tide. But few companies can hope to be part of that upturn without a helping hand from the Wall Street community and the people they influence who buy and sell stocks.

To get this assistance, however, is far tougher than it was back in the razzle-dazzle years of the 1960s. As Dr. Hammer's presentation suggests, Wall Street today is a much more serious and hardworking place. Along with the new economic attitudes fathered by a shattering recession, the security analysts themselves have gone through revolutionary changes. And those changes now make it more difficult than ever for a company to get the analyst's attention.

The most obvious and far-reaching change is that there are fewer faces in the crowd. When the series of brokerage house collapses and mergers began at the end of the Sixties, so did a significant shakeout in the ranks of security analysts. Although the New York Society currently has a membership list of 5,000, one analyst notes: "There are an awful lot of home addresses on the roster."

*From *Dun's Review,* July 1975, pp. 51–53. Reprinted by permission of the publisher.

Even more significant is the changing emphasis of the analysts' job. Until recently, the largest number of analysts worked on the "sell" side of the business; that is, in brokerage houses where they supply salesmen with evaluations of stocks, which the salesmen then sell to clients. But with the rising, and by now predominant, influence of institutions in the market, many analysts have switched to the "buy" side, working for the banks, insurance companies, pension funds and other institutions.

Because the institutions are interested almost exclusively in the top tier of stocks with huge amounts of shares on the market, the analysts have tended to focus their attention on fewer companies. Even Merrill Lynch has narrowed its interests drastically. A few years ago the giant retail brokerage firm kept track of 2,500 companies; today its analysts follow only 1,250, far more than any other firm but still only a fraction of all public companies. "It's very tough for small companies," concedes Merrill Lynch Vice President Robert L. Mentch. "It makes their stock less liquid, and it affects their ability to raise capital. We might go back to following more stock if the individual investors were to come back into the market in large numbers," Mentch adds. "But the way it looks now, the market will become more and more concentrated on a few issues."

With fewer issues to follow, an analyst can be more thorough and probing in his evaluation of a company. As a result, most consultants, editors and analysts themselves agree, the quality of security analysis has risen since the purge. "In the Sixties," says William Chatlos, principal partner of Wall Street consulting firm Georgeson & Co., "an analyst would walk through your door and ask what your annual growth rate was. If you said 10%, he'd walk out and go across the street where the growth rate was 11%. These days there is more emphasis on value."

Even some of the blue-chip companies that have traditionally been able to call their own tune with the financial community are now finding that it pays to be available to security analysts. When sugar prices skyrocketed last fall, for example, soft-drink analysts were understandably concerned about the impact on Coca-Cola Co. and rushed to their telephones. After a few days, Fillmore Eisenberg, Coke's executive vice president for finance, informed the analysts through a press release: "I have been getting sixty to seventy calls a day. Due to this volume, I am suspending all personal contact with analysts."

No company was in a better position to cut off communications with the financial community than Coke. The company is so cash rich it never has to borrow; and, far from suffering, Coke stock rose steadily after the severing of analyst relations. Still, in the spring Coke suddenly reversed its policy and notified analysts that it would talk to them once again. Eisenberg's explanation for the turnabout is that Coke stock is a favorite of pension funds and that Coke may be required to talk to analysts by the new pension reform act.

But one analyst thinks there may be an additional explanation for Coke's rapprochement. "With a company as large as Coke," he points out, "there are always sources of information, even when the company refuses to talk. You can talk to suppliers, competitors, former employees, and those 600 bottlers turned out to be a great source of what is really going on at Coke. In fact," the analyst concludes, "during the blackout I think analysts learned more about Coke then they ever had before."

## THE SPECIALISTS

Looking at the security analysts' hierarchy today, the most visible—and influential—is the small group of highly specialized analysts who track as few as half a dozen companies but know those companies—as well as the legal, economic and technological environments in which they function—thoroughly.

Not surprisingly, every company is eager to meet and impress the top analyst in its industry. That analyst not only has persuasive powers with the big institutional investors; when he delivers an opinion, other analysts generally listen.

But the elite are difficult to reach for all but the most prestigious companies. Their time is considered so valuable that their firms protect them from being pestered for advice by all but the biggest portfolio managers. They do not often attend the lunches and dinners at the New York Society, and when they do it is generally only to make certain that the company does not release any significant new information. For the most part, the top analysts already know the answers from private meetings with corporate officers.

To be sure, a New York Society lunch or dinner is not a waste of time. It at least exposes a company to a healthy mixture of inquisitive generalists as well as knowledgeable specialists. "It is a good way for a company to keep up with the passing parade, to catch the eyes of analysts who are switching specialties, from, say, real estate to energy," observes DeWitt C. Morrill, investor relations consultant at Carl Byoir & Associates.

Perhaps the most popular form of get-together is the small luncheon or cocktail party attended by a dozen analysts and several company officers. Most analysts prefer such gatherings to large meetings because of the greater opportunity for give-and-take. "I was at a small luncheon the other day and the chairman of a chain of department stores told us that he viewed the current year with 'suspended optimism,' " recalls William LeFevre, an analyst at Granger & Co. "I asked him what the hell that meant. He laughed and said he didn't know, but that his public relations department had thought it was a great phrase. It is hard to get candor like that at a large meeting."

It is always at least worth a try for a chief executive to invite a top analyst in for a talk. The analyst may well accept, if only for his own purposes. "Sometimes analysts just want to refine their technical knowledge and their vocabulary in an industry," notes Glenn Saxon, publisher of *The Saxon Report*, an investor relations newsletter.

It is up to the chief executive, of course, to turn such a meeting to his advantage. "By all means let the analyst pick your brains and answer his questions," Saxon goes on. "But don't let him get out of your office before you've had an opportunity to impress upon him the points about your company you wanted to make."

There is no question, though, that small and medium-sized companies have a difficult time getting analysts to listen at all—especially in New York. While any company eager to present itself might still be able to fill a dining room, the qualifications of the guests might be doubtful. One company hosted such a luncheon in New York not long ago, and when a vice president circulated among the dozen "analysts" in attendance he found that only four were bona fide analysts. The others were an assortment of brokerage house employees. "In times of economic distress," observes Jules Augus, an analyst for Moore & Schley, Cameron & Co., "a lot of guys show up at these lunches just to get a hot meal."

## GOING THE REGIONAL ROUTE

Because New York analysts are so tough to get to, many companies are now concentrating their efforts on regional brokerage houses around the country. Not only are they likely to get a more enthusiastic reception, a number of regional houses have sharply upgraded their research capabilities. Indeed, for food and beverage companies, the top analyst in the industry is now in Richmond, Virginia. Announcing that he was tired of New York City several years ago, John Maxwell left Oppenheimer & Co., moved down to Richmond and set up his own firm. Maxwell Associates, a division of Wheat, First Securities.

The growing importance of the regional houses is underscored by Georgeson's William Chatlos. "Ten years ago," says Chatlos, "I could not have recommended to a client that he go to the analysts anywhere but in New York, because there was so much leverage here. But now 80% of the meetings we hold are outside New York."

Consultant John P. Kehoe, who represents nine small-to-medium-sized companies, also does much of his work outside New York. "If my client is Amalgamated Mousetrap," Kehoe explains, "I know the company is too small for a consumer goods analyst at Paine, Webber, for example, to be interested in. I just want the analyst to be 'constructively passive' about the company. I talk to him over the phone to make sure he has heard of Amalgamated and agrees that it is a nice little company, although too small to justify a report."

Kehoe then takes his campaign for Amalgamated around the country. If the company has a plant in Charlotte, say, there is bound to be some local interest in the stock and so he runs a campaign in the local newspapers. And when the president of Amalgamated makes an inspection tour of the Charlotte plant, Kehoe arranges a lunch with the sales manager of the local Paine, Webber office. With any luck, some time after that lunch the sales manager will call the Paine, Webber analyst in New York and ask for his opinion of Amalgamated. The analyst will respond that it is a nice little company, and the sales manager will have clearance to sell the stock to his local clients.

As analysts become more expert and more sought after, they are just as likely to be company critics as company cheerleaders. They are also a lot more demanding of the companies they deal with than they used to be. Knowing from sad experience how rapidly corporate fortunes can change, these days analysts are very conscious of the quality of information they get from management, and they expect it to be honest information.

In fact, the worst mistake a company can possibly make, all analysts agree, is to be deceitful. Giving an analyst misleading information is a transgression not easily forgotten. "I've got a list of companies that have burned me at one time or another," admits analyst LeFevre. "They tried to cover up bad news or let it come out in dribbles."

Glenn Saxon recalls one classic example of just how poisonous even an innocent deception can be. Some years ago, Saxon says, the president of Singer Co. was invited downtown to Lehman Brothers to bring Lehman's analysts and some of its clients up to date on Singer's condition. Shortly before the meeting, the president became sick and sent along the executive vice president instead. That turned out to be a mistake.

The executive vice president was primarily a salesman, Saxon reports, and he did an excellent job of persuading the analysts of Singer's bright future, specifically in the upcoming quarter. But not long after the meeting, workers at Singer's Scotland plants went on strike, and as the strike dragged on it became clear that the company's earnings would suffer considerably.

It was not clear to the analysts, however. The item was too small to make the papers, and the executive vice president neglected to call them and revise his forecast. When the quarterly earnings were finally reported, they were well below the original estimate. "You can't really blame the vice president," argues Saxon. "Dealing with analysts was not his job."

Nevertheless, with that gaffe Singer became known as a company that would lead an analyst down the garden path. "You can tell Wall Street anything as long as you say it in the right way and soon enough," comments LeFevre. "The thing Wall Street can't stand is surprises."

## QUESTIONS

1. What is financial analysis?
2. Why are financial analysts important to users of financial statements? To accountants?
3. Where and how do the functions of an analyst and an accountant overlap?
4. How does an analyst feel about "future shock?"

# 123

# THE ACCOUNTANT'S ROLE IN LABOR RELATIONS*
Harold H. Jack

In the book *Horizons for a Profession*, which resulted from a study sponsored by the Carnegie Corporation of New York and the American Institute of Certified Public

*From *Management Accounting,* October 1970, pp. 57, 60, and 63. Reprinted by permission of the publisher.

Accountants, the conclusion is stated that with respect to accountants' services in labor relations, only arbitration, commerical or labor, appears to be of any significance at the present time, and this is limited to the larger public accounting firms. The same is true but to a lesser extent of collective bargaining and labor negotiation studies. While that study was limited to services performed by CPA firms, I believe we can say with a reasonable degree of assurance that the results of the study apply equally to licensed public accountants and to a lesser degree to accountants in industry.

I believe that this lack of participation by accountants in the collective bargaining process is unrealistic.

Certainly, as accountants, more than any other group, we can appreciate that accounting data constitutes an important segment of the total information which must be considered by both labor and management in the course of their negotiations. Almost without exception, labor negotiations involve more than hourly wage offers and demands (being a labor accountant, I prefer to think of the latter not as demands but as attempts to secure a fair share of the productive effort). Such matters as working conditions, pensions and profit sharing plans, holidays, vacation—and the list is long and impressive—have long been recognized as proper subjects of the collective bargaining process.

With rare exception, each item which is involved in the bargaining process whether it be offered by management—or demanded by labor—has a cost attached to it. Certainly we can agree that no one is better equipped to measure what the cost is than accountants. The feeling of responsibility to intelligently justify contract proposals probably bears more heavily on the union conscience than on management's. Since we make most of the suggestions we are expected to justify them. The day when the union takes as much or as little as it has the naked power to take has long since passed. In this age of highly integrated social and economic factors, there is a continuing demand that collective bargaining progress be related to community progress. Unions feel this keenly and, therefore, have for many years placed great emphasis on the accumulation and presentation of pertinent economic factors in support of its bargaining performance.

Thus it is not surprising to find a nationally-known corporate industrial accountant, Paul W. Demarest, writing in the August 1968 issue of *Management Accounting*:

"Union accountants have provided sufficient data to their management so that their union is in some cases better prepared than corporate representatives for negotiations."

## WAYS TO ASSIST MANAGEMENT

While the type of economic research and analysis required to determine the costs involved in a particular item might be different than anything you have previously dealt with, your background and training would enable you to develop reliable figures. Some of the particular areas in which you could assist management, either by computing projected costs or by furnishing background information which would assist it in the negotiations, include:

*areas for union accountant*

Costs of the proposals advanced by the labor negotiators;

Special productivity studies;

Analyses of profit margins to determine ability to pay;

Calculations of the effect of projected wage increases on profitability if prices cannot be increased;

Forecasts of profit margins based on sales forecasts and projected wage increases.

Historical summaries and analysis of employee wages and benefits could prove helpful. Such an analysis could take many forms. The amount of information which might be supplied is limited only by your imagination. For example, a historical tabulation of wage rates and benefits stated in total dollars, dollars per hour, and as a percentage of total sales and total costs could provide management with a meaningful guide against which present demands could be measured.

While some of the areas might be beyond those you are used to dealing with, I do not believe that a strong accountant need feel any trepidation about expanding his services to serve management needs.

From the standpoint of possible services which might be rendered to the labor side of the negotiations, consider these possibilities: Special studies of prevailing wage rates in the geographic area; special studies of contract settlements in comparable industries; special studies of cost of living index changes.

Again, these are only illustrations of possible areas of service. There are certainly many additional possibilities.

Those of you who are industrial accountants are probably not too interested in the possible areas of service to labor negotiators, but look again at the items above. Management has a vital interest in knowing how its offer compares with the wage rates in its area of operations, and further that its wage scale is comparable with its competitors, and further that, in relation to the change in price levels since the last contract was negotiated, its offer is fair.

Moreover, if you are dealing with a publicly held company it would be possible to develop important information from labor's standpoint by examination of published reports, SEC filings and other available information.

*management vs labor*

As you may have deduced, I believe the possibilities for an accountant rendering service in collective bargaining are greater on the management side than on the labor side. This naturally follows. An accountant cannot perform without information, and, without doubt, the amount of information readily available to the accountant makes his role as an advisor to management easier than when he is called upon to act as an advisor to labor. In most instances the information required to perform the various studies and projections which I have previously mentioned is available from the records of the company and need only be assembled and converted to understandable facts and figures. This is generally not true of the types of information required to produce meaningful information for the labor side in the collective bargaining process.

## HELPFUL GOVERNMENT SOURCES

Your search for information in this area should begin with the U.S. government. There is available a wealth of information which can be extremely useful. I am sure that you are all aware of the Bureau of Labor Statistics and the regularity with which it publishes the cost of living index, both on a national and local basis.

In addition, a number of publications are available at a nominal cost from the Government Printing Office. Examples of publications which could serve as possible sources of meaningful and helpful information are:

1. *Employment and Earnings and Monthly Report on the Labor Force.* This publication presents the most current information available on trends and levels of employment, hours of work, earnings and labor turnover. It gives not only overall trends, but also shows developments in particular industries in the States, and local metropolitan areas.

2. *Employment and Earning Statistics for States and Areas*—based on the 1957 standard industrial classification. This publication provides historical information on employment and earnings statistics.

3. *Monthly Labor Review.* This publication is the medium through which the Labor Department publishes its regular monthly reports on such subjects as trends of employment and payrolls, hourly and weekly earnings, weekly working hours, collective agreements, industrial accidents, industrial disputes and many others.

4. *Wages and Related Benefits.* This is a series of area wage surveys covering over 60 metropolitan areas.

As I stated earlier, many of you may feel that some of these areas lie outside the accountant's area of competence. While at present this may be, and in large measure is probably true, nevertheless, I don't believe any one of us is precluded from expanding his area of competence. If you will think about it for a moment, I am sure you will agree that each of the areas of possible service which I have suggested deals with facts and figures—and isn't that the meat and potatoes of our chosen field?

To those of you who have not been so involved in labor negotiations, may I suggest you consider getting involved. If you are in public practice, sell your clients—be they management or labor—on the idea that you have something to offer. If you are employed in industrial accounting, and your company is not getting this type of service from its accounting group, let it be known that management is missing a good bet.

The question arises: does the accountant even have to limit himself to merely furnishing facts and figures to the negotiating parties or can he also extend himself into active participation in the collective bargaining process? I personally feel that because of their background, training and broad exposure to people many accountants would make excellent negotiators. However, it would take time for accountants to adjust to the fencing exercises and apparent lack of progress which characterizes many collective bargaining sessions, but again his competence and background should stand the accountant in good stead.

We are determined as labor accountants to help in setting as high a standard as possible for our profession. There will be those who say it is perhaps the heat and the glare of the public spotlight, which seems to be kept well focused on labor unions, that helps to account for this attitude. Perhaps that is so. We also have professional pride.

*held in trust*

We think, for example, that this attitude of professionalism and conscientiousness had at least some part to play in the reduction of the premium for fiduciary bonds required of union officers and certain employees under federal labor law. The reduction was made by the insurance companies voluntarily and is the first such voluntary reduction in history.

Mr. Demarest, the corporate accountant to whom I referred to earlier, said this in that article,

The inconsistencies and inadequacies of corporate annual reports have frequently been mentioned in accounting literature. Corporate accountants could take a lesson from the Biennial Report of the AFL-CIO issued to their convention.

We are determined to maintain and improve the record as it stands, and we hope that more and more the scope and effectiveness of the magical collective bargaining process, which has helped make this nation and our system one of the wonders of the world, may be improved by virtue of a more intense interest on the part of the accountant as to the role he can play.

## QUESTIONS

1. What difference should it make to the certified public accountant as to how the user views certified accounting reports? Do you consider that a trade union leader looks upon a firm's accounting reports for use in collective bargaining in the same way as an investor does who is considering purchasing stock of the company? As a creditor does who is thinking about making a loan to the firm? As the government or the general public? As the management of the firm does generally or in collective bargaining?

2. How could the "extremely useful" information made available by the Bureau of Labor Statistics be adapted for inclusion in financial reports?

3. Do you agree with Mr. Jack's view that "the possibilities for an accountant rendering service in collective bargaining are greater on the management side than on the labor side?" Why?

# 124
# WHAT SHOULD BE THE FASB'S OBJECTIVES?*
William H. Beaver

Was the acrimony arising out of the investment tax credit much ado about nothing? Does it matter whether special gains and losses are reported in the ordinary income or in the extraordinary item section? When firms switch from accelerated to straight-line depreciation, what is the effect upon investors? Did the Accounting Principles Board allocate its resources in an appropriate manner? If its priorities needed reordering, where should the emphasis have been shifted? What objectives should be adopted for financial accounting standards?

To answer such questions, the Financial Accounting Standards Board plans to sponsor a sizable research program.[1] For this reason, now is an appropriate time to take stock of the current body of knowledge and assess its implications for the setting of financial accounting standards. This article summarizes the results of recent research that has explored several facets of the relationship between financial statement data and security prices. The findings have a direct bearing on the questions raised at the outset and suggest that our traditional views of the role of policy-making bodies, such as the APB, SEC and FASB, may have to be substantially altered.

Currently we have far too little evidence on important issues in accounting. However, given this paucity of knowledge, it would be unfortunate if we ignored the evidence that we do have. Aspects of this research have already had a considerable effect on the professional investment community. Yet there has been no awareness of this research in accounting at the practical level or in the setting of past standards, as reflected in the APB Opinions. If the hopes for success of the FASB are to be realized, it is imperative that we lead, not lag, in incorporating the current state of knowledge into the setting of standards. Regulating financial accounting standards in ignorance of this evidence makes the prospects for success dim.

## THE EVIDENCE

The behavior of security prices with respect to financial statement data is a widely discussed and hotly debated topic. The financial press is replete with articles of alleged effects of financial statement data on prices. In most cases, such allegations are not supported by any evidence. In a few cases, evidence of an anecdotal nature is offered. For example, the price of the stock of the ABC Company changed dramatically at approximately the same time the firm changed its method of depreciation to straight-line. Therefore, the cause was the change in accounting method. Such stories,

*From *Journal of Accountancy,* August 1973, pp. 49–56. Reprinted by permission of the publisher.

[1]"Recommendations of the Study on Establishment of Accounting Principles," *Journal of Accountancy,* May 72, pp. 66–71.

while often entertaining, hardly constitute convincing evidence for several reasons. First, such an approach may select only those cases which are favorable to the hypothesis of the author while ignoring those instances that would refute it. For example, an examination of the price changes of only one firm or a few hand-picked firms that changed depreciation methods is insufficient. An examination must be made for all firms that changed depreciation methods or at least a large, randomly selected sample. Second, the analysis explains price changes after-the-fact on the basis of a single factor. There may be many factors that cause a price change. Usually, little or no care is taken to account for these other factors.

Unfortunately, until recently such evidence was the only type available. However, the issue is far too serious to be left to casual empiricism. Security prices are of obvious importance because of their impact upon the wealth, and hence the welfare, of investors. This importance is formally recognized in SEC legislation. Recent cases arising out of Section 10b-5 testify to the fact that accounting practices are evaluated in terms of their effect on security prices.[2] Moreover, it is inconceivable that the FASB could set optimal financial accounting standards without assessing the impact of their actions on security prices.

The prevailing opinion in the accounting profession is that the market reacts naïvely to financial statement information. This view is reinforced by the anecdotal data of the sort described earlier, and by the obvious fact that the market is populated with several million uninformed, naïve investors, whose knowledge or concern for the subtleties of accounting matters is nil. However, in spite of this obvious fact, the formal research in this area is remarkably consistent in finding that the market, at least as manifested in the way in which security prices react, is quite sophisticated in dealing with financial statement data. One rationale for the observed sophistication of security prices is that the professional investors "make the market" and competitive bidding among one another for securities effectively makes the prices behave in such a manner that they reflect a considerable amount of sophistication. In any event, regardless of what the actual causal mechanism may be, there is considerable evidence that security prices do in fact behave in a sophisticated fashion. In the terminology of this literature, the securities market is said to be "efficient" with respect to financial statement data.[3]

A market is said to be efficient if security prices act as if they "fully reflect" publicly available information, including financial statement data. In other words, in

[2] For example, litigation is currently under way in the cases of **Memorex** and **Occidental Petroleum Corp.,** pursuant to SEC action under Section 10b-5. Brief summaries of issues appear in the June 25, 1971, and March 5, 1971, issues of **The Wall Street Journal,** respectively. In both cases, measures of damages being discussed are directly related to the effect of the firms' accounting practices on security prices.

[3] Three forms of efficiency have been delineated: (1) the weak form, which deals with efficiency with respect to the past sequence of security prices (e.g., the random-walk hypothesis), (2) the semistrong form, which concerns efficiency with respect to published information, and (3) the strong form, which involves all information including inside information. This article deals with efficiency in the semistrong form. There is also considerable evidence with respect to the weak form of efficiency, but it is beyond the scope of this article. For a summary of this literature, see W. Beaver, "Reporting Rules for Marketable Equity Securities," **Journal of Accountancy**, Oct. 71, pp. 57–61.

an efficient market the investor is playing a "fair game" with respect to published information. Specifically, this means no investor can expect to use published information in such a way as to earn abnormal returns on his securities. Each investor can expect to earn a return on a security commensurate with its risk.[4] All securities of the same degree of riskiness will offer the same expected return, regardless of what accounting methods are used and no matter how much time is spent gleaning the secrets of the financial statements hidden in the footnotes. Hence, no amount of security analysis, based on published financial statement data, will lead to abnormal returns. There are obvious implications for the community of professional investors, among others. However, there are also equally dramatic implications for the accounting profession. For this reason, the evidence, which has examined several aspects of market efficiency with respect to financial statement data, is summarized below.[5]

One aspect of efficiency is the speed with which security prices react to public information when it is announced. Empirical evidence indicates that prices react quickly and in an unbiased fashion to a variety of events, including announcements of stock splits, stock dividends, secondary offerings and rights issues, as well as both annual and interim earnings announcements. This finding is exactly what one would expect in a market where the security prices at any point in time fully reflect the information released. Moreover, the studies of earnings announcements find security prices anticipate earnings for several months prior to the announcement.[6]

[4] A detailed discussion of security risk and how it relates to expected returns is beyond the scope of the article. However, there has been a substantial amount of research in the portfolio theory and capital asset pricing literature dealing with this relationship. Briefly, the literature suggests that expected return must be commensurate with the risk incurred, in that securities with greater risk must offer higher expected return. Of course, the actual return in a given period may differ from expected return. For a more complete discussion of this issue in a nontechnical manner, see C. Welles, "The Beta Revolution: Learning to Live With Risk," *The Institutional Investor,* September 1971, pp. 21–64; W. Sharpe, "Risk, Market Sensitivity and Diversification," *Financial Analysts Journal,* January-February 1972, pp. 74–79.

[5] A more detailed summary of the literature is provided in the article by Eugene Fama, "Efficient Capital Markets: A Review of Theory and Empirical Work," *Journal of Finance,* May 1970, pp. 383–417. The implications of this literature for accounting also have been discussed in the following articles: W. Beaver, "The Behavior of Security Prices and Its Implications for Accounting Research Methods," *The Accounting Review* (Supplement, 1972), pp. 407–37; R. Ball, "Changes in Accounting Techniques and Stock Prices" (unpublished paper, University of Chicago, 1972); and N. Gonedes, "Efficient Capital Markets and External Accounting," *The Accounting Review,* January 1972, pp. 11–21.

[6] The studies referred to here are E. Fama, L. Fisher, M. Jensen and R. Roll, "The Adjustment of Stock Prices to New Information," *International Economic Review,* February 1969, pp. 1–21; M. Scholes, "The Market for Securities: Substitution Versus Price Pressure and the Effects of Information on Share Prices," *Journal of Business,* April 1972, pp. 179–211; R. Ball and P. Brown, "An Empirical Evaluation of Accounting Income Numbers," *Journal of Accounting Research,* Autumn 1968, pp. 159–78; P. Brown and J. Kennelly, "The Informational Content of Quarterly Earnings: An Extension and Some Further Evidence," *Journal of Business,* July 1972, pp. 403–21; G. Benston, "Published Corporate Accounting Data and Stock Prices," *Empirical Research in Accounting: Selected Studies, 1967, Journal of Accounting Research* (Supplement, 1967), pp. 1–54; and W. Beaver, "The Information Content of Annual Earnings Announcements," *Empirical Research in Accounting: Selected Studies, 1968, Journal of Accounting Research* (Supplement, 1968), pp. 67–92.

Another aspect is this: Does the market look behind accounting numbers or is it fooled by them? Does the market act only on reported accounting numbers or does it adjust for other information, such as the accounting method used to calculate those numbers? In other words, does the market use a broader information set than merely the reported accounting numbers? In this respect, there have been several studies of changes in accounting methods and the subsequent behavior of security prices.[7] All of these studies show essentially the same result. There is no increase in price by changing to an accounting method that reports higher earnings than would have been reported had no change been made. The market, as reflected in price behavior, is not so naïve as many people claim. Instead, it acts as if it looks beyond accounting numbers and takes into account the fact that earnings are being generated by a different method.

Further evidence compared the price-earnings ratios of firms that use accelerated methods of depreciation for both tax and reporting purposes (A/A group) with the price-earnings ratios of firms that use accelerated methods for tax purposes but straight-line for reporting purposes (A/S group).[8] The price-earnings ratio for the A/A group was larger than the price-earnings ratio for the A/S group. This finding is consistent with a market which recognizes that firms will report lower earnings under accelerated methods of depreciation than they would have under straight-line methods. Further analysis suggested that risk and growth could not explain the difference in the price-earnings ratios. In fact, the average riskiness and average growth rates were the same for both depreciation groups. However, when the earnings of the A/S group were converted to the earnings that would have been reported had they used an accelerated method for reporting, the price-earnings ratios of the two depreciation groups were essentially equal. In other words, when the firms were placed on a uniform accounting method, the price-earnings differences disappeared. Thus, the market appears to adjust for differences in depreciation methods among firms and, in effect, looks behind reported accounting data. Moreover, further testing found that changes in security prices more closely follow changes in certain nonreported forms of earnings than they do changes in reported earnings. This finding is consistent with a market where a broad information set is used in assessing price changes in contrast to one where there is sole, unquestioning reliance upon reported earnings.

In sum then, the evidence, across a variety of contexts, supports the contention that the market is efficient with respect to published information.

## IMPLICATIONS

This evidence, together with the evidence on the performance of mutual funds, has led to changes in the investment community.[9]

[7]The empirical studies referred to here include R. Kaplan and R. Roll, "Investor Evaluation of Accounting Information: Some Empirical Evidence," *Journal of Business,* April 1972, pp. 225–57; R. Ball, op. cit.; T. R. Archibald, "Stock Market Reaction to Depreciation Switchback," *The Accounting Review,* January 1972, pp. 22–30; and E. Comiskey, "Market Response to Changes in Depreciation Accounting," *The Accounting Review,* April 1971, pp. 279–85.

[8]W. Beaver and R. E. Dukes, "Depreciation Methods: Some Empirical Results," *The Accounting Review* (forthcoming).

[9]The empirical evidence finds that mutual fund returns fail to cover even research costs and brokerage commissions (let alone loading charges). After deducting these expenses, the net return

Many portfolio managers and their clients have moved away from a "beat-the-market," high-turnover philosophy to one where the emphasis is placed upon risk management and the minimization of operating costs. The Samsonite pension fund contract is but one recent example. Wells Fargo Bank has agreed to manage the Samsonite pension fund where the agreement stipulates the maintenance of a given level of risk within prespecified limits, a lid on the maximum amount of turnover that can occur and a restriction on the minimum number of securities comprising the fund.[10]

Given the practical impact that this research has had on the investment community, one might suspect that there are implications for the practice of accounting as well. In fact, there are several important implications for accounting in general and for the FASB in particular. However, there has been virtually no reaction on the part of the accounting profession. One reason is a general lack of awareness of this research, because its dissemination has essentially been restricted to academic journals. Another reason is that the anecdotal form of evidence discussed earlier continues to carry considerable weight among many members of the accounting profession. As a result, many readers may refuse to accept the evidence in support of market efficiency. But what if the mounting evidence in support of an efficient market finally becomes so overwhelming and compelling that it is accepted by all seven members of the FASB, all SEC Commissioners and staff, and all congressmen? What are the implications for the FASB? There are at least four major implications.

## First

Many reporting issues are trivial and do not warrant an expenditure of FASB resources. The properties of such issues are twofold: (1) There is essentially no difference in cost to the firm of reporting either method. (2) There is essentially no cost to statement users in adjusting from one method to the other. In such cases, there is a simple solution. Report one method, with sufficient footnote disclosure to permit adjustment to the other, and let the market interpret implications of the data for security prices.

Unfortunately, too much of the resources of the APB and others has been devoted to issues that warrant this straightforward resolution. For example, the investment credit controversy belongs in this category, as do the issues regarding the definition of extraordinary items, interperiod tax allocation, earnings per share computations

---

to the mutual fund shareholder is below the return that could have been obtained from a simple strategy of buying and holding a portfolio of the same degree of riskiness. In fact, only after all such costs were added back in computing the return is the average mutual fund performance approximately equal to (but not greater than) the return from random portfolios of the same degree of riskiness. Moreover, these results not only apply to the average performance of all mutual funds but additional tests also indicate that no individual funds were able to produce superior returns consistently. For example, past performance by a fund appeared to be of no value in predicting superior performance in the future. See M. Jensen, "Risk, the Pricing of Capital Assets, and the Evaluation of Investment Portfolios," *Journal of Business,* April 1969, pp. 167–247. See also M. Zweig, "Darts, Anyone? As Market Pickers, Market Seers, the Pros Fall Short," *Barron's,* February 19, 1973, pp. 11–25.

[10]C. Welles, op. cit.

involving convertible securities, and accounting for marketable equity securities. By contrast, the FASB should shift its resources to those controversies where there is nontrivial additional cost to the firms or to investors in order to obtain certain types of information (for example, replacement cost accounting for depreciable assets). Whether such information should be a required part of reporting standards is a substantive issue.

## Second

The role of financial statement data is essentially a preemptive one—that is, to prevent abnormal returns accruing to individuals by trading upon inside information. This purpose leads to the following disclosure policy: If there are no additional costs of disclosure to the firm, there is prima facie evidence that the item in question ought to be disclosed.

This relatively simple policy could greatly enhance the usefulness of financial statements. Many forms of information are currently being generated internally by the firm and could be reported with essentially no additional cost (e.g., the current market value of marketable equity securities). Such information, if not publicly reported, may constitute inside information. Merely because prices reflect publicly available information in no way implies that they also fully reflect inside information. One information cost that investors may be incurring currently is abnormal returns earned by those who have monopolistic access to inside information. Opponents of greater disclosure bear the burden of proof of showing that individuals can be prevented from earning excess returns with the undisclosed information or that the cost of disclosure exceeds the excess returns. Given the private incentives to trade on inside information, such a condition is very difficult to ensure.

Incidentally, efficient securities markets also have some important implications regarding the accountants' growing concern over legal liability. Accountants can be held legitimately responsible for insufficient disclosure. However, they should not be held responsible for using a "wrong" method (e.g., flow-through v. deferral) as long as they disclose the method that was used and sufficient data to permit adjustment to the nonreported method.

## Third

The FASB must reconsider the nature of its traditional concern for the naïve investor. If the investor, no matter how naïve, is in effect facing a fair game, can he still get harmed? If so, how? The naïve investor can still get harmed, but not in the ways traditionally thought. For example, the potential harm is not likely to occur because firms use flow-through v. deferral for accounting for the investment credit. Rather, the harm is more likely to occur because firms are following policies of less than full disclosure and insiders are potentially earning monopoly returns from access to inside information. Harm is also likely to occur when investors assume speculative positions with excessive transactions costs, improper diversification and improper risk levels in the erroneous belief that they will be able to "beat the market" with published accounting information.

This implies that the FASB should actively discourage investors' beliefs that accounting data can be used to detect overvalued or undervalued securities. This also implies that the FASB must not attempt to reduce the complex events of multimillion dollar corporations to the level of understanding of the naïve, or, perhaps more appropriately labeled, ignorant investor. We must stop acting as if all—or even most—individual investors are literally involved in the process of interpreting the impact of accounting information upon the security prices of firms.

An argument often advanced against fuller disclosure is that the increased disclosure will befuddle and confuse the naïve investor. A specific manifestation of this argument is that earnings under market value rules are more volatile and hence may lead to more volatile security prices. For example, the insurance industry currently opposes the inclusion of such information on marketable securities in the income statement, even though market values are already reported on the balance sheet. Given that market values on the balance sheet are already part of public information, it is absurd to think that there is going to be any further effect on security prices because of the income statement disclosure. Yet considerable resources of the APB, the insurance industry and others have been wasted on an attempt to resolve this issue. In the more general case where there is no reporting of market values, the efficient market evidence implies that the market is not reacting naïvely to the currently reported numbers but, rather, is forming "unbiased" assessments of the market values and their effects on prices. Since the market is currently being forced to assess the effects of market values indirectly, they are probably estimating the value with error. Hence, if anything, reporting the actual numbers may eliminate the estimation errors which may be one source of volatility in security prices.

Moreover, one message comes through loud and clear from finance theory. The investor is concerned with assessing risk as well as expected return. In this context, one role of financial statement data is to aid the investor in assessing the risk of the security. By presenting less volatile numbers, we may be doing him a disservice by obscuring the underlying riskiness of his investment. Hence, it is impossible to argue that less volatile numbers per se are better than more volatile numbers. Taken together with the evidence in the efficient market, this suggests that the market can decide for itself how it wishes to interpret a given piece of information. The same sort of reasoning should be applied to the currently hot topic of reporting and attesting to forecasts. In an efficient market, a paternalistic attitude is unwarranted; furthermore, operationally, if it is used to rationalize lesser disclosure, it is much more likely to result in the protection of management than in the protection of investors, which is its ostensible purpose.

### Fourth

Accountants must stop acting as if they are the only suppliers of information about the firm. Instead, the FASB should strive to minimize the total cost of providing information to investors. In an efficient market, security prices may be essentially the same under a variety of financial accounting standards, because, if an item is not reported in the financial statements, it may be provided by alternative sources. Under this view, which is consistent with the evidence cited earlier, the market uses a broad information set, and the accountant is one—and only one—supplier of information. One objective is to provide the information to investors by the most economical means. In order to accomplish this objective, several questions must be addressed: What are the alternative sources of information to financial statements? What are the costs of providing a given piece of information via the alternative source vis-à-vis the financial statements? Most importantly, do financial statement data have a comparative advantage in providing any portion of the total information used by the market, and, if so, what portion?

The nature of the costs has already been alluded to. One set of costs is the "cost" of abnormal returns' being earned by insiders because of monopolistic access to information. A second set of costs is excessive information costs. They can occur in two situations:

1. When the accountant fails to report an item that must be conveyed to the investing public through some other, more expensive source.

2. When the FASB requires firms to report an item that has a "value" less than its cost or items that could have been reported through other, less expensive sources of information. A third set of costs is incurred when investors erroneously believe that they can "beat the market" using published financial statement information. This set includes excessive transaction costs stemming from churning their accounts, improper diversification because of disproportionately large investment in "underpriced" securities and the selection of improper risk levels.[11]

## NATURE OF FUTURE RESEARCH

One of the objectives the FASB must face is the establishment of a research program. Several areas should be explored:

1. Although the evidence in favor of market efficiency with respect to published information is considerable, the issue is by no means closed and further work on the particular types of accounting information items is needed.

2. Much more research is needed regarding market efficiency with respect to inside information. Such research will help to specify what the costs of nondisclosure are.

3. Evidence is needed on how individual investors, as opposed to the aggregate prices, react to information. Specifically, what is the process or mechanism by which information reaches individuals and is subsequently impounded in prices? What evidence is there of excessive transactions costs' being incurred by investors who act on

---

[11]The costs of holding erroneous beliefs regarding market efficiency extend beyond investors. For example, consider the recent decision by Chrysler to change inventory methods because of alleged inefficiencies in the capital markets (both debt and equity markets). Even though Chrysler had reported supplemental statements in its previous annual reports, this was judged to be inadequate to overcome the inability of the capital market to look behind the reported numbers. The initial effect of a switch in inventory methods for both book and tax purposes was an incremental tax bill of approximately $50 million spread over a 20-year period. The efficient market evidence suggests that such a decision was a serious misallocation of resources. In fact, if anything, Chrysler is in worse economic position now because it is paying higher tax bills. For a summary of facts see "Chrysler Posts $7.6 Million Loss for the Year," *The Wall Street Journal,* February 10, 1971.

information that already has been impounded in prices? Research into volume activity, as opposed to price activity, may be particularly insightful here. What evidence is there that individuals incur improper selection of risk levels by taking speculative positions based on accounting data? There are currently research methods available in finance that can provide at least a partial answer to these questions. The application of behavioral science also offers promise here.

4. More research is needed regarding the association between certain specific financial statement items and security prices. For example, are there certain items that are now being reported which do not seem to be used by the market as reflected in security prices? Conversely, are there certain types of information which are not currently reported but, in spite of that fact, are reflected in security prices? In the former instance, such items are candidates for being considered for possible exclusion from currently reported items. With respect to the latter, such items are candidates for being considered part of currently reported items.

5. Further research is needed to examine to what extent financial statement data are helpful to individual investors assessing the risk of a security. In an efficient market, the usefulness of financial statement data to individual investors is not to find mispriced securities, since they are nonexistent. What then is the value, if any? The value lies in the ability of financial statement data to aid in risk prediction. Some recent findings in the area by Beaver, Kettler and Scholes are encouraging, but much more research is needed.[12]

## ERRONEOUS INTERPRETATIONS

The implications of market efficiency for accounting are frequently misunderstood. There are at least two common misinterpretations.

The first belief is that, in an efficient market world, there are no reporting issues of substance because of the "all-knowing" efficient market. Taken to its extreme, this error takes the form of asserting that accounting data have no value and hence the certification process is of no value.[13] The efficient market in no way leads to such implications. It may very well be that the publishing of financial statements data is precisely what makes the market as efficient as it is. As I was careful to point out earlier, merely because the market is efficient with respect to published data does not

[12]W. Beaver, R. Kettler and M. Scholes, "The Association Between Market Determined and Accounting Determined Risk Measures," *The Accounting Review,* October 1970, pp. 654–82.

[13]In this regard it is imperative to distinguish between two important aspects of information: (1) The first is to aid the market in arriving at a given set of security prices. One aspect of this role is to provide a market where the investors are playing a fair game with respect to some given information set (e.g., accounting data). (2) The second is to aid individual investors, who face a given set of prices, to select the optimal portfolio. One aspect of this role is the use of financial statement data in risk prediction. It is entirely possible that future research will discover that financial statement data have no role to play at the individual investor level and that the sole role is a social one. In any event, the social level is of paramount concern to a policy-making body such as the FASB. The distinction is made particularly clear in E. Fama and A. Laffer, "Information and Capital Markets," *Journal of Business,* July 1971, pp. 289–98; and J. Hirshleifer, "The Private and Social Value of Information and the Reward to Inventive Activity," *American Economic Review,* September 1971, pp. 561–74; see also, W. Beaver, op. cit., pp. 424–25.

imply that market prices are also efficient with respect to nonpublished information. Disclosure is a substantive issue.

A second erroneous implication is, simply find out what method is most highly associated with security prices and report that method in the financial statement. As it stands, it is incorrect for several reasons. One major reason is that such a simplified decision rule fails to consider the costs of providing information. For example, a nonreported method may be less associated with security prices than the reported method because the cost of obtaining the nonreported numbers via alternative sources is too high. Yet such information may be provided via financial statements at substantially lower costs. In another context, suppose the nonreported method showed the higher association with security prices; does it follow that the nonreported method should be reported? No, not necessarily. Perhaps the market is obtaining the information at lower cost via the alternative sources.[14]

Moreover, the choice among different accounting methods involves choosing among differing consequences, as reflected in the incidence of costs and security prices which affect individuals differently. Hence, some individuals may be better off under one method, while others may be better off under an alternative method. In this situation, how is the optimal method to be selected? The issue is one of social choice, which in general is an unresolvable problem because of the difficulty (impossibility) of making interpersonal welfare comparisons.[15]

There are certain specific issues (e.g., similar to those discussed in this article) which closely suggest a policy decision, if one is willing to accept the mild ethical assumption of Pareto-optimality.[16] However, such situations must meet a fairly specific set of conditions.

Regardless of the final resolution by the policy-maker, it is still possible to specify the types of evidence that are relevant to choosing among alternatives. In simplest terms, although evidence cannot indicate what choice to make, it can provide information on the potential consequences of the various choices. Without a knowledge of consequences (e.g., as reflected in security prices), it is inconceivable that a policy-making body such as the FASB will be able to select optimal financial accounting standards. In spite of the importance of a knowledge of consequences, currently too little is known about price behavior and virtually nothing is known about the magnitude of the three types of costs outlined earlier.

## CONCLUSION

Financial statement information is inherently a social commodity. However, it is clear that decisions regarding its generation and dissemination are of a much different

---

[14]These issues are discussed at greater length in R. May and G. Sundem, "Cost of Information and Security Prices: Market Association Tests for Accounting Policy Decision," *The Accounting Review,* January 1973, pp. 80–94.

[15]K. Arrow, *Social Choice and Individual Values* (Yale University Press, 1968). The issue has been discussed in an accounting context in J. Demski, "Choice Among Financial Accounting Alternatives" (unpublished, Stanford University, 1972).

[16]The concept of Pareto-optimality states that a society prefers one alternative to another, if at least some people are better off and no one is worse off.

nature than we have traditionally thought them to be. This change in the way we view the FASB is conditioned upon the assumption of market efficiency. While there is need for further future research in this area, there is sufficient credibility in the evidence to date that we should be prepared to face its implications:

1. Many reporting issues are capable of a simple disclosure solution and do not warrant an expenditure of FASB time and resources in attempting to resolve them.

2. The role of accounting data is to prevent superior returns' accruing from inside information and can be achieved by a policy of much fuller disclosure than is currently required.

3. Financial statements should not be reduced to the level of understanding of the naïve investor.

4. The FASB should strive for policies that will eliminate excessive costs of information.

5. The FASB should sponsor a full-scale research program in the areas indicated, so that it may have some evidence of the consequences of their choices among different sets of financial accounting standards.

## QUESTIONS

1. Why does Professor Beaver reject the prevailing opinion in the accounting profession that the market reacts naïvely to financial statement information?

2. What evidence does he provide to support his contention that the market is efficient with respect to published information?

3. If the market is efficient with respect to published information, what are four major implications for the FASB?

4. What are excess information costs, and how do they occur?

5. What are two common misinterpretations of market efficiency for accounting?

## SELECTED BIBLIOGRAPHY

Vasicek, Oldrich A., and John A. McQuown, "The Efficient Market Model," *Financial Analysts Journal*, September-October 1972, pp. 71-84.

# 125

## CPA UNIT PROPOSES RULES TO DETERMINE WHEN FAIR ISN'T FOUL*

Frederick Andrews

For decades, independent auditors have duly pronounced corporate financial reports as "fairly presented in conformity with generally accepted accounting principles." The phrase is a ritual stamp that caps an audit as definitively as a sheepskin crowns a college education, or as a marriage ceremony used to culminate a romance.

At length, the auditors are getting around to defining what their incantation means. To be sure, the record already reflects considerable learned discussion of what "generally accepted accounting principles," or GAAP, amounts to. But what of "fairly presented"? What does it mean? What does the phrase add, if anything? Is "fairly presented" something different from GAAP?

Today a committee of the American Institute of Certified Public Accountants made public for comment a proposal specifying four hallmarks of "fairly presented" financial statements in addition to general acceptance of the accounting principles. Significantly, the committee rejected the idea that "fairness" requires an auditor to make a separate judgment of fairness, "using personal criteria," apart from GAAP. The committee said that would detract from the usefulness of financial statements.

According to the committee, "fair presentation" also requires that:

The accounting principles must be appropriate in the circumstances.

The financial statements must be "informative of matters that may affect their use, understanding and interpretation."

The data must be presented and summarized "in a reasonable manner, that is, neither too detailed nor too condensed."

The financial statements must reflect "the underlying events and transactions" in a way that states the results within "a range of acceptable limits that are reasonable and practicable."

### THE ISSUE FORCED

Some critics unkindly liken the entire discussion to the medieval conundrum about how many angels might dance on the head of a pin.

In the landmark Continental Vending case, three auditors on trial for criminal fraud argued in vain that the disclosure of certain highly dubious transactions wasn't required by GAAP. They summoned eight expert witnesses who agreed with them. Nevertheless, the trial judge refused to instruct the jury that conformity with GAAP was a complete defense to the charge of fraud.

Another pressure on auditors has come from the Securities and Exchange Commission, whose officials have looked askance on the school of thought that GAAP

*From the *Wall Street Journal,* Mar. 6, 1975, p. 2. Reprinted by permission of the publisher.

statements are, by definition, fairly presented. The SEC has viewed that dubiously as an effort by auditors to hide behind a rulebook.

## SEC ACCOUNTANT'S VIEW

John C. Burton, SEC chief accountant, gave his views on "fairly presented" last month in delivering the Emanuel Saxe Distinguished Accounting Lecture at Baruch College in New York. Mr. Burton proposed three requirements and focused on the varying degrees of sophistication among users of financial statements.

The financial statements taken as a whole must present business results in a way that's understandable to persons generally familiar with "the accounting model." That model, Mr. Burton said, referred to the general framework of accounting (such as carrying assets at cost, or realizing income only when there's an arms-length transaction). A user should know something about accounting but needn't be an expert.

The financial statements mustn't lead users to make predictions or conclusions that the auditors know are unlikely or incorrect.

There must be enough disclosure for sophisticated users to understand the basis used in recording transactions. An example is adequate information about the method of valuing inventories.

## QUESTION

1. Compare the various meanings of "fairly presented."

# 126
# THE GAMES ACCOUNTANTS PLAY*
Abraham J. Briloff

A balance sheet is very much like a bikini bathing suit. What it reveals is interesting; what it conceals is vital.[1]

If there was a contest for the "Ralph Nader of the accounting field," a slim, unassuming—but outspoken—professor from the City University of New York would win it hands down. And you can be sure if the final tabulations in the contest did not check out, someone would speak up—Dr. Abraham J. Briloff himself.

*From *Management Accounting,* February 1973, pp. 57—58. Reprinted by permission of the publisher.

[1] Abraham J. Briloff, *Unaccountable Accounting,* Harper & Row, New York, 1972.

In his new book, *Unaccountable Accounting*,[2] Dr. Briloff analyzes some recent company fiascos and spotlights the role the auditors played. It is Professor Briloff's thesis that accounting is going through an identity crisis because in a number of celebrated instances the auditors did not blow the whistle on their client companies. He faults accountants on two counts: for not making sensible rules for the game and for not rationally interpreting principles already promulgated.

Most businessmen will recall the examples he cites in his indictment of the accounting profession. Those who read *Barron's National Business and Financial Weekly* regularly will recognize some of the material here and the breezy acerbic style of the author. In a series of articles for the financial weekly in 1968 and 1971, Dr. Briloff zeroed in on some of the questionable practices of companies who had found a gap in GAAP. Specifically, he took aim at the conglomerates, home-building industry, the leasing industry and land developers.

The pooling ploy has passed its heyday but the author shows how it was done at the height of the conglomerate frenzy. Dramatic improvements in the company's operations could be shown just by including earnings of the companies acquired during the year and comparing them with results the year before the conglomerator pooled. It worked for awhile, but then many people—including Author Briloff and the SEC—started blowing the whistle.

Another innovative bit of accounting noted by the author is that of leasing companies. They inflated income by picking up manufacturing revenues immediately despite short-term leases, the expenses involved in re-leasing or selling the equipment, idle capacity and other considerations.

The name of the game was earnings per share and before the bottom fell out, a number of companies excelled at it. The author mentions names and figures. He has done his homework well and when he concludes "The Emperor has no clothes," often as not he is right on the mark.

The burden of the responsibility for such distortion of accounting lies not with company managements—whom Dr. Briloff seems to expect to take advantage of every loophole—but with the CPAs who attest to the "fairness" of the statements. A CPA himself, Dr. Briloff has jousted with the companies involved and even with the former top rule-making body of the profession—the Accounting Principles Board. At one time, he was a co-defendant in a multimillion dollar suit brought by a company which he wrote about.

A considerable knowledge of accounting and a penchant for footnote-reading are prerequisites for reconstructing some of the earnings reports. As Dr. Briloff points out, even some professional accountants are unable to understand all the ramifications of some corporate financial statements.

But with an élan and color that belie the public image of fusty accountants and accounting, Dr. Briloff takes some financial reports apart and puts them back together. Here's a sampling of the chapter headings, illustrating a style which will help give the book a greater exposure than if it were in turgid academese: "Alice in GAAP Land," "A Look at Some Inflated Bosoms and Big Busts," and "A House Is Not a Home."

---

[2] Ibid.

In a final chapter, "Quo Vadis?", the author offers to the groups involved in financial reporting some prescriptions for corrective action. He suggests unless investors, analysts, business executives and accountants understand the implications of the crisis, "there is little hope for the survival of the corporation as a form of private enterprise." Challenging the accounting profession, he insists that "they must share with management the transcendent commitment to the total society and to posterity, they must manifest a realization that they are professionals, hence with the presumed commitment to an advancing body of knowledge, and a commitment to survive—and thereby forswear the coloration of a trade profession."

What Dr. Briloff is doing is sounding a call to accountants in public practice and in corporate offices. . . . The crisis may not be as deep and wide as the author believes, but the problems exist and, as a result, an upheaval is going on in financial reporting.

### QUESTION

1. Why is Professor Briloff perhaps the best-known critic of accounting practice today?

### SELECTED BIBLIOGRAPHY

Andrews, Frederick, "Abe Briloff Tees Off on Creativity in Accounting," *Wall Street Journal*, Mar. 13, 1973, p. 21.

North, S. L., "Three Faces of Accountants," *Accountants' Journal*, June 1972, pp. 381-388.

# 127
# THAT'S A LOT OF GAAP!*
Forbes

Here's a one-question quiz that could save you some money.

True or false: When outside auditors certify that a company's financial statements "present fairly the financial position" of the company, the investor has a guarantee that the books fairly present the financial reality.

Sad though it be, the statement is false. When you see the "presents fairly" phrase, the accountants are confirming no more than that the financial statements are "in conformity with generally accepted accounting principles." Thus the books of U.S.

*From "The Numbers Game," *Forbes,* Aug. 1, 1975, pp. 31—32. Reprinted by permission of the publisher.

Financial, Penn Central, National Student Marketing, Equity Funding and many more, all "presented fairly."

As Securities & Exchange Commissioner A. A. Sommer says: "The application of GAAP does not guarantee there will be a fair presentation."

Are you a bit confused at this point? We don't blame you. How can "presents fairly" be anything other than a fair presentation? Putting aside semantics, we can best illustrate with an example.

Remember Stirling Homex? It was going to do for housing what Henry Ford once did for cars. But only insiders got rich. Just 29 months after going public, Stirling Homex, folded leaving the investing public shortchanged by an estimated $100 million. Believe it or not, Stirling Homex' statements were stamped "presents fairly" and by no less an accounting firm than Peat, Marwick, Mitchell.

We dusted off Stirling's July 31, 1971 annual report—its last. Everything looked fine. Sales and earnings were up 63% and 60%, respectively. Working capital from operations more than doubled and shareholders' equity tripled. Wall Street was paying 250 times earnings for the stock.

The only hint of trouble was on the balance sheet. Current liabilities—mainly unsecured bank notes—nearly tripled, to $46 million.

But that hint of gloom was obscured by Peat, Marwick's certification letter. It clearly stated that Stirling Homex' statements ". . . present fairly the consolidated financial position of Stirling Homex . . . in conformity with generally accepted accounting principles. . . ."

Yet only 12 months later, the company was in receivership.

How can "presents fairly" present so unfairly?

The accountants mostly insist upon judging "fairness" in terms of an established framework of rules—generally accepted accountings principles. If a company's accounting policies conform to generally accepted accounting principles, the results automatically yield a fair presentation. "That makes the accountant's life easy," explains John Shank, associate professor of accounting and finance at the Harvard Business School, "because then the accountant doesn't have to apply any independent judgment to the situation. He only has to decide whether his judgment conforms to the rules." That's like following a cake recipe and worrying only about counting cups of flour—not about how it's finally going to taste.

## ACCRUING TROUBLE

The secret to Stirling Homex' rosy sales and earnings picture was a modern accounting concept known as "accrual accounting," which attempts to match income with expense. The minute a house rolled off the assembly line, Stirling Homex rang up a sale based on purported purchase contracts, even though the cash was a long way from the company till. The SEC charges 85.8% of Stirling Homex' 1971 sales were improperly recorded. But if you use accrual accounting the way Stirling Homex did, its numbers were "presented fairly."

To resolve the fair presentation problem, Commissioner Sommer and Chief Accountant John C. (Sandy) Burton of the SEC have recently urged accountants to take a broader approach to the phrase. Burton argues that GAAP is not the *only* important aspect of fairness. He suggests that GAAP rules should be part of a broad "accounting model" before the accountant approves a company's report. Accountants should realize they are talking to investors, not just to other accountants, and they must be responsible for making subjective judgments as to the overall fairness of the picture painted by corporate financial statements. As Sandy Burton puts it, accountants should be asking, "What is the *reality* behind a particular transaction?"

In the case of Stirling Homex, for example, this approach might have encouraged Peat, Marwick accountants to ask some tougher questions. Questions like: "Where is the cash behind those sales, *really*?" Or even "What *really* are the financial foundations of this company?"

If you want to make an accountant squirm, just suggest that this is the way it should be done. They have good reason to squirm. It would take them away from rules with which they feel safe and comfortable and throw them into a whole new world of subjective judgments—and, of course, of risk. For one thing, it would open up the possibility of getting into an argument with a good customer. He may want to handle a transaction in a certain way—as Stirling Homex did with accrual sales. Is the accountant then to append a note to his report suggesting that the client is hiding something? Hardly a way to keep the client happy.

And then, of course, there are the lawyers. Once judgment rather than fairly rigid rules enters into the picture, so does the possibility of lawsuits against the accountants. As Peat, Marwick's general counsel, Victor Earle III, puts it: "It's fine to talk about fairness and motherhood and all that. But what happens when a jury determines liability if they're allowed to do so on the basis of *their* view of fairness? What I don't want is a standard of liability that says even where the accountant in good faith followed all the accounting requirements and touched all the bases, he's still liable if the layman doesn't think his presentation was fair."

Earle is uncomfortably aware that the accountants are already seriously exposed.

Starting with the landmark Continental Vending case of 1969, the courts have, in most observers' opinions, consistently held that compliance with GAAP is not in itself a complete defense. According to the courts, when push comes to shove, the accountants *are* responsible for an overall fair presentation.

## REAL TIGER

Why all the fuss? Haven't most of the abuses been ended? Not necessarily. Many of the old GAAP-sanctioned practices that have led to abuses in the past are still available to the clever entrepreneur. Accrual accounting is just one of the ways reality can be distorted. Pooling—the simple addition of balance sheet items in the case of mergers—is another. It was pooling that allowed International Telephone & Telegraph to boost its pretax earnings from 1970 to mid-1974 by nearly $240 million, after its merger with Hartford Fire. According to pooling critics, the gain was illusory. According to GAAP, it was legitimate. . .

As John Shank says: "No matter how detailed the accounting rules, the mind of the enterprising entrepreneur can always conceive of a transaction consistent with the rules but inconsistent with the spirit behind them." In other words, crooks will be crooked.

Baruch College Professor Abraham Briloff, noted for his assaults on rigged accounting, puts the whole thing in witty perspective. If the accounts hide behind the rules, suggests he, the public may come to view generally accepted accounting principles—GAAP—"as cleverly rigged accounting ploys"—CRAP.

## QUESTIONS

1. Should accrual accounting always be followed to be in accordance with GAAP? Why?

2. How does the crux of many professional problems lie in making subjective judgments which are to be reviewed by nonprofessionals?

3. Do you think that users of financial statements understand that "no matter how detailed the accounting rules, the mind of the enterprising entrepreneur can always conceive of a transaction consistent with the rules but inconsistent with the spirit behind them?"

## SELECTED BIBLIOGRAPHY

Parker, John, "Income Reporting and the Canada-US Gap in GAAP," *CA Magazine*, May 1974, pp. 38-45.

# 128
## THREE-COLUMN STATEMENTS*
Robert Mautz, David Solomons, Robert Jaedicke,
Sidney Davidson, Herbert Miller, and Others

EDITORS' NOTE: The excerpt is from a conference held at Ohio State University in 1966 at which various types of users of financial statements explained how they used statements.

Professors Davidson and Miller have served on the AICPA's Accounting Principles Board at various times during the past decade. Professors Jaedicke and Solomons were Directors of Research for the AAA during the same decade. In 1966, the AAA (in *A Statement of Basic Accounting Theory*) recommended two-column statements (historical costs and current values). Professor Solomons has commented that users and accountants were "shackled to historical costs."

PROFESSOR ROBERT MAUTZ (Illinois): Why does Professor Solomons feel that we are "shackled to historical costs," when so many invitations have been issued to supplement historical costs with other data?

*From *The Use of Accounting Data in Decision Making*, T. J. Burns (ed.), Columbus, Ohio, The Ohio State University, 1969, pp. 64—68. Reprinted by permission of the publisher.

PROFESSOR DAVID SOLOMONS (Wharton): Perhaps the expression "shackled to historical costs" was unduly colorful, but at least it caught your attention. Second, if it is a matter of regret to Professor Mautz that more companies have not taken advantage of the opportunity to produce alternative statements, I share those regrets. I don't know that we ought to be particularly surprised, and I don't think it's convincing evidence ... that such statements would not have enough value to justify the cost of preparing them.

Recently the Accounting Principles Board produced its Opinion No. 6, including paragraph 19 which starts off with a flat reaffirmation of the principle of historical costs. There was one dissenting vote against that statement, by Professor Davidson. It is not surprising that in that kind of atmosphere, with the A.I.C.P.A. solidly for historical costs, not many companies think it worth the cost or time to prepare other statements. With the whole weight of organized professional opinion opposed it is quite clear that any alternative kind of information is going to have to occupy a low position in the scale of priorities.

PROFESSOR MAUTZ: It has taken me a long time as a conservative in accounting to recognize that price level changes are of some importance; to come here and find out that they're really not disturbs me a great deal.

PROFESSOR ROBERT JAEDICKE (Stanford): On the basis of the discussion here, that's an unwarranted conclusion as far as I'm concerned.

PROFESSOR MAUTZ: I hope it is. Several external users of accounting data today have not seemed to be concerned about the price level changes. This disturbs me. They are much more concerned with the influence of diversification and mergers and wanting product data and that sort of thing.

Yet I am very hopeful that we are near the point where we can do something useful about value changes. The reason I picked up Professor Solomon's expression "shackled to historical costs" is because I have the feeling that the difference between those who advocate historical costs and those who advocate current value of some kind has become largely an emotional one. We are fighting this out on an "I've got to win" basis, no matter what, rather than searching for a reasonable conclusion.

Now, it seems to me the most reasonable conclusion, and yet a very simple one, would be to present financial statements on two or more alternative bases. This is not particularly difficult or particularly expensive. I think it would pose no very real problems to auditors or to those who use the data. I see no reason why we couldn't have a set of statements with historical cost figures; then historical cost figures adjusted for some general price level index (and the A.I.C.P.A. Accounting Research Study No. 6 assures us that there is a useful index for this purpose);[1] and finally a third column which would be our best effort to approach current value. I am convinced that the users could use it effectively judging by the sophistication with which they use what we now present, as indicated by the authors present and their papers. Also, I don't think this would present any very real problem to auditors. Now, it might not solve the problem for those who just would do away with historical costs,

[1]*Reporting The Financial Effects of Price-Level Changes.* AICPA Accounting Research Study No. 6. American Institute of Certified Public Accountants, New York, 1963.

no matter what. Anyone who looks carefully at historical costs sees its deficiencies. I think anyone who looks carefully at current value, or the various proposals for current value—most of which have been completely untried—has a hesitation to rush into this.

Now, a period of trial where we would use the three together—which would let us unwind if we get ourselves in trouble—would let us discover which was the basic set of data and which was not. I don't think we have to put it on such a supplementary basis, Professor Solomons, that it would be lowered in priority. I think they could be equal. We could find ways to do this that would be an interesting experiment. And I have a notion that this might be brought about in the next few years.

PROFESSOR JAEDICKE: The reason for my concern is precisely the conclusion that you have indicated can be drawn. I was very intrigued by the roundtable discussion on accounting for fixed assets that was held at Harvard University a couple of years ago.[2] There is a statement in the proceedings where one of the participants used a statement out of Professor Horngren's research on the price level issue as strong evidence that analysts were not interested in adjustment for the general price level.

Now, what Professor Horngren reported was something like this: of all the analysts he talked to, he did not find any analysts using price level adjustments. How could he? They can't make them, and we don't make them, so where do such statements come from? But the point is that it was in print: "Security analysts don't use price level adjustment" or "don't make price level adjustments." And this statement came up 10 years later in a discussion of how to account for fixed assets as evidence that this really isn't useful information anyway. This is what I feared could happen here if you have five sophisticated users not mentioning this problem. But they've had no experience in using price-level adjusted statements because they don't have the data. Now, maybe it is true that the analyst does not want price level adjustments but I don't think so on the basis of what we have heard today.

PROFESSOR SOLOMONS: What advice do you think a company would get from its auditors if they were asked to advise the company on the preparation and publication of alternative forms of statements?

MR. J. B. GWILYM (Partner, Arthur Young & Company): If you remember that the senior partner of our firm, who retired one year ago, was one of the leading advocates of this kind of presentation on a supplementary basis, I might suggest that it was a good idea.

MR. L. L. HOPKINS (Partner, Coopers & Lybrand): I was very interested in the concept of a parallel reporting, and I think that my response to a client would certainly be in the affirmative. I myself would like to see a test period of this kind of information. Of course, we would have a struggle over the problem of the auditor's opinion.

---

[2]Robert T. Sprouse, reporter, "The Measurement of Property, Plant, and Equipment in Financial Statements," Harvard Business School Accounting Round Table, Harvard University Graduate School of Business Administration, Boston, 1964.

PROFESSOR MAUTZ: Dean Robert Roy, who has been in charge of the Common Body of Knowledge Study, uses an expression which I think is particularly useful. He says accountants deal with probabilistic phenomena in a deterministic manner.

I think it is very unlikely that soon we'll be saying there is an 80 per cent chance that the profit figure is within plus or minus 10 per cent, but we could indicate this if we gave a range. If we gave three columns, and we say, "Now, business is not simple, it's a complex matter; and you have to have at least this much data to begin to understand it. Now, it's somewhere within that range." If they asked me for that advice. Professor Solomons, I would recommend that they do it. I think that this would put the auditor himself in a better position when he says "present fairly." He would be a lot safer than he is now when he hangs it on one set of figures that everybody knows is not right.

PROFESSOR SIDNEY DAVIDSON (Chicago): Well, you know it's all well and good if the client comes to you and says, "Should I do this?" You give him your advice, or you talk about how Mr. Gwilym feels about this. But why should a client come to you, a client who is bidding for funds in the capital market against firms that do not present this kind of information, and say, "Should I present some information that's going to call my earnings figure into question?" Are we ever going to get this multiple-column presentation unless we tell firms, "You must present this or we will not certify it"? It's all fine and good for Professor Mautz to say, "Let's experiment." But unless we put some "muscle" behind it, . . . we are not going to get the experimentation. You aren't going to get that question from your client; you're going to have to ask him.

PROFESSOR HERBERT MILLER (Michigan State): Before we really get to the point of where we want to say we ought to prepare a variety of information, three columns or probabilistic, I think we ought to be sure we are prepared to cope with the universal question which will arise—which one is right? Which column is the right one? Otherwise, if we are not really well-organized to explain this and explain how these alternatives can be useful, we've missed our chance.

PROFESSOR JOHN WILLINGHAM (Texas): Which one is right now, Professor Miller?

PROFESSOR MILLER: We have only one.

## QUESTIONS

1. Professor Jaedicke argues that because users of financial statements do not request price-level-adjusted statements it does not mean they would not use them if they were available. He says it only means that they have not had any experience in using price-level-adjusted statements. If this argument is extended, what impetus for improving financial statements might be anticipated from users?

2. Of the following groups associated with financial statements—auditors, managers, investors, and creditors—which do you think might offer the most resistance to multicolumn statements, and why?

3. Why do you suppose recommendations for three-column statements or even two-column statements have not been implemented 10 years later?

# 129
## ALL THINGS TO ALL MEN? NO THANKS*
Geoffrey Holmes

It is now widely recognized that many classes of people look at published accounts—not merely existing shareholders, but trade creditors, banks, others who lend money, employees, trade unions, taxmen, and environmentalists.

I do not deny the need of these people to know a great deal about a company, but I believe it would be fundamentally wrong to try to cater for all of them in one set of accounts.

Accounts, as at present conceived, are a company's principal method of keeping in touch with its shareholders. They are not well-suited to the needs of lenders. They do not provide any real indication of break-up value; they are not intended to. A potential lender has other sources of information available to him before he makes the loan, and is, at that time, in a position to insist upon such continuing information as seems desirable to him.

Accounts do not provide any clear indication of taxable capacity. That again is not their purpose. The tax inspector has quite other means of obtaining data; and if government wishes to know more about the taxable capacity of industry, then it can take steps to obtain it, either using the power to collect statistics which it already possesses, or by seeking further statutory authority.

Accounts do not provide (except insofar as it is important to shareholders) a record of the company's employee relations policies, their costs, and their success—or lack of it; nor do they indicate the scope for improved pay or conditions. Perhaps they should say more about productivity, but not primarily in order to assist unions in framing wage demands, or devising means of restraining productivity unless they take a major part of productivity gains.

All these needs can be met. Most of them already are, by some form of ad hoc report.

Let us hope that the recently appointed sub-committee of the Accounting Standards Steering Committee which is at present considering the 'scope and aims' of published financial statements does not pay too much attention to the crackpots.

*From *Accountancy,* April 1975, p. 6. Reprinted by permission of the publisher.

Each of the special needs we have discussed can, and no doubt should, be met. The danger lies in our trying to meet them all in one document which, setting out to be all things to all men, will succeed in pleasing and enlightening no one.

## QUESTION

1. What uses of general-purpose accounts and statements are invalid?

**Part 7
The New
Accounting**

# 130
## WHAT'S AHEAD IN THE NEXT TEN YEARS*
Michael Chetkovich

Looking ahead to what might be expected in the field of accounting in the next decade, it is quite safe to begin with the prediction that there will be no slowdown in the pace of developments; if anything, we can look for acceleration. There is little likelihood, either, of any early end to controversy and criticism although one might hope, and possibly expect, that there will be some leveling off in volume and intensity.

With the creation of the FAF and the establishment of the FASB, there is a whole new approach to the development and/or delineation of accounting standards and concepts. While we have high hopes for the success of this new agency, it is unreasonable to assume that it can solve all the problems or satisfy all the critics. There is nothing like a state of perfection in the performance of this function and, even if there were, attainment of that state would not necessarily be so recognized and acknowledged on any widespread basis.

I believe strongly that the FASB can and will perform its task very creditably. Certainly, it would appear to present the best approach yet conceived for dealing with this most difficult responsibility, that of prescribing accounting standards. Because of the stature and quality of the members of the Board, the research capabilities supporting them, and the processes for achieving a high degree of input to and exposure of their proposed pronouncements, there is a good reason to expect that their statements will be sound. The true and difficult test will lie not so much in the quality of these statements, but in their general acceptance. We know, all too well, from all aspects of life, that the "right" answers are not necessarily the most popular ones, that the best medicine sometimes is the hardest to take.

There is considerable activity on the international scene, much more than ever before, and reason to expect some progress toward achieving a greater measure of uniformity in international accounting standards. Recognizing the great difficulty of achieving any high degree of uniformity within a single jurisdiction, we cannot anticipate rapid strides in this direction. The progress will be slow and painful. However, there is machinery in being, in the persons of the International Accounting Standards Committee (IASC) and the International Coordination Committee for the Accountancy Profession (ICCAC), whose commitment to and initial progress toward this objective are impressive and give promise of greater achievement. Certainly there is great incentive and need for attention to the international area, with the growth of multinational organizations, the increasing movement of capital across national boundaries, and the other developments shaping a global-economy.

The past decade has been a rather tumultuous one for accounting and for those who practice it. It is important to recognize that the attention focused on accounting, critical though much of it may be, is also a recognition of its great significance to the

*From *Accounting in Transition*, T. J. Burns (ed.), Columbus, Ohio, Ohio State University, 1974, pp. 237–239. Reprinted by permission of the publisher.

functioning of our system of free enterprise. In this context, of equal importance to the establishment of sound standards, and probably more difficult of attainment, is the need for a clearer understanding of the objectives and the limitations of accounting and, with such understanding, the achievement of a better balance between expectation and capability. This is a task we must address ourselves to energetically, even as we recognize that human nature being what it is, we can hope only to narrow the gap and not to eliminate it.

EDITORS' NOTE: Mr. Chetkovich is the managing partner of Haskins & Sells, one of the Big Eight firms.

## QUESTIONS

1. What are some limitations of accounting?
2. Why does Mr. Chetkovich expect the FASB to do well?
3. Why is there an increasing need to achieve greater uniformity in international accounting standards?

## SELECTED BIBLIOGRAPHY

Brummet, R. Lee, "Total Performance Measurement," *Management Accounting*, November 1973, pp. 11-15.

Chetkovich, Michael N., "Haskins & Sells at 80 Years," *H&S Reports*, Winter 1975, p. 12.

Crum, William F., "The European Public Accountant," *Management Accounting*, March 1975, pp. 41-44, 54.

# 131
# THE GOOD GUYS*
Newsweek

Over the years, accountants have acquired a public image as hardhearted fussbudgets who tend to their ledgers with Scrooge-like dedication and steer clear of controversial social issues. But Accountants for the Public Interest is out to change that. The San Francisco-based organization, composed of some 40 certified public accountants, provides free accounting and consulting services to community, environmental and consumer groups. As Morton Levy, API's executive director, explains: "Our point of

*From *Newsweek*, Jan. 7, 1974, pp. 56–57. Reprinted by permission of the publisher.

view is that financial data can be interpreted in a number of ways, but if one side of a particular controversy doesn't have access to accounting expertise, there may be only one interpretation available."

Since it was founded eighteen months ago, API has helped more than 24 carefully selected clients, ranging from a commuter group that is fighting an increase in Golden Gate Bridge tolls to a golfers' association protesting fees charged on a municipal course. In each case, API accountants analyzed the pertinent financial data and then explained it to their clients. "We don't advocate anything," says API president Esmond Coleman. "We just try to provide figures so people can make reasonable decisions." Still, the API program has achieved some noteworthy results. For example, a recent API study persuaded a judge in New Orleans to order three federally funded hospitals to provide free medical care to the poor.

API's volunteers include representatives from some of the largest CPA firms in the country. They try to maintain their objectivity, even if there is a conflict of interest with one of their employer's clients. "General Motors's outside accountants seem to be able to maintain their independence despite the obvious financial stake they have in the company's health," says Levy. "We do the same on our projects."

The organization is such a success that some 65 CPA's from across the country met recently in San Francisco to discuss how to set up other public-interest groups. They talked about how to screen candidates, attract volunteers and raise operating funds. API is funded entirely by foundations and hopes to operate this fiscal year on a $75,000 budget. As a result of the conference, public-interest firms are being opened in Portland and Los Angeles, with about eight to twelve other offices to be set up around the country by the end of the year.

## QUESTION

1. Can you make a case for accountants other than those who are members of the Accountants for the Public Interest being "the good guys?"

# 132
# PUBLIC ACCOUNTING IN TRANSITION*
The Arthur Andersen Chronicle

The decade of the 1970s has, from its earliest days, been marked by monetary and political crises. Those tremors have been felt not only in the United States, but worldwide. The current state of flux in which business and financial institutions find

*From *The Arthur Andersen Chronicle,* January 1975, pp. 4—9. Reprinted by permission of the publisher.

themselves is marked by a stage of transition as they seek new and more workable relationships.

Accounting, as a profession, has not been left untouched in the litigatious climate that seems to prevail. The present business recession has indeed focused more attention upon the accountant's role in controversies surrounding corporate financial reporting.

The key accounting issue in the current business climate is whether there is a need for a complete restructuring of corporate financial reporting, as practiced today, or can recognized deficiencies be corrected by reform of outmoded practices and application of new accounting and disclosure standards.

A sense of urgency and a desire for change now dominate the business sector which has witnessed immense corporate growth (sometimes fictitious), rapid technological change, unprecedented rates of acquisitions and mergers, and the appearance of untested forms of business combinations, all within the short span of the 1960s. Hand in hand with the rapid development of business came unorthodox methods of financial reporting, which were not always forthright in nature.

There is growing concern both outside and inside the accounting profession that inertia will eventually overcome attempts to secure meaningful professional reforms. If progress is not forthcoming from within the profession itself, there is a very real possibility of overt government involvement in the establishment of accounting principles. This, however, must be an alternative of last resort.

The American Institute of Certified Public Accountants (AICPA) organized several recent study groups to attempt to resolve the problems which accountants believed were confronting them. In early 1974, Arthur Andersen & Co. went further. It commissioned Opinion Research Corporation (ORC) to conduct a survey aimed at obtaining a full and objective appraisal of where the accounting profession stands today in the eyes of the constituencies it serves as well as in the eyes of accountants themselves. This independent study by the ORC also sought to assess where those same constituencies (or "key public" groups) believe the profession is heading.

Some of the questions which the study was designed to answer involved evaluating the kinds of changes that might be anticipated in corporate financial reporting, accounting policy, and the role of the independent public accountant.

This article is a summary of the study made by ORC and draws heavily from their report.

## AN EXPLORATORY PROGRAM

ORC, after preliminary discussion with Arthur Andersen & Co. personnel, determined that a "Phase One" exploratory research program should be conducted. This involved two major parts: (1) a series of exploratory interviews with several Arthur Andersen & Co. partners in offices throughout the United States; and (2) interviewing members of the "key public" groups which the accounting profession serves.

The Phase Two plan involved interviewing a "broader range of key publics and a national probability sampling of shareowners to determine the individual stockholder's impressions of the controversial issues surrounding the accounting profession." The study also called for interviews with key public chief executives and chief financial offices of a statistically random sample of the 1974 *Fortune* listing of the Top 1,000 Industrial Corporations in the U.S.

The term "key public" is best understood in terms of the key public groups interviewed. They included: corporate executives, professors (primarily in accounting), institutional investors and portfolio managers, stockbrokers and investment analysts, securities lawyers, certified public accountants, Federal government officials, business editors and writers, and corporate social activists.

The key public interviewing samples were viewed as "purposive" samples—that is, respondents were selected on the basis of their experience and reputation. Eighty-three percent of the key publics had some formal education or training in accounting and ninety-one percent owned stock in one or more companies; two percent of the respondents were women. The breakdown of the total number of interviews was: shareowners—404 and key publics—457 (including 262 corporate executives).

The ORC noted what it believed to be the major task confronting accounting today—restoration of the public's confidence in business and in corporate securities investments. The number of people believing that large company profits benefit everyone has declined from a high of 66% in 1965 to only 46% in 1973. In 1961, 61% of the total dollar trading volume on the New York Stock Exchange was by individual investors; today, the equivalent figure is less than 30%.

Among the objectives set up for the study, prime emphasis was placed on "gaining the respondents' overall assessment of the magnitude and seriousness of the problems that appear to be facing Wall Street and the accounting profession."

## RESPONSES

One question asked the respondents to rate the ethical and moral practices of seven occupational groups generally identified with business and financial affairs. The replies showed that Certified Public Accountants and bank executives are running "neck and neck for the highest ratings of their profession's ethical and moral practices." In fact, accountants received the best rating of any occupational group.

The high marks the accountants received on this particular question should provide a sound base from which the profession can begin to implement needed changes in its role and responsibilities. A recurring theme among the replies in the survey was the hope that accountants would become more aggressive in limiting the number of financial accounting alternatives available and in standing up to clients who press for favorable accounting treatment.

Desipte the generally high ratings on ethical and moral standards given to accountants, the key publics viewed loss of credibility and respect as the most serious problems facing them today. The key publics foresee the future as one marked by challenges to and changes in the traditional independent public accountant's role and feel that accountants are now entering a period of great professional change.

There were, however, among the favorable comments some dissenting ones which rated the profession unfavorably, thus clearly highlighting that the accounting profession is not without its problems despite the generally high esteem in which it is held.

## HIGHLY REGARDED

One of the strongest elements of the profession's reputation is the high regard given to its objectivity and independence. Eighty-one percent of individual shareowners agreed that public accounting firms exercise these traits in performing corporate audits, and 97% of corporate executives also expressed agreement.

Corporate executives and other key publics are virtually unanimous in their praise of the caliber of management and staff within the field. Usually, the general pattern of such ratings would show more disparity rather than such a high degree of consistency. Where there are opposing views, corporate social activists and the business press dominate the critical end of the spectrum, and accountants and securities lawyers are at the opposite end.

Eighty-two percent of the total key publics considered the range and value of services offered by large public accounting firms to be "excellent" or "good." The issue of fairness to the interests of all investors drew a similarly good response—785 respondents gave "excellent" or "good" ratings. Again, the critics were strongest among activist and business press respondents.

Public citizenship and the quality of on-going research were also rated. Those who were favorable and those who were critics again split along the expected lines. Corporate executives (96%) and most other key publics gave accountants favorable ratings on dependability and accuracy.

## RESPONSIBILITY

One characteristic in which accountants were rated lower than any other traits measured was in accepting responsibility for mistakes when they occur. Forty-five percent of corporate executives rated accounting firms as "only fair" or "poor" on this point. This is particularly significant in light of recent court cases involving members of the profession.

One of the central issues in the current spate of litigation is whether or not an accounting firm should be responsible for the detection of fraud—and the degree to which accountants may be held responsible for fraud apparently perpetrated by a company's management.

Accountants themselves have expressed concern that making them shoulder blanket responsibility for detection is too much to expect and that well-conceived fraud is difficult to detect solely by today's auditing standards. Among the professors and accountants interviewed by ORC for this study, most believe strongly that the detection of fraud is *not* the most important function of the outside auditor.

## ANNUAL REPORTS

The corporate annual report and whether it is doing its job was another focal point of the survey. Responses of the key publics indicated an undercurrent of dissatisfaction. The main criticism of the annual reports was that, too often, they are used for public relations purposes, and their usefulness as a decision-making tool is thereby jeopardized. Critics also charge that the range of optional accounting methods available tends to diminish the value of these reports.

Most of the respondents (58%) felt that annual reports should be targeted toward both the sophisticated and the average investor—and that it is possible to do so. Yet, readership of financial statements and the auditor's report within the annual report itself is not high.

The responsibility for the accuracy of financial information presented in an annual report was seen by most respondents as belonging to company management, not the outside auditor.

## DISCLOSURE

Corporate disclosure was another troublesome issue tackled by ORC—"Is *more* enough"? Generally, there was agreement that there is, in fact, more disclosure today than in the past five to ten years. The controversy arises over whether or not the information available is adequate for public and investor needs and whether it is in the form the average investor can understand and use. Key publics and individual shareowners want not simply more detail, but the kind of information that will help them evaluate a company's future prospects. Specifically, the information they want includes addition of Form 10-K Report information requiring companies to forecast future earnings and requiring auditors to certify quarterly reports.

## PERCEPTIONS OF RESPONSIBILITY

When key publics were asked what they considered the most important function performed by large public accounting firms when they audit public companies, there was basic agreement that the essence of the auditor's role was to provide an independent evaluation of the acceptability of the financial statement.

## UNIFORMITY

During the interviews, the key publics were asked to state what changes they would like to see in financial reporting in view of the current inflation rate. One of the main themes to appear was a desire for uniformity in accounting rules and procedures. Fifty-eight percent of the total key publics and 49% of the corporate executives believe that accounting principles and standards are *not* adequately defined, that there are too many options open in dealing with financial data.

Despite the obvious dissatisfaction with present accounting standards, there was considerable controversy over whether a uniform set of accounting rules and procedures *should* be adopted. The idea gained favor among many corporate executives (41%), institutional investors, government officials, and the business press but was not popular with the majority of corporate executives (56%), professors, securities lawyers, or accountants themselves.

The basic reason given for favoring uniform rules is that it would provide a clearer, more accurate, picture of corporate finance. Those who do not want to eliminate alternative forms argue that it would be impractical to do so and would lead to even further distortions.

There is much greater and more widespread support for uniformity in international accounting standards. Uniformity, it is felt, would facilitate the flow of capital and analysis of international corporations. Although international accounting is growing in significance and is becoming a major challenge for the profession, imposing uniform standards here is even more difficult than domestically, for the methods used should, to be effective, conform to local, legal, and traditional accounting in each individual country.

## IN SUMMARY

From the wealth of material gleaned during the ORC study, it can be seen that key publics do believe changes *are* needed in the accounting profession. The respondents believed, however, that the profession itself must assume the leadership role in solving its own problems and that, thus far, the profession has been able to regulate itself satisfactorily.

Whether the specter of stricter government regulation will evolve is an issue which cannot be quickly or easily dismissed. Time and again, the need for a self-examination by the profession was stressed. Adding impetus to this mood is the current atmosphere of rapid change, transition, and pressure in business.

The public not only wants, but is now demanding, better professional communication and a redefining of accounting roles and responsibilities. The public knows that time will be needed to do so, and also that time is growing short. The major issues that surfaced in the ORC survey were:

Reducing the number of accounting alternatives available and adopting new procedures to allow for the impact of inflation and a clear reflection of the financial status of multinational corporations.

Maintaining the auditor's independence in client relationships.

Achieving greater unity of purpose and viable self-regulation in the profession through an energetic Financial Accounting Standards Board.

Acknowledging that failure to accept responsibility for legitimate oversight in detecting fraud will undermine the profession and the corporate financial reporting process.

Promoting greater understanding of the scope and importance of the accountant's responsibilities.

The fact that the first serious piece of market research of the scope and detail of the ORC survey was commissioned by a public accounting firm should encourage confidence in the profession by many who view it with questions and reservations.

What changes the future holds for the accounting profession are not yet clear, but it is definitely a time for transition and changes.

To effect change, the findings cannot remain in a vacuum, they must be discussed and studied by the accounting profession, as well as by the business community and the investing public.

## QUESTIONS

1. Explain why accountants although receiving generally high ratings on ethical and moral standards have suffered a loss in credibility and respect.

2. Why are accountants rated low in accepting responsibility for mistakes?

3. What evidence was brought out in the survey in favor of continuing the policy of reducing optional accounting methods?

4. Do you feel that the survey results were somewhat contradictory in regard to annual reports and disclosures? Why?

## SELECTED BIBLIOGRAPHY

Beck, G. W., "Management Consulting by Public Accounting: An Inside and Outside View," *The Chartered Accountant in Australia*, May 1974, pp. 18-22.

Benjamin, James J., and Vincent C. Brenner, "Public Disclosure for CPA Firms," *Financial Executive*, August 1975, pp. 37-41.

Powers, James T., "Future Shock Jars Accounting World," *The New York Times*, June 2, 1974, p. 14F.

# 133

# ACCOUNTANTS WARY OF FINANCIAL MINEFIELD*
Russell E. Palmer

The road to economic reform has been marked by legendary frauds which have implicated the high and mighty, toppling governments and leading statesmen. Some of today's frauds ... also will become legends, but the people implicated are faceless entrepreneurs whose victims are the investing public.

All of us are affected by these frauds which in recent years seem to become more sensational. Who is responsible for detecting and preventing them? Who is responsible for protecting the public?

Recent publicity given to isolated instances of fraud by the management of large companies has created the erroneous impression that the public accounting firms are not carrying out their responsibilities in protecting the public. Reports of criminal actions against a few C.P.A.'s, injunctive proceedings against some firms, and sanctions against others alleging substandard audits leading to "false and misleading" financial statements unfortunately suggest that the Securities and Exchange Commission alone is protecting shareholders. This is a misconception, and a dangerous one because it

*From the **New York Times,** Apr. 6, 1975, p. F14. Reprinted by permission of the publisher.

tends to confuse the spheres of responsibility that the accounting profession and the Government have in protecting the public interest.

The S.E.C. has the responsibility of making certain that the shareholder—present and prospective—in reality the public, is properly informed about a company's activities. The S.E.C. has the authority by law to carry out this function. The independent accountant's responsibility to the users of financial statements is the same on a more limited basis—to ensure that financial statements, as a source of information about a company's economic activities, are fairly presented. These are distinct but shared responsibilities, but because of recent publicity, misconceptions are growing concerning what constitutes protecting the public interest. Within this shared responsibility, there is no provision or mechanism for the S.E.C. or the accounting profession to protect the shareholder from his greatest risk, which is the economic character of his investment.

While there really is no conflict as to objectives, there are differences in the way the two groups execute their responsibilities.

The S.E.C. investigates or audits on an exception basis, where there is a known or suspected problem. Such investigations are also conducted with the benefit of hindsight, with the full knowledge of the outcome of specific events or judgments. The accountant, on the other hand, operates in the present without such benefit. He approaches his task knowing that the statements are primarily the responsibility of management and that judgments and bias are involved, but that dishonesty is not presumed.

The problem is perhaps better understood by looking at the possible range of circumstances underlying the classic "false and misleading financial statements" charge—a charge which technically may be characterized as fraud under the Federal securities acts. Short of direct involvement of the accountants in the fraud, these circumstances can range from:

*Unintentional errors or omissions.* The responsibility for the accountant's failure to detect an unintentional error or omission is generally the easiest to resolve. In the absence of covert action to deceive the auditor it becomes a question of whether or not the auditor followed appropriate tests in the circumstances and whether such tests would have disclosed the irregularity.

*Error in judgment.* This is much tougher to evaluate in determining the auditor's culpability. One, two or three years after the fact it is relatively simple with hindsight to determine what the reserves for doubtful accounts, inventory obsolescenses and contingencies should have been. Here again we must distinguish between hindsight and foresight. The accountant's culpability must be determined based on the facts available to him at the time he had to evaluate the fairness of the judgment.

Furthermore, it is difficult to evaluate how apparent those factors were or should have been to the auditor at the time he made his evaluation.

*Intentional (fraudulent) errors and omissions.* These are the circumstances in which the errors and omissions are intentional, where fraud is involved in the moral as well as legal sense. The accountant's responsibility for detection of such fraud is currently a matter of deep controversy between the profession and the S.E.C., and the publicity over this controversy overshadows the far greater areas of collaboration and cooperation in which the public's interest is being served.

In those well-publicized cases where management fraud was charged, the Commission typically takes the position that the accountants should have uncovered the fraud. It has been argued by critics of the S.E.C. that it was trying to stretch the enforcement dollar by getting others to do the work. The idea is to make accountants in some way responsible for fraud committed by the management of the companies they audit in the hope that the result will be less fraud.

That is a fine objective, but it is essentially in conflict with the traditional audit approach which does not presume dishonesty. Our firm, and I am sure the same applies for most firms, will not undertake an audit where we have any reason to doubt the integrity of management. When the auditor approaches the engagement, he is alert to fraud opportunities but he does not expect to find fraud nor does he direct his primary efforts to search for it.

A dishonest management can subvert any system and the related internal-control features. Where there is a doubt, the auditor cannot rely on any reported facts or have any assurance that he will be able to determine all the relevant facts required for him to exercise a professional judgment.

The procedure is very different when an auditor takes a fraud investigation assignment, as Touche Ross did in the case of Equity Funding, after the massive fraud was discovered. Then the circumstances and the approach are more like those employed by the S.E.C. enforcement group when it investigates a suspected problem situation. In this fraud audit the auditor assumes the total adversary role. In those situations where fraud is known or suspected every transaction and every event are carefully scrutinized.

The question may be asked, wouldn't the public be better served if every audit were made in the total adversary mode? The answer is no. The cost of such audits is prohibitive and would far exceed the benefits in terms of the early fraud detections. Further, there is no assurance that even an exhaustive fraud audit will uncover all irregularities, particularly where company officers are in collusion with third parties outside the company, or where a secret contract is concealed in the president's wall safe at home.

In carrying out his normal responsibilities, the accountant does not have benefit either of hindsight or the power of subpoena as the S.E.C. does in its investigations, and his performance should be judged on what facts and circumstances were readily discernible to him at the time of his audit.

Under the circumstances, accountants cannot be held responsible for detecting all management frauds. Nevertheless, I believe that the profession does have a responsibility for developing techniques and practices within the normal audit that will make them alert to conditions which provide management with the opportunity for fraud. We have done so in developing and implementing an audit program which focuses attention on management involvement in material transactions.

Accountants have a professional responsibility and should be held accountable for their failure to meet standards established by the profession. The awards in, and costs of, civil litigation, however, provide more than enough incentive for all major firms to keep a heavy hand on the quality-control aspects of their practices. Moreover, the S.E.C. has the authority and an obligation to monitor the accountants' activities and take appropriate action where there is unprofessional conduct.

EDITORS' NOTE: Mr. Palmer is the managing partner of Touche Ross & Co., one of the Big Eight firms.

## QUESTIONS

1. What comparisons does Mr. Palmer make between the ways in which the SEC and the accountants execute their responsibilities?

2. What is the possible range of circumstances underlying charges of "false and misleading financial statements?"

3. Why do critics of the SEC argue that "it was trying to stretch the enforcement dollar by getting others to do the work?"

## SELECTED BIBLIOGRAPHY

Lamson, Newton W., "Peat, Marwick—The Auditor Gets Audited," *The New York Times*, November 23, 1975, pp. F1, 14.

Sansweet, Stephen J., "Mattel Ex-Aids Tried Cover-Up, Report Asserts," *The Wall Street Journal*, November 5, 1975, p. 18.

"The Touche Ross Manual for Spotting Fraud," *Business Week*, February 17, 1975, p. 52.

# 134

# UNITY IN THE ACCOUNTING PROFESSION*

James W. Pattillo

The discipline of accounting has always been characterized as one of logical and practical evolution, one in which changes are systematic and deliberate. This is as it should be. But where do we find ourselves today after a century of evolution and professional growth? We are a technical discipline still struggling with its theoretical foundations. We find a professional discipline still confronted with fundamental and complex questions of its practical superstructure. We find controversies in many

*From *The Journal of Accountancy,* July 1974, pp. 50–58. Reprinted by permission of the publisher.

current areas; further, we find many different opinions about the future direction of the profession.

AICPA Board Chairman Samuel A. Derieux[1] has said (*Journal of Accountancy*, Dec. 1973, p. 26):

". . . As I consider specific plans and programs, I keep coming back to one objective which seems to override all others—an objective which must be attained in order to achieve other goals. That objective is unity.

"Unity within the profession, and indeed within the entire business community, is essential if we are to fulfill our professional responsibilities. By unity, I do not mean that we must all be of one mind or one opinion on the many questions which confront us. . . . But unity does mean that we will work together with the highest possible degree of harmony in seeking solutions to the problems and questions which beset us all."

Those thoughts keynote the purpose of this article: to provide a perspective on the current state of the accounting profession. It is a "lean-back-and-put-your-feet-up-on-the-desk-and-think" perspective which tries to tie together a variety of problems, goals, organizational objectives and resources in a forward-looking context. It is a plea for cooperation where the opportunities exist or could be created. It is not a plea for one gigantic accounting organization in which there are pressures to conform or in which there is no room for debate of the issues.

In this spirit of perspective, many of the items to be touched upon in this article have been discussed before. But being reminded of these is perhaps healthful. The profession's problems will be identified and discussed and possible solutions will be advanced. In addition, some recommendations will be included, but these will be the author's opinion on how best to proceed.

## INTERESTS TO BE SERVED

Professional accountants serve diverse groups. Some serve single groups; others serve many groups. We can categorize these in several ways. For the present, let's identify them broadly as

1. *The general public.* These are the members of society in general and those who have social and economic rights and interests in the nation's entities:

Regulatory agencies, both public and private, are charged by law or agreement to protect the collective and separate rights and interests of the general public.

Stockholders and third-party information users are a major segment of the general public who have definite rights and interests in entities and claims to information about those entities.

Internal managers and information providers are in themselves a segment of the general public. Their individual lives and decisions are influenced by the welfare of the

---

[1]As of February 1, 1974, Mr. Derieux was redesignated chairman of the AICPA Board of Directors following an American Institute bylaws change. The bylaws revision transfers the title of president from the chief volunteer officer to the chief AICPA staff officer.

firm and, as such, they are consumers of the information that they themselves generate about the firm.

2. *Firms or other entities.* These are the members of firms or other organizations or individuals that generate information for the benefit of the segments of the general public:

Internal managers and information providers have a responsibility (among others) to supply the general public segments with the appropriate information to satisfy their collective and separate rights and interests in the firm.

Internal technicians aid the firm's managers by maintaining the firm's information system and by supplying the information appropriate to both internal and external decision-making.

External technicians aid the firm's managers and the general public with information appropriate for their decision-making.

From this delineation of interests in information, and of the professional accountants' service to these interests, we can identify related professional accountants' organizations.

Figure 1 depicts the groups identified above as respective "spheres of influence" within the two general interests to be served. Related to each of these spheres are several professional groups which can be identified either as interested in their activities or as having interested employees on their membership rolls.

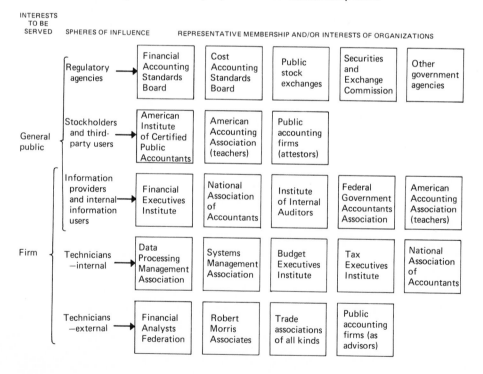

**Figure I**

Obviously, not all of the organizations operating within the particular spheres of influence are listed; the inclusions are merely examples. Also, some organizations' objectives and policies overlap into areas other than where they were listed; only the major thrusts were categorized for simplicity.

## AREAS OF PROFESSIONAL RESPONSIBILITY

Each of these groups has a place in serving the general public and the individual firms. And each has a stake, either direct or indirect, in fostering accounting as a professional discipline. These similarities lead us to identify common areas of responsibility. Perhaps there are others, but the following are evident:

COMMON AREAS OF PROFESSIONAL RESPONSIBILITY

| Technical | Accounting and reporting standards<br>Professional education and training<br>Professional programs' accreditation | Joint responsibility |
|---|---|---|
| | Professional certification and specialization<br>Research | Joint and individual responsibility |
| Practical | Codes of professional conduct<br>Recruitment and career fostering<br>Social service and legislation | Individual responsibility |

The accounting discipline is rapidly being pushed into a new era of technical content and professional practice. Internal and external forces are being exerted that will have profound influence on the profession in both the near and distant future. Each of the above areas of responsibility will be affected by these forces. Let's survey each of these areas. To explore each area in depth is not needed, for the issues involved have been debated before in the professional literature.

## ACCOUNTING AND REPORTING STANDARDS

The formation of the Financial Accounting Standards Board has been heralded as a momentous event in the accounting profession. For the first time in the profession's history, the need for a separate and independent group to research and establish financial accounting standards has been recognized and met. . . .

The FASB is authorized to issue Statements of Financial Accounting Standards and Interpretations of Financial Accounting Standards. These are designed to establish or improve standards of financial accounting and reporting for the guidance and education of the public, investors, creditors, preparers and suppliers of financial information, reporting entities and public accountants.

The function of establishing or improving financial accounting standards was previously the domain of the Accounting Principles Board. While the APB represented a wide range of backgrounds and experiences, it was in the final analysis an entity created by, supported by and answerable to the AICPA. Thus it was looked upon as overemphasizing the viewpoint of the independent auditor and not adequately reflecting the interests of the other members of the financial community (in effect, all the groups and organizations reflected on Figure I). Whether justified or not, that criticism probably was a major one contributing to the APB's demise and the creation of an independent FASB to oversee the area of financial accounting and reporting standards.

Now, the AICPA serves principally the interests of its members by providing input to the FASB's deliberations. Although a power base has been shifted, all the financial community and the professional accounting organizations stand to gain by the creation of FASB. The existence of the Board and the pledges of support by the SEC, the New York Stock Exchange and the various accounting organizations represent a giant step toward unity within the accounting profession.

Opinion seems divided on the question of whether the creation of the federal government's Cost Accounting Standards Board represents a step toward unity or whether it is a divisive influence. The CASB has five members and an executive secretary. Its staff reflects a broad composition: seven members are from industry, two from public accounting, three from academia and nine from government. Four part-time consultants assist the staff and Board. The CASB staff is full-time; the Board itself is part-time.

The CASB was created in 1970 by Congress to promulgate cost accounting standards to be followed by prime contractors and subcontractors in the pricing, administration and settlement of negotiated defense contracts over $100,000. . . .

The CASB's creation and existence is a positive step toward professional unity because it marks a trend toward developing greater interest and minimizing differences in managerial and cost accounting. Also, the Board's activities are forcing all the professional accounting organizations, industry associations and individual contractors to work separately and collectively in providing positive input to the CASB's deliberations. The attitude now seems to be that "the CASB is here; let's at least provide constructive input to assist in obtaining output we can live with." Hopefully that constructive attitude will grow and bear more positive results.

The report of another organization is certain to help the profession toward unity, and that is the Trueblood Commission's report on the objectives of financial statements. While some of these objectives may be controversial, overall they will provide a basis for discussions of the separate organizations' objectives. In the final analysis, the majority of the profession will come to see the wisdom of the objectives and the simplicity and the accuracy of their language. This will result in widespread support which will also foster unity within the profession.

## PROFESSIONAL EDUCATION AND TRAINING

The area of professional education and training is second in importance only to that of establishing technical standards. Education is the cornerstone of the technical and practical structure of the profession.

Three distinct areas of educational responsibility can be identified: preprofessional education, professional education and continuing education. Preprofessional education is obtained largely in colleges and universities and consists of the nonbusiness, business and basic accounting subjects as outlined in *Horizons for a Profession.*[2] Professional education consists of the formal study of advanced accounting subjects and the in-house and on-the-job training provided by public accounting and private industrial firms; it also includes the advanced and specialized accounting education and training acquired after the initial and basic exposure. Continuing education consists of all the formal and informal study a professional accountant does once he has entered the profession. Professional and continuing education is acquired from various sources: colleges and universities, accounting firms, industrial firms and accounting and professional organizations such as the AICPA's continuing professional education program.

Over the years there have been discussions of "who should do what." But the sad thing is that these discussions have been counterproductive. Because of the fear of offending colleagues, of overrunning traditional boundaries and of rushing into unknown areas too fast, the profession seems to have made limited advances in its professional education programs.

Accountants in public practice and in industry have been reluctant to voice their collective opinions on the nature of the professional education and the desirable characteristics of that process. Some contend it's not their business. But it is, because they hire the product of the educational process.

The practitioners' reluctance to state their views may be waning. The first significant pronouncements were the Roy/MacNeill *Horizons for a Profession* study and the report of the AICPA committee on education and experience requirements for CPAs. While the program it outlined has not escaped controversy, publication of the report has spurred greater cooperation among practitioners and academicians toward the objective of improving the accounting curriculum.

A further waning of this traditional reluctance is evidenced by some recent developments. A growing interest for professional schools of accounting is developing. Perhaps these schools should be similar in concept to the separate professional schools of law and medicine. In July 1973 a joint committee of the AICPA and the National Association of State Boards of Accountancy issued its "Report on Professional Recognition and Regulation." The report recommended that the AICPA and NASBA encourage the establishment of professional schools of accounting at qualified and receptive colleges and universities and that state CPA societies and other segments of the accounting profession join in this effort to provide financial support to the fullest extent possible. And last, it recommended that a committee be formed to develop

[2]Robert H. Roy and James H. MacNeill, *Horizons for a Profession* (New York, N.Y.: AICPA, 1967).

standards for professional schools and to identify the means for translating the recommendation into action.

The September 1973 *Journal of Accountancy* (p. 20) carried the notice that the AICPA Board of Directors had authorized the publication of a position statement regarding professional schools of accounting. This statement said, in part, that ". . . the Institute endorses and encourages the establishment of professional schools of accounting at qualified and receptive colleges and universities." Currently, several of the AICPA committees are concerned with various aspects of professional education and training.

There is no doubt that these activities, in particular the movement toward professional schools of accounting, could also be a positive force toward unity within the profession. They will force greater cooperation between the public and private practitioners and the accounting academicians.

The American Accounting Association has traditionally served as a forum for exchange of ideas and at this point does not speak "as an association." Over the years its committees have studied various educational policy issues, but these reports have had relatively little long-range impact upon professional accounting education. While academic freedom and flexibility are highly desirable, the accounting profession needs the official guidance of its academic arm. Further, that arm should be strong and able to carry its own weight by the quality and content of its pronouncements.

One of the American Accounting Association's most significant acts to promote professional education could be that of leading a movement toward forming an FASB-like organization—call it (say) the Accounting Education Standards Board. The mandate to the board would be to foster professional accounting education and training at all levels and in whatever way feasible. This involves establishing standards for accounting education and training at the preprofessional, professional and continuing education levels.

This board should contain representatives of all groups concerned, be reflective of their interests, but be dominated by no one. It should be a private voluntary organization with no legislative authority to promulgate standards. The acceptability of the guidelines and standards would be determined by the quality and soundness of the standards. Such a move might assist in integrating the academic arm into the professional mainstream as well as boosting the unity within the accounting profession generally.

## PROFESSIONAL ACCOUNTING PROGRAMS' ACCREDITATION

The move toward professional schools of accounting also will inevitably involve a move toward some form of official accreditation of professional accounting programs. In the past the AAA, AICPA and AACSB (American Association of Collegiate Schools of Business) have for various reasons been reluctant to accredit professional accounting programs, although the AACSB does accredit business schools' undergraduate curriculums as a whole, and masters' programs.

More than 33,000 candidates took the November 1973 CPA examination. In the recent past, almost all the candidates had attended college or had some advanced accounting education. NASBA estimates that more than 60 percent had degrees with a concentration in accounting from the more than 700 colleges and universities that offer an accounting curriculum.

Today the state boards of public accountancy have the responsibility for determining whether candidates have satisfactorily fulfilled the statutory requirements for an accounting education. Complicating the problem is that, of the 53 jurisdictions, few have the same standards. Accounting professors could help alleviate this problem as members or consultants to the state boards.

The existing situation, that of the accounting profession's playing no official role in accrediting the education process, contrasts with that in the other professions. Other professions' involvement in the accreditation process for entrance into the profession is well documented. Law, medicine, engineering, architecture and theology are prime examples.

The accounting profession should take bold steps in this area. Program accreditation should be accomplished through the proposed Accounting Education Standards Board, as outlined above. Voluntary participation by all interested segments of the profession in such an independent body could easily remove the stigma of unilateral action by any single group. Perhaps the American Accounting Association should take the lead in establishing this independent board and, after its establishment, fully cooperate with it.

## PROFESSIONAL CERTIFICATION AND SPECIALIZATION

Another area of current controversy within the accounting profession is that of professional certification and specialization. The objectives, content and adequacy of the CPA examination have been studied many times in the past. Perhaps now is the time to look to future developments regarding the general and specialty practice of the "professional accountant" in the broader sense.

*Horizons for a Profession* called for the CPA examination to be a threshold examination—the passing of which would signify the candidate's entrance into the accounting profession. The current AICPA policy reflects this position: that the CPA certificate is evidence of basic competence of professional quality in the discipline of accounting. This broad interpretation recognizes that CPAs are involved in both public and private practice. Nevertheless, because of its history, the "CPA" is still generally associated with professional practice as a public accountant.

Perhaps as the CPA examination evolves toward inclusion of the appropriate areas mentioned in *Horizons* and toward implementing the recommendations of the Beamer and Littler committees,[3] we will detect a broadening of its content. However, over the years the CPA examination has tended toward the practice of public accounting, and it will probably continue to do so in the future. One of the main reasons for this is the body of legislation that has been built which ties passing the CPA examination with the granting of a license to hold oneself out as a public accountant. The CPA

[3]Respectively, the "Report of the Committee on Education and Experience Requirements for CPAs" (New York, N.Y.: AICPA, March 1969); and "Report of the Committee to Study the Content of the CPA Examination," see *Journal of Accountancy*, July 71, p. 61.

examination, therefore, must test auditing capabilities as well as other skills directly associated with public practice.

In order to demonstrate a candidate's abilities in areas of professional accounting other than public practice, two other examinations have emerged. The National Association of Accountants has established the Institute of Management Accounting to prepare an examination and to issue a certificate in management accounting (CMA). Also, in a similar program the Institute of Internal Auditors issues a certificate in internal auditing (CIA). Both of these promote the recognition of the candidate's acquisition of professional-level education and experience in a particular area of the accounting profession. The impact of these examinations will likely be divisive rather than unifying.

A unifying move would encompass viewing the whole area of professional certification and specialization in a slightly different way then we now do. This view would correspond to the professional education and training discussion above. Figure 2, this page, depicts the correlation between the proposal for professional education and professional certification. The content of the preprofessional and the advanced professional education would be the basis for a designation of "certified professional accountant."[4] Additional education, training and experience would be the basis for one or more of the various specialty designations. Beyond that, professional continuing education programs would be the basis for maintaining one's certificates in force. This same basic structure has proved valid for other professions; it should also be a workable system for professional accounting.

In 1970, then-AICPA President Louis M. Kessler called upon the profession to consider the possibility of a national CPA certificate. In the same manner, the

[4] This was proposed in C. Aubrey Smith, "The Certified Public Accountant Not in Public Practice," *Journal of Accountancy*, Dec. 1968, pp. 52–56.

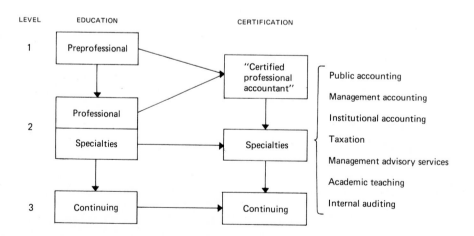

Figure 2

certification program advocated above accommodates such a proposal. Beyond the uniform national "certified professional accountant" designation, individual jurisdictions could still issue licenses to practice as a public accountant or in any other specialty, following whatever criteria were deemed desirable. Such a national certification program would require a central body to administer it. The reasonable approach, since all professional organizations have a vital interest, would be to join in a collective group effort similar to the proposed Accounting Education Standards Board as outlined above. Perhaps it could be called the Professional Accounting Certification Board. Its only jurisdiction would be in the area of the national certificate. The separate organizations would then be encouraged to administer their own specialty examinations and to issue specialty certificates in a manner similar to the three mentioned. True, laws would have to be changed to accomplish all of this; while difficult, it should not be impossible. We are a nation of laws, and we should see that those laws that affect us change with the times and with the dynamics of the profession.

Such cooperation and coordination among the various accounting organizations would certainly promote unity within the accounting profession. It would also promote a better image of the professional accountant in whatever area of accounting he may work.

## RESEARCH

Research within the profession has both technical and practical facets. And, like professional certification, research is the joint and individual responsibility of all the professional organizations.

Professional research rightfully comprises several different levels. First, there is the survey and tabulation of the application of standards, techniques and procedures that exist currently in practice. The AICPA's annual publication, *Accounting Trends & Techniques*, is an example of this. Second, there is the discovery of and refining of standards, techniques and procedures applicable to current practice. The FASB Statements will be largely of this nature. Third, there is "pure theory," the discovery of standards, techniques and procedures that are not necessarily applicable to current practice. The AICPA Accounting Research Studies Nos. 1 and 3 are of this nature. Each level of research has its place in the profession, and each must be done if it is to progress technically and practically.

Currently the directors of research of several of the accounting organizations meet intermittently to interchange ideas and "talk shop." An expanded interchange would advance professional unity. Each organization has its own separate research interests roughly corresponding to its sphere of influence outlined in Figure 1 and will continue to have these interests. And these different interests are fine. But the profession as a whole would benefit by a closer coordination of projects, and by each organization's devoting a larger budget to research efforts. "Progress through research," says one company's slogan. It is no less applicable to professional accounting.

## CODES OF PROFESSIONAL CONDUCT

Up to now the most notable code of professional conduct has been that of the AICPA, the associated codes of the state boards of public accountancy and the state CPA societies. While differences do exist, for all practical purposes these are similar and are directed to practice as a public accountant.

The official recognition and acceptance of the accounting profession as consisting of professionals in several pursuits, and the recognition of the realities of existing and future specialties, would require a structuring of an appropriate code of professional conduct. It is not inconceivable that there could exist a basic code governing the activities of the "certified professional accountant" and separate codes appropriate for each specialty designation. Each professional organization representing a particular specialty would be charged with structuring its own code of professional conduct. A joint effort by all concerned, perhaps through the Professional Accounting Certification Board mentioned above, would have to be responsible for the basic code.

This proposal, like most of the proposals mentioned above, are beset with problems of implementation. Obviously these problems need to be studied and debated, and solutions need to be tried. One knotty problem is that conceivably a person could be subject to the basic code and several specialty codes. An oversimplified solution could be that every professional would be subject to the basic code as well as that specialty code that covers his primary professional specialization area.

The recognition of the accounting discipline as a true profession requires that a suitably broad code of professional conduct be established. Such a move toward a general code for all professionals plus separate codes for various specialists would be another step toward unity.

## RECRUITMENT AND CAREER FOSTERING

While progress in technical standards, education and research is required for a growing profession new recruits into the profession are the lifeblood of its existence. And therein lies a problem that the profession has not heretofore realistically faced.

The problem is basically one of image. The accountant is often cast as a policeman-type—one who looks for faults in people and their work and who causes them concern and pain when they are around. Also, he is frequently cast as a conniver, usually introverted and generally obnoxious. In total, his general image is a negative one.

Committees have studied the twin problems of image and recruitment over the years. During the early 1960s, there was cooperation among five accounting organizations in establishing an Accounting Careers Council to foster careers in accounting. However, along with other problems, the climate for such cooperation was not right, and the ACC dissolved. But the failure of some 10 years ago should not portend doom for all current or future efforts.

High school and college students today are even more highly career conscious. The accounting profession should make every effort to identify and reach these potential professionals and to steer them in the right direction early in their career planning process. There is a great need to "sell" the general notion of "be a professional accountant" to the lower division college student, the high schooler and even the pre-high schooler. Such a general approach should be the combined responsibility of all accounting organizations and individual accounting professionals. Likewise, there is a great need also to sell the notion of "here's a profession in which you may specialize." The professional organizations representing such specialties should be the primary ones to do this task. Since usually the specialists go through the generalist route first, the specialty organizations have a responsibility to recruit also for the generalists' ranks. All organizations should take another look at formal cooperation in fostering new recruits for the accounting profession. This cooperation would indeed be a step toward unity within the profession. Short of that, a minimum effort would dictate that each organization do its share toward both upgrading the profession's image to a positive one and fostering new recruits for the profession.

## SOCIAL SERVICE AND LEGISLATION

A long-time problem, probably related to that of the profession's image, is that accountants have traditionally kept out of the limelight. The accounting profession is not a "high visibility" profession like law or medicine. Accountants have not traditionally been associated in people's minds as defenders of justice or curers of all ills. Accountants have traditionally not entered politics or established avenues to aid people and firms that need financial advice.

Inroads in all these areas are being made, such as the establishment of the Accountants for the Public Interest organization in California. These efforts are most commendable. The profession may be at a turning point. The time seems right politically and socially to project ourselves collectively and individually to be a positive social force in our communities and nation. Accountants must do their share as individual citizens and as a nationally recognized and responsible profession to help mold society. The bad news will always get reported in the press; but bad publicity may be offset through positive local and national efforts. . . .

## CONCLUSION

The accounting profession is indeed on the brink of a new era. It's an exciting time to be an accountant. Depending upon the collective and individual efforts now and in the next few years, the profession will either be a unified positive force in our society or a group of fragmented self-serving organizations. The choice is ours.

## QUESTIONS

1. Why does Professor Pattillo argue for "unity" within the profession and the business community?
2. What kinds of professional unity should be achievable? Not achievable? Why?
3. How could accountants become a more positive social force in the nation?

## SELECTED BIBLIOGRAPHY

Biagioni, Louis F., "Roles and Rules for Accountants," *Business Horizons*, February 1975, pp. 67-75.

# 135
## ACCOUNTANCY WAS MY LIFE*

Accountancy was my life
Until I discovered Smirnoff
. . . The effect is shattering

# 136
## THE SOOTHSAYERS†
Liz Roman Gallese

Joseph L. Shapiro spends a good deal of time in his sunny office in the planning department of Gillette Co. here contemplating what the changing role of women might bring about for the family in the decades ahead.

He isn't exactly sure what that has to do with selling Gillette's razor blades and toiletries, if anything. No matter. As the company's resident crystal-ball gazer, he isn't paid to come up with the answers but rather to raise the questions.

Mr. Shapiro's official title at Gillette is director of commercial research. Informally he is called a "futurist" or a "soothsayer." And he is one of a proliferating breed of corporate officials around the country who are paid by companies like Shell Oil, American Telephone & Telegraph and General Electric to try to discern the future implications of past and present trends.

The particular trend toward soothsayers on corporate payrolls is currently under study by James B. Webber, a director at Cambridge Research Institute in Cambridge, Mass. Mr. Webber, a consultant, is working with six firms, three hospitals and a

*From advertisement for vodka.

†From the *Wall Street Journal*, March 31, 1975, pp. 1 and 11. Reprinted by permission of the publisher.

government agency. He says that as many as one out of five of the "Fortune 500" companies now have employes who "play the genie in a practical sense, keeping firms abreast so they don't get caught short."

Wayne Boucher, secretary of The Futures Group, a research and consulting firm in Glastonbury, Conn., believes that more and more companies will be hiring futurists in the coming months as they try to brace themselves for the crises that have been catching them off guard in recent years—the energy shortage, wage and price controls, the environmental outcry. "Times are perilous," Mr. Boucher says. "It's a crisis with a capital C (for industry) . . . And the changes will accelerate."

## GOING BEYOND PROFIT

Corporate planning departments of old are far from adequate today, Mr. Boucher says. Using economic data, marketing statistics and a smattering of demographic information, they merely estimated the profit potential of new products over a future of no more than five years. As Mr. Boucher puts it: "They looked at birth rates without considering birth-control pills."

Futurists, on the other hand, try to peer as far as 30 years into the future and bring a host of social and political factors to bear on a number of corporate problems. Usually trained as economists or market researchers, they are apt to be voracious readers who have an ability to develop contacts and to spot trends. Their function, though not yet formally named at many companies, is beginning to be called "social and political forecasting," "environmental scanning" or "early warning systems."

Whatever the name, the futurist often works by himself or with one other person, either independently or affixed to the planning department. However, this varies considerably. Shell Oil, for example, has a team of six working within its 40-man planning department. And American Telephone & Telegraph Corp.'s planning division has eight individuals with an "artistic temperament" or a background in history, literature or journalism working alongside its 40 economists and statisticians.

Since they rarely have real authority, futurists are apt to be wily in the ways they get their points across to top management. Cambridge Research's Mr. Webber says one futurist often sneaks his ideas into speeches that he ghostwrites for top executives, hoping that the executives will begin to think of the ideas as their own. The same futurist is also said to build qualitative forecasts around hard economic data on the theory that executives readily understand economics.

## FRIENDLY PERSUASION

Gillette's Mr. Shapiro is also adept at friendly persuasion. "He does it so subtly that often people aren't even aware he's doing it. Sometimes they think they've come up with the ideas themselves," an executive says. Indeed, Mr. Shapiro's powers of persuasion may be one of the reasons that he's already getting results.

A 62-year-old economist, Joseph Shapiro formerly did social and statistical research for the Social Security Administration and marketing research for several firms, among them Gillette's former Toni division (now the personal care division). In 1968, Vincent

C. Ziegler, chairman and chief executive, asked him to return to Gillette's planning department, whose four other members deal largely with specific short-term planning.

Mr. Shapiro's first project was a report outlining the pitfalls and prospects for the company in the year 2000. One of the prospects was the opportunity to get into service-oriented businesses, he wrote. And conversely, one of the pitfalls would be a failure to do so. One reason behind this thinking, he says, was that he spotted a stabilizing population that would need a lesser rate of new products. Given Gillette's current rate of growth, he says, "We'll be approaching $3 billion in sales by 1980, up from $1.2 billion now. And when you think about it, where else will that type of growth come from" but services?

A few years after Mr. Shapiro's project, Gillette took its first cautious steps in the service area with acquisitions of Welcome Wagon International Inc. in 1971 and Jafra Cosmetics Inc. in 1973. (The former is the well-known community greeting service, and the latter makes a cosmetic line sold in the home by beauty consultants.) "We did it largely on the basis of Joe's information," Mr. Ziegler says. "Both businesses are doing well. And by 1980 services should be a significant part of our business."

Mr. Ziegler often asks Mr. Shapiro to accompany Gillette executives to acquisition discussions so that Mr. Shapiro can ask the pertinent questions about future potential. The chairman also asks his futurist a number of specific questions. For example, Mr. Shapiro was asked to investigate what the rising average age of the U.S. population might mean for Gillette. Mr. Shapiro's answer was a recommendation that the company design and market more products aimed at the previously ignored over-55 age group.

Mr. Shapiro is currently updating his report on the year 2000. As with most projects, he begins by formulating a hypothesis, in this case that the family structure will be profoundly affected by the changing role of women. From the three newspapers he reads each day and the 30 to 40 magazines and journals he gets each month, he tries to pick up clues about the future. He puts trends in historical perspective and further tests ideas by talking to visitors and colleagues. (Could one person's observation that few families eat meals together anymore mean that household items like fancy dishes won't be selling as well?)

Gillette's futurist rarely interviews outsiders because he doesn't want to tip the company's hand. "Like Lady Shalott (in Tennyson's poem), I know the outside world from a mirror," he says. "I read and read and read, and at some point I come through the critical mass, the facts either filling in or disclaiming my hypothesis."

Futurists say they can't provide specific answers to what the future holds but that they can ask the right questions about its possibilities. One such questioner is Ian Wilson, General Electric futurist since 1967. Mr. Wilson is currently studying the possible impact of today's energy situation on the 1980s. One possibility, he says, is that consumers will be deeply concerned about energy conservation, meaning that General Electric might have to develop products that use less energy.

"Presenting alternatives gets executives to do 'what if . . .' thinking," Mr. Wilson says. "If that's the only way to forecast now—and it is—so be it. We simply can't do without it."

Mr. Wilson first got involved in "what if . . ." thinking in 1967, when he did his first general study of the future and failed to take into account the student riots that occurred just one year later. Reexamining conversations with people he had interviewed, he realized that they had mentioned all of the factors that had contributed to the uprisings. "We learned that we had to see trends in synoptic and interacting modes, not in isolation," he says.

By asking "what if . . ." questions a year later, Mr. Wilson was able to reason that the minority-rights movement could spread to other groups, specifically women. That reasoning, he says, enabled the company to set up affirmative-action guidelines a year before the federal government required them.

## "FUTURE SHOCK"

As futurist departments go, GE's operation is fairly old. Neither Shell Oil nor AT&T set up social and political forecasting units until 1972, when each hired a team of individuals with divergent specialties. In Shell's case, the company was responding to an outside factor: the possibility of becoming more dependent on foreign crude oil. "Future shock hit us," says Rene Zentner, manager of Shell's futurist team. "As the world changed, we realized we couldn't continue to follow constant trends and count on a 5% annual growth rate."

An arm of the planning department, Shell's team consists of Mr. Zentner, two economists, a lawyer, the holder of a master's degree in business administration, and a sociologist, all of whom work individually on specific projects. The lawyer is following the development of energy policy, for example, and the MBA is covering political and economic developments in foreign countries.

AT&T's corporate planning division is an outgrowth of the management sciences division formed in 1968. Unlike the Shell unit, the department's eight humanities-oriented people work jointly with its 40 economists and statisticians on projects in a handful of areas, such as regulatory trends. "Working separately sets up artificial barriers," says Henry Boettinger, director of corporate planning.

In at least one instance, a whole group of companies has access to a futurist team. This is the case with the 200 firms belonging to the Institute of Life Insurance, a New York trade group. Three times a year, the institute publishes "Trend Analysis Reports" that cover new developments in science and technology, social sciences, business and economics, and politics and government. Coordinated by Edith Weiner, the program was begun in 1970. Ninety volunteers from the institute's member firms monitor 60 publications each month. A committee of top executives then puts together the reports, each one wrapping up trends in specific areas.

## STUDYING THE LIFE CYCLE

A recent institute report, entitled "The Life Cycle," showed that the rigid pattern of most people's lives—formal education, followed by career, followed by retirement—could give way to a less structured system. Bankers Life Co. in Des Moines was so taken by that report that executives designed a "life cycle" policy, in which holders can scale premium payments up and down throughout a lifetime to reflect changes in work status. The company is currently trying to get state regulatory agencies to approve the concept and hopes to introduce it within five years.

Equally impressed with the reports, Equitable Life Assurance Society in New York spotted an opportunity to sell to a whole new segment—two-income families. "Agencies never approached women before," says Anna Rappaport, vice president and associate actuary for marketing. "But now families need insurance on both spouses."

Of course, not all companies take to social and political forecasting. Many executives frown on the whole area because they don't see immediate results; others find that futurists tend to voice ideas that grate on nerves. Jay Mendell, who now is teaching at Florida International University in Miami, says he tried for a year to convince the Pratt & Whitney Aircraft division of United Aircraft Corp., where he once worked in the marketing department, to use the unit he had set up. On his own, he drew up a list of areas which he thought the company should follow: legislation, opportunities in civil technology, places where funding was drying up. But, he says, he merely annoyed his superiors, who thought he should concentrate on the job he was hired to do. "While Pratt was competing for the SST engine," he explains, "I was saying, 'Why would people want to fly so fast?' "

John Marshall of Pratt & Whitney's marketing department and the man who was Jay Mendell's boss, says, "In part, Jay is somewhat right. His plan was a little grandiose, and these are hard times. It got lost because of economics. But we are pursuing some of the activities he set up." (The division currently has a subgroup in its business planning department that keeps an eye on what it calls "geopolitical, economic and transportation research"—but only as such research relates to Pratt & Whitney's products.)

While the whole area of social and political forecasting is relatively new, technology forecasting—or predicting what the technology of the future will be—goes back to studies by the federal government in the 1930s. Over the years, technology forecasting proved to be eminently useful. In the early 1960s, for example, Richard Davis, of Whirlpool Corp., spotted the coming of permanent-press fabrics, thereby enabling the company to be the first on the market with washers and dryers that accommodate such materials.

But Mr. Davis, whose title is staff technological forecaster, says that he has since become more dependent on social, political and environmental factors. So while he is trying to determine where there are shortages of potable water, he is also keeping an eye on what he calls "human values." Working mothers, fewer children and the use of paper as opposed to cloth could mean, for example, a need for smaller washers and dryers. "Anyone who ignores these factors does so at his own peril," he cautions.

## QUESTIONS

1. Who are "the soothsayers?"
2. How do their duties relate or not relate to accounting?
3. What are the implications of the soothsayers for the education of accountants?

## SELECTED BIBLIOGRAPHY

Lacey, Frederick B., "How Accountants Can Fight Organized Crime," *World*, Summer 1970, pp. 3, 5.

# 137
# OFFICE IN MOSCOW*
Theodore Shabad

One of the largest accounting firms in the United States is expected to open an office in Moscow soon as part of a broad-ranging agreement with the Soviet Government in auditing, international taxation and management services.

The firm, Arthur Andersen & Co. of Chicago, will become the first American company to work closely with the Russians in the field of Western management techniques as the Soviet Union expands its worldwide commitments. A final accord is expected next month, according to American business sources.

## EXCITING CHALLENGE

Harvey E. Kapnick Jr., chairman of Andersen, declined to disclose details of the negotiations pending an agreement.

"We are moving along on schedule," he said by telephone from Chicago, "and hope that the talks will culminate in our presence in Moscow in the near future."

Describing the prospective arrangement as an "exciting challenge in East-West economic relations," the 48-year-old Mr. Kapnick said:

"We believe that our cooperation with the Soviet Union will help foster East-West trade by helping each side understand the business practices and philosophy of the other."

Mr. Kapnick, who became chief executive in 1970, has been described as something of a "whiz kid" at Andersen. Raised on a Michigan farm, he went to work in the firm's Chicago office in 1948, rising to the rank of partner in eight years; ordinarily it takes about a dozen years to get that far.

On the Soviet side, too, a "whiz kid" has been the moving force behind the project. He is Dzhermen M. Gvishiani, the 45-year-old deputy chairman of the State Committee for Science and Technology, who has been in the forefront of Soviet efforts to use Western management techniques to the extent that they are compatible with Marxist ideology.

*From the *New York Times,* Mar. 19, 1974, pp. 47, 59. Reprinted with permisssion of the publisher.

## REORIENTATION STRESSED

Only last week, Pravda, the Communist party newspaper, stressed the need for a psychological reorientation in economic management. In an editorial criticizing delays in establishing a new system of Soviet state corporations known as production associations, it said:

"The modern executive must be familiar with the science of management, broaden his horizons, be able to improve the planning and organization of production, and adopt a party-oriented approach to any problem."

Mr. Gvishiani, who is Premier Aleksei N. Kosygin's son-in-law, has long favored economic reforms that would shift short-term decision-making from central ministries to the new state corporations.

Mr. Gvishiani played a key role in the organization in 1972 of the International Institute of Applied Systems Analysis in Laxenburg, Austria. The institute, an international "think tank" sponsored by a dozen nations, will study pollution control, urban growth and other problems of industrial countries.

A specialist in American management science, Mr. Gvishiani has also led a drive for training Soviet economic executives in modern management information and control systems. A high-level business administration school, known as the Institute for Management of the National Economy, opened in Moscow in February, 1971.

In Arthur Andersen, the Soviet Government will have the services of an accounting firm that serves more companies listed on the New York Stock Exchange than do any of its rivals. Among the companies served by Andersen are Tenneco, Inc., and the Occidental Petroleum Corporation, which have plans for bringing Soviet liquefied natural gas to the United States, and the General Dynamics Corporation, which builds ships for the transportation of liquefied gas.

Another Andersen client is Combustion Engineering, Inc., whose Lummus unit is doing engineering and construction for the Soviet chemical industry.

The accounting firm is expected to advise its American clients on the Soviet Union's industrial and trade program and to assist Soviet officials in dealing with the wide range of business procedures and practices encountered in expanding foreign operations.

The Soviet Union is also expected to benefit from Andersen's personnel-training program, which has made use of advanced audio-visual techniques for instruction in the firm's worldwide network of offices. Soviet officials may also attend the firm's training center, with accommodations for 600 people, at St. Charles, Ill., west of Chicago.

The firm's approaches to the Soviet Union began in 1972 when it filed an application for permission to establish an office in Moscow.

## QUESTIONS

1. What are the possible accounting implications of a Western public accounting firm opening an office in Moscow? If one is opened in China?
2. What is the social significance of this event?

# 138

## ... ACCOUNTING FIRM ... ANNUAL REPORT ...*

Frederick Andrews

Arthur Andersen & Co. has become the first accounting firm to publish an annual report, providing an unprecedented look into the structure and finances of a huge, world-wide accounting partnership.

The annual report, a 36-page, four-color document published in five languages, is being distributed to Andersen's 11,400 partners and staff members and its 50,000 clients. Professional ethics bar the Chicago-based firm from open distribution of its report, but Chairman Harvey Kapnick said a copy would be given to "anyone with a legitimate interest." He specifically included shareholders of publicly held clients of Andersen.

Traditionally, the accounting profession, which sets disclosure requirements for all publicly held companies, has disclosed very little about itself. In part, this posture is rooted in professional bars against self-promotion. In addition, the auditors have never shown great interest in disclosing how much money they make.

A decade ago, the Andersen firm, which enjoys a reputation as a maverick, urged accounting authorities to collect financial data from CPA firms. Later it volunteered to file financial information with the Securities and Exchange Commission, but its offer wasn't taken up.

"Investors should have a way of finding out what an accounting firm is all about," Mr. Kapnick said in an interview. In his view, disclosure of financial data will counter skepticism that auditors can't stand up to client companies because they are dependent upon them for fees. "With a knowledge of our world-wide fees and financial resources, you can better understand why we are able to resolve major issues with any client with complete independence and objectivity."

According to Mr. Kapnick, the report has been in circulation since last Thursday, and thus far hasn't generated any criticism from other accounting firms. "Ethics today are changing," he said, "and anyone who questions (such disclosures) must justify why the (traditional) ethical rules are in the public interest."

Among the report's disclosures were:

In the year ended March 31, an Andersen partnership was worth, on average, $215,000 to the firm's top 20 partners. Total distribution to the firm's 749 active partners came to $55.8 million and averaged $74,500, up 6% from the year before. In addition, 87 retired or former Andersen partners or their estates received $10.7 million. In the interview, Mr. Kapnick declined to disclose how much was paid to the partner with the highest profit participation.

The annual report was quick to explain that these distributions aren't comparable to salaries of corporate executives, who also receive fringe benefits and possibly stock options. Partners must provide their own retirement and fringe benefits, it said.

*From the *Wall Street Journal*, June 14, 1973, p. 4. Reprinted by permission of the publisher.

The firm's partnership capital stood at $75.6 million March 31, up from $69.3 million a year earlier. The Andersen partners all share in its world-wide income, in proportion to their capital in the firm. The average active partner's capital share was $85,000 and the top 20 partners averaged about $280,000.

The partnership units are divided into world-wide units," comparable to shares of stock. All new partners are admitted with the same number of units, regardless of where they work, and the units are adjusted annually to reflect changes in exchange rates and inflation. There is also a system for awarding "merit" units to exceptional partners. Almost all taxes on Andersen's earnings are paid by the individual partners.

New partners must contribute capital when they join the firm. Normally, they have no difficulty borrowing money to make this contribution, Mr. Kapnick said.

In fiscal 1973, the Andersen firm, which operates in 27 countries, took in $271.5 million in world-wide fees, up 11% from $244.5 million a year earlier. In 1964, the firm, with about 21,000 clients, earned about $55 million in fees. According to the report, Andersen audits about 250 companies listed on the New York Stock Exchange, more than any other accounting firm, Andersen said.

The report said in fiscal 1973, 69% of Andersen's fees came from auditing and accounting, 18% from its tax practice, and 13% from management consulting. Mr. Kapnick said these proportions have remained roughly the same over the years. There was no breakdown of fees by country.

In fiscal 1973, more than $214 million went for the payroll, including distributions to partners. Payments to nonpartners included $41.1 million to its 1,600 "managers," $87.7 million to its 6,400 other professionals, and $18.9 million to 2,200 others on the office staff. According to Mr. Kapnick the ratio of partners to staff runs about one-to-15, a key measure of both the quality of a firm's supervision and the size of its partners' share.

Nonpayroll expenses were $57.2 million, including $4.5 million in insurance premiums and provisions for uninsured risks.

On March 31, the Andersen firm had lawsuits pending against it involving 28 client companies or former clients, in addition to the three Andersen auditors under indictment on fraud charges involving the former Four Seasons Nursing Centers of America Inc. (The three men and the firm have vigorously denied any wrongdoing.)

The report didn't disclose, however, any sums Andersen might have paid in the past to settle or avoid lawsuits, such as its recent payment of $875,000 to Whittaker Corp. in connection with a $6.3 million inventory shortage. In the report, Mr. Kapnick said there was "a tremendous increase" in stockholder or creditor suits against accountants throughout the profession and estimated that such litigation involving more than 500 companies was pending.

"We inevitably will be a legal target for those who seek to salvage something from their investment or creditor position," he contended.

Andersen's main need for cash is to finance work in progress until clients pay fees. In recent years, working capital has averaged about 30 cents for each $1 of fees. At March 31, current assets amounted to $103.4 million (including $79 million in receivables), and current liabilities were $27.9 million. Working capital, thus, came to $75.5 million.

Andersen said it "avoids" tapping short-term credit for working capital, though it has a line of credit with a "major nonclient bank" and $500,000 in short-term bank loans outstanding outside the U.S. Its long-term debt amounts to $26.9 million, mainly an unsecured note for $21.5 million payable, at 7.25% interest, to an insurance company, also not a client.

The firm has $27 million invested in property, but usually leases its office premises. Its lease commitments total $104.6 million, including $10.9 million payable in fiscal 1974.

The firm admitted 84 new partners last April 1, bringing the current total to 826, including 137 non-U.S. nationals. Accounting sources say the firm has grown so large it has difficulty finding a hotel to accommodate a convention of all the partners. All the partners are men, but according to Mr. Kapnick, "a good portion" of the professional staff are women, some of whom will, in time, become partners.

Every partner has one vote, but the firm is run by an 18-member board of directors, with Mr. Kapnick as chairman and chief executive. Andersen stresses a "one-firm" concept, which it says involves having experts in Chicago readily available to help local offices. Other accountants say that Andersen is noted for strict control from the home office. They also say its system of having all partners share in world-wide income, rather than simply profits from their country or area, is unique.

Andersen also is known for aggressive growth, in particular for systematically obtaining young companies as audit clients, with an aim to growing with them. In the report, Mr. Kapnick defended this approach, which in some instances has led to woes.

"In a private enterprise system, a substantial number of companies that begin as new ventures are likely to fail," he said. "We have no crystal ball to tell which will succeed and which will fail, and we don't believe it is in the public interest for auditing firms with established reputations to decline those engagements."

EDITORS' NOTE: In 1975 Arthur Andersen issued its third annual report. It expanded its disclosures to include a full set of financial statements, which it described as equivalent to an external audit, except for being performed by an Andersen team. For 1975, AA's fee revenue was up 16 percent to $386.3 million. The growth was attributed to a 4.5 percent growth in hours of client work and to higher fees (8.5 percent higher in the United States and 14.7 percent higher abroad). Earnings rose 14.1 percent to $90.8 million. Earnings per active partner were up 5.1 percent to $95,152 (based on 844 partners). Total partners' capital rose to $100.6 million; no partner has a stake larger than 0.5 percent in earnings or capital.

## QUESTIONS

1. What information about this firm is disclosed in its annual report?

2. Why have public accounting firms (along with other professional firms) resisted attempts to encourage them to publish annual reports?

3. Why should a professional firm publish financial statements annually?

## SELECTED BIBLIOGRAPHY

Allan, John H., "Maverick of Ledgerland," *The New York Times*, June 24, 1973, p. F5.

Andrews, Frederick, "Audacious Auditor," *The Wall Street Journal*, October 2, 1975, pp. 1, 14.

"Auditing the Auditors," *The New York Times*, Nov. 5, 1973, p. 8C.

Benjamin, James J., and Vincent C. Brenner, "Public Disclosure for CPA Firms," *Financial Executive*, August 1975, pp. 37-41.

Kapnick, Harvey, "Accountants Are Sitting on Their Hands," *The New York Times*, November 23, 1975, p. F14.

# 139

## PUBLIC REVIEW BOARD*

Harvey Kapnick

We are pleased to announce that our firm is establishing a Public Review Board. . . . A public accounting firm has a significant responsibility in the private sector of our economy not only to clients but also to investors and creditors and to the public generally. We are dedicated to fulfilling this responsibility and to improving the effectiveness of our free enterprise system in the public interest. We believe that the establishment of this Board is a constructive and beneficial step that should enhance the efforts of our firm to carry out its function in the business and financial community in the best possible manner.

The general purpose of this Board is to review the professional operations of our firm, including the manner in which our firm is managed and financed, the scope of our practice and how the quality of our work is controlled.

Initially there will be five members of the Board, who will serve on a part-time basis. . . . As additional members are selected, they will be announced at that time. The present members are as follows:

William L. Cary   Dwight Professor of Law at Columbia University; Counsel, Patterson, Belknap & Webb; former Chairman of Securities and Exchange Commission

James Don Edwards   Research Professor at University of Georgia; Past President of American Accounting Association; Member of AICPA Study Group on the Objectives of Financial Statements

Newton N. Minow   Partner, Sidley & Austin; former Chairman of Federal Communications Commission

*From *Arthur Andersen Co. Executive News Briefs,* June 1974, p. 1. Reprinted by permission of the publisher.

George Romney Chairman of National Center for Voluntary Action; former Chairman of American Motors Corporation; former Governor of Michigan; former Secretary of Housing and Urban Development

Randolph William Thrower Partner, Sutherland, Asbill & Brennan; Chairman, American Bar Association Planning Committee; former Commissioner of Internal Revenue Service

Newton N. Minow will act as the initial Chairman.

The broad and diverse backgrounds of the members of the Board give them unique qualifications to evaluate our firm from the standpoint of the public interest, with particular reference to the performance of our professional services.

The members of the Board will establish their own program for reviewing and considering the operations of our firm. They will have access to all information that is necessary to accomplish their objectives.

The Board will be expected to submit comments and suggestions from time to time to the management of our firm. Also, it is contemplated that the Board will make an annual report that will be published by the firm.

We believe that this Board will bring an outside viewpoint to our professional practice, particularly with respect to our public responsibilities as independent accountants and auditors.

EDITORS' NOTE: Mr. Kapnick is managing partner, Arthur Andersen & Co., one of the Big Eight firms. The "Public Review" board's first report was included in Arthur Andersen's 1975 Annual Report. The board recommended that: (1) the firm should retain a financial analyst as an advisor to keep it up to date on what information security analysts and other users need in financial statements; (2) partners should rely less on staff accountants and assume a larger role in detailed audit work and, in particular, in the firm's tax work, including better training and supervision of junior tax accountants; (3) the firm should volunteer its services without charge to help the Federal Elections Commission develop accounting standards and ways to monitor political financing; (4) the firm should consider hiring another accounting firm to audit Andersen's financial results. The board also had some approving words for class-action lawsuits which "do encourage attentiveness and care in the conduct of audits and needed disclosures in financial statements."

## QUESTION

1. How does the naming of a public review board by this firm integrate with the increasing acceptance by accountants of their accountability to the general public?

## SELECTED BIBLIOGRAPHY

Andrews, Frederick, "Arthur Andersen Generally is Praised in 'Public Review' Board's First Report," *Wall Street Journal*, November 12, 1975, p. 17.

# 140

## COMPANY WATCHDOGS*

George Melloan

The company auditor, whose job once was confined to poring over financial ledgers, is now becoming a combination private detective, credit sleuth, cost-cutter and all-round trouble shooter.

Auditors who work for corporations still check books for errors or signs of chicanery. But they also are moving into new areas of responsibility that bear little relation to their traditional tasks. They are reviewing price policies for possible antitrust violations, investigating outside activities of company officers to spot conflicts of interest, checking credit of suppliers, customers and potential merger partners and roaming plants and offices in search of inefficiency.

Thus an auditor from Pacific Telephone & Telegraph Co. visited a San Francisco couple to inquire about the quality of service when a phone was installed recently. And at the Louisville works of International Harvester Co. two auditors in white shirts and ties poke into piles of rusty scrap and surplus parts looking for waste.

### HARVESTER'S SAVINGS

There's evidence that the new look in auditing pays off. Harvester auditor John D. Bergerson, for example, spotted the fact that two different size bolts were used on one of the company's disc harrows. He asked if the smaller bolt could be used exclusively. Engineers decided it could, saving Harvester $19,000 a year. Another sharp-eyed Harvester auditor touring a plant suggested that, in view of capabilities of new steel rolling mills, steel sheets could be ordered by Harvester to closer thickness tolerances. Such orders, which insure that the company now gets the maximum number of sheets per ton, save over $200,000 a year at one plant and could save up to $1 million a year if all Harvester divisions adopt the practice, an official says.

This broadening role of the auditor as the eyes and ears of top management is a relatively new one. It comes about largely because many U.S. companies have grown so complex and far-flung that the people who run them can never be wholly certain that they know about important things that are happening at lower levels. These managers often find it highly useful to have a reasonable objective and independent branch to look into situations that other subordinates might be reluctant to report, or the significance of which they might not understand.

Auditors can expand their role because office automation is freeing them from much of their traditional routine paper work. Edward A. Johnson, assistant general auditor for Minnesota Mining & Manufacturing Co., notes that a computer can scan through credit accounts in a few hours in search of any that are dangerously overdue. Before automation the job required several hundred man-hours of auditing department time.

*From the *Wall Street Journal,* Oct. 26, 1969, p. 1. Reprinted by permission of the publisher.

## "OPERATIONAL AUDITING"

Lockheed Aircraft Corp. has expanded its auditing staff to 112 persons today from 14 in 1949, says Frederic E. Mints, resident internal auditor at the Lockheed-California division. But only about 30% of the man-hours of the department today are expended on financial auditing, he says. The rest are devoted to broader "operational" auditing, involving such things as surveying the efficiency of aircraft assembly lines.

A survey of auditing practices by the National Industrial Conference Board (NICB), a non-profit business research institution, confirms this trend. Over 60% of the 177 companies checked had made a significant move toward broadening auditors' duties in the last five years.

As auditors tackle new jobs, many concerns are drawing recruits for their auditing departments from fields other than accounting. John M. Schulz, general auditor at Atlantic Refining Co., started his career as a chemical engineer and has never had any formal training in accountancy.

"A few years ago most people were drawn from accounting but today we just look for brains," says Robert L. Richmond, general auditor at B. F. Goodrich Co. At Shell Oil Co., promising men are given two or three years in internal auditing as a means to train them for top management posts. Since auditors see all phases of a corporation some executives think it is an ideal training ground.

## DEMAND AND PAY ARE UP

Demand for company auditors who can fill more "sophisticated" jobs is growing and salaries are rising, says Robert C. Zabor, vice president of Heidrick & Struggles, a New York executive recruiting and management counseling firm. Managers of internal auditing now can command salaries ranging from $20,000 to $30,000 a year, he notes. Four or five years ago the range was more likely to be $18,000 to $22,000, he says. "There's a general upgrading of the field," says Mr. Zabor. "The man who goes into it is required not only to be a good auditor but a potential executive."

Archie McGhee, managing director of the Institute of Internal Auditors, a professional association, says one large company now hires new auditors at $10,000 a year or more, compared with about $8,000 a few years ago. The Institute also reports a higher turnover in auditing jobs; 14% of jobs changed hands last year, according to a survey, compared with a "normal" level of 11%. Mr. McGhee says higher turnover often reflects higher salaries that induce auditors to change jobs.

Broader assignments for auditors often reflect the concern of management over dangers of fraud and overextended credit. The well-publicized "salad oil scandal," in which perhaps $150 million in edible oils proved to be fictitious, spurred the auditor of one petroleum pipeline company to study his own firm's techniques of checking what is in its storage tanks.

At another large concern, the president recently called in auditors and asked them to give credit checking procedures a close scrutiny. The move was prompted by word that a finance subsidiary of Whirlpool Corp. had been forced to set up a $21,376,000 reserve to cover uncollectible receivables, which resulted partly, according to Whirlpool, from inadequate checking of credit. "Fortunately, we found our control systems were working well," says the auditor.

A large Midwest concern not long ago took a loss of some $1 million when a customer that owed it that sum went broke. According to the concern's auditor, the report of a public accounting firm erroneously showed that the customer was in sound condition with net assets of nearly $2 million just before it collapsed. The Midwest company now has its own auditors check over the books of its big credit customers, making it clear to the customers that this is one of the conditions of obtaining credit.

About one-third of the companies surveyed by the NICB now have their own auditors investigate other companies they deal with. These include organizations being considered for acquisition, concessionaries, licensees, subcontractors, sole suppliers of a vital material, dealers and advertising agencies.

About half of the 151 companies in the NICB survey that engage in operational auditing have their auditors check whether their respective companies are complying with Federal, state and local laws and rules of regulatory bodies. This ranges from determining if a refinery is complying with local fire ordinances to checking whether branch offices are violating the Robinson-Patman Act by making price concessions to some customers and not others, says a major oil company auditor. Checking for collusion that might run the company afoul of antitrust laws is one of the toughest jobs he says. "What you are really dealing with there is collusion among salesmen and that can be very difficult to detect," he says.

## SMOKING OUT CONFLICTS OF INTEREST

According to the NICB study, conflicts of interest, in which some company executives "may have outside business interests that adversely affect the fulfillment of their obligations to their principal employers," are another concern which managers are turning over to their auditors. "At times the auditors go so far as to obtain retail credit reports and Dun & Bradstreet reports on individuals who appear to be living beyond their company salaries," the report says.

A general auditor at a big chemicals producer recently made his first report to the board of directors on possible conflicts of interest in his company. Though neither the auditor nor the directors have reason to suspect any wrongdoing, the new policy was begun as a precautionary step.

In a few companies the general auditor reports to the board at all times. Such is the arrangement at New York Life Insurance Co., a mutual insurance firm with assets of some $7 billion. New York Life's general auditor has authority to make audits and examinations of company affairs on his own initiative and report directly to the board. The company says it believes it is necessary for the auditor to report to a level beyond that of the executives whose activities are audited.

## "PLAY GOLF WITH SALES MANAGER"

As their authority broadens, auditors find new demands being made upon them to develop outgoing personalities, as well as to show considerable tact. At the annual convention of the Institute of Internal Auditors in Houston this summer, Clyde Skeen, executive vice president of Ling-Temco-Vought, Inc., urged auditors to unbend a bit in dealing with other company workers so that management won't be faced with protests from sales managers and engineering department heads about second-guessing from the auditors. "Put on a sports shirt and go out and play golf with the sales manager—it won't hurt you," Mr. Skeen advised.

An auditor for Vickers division of Sperry-Rand Corp., Robert M. Miller, suggests that auditors avoid disagreeing with a manager "when he (the manager) is feeling depressed, irascible or ill." Mr. Miller, in an article in an auditing journal, adds, "Train yourself to be sensitive to storm signals of facial expression, posture, tone and voice" and don't press a manager "for an unmistakable statement that he has reversed himself."

Most auditors contend they try to sell themselves to the people whose activities they're inspecting. For one thing, says one auditor, a friendly, relaxed approach often allows the auditor to pick up gripes or information that might be important to his investigation. But another remarks, "You can't be out trying to make yourself popular. In the final analysis we have to be on management's side and we have to deal with some very hard questions."

## QUESTIONS

1. Why has the role of the internal auditor been broadened?

2. Of the various activities now being undertaken by company auditors, do you feel that there are any that they should not undertake? Why?

3. It has been said that accountants are like the Lord in the Bible, where it is written that "a thousand years are in His sight as yesterday," in the sense that every figure is equally important to them. What implications do you see in this observation for a company auditor?

4. The Institute of Internal Auditors now certifies internal auditors who pass a written examination and meet other criteria. A certified internal auditor is referred to as a CIA. What may be the impact of this development on internal auditing?

# 141

## PROFESSIONAL FOOTBALL AND INFORMATION SYSTEMS*

Frank Ryan, Arthur J. Francia, and Robert H. Strawser

During a National Football League game between the New York Jets and Cleveland Browns, in the second quarter the Browns needed seven yards on third down. Wide

*From *Management Accounting,* March 1973, pp. 43–47. Reprinted by permission of the publisher.

receiver Gary Collins raced down the right sideline, trying to elude the two Jet defenders who were double-covering him, when suddenly his teammate, tight end Milt Morin, curled over the middle to take the pass and make the first down with several yards to spare. After the play had ended, it was obvious to nearly everyone watching that Collins was in fact a decoy and Morin had been the intended receiver all along.

A thorough analysis of the Browns' tendencies by the Jets could possibly have nullified the completion. The Browns at the time were primarily a pattern team, executing most of their pass plays according to predetermined plans, which incorporated their field position, the down, the yardage needed to gain a first down, the game situation, and anticipated defense. If the Jets had sufficiently familiarized themselves with the Browns' *modus operandi*, they would have known that the Browns, who led by a touchdown at the time, rarely use the long pass on third down, instead relying on short passes to the backs and to the tight end. With this knowledge, the Jets could have played percentage ball by assigning a single man to cover Collins, thus freeing the other defensive back to assist in the coverage on Morin.

This situation illustrates a fact of modern football life. The sport is structured in such a way that careful acquisition and evaluation of the observable details associated with each play can lead to meaningful trends analysis. In fact, most coaches, on all levels of the sport, compile some statistics or frequency counts which convey information on their opponents as well as themselves. Unfortunately, to accomplish this task manually in a thorough and complete manner is time consuming to the extent of being impossible in the practical world of winning football.

The application of data processing to professional sports is developing quite rapidly.[1] In football, computer technology finds an opportunity to provide a practical and valuable assist to the coaching method in the area of strategy preparation. While it is standard operating procedure to review the films of previous games and to chart tendencies in a variety of situations, data processing methods can nevertheless lead to inadequate and even misleading information. The purpose of this article is to compare certain accounting and information systems concepts with analogous concepts in professional football. The authors feel that fundamentally the basic problems of data accumulation and retrieval in business and professional football are very similar.

## THE REPORTING FUNCTION

... Implicit in [accounting] statements is the importance of the accountant's reporting function. The task of the accountant is to observe, interpret, summarize, and communicate data in a form which will enable the user of the data to evaluate, control, plan, and even predict performance.

Exhibit 1 presents a "matrix of communication"[2] developed on the premise that accounting is a function of communication processes. Although this model was

[1]For a review of several computer applications in athletics, see J. Gerry Purdy, "Sports and EDP ... It's a New Ball Game," *Datamation,* June 1, 1971.

[2]Norton M. Bedford and Vahe Baladouni, "A Communication Theory Approach to Accountancy," *The Accounting Review,* October 1962, p. 653.

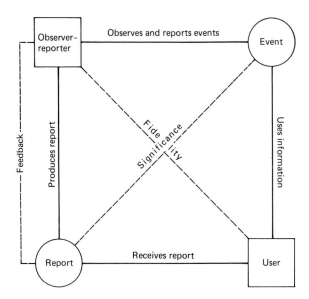

**Exhibit 1**    The matrix of communication.

originally developed as a description of the financial reporting process, it is applicable to the management accounting process and the game of football as well. In its original form, the model stresses the importance of the accountant's reporting function. It is the task of the accountant to prepare accounting reports which will transmit meaningful data to decision makers. To accomplish this purpose, the accountant must first ascertain the type of data required by the users of the reports. The needs of these users must be the guiding principle for the accountant in the preparation of his report.

These same concepts are also applicable to professional football. The scout observing a future opponent gathers information which can be used to prepare meaningful reports. These reports transmit informative data to the coaching staff, who use them in planning for the next game. In order to accomplish this purpose, the scout must also first ascertain, in some detail, the information needs of the coaching staff. As in the case with accounting statements, the needs of users must be the guiding principle in the preparation of the report. The parallel relationship of the information needs in a business situation and in professional football are presented in outline form in Exhibit 2.

## THE PROBE CONCEPT

To meet the information needs of football coaches, PROBE was conceived as a means of utilizing the computer to process and evaluate football data.[3] It is a generalized report generating system for application in football strategy analysis. This concept is

---

[3]The system was developed by Frank Ryan Computer Services in conjunction with the Chi Corporation of Cleveland, Ohio.

**Exhibit 2  Parallel Relationship of Information Needs**

| MATRIX COMPONENT | BUSINESS | FOOTBALL |
|---|---|---|
| 1. The matrix of communication situation | This represents the composition and workings of the economic system (both within and without the firm) in which the communication situation of accountancy takes place. | This represents the composition and workings of football in which the communication of information takes place. |
| 2. The four basic elements of the communication situation | | |
| a. The event circle | This circle represents the world of economic events of a business enterprise. | This circle represents a football game (or games). |
| b. The observer-reporter square | This square represents the accountant. The accountant is to be thought of as comprising the entire accounting staff of the firm as well as the firm's external auditors. | This square represents the scout. The scout is to be thought of as representing the entire coaching staff of a team. |
| c. The report circle | This circle represents the accounting reports and financial statements of a firm. | This circle represents the scouting reports of a team. |
| d. The user square | This square represents the user of accounting statements both internal and external. | This square represents the user of the scouting reports, the coaching staff. |
| 3. The direction of information flow | The direction of information flow is indicated by the arrows along the horizontal and vertical lines (counter-clockwise). | The direction of information flow is indicated by the arrows along the horizontal and vertical lines (counter-clockwise). |
| 4. The relationships among the elements | | |
| a. Event to observer-reporter | This is the relationship between the accountant (observer-reporter) and the world of economic events (event) of a business enterprise. | This is the relationship between the scout (observer-reporter) and the football game (or games) (event). |
| b. Observer-reporter to report | This is the relationship between the accountant (observer-reporter) and the accounting statements (report). | This is the relationship between the scout (observer-reporter) and the scouting report (report). |

| | Accounting | Scouting (football) |
|---|---|---|
| c. Report to user | This is the relationship between the user of accounting statements (user) and the accounting statements (report). | This is the relationship between the user of the scouting report (user) accounting statements and the scouting report (report). |
| d. User to event | This is the relationship between the user of accounting statements (user) and the world of socio-economic events (event) of the related business enterprise. | This is the relationship between the user of the scouting report (user) and the subsequent football game (or games) (event). |
| 5. Fidelity | This is the correspondence between what is understood by the user of accounting statements (user) with what the message(s) is (are), or is (are) intended to be, expressed by the accountant (observer-reporter). | This is the correspondence between what is understood by the coaching staff (user) with what the message(s) is (are) or is (are) intended to be, expressed by the scout (observer-reporter). |
| 6. Significance | This is the degree of relevance and adequacy which accounting statements (report) have in relation to the world of economic events (event) they represent. | This is the degree of relevance and adequacy which the scouting reports (report) have in relation to the football game (or games) (event) they represent. |
| 7. Feedback | The accountant (observer-reporter) can accomplish feedback and correction by interpreting to himself the accounting statements (report) he has encoded but not yet released. | The scout (observer-reporter) can accomplish feedback and correction by interpreting to himself the scouting report (report) he has encoded but not yet released. |

Columns one and two of this Exhibit were adapted, with permission, from Norton M. Bedford and Vahe Baladouni, "A Communication Theory Approach to Accountancy," *The Accounting Review*, October 1962, p. 54.

based on the fact that football possesses a great number of easily identifiable characteristics, such as down, distance, field position, relative score, offensive formations, defenses, weather, personnel, etc., all of which are directly related to the decision-making processes of the game. These factors must be evaluated relative to one another in order that new information results.

The system is effected as a multistep operation. First, the coaching staff must define in a precise and consistent fashion the complete terminology that it requires to describe the football events that confront the coaches. Terminology varies from team to team, and in fact the basic structure of football ideas changes from coach to coach. For the main part these terminology schemes are incomplete, serving only to describe what the coach's own team does, not in general what the opponents do. It is not an easy task to establish a precise terminology base which is rich enough to describe all football maneuvers, and which is simple to use in practice.

An input form is prepared which includes all of the basic play terminology required to describe the football factors being analyzed. The design of this input document is critical because of the timing problems involved. Obviously, the more information desired, the more time is required to encode the data. Since the time of the coach or scout encoding the information is limited, it is essential that the input document allow him to gather all of the information needed in the minimum time possible.

The basis of football analysis is the study of game films in which each play is recorded in detail on a separate input form. A professional game will normally include anywhere from 100 to 150 plays, offensive and defensive combined. Films are viewed by a coach (or coaches) and each play is analyzed and recorded. Items which might be included among the encoded information are the following:

1. The number of the play (all plays in the game are numbered sequentially)
2. The down
3. The yardage necessary for a first down
4. The field position
5. The type of formation
6. The type of play
7. Fakes
8. Backfield action
9. Blocking action
10. Patterns run by receivers
11. The configuration of the defensive line
12. The shifting patterns of the defense
13. The operational defensive actions that are repeated
14. The nature of the pass coverage
15. The result of the play
16. Weather
17. Personnel

The information recorded on each input sheet can be transformed in a variety of ways to machine readable form, thus creating a football data base. Each week data is added to the information bank, updating the data base.

At this point it should be noted that the scouting function is often also performed "live." Usually a coach will send one of his assistants to scout a game which involves a future opponent. While this phase of scouting lacks much of the precision found in extracting data from films, it frequently provides an important supplement to the analysis of game films. For example, it provides information on weather, tempo, mood, sideline signals, etc. It should be noted that while "live" scouting depends on the intuitive grasp or feel of the scout, for many years it was the only method teams had of scouting an opponent.

The overall purpose is, of course, to obtain as much information as is possible concerning the specific strengths and weaknesses of an opponent. While each play in a football season is an event that will never specifically recur, the strengths and weaknesses of a team do recur in well defined statistical patterns which are particularly susceptible to trend analysis. Simply put, most football teams normally follow similar patterns of play when confronted with similar situations, modified by predetermined strategies. Thus, for planning purposes in football it is important that detailed information concerning both your opponent and your own team be known to management, i.e., the coaches.

The information desired by the coach should, of course, determine the manner in which the data will be manipulated and also the format of the subsequent report generation. The analysis technique developed must be flexible enough to allow the report to provide answers to the "usual" football analysis questions with minimal effort. It should also be flexible enough to retrieve "unusual" information on command as it is required. Just as is the case in a business situation, the report should fit the needs of the user, rather than fitting the user to the report.

There is the need for a general purpose "standard" report which shows the overall tendencies of, e.g., running game, passing game, and use of personnel. This general report should be sophisticated enough to indicate a profile of the team's operational decisions and tendencies. This type of information depends on the reliability of the football data base. As an example of the type of information that may be learned, the analysis of several games of one team revealed that whenever it encountered a third down situation with the ball between its own fifteen and twenty yard lines on the right side of the field it ran its fullback on a draw play. If this information were available to its opponent, the linebackers could "key" on the fullback in this (and perhaps similar) situations to stop the play before it got started.

In addition to the standardized type of report described above, special reports may be requested according to the relevant needs of the moment. For example, if a coach wished to know by field position, down, and the distance for a first down, where the San Francisco Forty-Niners most frequently throw the screen pass, PROBE could provide the answer in a matter of seconds.

A critical aspect of the report generation phase is the determination of the optimal manner of presenting the information to the user. One coach may prefer a graphical description of the data while another may prefer a detailed listing of successive events that occurred (such as all third down plays, in sequence, run from the left hash mark).

An ideal data bank would be one which includes all aspects of a game, both offensively and defensively, and which could be accumulated with appropriate weighting factors for data acquired in nonstandard situations. Weighting is necessary because a team may appear to have a strong passing attack when playing another team which has a weak pass defense or which has injured players. Another team may appear to be a blitzing team only because its opponent is particularly vulnerable to blitzing. The number of combinations of apparent strengths and weaknesses is large if a specific team is considered in the perspective of its play against other teams. All of these factors should be taken into consideration if accurate analysis is desired. Weighting would be an attempt to provide a standardization of all data accumulated on a specific team against all of its opponents.

Of course, the raw data without weighting would also be available for those coaches who desire it. It does provide a measure of reliable "gross" information. Any football information system should have the capacity to permit the retrieval of the tendencies of a team in a particular situation and to calculate the probability of success or failure based upon previous attempts in the same or similar situations. External factors such as weather, injuries, and other exogeneous playing conditions must also be considered. This type of information requires the continuous analysis of games in order to maintain an information bank which is always current.

As an alternative to using a "query" system which can be specialized from team to team and from report to report, a team might rely on the same "standard" set of reports for analyzing every opponent. If this alternative is chosen, a great deal of care must be exercised because the same reports will be produced each week without regard to the nature of the opponent of the team being scouted or to the specific requirements of the coach. For example, standard reports might be used to describe a team's offensive tendencies without taking into account the defenses upon which the offensive tendencies were shaped. In effect, little emphasis would be placed on different circumstances with misleading information as a possible result. This danger may be compounded if a coach is influenced by the results of a specific report one week because of the favorable results obtained from its use. The use of this report may well yield marginal or even poor results in the future, however, because the future analysis would be based on different criteria.

## CONCLUSION

Just as the impact of the computer has been felt by almost every business in the last two decades, the application of data processing to professional sports has developed quite rapidly in recent years. The computer has been used in professional football in processing scouting reports for individual players (for the pro draft of college players) and for teams (strategy analysis as described above). As is the case in most business-oriented decision situations, the present philosophy of planning in professional football is one of user-preparation of statistics (that is, preparation by the coaches themselves) and subjective decisions which are sometimes based on minimal information. In most business firms, managers have increased their demands for data from the company's information system. More detailed reports are often requested at more frequent time intervals. A parallel situation exists in football: it appears that there is in general a definite need for a more sophisticated football data bank and professionally prepared reports for the use of coaches in their decisions. Just as the manager relies on the information system to collect and process data for decision making (his major function), the football coach would be free to coach without spending time collecting data and preparing reports with a data bank which has been transcribed by an assistant. This would eliminate a substantial part of the timing problem in getting information to the players just as it enables the manager to make his decisions on a timely basis.

## QUESTIONS

1. Recently many university departments of accounting have been renamed to include information systems in their title. What do you think is included in information systems that is not included in accounting?
2. With automation, which accounting records will become less necessary? Why?
3. What is a data bank? What are its merits and its shortcomings?
4. How are the information needs of a football team similar to those of a business?

## SELECTED BIBLIOGRAPHY

"Accountants Losing Ground in EDP," *Accountancy*, April 1975, p. 5.

Clowes, Kenneth W., "Computers and Information Technology," *Management Controls*, July-August 1975, pp. 114-118.

# 142
# ELECTRONIC FUNDS TRANSFER SYSTEMS*
Peter D. Louderback

Electronic Funds Transfer Systems (EFTS) continue to be the glamour baby of the financial industry. The popular acronym has come to be a catchall for almost anything vaguely related to automated processing of financial transactions.

When most people talk about EFTS development, however, they are referring to three basic approaches.

In the banking industry *automated clearing houses* (ACHs) accomplish electronically what Clearing House Associations have been doing manually for years. For instance, when a consumer pays a bill by check, the company's bank that receives the check—if different from the consumer's bank—must deliver the physical document to the consumer's bank in order to receive credit for the funds involved. In many cities,

*From **World**, Spring 1975, pp. 9—14. Reprinted by permission of the publisher.

representatives from all major banks actually sit down several times each day to exchange bundles of checks that are drawn on each other's banks. ACHs are organized to accomplish this check clearing process electronically, rather than through a paper exchange. This expanded use of automation for transaction clearing also allows banks to offer highly automated services to their customers such as direct deposit of payroll, preauthorized payments, and "bill-check," all of which will be explained later in more detail.

Although volume buildups have not been overwhelming, ACHs have their sights set on a specific course. Five ACHs are currently in operation and several more are in the formative stages. A national organization—NACHA (National Association of Automated Clearing Houses)—exists for exchanging standards and enhancing the basic ACH computer programs, as well as providing a communications and guidance vehicle. In time, NACHA—which has recently signed up its 19th regional member—may well provide the communications switching network, to tie the regional ACHs together, though for now, inter-regional transactions data are distributed on magnetic tape, via courier.

*Automated teller machines* (ATMs) are currently being investigated by all segments of the financial industry. ATMs provide the means for consumers to execute various transactions on their accounts without the need for a human teller. These devices range in complexity from a simple Money Machine that dispenses cash when an acceptable plastic card is inserted to multi-transaction on-line minicomputers that actually access and post the appropriate accounts at the customer's direction.

*Point-of-sale* (POS) implementation is perhaps the most revolutionary approach since it offers the opportunity for the consumer to do his banking as he shops—at the supermarket, the pharmacy, or the hardware store. It encompasses anything from the use of a simple touchtone telephone terminal for check or credit authorization to a far more complex system that completes the posting of debits and credits directly from a cash register location. A wide range of businesses may be affected by this development.

Of the three basic categories, the ACH movement seems to be making the greatest headway. The other two approaches still lack definition and direction but should pick up steam significantly toward the end of 1976. This assumes that proposed legislation which would impose a two year moratorium on all new EFTS projects is not enacted.

## AUTOMATED CLEARING HOUSE MOVEMENT

The ACH movement grew out of initial efforts by the major banks in California. As far back as 1966-67, people were talking about a checkless, cashless society, and banks became interested in trying to bail themselves out of the never-ending growth—estimated by some at 7% a year—in the volume of paper checks being processed. Given additional impetus from the Treasurer of Santa Clara County who wanted to implement direct payroll deposit for all County employees, 10 banks sat down and put together a plan for developing a statewide automated clearing house.

In August of 1972, CACHA (California Automated Clearing House Association) was incorporated, covering both of the existing California-based Clearing House Associations—in San Francisco and Los Angeles. After a year and a half of negotiating, the Federal Reserve, the government arm with overall responsibility for the clearing of checks, reluctantly agreed to participate in the project but only with certain stipulations. They were: that all commercial banks in California had to be invited to join, regardless of whether they had computers; that the computer programs had to be made available to any other groups that might express an interest, and that "on-us" transactions, where both the debit and the credit involved only one bank, need not be transmitted to the ACH.

A special committee—called the SCOPE (Special Committee on Paperless Entries)— was established to contract for and provide guidance in development of computer programs and procedures to be used by the ACH. That computer package—also called SCOPE—has become the standard base for all subsequent ACH operations.

At the moment, there are said to be 38 groups nationwide which are in various stages of ACH implementation and planning. After California, the movement spread into Georgia, New England, and the Upper Midwest (specifically, Minneapolis, St. Paul). The most recent arrivals on the scene are Columbus, Kansas City, and Baltimore. The Baltimore group—called the Mid-Atlantic ACH—was the first to invite mutual savings banks to join. Savings and loan associations will seek memberships when and if they are permitted to offer checking account services—a privilege sought by many.

Although the number of transactions to date has been relatively small, the ACH movement is beginning to develop momentum. Member banks appear to be taking greater interest in marketing the services made possible by ACHs. The real payoff is in automating those activities with high check volumes and low average dollar values— payroll, consumer bill paying, etc. rather than transactions that occur less often such as only those among business concerns. The major cost to the participating banks is their own marketing campaigns. Other EFTS approaches require an investment in hardware and systems development as well as marketing.

As regional ACH operations grow, the framework is already in place for eventual electronic clearing on a national basis. NACHA is currently providing a communication vehicle for advising all interested parties on new developments and software changes.

At the moment, ACH members are pushing three basic types of services:

*Direct deposit of payroll (DDP)*—In its conceptual form the employer obtains authorization, bank name, and account number from each of his participating employees and enters them into the system via his bank—the originating bank. At a designated time before payday, the employer delivers a magnetic tape of payroll data for all employees whose accounts are to be credited directly. (He also continues to deliver earnings statements to all his employees on payday, regardless of whether or not they participate in the DDP program.) The originating bank automatically debits the employer's account for the total amount of his DDP payroll; credits those employee accounts that reside at that bank, and generates a new tape of data for all the banks involved, along with authorization to debit the originating bank's reserves. It then delivers the tape to the ACH—located at a Federal Reserve computer processing center. The ACH generates new tapes or computer listings for all banks involved in that particular payroll, having sorted the data appropriately so that each bank receives its own data as well as data for its correspondent banks. The employee receives no deposit receipt except for the entry on his normal monthly bank statement.

One of the problems (and the reason the method has not had overwhelming success) is that most of the benefit in DDP accrues to the banks, and some to the employees. The employer realizes only a slight payoff in savings that many perceive as not offsetting what is known as the lost "float." Normally, when an employer issues paychecks he calculates the percentage of total payroll that will remain uncashed for each day thereafter, thus remaining in the employer's account as float on the checks he has issued. DDP eliminates that float because the employer's account is debited immediately and credited to the employees' accounts at their respective banks. The banks thereby gain the float that the employer has lost.

Some of the other stumbling blocks for employers revolve around the need to continue operating the traditional check payroll system as well. Not all employees choose to participate in a DDP program; in fact, participation rates are generally well below 50%. And not all employees' banks are ACH members, for one reason or another, so the employer is often unable to offer DDP to all employees without utilizing a third system—the mail.

The real impetus for DDP has come from the Federal government. The Air Force, for example, has been the pioneer in the area. It began offering a DDP program about 15 to 20 years ago and has been emphasizing it even more since 1971. Current participation is 48% of the military and 53% of the civilian payroll, with the entire operation centralized in Denver. The Air Force is currently changing its DDP distribution vehicle from the U.S. Postal Service to the Federal Reserve System. With 51,000 active duty pay accounts currently opting for the DDP program, the Air Force hopes to make this sytem mandatory at some point which would—even at the current participation level—save an estimated $1 million a year on payroll distribution.

The Treasury Department is following the Air Force's lead by starting implementation of Social Security benefit payments in the same fashion. In November 1974, the Treasury began a pilot operation in Georgia by inserting notifications in the Social Security checks describing the benefits and procedures for having the checks deposited automatically in a check or savings account. While the response was lower than expected, Treasury is going ahead as planned and will expand the project to other areas of the country this summer. The system will not be automated electronically until late 1975 or early 1976. The payoff in this particular case is as much in curtailing the number of lost and stolen Social Security checks as it is in reducing check processing and mailing expenses.

The government is definitely espousing the direct deposit idea. Plans are to expand from Social Security and the Air Force to other government payrolls—Civil Service retirement, Veterans Administration benefits, railroad retirement payments, and so on down the list, even, hopefully, to welfare. In total, the U.S. government is currently producing some 40 million checks each month.

The ultimate effect of all these DDP programs may well be to increase the number of people who have checking accounts. This, too, offers benefits to the financial institutions and the banks are really looking to the government for leadership in direct deposit of payroll.

*Preauthorized payment services*—with the exception of mortgage and loan payments, which banks have long offered as automatic internal debits, the only area where preauthorized payments are beginning to catch on is insurance. The leader is The Equitable Life Insurance Society which has been automating a preauthorized payments system that it already used for its 600,000 life insurance premium accounts. Working with the Chase Manhattan Bank, Equitable now processes 27,000 preauthorized debit transactions monthly. The participating banks—those holding Equitable accounts—generate magnetic tapes containing the preauthorized insurance payments each month and send them to Chase, which removes and posts the data for its own customers' accounts and generates new tapes for three other banks in New York and for three ACHs which are involved.

According to one source, working out the original software package and the mechanics of the whole operation with Chase took only eight months from initial discussion to the processing of the first 6,000 transactions in June of 1973. Equitable estimates that the breakeven point should come sometime in the third quarter of this year when it expects to reach 80,000 electronic debits a month. Total development cost to that point will have been $100,000 to $125,000 for Equitable.

The insurance giant justifies this pioneering effort on the basis of potential cost savings, smoother flow, and improved public relations. Other companies are beginning to follow in Equitable's footsteps. The best candidates are those who already have some established preauthorized payments system that can simply be automated. Here, as elsewhere in EFTS, no one is yet willing to embark on a vast program of consumer education. A dynamic marketing program is also needed but not yet emphasized.

*Bill-check*—This system has had little success so far and there are many who do not consider it a viable approach. A major example of this approach is The South East Bankcard Association. SEBA began by capturing its customers' bank account numbers during the normal payment process one month. It then included, in the next month's statements, an explanation of the bill-check process and requested verification of the bank account data it had collected. The participating consumer now receives his bill each month with a space for indicating the amount to be paid and his signature and can simply return this portion of the bill without including a check. The credit company then credits the customers' accounts as it normally would and generates a magnetic tape for its bank. This originating bank posts the debits to its customers' accounts and generates a new tape for the ACH, in a manner similar to the DDP process.

The primary problems of the method have been twofold. Large national companies who might be expected to lead such a trend are not interested in doing it in only one or two isolated states and small companies cannot afford to take on the massive job of consumer education. And, the benefits of a bill-check system appear to, again, accrue primarily to the banks, leaving the companies that might use it with little motivation to undertake such a project.

## AUTOMATED TELLER MACHINES

In contrast to the quietly forward-moving ACH sector of the EFTS evolution, the once frantic move by banks and savings and loan association to install ATMs is now at something of a standstill. With approximately 2500 ATMs and cash dispensers installed to date, even the suppliers admit they expect no spectacular growth in this area for 1975.

At more than $30,000 a unit just for the equipment, such an investment requires significant justification, especially in the hard times of today's economy. Those currently installed have primarily served as marketing gimmicks for the banks, but few banks have honestly convinced themselves that any new business has resulted from their expenditure.

The real advantage of ATMs is the ease with which a bank can extend at least some of its services to locations more convenient for its customers—at far less cost than the bricks and mortar investment involved with establishing a conventional branch. Current controversy on whether the installation of such a remote terminal constitutes a branch or whether it is merely an extension of a bank's services must be resolved before large numbers of such installations will appear.

Some say the ultimate impetus to increasing the use of remote ATMs will be the sharing of these devices among several financial institutions at places like airports, subway stations, shopping centers and so on. Although large commercial banks will merely view this phenomenon as wiping out the marketing advantage they might have gained by peppering the countryside with ATMs, sharing of these facilities will make participation much more affordable for the smaller banks and thrift institutions. But if the establishment of remote ATMs is controversial at the outset, sharing of these facilities is even more so. The several existing joint pilot installations—primarily operated by thrift institutions—are under constant attack from the competition.

Total on-line ATM implementation requires a number of significant phases:

Customer held posting records such as the savings passbook must be replaced by a statement prepared at regular intervals by the computer. ATMs do not accommodate a passbook.

A Central Information File (CIF) must be developed and this can take several years. This project is akin to other businesses' projects to implement data base management systems. Most commercial banks—except for some large or highly innovative medium-sized ones—are still in the pre-CIF development stage.

If ATMs are a definite part of the total plan, the financial institution should be undertaking the process of introducing debit or credit plastic cards and building up some use for them. This step alone can take many months because a whole marketing campaign is involved. It is interesting to note that banks that have strongly opposed the plastic card in the past are now getting on the band wagon and offering one. It has now become a necessary service for an aggressive financial institution. Most existing ATMs are off-line and thus not connected with the computer.

Terminals must be installed at human teller locations and this perhaps is another one-year effort. Not only must the bank invest in hardware, but it has to delve into the whole data communications area. And the installation of terminals require significant training time, not to mention all the bugs that don't show up until regular daily use begins.

The problems with ATM market growth are economic and legal. Commercial banks for the most part have little desire to make the kind of investment involved in this effort. They look for significant return in terms of cost savings from terminal installations at teller windows, but have seen no real savings to date. Their moves in the direction of ATM installation are primarily reactions to the competition they are experiencing or anticipating from S&Ls and other commercial banks in their own areas of operations. Thrift institutions in general are much further down the on-line systems development road and see ATMs as a means of getting around their legislated inability to offer demand deposit accounts. To the extent that they can increase their deposit base by attracting new accounts through the convenience of ATMs, they are aggressively pursuing this approach—primarily at the expense of their counterparts in commercial banking.

Several recent experiments in ATM implementation are of particular note:

First National City Bank in New York, the nation's second largest bank with assets of about $55.5 billion, began customer education by issuing plastic cards and installing machines for account balance inquiries. Surprisingly, they observed a number of people who seem to make special trips to the bank just to look at their bank balances. People seem to be intrigued with this capability.

City National Bank in Columbus, Ohio, opened a totally automated branch in a new office building. Its experience with cash dispensers began in the Spring of 1970 when it installed one in each of its branches. These went on line in late 1972 and this latest move utilizes two kiosks with four ATMs each—all four operating from one controller—and four more outside the bank for 24-hour service. Human tellers have moved from behind-the-counter, stand-up, clerical positions to desk locations as "financial advisers." City National will extend this concept to its other branches in the next few months and hopes to be able to install units in free-standing locations like factories as well.

Chase Manhattan Bank has installed an ATM in its branch at Grand Central Station in New York and feels that convenience of location is a particularly important factor in building up use of the devices.

The Wilmington Savings Fund Society, a mutual savings bank, has installed cash dispensers as part of an overall program. WSFS's own plastic card can be used not only at the bank's own 18 dispensers but also at 18 others installed by the Delaware Trust Company through a reciprocal agreement.

The Exchange Systems, Inc., a corporation owned by 16 S&Ls and mutual savings banks in Washington state, has an experimental shared ATM installation in a shopping center in Bellevue, Washington. Washington is one of the most liberal banking states, specifically permitting both statewide branching and shared remote facilities. In addition, mutual savings banks are permitted and have full consumer lending power though, as yet, they cannot offer third-party payment facilities. State-chartered S&Ls are allowed both consumer lending and third-party payment facilities.

## POINT-OF-SALE IMPLEMENTATION

If the name of the EFTS game from the banks' point of view is to cut down on paperwork, shift the data entry burden to someone else, and increase convenience (in hopes of adding new customer accounts at the lowest possible cost), then the real EFTS payoff is at the point-of-sale (POS) terminal.

Grocers and other retailers cash more checks every year than banks do, so the bulk of the paperwork begins there. By using plastic cards, the bank can have the retail organization's employees enter the credit or debit data at the checkout counter or check cashing stand. The notion is that consumers will find it more convenient to do simple banking functions at the store rather than making a trip to the bank.

One of the most interesting experiments in this area involves the First Federal Savings and Loan of Lincoln, Nebraska, which has installed very simple terminals in all five Hinky Dinky grocery stores in Lincoln. The institution's cardholding customers can cash checks and make deposits at any of these Hinky Dinky locations.

The customer presents his card and fills in a transaction form at the check-cashing counter. The store's employee then connects the terminal to First Federal, has it read and transmit data from the card's magnetic stripe, enters the type of transaction and amount, and waits for an audio response verification and authorization. First Federal's computer meanwhile transfers the amount given from the consumer's account to Hinky Dinky's—in the case of a withdrawal—or vice versa for a deposit. The store honors the transaction, confident that it is valid. Hinky Dinky is by far the largest grocery chain in Lincoln, and First Federal claims to have added a significant number of new accounts as a result. The project acts as a very cheap way of branching for First Federal without really adding more than a $500 terminal and some software and communications lines. The next phases will add both new locations and new services, such as bill paying.

Other POS experiments relate primarily to credit card use. Four large New York banks, for example, have collaborated on an experimental switch for their Bank-Americard and Master Charge credit authorization.

Many others are already poised, ready for action, in this area. Western Savings in Phoenix and Gem City Savings in Dayton, Ohio, have established complete branches in local supermarkets. Out in Portland, Oregon, Fred Myer, owner of Fred Myer, Inc., a retail chain dealing in everything from food to toys, bought a $3 million S&L last spring, which he renamed Fred Myer Savings and Loan. The former three-man, one-branch, institution now has five more locations—four of them in retail outlets—and has already grown to $10 million in assets. Sears also has an S&L in one of its Chicago stores and has been a part of the financial services market for years.

## THE ROADBLOCKS

The EFTS evolution is an inevitability. Almost anyone in or close to the banking and retail industries will agree that the wheels are irrevocably in motion. (To quote Michigan's Bank Commissioner Richard J. Francis, one of the more knowledgeable opponents of the uncontrolled spread of EFTS, "How do you unscramble an egg after the omelet has been made?") But a number of roadblocks must be circumvented or eliminated before unhindered forward progress can proceed.

The problems are not technological. ACHs can operate and are operating smoothly. ATMs—branches or free standing—are an established fact. POS data capture has been done for credit as well as debit transaction substitutes for cash without too much difficulty. The equipment, communications, software, and plastic card technology are all here.

What's standing in the way is primarily a fearful anticipation regarding the changes EFTS may effect on the nation's banking structure—perhaps, even the whole structure of the American economy.

At the moment, it is apparent that EFTS is taking off in all directions at once and that sufficient roadblocks exist in the ATM and POS areas to keep widespread growth at a minimum for at least the next year or two. Even without all the regulatory and legislative hangups EFTSs will face, consumer education will still cause progress to be extremely slow.

## QUESTIONS

1. What are ACHs, ATMs, and POS?
2. What are the effects of automation on control?
3. In an automated system how will end-of-period adjustments be prepared? Trial balances? Financial statements? How will subsidiary ledgers be proved?
4. What is the EFTS evolution?

## SELECTED BIBLIOGRAPHY

Walsh, J. P., "Computers, Privacy and the Law," *The Australian Accountant*, October 1975, pp. 537-544.

# 143
# TOWARDS THE PREVENTION OF FRAUD*
Helen Fearnley

EDITORS' NOTE: This selection complements Selection 133.

Although most American certified public accountants (like many of their British colleagues) insist that top management fraud is virtually impossible to detect, because the outside auditor's work *depends* fundamentally both on management integrity and

*From *Accountancy,* April 1975, p. 4. Reprinted by permission of the publisher.

co-operation, there is no doubt that in the wake of recent scandals such as Equity Funding they now put their case somewhat less convincingly.

Using attack as one of the best means of defence, they maintain that an audit designed to achieve such an (impossible) degree of detection would be prohibitively time-consuming and expensive. But that is what the man in the street believes an audit provides—a system which detects and prevents fraud. And danger lies in a profession failing to live up to public expectations. Touche Ross & Co, in America one of the big eight accounting firms, has done something to grapple with the problem. It has published a set of SEC-approved guidelines as to the sort of situations most likely to foster (or hide) fraud of various kinds. The guidelines include a list of 12 points— special business conditions or economic factors—that might encourage management to present a falsely optimistic picture of transactions. Among them are: insufficient working capital or credit; an urgent desire for good earnings to support a company's share price; dependence upon few products, customers or transactions; management domination by one man or a few individuals; inadequate internal audit staff and controls; and highly diversified operations, each division having its own accounting system.

According to Mr. Robert S. Kay, Touche Ross & Co's director of accounting and professional standards: in 99% of cases where management might have a vested interest in certain transactions, there is no deliberate attempt to mislead the auditors. But the remaining 1% includes those scandals which have shaken—and some which may still severely try—people's faith in auditors and audit methods.

Nor does Touche Ross regard as exhaustive the measures set out. 'We are not trying to peel every grape', says Touche Ross partner Mr W. Donald Georgen, 'but we will be looking at all material transactions in greater depth'. Which is quite understandable, since Touche Ross, as auditor of US Financial, the big Californian financial conglomerate and real estate developer, came in for some criticism from the SEC when the US Financial former top officers were charged last year with fraud. The firm agreed to submit to a national 'peer review' of its methods by a panel of CPAs. It also agreed to speed up work on formal procedures for cases where management might have an undisclosed interest in transactions. The guidelines are the result.

Under them, in cases of possible vested interest, where the company's board of directors are all insiders, Touche Ross suggests that an outside legal opinion would be needed. In cases where companies change accountants, or where two or more firms are used to audit different branches of the business (Equity Funding provides a glaring example of both), Touche Ross will insist that the accountants ask each other about management involvement. And where Touche Ross tax or management services are used by the corporation, the firm's personnel will also be questioned about potential conflict situations.

A review of the effectiveness of the measures will be made after they have been tested in operation. And Touche Ross are right, for unless the profession as a whole does adopt this ever-vigilant approach—unless it takes its responsibility to detect and prevent fraud seriously—it will lose face in the business community.

## QUESTIONS

1. What are the Touche Ross & Co. guidelines for detecting management fraud?
2. According to the guidelines, what should an auditor do in the following situations:
   a. All company directors are insiders.
   b. The company uses the auditing firm's tax and management services.
   c. Two or more auditing firms audit different branches of the division.
3. What is "the man in the street's" belief about an audit and fraud?

# 144

## UNSAFE COMBINATION
### Crooks and Computers*
N. R. Kleinfield

A story in this newspaper two years ago reported that what bothered many people about computer-assisted thefts was the simplicity of the fraud schemes that had then come to light. Brandt Allen, an associate professor in the University of Virginia graduate school of business, was quoted as saying:

One cannot help but wonder what the really clever people are doing.

Well, now we know.

The Equity Funding scandal, probably the biggest fraud involving a computer in business history, focuses new attention on an uncomfortable fact of life in today's business world: Computers make fraud easier to commit—for someone who controls them or knows how to run them—because computer fraud is harder to detect than the old-fashioned kind.

Furthermore, "a virtually unlimited amount of money can be taken without any increase in the danger of being detected," says Donn Parker, a computer-crime student at Stanford Research Institute in California.

### THE OPEN WINDOW

"Once you've built a window into a system," Mr. Parker explains, "It's there permanently, and large amounts or small amounts of money can pass through that window over a period of time without any change in risk. The level of controls is the same regardless of the amount involved."

*From the *Wall Street Journal,* Apr. 26, 1973, pp. 1 and 15. Reprinted by permission of the publisher.

When more crooks realize this, computer-security experts figure, the thefts are going to get larger. Joseph Wasserman, head of Computer Audit-Systems, Inc., a consultant firm in New Jersey, says:

"As computer systems grow more sophisticated, and as it takes more know-how, those who can pull off a theft are going to dip in for bigger and bigger amounts."

The booty already includes some large sums and some interesting techniques:

In the Equity Funding case, it now appears, phony customers' pledges of phony mutual-fund shares as collateral for phony loans to finance the purchase of many millions of dollars in phony insurance ultimately became numbers on a computer tape, which then printed out phony assets, enabling the company to report steadily increasing earnings.

Only a few weeks before the Equity Funding case broke, the chief teller at a branch of the Union Dime Savings Bank in New York was charged with stealing more than $1.5 million from the banks deposits. He allegedly shuffled hundreds of accounts and fed false information into the bank's computer so that the accounts appeared untampered with whenever quarterly interest payments were due.

A clerk at Morgan Guaranty Trust Co., New York, was convicted in June 1971 of embezzling $33,000. He had directed the bank's computer to issue dividend checks in the names of some former shareholders who had sold their stock in corporations for which Morgan acted as transfer agent. The checks were all sent to the address of an accomplice, who deposited them. The computer was used again to erase all record of the dividend checks having been issued.

Just how many cases of computer theft haven't been detected is, naturally, unknown. And while there are no definitive statistics on the detected cases, they are reported by security experts to be on the rise everywhere, often eating into the cost savings that computers provide. Donn Parker, the computer-crime researcher, says, "Business has probably never been so vulnerable to theft."

It isn't defenseless, however. The security experts recommend a number of counterattacks, including care in hiring.

## WHY IT'S EASIER

Computer theft is easier than the old-fashioned kind because, in places where computers are used, many of the bookkeeping procedures that used to help trip up swindlers don't exist any more. Not on paper anyway. The computer itself performs a lot of them—with the aid of a kindly, or perhaps felonious, programmer.

A programmer is someone who writes, in computer language, a series of instructions that, when fed into a computer, cause it to perform a series of operations. In short, a programmer sets up a computer to do what it's supposed to do when a computer operator, who may or may not be the programmer, operates it.

Now, a computer leaves a printed record of its activities, called a printout, and it is printouts that accountants rely on in auditing the books. But as computer systems operate faster and faster, telescoping several operations into one, they produce fewer and fewer printouts.

Therefore, much of what goes on inside a computer never appears on a printout. If a computer's program is changed to include, say, a fraudulent $2,000 payment to John Doe, and then is changed back to the original program, there will be no printed record that the program was ever changed.

## PROGRAMMING FOR DARKNESS

Even if it isn't changed back, the auditor may not detect that the change wasn't legitimate. And even the original program could have been faulty, intentionally or not. The average auditor will be able to see that a computer was told to do something and that it did it. But that in itself won't tell him whether the computer *should* have been told to do it.

What's more, a computer can be programmed to keep an auditor in the dark. A computer at Equity Funding's life-insurance subsidiary was reportedly programmed to overlook fictitious policies on some of its runs.

Moreover, it is known that just before authorities swooped down to seize the insurance subsidiary, someone reprogrammed the computer to switch the designation of bogus accounts and mislead investigators. Former Equity employes had told investigators to check into "Department 99." But as a result of the computer manipulation, within minutes some 56,000 false insurance policies were swept from Department 99 into Department 92. The result was to steer examiners away from the connection between the parent, which recorded phony loans to nonexistent policy-holders, and the insurance subsidiary, which wrote phony policies.

It was true even in the days before computers that auditors could be misled or kept in the dark. But there were more double-checks then—ledgers here, ledgers there, written records of supplies coming in and cash going out, perhaps an occasional erasure. (One double-check then that is still fully available now is the spot check on the existence or nonexistence of claimed assets, a tool that some accountants say might have proved useful in the case of Equity Funding.)

The security experts say that so many of the double-checks have been eliminated today and so much of the record-keeping is centralized in the brain of the computer, that a crook can perpetrate a major theft armed with nothing but a few seconds' access to a computer and the ability to tell it what to do. He doesn't even need a pencil.

It is such a clean operation that the vast majority of detected thefts involving computers have been detected more by accident than by design. For example:

A former employe evidently sounded the alarm on Equity Funding. If he hadn't, the maneuvers might have gone undetected for years, as the manipulators thought they would.

The Union Dime teller, Roswell Steffen, was a heavy bettor on professional basketball games and horse races, the police say, and he happened to place his bets with a bookmaking operation that later came under police investigation. During a raid, detectives confiscated records showing that the teller was betting $30,000 a day. So they kept an eye on him.

The Morgan Guaranty clerk, Thomas Potocnie, and his accomplice, Frederich Otto, tripped themselves up when, still using former shareholders' names and Otto's address, they issued themselves Johnson & Johnson stock after the firm declared a stock split. They then sold the stock, and when the canceled shares came back to the bank—the transfer agent—someone noticed that the new Johnson & Johnson stock had been sent to a "shareholder" who had sold his stock before the split was declared and therefore didn't qualify to participate in the split. An investigation into this happenstance uncovered the fraud. If Potocnie and Otto had settled for dividends instead of selling the stock, they might never have been caught.

## CONDUCTING THE DEFENSE

To make things tougher for crooks, the computer specialists recommend a variety of safeguards. They include the following:

1. Closely screen applicants for jobs as programmers. This is particularly important today, the experts say, when the demand for programmers is increasing.

2. Don't let a computer's programmer be its operator too. The reasoning here is that a crook is less likely to succeed if, after programming a machine for fraud, he must rely on another operator's allowing the machine to slip him money.

3. Segregate computerized check-writing operations from the departments that authorize checks, thus making it tougher for an embezzler to convert fake data into checks.

4. Frequently switch both programmers and operators to different machines and programs. The security experts say an employee may decide against undertaking a fraud if he knows he won't be working on a machine long enough to drain it of very much money.

Whatever slips through such safeguards is supposed to be caught by auditors. But, according to data-processing specialists, crooks won't find it hard to fool any auditor who doesn't understand computers. These specialists urge, therefore, that companies rely on "computer auditors"—auditors who have been trained as programmers—to inspect their books. Such auditors wouldn't simply use printouts. They would start from scratch in checking the accounts.

Perhaps a dozen computer-security firms each have a few of these computer auditors. Most auditing companies also have a few. At the moment, then, there are far from enough to meet the potential demand.

## A CHANGE IN PROGRAM

Perhaps the toughest chore confronting auditors is determining whether a computer program has ever been changed dishonestly, then changed back. Research is being conducted on this problem. Meanwhile, security specialists suggest techniques that might spot dishonest changes that haven't been changed back.

One technique is to program a computer to spot a certain type of irregularity—any transaction, say, larger than a particular amount—and to immediately print out a copy of the transaction for auditors to inspect.

Another technique is to feed a fictitious account into a computer and keep an eye on it. This would guard against someone's siphoning off money from all accounts but wouldn't guard against theft from just certain accounts unless a crook was unlucky enough to pick the fictitious account to loot.

Security experts say that computer manufacturers have failed to incorporate enough security checks into their systems and that the manufacturers are thus partly to blame for computer vulnerability. Some manufacturers now have begun to give the subject more attention.

International Business Machines Corp., the largest computer manufacturer, began a $40 million research program last May and says it will report its initial findings this June.

One form of computer that is especially vulnerable to outsiders is the "time-sharing" unit used by many customers. To try to curb this deficiency, Honeywell Inc. last January introduced a new version of its Multics time-sharing system, a version that it calls the most secure computer system available.

Under the system, a company controls, by a method of its own devising—say a combination of passwords and account numbers—the accessibility of its Multics file segment to another user. And a user is continuously monitored to make sure he is tapping into the proper segment. The first commercial shipments are scheduled early next year.

## QUESTIONS

1. Why is it easier to conceal theft with a computer than with a manual bookkeeping system?

2. Give illustrations of computer thefts that have been uncovered.

3. What are four safeguards against computer theft?

4. Why is a "time-sharing" computer particularly vulnerable to theft?

## SELECTED BIBLIOGRAPHY

"Computer Security," *ELE*, Summer 1974, pp. 2, 4, 5, and 7-9.

"Computer Security," *World*, Spring 1974, p. 57.

"Fraud: Conning by Computer," *Newsweek*, Apr. 23, 1973, pp. 90 and 93.

# 145

## PUTTING PIZZAZ IN OUR PROFESSION*
Roger F. Pickering

Dear Mr. Editor:

In his recent report, Elmer Otte, our public relations consultant, states that we need more contact with the press, educators, and the general public. His conclusions should come as no surprise to the profession. The generally accepted version of the accountant is almost classic; unimaginative, flinthearted, pot-bellied and penurious, but a whiz at figures!!

The prototype is, of course, Ebenezer Scrooge, the surviving partner of the Counting House of Scrooge and Marley, whose image was scarcely redeemed by his turnabout on Christmas morning. The Scrooge image of the CPA has been nourished ever since Dickens, by countless authors and playwrights who find it convenient, if not derigueur, to use an accountant when they need a character that is, well—a clod.

When it comes to PR, other professions back accountants right off the map. On TV, for example, you can hardly turn on your set without finding a show based on medicine or law. What we need is a TV series in which a CPA is the central figure, a la Marcus Welby, M.D. or Owen Marshall.

In the show I envision, our hero, a CPA, would be presented a difficult situation and in 60 minutes, with time out for commercials, would carry the day. A typical plot would have our man (probably played by Paul Newman) saving a company treasurer from divorce, alcoholism and the axe by reorganizing the accounting department and chopping out 17 jobs. In the closing scene, the President, Treasurer and our Star toast the New Year with *lemonade* at the office Christmas party as dismissal notices are passed out to the displaced employees.

If this surefire concept could not be sold in prime time, perhaps a more modest start could be made on daytime TV, with a soap opera format and a CPA firm setting. The typical sequence would have Ms. Peabody, a junior, and the managing partner, Mr. Winkle, falling in love while amortizing good will. Mr. Winkle is about to leave his wife for Ms. Peabody when she turns up pregnant.

But, wait a minute, Mrs. Winkle has been seeing the tax man, Mr. Keystone (hint, hint) and it looks like the old switcheroo is coming up. Then Keystone splits for New Zealand and . . .

You get the idea.

Space does not permit a discourse on other image building ploys, such as adding Golf as a fifth part to the CPA exam. (In case you haven't noticed, our golf outings are an encyclopedia of shanks, slices, duck hooks and other public displays of ineptness.) If we put our minds to it, surely we can raise the status of our profession to a point where at least some of our members can evoke such remarks as "Isn't that what's-his-name, the CPA?"

*From *Wisconsin CPA,* December 1974, p. 29. Reprinted by permission of the publisher.

QUESTION

1. Relate what Mr. Pickering says about "image" to the comments of Professor Pattillo (Selection 134).

# 146
## PROFESSIONAL PROBLEMS*
Walter E. Hanson

EDITORS' NOTE: Mr. Hanson is managing partner of Peat, Marwick, Mitchell, the largest of the Big Eight firms. He left the firm to go into industry and then returned to the firm.

Q: What do you consider to be the major problems confronting the accounting profession?

A: One of the greatest is simply getting the various firms to work together on the solution to problems of the profession. In the past, everyone has gone in their own direction with not enough concern for what is best for the profession over the long term. That's one of the reasons for the demise of the Accounting Principles Board; there was a lack of cooperation between the Big Eight firms themselves.

Another major problem is legal liability. There has to be some limitation or the profession is in real trouble. This is not at all to say that any of us feel we should have *carte blanche.* Obviously, if we make a mistake we should pay for it. But there has to be some relationship between the fee involved, the magnitude of the engagement, and the liability.

Q: Doesn't this sword of liability hanging over your heads make you want to reduce the amount of required work?

A: A lot of people in the profession don't want to take on additional responsibility for fear of liability. I don't view it that way personally. I feel we should expand our professional responsibility and try to make people understand what we do. If they have a better understanding of what a review is, or what an audit is, then we'll reduce our liability as this becomes known. Just to sit in fear and do nothing seems to make no sense at all to me.

Again, it goes back to the idea of reducing the liability. Accounting firms find themselves in a position where they may have received a fee of $3,000 and have $300 million worth of exposure. There's no rationale for that sort of thing. One way of attacking it would be to put some restriction on the class-action suit. We don't want to

*From *World,* Summer 1975, pp. 24–25. Reprinted by permission of the publisher.

stop people from suing if they've been damaged, but there should be some responsibility on their side, such as a system like they have in the U.K. where the loser of a suit pays the expenses. That would cut down on the totally frivolous suits. Frankly, a good many of the suits the profession has result from a lawyer cutting something out of *The Wall Street Journal* and typing up a complaint. He has no idea whether the facts are substantive or not, but it's a nice free ride toward a possible contingent fee. Fortunately, people win these sorts of suits very seldom but it costs us money to defend ourselves from this sort of thing.

Q: How do you foresee the long-term growth potential of accounting in terms of quarterly audits and other areas?

A: I think almost immediately we're going to be involved in quarterly *reviews*, not audits. We're doing so already for a number of our clients. What all this means is the constant involvement of a CPA firm, an idea that has a tremendous amount of merit in my view. We are doing it now in our banking practice—PMM has by far the largest banking practice of all the firms. A bank is different from a typical corporation in that they have in place a very substantial internal audit or inspection team. As we work with the banks, we've developed a program of "round the clock auditing," where we coordinate directly with this large inspection force. We are really—without adding a great amount of work—able to, in effect, bless the quarterly figures because of that total involvement throughout the year and do very little "detail auditing" at the year end. We think this concept can flow very well over to the corporate environment, particularly to companies that have a large, sophisticated internal audit group.

Q: Why do you feel the FASB will succeed where the APB did not?

A: There's no guarantee that it will succeed but I think it will if we all support it. If the APB had functioned from the beginning the way it did its last two years, it probably would have succeeded. The APB got a bad reputation as it worked hurriedly to restructure and do a better job. But, if you look at the last couple of years of the APB, it was turning out a lot of valuable product. By then, it was just too late.

The independence of the FASB takes it a little further away from the pressures of the individual firms and also the people are full-time. When you consider that all the people on the APB had other responsibilities, it's amazing they did as much as they did in the latter years.

Q: What educational background should a person possess before he enters accounting today?

A: I feel very strongly about the value of a broad-based liberal education at the undergraduate level and then graduate school as a way of focusing on a career. . . . Our proportion of MBAs is growing every year and I think down the road it may well be a requirement to have an MBA. Business is getting more complex and a broader background and advanced education is really necessary.

Q: What words of advice would you give to accounting and business students?

A: I think patience is a virtue to a certain degree. The quality of students coming out of college now is much higher than it has ever been. They're highly motivated and they want to conquer the world tomorrow. Sometimes, I think, through over-anxiousness, they miss a base of experience that is necessary to sound business judgments. The people who become partners in our firm must have this necessary base of experience. When one of our partners signs Peat, Marwick, Mitchell & Co. on a report, he's speaking for over 900 of us. Unfortunately, the more capable and motivated a young man is, the less he is inclined to wait. I say this, of course, as one who jumped the traces and went into industry so I do recognize that patience has its limits, too.

EDITORS' NOTE: An alternative approach to the one described in Selection 139 is that of "peer review," where one public accounting firm audits another to its standards and performance. In 1975 Arthur Young conducted a peer review of Peat, Marwick, Mitchell & Co., which consisted of 12,000 hours of work by 150 CPAs. This firm has been subject to SEC pressure since it was the auditor for several companies (including Stirling Homex in Selection 127) which experienced unexpected financial collapses.

## QUESTIONS

1. Compare Mr. Hanson's comments to those of Mr. Chetkovich (Selection 130), Mr. Palmer (Selection 133), and Mr. Kapnick (Selection 138). Compare to those of Professor Pattillo (Selection 134) and Mr. Wriston (Selection 118).

2. How do you react as an accounting student to his advice about the virtue (to a point) of patience and the value of experience?

## SELECTED BIBLIOGRAPHY

"The Scramble for MBAs," *Dun's Review*, June 1975, pp. 87-88.

# 147
## CATCH-22*
Newsweek

Among the shoddy practices of the Committee for the Re-election of the President was its success in pressuring big corporations to make illegal campaign contributions. Beyond the disturbing moral and legal issues these acts raise lie some less obvious though equally troubling questions. All of the companies involved—so far nine have pleaded guilty and two more are under indictment—are publicly held corporations whose finances are audited by outside accounting firms. The auditors are supposed to protect the investing public by trying to make sure that a company does not

*From *Newsweek,* Apr. 22, 1974, pp. 88 and 91. Reprinted by permission of the publisher.

misrepresent its fiscal state of affairs. How, then, did these companies manage to funnel their funds into illegal channels without the auditors finding out? And if companies can fool accountants on this, what else might be hidden?

The "how" turns out to be quite simple. A corporation can resort to a variety of dodges. American Airlines, for instance, had a Lebanese broker send it a phony bill. American's accountants didn't know the $55,000 it paid to cover the bill actually wound up with CREEP.

This use of a bogus invoice is perhaps the most popular ploy. But there are others. Ashland Oil, whose books are audited by Ernst & Ernst, drew $100,000 from a subsidiary in Gabon. The money was "laundered" by passing it through a Swiss bank. Finally, it was delivered to the Nixon campaign. American Ship Building Co. is charged with awarding phony "bonuses" to eight trustworthy corporate officials—together with a list of GOP committees to give the money to. "There are a hundred ways this can pass by an auditor," says Phillip Moore of the Washington-based Project on Corporate Responsibility. "I'm sure that there are thousands of corporate campaign contributions that will never be known."

## EXCUSE

These schemes work because $100,000 is not very much by corporate standards. "We've long taken the position that we're not responsible for the detection of fraudulent or illegal activities unless they're so large as to materially affect a company's financial statement," says Thomas Flynn, a partner in Arthur Young & Co. Flynn's firm audited Phillips Petroleum, which gave a total of $100,000 to CREEP, and American Airlines. Flynn's may seem a narrow view of the accountant's responsibility. But, in fact, the auditor's job is merely to give an opinion on whether a company has fairly stated its financial situation.

To arrive at this opinion, the auditor doesn't check over every item in the company's books—that's impractical—but instead concentrates on items that are particularly big or that seem suspicious, and randomly tests the rest. Because of this, dodges like the phony-invoice scheme will almost always succeed.

"If I see a payment of $50,000 that has been approved by the chairman of the board, the president and the financial vice president, I am less likely to question it than if it was approved by a clerk," notes Thomas A. Ganner, director of U.S. operations for Price Waterhouse & Co. Among Price Waterhouse clients are Carnation Co., Goodyear and Gulf Oil; the three illegally gave a total of nearly $174,000 to political causes in 1972. When top officers get together to do something with $50,000 of the company's money, "they're going to get away with it," Ganner says flatly.

Indeed, many accountants maintain that even if they stumble across an improper action, their duty is to take their discovery no further than the company's board of directors. Arthur Andersen & Co., which audited American Ship Building, had heard rumors of the company's allegedly phony bonus scheme. But the accounting firm says that it did not pursue the matter after American Ship Building attorneys assured it that everything was legal.

Should Arthur Andersen have gone further? Most accountants think not. "We're not a law-enforcement profession," says Kenneth Stringer of Haskins & Sells. The firm audits Braniff Airways, Diamond International and Minnesota Mining & Mfg., which among them gave a total of $75,000 to the Nixon effort. "We have no duty beyond that of the citizen to report a crime," Stringer insists. "Just because there is a violation of the law per se is not enough for us to make it public unless [the violation] will expose the company to serious financial impact."

## RESIST

Still, auditors are coming under increasing pressure to recognize wider legal and ethical obligations. They are resisting, mainly on practical grounds. "If the public demands finding a $30,000 figure in a billion-dollar company, we can do it," Stringer says. "But it might cost $3 million for every $30,000 found."

Current auditing procedures are adequate, accountants argue, as long as the company they are auditing is reasonably honest. "If you can't believe the representations of your client, you can't audit him," says Flynn of Arthur Young. "We think we are pretty smart, but we've never thought we were smart enough to audit a crook." There is a logic to this widespread belief but it smacks of Catch-22. For, as most accountants agree, it is the crooks who need auditing the most.

EDITORS' NOTE: Selections 133 and 143 complement this selection.

## QUESTION

1. Why are accountants accused of "Catch-22" logic when they argue you can't audit to catch crooks?

# 148
# ODE TO AN ASPIRING EXECUTIVE*
T. D. L.

Ye lads an' lassies, yin an' a',
Wha ken aboot accounts an' law
Wi' vast know-how for a' tae see,
Promoted ye may never be.

And lads an' lassies, a' intent
On stern career development,
Effective leaders tae a tee,
A partner yet ye ne'er may be.

*From *The Accountant's Magazine,* December 1974, p. 471. Reprinted by permission of the publisher.

Aye, lads an' lassies, fu' o' wits,
Wha maister taxes and audits,
Wha' canna find the time for tea,
A partner, yes, ye maun can be.

And lads an' lassies, fu' o' tact,
Wi' winsome weys that aye attract
The client wi' a muckle fee,
A partner, well—ye just may be.

But lads an' lassies, ye who snooze
An' haud yer Scotch an' ither booze,
Ah hae a message for a' ye,
A partner ye are sure tae be.

# 149
## NONPROFIT ACCOUNTING
## A Revolution in Progress*
Malvern J. Gross

"Anything goes!" That seems to have been the rule for nonprofit organizations in the past—for until recently there were relatively few "rules." But now, in less than 18 months, the accounting profession has laid down some very specific rules for the three most important sectors of the broad category referred to as nonprofit organizations. As a result, nonprofit organizations suddenly find themselves catapulted from an era of permissiveness to an era where the accounting and reporting requirements are spelled out in great detail. For them, it's a period of revolutionary change.

The nonprofit organizations category includes colleges and universities, hospitals, voluntary health and social welfare organizations, museums, membership associations, country clubs and the like. As a group, they have tremendous influence on our society and on the way we solve the problems of our times.

Why then have there been so few accounting rules for these organizations? Basically, the answer is that only recently has the accounting profession devoted any significant attention to the accounting and reporting procedures these groups follow. Historically, their procedures were tied to the stewardship concept (that is, the accountability for funds received and disbursed). This type of accounting is usually referred to as fund accounting. Unfortunately, fund accounting can get very compli-

*From *Price Waterhouse Review,* No. 3, 1973, pp. 43–50. Reprinted by permission of the publisher.

cated—not because the underlying principles are complicated but because of the dozens of different "funds" some organizations tend to set up. Typically, each fund is accounted for as though it were a separate entity. As a result, it is usually hard to get an overall picture of an organization's activity.

## THREE AUDIT GUIDES

About 18 months ago the American Institute of Certified Public Accountants (AICPA) issued the first of three audit guides. It dealt with hospitals. The second guide, issued last summer, pertained to colleges and universities. The third, issued last fall, applied to voluntary health and welfare organizations. Obviously, these guides have affected the specific organizations to which they were addressed. But their cumulative effect is also being felt by all other types of nonprofit organizations because the guides express opinions about appropriate accounting and reporting principles for transactions that are common to most nonprofit groups.

## WHAT IS AN AUDIT GUIDE?

Audit guides provide direction to AICPA members in examining and reporting on financial statements. They set forth the considered opinion of knowledgeable accountants and, as such, represent the best thoughts of the accounting profession. The guides deal not only with the actual conduct of the audit but also the appropriate accounting and reporting principles. It is in the discussion of these principles that the guides will have the most impact on nonprofit organizations. A CPA who deviates from the principles outlined in these guides may very well be forced to justify such departures. Effectively, then, the guides constitute an authoritative pronouncement on appropriate accounting and reporting principles.

## CONSISTENCY AMONG THE GUIDES

Three separate committees were involved in writing these guides. Some attempt was made for conformity among them but differing industry practices and customs and the differing perspectives of the committees resulted in a number of principles that are not completely consistent. On some points, however, the guides are consistent. On others, two of the three guides are in agreement, therefore suggesting how a particular issue is likely to be resolved eventually. Exhibit 1 summarizes the major accounting and reporting principles and the position taken in each guide.

There are six areas where the guides will have particular significance for all nonprofit organizations. I will discuss each of these. I will also highlight the several inconsistent areas which will affect many types of organizations.

### 1. All Legally Unrestricted Contributions Reported in a Single "Income" Statement

The most important and far-reaching change is that each of the three guides now requires nonprofit organizations to record all legally unrestricted contributions in a

**Exhibit 1    Comparison of Accounting and Reporting Principles Prescribed in the New Audit Guides**

| | HOS-PITALS | COL-LEGES | VOLUNTARY HEALTH AND WELFARE |
|---|---|---|---|
| 1. Accrual basis accounting required | Yes | Yes | Yes |
| 2. Use of separate board-designated funds allowed in the income statement | No | Yes | No |
| 3. Unrestricted contributions must be reported in income statement | Yes | Yes | Yes |
| 4. Current restricted contributions reported in full in year received rather than in year expended | No | No | Yes |
| 5. Pledges *must* be recorded if material | Yes | No | Yes |
| 6. Contributed services must be recorded under certain circumstances | Yes | No | Yes |
| 7. Unrestricted dividend and interest income must be reported in the income statement | Yes | Yes | Yes |
| 8. Capital gains on legally unrestricted investment funds must be reported in the income statement | Yes | No | Yes |
| 9. Transfers between funds reported in the income statement | No | Yes | Yes[a] |
| 10. Use of a separate fixed asset or plant fund allowed | No | Yes | Yes |
| 11. Fixed assets must be capitalized | Yes | Yes | Yes |
| 12. Fixed assets must be depreciated and the depreciation charge reported in the income statement | Yes | No | Yes |
| 13. Appropriations or encumbrances can be charged against expenses | No | No | No |
| 14. Appropriations or encumbrances can be reported as a liability on the balance sheet | No | No | No |
| 15. Transfers under the "total return" concept of reporting endowment fund gains must be reported as a transfer after the excess of income caption | Not discussed | Yes | Yes |

[a]But only after the caption, "excess of income over expenses."

single income statement so that the reader can see the total amounts received. Previously, it was common for boards of trustees to "designate" certain categories of legally unrestricted contributions for some specific purpose and then disclose them only in separate income statements for the "designated" funds. As a result, the casual reader who was unaware of this bookkeeping maneuver would see a bleak picture when he looked at what passed for an income statement. In fact, the organization may very well have received substantial amounts which the board had designated for some other purpose and thus not included in the main income statement. Now, all unrestricted contributions must be reported in the general fund income statement.

Of course, if a donor designates in a legal fashion that he wants his contribution used only for an endowment fund or for some other restrictive purpose, these amounts will be recorded directly in that particular fund. But the board cannot assume this is the donor's intention. It has to be a legally binding action of the donor.

## 2. Summarizing All Other Unrestricted Activity on One Statement

Each of the three guides also requires that all other unrestricted income and expenses be reflected in this single income statement. There are three different styles of statement formats but each attempts to tell the reader what the excess of unrestricted income (revenues) over expenditures was for the year.[1]

Perhaps it is not so obvious but, in including all categories of unrestricted income, these guides are saying that investment income (dividends and interest) must also be reported in this "income" statement. In the case of hospitals and voluntary health and welfare organizations, capital gains arising from unrestricted investments must be included too. This will be a significant departure from past practices for many organizations.

## 3. Fixed Assets and Depreciation Accounting

The recording of fixed assets in the financial statements and the taking of depreciation have stirred up controversy in nonprofit accounting for years. All three guides now require that fixed assets be recorded and reported in the balance sheet, and two of the guides (hospitals and voluntary health and welfare organizations) require that fixed assets be depreciated over their useful lives. The college guide requires capitalization of fixed assets but does not require depreciation. Even in this guide, however, there is permissive language allowing depreciation in the plant fund column of the statement of changes in fund balances. The acceptance of depreciation accounting by two of the guides and the emphasis on cost of services (discussed below) will put increased pressure on colleges to follow depreciation accounting in the future.

[1]In the hospital audit guide, the statement comes down to the caption, "excess of revenues over expenses." In the voluntary health and welfare guide, the caption reads, "excess of public support and revenue over expenses." The college audit guide is not quite as clear cut because the accounting principles are still basically a stewardship type of reporting. Nevertheless, even in the college guide there seems to be a trend toward telling the reader what the net results of operation were for the year.

## 4. Carrying Investments at Market

Significantly, both the college and the voluntary health and welfare guides state that investments may now be carried at market or fair value. This is not a mandatory requirement but rather an acceptable alternative to carrying investments at historical cost. Many institutions with large endowment funds may find carrying investments at market value is more meaningful than cost. The hospital guide does not provide for carrying investments at market value. However, the subsequent release of the other two guides would seem to give the green light to hospitals (as well as other nonprofit organizations) to do so too.

## 5. An Increased Emphasis on Programs of the Organization

Traditionally, nonprofit organizations have reported in terms of the amounts spent for salaries, rent, supplies, etc. The voluntary health and welfare guide takes a major step forward when it states that the organization exists to perform services and programs and therefore should be reporting principally in terms of its individual program activities or functions. Exhibit 2 is an example of an organization reporting on a functional basis. This type of presentation forces management to tell the statement reader how much of its funds were expended for each program category and the amount spent in supporting services, including fund raising.

In addition to this statement, these organizations are encouraged to prepare a statement of functional expenses, which analyzes the costs of each program category. Exhibit 3 is an example of this kind of statement. Between these two statements, the reader is given a great deal of information.

Neither the hospital guide nor the college guide requires this reporting on a program (functional) basis. But, because of the large number of voluntary health and welfare organizations, the requirement for functional reporting will have wide impact. Also, once the effective date of this guide passes (for years beginning after July 1, 1974), organizations requiring a CPA's opinion will have to follow this format if they want an unqualified opinion from their CPA.[2] For many organizations, this expanded format will require significant changes in bookkeeping procedures in order for them to know how much of their costs relate to each program.

## 6. Internal Control over Contributions

A little noticed (but very important) section of the voluntary health and welfare guide is a statement about the organization's responsibility to take all practical steps to assure adequate internal control over contributions. For example, the guide observes that, when an organization solicits funds through a direct mail campaign, two employees should be assigned the function of jointly controlling incoming mail and

---

[2]The laws of New York, Pennsylvania, Georgia, Connecticut, Illinois, Wisconsin and Minnesota have reporting requirements for organizations soliciting funds within these states. These requirements include an opinion by a CPA.

**Exhibit 2    National Association of Environmentalists**
**Statement of Income and Expenses for the Year Ended December 31, 1973**

| | | |
|---|---:|---:|
| Income: | | |
| Membership dues | $233,550 | |
| Research projects | 127,900 | |
| Contributions and bequests | 91,500 | |
| Advertising income | 33,500 | |
| Subscriptions to nonmembers | 18,901 | |
| Investment income | 14,607 | |
| Gains on sales of investments | 33,025 | |
| Total income | | $552,983 |
| Expenses: | | |
| Program services | | |
| "National Environment" magazine | 110,500 | |
| Clean-up month campaign | 126,617 | |
| Lake Erie project | 115,065 | |
| Total program services | | 352,182 |
| Supporting services | | |
| Management and general | 33,516 | |
| Fund raising | 5,969 | |
| Total supporting services | | 39,485 |
| Total expenses | | 391,667 |
| Excess of income over expenses | | $161,316 |

preparing a record of amounts received. The guide also discusses the appropriate level of internal control over door-to-door solicitation. Many organizations—particularly smaller ones—do not provide the appropriate control. In the absence of adequate internal control, the CPA must qualify his opinion.

## SIGNIFICANCE OF THESE CHANGES

All of these major accounting and reporting changes give recognition to the importance of nonprofit organizations in our society. At a time when their influence was relatively narrow and the principal persons concerned were usually knowledgeable contributors, the reporting and accounting principles they followed were of less importance. Today, an increasing portion of society's activities are carried out by nonprofit organizations, and both the accounting profession and the leaders of these organizations recognize that, if their role is going to continue to expand, complete and straightforward reporting must take place. These three guides—which were the result

**Exhibit 3  National Association of Environmentalists**

**Analysis of Functional Expenses for the Year Ended December 31, 1973**

| | TOTAL ALL EXPENSES | PROGRAM SERVICES | | | | SUPPORTING SERVICES | | |
| --- | --- | --- | --- | --- | --- | --- | --- | --- |
| | | "NATIONAL ENVIRON-MENT" MAGAZINE | CLEAN-UP MONTH CAMPAIGN | LAKE ERIE PROJECT | TOTAL PROGRAM | MANAGE-MENT AND GENERAL | FUND RAISING | TOTAL SUP-PORTING |
| Salaries | $170,773 | $ 24,000 | $ 68,140 | $ 60,633 | $152,773 | $15,000 | $3,000 | $18,000 |
| Payroll taxes and employee benefits | 22,199 | 3,120 | 8,857 | 7,882 | 19,859 | 1,950 | 390 | 2,340 |
| Total compensation | 192,972 | 27,120 | 76,997 | 68,515 | 172,632 | 16,950 | 3,390 | 20,340 |
| Printing | 84,071 | 63,191 | 18,954 | 515 | 82,660 | 1,161 | 250 | 1,411 |
| Mailing, postage and shipping | 14,225 | 10,754 | 1,188 | 817 | 12,759 | 411 | 1,055 | 1,466 |
| Rent | 19,000 | 3,000 | 6,800 | 5,600 | 15,400 | 3,000 | 600 | 3,600 |
| Telephone | 5,615 | 895 | 400 | 1,953 | 3,248 | 2,151 | 216 | 2,367 |
| Outside art | 14,865 | 3,165 | 11,700 | – | 14,865 | – | – | – |
| Local travel | 1,741 | – | 165 | 915 | 1,080 | 661 | – | 661 |
| Conferences and conventions | 6,328 | – | 1,895 | 2,618 | 4,513 | 1,815 | – | 1,815 |
| Depreciation | 13,596 | 2,260 | 2,309 | 5,616 | 10,185 | 3,161 | 250 | 3,411 |
| Legal and audit | 2,000 | – | – | – | – | 2,000 | – | 2,000 |
| Supplies | 31,227 | – | 1,831 | 28,516 | 30,347 | 761 | 119 | 880 |
| Miscellaneous | 6,027 | 115 | 4,378 | – | 4,493 | 1,445 | 89 | 1,534 |
| Total | $391,667 | $110,500 | $126,617 | $115,065 | $352,182 | $33,516 | $5,969 | $39,485 |

of joint efforts by CPAs and the leaders of each type of organization—are designed in large part to help eliminate the credibility gap that many feel now exists.

These objectives are relatively clear—but implementing them is not going to be easy. The past permissiveness in accounting allowed some organizations effectively to conceal part of their assets. The new changes will result in full disclosure and will cause many organizations to reexamine their objectives and needs. Boards of trustees may have a hard time justifying a request for increased contributions if their financial statements show a surplus. But this is probably as it should be. If an organization cannot justify continued support or an increased level of support, then under our system the organization should not be able to raise these funds. Society gives nonprofit organizations a significant advantage in tax concessions and society has a right to insist that these organizations do, in fact, respond to public needs.

Many organizations are going to find that their bookkeeping costs will grow, as will their professional fees for auditing. The increased level of reporting along with an increased level of internal control over contributions will be expensive.

I believe these changes and the trend they indicate are clearly in the public interest. For many, greater disclosure will be a traumatic experience, and for some it may have an immediate negative financial impact. But where this happens board members will have to face up to the fundamental question: Is the organization providing a service which is needed by the public at a cost which is appropriate? The accounting and reporting principles in the new audit guides will help the public make an informed judgment. For this reason, the guides are a major contribution.

## QUESTIONS

1. What is the nonprofit accounting revolution?

2. What are nonprofit organizations? Of what significance are they in our economy?

3. What is the single most important change in accounting for nonprofit organizations? Why?

4. What has the change in depreciation for nonprofit organizations?

## SELECTED BIBLIOGRAPHY

Boyles, Harlan G., and Randall P. Martin, "A Statewide Accounting System for Local Government," *Management Controls*, June 1975, pp. 93-95.

Hensler, Emil J., Jr., "Accounting for Small Nonprofit Organizations," *Management Accounting*, January 1973, pp. 41-49.

Keister, O. R., "Internal Controls for Churches," *Management Accounting*, January 1974, pp. 40-42.

# 150

## DOLLAR VALUES IN THE SOCIAL INCOME STATEMENT*

Lee J. Seidler

Are the profits of a corporation fairly measured if no expense is shown for the air or water pollution it causes? Are the limited and finite funds available better spent on job training for disadvantaged minority groups or on high school dropout prevention programs? Should we build more superhighways or improve mass transit systems?

Such questions suggest the necessity for new methods of accounting to support better policy decisions. Conventional accounting techniques, based largely on the existence of reasonably established and verifiable market prices are of little use when large portions of both inputs and outputs lie outside the normal price system. Thus, the repeated calls for improvements in measurement techniques and quite logically, for the development of some forms of social accounting.

The keynote speaker at the 1969 annual meeting of the American Accounting Association called upon accountants to assist in the development of socially based income concepts.[1] Both the AICPA and the AAA established committees on Socioeconomic Accounting. The *Journal of Accountancy* has featured articles on the social aspects of accounting, as have *The Accounting Review* and other publications.[2] The AICPA has published a volume, *Social Measurement.*

From all this activity it might appear that accountants are making significant progress in the development of principles and practices applicable to social measurement. A closer look suggests a less optimistic view. The articles, papers, and the book are either exhortations to action, calls to accountants to assume their "social responsibility," or discourses on the difficulties of performing social accounting, but they are pitifully short on examples of actual technique. The evidence of significant progress is at best, limited.

Does this mean that no progress is being made in the measurement and evaluation of social inputs and outputs? Fortunately for American society, if not for the accounting profession, some advances are being made in the development of techniques of social accounting, but not by accountants.

In 1965, The Brookings Institution published *Measuring Benefits of Government Investments*, a collection of case studies involving the measurement of costs and

---

*From *World,* Spring 1973, pp. 14—23. Reprinted by permission of the publisher.

[1]Mancur L. Olson, "Measurement Problems in the Social Accounts" (unpublished).

[2]See, for example, D. F. Linowes, "Socio-Economic Accounting" (J. of A., Nov. 1968); B. G. King, "Cost-Effectiveness Analysis: Implications for Accountants" (J. of A., March 1970): Bruns and Snyder, "Management Information for Community Action" (*Management Services*, July-August, 1969), Sybil Mobley, "The Challenges of Socio-Economic Accounting" (*Accounting Review*, October, 1970).

benefits of nine separate socially oriented projects.[3] Not one accountant, academic or professional, can be found among the writers of the cases. In 1969, the Joint Economic Committee published a three volume collection, *The Analysis and Evaluation of Public Expenditures*, composed of papers by a total of 57 authors.[4] The work is concerned with the theory and practice of social accounting. Not one of the authors is an accountant; virtually all of the academic contributions are the work of economists.

More exhaustive examples may be cited, but the general points are clear: (1) there is considerable interest, at private and public levels, in performing social measurements and, (2) accountants are making little tangible progress in the area.

Even with the logical difficulties inherent in determining causes for *inaction*, we can postulate several possible explanations for the present lack of accounting contributions. A simple explanation, perhaps more associative than causal, is that accountants have not in the past shown any significant interest in applying their skills to areas outside normal enterprise accounting. Quite possibly that limited interest is due to the lack of a link between the apparently concrete aspects of conventional enterprise accounting and the amorphous, elusive ideas inherent in accounting for social costs and benefits.

One possibility of establishing such linkage, and thus of providing a central focus for accounting efforts in the social dimension would be the establishment of at least a tentative accounting concept of social profit. Clearly, a major part of the development of financial accounting theory and practice has centered around efforts to improve income determination. The purpose of this article is to offer a similar central focus in social accounting, with the goal of finally increasing the *active* interest of accountants in the subject.

The concepts and the underlying assumptions which follow are highly tentative: they are proposed only as a starting point for future development.

The short-lived Socioeconomic Accounting Committee of the American Accounting Association spent the better part of its one year existence (1969-1970) attempting to construct a clear and valid definition of social accounting. One rather promising effort suggested that no new definition was actually necessary: all accounting is for socioeconomic purposes. It was suggested that the definition of accounting itself should be essentially that: *Accounting is the art and/or science of measurement and, interpretation of activities and phenomena which are essentially of a social and economic nature.*

Such a definition would exclude a primary concern with the measurement of purely physical phenomena, such as hardness, color, time or distance, although related measurements might enter into accounting calculations. Similarly, accounting is not concerned, at a primary level, with measurements of such human, but non-economic activities as individual attitudes, although again, such measurements might enter into accounting calculations.

---

[3] Robert Dorfman, ed. *Measuring Benefits of Government Investments* (Washington, The Brookings Institution, 1965).

[4] *The Analysis and Evaluation of Government Expenditures* (3 vols.), papers presented to the JEC of the U.S. Congress, 1969.

Clearly, the operations of business enterprises would constitute relevant phenomena under this definition, whether considered in terms of the enterprise as a whole (conventional financial accounting) or in its constituent parts (conventional managerial accounting).

Thus, so called conventional "accounting" appears as a subset in this rather more encompassing definition of accounting. National income accounting would also obviously fall under such a definition. Here, we encounter a difficulty, since virtually all those who perform this type of macro-accounting style themselves as economists or statisticians. National income accounting, thus far, has been almost exclusively concerned with simple economic or financial measurement, with almost no attention paid to social or qualitative aspects of inputs and outputs.

Current conventional accounting focuses around two entities, the business enterprise (financial and managerial accounting) and the nation state (national income accounting). "Social accounting" as used in this article, deals with an area, which constitutes somewhat of a middle ground between these two.

In social accounting, measurements would be made from the point of view of society, or some subset of society, such as a particular government body or a given group in the population. In enterprise accounting the entity is the focus of measurement. However, in social accounting the undertaking is not necessarily a specific business enterprise, as in conventional accounting. The definition of the entity is flexible; it will vary with the circumstances and with the definition of "society." It may be a company, an area or a project, such as a government experiment in job training.

Another distinction in this form of social accounting lies in the terms of measurement. Rather than concern with the changes in the economic resources of a group of shareholders, social accounting measures the change in the "general welfare" resulting from the activity being measured.

Some examples of this social accounting would include the so-called, but misnamed "social audit" of a business corporation. In such a context the business entity remains the focus of the accounting, but the inputs and outputs are defined as consumption of and additions to society's resources, rather than only those resources that the firm pays for or receives in money. Therefore, pollution caused by the firm is an additional cost; socially desirable outputs would be revenues.

Another use for social accounting would be to measure the effectiveness of certain programs undertaken by government bodies. The social costs of a program, principally taxes, would be compared with the social revenues, the improvement in the general welfare, which it generates. The clear definition of the effects to be measured obviously constitute one of the principal problems of the field.

Sartre, in *Existentialism*, postulates that man is condemned to continuous decision-making. This process of decision-making is unavoidable; it is the essence of existence.

Consider the accountant in this context. His work is to produce measurements, estimates, and usually financial statements. If he does not produce these results, if he tells his client that the theoretical complexities of the situation preclude a judgment, his very reason for existence ceases. Like Sartre's man, the accountant is thus condemned to make decisions. He must produce annual financial statements, even though it is clear to him (and his critics) that there are theoretical deficiencies in his methodology.

How does the accountant exist under such an imperative? He does so, as George O. May noted, by establishing conventions. Where theoretical limitations preclude "truth" in an answer which *must* be given, the accountant develops some (hopefully logical) arbitrary compromise. To the extent that he convinces other accountants and users to accept such simplifying compromises, they become accounting conventions.

The accountant is not so naive as to believe that productive assets actually lose their revenue producing potential in exactly equal fractions of their original cost each year, or in accordance with any other arbitrary curve of decay. He recognizes that he is incapable of attributing the joint cost of equipment in any theoretically defensible way to the revenues of the periods in which the asset is used. But, he *must* produce an income figure at the end of the year. Therefore, he adopts the simplifying convention of straight-line depreciation or of some other usage curve. The accountant knows that it is not a "correct" portrayal of the circumstances; (hopefully) the user also understands. They have agreed on a convention permitting the accountant to produce a result, which although not perfectly correct, appears to provide information that users have found to be worth its cost.

It is quite fashionable for economists and mathematicians to criticize the way in which accounting calculations are performed. The adherence to original cost, overhead allocations, depreciation methods, etc. are all apt targets which have allowed members of these other honored disciplines (and numerous accountants) to demonstrate their intellectual superiority over mere bookkeepers at scores of academic meetings and in the endless pages of academic journals.

It takes no great skill to demonstrate the theoretical errors of most accepted accounting conventions; it requires considerably more ability to offer alternative conventions which will better satisfy the totality of the needs of those who must use financial statements.

Similarly, it is not possible to make theoretically defensible calculations of a social nature with our presently available information and limited perceptions of human behavior and motivations. However, given our environment and the problems now facing us, a more rational basis for the allocation of scarce funds is imperative.

The device which will allow such calculations will be the development of social accounting conventions, i.e. agreed upon compromises and simplifying assumptions which will allow practicing accountants to make reasonably useful social calculations.

An example of the type of issues or problems which might lend themselves to a social accounting approach may provide a better focus.

Consider a project now being attempted at New York University. This institution, like many other private universities, suffers from a large operating deficit and resulting financial difficulties.

When we speak of the "deficit," the context is that of conventional accounting. The revenues of the University come principally from tuition, research and (nominal) state aid. The major cost categories are instruction, research, libraries, student-aid and overhead. (There are also substantial costs and revenues associated with real estate, hospital operations, and similar activities which are ignored, for simplicity, in this discussion.)

Conventional matching of these costs and revenues under enterprise accounting principles shows the University in a deficit.

The University might also be viewed in a social accounting context: what does its operation cost society, and what benefits does it produce for society? In this light, we might reverse the normal income statement of the University. The amounts shown as revenues to the University actually represent "costs" to society; the payments which society gives the University for its services. The University's costs represent the services it has performed, such as research and teaching; "benefits" to society. The two income statements might appear as shown in Figure I.

The preparation of the social income statement will essentially be a process of attributing values to the various captions. Consider the revenues.

From a social view, the educational outputs of the University consist of citizens, presumably better educated when they leave the University than when they arrived, and therefore of greater value to society.

The attribution of value to this output, however, involves a number of problems. There are reasonably good figures to indicate that the incomes of graduates exceed those of non-graduates. One could therefore compute the present value of the net increment supposedly due to education. Of course, there is the rather fundamental question of whether it is the education that caused some or all of the difference in incomes, e.g., that changed the people, or is the result to some extent merely associative.

We then face issues of attribution of the net income increment to the various parties benefiting from it. "Social" benefits would seem to imply benefits to society as a whole; but a large part of the increment in income due to education is internalized by the student himself. For him, education to a great extent is a market transaction.

**Figure I**

| CONVENTIONAL INCOME STATEMENT | SOCIAL INCOME STATEMENT |
|---|---|
| Revenues: | Revenues: |
| Tuition paid to university | Value of instruction to society |
| Research grants[a] | Value of research to society |
| State aid | |
| Less costs: | Less costs: |
| Instructional | Tuition paid to university |
| Research costs[a] | Cost of research |
| Student aid | State aid |
| Overheads | Other—Lost production, etc. |
| Result: | Result: |
| (Deficit) | Profit |

[a] Research is shown as the same figure in both parts of the conventional statement, at the amount received and expended.

Society will also benefit from the assumed increased social and intellectual productivity of the graduate.

Then there is the question of which society will benefit. Is "society" to be regarded as New York City? In that case, in or out migration of graduates will have some effects. If "society" is the United States, NYU's high proportion of foreign students may also have some very substantial effects.[5]

The research output would also have to be valued in social terms. Some amount of work has been done in this respect, particularly under National Science Foundation sponsorship, to estimate the rate of return from investments in various categories of research.[6] The valuation of the research output would include such items as increased productivity due to research, lives saved, health improved, etc. In NYU's case, about two-thirds of the research is biomedical, where payoffs can be reasonably estimated. The assigning of specific values to other categories of research; historical or even that in accounting, might be rather more difficult.

On the cost side, the accounting appears less difficult. Payments for tuition, research and state-aid are denominated in cash. Nevertheless, some problems remain. Payments for research and state-aid comes from governments or government funded agencies; they are a direct cost to society. Tuition payments, however, come from individuals, who personally pay for and personally receive and internalize the benefits of education. This, of course, is the same question which was raised in connection with outputs. It will be discussed below in the context of the "matching concept."

There would appear to be several uses for calculations of this nature. Immediately, and assuming that the social income statement shows a substantial "profit," as contrasted with the conventional statement, such a calculation should have value as a fund raising device. In the broader sense, estimates of the relative social productivity of the institution should be of considerable value as questions of state support to cover deficits become critical.

In conventional enterprise accounting the determination of the amount to be labelled "net income" has been the central focus of virtually continuous debate. The contentious issues, however, have really not involved the nature of profit; virtually all of the controversy has been over the timing of the recognition of profits. Ultimately all elements of gain or loss, recurring or non-recurring, those recognized at point of sale, or through accretion, will find their way to the equity section of the balance sheet, to show as an increase in the wealth of the firm.

Unfortunately, this would not be the case in accounting in a social vein. Conventional enterprise accounting measures money flows (present, past, or future) in and out of the enterprise. Resource flows which do not have a money cost to the firm (or yield a revenue) are ignored, although ignoring them may actually result in the recording of a profit. For example, a factory which manages to dispose of an effluent

---

[5] These questions are discussed in greater detail in Hansen and Weisbrod, *Benefits, Costs and Finance of Public Higher Education* (Chicago, Markham, 1969).

[6] National Science Foundation, *A Review of the Relationship between Research and Development and Economic Growth,* February, 1971. In particular, see Zvi Griliches, "A Memorandum on Research and Growth."

by dumping it in the local river will show no expense for this disposal. Another enterprise, located inland, which must pay for the disposal of its waste will show a lower profit. Thus, the factory which is "appropriating" a public resource, the river, will show a higher profit for doing so. This may be logical from a financial accounting view, but it seems socially counterproductive.

In social accounting, profit must be determined in relation to some concept of social gain. There is no neat market system, or clearly defined money flows to determine social revenues and costs. While some of those committed with excessive zeal to the causes of ecology and anti-pollution would appear to have an absolute set of values as to what is good and bad, it takes little imagination to suggest that precisely what is socially desirable and what may not be could be the subject of some debate.

At the broadest level, there are issues as to "what is good for people." Ideas of individual freedom may clash with concepts of national commitment and discipline; concepts of the sanctity of private property with desires to improve the distribution of wealth, etc.

At a more operational level, there may be conflicts between two apparently desirable and relatively uncontroversial social actions. Recently, the New York City Council considered legislation which would require that supermarket meats be completely packaged in transparent materials. This would permit the purchaser to see the underside of the meat which is normally concealed by the usual opaque paper tray. Only a butcher intent on defrauding the consumer (or a paper manufacturer) could oppose the suggestion; it clearly seemed socially desirable.

At the same time, anti-pollution groups were attempting to reduce the use of plastic packaging materials, on the quite correct grounds that they were not biodegradable and hence, when discarded, remained to blight the landscape. Similarly, if burned in the City's incinerators, plastic produces far more toxic fumes than paper.

Obviously, the two apparently desirable proposals are in conflict with each other. The situation also demonstrates that even quite desirable social programs have negative social aspects. This is in contrast (or possibly in addition to) negative economic aspects, e.g., damage to paper or plastic producers. And, if the economic costs to the respective manufacturers result in reduced employment, we continue on to a new level of social costs.

Recall the early example of social accounting, evaluating New York University in a social context. Assume that a study indicates that the present value of the total future earnings of a New York high school graduate, starting from a point four years after his high school graduation, is $100,000. Assume that the present value of the total future earnings of a comparably endowed, but NYU educated student at the same date is $150,000. Assume that the degree cost the NYU graduate $20,000 (including earnings foregone). Thus, the profit to the student, inherent in the education, is $30,000. Like all profits, it will eventually be taxed, let us say, at $5000. Therefore, the net gain to the student is $25,000.

Clearly, the $5000 to be paid in taxes is a second order social benefit, assuming that the "state" is considered society. The treatment of the $25,000 of benefits to the student is less clear. These benefits are appropriated or internalized by the graduate. From the graduate's (or his family's) point of view, the education is very much a market transaction. Tuition has been paid to purchase the benefits which will flow from education. There seems to be little difference between this transaction and any other market purchase of services other than that the activity is carried out by a socially desirable institution. Is it then logical to consider the additional earnings of the graduate, a private gain, as a "social" gain?

Let us consider a slightly different example. A national park, such as Yellowstone, would seem to be a prototype "social institution," and its use would logically be considered socially beneficial. However, the park is used by individuals, who like the NYU graduate, internalize the benefits.[7]

If we exclude the benefits that are appropriated by individuals from being denoted as social benefits, then we encounter a rather paradoxical result. The more the park is used by individuals, the greater will be its cost, but the lower will be its social benefit. This does not seem entirely logical. Yet, the only difference between the park and the University, both social institutions, is that in the latter case the benefits are directly received in an aesthetic sense, while those from the University include a large element of hard cash.

American history may provide direction for a solution to this issue. The fundamental idea of the social contract which sharply influences the thinking of those who framed the constitution is that government acts to improve the condition of individuals, not of "society." The history of federal legislation suggests, even more strongly, that the trend of American social legislation has been that of collective (government) action to affect the circumstances of individuals. To the extent that the chosen individuals receive the intended benefits, the legislation *is* performing its function. Thus, it would seem appropriate not to exclude those social benefits which are appropriated by individuals, *if they are the intended recipients of the particular social program.*

This last conclusion points up a required preliminary step in making social accounting determinations; the social purpose (or purposes) of the entity under examination must be postulated as a preliminary to any social calculation. Effects which correspond to the purpose or logically flow from it, should be considered social benefits; effect which tend to thwart the purpose of the project should be considered as costs.

This last point suggests a possible format for social evaluation of profit seeking corporations, as contrasted with the model of the non-profit organization offered earlier.

There would be general agreement that the production of a drug company manufacturing antibiotics would be socially desirable. By contrast, the production of illicit narcotics, stimulants, depressants, or other drugs leading to addiction would be considered socially undesirable. Ineffective, but harmless patent medicines might lie socially somewhere between these two extremes. We need add only a few other examples to indicate that any attempts to directly evaluate the social desirability of the production of various products would certainly be bogged down in a mass of contradictory value judgments.

---

[7]It should not be particularly difficult to price up the value of the direct benefits, using some form of analysis based on the cost of alternative available recreational facilities.

Therefore, why not, as suggested to me by Professor David Solomons, adopt the convention that all production, as long as it can be freely sold in the market, is socially desirable. Instead of evaluating the social merits of the production, measure the favorable or negative social effects that flow from the production process. This analysis would suggest an alternate form of social income statement, for profit seeking enterprises, as noted in Figure II.

The caption "Socially desirable outputs not sold" would include such benefits as job training, health improvement of workers and the deliberate employment of disadvantaged minorities. Socially undesirable effects not paid for could include air and water pollution generated by the company, health problems caused by use of its products, etc. The resulting net social profit or loss figure would be capable of manipulation comparable to that performed on conventional financial data.

There has been no indication in this paper thus far that the measurements in social accounting are contemplated in any unit other than money. Obviously, we are not condemned to postulate social accounting in monetary terms; social inputs and outputs could be measured in ergs, dynes, utils, or perhaps most appropriately, "plaisirs." Whatever unit happens to strike the fancy of the particular author could be adopted. We are breaking new ground and there is no necessity to be tied to hoary and perhaps materialistic accounting traditions. Indeed, among the students in my social accounting course there is invariably a feeling that expressing social measurements in terms of dollars is, in some sense, obscene.

Of course, such ideas are not new. In the period following the revolution, the Russians theorized that measurements in money terms were vestiges of the old system. Attempts were made to develop systems of value measurement in terms of "socialist utility." They were not successful, however, and the communist planners reluctantly returned to money terms.

It is difficult to see why any measurement unit, other than money, should have any particular attraction, except for semantic or aesthetic connotations. Money is merely a common denominator; the same would hold for any other postulated unit of welfare, pleasure or satisfaction. Money has the advantage, however, that reasonably realistic values for many inputs and outputs have already been stipulated by the "market." Any other system would require substantially greater effort to apply values to a wide variety of costs and benefits.

There is an obviously difficult problem in attributing values to some of the highly subjective phenomena that would be encountered in any social accounting system. These difficulties have led to the suggestion that absolute numerical values, whether

**Figure II    Social Income Statement of a Profit-seeking Organization**

| VALUE ADDED BY PRODUCTION OF THE ENTERPRISE |
| --- |
| +  Socially desirable outputs not sold |
| −  Socially undesirable effects not paid for |
| =  Net social profit (or loss) |

expressed in dollars or any other unit, might not be necessary. At this stage, and probably for the foreseeable future, many of the elements which will be required in social accounting determinations do not appear to be susceptible to specification in cardinal numerical terms. It may be possible, however, to quantify some of these factors, such as satisfaction, on some ordinal scale, such as a ranking system. While there seems to be general agreement that the ultimate goal of a social accounting system ought to be to make monetary or at least unitary determinations, perhaps a useful intermediate step would be to utilize rather more simple, but usable ordinal systems.

It is difficult to argue with such contentions, particularly since they appear to promise some acceleration in the ability of the accountant to measure social phenomena. Nevertheless, all such alternative number systems suffer from one rather compromising flaw; they are typically comprehensible only to those who invent or at least constantly work with them. Bidding systems for the game of bridge are an excellent analogy.

Certain professionals, such as doctors and lawyers, enjoy one significant advantage over accountants; they are required to communicate the technical details and nuances of their profession only to other initiated members. Outsiders, clients and patients, tend to demand results rather than comprehension. Thus, lawyers and doctors are quite free to develop elaborate jargons which are comprehensible only to the practitioners of the art. Aside from providing a pleasant sense of camaraderie such specialized languages have the additional desired effect of excluding lay practitioners of the art.

But social accounting results, like the outputs of the conventional accounting process, must be communicated to the uninitiated—to the non-accountant. Indeed, the best use which can be made for social accounting calculations would be their adoption by politicians, whose ranks include few accountants. Money measurements are the most common language of most people; they would be most useful in social accounting.

As in any new area, and social accounting is no exception, there are evangelists and sceptics. Those less enthused about the possibilities of social accounting generally raise certain objections, which might be considered at this point.

The most common objection is that it is not possible to make valid social accounting calculations; there are too many areas involved.

In response, consider the problem of measuring the net income of a complex corporation, such as a major oil company—for the first time. It would take but a few moments to list the problems—joint product costs, depreciation, valuation of mineral reserves—which make it impossible to determine income for any one year on a theoretically justifiable basis.

Of course, accountants do determine the income of such complex businesses every year, and they have been doing so for some time. Such determinations involve a process of compromise with theory and the evolution of a set of agreed upon simplifying conventions. As noted earlier, accountants are virtually "condemned" to make annual income determinations and they do so, albeit sometimes with a good deal of inaccuracy. Certainly, the complexities of social measurements do not appear much more foreboding than those of an international oil company; practice should yield some reasonably accepted results.

Nevertheless, one must admit that there are some rather awesome problems associated with making many social accounting determinations. For example, how are we to attribute a value to increases in human self esteem and dignity associated with job training or educational programs. Behavioral psychologists admit that they have made little progress in quantifying or determining attitude changes.[8]

Once again, the writer retreats to conventional financial accounting. In that mundane discipline, there are analogous situations. Consider, for example, the valuation of "proven" mineral reserves. It is obvious that proven reserves have a real and significant value, rarely bearing any relation whatsoever to the historical cost of finding them. Nevertheless, accountants have strongly resisted suggestions that they attempt "discovery value" accounting. Instead, conventional accounting resorts to recording the arbitrary and absolutely illogical, historical cost.[9]

With the equally elusive "goodwill" of a going firm, accountants do not even attempt to put an arbitrary, unrelated figure on the balance sheet, unless zero can be considered to be an arbitrary value. No attempt is made to account for such values.

Thus, the conventional accounting often avoids those areas where it is not practicable to tread. While other instances of this "discretion" such as the failure to recognize the effects of inflation, have produced a great deal of criticism of conventional accounting, it has by no means been rendered useless.

While the above should not be taken to excuse the sloth of our professional accounting rule making bodies, it does suggest that it will not be necessary to solve all the problems of social accounting before practice can be undertaken. There will be flaws theoretically and practically in social accounting determinations. Such flaws will constitute a valid criticism only if they result in answers which are less valid than no answers at all, or if practicing social accountants fail to modify their techniques as knowledge increases.

### QUESTIONS

1. What is social accounting, and how does it differ from financial and managerial accounting? From national income accounting?

2. What is a "social audit" of a business corporation?

3. Construct a hypothetical social income statement for your college or university.

4. What would be a social income statement for a profit-seeking enterprise?

5. What arguments does the author advance for practicing social accounting even if all problems with it are not solved?

---

[8]See, for example, P. Zimbardo and F. Ebbesen, *Influencing Attitudes and Changing Behavior* (Massachusetts, Addison-Wesley, 1970) p. 25. The authors note that attitudes which have been measured experimentally, ". . . are rarely socially significant ones . . . ."

[9]The practice followed by most major companies, expensing unsuccessful exploratory costs, produces a balance sheet valuation for reserves which is totally unrelated to reality. So-called "full costing" which also avoids any attempts at valuation is, at least, closer to discovery value, in absolute terms.

## SELECTED BIBLIOGRAPHY

Barnett, Andrew H., and James C. Caldwell, "Accounting for Corporate Social Performance: A Survey," *Management Accounting*, November 1974, pp. 23-26.

Churchill, Neil C., "Toward a Theory for Social Measurement," *Sloan Management Review*, Spring 1974, pp. 1-17.

Elias, Nabil, and Marc Epstein, "Dimensions of Corporate Social Reporting," *Management Accounting*, March 1975, pp. 36-40.

# 151
# MEASURING THE QUALITY OF LIFE*
Robert K. Elliott

Social accounting is a concept in search of a workable method. Clearly, it is an idea whose time has come. Not so clear are the objectives and limitations of social accounting and the standards and methods needed for its performance. Academic accountants are now involved in an energetic drive to develop such principles.

This intellectual search, however, is painfully slow. In the meantime, various decision makers are demanding information on social effects, and the practicing accounting profession is simply plunging into social accounting. Although the reports developed could be more elegant if solidly based on a neat set of principles, they nevertheless have the important advantages of timeliness and relevance.

In taking this pragmatic approach, the profession has been putting social accounting to work in such projects as analyzing nonfinancial data for grant receiving organizations, input/output factors in community welfare programs, cost/benefit measures for pollution control, urban renewal, crime, mass transit and traffic problems. The General Accounting Office (the Federal watchdog agency responsible directly to the Congress) has been active in the field for a decade, measuring benefits—not just costs—of various Federal programs. The experience gained in these endeavors is helping to form the necessary definitions and guidelines and is helping to alert business leaders to the importance of social measurement. The purpose of this article is to disclose some of the implementation problems facing the social accounting practitioner and to explain how and why the accountant fits into social accounting. But before considering these subjects, it is desirable to establish the need for social accounting and to provide at least a provisional definition of it.

Social accounting is necessary because there is a tremendous need for information to solve the problems of unbridled growth of population and of per capita consumption that already are placing severe strains on the environment and exhausting the

*From *World,* Spring, 1973, pp. 15, 24—29. Reprinted by permission of the publisher.

world's natural resources. Although new power sources, alternate raw materials, and efficient recycling may help, it is nevertheless obvious that there is a physical limit to growth potential. Computer simulations using a number of alternate assumptions have indicated that unless economic growth is halted, there will be an economic and ecological crash within 50 to 100 years. Some have disputed the assumptions and the model used, but there is widespread agreement on the existence of a severe problem. And that is only part of our social concern. It also includes the problems of racial and religious equality, urban blight, the breakdown in the transportation system, unemployment, welfare, old age support, health, and education. As if these were not problems of sufficiently staggering magnitude, technology continues to introduce brand new areas of trouble. For example, as more and more jobs are automated, huge masses will be unemployed, or the work will spread around so that most people will be underemployed.

In order to solve these immense social problems we must operate with a reasonable degree of efficiency, and this can only be done in the presence of vast quantities of useful information. That information will be the product of social accounting. The fact is that social progress will be hindered until there are adequate measures of progress toward social goals.

Social accounting can be defined as the reporting of accountability for *all* resources used by a corporation (or, for that matter, any entity). Typically, corporations have reported on the use of financial resources to the suppliers of those resources—owners and creditors. In a social accounting, the corporation reports on its use of human and natural resources to the suppliers of those resources, who are—in the broadest sense—the general public. The concerns giving rise to the pressures for social accounting, and the most relevant terms in which to report this accountability, all boil down to one concept—"quality of life." Social accounting is simply concerned with the corporation's impact on quality of life.

In actual application, this vague abstraction must be made operational. In practice, the social accountant must analyze the various "constituencies" of the corporation—that is, those groups that have a distinct and identifiable interest in corporate activity—and then analyze just how the corporation affects their quality of life. For a manufacturing concern, the constituencies and impacts to be measured might be as follows:

| CONSTITUENCIES | IMPACTS TO BE MEASURED |
|---|---|
| Employees | Product performance |
| Dealers | Economic performance |
| Customers | Development of human resources |
| Suppliers | Use of environment |
| Communities | Community welfare |
| Public | Government relations |
| Government | |
| Creditors | |
| Owners | |

As an example of this form of analysis, we could consider the effect of a manufacturing plant on the community in which it is located. General Motors has a vehicle assembly plant in Wilmington, Delaware. This plant consumes space, air, utilities, and has various other effects upon the community. A citizen of Wilmington (as a citizen, that is assuming he is not an employee, customer, investor, etc.) has little immediate interest in the overall social performance of General Motors; he is mainly interested in the company's performance in Wilmington. Specifically, he would like to know such things as the long-term viability of the Wilmington operation; stability of employment levels; local taxes paid; contributions to local charities; labor relations; hiring, promotion, and pay practices; air, water, and noise pollution; power and water consumption; plant appearance; traffic flow; impact on local politics; and general corporate citizenship. A report on these matters to the community of Wilmington would constitute one element in the overall social accounting of General Motors.

Such a report would not only be useful to members of the community in assessing corporate performance, but would also help management establish goals by assuring that a more complete consideration is given to total business needs and public expectations. Also the preparation of such a report would help management to think through the total consequences of their actions, thus resulting in better decisions.

Recently, a number of corporations have devoted part of their annual reports to stockholders to the area of social responsibility. It is clear, however, that these corporate reports, while salutary, are *not* social accounting. The reason is that they are still essentially oriented to financial accounting. After all, a corporation must be somewhat socially responsible just to survive. In effect these companies are telling their stockholders that they are not behaving in an antisocial way that might endanger their fiscal health—a result that could ensue if they were boycotted for discriminatory hiring, or closed down for excessive pollution. Even if these possibilities are not imminent, the company may still reap long-term financial benefits by improving its public image, thus enhancing, for example, sales and personnel recruitment.

It comes down to this: real social accounting must report to the suppliers of resources—and stockholders are not the suppliers of human and natural resources to the corporation.

Perhaps the most difficult and important decisions to be made about social accounting are practical ones: what is to be measured and what is the unit of measurement? There is a tendency to measure costs instead of benefits. For example, many persons are quite concerned over the staggering costs of welfare programs in New York. Few measure the programs in terms of the benefits they bring, whether they are to rehabilitate people and put them to work or simply to support lives that otherwise would be lost. Cost gives no indication of these benefits and some people apparently believe there are no benefits. But, in social terms, most reasonable people would agree that even if human beings are simply prevented from starving, that is a useful, measurable benefit.

It is not, however, a benefit that can be measured in dollars. We cannot say a human life prevented from starving is worth $50,000. We can say that for $x$ billion dollars spent we supported $y$ number of lives. That is a useful type of cost/benefit measure, even though not expressed completely in dollars.

The conclusion that quality of life cannot be reduced to dollar measures also has support in other professions, as illustrated in the following quote from a well known political scientist:

"In short, national economic accounting has promoted a 'new Philistinism'—an approach to life based on the principle of using monetary units as the common denominator of all that is important in human life. The 'new Philistinism' shows up in different forms:

The cost-benefit analysts who recognize no benefits (or disbenefits) that cannot be expressed in dollars and cents.

The econometricians still operating on the ludicrous premise that there is, or should be, a 'single-valued, objective welfare function' by which one could judge alternative courses of action.

The pathetic effort in the United States to debate policies for the 'Great Society' and the 'quality of life' on the basis of concepts developed decades ago to fight depression and provide minimum material sustenance for the population.

"This bias can be overcome only by persistent efforts to develop broader models that include many more variables than those thus far used by economists."[1]

Measuring in terms of costs has great appeal to accountants precisely because such measurements are expressed in dollars and already appear in the regular books of account of the disbursing organization. These are terms that accountants are accustomed to dealing with. Unfortunately, costs are much more relevant to the disbursing organization than to the social constituency which is the intended user of the information. Furthermore, costs tend to become merged over the years and are difficult to identify and allocate, and often cannot be separated from economic costs. For example, providing a pension plan for retiring employees is socially beneficial. It gives them security in their old age. But, it is also an economic cost because in order to attract employees at all, the company must be competitive in its employee benefit plan.

Costs are rather poor measures of effectiveness anyway. For example, one could present simply the cost of providing hospital service. The uninformed user of this information might deduce that a hospital that is spending more to provide service is providing greater social benefit than one that is spending less, since costs are the only measurement at hand. The social benefit from hospitals is improved health. Therefore, the benefit measure should be cast in terms of health, not costs.

Instead of costs, social accounting must measure social impacts, whether they be social benefits or social detriments. Which, of course, again raises several problems. Should the social accountant measure only the side effects of corporate action, or should he measure all the effects, including the mainstream effects? With an automobile manufacturer, for example, the side effects include the pollution created by producing automobiles and by operating them after they are manufactured, as well as traffic injuries and fatalities. Long-range side effects—the result of putting millions of cars on the roads—include increasing urbanization. The mainstream effect is the

[1]Bertram M. Gross, "The State of the Nation: Social Systems Accounting," in *Social Indicators,* edited by Raymond A. Bauer, The M.I.T. Press, Cambridge, 1966, pages 167–168.

automobiles themselves, which are a desired means of personal transportation. Some economists and social accountants maintain that mainstream effects are best measured in the marketplace. If, they say, the market is willing to spend $3,000 for an automobile, that is an excellent indication of its social utility.

But, that is simply not true, because individual decisions are usually short term. When one person buys a car, he is merely looking for personal transportation. Multiply that decision by the millions who purchase cars and not only is there an increase in personal transportation, but the side effects of mounting urbanization and pollution. So to say that the market should value mainstream effects is not adequate because the aggregate effects are much greater than the sum of the individual decisions. Probably most persons would agree that the market does a poor job of measuring the social utility of, say, Saturday night specials or heroin.

In addition, if social accountants measure only side effects, there is a serious problem of distorting decisions, because often the side effects will be mainly negative. If the social reporting does not also measure the mainstream effects, which are often positive, a lopsided picture will emerge. Ideally, therefore, the social accountant would measure all social effects.

Obviously, there are limits to what can be measured. Often the ripples going out from mainstream effects are endless. What, for example, is the ultimate social impact of the economic decision to import slaves three centuries ago? We will never know. So, the task of the social accountant will be to measure as far out from the mainstream effects as he can; in effect, as far as the measurement techniques will allow. Presumably, as these techniques improve, the radius of useful measurement will expand.

The next question concerns the unit of measure to be used. In financial areas, it is easy to get agreement on the unit of measure because commercial organizations are formed to maximize the return of dollars. The dollar is therefore an obvious unit of measure. In social areas, however, the quantity to be maximized is quality of life. Some day it may be possible to develop a quality of life measurement unit; but, for now, this is not a realistic possibility. Therefore, what the social accountant must do is break down quality of life into constituent elements and use surrogate measures. For example, one does not have much quality of life if his personal safety is threatened, so a surrogate measure might be the crime rate. Pollution diminishes quality of life; therefore a surrogate measure would be pollution rates. An adequate income is necessary for quality of life, so a surrogate measure would be the level and distribution of personal income.

The difficulty with using these surrogate measures is that, since they are not expressed in common measurement units, it is difficult to make rational choices based on them. Should the Federal government, for example, allocate marginal resources to cancer research or to raising the reading ability of ghetto children? If the benefits are expressed in different units the choice is not obvious. Those who would express everything in dollars might say cancer has a benefit of $1 billion and reading has a benefit of $2 billion; therefore, reading wins. Most likely, though, the public would simply reject those dollar measures as being quite arbitrary, and revert to qualitative measures. The existence of objective information, even though in different units, should improve the decision process from the way it functions today. No matter what improvements are made in social accounting, however the choice between cancer research and reading ability will probably always remain a societal decision.

For the accounting profession, the major question concerns the extent to which accountants should become involved in social measurement. Other professions—sociology, economics, ecology—would seem to have primary competence in social accounting. What expertise can the accountant bring? The answer to this question is two-fold: first, the accountant can design social information systems, and second, he can attest to reported information.

In the design area, accountants are experienced designers and operators of large-scale information systems and, in fact, are uniquely qualified to assemble and validate quantitative information. There is really no reason the accounting profession cannot broaden this expertise from the financial area into social accounting.

In addition to designing these information systems, the accountant can attest to their reliability. The public accountant's reputation for independence and integrity qualifies him for this task. After all, if information is developed and is not in some way validated, its limited credibility will diminish its usefulness for decision-making.

In any case, as pointed out above, accountants have already become involved in the field.

There are plenty of accountants who believe that we should put our financial house in order before reaching out to embrace new, and perhaps more difficult, problems. Unfortunately, financial accounting is such a complex subject that we shall probably never reach ultimate solutions to financial problems. The danger is that we may commit the resources of the profession to a perpetual quest for truth in an area of declining (and perhaps disappearing) relevance, while failing to make any useful progress on a crucial problem of increasing relevance.

Interestingly, the authoritative literature of accounting gives implicit support to the extension of the scope of accounting practice into social measurement. For example, this passage adopted in 1939 seems prophetic when placed in a social accounting context, rather than the more familiar financial accounting context:

"The committee regards corporation accounting as one phase of the working of the corporate organization of business, which in turn it views as a machinery created by the people in the belief that, broadly speaking, it will serve a useful social purpose. The test of the corporate system and of the special phase of it represented by corporate accounting ultimately lies in the results which are produced. These results must be judged from the standpoint of society as a whole—not from that of any one group of interested parties.

"The uses to which the corporate system is put and the controls to which it is subject change from time to time, and all parts of the machinery must be adapted to meet such changes as they occur."[2]

Although there are no theoretical reasons that CPAs cannot become involved with social accounting, there are some very practical constraints which would hamper the

---

[2]Accounting Research Bulletin No. 1, American Institute of Certified Public Accountants, 1939, incorporated into Accounting Research Bulletin No. 43, which is still in effect today.

profession at this point. They fall into three classes: the level of skill within the profession, entrance requirements to the profession, and the problem of legal liability.

First, certain skills essential for social accounting are underrepresented in the profession today. These include economics, engineering, mathematics, law, sociology, and behavioral science, among others.

Second, in terms of entrance requirements, the profession persists in the "myth of the generalist." It recommends a single formal education program as preparation for becoming a CPA, and administers a single, general qualifying examination. Once a person clears these formal hurdles, he is deemed to be competent in any of the many facets of accounting. In fact, the profession forbids formal designated specializations. As a result of this series of formal hurdles for admission to the profession and the lack of recognition for special expertise, many types of persons urgently needed in the profession are effectively screened out. They do not desire, or are not able, to meet these mechanistic requirements (of little or no relevance to their intended field of specialization) and could achieve no professional recognition if they did gain admittance.

The third practical problem is that of legal liability. The present potentially ruinous levels of liability have already made the CPA sufficiently defensive that he is hesitant to accept new responsibilities. In an uncharted area such as social accounting, the legal threat is unknown and, hence, foreboding.

Our social problems will not go away. To hold them in check, let alone to ameliorate them, we will require vastly greater amounts of objective social information. Accountants can, and should, be involved in creating this information. But to become effectively involved, accountants must take some positive actions.

Academic accountants must

attract into accounting promising candidates outside the traditional mold, that is, conceptual, verbal, socially oriented persons,

broaden the accounting curriculum to include newly required skills,

establish links with other professions to assure an interchange of relevant information,

establish research programs in social accounting, and develop courses to update current practitioners on social accounting.

Public and corporate accountants must

change their self-image from communicators of *financial* information to communicators of *decision-making* information,

become acquainted with social accounting,

hire and welcome into the profession those who will be able to cope with the ambiguous social data,

become acquainted with effectiveness measures used in other professions,

support academic accountants in this area,

experiment with social accounting,

install effectiveness measures instead of just cost measures in their own spheres of influence, and begin to look beyond financial statements and operations to their impact on all corporate constituencies.

If the profession implements these recommendations and begins to move vigorously toward the goals of social accounting, then it could find itself in a leadership position in this vital and fascinating area with its inherent opportunities to provide a highly useful and laudable service to society.

## QUESTIONS

1. Why is there a tendency in social accounting to measure cost instead of benefits?
2. Why are costs poor measures of effectiveness?
3. Why does the author regard a quality of life measurement as not now a realistic possibility?
4. What are the three classes of practical constraints which hamper accountants in practicing social accounting?
5. What must academic accountants, public accountants, and corporate accountants do to become actively involved in creating objective social information?

## SELECTED BIBLIOGRAPHY

Alexander, Michael O., "Social Accounting, If You Please," *Canadian Chartered Accountant*, January 1973, pp. 21-30.

Beresford, Dennis R., "How Companies Are Reporting Social Performance," *Management Accounting*, August 1974, pp. 41-44.

# 152
# A STUDY OF TRIBAL SUB-GROUPS
The Accountants*

Ivor E. Tower

Late in 1970, I received a grant from the Pierpont Morgan Foundation to continue my fieldwork among the Babiras in the Epulu Valley.[1]

In 1968/69, when I spent eighteen months among the tribe, I had made some superficial observations on a separate group within the tribe, called the Accountants.

*From *The Australian Accountant,* June 1975, p. 308—310. Reprinted by permission of the publisher.

[1]This article summarizes my research findings which were first published in the *Journal of the Royal Anthropological Institute,* July 1974.

This group uses a special language and adheres to customs which deviate considerably from those of the rest of the tribe. I felt that this group, the Accountants, merited closer investigation.

In February 1971, I went back to the Epulu Valley. The tribe was still relatively isolated from its neighbours and customs had therefore not changed. I was fortunate to find that Tom, my interpreter of the 1968/69 field trip, was again willing to assist me. There were, however, this time special problems—I found that Tom's English, learnt at the mission school, was often inadequate with regard to the Accountants' terminology.[2]

Blending in with the Accountants was initially difficult. The qualifications of each member of the group are apparently always closely examined; mine were found to be inappropriate. After some months, however, I was able to establish a reasonable working relationship.

I decided to study the group in the following ways: general observation of its physical characteristics; a study of its social organization; a tabulation of differences from the rest of the tribe; a discussion of old age and retirement; a study of the behaviour of its women. For this I made use of my wife's notes.

## PHYSICAL CHARACTERISTICS

In build and diet, Accountants do not differ in any significant way from the rest of the tribe. However, constant and obsessive preoccupation with symbols results in lack of exercise and most Accountants therefore have poor muscle tone. A protruding stomach, which occurs in many individuals, seems in some way connected with a large intake of the local brew, claimed by some to be nourishing.

The group dresses conservatively; very few beads or feathers are worn. I noticed that some of the younger members of the group, who wish to conform with their peers in the tribe, are subject to considerable pressure to discard vivid colours.

In regard to physical characteristics, Accountants might easily be mistaken for the group which is involved with big business,[3] although the latter is prone to excess weight, perhaps due to large midday meals.

I have observed that the two groups have particular interests in common: *taxes*[4] and tax deductions. It seems that some Accountants have acquired great skills justifying tax deductions where no logical grounds exist—the so-called "rope trick". Their advice is often sought by members of Big Business. Tax experts are thus comparable in status to the medicine men of the Bariras.

---

[2]For example, it took me several months before I understood that the words *fund flow* did not refer to a river. My interpreter is uncertain as to what they *do* mean.

[3]See the paper, "Big Business and Deprivation in Infancy", which I presented at the Seminar of the Alaskan Anthropological Society, Anchorage, December 1973. I reported my findings on the conceptual chain: Big Business—Monkey Business—Fraud—Freud. There is no etymological link between Fraud and Loss, although there is a clear connection between early deprivation (loss) and sexual frustration. The paper was published in the *Journal of the Royal Anthropological Institute,* March 1974.

[4]See Glossary for a definition of terms appearing in italics.

## SOCIAL ORGANIZATION

On the surface, Accountants appear to be a close-knit group. Further study made it clear to me, however, that considerable tensions exist. I found that some of these tensions are connected with the fact that two sub-groups fulfil separate functions: one group specializes in practice and the other in teaching. The first group earns more, the second group carries more status. Neither group takes the other seriously, but a united front is usually presented when dealing with the rest of the tribe.

In the three years I lived with the Accountants, I discovered that the practitioners strongly believe in magic. I observed an important social mechanism called "green ticking", which is usually accompanied by shouting (called "hollering"—presumably a call to the deity)[5]; by performing these rites, everything appears to come out right.

The practitioner sub-group is strongly traditionalist and regards the teachers as being out of touch with reality. For example, the practitioners allege that the teachers are unaware of the sacredness of a book of rules, called *G.A.A.P.* These rules were apparently revealed to an important group of practitioners who had camped temporarily on the top of a mountain. The view they received on this occasion was said to be "true and fair".[6]

Feelings run high about a rite called *revaluation of assets* which is in some way connected with *depreciation.* In the opinion of the teachers, the rite, as carried out by the practitioners, is quite primitive if not barbaric. They reason that *the books*, which are sacred, often do not show the *real financial position.* The practitioners, on their part, argue that the real financial position is too obscene to be shown. In 1972, during the second year of my stay in the Epulu Valley, two members of the teaching group had heart attacks because they were involved in a controversy on this matter. I concluded that many taboos are involved.

There is a strongly defined hierarchy in the teacher sub-group. I tape-recorded interviews with a select few, the holy men, whom I will call gurus for want of a better word.[7] One of the most highly respected gurus was reputed to have had a genuine vision in the late 1960s. He has since collected a band of devoted followers and I found his reputation of omniscience had spread as far afield as the neighbouring valley. When the vision was described to me, the letters *C.C.E.* were repeatedly uttered. Their apparent meaning gives no hint of the emotions aroused when the letters are uttered. I therefore suspect that there is a hidden reference to demonic forces.

Just before I left the valley a group of young Turks was sighted, noisily promoting a new form of soothsaying called "efficient market hypothesis". They prefer to read omens in shell transfers, instead of combining, as is customary, the interpretation of symbols with the reading of entrails. I observed that the younger group's

---

[5] I tried to find links with other religious practices of the group. It is however an isolated phenomenon.

[6] The letters G.A.A.P. were frequently cited and apparently refer to principles. My interpreter assured me that these letters denote the strong moral stance of the Accountants. The expression "true and fair view" would support this.

[7] Amongst practitioners there is also a select few known as Councillors. They are known colloquially as Top Dogs.

method of soothsaying generated much hostility, even hysteria. The fact that the method originated in the neighbouring valley—where the group had been prepared for initiation—may have aggravated the hostility.

During my stay in the valley, shells fell dramatically in barter value. This increased the tension between the two sub-groups. Revolutionary methods for notching counting sticks were proposed by the teachers. These methods were opposed by the practitioners, who again appeared to rely on magic.

## OLD AGE AND RETIREMENT

The Accountants, in contrast with other members of the tribe, are not made to feel redundant when they are past sixty. The ability to interpret symbols often leads to invitations to join boards of directors; if they accept such invitations, they can spend many pleasant hours in comfortable chairs at board meetings.

There is also the stimulating pastime known as "looking after one's investments". I observed that this activity kept the older members of the sub-group alert and cheerful. Concern about the capital gains tax may, however, lead to severe depression.

Provided a person is still in good condition, he can take part in the ceremonies[8] called conferences. The elders appear to enjoy the singing and dancing on these occasions, although this requires more stamina than the discussions.

As I hope to have made clear in this analysis, the Accountants are a sub-group whose customs were preserved from too much contact with civilization and which were therefore worthy of such a thorough anthropological study. At the Winter Seminar of the Royal Institute, I will present the results of my study of the behaviour of the women of this subgroup.

## GLOSSARY

*Asset*  pig
*Audit*  generic title covering the various rites during which practitioners nervously tick and holler
*Accounting Profit (Prophet?)*  tribal elder
*Balance Sheet*  listing of old shells used in exchange
*Big Business*  pig traders
*Board of Directors*  big business equivalent of Top Dogs
*The Books*  collection of secret symbols
*C.C.E.*  current cockle equivalents; cockle shells are the basic medium of exchange
*Depreciation*  result of starvation of asset
*Financial Position*  quantity of assets (pigs) expressed in shells
*Real Financial Position*  naked pigs
*Financiers*  shell collectors
*Fund Flows*  tidal movement of cockle shells

[8] I attended several of these ceremonies. The tape-recordings of the discussions were unsatisfactory; the participants were often in a trance for the duration (perhaps induced by the local brew), which resulted in slurred speech and incoherence.

*G.A.A.P.*    generally avoided accounting principles
*Professional Year*    period of practising rites prior to initiation into the group
*Revaluation*    recognition of increase in weight of assets
*Stock Exchange*    tree under which transfer of cockle shells takes place
*Taxes*    the procedure of bloodletting at regular intervals; sometimes from stones obtained

## QUESTION

1. Of the various professors whose articles are reprinted in this book, which one does Mr. Tower regard as a "guru?" Which one is a "young Turk?"

# 153
## LIVE — I AM COMING
Oliver Wendell Holmes

... The riders in a race do not stop short when they reach the goal. There is a little finishing canter before coming to a standstill. There is time to hear the kind voices of friends and to say to oneself: The work is done. But just as one says that, the answer comes: "The race is over, but the work never is done while the power to work remains. The canter that brings you to a standstill need not be only coming to rest. It cannot be, while you still live. For to live is to function. That is all there is to living."

And so I end with a line from a Latin poet who uttered the message more than fifteen hundred years ago, "Death plucks my ear and says: Live—I am coming."

EDITORS' NOTE: The above is attributed to Oliver Wendell Holmes on his ninetieth birthday. For more than 50 years, he was a member of the Supreme Court of the United States. Justice Holmes spoke extemporaneously following a national radio program (March 7, 1931) of tribute.

# INDEX